Economic Report of the President

Transmitted to the Congress
February 2006

together with
THE ANNUAL REPORT
of the
COUNCIL OF ECONOMIC ADVISERS

UNITED STATES GOVERNMENT PRINTING OFFICE

WASHINGTON : 2006

For sale by the Superintendent of Documents, U.S. Government Printing Office
Internet: bookstore.gpo.gov   Phone: (202) 512-1800   Fax: (202) 512-2250
Mail Stop: SSOP, Washington, DC 20402-0001

ISBN 0-16-075418-6

C O N T E N T S

* For a detailed table of contents of the Council's Report, see page 11

ECONOMIC REPORT
OF THE PRESIDENT

ECONOMIC REPORT OF THE PRESIDENT

To the Congress of the United States:

The United States economy continues to demonstrate remarkable resilience, flexibility, and growth. Having previously endured a stock market collapse, recession, terrorist attacks, and corporate scandals, this year the economy showed strong growth and robust job creation in the face of higher energy prices and devastating natural disasters. This is the result of the hard work of America's workers, supported by pro-growth tax policies.

In 2005, the Nation's real gross domestic product (GDP) grew 3.5 percent for the year, above the historical average. About 2 million payroll jobs were added in 2005, and the unemployment rate dropped to 4.7 percent last month, well below the averages of the 1970s, 1980s, and 1990s. Real disposable personal income increased, and real household net worth reached an all-time high. This growth comes on top of an already strong expansion. More than 4.7 million payroll jobs have been added since August 2003.

Compared with the performance of other nations' economies, our economic growth is especially impressive. The United States has added more jobs in the past two-and-a-half years than Japan and the European Union combined. Real GDP growth in the United States has been faster than in any other major industrialized country since 2001, and America is forecasted to continue as the fastest-growing country over the next two years.

Our economy's fundamental strength comes from the ingenuity and hard work of our workers. Productivity—how much workers produce per hour—has accelerated since 2000. In the past five years, productivity has grown faster than in any other five-year period since the mid-1960s. The productivity of the United States is increasing faster than any other major industrialized country.

Productivity growth raises our standard of living and plays a central role in our competitiveness in the worldwide economy. Productivity growth will be even more important as new technologies accelerate global economic integration and as the American population ages.

We must now build on this fundamental strength by making robust investments in physical sciences, improving private incentives for research and development, and boosting math and science education and worker training. The American Competitiveness Initiative will help us remain a world leader in science and technology, which means good high-paying jobs for the American people.

We must also continue to pursue pro-growth economic policies and foster a culture of entrepreneurship. To adopt innovations effectively, our companies and workers need the incentives and flexibility that support a thriving free-market economy.

Maintaining a low tax burden is essential for our economic growth and competitiveness. Tax relief has helped our economy, and raising taxes will increase the burden on our families and small businesses. To keep our economy growing, Congress needs to make the tax relief permanent.

Two years ago, I called for cutting the budget deficit in half by 2009 by restraining spending and spurring economic growth. Every year of my presidency, we have reduced the growth of non-security discretionary spending, and last year Congress passed bills that cut this spending. This year, my budget will cut it again, and it will reduce or eliminate more than 140 programs that are performing poorly or not fulfilling essential priorities. By passing these reforms, we will save the American taxpayer another $14 billion next year, and we will stay on track to cut the deficit in half by 2009.

Controlling discretionary spending alone is not enough, however. We have recently passed significant savings in mandatory spending programs. We need to do more because the only way to solve our Nation's fiscal challenges is to address the explosions in growth of entitlement programs like Social Security, Medicare, and Medicaid. I have called for a bipartisan commission to examine the full impact of the Baby Boom retirement and help us come up with bipartisan answers. The longer Congress waits to act, the more difficult the choices will become.

Working together, we accomplished other significant pro-growth reforms that will help our Nation's economy grow stronger and create more jobs. More remains to be done.

Growth in spending on health care has been more rapid than general inflation, straining consumers, employers, and government budgets. Two years ago, we created Health Savings Accounts (HSAs) to help give patients more control over their health care decisions and to make health care more available and affordable. This year, I am proposing to enhance HSAs to make them more widely available, valuable to consumers, and attractive to small businesses—and to make it easier for people to keep their insurance policies when they change jobs. Last year, we worked with Congress to pass a patient safety bill that will help reduce medical errors. Getting doctors and patients the information they need on the quality, cost, and effectiveness of different treatments will help Americans get the highest quality and highest value care. This year, my Administration will push to make more information about price and quality available to consumers, and move forward on these and other policies to lower the cost of health care.

Our Nation's liability laws allow too many frivolous lawsuits and raise costs for consumers and businesses. A year ago, we worked with Congress to pass bipartisan class action reform to help curb lawsuit abuse. I urge Congress in the coming year to pass other essential legal reforms, including asbestos and medical liability reforms.

Energy prices have risen in the last year, but the underlying causes of high prices are long-standing. Last year, we passed the first major energy bill in over a decade. It encourages new technologies and updates government regulations. Over time, the new law will help increase the reliability of our energy supply and the efficient use of the energy we have. We must continue to find new ways to diversify our sources of energy. I have proposed the Advanced Energy Initiative to help increase research in alternative energy sources and technology and to make America less dependent on foreign sources of energy.

Because 95 percent of the world's customers live outside of our borders, opening international markets to our goods and services is critical for our economy. My Administration will continue to work tirelessly to open markets and knock down barriers to free and fair trade so that American farmers and workers can compete on a level playing field worldwide.

These and other issues are discussed in the 2006 Annual Report of the Council of Economic Advisers. This report is prepared by CEA to help policymakers understand the economic context of a variety of issues and trends as our Government makes decisions regarding our economic future. By adopting sound economic policies that build on our strengths, we will keep our economy moving forward and extend prosperity for all Americans.

THE WHITE HOUSE
FEBRUARY 2006

THE ANNUAL REPORT
OF THE
COUNCIL OF ECONOMIC ADVISERS

LETTER OF TRANSMITTAL

COUNCIL OF ECONOMIC ADVISERS,
Washington, D.C., February 13, 2006

MR. PRESIDENT:

The Council of Economic Advisers herewith submits its 2006 Annual Report in accordance with the provisions of the Employment Act of 1946 as amended by the Full Employment and Balanced Growth Act of 1978.

Sincerely,

Katherine Baicker
Member

Matthew J. Slaughter
Member

CONTENTS

Overview

The expansion of the U.S. economy continued for the fourth consecutive year in 2005. The President has laid out an agenda to maintain the economy's momentum, foster job creation, and ensure that America remains a leader of the global economy.

The President is advancing plans to make tax relief permanent; restrain government spending to reduce the budget deficit; strengthen retirement systems; make health care more affordable and accessible; create an economic environment that encourages innovation and entrepreneurship; enhance private incentives for research and development; boost math and science education and worker training; reform the immigration system and strengthen our borders; continue to open markets to American goods and services; and reduce America's dependence on foreign oil by diversifying our energy supply.

This *Report* reviews the state of the economy and the economic outlook, and discusses a number of economic policy issues of continuing importance. The *Report* highlights how economics can inform the design of better public policy and reviews Administration initiatives.

The Year in Review and the Years Ahead

The economy has shifted from recovery to sustained expansion, having absorbed the effects of the Gulf Coast hurricanes and large increases in energy prices in 2005. Chapter 1, *The Year in Review and the Years Ahead*, reviews the economic developments of 2005 and discusses the Administration's forecast for the years ahead. The key points of this chapter are:

- Real GDP grew strongly during 2005. Most components of demand that accounted for growth in 2004—consumer spending, business investment in equipment and software, and exports—continued to do so in 2005.
- Labor markets continued to strengthen. Employers created 2 million new jobs in 2005, and the unemployment rate dropped to 4.9 percent by year-end.
- Productivity growth remained well above its historical average in 2005.
- Inflation rose substantially at mid-year, but came down by year-end as it reflected the movement of energy prices. In contrast, inflation in the core consumer price index (CPI) (which excludes food and energy prices) has remained in the moderate 2-percent range.
- The Administration's forecast, consistent with consensus private forecasts, shows the economic expansion continuing for the foreseeable future.

19

Skills for the U.S. Workforce

Chapter 2, *Skills for the U.S. Workforce*, discusses the economics of education, immigration, and job training. The key points are:

- Education is a key contributor to economic growth and individual income.
- Advances in education levels have slowed over the past 25 years. The No Child Left Behind Act is working to reverse this trend by making schools more accountable. If, however, we do not continue to improve our schools, the U.S. standard of living could be jeopardized in years to come.
- High-skilled immigrants make up a vital part of the U.S. economy, particularly in the science and engineering sectors.
- Workers need to upgrade their skills continually to adapt to and take part in an ever-changing economy.

Promoting a flexible and skilled labor force—through improved access to high-quality primary, secondary, and post-secondary education, through policies that attract the world's best and brightest to our shores, and through investment in the continuing education and training of our mobile workforce – will ensure that the United States remains a competitive leader in this rapidly changing world economy.

Saving for Retirement

Over the past few decades, concerns have mounted that Americans have been preparing inadequately for retirement. The main points of Chapter 3, *Saving for Retirement*, are:

- Most working-age Americans are on track to have more retirement wealth than most current retirees. It is inherently difficult, however, to assess whether these preparations are adequate for most households.
- The decline in an often-cited aggregate personal saving rate may not be cause for much alarm for retirement preparedness. Much of this decline can be attributed to spending triggered by wealth increases from capital gains on housing and financial assets.
- There are, however, a number of risks to the retirement preparations of Americans. People today are living longer and could face higher health-care costs in retirement than members of previous generations. In addition, Social Security and many defined-benefit pension plans are at risk.
- Both defined-benefit pensions and Social Security suffer from fundamental financial problems that expose not just retirees but all U.S. taxpayers to risk of substantial losses. The Administration is focused on addressing these problems and protecting the Nation's retirement security.

Improving Incentives in Health Care Spending

Health care spending in the United States has increased rapidly over the past several decades, rising 44 percent in real per capita terms in the past ten years alone. Some of the reasons for this marked rise reflect higher-quality health care, such as improved technological options for enhancing health and quality of life. Other factors, however, such as poorly functioning markets for health care, may have led to excessive spending and inefficient patterns of medical care utilization.

Chapter 4, *Improving Incentives in Health Care Spending*, reviews the causes and consequences of health care spending growth and discusses how the President's consumer-driven proposals can improve the health care system. The key points are:

- Growth in spending on health care has been much more rapid than general inflation, straining consumers, employers, and government budgets.
- Perverse tax and insurance incentives have led to inefficient levels and composition of spending on health care.
- Promoting a stronger role for consumers is a promising strategy for improving health care value and affordability.

The U.S. Tax System in International Perspective

All governments face two important decisions. They must choose the scope and scale of public goods and services to provide for their citizens, and they must also decide how to collect the funds to finance those public services. Chapter 5, The U.S. Tax System in International Perspective, examines U.S. choices in the context of other countries. It makes three key points:

- Fundamental choices about tax systems matter because they affect the living standards of citizens.
- The United States has made different choices from other countries. The United States has a relatively low tax burden compared to the rest of the world, and we finance more of that burden with a tax on personal income instead of consumption.
- When viewed in an international perspective, the U.S. system has been significantly improved in recent years but could benefit greatly from additional reforms, particularly those focused on the taxation of capital income.

The U.S. Capital Account Surplus

The United States conducts an enormous number of trade and financial transactions with other countries. In 2004, the U.S. ran a current account deficit of $668 billion. This deficit meant the U.S. imported more goods and services than it exported. The counterpart to the U.S. current account deficit was a capital account surplus of an equal amount. This surplus meant that foreign investors purchased more U.S. assets than U.S. investors purchased in foreign assets, and the U.S. received net foreign capital and financial inflows. Chapter 6, *The U.S. Capital Account Surplus*, makes several key points:

- The size and persistence of U.S. net capital inflows reflects a number of U.S. economic strengths as well as some shortcomings.
- The recent rise in U.S. net capital inflows in part reflects global economic conditions as well as policies in some Asian countries and weak growth in several European economies that led to greater net capital outflows from these countries.
- Encouraging greater global balance of capital flows would be helped by steps in several countries, such as higher domestic saving in the U.S., stronger economic growth in Europe and Japan, and greater exchange rate flexibility and financial sector reforms in Asia.

The History and Future of International Trade

While economic research and historical evidence show the benefits of trade outweigh the costs, trade liberalization has always brought anxieties in the United States and throughout the world. There have always been temptations to retreat to economic isolationism, but the Administration rejects that notion. The key points in Chapter 7, *The History and Future of International Trade*, are:

- Over the past 70 years, policymakers across political parties have consistently recognized the importance of international commerce, and have achieved major trade liberalization both here and abroad.
- The net payoff to America from these achievements has been substantial. For example, studies have estimated the annual payoff from U.S. trade and investment liberalization thus far averages $5,000 per American.
- A number of barriers to trade remain, especially in services, and the benefits of eliminating these barriers are significant. One study found removing all remaining barriers to trade in services would lead to an additional $7,000 in annual income for the average American family of four. The Administration is working to open these markets in global, regional, and bilateral negotiations.

The U.S. Agriculture Sector

In 2005, the Federal government spent approximately $20 billion on agricultural support payments in a sector forecast to produce approximately $270 billion of output. In addition, the United States maintains barriers to the import of some commodities, and these barriers raise the domestic prices of these commodities relative to world prices. To what extent do these many payments and trade barriers serve a public purpose? Are they needed to maintain a healthy U.S. agricultural sector? Could alternative policies achieve this goal? Chapter 8, *The U.S. Agricultural Sector*, addresses these and other questions. The key findings of this chapter are:

- Most farmers do not benefit from commodity subsidies.
- Support to agriculture can be provided in many forms that are potentially less market- distorting than existing commodity subsidies.

The U.S. Financial Services Sector

Most people interact regularly with the financial services sector, such as when they make deposits at banks or obtain loans from them. Nevertheless, understanding what this sector does can be difficult. Why do individuals go to intermediaries like banks for mortgages, rather than skip intermediaries and deal directly with savers? And why do financial service firms ask for so much information before making a loan and, afterward, place so many restrictions on borrowers?

Chapter 9, *The U.S. Financial Services Sector*, explores what financial services do for an economy, how financial development relates to economic performance, and how financial services can be effectively regulated. The key points are:

- The U.S. financial services sector addresses informational problems that can otherwise keep financial capital from finding productive uses. The sector tends to deliver these services in a cost-effective manner.
- Financial services facilitate innovation and thus encourage economic growth. They might also bolster economic stability.
- Financial regulation should protect consumers and ensure the system's safety and soundness. Moving too far in the direction of public regulation, however, can stifle the productivity and innovation necessary for the economy to enjoy fully the benefits of financial services. An effective financial regulatory system appropriately balances the costs and benefits of public regulation.

The Role of Intellectual Property in the Economy

The founders of this country believed that intellectual property was so important that one of the grants of power to Congress under the Constitution was "To promote the Progress of Science and the useful Arts, by securing for limited Times to Authors and Inventors the exclusive Right to their respective Writings and Discoveries." Economic research over the past two centuries confirms the importance of intellectual property. The key points of Chapter 10, *The Role of Intellectual Property in the Economy*, are:

- Intellectual property rights create incentives for individuals and firms to invest in research and development, and to commercialize inventions by allowing them to profit from their creations.
- Well-defined and enforced intellectual property rights are important to economic growth.
- The Administration continues to enforce vigorously the rights of American intellectual property owners.

Recent Developments in Energy

Chapter 11, *Recent Developments in Energy*, discusses energy markets— systems that connect consumers and suppliers of energy products, where prices are determined by what buyers will pay and what sellers will accept. The chapter reviews developments in markets for crude oil, refined petroleum products, and natural gas, as well as developments in the electricity-generation sector. The key points are:

- Increased scarcity and rising prices over time will encourage conservation, increase incentives for exploration, and stimulate the development of new, energy-efficient technologies and alternative energy sources.
- In the near term, unexpected disruptions to energy supply and distribution networks may continue to affect consumers and businesses. Hurricanes Katrina and Rita demonstrated that competitive markets play a central role in allocating scarce energy resources, especially during times of natural disaster or national emergency.
- The continued expansion of energy markets through regional and global trade can further increase our resilience to energy supply disruptions.
- Policies that reduce U.S. vulnerability to energy disruptions, encourage energy efficiency, and protect the environment can be beneficial supplements to markets. These policies can be made more effective and less costly when designed based on economic incentives.

CHAPTER 1

The Year in Review and the Years Ahead

The expansion of the U.S. economy—having gathered momentum in 2003 and 2004—continued for its fourth full year in 2005. Economic growth was solid, with real gross domestic product (GDP) growing 3.1 percent during the four quarters of 2005 and 3.5 percent for the year as a whole. Near-record prices of energy and damage from several powerful hurricanes threatened to derail the expansion, but growth was well maintained in the face of these shocks and a long series of rate hikes by the Federal Reserve. Productivity growth remained well above its historical average.

This chapter reviews the economic developments of 2005 and discusses the Administration's forecast for the years ahead. The key points of this chapter are:

- Real GDP grew strongly during 2005. Most components of demand that accounted for growth in 2004 continued to do so in 2005: consumer spending, business investment in equipment and software, and exports.
- Labor markets continued to strengthen. The unemployment rate continued to decline, and employers created another 2 million jobs.
- Inflation rose substantially at mid-year, but came down by year-end reflecting the movement of energy prices. In contrast, inflation in the core consumer price index (CPI) (which excludes food and energy prices) has remained in the moderate 2-percent range, and inflation expectations for the period beyond a one-year horizon remain moderate and stable.
- The Administration's forecast calls for the economic expansion to continue in 2006, with real GDP growth close to its post-World War II average rate and the unemployment rate stable at about its current level. This is expected to continue in subsequent years.

Developments in 2005 and the Near-Term Outlook

Despite the impacts of rising energy prices and a devastating hurricane season (see Box 1-1), the U.S. economy continued to expand at a solid pace in 2005 and inflation pressures remained contained.

Consumer Spending and Saving

Consumer spending continued its strong growth in 2005, rising faster than disposable income over the past decade and a half. As a result, the personal

Box 1-1: Economic Impact of the 2005 Hurricanes

In addition to the tragic loss of life and the massive destruction of personal property, the two major hurricanes (Katrina on August 29 and Rita on September 24) damaged the productive capacity of the American economy. Hurricane Wilma (October 24) also caused sizable losses to life and property, but the damage to the economy as a whole was much less. Both Hurricane Katrina and Hurricane Rita passed through offshore areas where oil and natural gas platforms are concentrated and then struck on-shore areas where petroleum is refined and natural gas is processed. In addition to the damage to equipment and structures, the hurricanes separated at least 782,000 workers from their jobs (and displaced many more from their homes).

The direct damage to the capital stock and the displacement of labor probably cut real GDP growth by about 0.7 percentage point at an annual rate in the third quarter. Most of this GDP loss was the direct result of destruction of oil and natural gas operations. Although rebuilding of petroleum and natural gas operations was well under way in the fourth quarter, the continuing disruptions likely subtracted about 0.5 percentage point from the annual rate of real GDP growth in that quarter. Hurricane Katrina shut down about 1.4 million barrels per day of oil extraction and 8.8 billion cubic feet per day of natural gas production when it passed through on August 29. Those operations were well on their way to recovery when Hurricane Rita came along for a second strike on September 24, erasing the recovery efforts up to that date (see the chart below). From Katrina's approach through the Gulf of Mexico until the end of the third quarter, oil extraction was cut by an average of 1.08 million barrels per day below normal levels and by an average of 0.7 million barrels per day during the fourth quarter. Similarly, natural gas production was reduced by an average of 5.4 billion cubic feet per day (roughly 10 percent of U.S. output) from Katrina's approach through the end of the third quarter and by an average of 4.0 billion cubic feet per day in the fourth quarter. Damage to refineries cut output by an average of about 2 million barrels per day during September and forced the demand for refined petroleum products to be met by higher imports and a liquidation of inventories. Most refinery output was restored by early-November, however. (Recent energy developments are discussed further in Chapter 11.)

About 782,000 workers filed claims for unemployment insurance (UI) benefits because of the hurricanes (604,000 under the regular UI program and another 178,000 under the Disaster Unemployment Assistance program). The lost production from these workers also subtracted from real GDP growth in the third quarter (after making an allowance to avoid double counting the lost production of

Box 1-1 — *continued*

Oil and Natural Gas Production since Recent Hurricanes
Hurricanes Katrina (8/29) and Rita (9/24) shut down major amounts of crude oil and natural gas production, and the damage took a long time to repair.

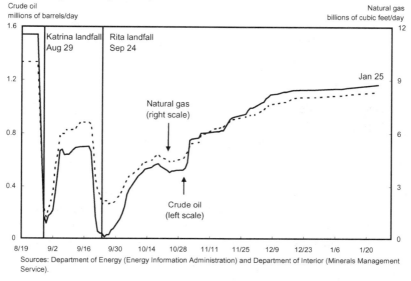

Crude oil
millions of barrels/day

Natural gas
billions of cubic feet/day

Sources: Department of Energy (Energy Information Administration) and Department of Interior (Minerals Management Service).

workers in the petroleum and natural gas industries noted earlier). Data from the Current Population Survey indicate the unemployment rate among evacuees was about 12 percent by year end.

According to a Red Cross damage assessment, the three hurricanes destroyed an estimated 213,000 housing units; most of this damage was done by Katrina. Furthermore, 169,000 units suffered major damage (enough to make them uninhabitable), 220,000 had minor damage, and another 235,000 had extremely minor damage. The Bureau of Economic Analysis estimates the loss of residential capital stock at about $67 billion—about $37 billion of which was insured. The insured structures are likely to be rebuilt (although not necessarily in the same location), and many of the uninsured structures may be rebuilt as well. The pace of reconstruction is uncertain but is likely to take place over a period of three years or so.

In the aftermath of the hurricanes, the President and Congress worked together to provide disaster relief for the affected areas. Two emergency spending bills provided for $62 billion of disaster relief, including transfer payments to persons and businesses in the affected areas, direct government purchases of goods and services, and grants to State and local governments. These bills also included funding for the Defense Department and the Corps of Engineers to rebuild military facilities and levees in New Orleans and the Gulf Coast. Additional legislation authorized a reallocation of about $6 billion from other programs to disaster relief, established $17 billion of additional borrowing authority for Federal flood insurance programs, and provided about $15 billion of tax relief for the affected areas.

In the fourth quarter, the Federal disaster spending together with private rebuilding may have partially offset the still-negative effects of petroleum and natural gas operations. By the first quarter of 2006, these post-hurricane effects are expected to combine to produce a clearly positive contribution to real GDP growth.

saving rate fell to a postwar low this year, turning negative in the second quarter and remaining negative through the fourth quarter. A number of factors contributed to growth in consumer spending in 2005; the most important was the increase in energy prices including the transitory post-Katrina surge. Other factors with sizable effects in particular quarters were motor vehicle incentive programs and the loss of rental income from the hurricanes. Rising household net worth during the late 1990s and again over the past two years has provided a more-persistent boost to consumer outlays relative to after-tax income.

Energy Expenditures

Consumer budgets continued to be stretched by higher energy prices in 2005. Consumer energy prices increased about 21 percent during the four quarters of 2005, following an 18-percent increase in 2004 (as measured by the consumption price index in the national income and product accounts). Real consumption of energy was fairly flat in 2005, but because of the higher prices, the share of household income allocated to energy purchases increased sharply. Spending on energy goods and services jumped from 4.2 percent of disposable personal income in 2002 to about 6 percent in October and November of 2005 as the average household's energy budget rose by about $700 during 2005.

Light Vehicle Expenditures

While annual average sales of cars and light trucks have been remarkably stable over the past six years, much of the quarter-to-quarter volatility in consumer spending generally comes from motor vehicle purchases. Quarter-to-quarter variability in light vehicle sales was particularly evident in 2005. In

July, when General Motors, Ford, and Chrysler each introduced incentive programs on 2005 models, the sales of light vehicles peaked at 20.7 million units at an annual rate. However, motor vehicle sales dropped off in the fourth quarter to 15.8 million units at an annual rate with the removal of the incentive programs. Light vehicle sales for the year as a whole averaged 16.9 million units, however, almost identical to the average pace during the 2000-to-2004 period.

Personal and National Saving

Meanwhile, real purchases outside of energy and motor vehicles grew at their long-standing trend of about 3½-percent growth per year. With energy prices up and other consumption on an unaltered trajectory, most of the funds for these higher-cost energy purchases came from reducing saving. The personal saving rate, which had been generally falling during the preceding 15 years, fell to -0.5 percent for 2005.

Personal saving is only one part of national saving. The personal saving rate does not include corporate saving in the form of retained earnings; but corporate saving adds to the wealth of corporate shareholders and supplies funds for investment. Net private saving, which includes corporate saving as well as household saving, was 4.3 percent of net national income in the first half of 2005, down from 7.4 percent in the 1990s. A still broader measure of saving, national saving, subtracts dissaving by Federal, state, and local governments (in the form of government budget deficits) from private (public plus corporate) saving. The national saving rate was 1.7 percent in the first half of 2005. (Personal and national saving are discussed further in Chapter 3, Saving for Retirement; the international aspects of saving are discussed in Chapter 6, The U.S. Capital Account Surplus.)

Wealth Effects on Consumption and Saving

A strong rise in household net worth during the late 1990s and again during the past two years coincided with a sizable increase in consumer spending relative to disposable personal income (Chart 1-1). From 1995 through 2000, in large part because of a booming stock market, the wealth-to-income ratio rose well above its historical range, eventually reaching 6.15 years of disposable income, and the fraction of disposable income spent by consumers rose to new heights as well. The wealth-to-income ratio fell sharply in 2001 and 2002 due to the stock market decline. Since its low point in the third quarter of 2002, the wealth-to-income ratio has again risen sharply. By the third quarter of 2005, it had recovered to about 5.6 years of disposable income, well above the historical average of 4.8. Gains in the stock market accounted for about half of the recovery while increases in net housing wealth accounted for another third.

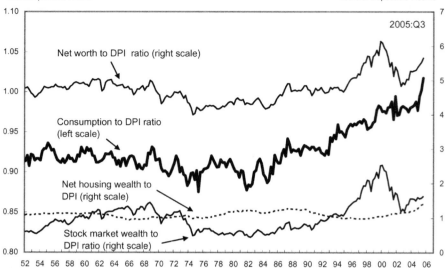

Chart 1-1 Consumption & Net Worth (Relative to Disposable Personal Income)
Consumption gains in 2004 and 2005 were partly supported by increases in wealth, with increases in housing and stock market wealth accounting for most of the increase.

Consumption/DPI Ratio   Years of disposable income

2005:Q3

Net worth to DPI ratio (right scale)

Consumption to DPI ratio (left scale)

Net housing wealth to DPI (right scale)

Stock market wealth to DPI ratio (right scale)

52 54 56 58 60 62 64 66 68 70 72 74 76 78 80 82 84 86 88 90 92 94 96 98 00 02 04 06

Sources: Department of Commerce (Bureau of Economic Analysis), Federal Reserve Board, and Council of Economic Advisers.

Looking ahead, real consumption growth during the four quarters of 2006 is expected to be somewhere around the 3½-percent trend rate measured during the past three years. Over the near term, the personal saving rate is expected to increase. If energy prices decline in 2006, consumer spending should decline relative to income; to the extent that energy prices remain high, consumer spending may still decline relative to income as consumers reduce energy use and substitute energy alternatives.

Housing Prices

During the past five years, home prices have risen at an annual rate of 9.2 percent. This increase was largely supported by two factors: first, an increase in housing demand, driven by a rise in nominal per capita disposable income of 3.4 percent per year; second, a decline in the cost of financing house purchases, due to a drop in the monthly payment on 30-year fixed-rate mortgages of 4.3 percent per year. Housing demand was also boosted by increased household formation and a strengthening job market. Supply constraints, due to limits on the supply of buildable land in some areas, also contributed to rising prices over the past five years. After falling during 2004, mortgage rates were roughly flat at 5¾ percent in the first three quarters of 2005, and then edged up along with other long-term interest rates in the fourth quarter. As a result, a well known measure of housing affordability has now fallen to about its average level over its 34-year history.

To gauge the extent to which house price increases have reflected fundamentals, some studies compare housing prices to rents. The rent-to-price ratio is a real rate of return on housing assets in the same way that the earnings-to-price ratio measures the real rate of return on corporate stocks. Viewed as an asset, a home should bear a real return similar to the real return available on alternative assets, such as stocks and bonds. As real interest rates have fallen in the United States and in most other Organization for Economic Cooperation and Development (OECD) countries, the rent-to-price ratio for housing has likewise fallen across a broad range of OECD countries. A recent OECD paper concluded that the decline in the rent-to-price ratio in the United States from 2000 through 2004 was roughly consistent with the decline in interest rates over the same period.

Residential Investment

In response to strong demand and the consequent rise in prices, builders began construction on more than 2 million new homes during 2005, one of the highest rates of homebuilding on record. Similarly, residential investment, at 6 percent of GDP in 2005, was at its highest level since 1955. During 2005, growth of residential construction contributed about half a percentage point to real GDP growth. Homebuilding in 2005 was slightly in excess of the pace of about 1.9 million starts per year that some economists have estimated is compatible in the long run with U.S. rates of household formation and other demographic influences.

During the next five years, the Administration expects the pace of homebuilding to decrease gradually because of demographic trends and slowly rising long-term interest rates. A gradual slowing of homebuilding appears more likely than a sharp drop because the elevated level of house prices will sustain homebuilding as a profitable enterprise for some time. On balance, residential investment is not projected to contribute to real GDP growth during the four quarters of 2006; in subsequent years, it is expected to subtract a bit from overall growth.

Business Fixed Investment

Real business investment in equipment and software grew 8 percent during the four quarters of 2005. This growth is down from the 14-percent year-earlier pace, which was boosted by the end-of-2004 termination of the bonus depreciation provisions of the Jobs and Growth Tax Reconciliation Act. Equipment purchases grew rapidly in mining and oilfield machinery (18 percent) in response to higher prices for oil and natural gas and the need to replace hurricane-damaged rigs in the Gulf of Mexico. Equipment investment also grew rapidly in the high-tech fields of computers, software, and communications equipment. Investment in industrial and construction equipment grew only moderately (6 percent and 4 percent, respectively). Investment in light trucks was strong through the third quarter, but fell back in the fourth.

In contrast to equipment and software, investment in structures was weak, growing only 1 percent during 2005, after 2.8-percent growth in 2004. Strong growth in the construction of hospitals, shopping centers, and mines (including oil and natural gas rigs) has been offset by declines in the building of electrical power stations, hotels and motels, and amusement and recreation facilities. Office construction fell for the fifth year in a row; however, the 2005 decline was smaller than previous years as office occupancy rates have begun to increase.

The accumulation of internal funds has been more than sufficient to finance business investment during this expansion (Chart 1-2). These funds, also known as *cash flow*, are the sum of undistributed after-tax profits and depreciation. In general, funds for business investment can be generated through borrowing (typically from the bond market, commercial paper market, or banks), issuing new stock, the drawdown of liquid assets, or tapping into cash flow. Historically, business investment has been about 21 percent higher than cash flow, with firms raising most of the extra funds in credit markets. In contrast, business investment during this expansion has not kept pace with cash flow. As a consequence, corporate liquid assets have now built up to levels that are well above any that have been seen during the past decade and a half. This buildup in liquid assets implies that financing for future investment should be readily available. However, the buildup may reflect greater overall caution among business executives and owners, a shift in sentiment that could dampen future investment.

During the next couple of years, investment in equipment and software is likely to maintain the same rapid growth as in 2005, as output continues to grow and businesses remain flush with cash. Investment in business structures is projected to accelerate as new oil and gas rigs are built and as continued declines in vacancy rates support the construction of new office buildings.

Business Inventories

The pace of inventory investment in 2005 was below the 2004 pace and on average subtracted from overall GDP growth during the first three quarters of the year. As sales grew during the year, the inventory-to-sales ratio continued to decline. Indeed, the inventory-to-sales ratio has fallen considerably since the mid-1980s. In 2005, businesses held inventories equal to about 27 business-days' worth of sales—about three days' worth of sales less than they held in 2000, and about seven days' less than in 1985. The trend toward leaner

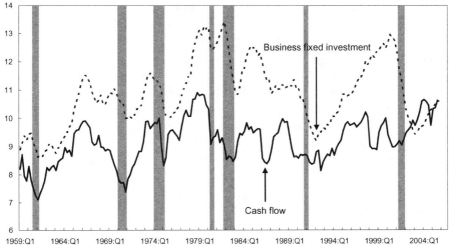

Chart 1-2 **Business Fixed Investment and Cash Flow**
Business fixed investment and cash flow tend to move up and down together, although BFI usually exceeds cash flow. During this expansion, in contrast, BFI is not higher than cash flow.

Share of Potential GDP

Business fixed investment

Cash flow

Note: Potential GDP is the level of GDP consistent with full employment. BFI data available through 2005:Q4; cash flow data available through 2005:Q3. Shaded areas indicate recessions.
Sources: Department of Commerce (Bureau of Economic Analysis) and Congressional Budget Office.

inventories has been evident in manufacturing since the mid-1980s, and has appeared in retailing and wholesaling since at least 2000. Leaner inventories suggest that new business practices such as just-in-time inventory control in manufacturing and computer- and Internet-assisted supply-chain management continue to become more popular among supply managers.

Inventory investment generally makes little contribution to real GDP growth when the growth of final sales is roughly stable from year to year. (In contrast, inventory investment *is* important in the early phases of business-cycle recessions and recoveries.) With the economy in the midst of an ongoing expansion, and the Administration expecting fairly smooth growth of final sales during the next several years, inventory investment is not anticipated to be a major contributor to annual GDP growth. The economy-wide inventory-to-sales ratio is expected to trend lower over the projection period.

Government Purchases

Federal Government purchases as well as transfers and grants (such as Social Security, Medicare, and Medicaid) contributed to real GDP growth during 2005. Federal purchases contributed 0.2 percentage point at an annual rate to real GDP growth in the first half of the year, and about 0.5 percentage point in the third quarter. Almost all of these contributions were from the defense budget, largely a by-product of the reconstruction and military operations in

Iraq and Afghanistan. Despite the developments in Iraq and the hurricane-relief efforts, however, Federal spending in fiscal year 2005 (which runs from October 2004 to September 2005) was $7 billion below last year's projection in the FY 2006 budget. An additional $62 billion has been authorized so far for hurricane-disaster relief. Although these funds were authorized in FY 2005, the hurricanes struck near the end of the fiscal year, and so most of the funds will be disbursed in FY 2006 and beyond.

Federal Government purchases and the consumer spending that results indirectly from Federal transfers will add to real GDP growth in early 2006. Federal outlays for FY 2006 are likely to increase largely due to hurricane-disaster relief and because of additional funds for reconstruction and counterinsurgency in Iraq.

From FY 2007 forward, however, the impact of Federal outlays is projected to move sharply toward restraint. For example, Federal outlays are projected to shrink by 0.7 percentage point of GDP in FY 2007. The shrinking of the Federal Government's claim on resources should allow private economic activity more room to grow.

Exports and Imports

Real exports grew 5¾ percent during the four quarters of 2005, about the same as export growth in 2004. This reflects the interaction of two offsetting influences: the somewhat faster growth of our trading partners in 2005, which tends to increase the demand for U.S. exports, and the increase in the exchange value of the dollar, which tends to dampen export demand by making U.S. goods relatively more expensive. Real GDP growth among our OECD trading partners picked up a bit to 2.6 percent during the four quarters of 2005 from a 2.1-percent pace in 2004, as computed from the latest OECD projections. Offsetting the effect of stronger foreign growth on our exports was a 7-percent rise in the value of the dollar against major currencies over the 12 months of 2005.

Data on the destination of U.S. exports show the fastest export growth to the most rapidly developing countries and regions such as Asia and Africa. Nevertheless, our OECD trading partners still account for more than two-thirds of our exports.

Growth of our real exports in 2006 and 2007 is likely to be similar to that in 2005, because economic growth in our export markets is likely to be about the same as in 2005. The OECD projects that real GDP growth among our OECD trading partners (2.6 percent during the four quarters of 2005) will be 2.5 percent and 2.8 percent in 2006 and 2007, respectively. Growth of real exports to rapidly developing countries in Asia and Africa will likely continue to be healthy over the next two years as their economic expansion leads them to demand more goods and services from abroad.

Growth in real imports slowed substantially during the four quarters of 2005 to 4.6 percent from 10.6 percent in 2004. Imports grew more slowly than exports during 2005. Import growth was particularly weak in the second and third quarters and was fairly widespread, affecting imports of consumer goods, non-auto capital goods, petroleum products, and services. Imports picked up in the fourth quarter, particularly for petroleum products to replace domestic production lost because of the damage caused by the hurricanes.

The current account deficit (the excess of imports and income flows to foreigners over exports and foreign income of Americans) averaged 6.4 percent of GDP ($790 billion at an annual rate) during the first three quarters of 2005, up from 5.7 percent of GDP during 2004. Recent increases in the deficit reflect faster growth in the United States than among our trading partners, making our imports grow faster than our exports. The longer-term trend also reflects faster growth of domestic investment than domestic saving with foreign saving filling in the gap in financing.

The United States has been able to buy more goods and services than it sells because foreigners have been investing in the United States. The current account deficit of $790 billion also represents the net increase in foreign holdings of U.S. assets (either financial assets or direct ownership of corporations) relative to U.S.-owned assets abroad. In the future, the returns from these foreign-owned U.S. investments (that is, interest, dividends, and reinvested earnings) will themselves add to the current account deficit. These ideas are explored more fully in Chapter 6, The U.S. Capital Account Surplus.

Employment

Nonfarm payroll employment increased by 2.0 million during the 12 months of 2005, an average pace of 168,000 jobs per month. The unemployment rate declined by 0.5 percentage point to 4.9 percent during the 12 months of the year. The average unemployment rate in 2005 (5.1 percent) was below the averages of the 1970s, the 1980s, and the 1990s. During the first eight months of 2005, employment growth averaged 196,000 per month, but dropped to only 21,000 per month in September and October immediately after the hurricanes. The Bureau of Labor Statistics expects a slight downward revision to employment growth over the 12 months ended in March 2005.

Job gains were spread broadly across major industry sectors in 2005. The service-providing sector accounted for 88 percent of job growth during the 12 months of the year, a slightly larger contribution than would be suggested by its 83 percent of overall employment. The goods-producing sector accounted for the remaining 12 percent of the gains, notably weaker than its 17-percent share of overall employment. Within the goods-producing sector, over-the-year employment growth was concentrated in construction and mining, while manufacturing employment decreased for the seventh time in the past eight years.

By educational attainment, the drop in the unemployment rate during 2005 was most pronounced among those without a high school degree; the jobless rate in this group tumbled 0.7 percentage point during the 12 months of the year. By race and ethnicity, the unemployment rate fell the most among blacks and Hispanics, (1.5 and 0.5 percentage points, respectively), in contrast to 0.3 percentage point for whites. By age, the jobless rate fell most among teenagers 16 to 19 years old. By sex, the jobless rate fell more among adult men than adult women. The median duration of unemployment, an indicator that typically follows the business cycle with a substantial lag, declined from 9.4 weeks in December 2004 to 8.5 weeks in December 2005. In general, unemployment rates fell the most in 2005 among those groups with the highest rates at the end of 2004.

The Administration projects that employment will increase at a pace of 176,000 per month on average during the 12 months of 2006—roughly in line with the Philadelphia Federal Reserve Bank's survey of professional fore-casters. The Administration projects the unemployment rate will remain at about 5.0 percent throughout 2006.

Productivity

Labor productivity growth in the nonfarm business sector has been exceptionally vigorous, exceeding the forecasts of most economists. Productivity (real output per hour worked) grew at a 3.4-percent annual rate during the first three quarters of 2005, following similar or higher growth rates during the three preceding years. Since the business-cycle peak in the first quarter of 2001 (a period that includes a recession and a recovery), productivity has grown at an average 3.6-percent annual rate, notably higher than during any comparable 4½-year period since 1948 (Chart 1-3). Although 1995 has been regarded as a watershed year for productivity because of the acceleration of productivity from a 1.5-percent to a 2.4-percent annual rate of growth, the further acceleration to a 3.6-percent annual rate of growth during 2001 to 2005 is even more striking (the precise time periods are shown in Table 1-2, later in this chapter). The 1995-2001 acceleration may be plausibly accounted for by a pickup in capital services per hour worked and by increases in *organizational capital*, the invest-ments businesses make to reorganize and restructure themselves, in this instance in response to newly installed information technology.

In contrast, capital deepening (the increase in capital services per hour worked) does not explain any of the post-2001 increase in productivity; in fact, the growth of capital services per hour worked appears to have fallen off slightly in this period. The post-2001 acceleration in productivity, therefore,

Chart 1-3 **Productivity Growth During Cyclically-Comparable Business Cycle Intervals**
Productivity growth during the first 4½ years since the 2001:Q1 business-cycle peak is as high or higher than during any cyclically-comparable period during the postwar era.
Percent change, annual rate during the 4 ½ years beginning wth each business-cycle peak

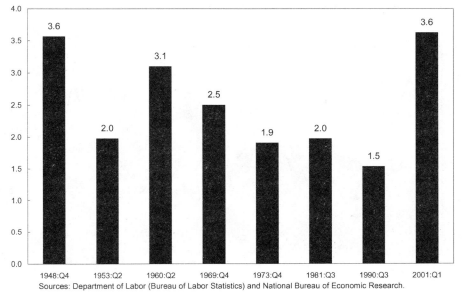

Sources: Department of Labor (Bureau of Labor Statistics) and National Bureau of Economic Research.

appears to be accounted for by factors that are more difficult to measure than the quantity of capital, such as continuing improvements in technology and in business practices.

One curious aspect of productivity acceleration has been its limited spread. Business-sector productivity growth has been higher in the United States than in any other major industrial economy. (Business-sector productivity growth has also been rapid in Ireland, Greece, Korea, Turkey, the Scandinavian countries, and several transitional east-European countries.) As every industrial economy has access to the same technology, the strong U.S. performance suggests that other structural features of the U.S. economy may also play an important role in productivity growth. Some research suggests that, all else equal, countries with more-flexible, less-heavily regulated product and labor markets are better able to translate technological advances into productivity gains.

Rather than assume that the recent remarkable pace of productivity growth will continue, the Administration believes it is prudent to build a budget based on a forecast somewhat lower than the 3.6-percent pace of productivity growth since 2001. Productivity is projected to average 2.6 percent per year during the six-year span of the budget projection—roughly equal to the average annual pace during the past decade.

Chart 1-4 **Inflation**
Core CPI inflation (which excludes food and energy) has remained moderate and stable in the face of the recent uptick in overall CPI inflation.

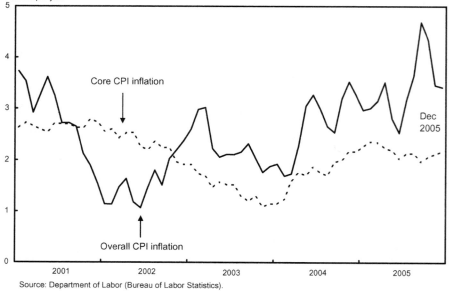

Percent per year

Source: Department of Labor (Bureau of Labor Statistics).

Wages and Prices

As measured by the Consumer Price Index (CPI), overall inflation increased in 2005 to 3.4 percent from 3.3 percent during the 12 months of 2004. Rapid increases in energy prices (16.6 percent and 17.1 percent in 2004 and 2005, respectively) elevated the level of overall inflation in both years. The four major energy subindexes (gasoline, fuel oil, natural gas, and electricity) all posted large increases in 2005, with prices of natural gas and electricity advancing faster than in the preceding year. Food price inflation, at 2.3 percent, was moderate and little changed from the year-earlier pace. Core CPI prices (which exclude the prices of food and energy) increased 2.2 percent during 2005, substantially below the overall inflation rate and the same as the year-earlier pace.

Labor costs (which comprise about 62 percent of the costs of nonfarm business) have been stable, or possibly trending lower. Hourly compensation for workers in private industry increased at a 3.0-percent annual rate during the 12 months ended in September 2005 down from 3.7 percent during the year-earlier period according to the Employment Cost Index (ECI), which is compiled from the National Compensation Survey (NCS). The deceleration occurred in both wages and salaries (with growth down to 2.2 percent from 2.6 percent in the year-earlier period) and hourly benefits (which slowed to 4.8 percent from 6.8 percent). The slowing in hourly benefits was accounted for primarily by smaller increases in contributions to defined-benefit pension programs in 2005 than in 2004 according to other tabulations from the NCS. Hourly benefits have increased notably faster than hourly wages and salaries in each of the past four years. Another measure of hourly compensation published by the Department of Labor and derived from the national income and product accounts (NIPA) has increased notably faster than the ECI measure, rising 5.0 percent during the four quarters ended in the third quarter of 2005. The difference between these two measures may be partly attributable to the exercise of stock options which are included in the NIPA-derived measure at the time they are exercised, but are not recorded by the NCS.

With hourly compensation growing in the 3.0 percent-to-5.0 percent range (depending on the index) and labor productivity growth at about 3.0 percent, trend unit labor costs have barely changed, with increases in the range from 0 percent to 2 percent. Because unit labor costs have increased by less than the 2.9-percent increase in the GDP price index during the four quarters through the third quarter of 2005, labor costs do not appear to be putting upward pressure on inflation.

An important determinant of inflation during the next year is likely to be energy prices, whose run-up during the past two years has been the main reason for the increase in inflation. Futures markets suggest roughly stable oil and natural gas prices, which (if they come to pass) will remove some of the upward pressure on the overall inflation rate.

Although some measures of short-run inflation expectations increased around the third quarter of 2005, they fell back later in the year. More importantly, a variety of longer-term measures of inflation expectations have been approximately stable during the past two years, including those derived from the market for Treasury Inflation-Protected Securities (TIPS) and the University of Michigan consumer survey (Chart 1-5). History suggests that the stability of inflation expectations promotes stability in actual inflation as well as in the overall economy.

The Administration expects CPI inflation to stabilize at 2.4 percent during the next several years, up only slightly from the 2.2 percent increase in the core CPI during the 12 months through December. The projected path of inflation as measured by the GDP price index is similar, but a bit lower. Inflation by this measure is projected at 2.2 percent during the four quarters of 2006 and 2007, down from the 3.0-percent increase during 2005. These inflation projections are very close to those of a year ago, and are also very close to those of the consensus of professional forecasters.

The "wedge," or difference, between the CPI and the GDP measures of inflation has implications for the Federal budget projections. A larger wedge (with the CPI rising faster than the GDP price index) raises the Federal budget deficit because cost-of-living programs rise with the CPI, while Federal revenue tends to increase with the GDP price index. For a given level

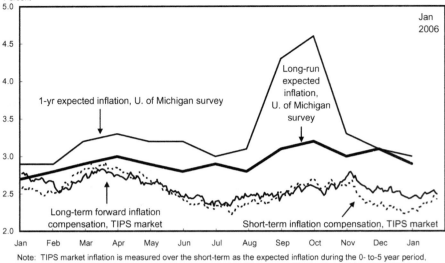

Chart 1-5 **Survey and Market Measures of Expected Inflation in 2005 and 2006**
Although 1-year consumer expectations spiked around October, consumers' long-term expectations and expectations derived from the TIPS market remained moderate and stable.

Note: TIPS market inflation is measured over the short-term as the expected inflation during the 0- to-5 year period, and long-term forward inflation is measured from 5 years out to 10 years out. The long-term University of Michigan expectation is from 0 to 5-10 years out.
Sources: Federal Reserve and University of Michigan survey of consumer sentiment.

of nominal income, increases in the CPI also cut Federal revenue because they raise income tax brackets and affect other inflation-indexed features of the tax code. Of the two indexes, the CPI tends to increase faster in part because it measures the price of a fixed basket of goods. In contrast, the GDP price index increases less rapidly because it allows for households and businesses shifting their purchases away from items with increasing relative prices and toward items with decreasing relative prices. Among other differences, the GDP price index places a larger weight than does the CPI on computers, which tend to decline in price (on a quality-adjusted basis). In addition, the CPI places a much larger weight on energy.

During the 13 years ended in 2004, the wedge between inflation in the CPI-U-RS (a historical CPI series designed to be consistent with current CPI methods) and the rate of change in the GDP price index averaged 0.36 percent per year. The wedge was particularly high during the first three quarters of 2005 when the CPI increased 1 percentage point faster than the GDP price index; this difference reflected the roughly 50-percent annual rate of increase in crude oil prices, which have a larger weight in consumer prices than in GDP as a whole. Since domestic production accounts for only about 35 percent of U.S. oil consumption, the weight of oil prices in GDP is roughly one-third of its weight in consumption. As this boost from higher oil prices unwinds over the next couple of years, the wedge between the CPI and GDP inflation is likely to be lower than average. From 2008, the wedge is projected to average 0.3 percentage point.

Financial Markets

The Wilshire 5000 (a broad stock price index) increased 4.6 percent during 2005, the third consecutive year of stock market gains following three years of declines. The 2005 increase was well below the gains of the two preceding years.

Short-term interest rates increased during the year as the Federal Reserve's Open Market Committee raised the target Federal funds rate by 25 basis points at each of its eight meetings. As a consequence, rates on 91-day Treasury bills rose 1.7 percentage points during the year.

Despite the increases in short-term rates, yields on 10-year Treasury notes remained low, increasing only 24 basis points during the 12 months of 2005 (Chart 1-6). The low level of long-term interest rates was due, in part, to low and stable long-run inflation expectations. At the end of 2005 the gap between the yield on 10-year Treasuries and the rate on 91-day Treasury bills was only about 0.6 percentage point, noticeably lower than its historical average. (The yield on longer-term Treasury notes is usually higher than on shorter-term notes because the market compensates investors for the extra risk of holding longer-term securities.)

Chart 1-6 **10-Year Treasury Yield**
Yields on 10-year Treasury notes remained near decade lows during 2005 in the face of sharp increases in short-term rates.
Percent per annum

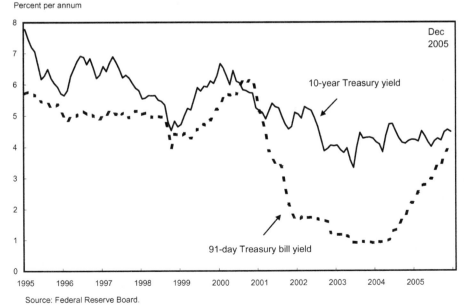

Source: Federal Reserve Board.

Yields on corporate bonds also remained low and the spread between yields on corporate bonds (which carry more risk) and the yields on more-secure obligations of the U.S. Treasury remained small. Measured relative to Treasury obligations of similar maturities, the yields on corporate bonds rated "BAA" (about average quality) by Moody's Investor Services remained near their lowest levels over the past decade (Chart 1-7). This suggests that the perceived default risk of U.S. corporations remains low.

The Long-Term Outlook Through 2011

The U.S. economy continues to be well positioned for long-term growth. The Administration projects that real GDP will expand at about its potential rate (between 3.1 percent and 3.3 percent per year) through 2011, inflation will remain low and stable (with the CPI increasing at around 2.4 percent per year), and the labor market will remain firm (Table 1-1). The forecast is based on conservative economic assumptions that are close to the consensus of professional forecasters. These assumptions provide a prudent and cautious basis for the Administration's budget projections.

Chart 1-7 **Corporate Bond Yield Spreads**
In 2005, the spread between the yield on average quality (Baa-rated) corporate securities and Treasury notes were at the low end of the past decade's range.

Percentage points per annum

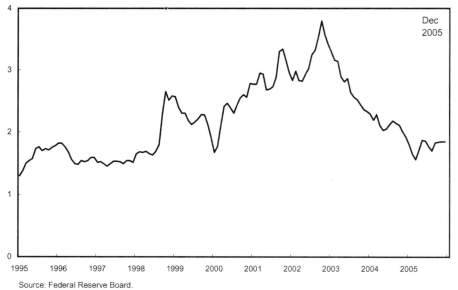

Source: Federal Reserve Board.

TABLE 1-1.—*Administration Forecast* [1]

Year	Nominal GDP	Real GDP (chain-type)	GDP price index (chain-type)	Consumer price index (CPI-U)	Unemploy-ment rate (percent)	Interest rate, 91-day Treasury bills [2] (percent)	Interest rate, 10-year Treasury notes (percent)	Nonfarm payroll employ-ment (millions)	Nonfarm payroll employ-ment (average monthly change, Q4-to-Q4 thousands)
	Percent change, Q4-to-Q4				Level, calendar year				
2004 (actual)...	6.8	3.8	2.9	3.4	5.5	1.4	4.3	131.5	178
2005	6.4	3.5	2.8	3.8	5.1	3.2	4.3	133.6	160
2006	5.6	3.4	2.2	2.4	5.0	4.2	5.0	135.5	176
2007	5.6	3.3	2.2	2.4	5.0	4.2	5.3	137.4	140
2008	5.4	3.2	2.1	2.4	5.0	4.3	5.5	139.0	139
2009	5.3	3.1	2.1	2.4	5.0	4.3	5.6	140.7	132
2010	5.3	3.1	2.1	2.4	5.0	4.3	5.6	142.2	127
2011	5.3	3.1	2.2	2.5	5.0	4.3	5.6	143.7	126

[1] Based on data available as of November 15, 2005.

[2] Discount basis.

Sources: Council of Economic Advisers, Department of Commerce (Bureau of Economic Analysis), Department of Labor (Bureau of Labor Statistics), Department of the Treasury, and Office of Management and Budget.

Growth in GDP over the Long Term

The Administration projects that real GDP will grow at a slowly diminishing rate from 2005 through 2009, decelerating year by year from a forecasted 3.5-percent rate during the four quarters of 2005 to 3.1 percent in 2009, roughly in line with the consensus forecast for those years. The year-by-year pace is close to the estimated growth rate of potential real GDP growth (a measure of the rate of growth of productive capacity). The unemployment rate is projected to remain flat at 5.0 percent. As discussed below, potential GDP growth is expected to slow in the near term as productivity growth reverts toward its long-run trend, and potential GDP is expected to slow further during the 2007-to-2011 period as labor force growth declines.

The projected growth of potential real GDP, 3¼ percent during the next two years, is in line with recent experience. Potential growth is the rate of real GDP growth that can be achieved while the unemployment rate remains stable. For example, during the past four years (from the third quarter of 2001 to the third quarter of 2005) real GDP growth was 3.22 percent at an annual rate while the unemployment rate was unchanged—on net—at about 5 percent.

The growth rate of the economy over the long run is determined by its supply-side components, which include population, labor force participation, the ratio of nonfarm business employment to household employment, the workweek, and the growth in output per hour. The Administration's forecast for the contribution of the growth rates of different supply-side factors to real GDP growth is shown in Table 1-2. As can be seen in the fourth column of the table, the mix of supply-side factors determining real GDP growth has been unusual since the business-cycle peak at the beginning of 2001, with the exceptionally high productivity growth (3.6 percent at an annual rate) partially offset by declines in the participation rate (line 2) and the workweek (line 8). Also puzzling is the large decline in the ratio of nonfarm business employment to household employment (line 6). This unusual decline reflects the slow growth of employment

TABLE 1-2.— *Supply-Side Components of Real GDP Growth, 1953–2011*

[Average annual percent change]

Item	1953 Q2 to 1973 Q4	1973 Q4 to 1995 Q2	1995 Q2 to 2001 Q1	2001 Q1 to 2005 Q3	2005 Q3 to 2011 Q4
1) Civilian noninstitutional population aged 16+[1]	1.6	1.4	1.2	1.2	1.1
2) Plus: Civilian labor force participation rate	0.2	0.4	0.1	-0.3	-0.1
3) Equals: Civilian labor force[2]	1.8	1.8	1.4	0.9	1.0
4) Plus: Civilian employment rate	-0.1	0.0	0.3	-0.2	0.0
5) Equals: Civilian employment[2]	1.7	1.8	1.7	0.7	1.0
6) Plus: Nonfarm business employment as a share of civilian employment[2][3]	-0.1	0.1	0.4	-0.8	0.1
7) Equals: Nonfarm business employment............................	1.6	1.9	2.0	-0.1	1.0
8) Plus: Average weekly hours (nonfarm business)...............	-0.3	-0.3	-0.1	-0.3	-0.1
9) Equals: Hours of all persons (nonfarm business)................	1.3	1.6	1.9	-0.4	1.0
10) Plus: Output per hour (productivity, nonfarm business)	2.5	1.5	2.4	3.6	2.6
11) Equals: Nonfarm business output......................................	3.8	3.1	4.3	3.2	3.6
12) Plus: Ratio of real GDP to nonfarm business output[4]	-0.2	-0.2	-0.5	-0.4	-0.4
13) Equals: Real GDP	3.6	2.8	3.8	2.8	3.2

[1] Adjusted by CEA to smooth discontinuities in the population series since 1990.

[2] BLS research series adjusted to smooth irregularities in the population series since 1990.

[3] Line 6 translates the civilian employment growth rate into the nonfarm business employment growth rate.

[4] Line 12 translates nonfarm business output back into output for all sectors (GDP), which includes the output of farms and general government.

Note: 1953 Q2, 1973 Q4, and 2001 Q1 are NBER business-cycle peaks. Detail may not add to total because of rounding.

Sources: Council of Economic Advisers, Department of Commerce (Bureau of Economic Analysis), and Department of Labor (Bureau of Labor Statistics).

as measured by the payroll survey (which asks employers to report the number of employees) relative to the more-rapid growth of employment as measured by the household survey (in which people report the employment status of their household members)—a disparity that has not yet been explained.

The participation rate fell from 2001 to 2005, and is projected to trend lower through 2011. The recent behavior stands in contrast to the long period of increase from 1960 through 1996 (Chart 1-8). The participation rate appears to have topped out in 1997-2000 before declining. The reversal of direction reflects nothing new about the participation rate for men, which continued a downward trend that began shortly after the end of World War II. Rather, the new factor at play is the change in the trend in the female participation rate, which has edged down on balance since 2000 after having risen for five decades.

Another factor in the decline in the labor force participation rate has been the increase in the number of workers collecting insurance for disability retirement. The 0.5-percentage point increase (as a share of the working-age population) since 2000 accounts for about half of the overall decline, and appears to be largely a reflection of increases in the number of workers entering high-disability ages (50+ years old).

Chart 1-8 **Labor Force Participation Rate and Disabled Workers Relative to Population**
Female particpation rates have peaked, while men's rates continue downward. Increases in disability account for some of the recent decline in the overall participation rate.

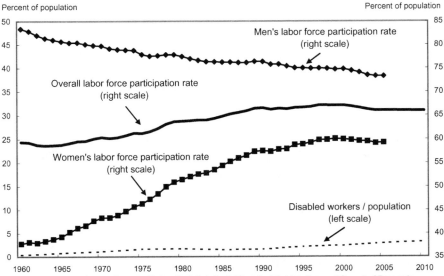

Sources: Department of Labor (Bureau of Labor Statistics), Social Security Administration, and Council of Economic Advisers.

Looking ahead, the participation rate is projected to decline slowly, reflecting the aging of the baby-boom cohorts, leading to more retirements and a likely increase in the share of disabled workers. Baby boomers are currently in their forties and fifties, and over the next several years they will move into older age brackets which typically have lower participation rates. The decline in the participation rate may quicken after 2008 when the first baby-boom cohort reaches Social Security's early retirement age of 62.

Interest Rates over the Near and Long Term

The Administration forecast of interest rates is based on financial market data as well as results of a survey of economic forecasters. As of November 15, 2005, the date that the forecast was finalized, trading in financial futures suggested that market participants expected short-term interest rates to rise a bit further, and the Administration's interest-rate projections reflect those views. Taking its cue from financial futures markets, the Administration projects the rate on 91-day Treasury bills to increase to about 4.2 percent by 2007 and to about 4.3 percent from 2008 to 2011. At that level, the real interest rate on 91-day Treasury bills will be close to its historical average.

The yield on 10-year Treasury notes on November 14 was 4.61 percent, just 68 basis points above the (discount) rate on 91-day Treasury bills. This difference was very low relative to its historical average, and the Administration expects it to increase gradually during the six-year forecast period. As a result, yields on 10-year notes are expected to increase somewhat further, reaching a plateau at 5.6 percent from 2009 onward.

The Composition of Income over the Long Term

A primary purpose of the Administration's economic forecast is to estimate future government revenues, which requires a projection of the components of taxable income. The Administration's income-side projection is based on the historical stability of the long-run labor compensation and capital share of gross domestic income (GDI). (GDI is the sum of all income components and differs from GDP only by measurement error—which can be substantial.) During the first three quarters of 2005, the labor compensation share of GDI was 57.6 percent (according to the advance data available when the projection was finalized), slightly below its 1963-2004 average of 58.1 percent. From this jump-off point, the labor share is projected to slowly rise to 58.1 percent by 2011.

The labor compensation share of GDI consists of wages and salaries (which are taxable), nonwage compensation (employer contributions to employee pension and insurance funds—which are not taxable), and employer contributions to social insurance (which are not taxable). The Administration forecasts that the wage and salary share of compensation will be roughly stable during the budget window. One of the main factors boosting nonwage compensation during 2002-2004 was employer contributions to defined-benefit pension plans. As noted earlier, the National Compensation Survey for 2005 shows a moderation of these contributions, suggesting that the period of very rapid catch-up contributions may be behind us.

The capital share of GDI is expected to edge down from its currently high level before stabilizing near its historical average. Within the capital share, depreciation is expected to increase (a result of the strong growth of investment during the past three years). After adjusting for the temporary effects of the hurricanes, profits in the third quarter of 2005 were about 11.6 percent of GDI, well above their post-1959 average.

Book profits (known in the national income and product accounts as "profits before tax") jumped up in the first quarter of 2005 in large part because of the termination of the temporary provision for expensing of equipment investment under the Job Creation and Worker Assistance Act of 2002 and the Jobs and Growth Tax Relief and Reconciliation Act of 2003. These expensing provisions reduced taxable profits from the third quarter of 2001 through the fourth quarter of 2004. The legacy of these expensing provisions increases book profits from 2005 forward, however, because investment goods expensed during the three-year expensing window will have less remaining value to depreciate. The share of other taxable income (the sum of rent, dividends, proprietors' income, and personal interest income) is projected to fall in coming years, mainly because of the delayed effects of past declines in long-term interest rates, which reduce personal interest income during the projection period. In addition, rental income has been—and is projected to continue—trending down as a share of GDI.

Conclusion

The economy has shifted from recovery to sustained expansion, having absorbed the effects of the third-quarter hurricanes and large increases in energy prices. The economy is projected to settle into a steady state in which GDP grows at its potential rate, the unemployment rate remains flat at a low level, and inflation remains moderate and stable. Consumer spending remains strong, businesses are continuing to invest, and exports are growing faster than domestic production. Having said this, we must remember that economic forecasting is difficult, and no doubt unforeseen positive and negative developments will affect the course of the economy over the next few years. Given the economy's fundamental strengths, however, prospects remain good for continued growth in the years ahead. Nevertheless, much work remains in making our economy as productive as possible. Later chapters of this *Report* explore how pro-growth policies, such as improving incentives in health care, promoting free trade, reforming our retirement and tax systems, and boosting the skills of the U.S. workforce can enhance our economic performance.

CHAPTER 2

Skills for the U.S. Workforce

A strong U.S. economy requires a skilled and well-educated workforce that is prepared to meet the challenges presented by a rapidly changing world economy. Research has found, for example, that countries with higher levels of education and higher average math and science test scores experience faster economic growth. For more than a half-century, the United States experienced an extraordinary rise in education levels and still maintains one of the best-educated populations in the world. But in recent years, improvements in educational attainment have slowed. Today, for example, younger Americans are less educated, on average, than their counterparts in a number of advanced countries. In addition, U.S. high school students also score below students in most other advanced countries in their math and science skills. To remain competitive in the global economy, the United States needs to improve the education and skills of its residents and prepare them for jobs that will be available in the future.

This chapter discusses the importance of the education and skill levels of the U.S. workforce, the contributions of legal immigrants to the skills of the U.S. workforce, and the importance of upgrading workforce skills through job training. The key points of this chapter are:

- Education is a key contributor to economic growth and individual income.
- Advances in education levels have slowed over the past 25 years. This slowdown could jeopardize the U.S. standard of living in years to come.
- Legal immigrants make up a vital part of the U.S. economy, particularly in the science and engineering sectors.
- Workers need to continually upgrade their skills if they are to adapt to and take part in a continually changing economy.

By setting its sights on improving the education and skills of U.S. workers, the United States can create a workforce that will thrive in the fast-changing world economy.

Educational Achievement in the United States

Both economic research and common sense suggest that workers' skills play a critical role in economic growth and individual well-being. In the past, rapid increases in schooling levels helped to raise the U.S. standard of living, but in recent years improvements in educational attainment have slowed. Unless the United States can improve the educational achievement of its residents, it may be difficult to sustain rapid economic growth in the future.

Workforce Skills and the U.S. Standard of Living

Education and Income

Economic research suggests that educational attainment and test scores are important at both the individual and the national level. At the individual level, people with higher levels of education have higher earnings than people with less education. In 2004, workers with a bachelor's degree only (no advanced degree) earned almost $23,000 more per year on average than workers with a high school degree only (see Table 2-1). These differences have grown over time: In 1975, workers with only a bachelor's degree earned $14,220 more per year (in 2004 dollars) than high-school educated workers. According to a U.S. Census Bureau study, over his or her lifetime, a worker with only a bachelor's degree earns nearly $1 million more (in 2004 dollars) than a worker with a high school degree only.

In addition to income, schooling levels are associated with other positive economic and social outcomes. More-educated adults are less likely to be unemployed or incarcerated than less-educated adults. More-educated adults are healthier and have lower mortality rates than less-educated adults. They are also more likely to have college-educated children, thereby passing the benefits of higher levels of education on to future generations.

Studies have also shown that higher test scores are associated with higher wages and more years of schooling. High school students with higher test scores are more likely to attend college and, if they attend, are more likely to graduate. Controlling for individuals' educational attainment and family background, those who score higher on achievement tests in high school have higher wages later in life.

TABLE 2-1.—*Average Annual Earnings by Education (2004 dollars)*

	1975	1990	2000	2004
Bachelor's degree only	39,065	43,591	54,396	51,568
High school degree only	24,845	24,968	28,179	28,631
$ difference	14,220	18,623	26,217	22,937
% difference	57%	75%	93%	80%

Note: Data refer to all workers aged 18 and older.
Source: Department of Commerce (Bureau of the Census).

Education and U.S. Standard of Living

Higher schooling levels and test scores do not just improve individual outcomes, they also raise the standard of living for the country as a whole. More-skilled workers are typically better at identifying, adapting, and implementing ideas that lead to higher productivity growth. Productivity growth raises the standard of living because it leads to real increases in workers' wages. Research has found that, all else equal, countries with higher levels of education and higher average math and science test scores experience faster economic growth. A recent study of U.S. growth between 1950 and 1993 found that one-third of productivity growth over this period was due to increased levels of education.

Education and skills are critical for economic growth, but other factors, such as openness to trade and government institutions that protect private property, are also important. The United States tends to score highly in these areas compared with its international peers, which may help to explain why the United States has experienced faster economic growth than most other advanced countries over the last decade.

Educational Attainment

For more than a half-century, education levels have been rising in the United States. In 2004, about 85 percent of adults aged 25 and older reported that they had completed high school; 28 percent of adults had attained a bachelor's degree or higher (see Chart 2-1). This is an extraordinary rise since the mid-twentieth century, when only about 36 percent of adults had a high school diploma and around 6 percent had a bachelor's degree or higher.

This rapid rise in educational attainment came about mainly because, for many years, each generation was more educated than the one before: Each generation was more likely than the previous one to have completed high school or attained a bachelor's degree. As older, less-educated workers retired and younger, more-educated workers entered the workforce, the overall education level of the U.S. workforce grew rapidly.

Over the past 25 years, however, this pattern has changed. According to some measures, younger generations have been no more educated than previous ones. The share of U.S. residents aged 25–29 who have completed high school has remained relatively constant over this time, staying within a range of about 85 percent to 88 percent (see Chart 2-1). Over the same period, the manner in which people complete high school has changed. People counted as having completed high school include both those who graduate from high school and those who receive a General Education Development (GED) certificate or another alternative to a regular high school diploma. (The GED is a certificate awarded to applicants who pass a specific, approved, high-school equivalency exam.) Over time, GED recipients have made up an increasing share of this group. In 1999, of 18- to 24-year-olds who had completed high school, about 11 percent obtained a high school credential via a GED, up from 5 percent in 1988. While GED recipients are counted as people who have completed high school, studies suggest that they are not equivalent to high school graduates in their economic outcomes. For instance, GED recipients have lower earnings and are less likely to obtain post-secondary education than are high school graduates. These differences in economic outcomes are of concern given that GED recipients make up an increasing share of those who have completed high school.

Unlike the share of people who have completed high school, the share of people aged 25–29 who have a bachelor's degree or higher has continued to rise. This share, however, is rising more slowly than it was 25 years ago. Over the past 25 years, it rose 6 percentage points, from 23 percent in 1979 to 29 percent in 2004. In contrast, in the 25 years prior to 1979, it increased by about 13 percentage points, or more than twice as much.

Although schooling levels, already relatively high in the United States, cannot grow indefinitely, international comparisons of educational attainment suggest that the United States still has great potential for increases in the schooling levels of its residents. These comparisons show that younger U.S. residents have lower levels of education than their counterparts in a number of other advanced

Chart 2-1 **Educational Attainment by Age, 1947–2004**
Schooling levels are no longer rising as quickly as in the 1950s and 1960s among people aged 25–29.

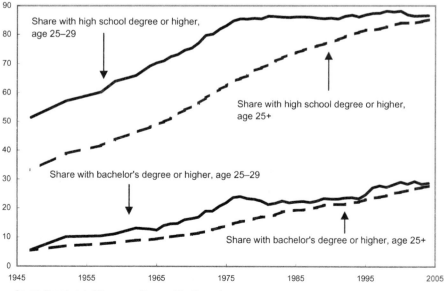

Source: Department of Commerce (Bureau of the Census).

countries. In 2002, for example, half of young people in Canada and Japan had attained a college degree (an associate's or bachelor's degree or higher), compared with 39 percent of young people in the United States.

Many students exit college without obtaining a bachelor's degree. In 2004, about one-quarter of adults had attended a post-secondary institution but had not completed a bachelor's degree. People who complete some college without obtaining a bachelor's degree are a diverse group. Some attain an academic or vocational associate's degree or certificate, while others drop out of college without completing a single semester. Some attend a four-year college, while others go to two-year community colleges. Among those with some college but no bachelor's degree, many began college immediately after completing high school, while others are older workers who return to school for additional training.

Educational Attainment by Race, Ethnicity, and Gender

Women tend to be more educated than men. Women are more likely to have completed high school or obtained a bachelor's degree or higher. In 2004, for example, about 31 percent of 25- to 29-year-old women had a bachelor's degree or higher, compared with 26 percent of their male counterparts (see Table 2-2). This is a fairly recent trend: Until 1991, men in this age group were more likely than women to have a bachelor's degree or higher.

Educational attainment differs widely by race and ethnicity. More than 90 percent of non-Hispanic white and Asian 25- to 29-year-olds have completed high school, compared with 88 percent of blacks and 62 percent of Hispanics in that age group (see Table 2-2). Racial and ethnic differences are even larger for college completion: Among 25- to 29-year-olds, about 61 percent of Asians have a bachelor's degree or higher, compared with 35 percent of non-Hispanic whites, 17 percent of blacks, and 11 percent of Hispanics.

TABLE 2-2.— *Educational Attainment by Race, Ethnicity, and Gender, 2004*

	Share with high school degree or higher	Share with bachelor's degree or higher
Total	87	29
Non-Hispanic white	93	35
Black	88	17
Hispanic	62	11
Asian	96	61
Men	85	26
Women	88	31

Note: Data refer to noninstitutionalized population aged 25–29. Since data exclude incarcerated population, they likely overstate educational attainment of U.S. residents.

Sources: Department of Commerce (Bureau of the Census).

Schooling levels differ between natives and immigrants. In 2004, for example, half of all adult Asian immigrants had completed a bachelor's degree or higher, compared with 28 percent of the overall adult U.S.-born population. Latin American immigrants tend to have lower levels of schooling while their children tend to improve upon the education attained by their parents. According to the National Center for Education Statistics, for example, about 50 percent of Latin American immigrants aged 18–24 had completed high school, while the high-school completion rate was 78 percent among their U.S.-born children of the same age.

Math, Science, and Reading Skills in the United States and Around the World

Educational attainment is an important measure of the preparedness of a nation's workforce, but it does not tell the whole story: Two people with the same level of education may have very different skill levels. Similarly, a high school diploma may not ensure that a student is competent in all areas. The fact that growth in schooling has slowed in the United States might be less worrisome if it were balanced by an improvement among the U.S. population in other measures of skills.

One way in which the United States monitors the academic preparedness and skills of its students is through standardized tests of math, science, and reading. The United States participates in several national and international tests for elementary and high school students. These tests shed light on how the math, science, and reading skills of U.S. students compare to those of students in other countries.

Table 2-3 ranks advanced countries by students' scores on math and science tests at different ages. The countries are ranked by average score, with the highest scorers at the top. Not all countries participate in every test. So that the country rankings can be compared at different ages, only countries that participated in at least half of the tests are included in the table.

As the table shows, older U.S. students do worse relative to other advanced countries than younger U.S. students do. At ages 9 and 13, the United States generally places above the middle of the rankings on math and science tests. By age 15, however, U.S. students are outperformed by most of their international peers. Among students in their last year of secondary school, U.S. students are at or near the bottom of the rankings. Country rankings from international tests in reading, not shown in Table 2-3, are only available at ages 9 and 15. In rankings of advanced countries similar to those shown in Table 2-3 for math and science, U.S. students score above the middle of the rankings in reading at age 9 but fall below the middle by age 15.

TABLE 2-3.— *Rankings of Selected Advanced Countries by Average Score on International Tests*

Age 9		Age 13		Age 15		Last year of secondary school	
Math	Science	Math	Science	Math	Science	Math	Science
Hong Kong	Japan	Hong Kong	Hong Kong	Hong Kong	Japan	Netherlands	Sweden
Japan	Hong Kong	Japan	Japan	Netherlands	Hong Kong	Sweden	Netherlands
Netherlands	**USA**	Netherlands	Netherlands	Japan	Australia	Norway	Norway
USA	Netherlands	Australia	**USA**	Canada	Netherlands	France	Canada
Italy	Australia	**USA**	Australia	Australia	New Zealand	New Zealand	New Zealand
Australia	New Zealand	Sweden	Sweden	New Zealand	Canada	Australia	Australia
New Zealand	Italy	New Zealand	New Zealand	France	France	Canada	Germany
Norway	Norway	Italy	Norway	Sweden	Sweden	Germany	France
		Norway	Italy	Germany	Germany	Italy	**USA**
				Norway	**USA**	**USA**	Italy
				USA	Italy		
				Italy	Norway		

Note: The last year of secondary school is 12th grade in the United States but varies in other countries. In countries that track students, students in all tracks were tested in their last year of secondary school; the last year may differ within countries for students on different tracks. Students who dropped out of school before the last year of secondary school were not tested. Data are for 2003 except for last year of secondary school (1995).

Source: Department of Education (National Center for Education Statistics).

The United States has also conducted tests of its 9-, 13-, and 17-year-olds in math and reading going back to the early 1970s. These test results show that elementary school student scores have improved since the early 1970s, especially in math, but the math and reading scores of 17-year-olds are essentially unchanged. This discrepancy means that the United States has failed to translate test-score gains among younger students into higher scores among older students. There is little consensus as to why test scores have not improved more among older students, but understanding the mechanisms would be an important step in raising their educational achievement.

School Accountability and No Child Left Behind

In recent years, as a result of state initiatives and the No Child Left Behind Act, states have implemented plans to enhance school accountability, with the aim of improving student achievement. Under these "strict accountability" plans, schools can be sanctioned (such as through loss of funding or mandatory restructuring) if their students do not meet performance standards. In order for school accountability to work, student achievement must be measured in a quantifiable way that is comparable across students and schools. This measurement is normally done through standardized tests, which are used to quantify school quality in order to identify low-performing schools. These tests allow parents to make meaningful comparisons between schools and make informed decisions about the schools in which to enroll their children.

Rigorous research into the effects of school accountability on student performance is limited, but the results are promising. For instance, a 2004 study found that states implementing school accountability during the 1990s experienced greater increases in students' test scores afterward than states without accountability. This study further found that only strict school accountability led to higher student achievement.

In January 2002, the President signed into law the No Child Left Behind (NCLB) Act, with the purpose of improving the performance of U.S. students. NCLB aims to make schools more accountable for the performance of their students. Under NCLB, each state sets standards for what students in grades 3–8 should know in math and reading. (Science assessments will be added by the 2007–2008 school year.) States must measure students' progress toward those standards through standardized tests. Schools must meet not only an overall annual performance goal but also specific performance goals for subgroups of students, such as racial, ethnic, and income groups. Schools that do not eventually meet performance goals must allow students to transfer to another public school, including charter schools, within the school district and must offer supplemental educational services to students attending schools in need of improvement.

NCLB accountability based on test scores mostly applies to grades 3–8. Testing is now required only once in high school. The President has proposed expanding accountability in high schools by requiring assessments in reading and math for students in grades 9, 10, and 11. Expansion of testing in high schools could help our high school students improve their performance relative to their counterparts in other nations.

Immigrants in the U.S. Workforce

Legal immigrants are a critical part of the U.S. workforce. Although both low- and high-skilled immigrants contribute to the U.S. economy, this chapter focuses on high-skilled immigrants. Chapter 4 of the 2005 *Economic Report of the President* covered immigration in greater depth, with a particular focus on illegal immigrants, who tend to be low-skilled, as well as the fiscal impact of immigration, immigrants and the U.S. labor market, and immigration policy and the enforcement of immigration laws.

Immigrants living in the United States can be divided into four groups: *naturalized American citizens*, immigrants who have become citizens by passing a citizenship test and fulfilling other requirements; *permanent residents*, immigrants who have "green cards" and the legal right to reside permanently in the United States but have not become naturalized citizens; *temporary residents*, people admitted to the United States temporarily for a specific purpose, including visitors, students, and temporary workers (referred to as *nonimmigrants* by immigration authorities); and illegal immigrants, people residing in the United States illegally. This chapter uses the terms *immigrant* and *foreign-born* according to the Census Bureau's definition: Any person who is in the United States who was not a U.S. citizen at birth, that is, was not born in the United States or of U.S. parents.

Immigrants are prevalent in every education group but are particularly represented among the least-educated workers (those with less than a high school degree) and among the most-educated workers (those with a doctoral or professional degree). As U.S. workers have become more educated and increasingly work in jobs requiring higher education levels, many low-skilled jobs continue to be filled by immigrants. At the same time, high-skilled immigrant workers are a significant part of the skilled U.S. workforce, especially in the science and engineering fields. Many of the nation's university and private research laboratories rely heavily on immigrant graduate students, post-doctoral students, and researchers.

Immigrants in Science and Engineering

Innovation is crucial to U.S. economic growth and competitiveness, and the United States is a leading innovator. Innovation depends, in part, on scientific research, which in turn requires smart, creative people proficient in science and technology. One way in which the United States is able to maintain its position as a leader in innovation is by attracting the best and the brightest from around the world. Policies that welcome the world's "best and brightest" can contribute to future U.S. competitiveness. More than one-fifth of America's scientists and engineers come from abroad.

Chart 2-2 shows the share of immigrants among scientists and engineers aged 25–44 by education in 1996 and 2002. Immigrants tend to come to the United States as young adults, not as older workers. As the younger, more-recent immigrants age, they should make up a larger share of older workers as well. Thus, restricting Chart 2-2 to workers aged 25–44 provides a glimpse at the future of the U.S. scientific workforce.

Immigrants make up an increasing share of the scientific workforce (see Chart 2-2). In 2002, immigrants made up about 24 percent of scientists and engineers aged 25–44, an increase from 17 percent in 1996. The higher the education level, the larger the share of immigrants: Among scientists and engineers with only a bachelor's degree, 17 percent were immigrants (up from 11 percent in 1996), while among those with doctoral or professional degrees, 43 percent were foreign-born (up from 38 percent in 1996). Immigrants are especially prevalent in the fields of engineering and math/computer science and in the physical/biological sciences. Among those aged 25–44 with professional or doctoral degrees and working in these fields, immigrants made up about half of workers.

Chart 2-2 **Foreign-born Share of Employment by Education among Scientists and Engineers, 1996–2002**
Immigrants are over-represented among scientists and engineers.

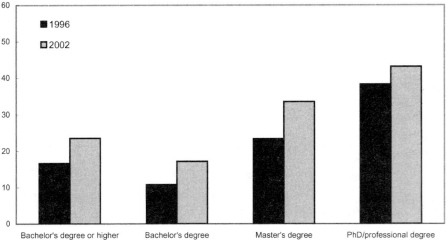

Percent

Note: Data refer to people aged 25–44 and exclude post-secondary teachers. The ending year for this chart is 2002 because occupational definitions were changed after 2002; the post-2002 occupational categories are not comparable to earlier data.
Source: Department of Labor (Bureau of Labor Statistics).

International Science and Engineering Students

The United States is a top destination for science and engineering students from around the world. In 2003, almost 150,000 students from abroad were enrolled in science and engineering graduate programs at U.S. universities. Nonetheless, new enrollment of such students has been falling. Between 2001 and 2003 (the latest year available), first-time international graduate student enrollment in U.S. science and engineering programs declined by 13 percent. This decline may be the result of increased training opportunities in other countries and visa restrictions for foreign students and scholars put in place in the United States following the September 11, 2001, terrorist attacks.

After completing their studies in the United States, some students return to their countries of origin and others join the U.S. workforce. According to the National Science Foundation, about three-quarters of non-U.S. citizens who obtain science and engineering doctorates from U.S. universities plan to stay in the United States, at least for the short term. In order to remain and work in the United States, these students must get temporary work visas or become permanent residents. This process is described in more detail in the section below.

Regulation of Legal Immigration

The H-1B Program

Temporary work visas allow foreigners to work in the United States for a limited period of time. A commonly used temporary work visa for high-skilled foreigners is the H-1B visa. The visa lasts for three years and is renewable once, for a total stay of up to six years. U.S. employers hiring H-1B workers must attest that they will pay the H-1B workers at least as much as similarly employed U.S. workers and that the working conditions of such workers will not be harmed. In order to hire an H-1B worker, U.S. employers must also pay government fees of $1,435 to $2,185, depending on the size of the firm, plus an additional $1,000 fee for faster processing of the H-1B application. These costs help to ensure that employers are unlikely to hire H-1B workers unless suitable U.S. workers are not available.

Almost all workers with H-1B visas have at least a bachelor's degree, and half have an advanced degree. H-1B visas have been particularly important to the high-tech sector, with over half going to scientists, engineers, and people in computer-related occupations. According to one study of H-1B workers, many such workers do not come to work from abroad but are hired as they graduate from U.S. universities.

The number of high-skilled temporary workers is constrained by the caps on the H-1B program. The number of H-1B visas is capped at 65,000 annually for private companies seeking to hire high-skilled foreign workers, after having been temporarily raised to 195,000 during 2001–2003. Since May 2005, an additional 20,000 visas have been available each year for foreigners who have a U.S.-earned master's degree or higher. H-1B workers are not subject to the cap if they are employed at institutions of higher education, or at nonprofit or governmental research organizations.

Since reverting to 65,000, the H-1B cap has been reached earlier and earlier with each fiscal year. The cap for fiscal year 2004 was reached less than five months into the fiscal year. The cap for fiscal year 2005 was filled on the first day of the fiscal year, and in fiscal year 2006, the cap was reached almost two months before the year even started. That the H-1B cap has been reached so quickly suggests that it is no longer sufficient to meet U.S. demand for high-skilled workers.

Some have proposed to increase the number of high-skilled workers by replacing the current H-1B cap with a market-based cap. A market-based cap would increase or decrease with demand for H-1B workers. If the cap were reached in one year, the cap would be increased by a set percentage—say, 20 percent—the following year. If the cap were not reached in a given year, it would fall by a similar amount the next year. In this way, the number of H-1B workers would depend on demand for such workers. Any such change would require congressional action.

Employment-Based Green Cards

A temporary visa allows a foreigner to remain in the United States for a specified period of time. To stay permanently requires becoming a permanent resident. In determining who can become a permanent resident, U.S. immigration law prioritizes family- and employment-based immigration. Under family-based immigration, new permanent residents must be sponsored by family members who are themselves U.S. citizens or permanent residents. Under employment-based immigration, most workers must be sponsored by their employer and have at least a bachelor's degree. From 2000-2004, about two-thirds of new permanent residents received their green cards through family-based immigration, about 15% through employment-based immigration, and the remainder through various other programs such as those for refugees.

Caps on employment-based green cards limit the number of high-skilled foreigners who can become permanent residents. The cap is set at 140,000 visas per year, including visas for the workers' spouses and children. Each country's nationals can make up no more than 7 percent of total immigrant visas. These caps have led to long delays for applicants, especially for workers from over-represented countries. For instance, some workers who became eligible in January 2006 for EB-2 employment-based green cards (for workers with advanced degrees or persons of exceptional ability) had applied for permanent residence five years earlier.

A variety of proposals have been advanced for permanent employment-based immigration to allow for more high-skilled workers and to reduce wait times. Any changes to the cap on the number of employment-based green cards would require legislative action. First, workers' spouses and children could be exempted from the cap, as is currently done for the H-1B program. Spouses and children make up about half of the recipients of employment-based green cards, so this change would roughly double the number of workers able to get employment-based green cards. Second, the fixed 140,000 cap could be replaced with a flexible market-based cap that would increase or decrease with demand for workers eligible for employment-based green cards. Finally, under current policy, nationals of no single country can receive more than 7 percent of green cards. This share could be raised to reduce the long delays for employment-based green cards for applicants from countries with large numbers of desirable, high-skilled workers. Careful enforcement of limits on foreign nationals' access to sensitive technology would provide continued protection for our national security.

Skilled Immigration and Innovation

Legal skilled immigrants play an important role in the U.S. economy. They add to the process of scientific discovery, technology development, and innovation, which in turn lead to greater productivity growth. Greater productivity growth improves the standard of living for the U.S. population as a whole.

A recent World Bank study attempted to quantify immigrants' contributions to innovation and the generation of new ideas, as measured by the number of patents applied for or received in a given year. (Patents are a commonly used proxy in studies of innovation.) According to the study, a 10 percent increase in the number of graduate students from abroad, as a share of total graduate students, increases the number of patents granted to U.S.-based universities, firms, and other institutions by about 6–7 percent. Skilled immigrants overall have a smaller but still positive effect: a 10 percent increase in the number of skilled immigrants, as a share of the U.S. labor force, raises the number of patents granted to U.S.-based institutions by about 1 percent. The results of this study may be partly due to a higher concentration of foreign graduate students in the science and engineering fields, as compared to domestic graduate students who are found in a wide variety of fields including humanities and liberal arts.

Skilled immigrants not only contribute to the innovation process themselves, they also help train our own future innovators. The foreign-born make up about one-fifth of science and engineering faculty at U.S. universities, including more than one-third of engineering faculty. As faculty, they teach both undergraduate and graduate students, training the next generation of U.S. scientists and engineers.

U.S. immigration law, by restricting the number of high-skilled immigrants authorized to work and settle in the United States, limits how many foreigners can contribute to the innovation process. Increasing the caps on the H-1B program and on the number of employment-based green cards would allow more high-skilled immigrants into this country. By welcoming more of the best and the brightest from around the world, these changes to the caps would enhance U.S. competitiveness and result in productivity gains for both immigrants and natives, raising the standard of living for the population as a whole.

Job Training

Education and learning do not stop when someone leaves school. Workers need to continually upgrade their skills if they are to adapt to and take part in a continually changing economy. Skills originally learned as a teenager or young adult in high school or college can quickly become outdated. To remain competitive, workers need to keep their skills relevant, and job training can be a useful way of doing that.

Job training comes in many forms. Often it occurs on the job, either through formal programs run by the employer or through informal learning. Some employers may also send their workers to post-secondary institutions to receive training. Other workers will attend such institutions on their own to keep their skills fresh for their current job, to improve their skills in order to land a better job, or to upgrade their skills after being laid off.

The Role of Community Colleges

Workers often obtain training at community colleges, generally two-year post-secondary institutions that offer certificates and associate's degrees. Community colleges play an important role in providing training to workers, both directly and through employers. Of individuals age 30 and older attending college, about half go to a community college, compared with one-third of students of traditional college age. Some employers may reimburse workers for regular courses taken at community colleges, while other employers may contract with community colleges to offer courses tailored to the employers' needs. Workers may also attend community colleges on their own, especially after a job loss. According to one recent study, about 15–20 percent of long-tenured, laid-off workers complete at least one community college course around the time of their job loss.

Given that so much job training and retraining occur at community colleges, it is important to know whether or not community colleges actually help workers raise their earnings. Recent studies have found that community colleges do contribute to workers' earnings. A year of community college raises real annual earnings by around 6 percent. Community college also helps laid-off workers. According to one study, in the long term, a year of community college raises the earnings of long-tenured, laid-off workers by about 7 percent for men and even more for women, compared to similar workers who do not enroll in community college classes. The earnings gains are higher for workers who take technical, scientific, or health-related courses, and lower for workers who take less quantitative courses.

One of the major sources of financing for community college students is the Pell Grant program, a Federal government program that helps low-income students attend college. In 2005, the Federal government spent about $7 billion on Pell Grants for students in community colleges. In addition, in 2005, in order to help community colleges provide worker training, the President proposed and Congress approved the creation of Community-based Job Training Grants. The program has continued in 2006 with $124 million in funding.

Job Training Funding

In 2005, the Federal government spent nearly $15 billion (excluding Pell Grants) on job training and employment programs. These programs assist many workers in getting the training and other services they need to advance their careers. However, these programs can be strengthened. The $15 billion in job training money is spread among 9 different government agencies and more than 40 different programs, most with their own rules, eligibility requirements, administrative staff, and overhead costs. Much of this money is not used to support job training programs but instead funds job referral services or job search assistance.

To get more job training dollars into the hands of workers, eliminate unnecessary duplication of services, and improve accountability, the President has proposed consolidating several large job training and employment programs into a single grant that would be used to provide job training vouchers. These vouchers, known as Career Advancement Accounts, would be administered by each state but controlled largely by the worker, who could use the account to pay for education and training. The education and training could take place either at post-secondary institutions or through apprentice-ships or other work-based training. These accounts would complement, but not duplicate, Pell Grant resources available to help workers further their career education. States would be required to achieve Federal accountability standards for job placement, employment retention, and earnings. By reducing administrative costs and redirecting more money into job training programs, the Career Advancement Accounts proposal would increase the number of workers who receive the job training they need to upgrade their skills and improve their employment prospects. Career Advancement Accounts would also allow workers the flexibility to choose the training that best suits their needs. They would not tie workers to any particular training provider or location, thus providing workers with maximum flexibility.

Conclusion

Historically, high levels of education and skills in the United States have boosted earnings for individual workers and fueled one of the most dynamic, innovative economies in the world. In recent years, though, educational attainment among young people has, by some measures, leveled off. The rapid growth in schooling in the 1950s and 1960s, and the higher levels of education attained by the younger residents in some of our international competitors, prove that the United States can do better. Promoting a flexible and skilled labor force—through improved access to high-quality primary, secondary, and post-secondary education, through policies that attract the world's best and brightest to our shores, and through investment in the continuing education and training of our workforce—will ensure that the United States remains a competitive leader in this rapidly changing world economy.

Saving for Retirement

Over the past few decades, concerns have mounted that Americans have been preparing inadequately for retirement. Recent newspaper headlines suggest that Americans have stopped saving and are at risk of sharp reductions in both their private and public pension benefits. To be sure, these concerns have some basis: The aggregate personal saving rate published in the National Income and Product Accounts (NIPA) turned negative in 2005; high-profile bankruptcies in airlines and other industries have led to substantial reductions in retiree pension benefits; the collapse of technology stocks in the early 2000s left many defined-benefit pension plans underfunded; and promised Social Security benefits vastly exceed forecasted revenues. Understanding how these events relate to retirement security is important if public policy is to respond productively. This chapter builds such an understanding. The main points are:

- Most working-age Americans are on track to have more retirement wealth than most current retirees. However, it is inherently difficult to assess whether these preparations are *adequate* for most households, given that incomes have also grown over time and people may have markedly different plans for their retirement length and standard of living.
- The decline in an often-cited aggregate personal saving rate may not be cause for alarm. Much of this decline can be attributed to spending triggered by wealth increases from capital gains on housing and financial assets.
- There are, however, a number of risks to the retirement preparations of Americans: People today are living longer and could face higher health-care costs in retirement than members of previous generations. In addition, Social Security and many defined-benefit pension plans are at risk.
- Both defined-benefit pensions and Social Security suffer from fundamental financial problems, which expose not just retirees but all U.S. taxpayers to risk of substantial losses. The Administration is focused on addressing these problems and protecting the Nation's retirement security.

What Does "Retirement Preparedness" Mean?

Retirement preparedness is defined here as the accumulation of wealth necessary to maintain a desired standard of living in retirement. Economists tend to agree that individuals want to *smooth consumption* in retirement (i.e., limit the extent to which retirement will decrease their consumption). However, individuals may have disparate views about how much they want to smooth consumption, when they plan to retire, and how much they intend to work in retirement. Thus, two individuals, even with the same preretirement standard of living, may have markedly different views about how much wealth accumulation is adequate.

For the purposes of this discussion, we divide the wealth that individuals can draw on in retirement into three categories: personal net worth, including defined-contribution pension plans; employer-sponsored defined-benefit pensions; and Social Security. (Retirement wealth also includes other expected benefits, such as retiree health care from employers and Federal programs, but such benefits fall outside the scope of this chapter.) Personal net worth is the sum of the value of financial assets (e.g., stocks and bonds held in and out of retirement accounts such as 401(k) plans, and savings accounts) and durable goods (e.g., houses and cars) less the value of liabilities (e.g., credit card debt, mortgages, and car loans). Net worth grows in part from personal saving—the excess of after-tax income over consumption—and in part from inheritances and capital gains on assets already owned. Some portion of current workers' net worth, however, may be drawn down before retirement. For instance, households may liquidate financial assets or take out home-equity loans to make tuition payments, pay health-care expenses, or offset negative income shocks.

The other two sources of retirement wealth, employer-sponsored defined-benefit pensions and Social Security, are sometimes referred to as retirement income, since payments from both sources are periodic. Employer-sponsored defined-benefit pensions generally increase with years of employment and salary levels, while Social Security payouts tend to increase with retirement age and average lifetime earnings.

The next section of this chapter considers how prepared households are for retirement. Because the definition of retirement adequacy is somewhat subjective, we focus primarily on cross-generational comparisons of retirement-wealth accumulation. Cross-generational comparisons do not speak directly to the adequacy of retirement preparations, but do shed light on the related question of whether retirement preparations have deteriorated.

Estimates of Retirement Preparedness

This section begins with a brief description of the results from studies that directly address the difficult question of whether retirement preparations are adequate. The section then discusses cross-generational comparisons, beginning with comparisons of net worth and ratios of net worth to income, and then turning to comparisons of retirement income from defined-benefit pensions and Social Security. The section concludes with a discussion of the key limitations of cross-generational approaches.

Studies that directly address the question of retirement adequacy typically define adequate wealth accumulation as essentially that which is expected to smooth consumption according to a particular model of individual preferences. Given that these studies make different key modeling assumptions, and in some cases include different components of expected retirement wealth, they have generated a wide range of results. Nevertheless, some recent studies find that most baby-boom households have been preparing adequately. In any case, conclusions about retirement adequacy based on these studies should be regarded as suggestive only, given the inherent uncertainty surrounding predictions of how much wealth is enough.

Comparing retirement wealth across generations, unlike evaluating the adequacy of any one generation's preparations, can be done without reliance on subjective assumptions. One such cross-generational study of retirement wealth contrasts the net worth (defined as above) of households in the baby-boom generation (individuals born between 1946 and 1964) and generation X (headed by individuals born between 1965 and 1976) with that of households in the pre-baby boom generation (headed by individuals born between 1925 and 1945). The study considers the net worth of the heads of these households when they were between 25 and 34 years old. Controlling for age is essential given that individuals tend to save at different rates over their lifetimes.

The study finds that baby-boom and generation-X households tend to have more net worth than pre-baby-boom households had when they were roughly the same age. As shown in Table 3-1, the median net worth of pre-baby-boom households at ages 25-34 was $6,072 in 1998 dollars. In contrast, the median net worth of baby-boom and generation-X households was, respectively, $19,504 and $15,500 in 1998 dollars. The somewhat lower median net worth of generation-X households mainly reflects their higher debt burdens. The table also reveals that baby-boom and generation-X households with heads of all types—low or high education, married or single—were better off than pre-baby-boom households.

We might also want to compare household net worth to income for each generation to see whether saving rates have kept pace with increases in income. Intuitively, households with greater wealth-to-income ratios will be better able to maintain preretirement living standards when they retire. As shown in Table 3-2, the same study also finds that median net worth-to-income ratios are higher for the baby-boom and generation-X households than for the pre-baby-boom households, and these gains were experienced by a wide range of demographic groups.

Finally, we can compare the median expected retirement income of baby-boom households with that of generation-X households. The study finds that median expected retirement income (including predicted defined-benefit pension and Social Security payouts in inflation-adjusted dollars but not personal net worth) for generation-X households is greater than that for

TABLE 3-1.— *The Median Value (in 1998 dollars) of Net Worth for Households Headed by a 25- to 34-Year Old— Differences by Homeownership, Marital Status, and Education*

	Median		
	Pre-Baby Boom	Baby Boom	Generation X
Homeowners	$25,594	$60,521	$43,100
Nonhomeowners	982	4,699	3,300
Less than high school	815	4,658	2,500
High school graduate	10,044	17,195	17,920
College graduate	23,953	36,569	30,020
Married	9,165	31,677	34,501
Not married	0	7,160	5,750
All households	**$6,072**	**$19,504**	**$15,500**

Note: Government Accountability Office analysis based on data from the Survey of Consumer Finance. Households between the ages of 25 and 34 in 1962, 1983, and 1998 belong, respectively, to the "Pre-Baby Boom," "Baby Boom," and "Generation X."

Net worth is equal to assets minus liabilities. Assets include IRAs, 401(k)s, 403(b)s, and other thrift-type plans, as well as savings accounts, mutual funds, stocks, bonds, and durable goods. Liabilities are from credit card debt, installment loans, and housing debt.

Source: Federal Reserve Board.

TABLE 3-2.— *Median Value of Wealth-to-Income Ratios for Households Headed by a 25- to 34-Year Old— Differences by Homeownership, Marital Status, and Education*

	Median		
	Pre-Baby Boom	Baby Boom	Generation X
Homeowners	0.641	1.343	1.044
Nonhomeowners	0.052	0.167	0.151
Less than high school	0.029	0.216	0.159
High school graduate	0.278	0.525	0.586
College graduate	0.510	0.799	0.743
Married	0.261	0.755	0.742
Not married	0.000	0.299	0.268
All households	**0.214**	**0.562**	**0.523**

Note: Government Accountability Office analysis based on data from the Survey of Consumer Finances. Households between the ages of 25 and 34 in 1962, 1983, and 1998 belong, respectively, to the "Pre-Baby Boom," "Baby Boom," and "Generation X."

Net worth is equal to assets minus liabilities. Assets include IRAs, 401(k)s, 403(b)s, and other thrift-type plans, as well as savings accounts, mutual funds, stocks, bonds, and durable goods. Liabilities are from credit card debt, installment loans, and housing debt.

Source: Federal Reserve Board.

baby-boom households. A second, less sanguine, result is that if the Social Security system's expected funding shortfalls are resolved by gradually reducing retirement benefits (notably, not the Administration's proposed solution) and thus lowering benefits for generation X more than for the baby boomers, then the median expected retirement incomes of generation-X and baby-boom households are about the same. This implies that, in terms of retirement income relative to preretirement income, generation-X households have not kept pace with the baby boomers.

The results shown above have a few important limitations. First, cross-generational comparisons fail to adjust for the possibility that current generations may live longer and could face higher health-care costs in retirement than previous generations. As a result, current workers may need more retirement wealth than previous generations. On the other hand, longer life expectancies may encourage current generations to work longer than previous generations, which, all else equal, would lower retirement-wealth needs.

Another limitation of these cross-generational comparisons is that they consider only a relatively early period in each generation's lifecycle (although they allow the inclusion of more recent generations). However, studies that compare somewhat older households from the baby-boom generation to recent retirees find similar conclusions. Nevertheless, retirement preparations of today's Americans may veer off track as they age if they stop saving or if financial-asset returns, house-price gains, or defined-benefit pension and Social Security payouts turn out to be less than expected. The next section of this chapter addresses some of the key risks to retirement preparations.

The Risks to Retirement Preparedness

Three risks to retirement wealth are discussed in this section: first, the risk to household net worth created by the negative level of the personal saving rate, as measured in the National Income and Product Accounts (NIPA); second, the risk to defined-benefit pension plans created by underfunding, in part due to investments in risky assets; third, the risk to Social Security from the aging of the population and other structural problems.

Are Low Saving Rates Putting Household Net Worth at Risk?

The NIPA personal saving rate is the difference between the *household sector's* after-tax personal income *(disposable income)* and personal consumption, expressed as a percentage of disposable income. As a technical matter, the household sector includes nonprofit institutions. The NIPA personal saving rate was constructed as a measure of the household sector's contribution to *national saving*—funds set aside from the economy's current production to finance investment (see Chapter 1, entitled The Year in Review and the Years Ahead, and Chapter 6, entitled The U.S. Capital Account Surplus, for more discussion of the national saving rate). However, the NIPA personal saving rate is widely cited in newspapers as a gauge of retirement preparedness. The discussion here details the NIPA saving rate's limitations as a measure of the extent to which households are adding to their retirement wealth. The goal of the discussion is to assess whether the decline in the NIPA personal saving rate reflects a widespread deterioration in household retirement preparations.

Chart 3-1 illustrates the decline in the NIPA personal saving rate. The saving rate is volatile from quarter to quarter but has been trending down at a relatively constant rate of about 0.5 percent per year since the early 1980s. In the fourth quarter of 2005 (the most recent quarter for which data are available), the NIPA personal saving rate was -0.4 percent, not far above the post-World War II low observed in the third quarter.

Chart 3-1 **Personal Saving as a Percentage of Disposable Personal Income**
The saving rate has declined from 10 percent to a bit below zero over the past 25 years.

Personal saving, percent of disposable personal income (seasonally adjusted)

Note: Shaded areas indicate recessions.
Source: Department of Commerce (Bureau of Economic Analysis).

However, the relationship between the personal saving rate and households' wealth accumulation is not always close. Household net worth is what matters for retirement, but the NIPA personal saving rate is not equal to the change in household net worth. First, the NIPA personal saving rate excludes the acquisition of consumer durables, a component of household net worth. Second, while business saving (such as businesses' retained profits) is ultimately owned by households, it is also excluded from NIPA personal saving. Third, and arguably most important, the NIPA personal saving rate excludes capital gains on financial and other assets (e.g., the increase in the value of a house); however, taxes on capital gains, which reduce the saving rate, are included in the computation of personal saving. The exclusion of capital gains is particularly problematic because capital gains may encourage households to consume more, which in turn drives down the measured saving rate. In other words, capital gains may be reflected in the data as reductions in saving, even though these gains add to household wealth on net—though some might argue that these gains can be illusory.

Do Wealth Gains Explain the Decline in the NIPA Personal Saving Rate?

The *consumption-wealth effect* (i.e., the tendency to consume more as wealth increases) has been the subject of numerous empirical investigations. Studies find that an additional dollar of wealth tends to lead to a permanent rise in the level of household consumption of about 2 to 5 cents. The link between aggregate wealth and spending has proved to be one of the more enduring relationships in macroeconomics.

Estimates of the consumption-wealth effect suggest that it can explain a sizable portion of the decline in personal saving since the mid-1990s. As shown in Chart 3-2, the ratio of household net worth to disposable income has risen from about 440 percent in the early 1980s to about 550 percent in the third quarter of 2005. This measure of household net worth, obtained from the Federal Reserve's Flow of Funds Accounts, is the difference between household assets—including defined-benefit pension wealth—and household liabilities. The ratio moved up and down with the rise and collapse of the stock market in the late 1990s and early 2000s and then rebounded more recently along with rising house prices and stock market gains. An estimate of the impact of these wealth gains on the NIPA personal saving rate is shown below in Chart 3-3. Under the assumption that an additional dollar of wealth leads to a $0.035 permanent rise in the level of consumption (the middle of the range cited above), the chart shows that the personal saving rate would have declined about half as much since 1980 if household wealth had grown at the same pace as disposable income (keeping the ratio constant) over that period.

Chart 3-2 Household Net Worth as a Percentage of Disposable Income

Since the mid-1990s, net worth has increased on balance relative to disposable income.

Percent

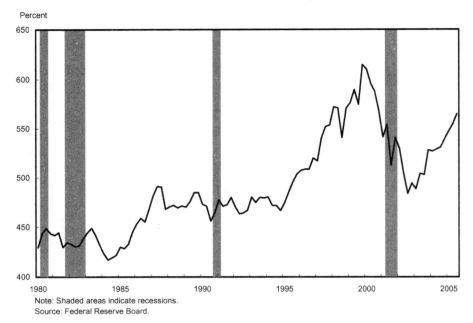

Note: Shaded areas indicate recessions.
Source: Federal Reserve Board.

Chart 3-3 Household Saving Rate as a Percentage of Disposable Income

If wealth only grew as much as disposable income since 1994, the saving rate would have declined substantially less.

Percent of disposable income

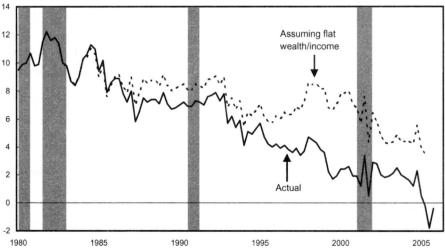

Note: Shaded areas indicate recessions. The difference between the two lines reflects additional consumption triggered by wealth gains. The calculation assumes that a $1 change in wealth leads to a total of $0.035 change in consumption over a two-year period.
Sources: Department of Commerce (Bureau of Economic Analysis) and Federal Reserve.

Are Saving Rate Declines Widespread?

Yet another limitation of the NIPA personal saving rate as a measure of households' wealth accumulation is its aggregate nature; as such, it masks possible differences in behavior by households at different income levels. Understanding the saving dynamics in different parts of the income distribution requires household-level data on saving.

However, household wealth at the individual level is difficult to track over time. One study thus employed an innovative approach to circumvent various data problems and found that the saving rate, using NIPA definitions, for households in the upper two-fifths of the income distribution declined over the 1990s, while the saving rate for households in the middle fifth remained relatively steady, and the saving rate for households in the bottom two-fifths actually increased. Given that high-income households almost certainly experienced the majority of capital gains in the 1990s, these results suggest that the net worth component of retirement wealth may not be at risk. Relatively high-income households may have accumulated net worth from capital gains, while other households may have accumulated net worth by saving.

Overall, the above discussion of household saving suggests that the net worth component of retirement preparedness may not be in jeopardy. The NIPA personal saving rate is a potentially misleading measure of households' wealth accumulation. Moreover, much of the recent decline in the NIPA personal saving rate may reflect consumption increases that were triggered by capital gains on stocks and real estate. Finally, some evidence suggests that the decline in household saving rates has not been widespread but may have been concentrated among higher-income households.

Policy Reforms

While the net worth component of retirement wealth does not appear to be in jeopardy, policy reforms can still productively reduce impediments to saving. Under current law, interest income is taxed, creating a disincentive for households to set aside funds for retirement. This disincentive is mitigated to some extent by policies that afford favorable tax treatment to various types of retirement accounts (e.g., IRA and 401(k)). However, restrictions on these accounts limit their value as retirement-saving vehicles. To make these accounts more effective, Congress passed legislation that increases contribution limits and makes retirement assets more portable. In addition, the Administration has proposed simplifying the retirement account system in two important ways: (1) creating a single Retirement Savings Account (RSA) to replace the three types of Investment Retirement Accounts (IRAs) currently in place; and (2) creating a Lifetime Savings Account (LSA) that could be used for a variety of purposes, including retirement saving (see Chapter 5, entitled The U.S. Tax System in International Perspective, for additional discussion of tax recommendations in the President's Budget). Another impediment to saving may be limited financial knowledge. The Department of the Treasury is actively engaged in campaigns to improve financial literacy. In addition, the President has instructed the Federal Deposit Insurance Corporation (FDIC), the Small Business Administration (SBA), and the Treasury Department to work with consumer groups to ensure that financial literacy is widespread.

Defined-Benefit Pensions

Historically, *defined-benefit* pension plans have been an important part of retirement preparedness. These employer-sponsored plans compensate retirees through a specified monthly benefit, which tends to vary with salary and years of service. In addition, most plans sponsored by private employers are guaranteed in part by the Pension Benefit Guaranty Corporation, and those sponsored by public employers are ultimately backed by the ability of states to levy taxes. As such, "DB" plans may appear more stable than increasingly prevalent "defined-contribution" plans (such as 401(k) plans), which explicitly depend on employee contributions, tie benefits more directly to market performance, and may expose retirees to longevity risk (the risk of outliving retirement resources).

Defined-benefit plans can, nevertheless, carry considerable risk. This risk comes from employers (1) contributing less to plans than what is promised to employees *(funding risk)*, (2) investing contributions in a hazardous manner *(portfolio risk)*, and (3) encountering financial distress *(bankruptcy risk)* in the case of private employers. When these risks are realized, beneficiaries and taxpayers can be exposed to substantial and oftentimes unanticipated losses.

An early example of these problems comes from the 1960s landmark case of Studebaker Corporation. When this former carmaker defaulted on its defined-benefit plan, it left about 11,000 participants without most or any of their pensions. These losses eventually led Congress to set minimum standards for private pension plans via the Employee Retirement Income Security Act (ERISA) in 1974.

ERISA gave rise to the Pension Benefit Guaranty Corporation (PBGC), which now partially insures the pensions of over 34 million workers and retirees. The PBGC largely funds itself with premiums from private-sector sponsors of defined-benefit plans (i.e., employers). When an employer becomes financially distressed, the PBGC may take control of the plan's management and use the plan's assets and its own funds to pay retirees a capped portion of their promised benefits. Employees in contemporary cases like the bankruptcy of United Airlines filed in 2002 are thus less exposed to defined-benefit risks than were employees in cases like Studebaker.

Despite this insulation, employees with defined-benefit pension plans sponsored by private employers remain exposed to considerable risks. As of 2005, for example, the limit on PBGC insurance increased with retirement age, and topped out at about $46,000 per year. Employees whose plans default can thus incur considerable losses when their promised benefits exceed these limits. United's workers, for example, expect to receive about 80 percent of their earned benefits, and thus stand to lose more than $3 billion of total promised benefits. In addition, as the following sections show, the combination of inadequate protections and a series of pension defaults has left the PBGC with insufficient funds for paying even these limited claims. Consequently, if losses overwhelm the pension insurance system, Congress may step in and pass the bill to taxpayers.

For defined-benefit plans sponsored by public employers, the taxpayer exposure is even more direct. Recall that the PBGC only insures plans sponsored by private employers. In the event that a publicly sponsored plan's assets are insufficient to pay benefits, absent renegotiation of benefits, such plans could only be made whole with the support of state-level tax revenues.

Employee Exposure to Defined-Benefit Risks

Recently, market fluctuations and the rules that govern how employers participate in the defined-benefit system appear to have turned risks into reality. Decreasing interest rates and stock market valuations, coupled with the exposure of pension plan assets to market fluctuations, coincided with a marked increase in the underfunding of defined-benefit plans. Underfunding, in turn, increased expected defaults on pension obligations, putting both workers and the pension insurance program into jeopardy.

In the case of privately sponsored pensions, the value of assets set aside to fund retirement obligations began to decrease in 2000 while the value of promised benefits began to increase. The total underfunding of private pension plans grew from less than $50 billion at the end of 2000 to over $400 billion today. At the same time, as Chart 3-4 illustrates, PBGC's capacity to insulate workers from employer defaults turned from a $10 billion surplus in 2000 into a deficit that now totals more than $20 billion.

This deterioration can plausibly be attributed to the exposure of pension plan portfolios to coincident decreases in both interest rates and stock market valuations. A decrease in interest rates can contribute to this problem by increasing the measured *present value* of a pension plan's promised benefits. A decrease in stock market valuations can further contribute by weakening the ability of plan investments to pay benefits.

To see this relationship, suppose that an individual wants to buy a new appliance next year for $500, and consider how much must be saved today to

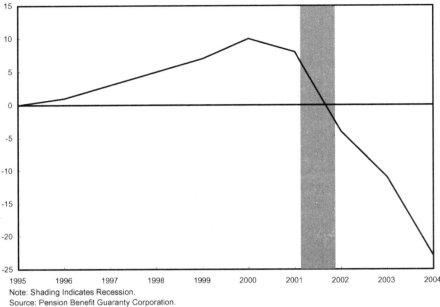

Note: Shading Indicates Recession.
Source: Pension Benefit Guaranty Corporation.

fund this purchase. The answer depends on how much interest these savings will earn: As this interest increases, the savings that are necessary to fund the future purchase decrease. Extreme cases are illustrative: One would have to save $500 today if the interest rate is 0 percent, but only $250 if it is 100 percent. This example reflects a more general relationship: When interest rates decrease, the present value of future obligations increases.

For pensions, this relationship implies that employers must set aside more funds to meet pension obligations when interest rates decrease. The decrease in interest rates that started late in 2000 thus threatened the funding status of defined-benefit pension plans.

A simultaneous decrease in stock market valuations from the peaks of the late 1990s appears to have furthered this threat. At the same time that interest-rate changes were increasing the value of employers' obligations, a decrease in stock market valuations was diminishing the value of assets that employers had set aside to fund those obligations. Together, these changes coincided with the marked weakening in the funding status of both defined-benefit plans and the PBGC.

While market fluctuations appear to have been an important contributor to these woes, they could be made less so. To see why, recall from above that the PBGC manages the pension plans it receives from financially distressed employers. In doing so, it reduces exposure to interest-rate fluctuations by matching investment payoffs with the timing of employee benefits. The value of plan assets and liabilities will tend to move more closely together under this strategy of duration matching than they would under the strategies that employers appear to have used.

Taxpayer Exposure to PBGC's Deficit

The recent spike in underfunding has also exposed taxpayers to the prospect of making up for the PBGC's deficit (recall that this exposure is more immediate for publicly sponsored plans). While the PBGC's liabilities are not explicitly backed by the Federal government, a future Congress might decide that a taxpayer bailout is preferable to a PBGC default. Indeed, taxpayers' exposure to the PBGC's deficit is especially concerning since the manner in which it evolved mimics how the 1980s savings and loan (S&L) crisis developed.

Like the insurance that PBGC offers, the insurance offered to depositors at financial institutions can provide important benefits. But if they are not prudently managed, these insurance programs can fall prey to moral hazard (explained in Chapter 9, The U.S. Financial Sector) and thus expose taxpayers to an undue liability. In the 1980s, for example, loose regulatory oversight let savings and loans overly expose themselves to market fluctuations (such as changes in real-estate values and interest-rates) and ultimately left insufficient funds for paying off depositors. Depositors did not fully bear the burden of this underfundng, however. Instead, the Federal Savings and Loan Insurance Corporation (FSLIC) insured depositors in much the same way that PBGC covers retirees.

In an analogous manner to the current pension situation, market fluctuations and regulatory difficulties not only helped increase the rate at which depositors drew on this insurance, they also compromised FSLIC's capacity to pay insurance claims. Like the PBGC, FSLIC was structured to be self-financing. Nevertheless, taxpayers ultimately paid about $150 billion for the financial losses of failed institutions.

The PBGC faces a situation that is similar to what plagued FSLIC. Waiting to implement productive reforms magnified taxpayers' burden in bailing out the S&L industry. Postponing the issue of underfunded pension plans can likewise make matters worse for pensioners and taxpayers. According to testimony by the PBGC's executive director, the PBGC's present $23 billion deficit could grow toward $80 billion over the next ten years. Without prompt and effective action, taxpayers may thus find themselves bailing out yet another "self-financed" public insurance program.

Policy Reforms

Prompt action, grounded in good economics and informed by lessons learned from similar financial crises, can keep the current pension problem from becoming even more burdensome. To help the private pension system move in this direction, the administration has proposed to strengthen the requirements for funding privately sponsored pension plans and improve the manner in which plan sponsors disclose information. State-level policies that would address the problems with plans sponsored by public employers are at an earlier stage of development.

Current funding and disclosure rules can allow privately sponsored pension plans to appear healthier than they actually are. Reforms such as restricting the use of "credit balances" could help enhance funding adequacy and transparency. Under present law, employers receive credit for contributions that exceed minimum requirements and can later use those credits in lieu of actual contributions. This treatment is problematic. For example, excess contributions are characterized as earning interest even if the assets in which those contributions were invested lose value. Moreover, credit balances can delay plan sponsors from addressing funding problems and thus let even grossly underfunded employers forgo actual contributions.

Limiting private employers' ability to use an average interest rate to value plan liabilities could also strengthen funding and improve transparency. Recall that, as interest rates decrease, the present value of an employer's pension obligations increases. Current law lets employers use a moving average of these rates spread out over several years, however, and thus mutes the near-term effect of an interest-rate decrease on an employer's contribution requirements.

To see this effect, suppose that employers can use a two-year average, and that interest rates decrease from 6 percent to 5 percent. Using an average rate, employers could discount their future obligations at 5.5 percent. But if employers had to use the current rate of 5 percent, they would have to increase contributions by more, and do so more quickly. Averaging the discount rate can thus cloud the picture of a plan's status.

The Administration has similarly proposed limits on the ability of private employers to smooth reported fluctuations in the value of their plan-assets. Coupled with the related proposal for plans to accurately address the timing of benefit payments, this reform could reduce the portfolio risks that are characterized above as the proximate cause of the system's weakened funding status.

Finally, the administration has proposed to increase funding targets, measure the performance of plans in a uniform manner, and update assumptions like those of mortality. These reforms, like the others discussed above, would enhance the integrity of the defined-benefit system, and should be uniformly applied across plan sponsors. Doing otherwise would give some economic sectors, or firms within a sector, an artificial advantage. Economic performance could deteriorate as scarce resources flow not to their most productive uses, but to their most politically-favored uses. In addition, exempting certain sectors or firms could exacerbate the underfunding problem by breathing artificial life into risky plans and thus further exposing workers, retirees, and taxpayers to economic risk.

Social Security

Along with personal savings and employer-provided pension plans, Social Security has long stood as a pillar of retirement security. A response of Franklin D. Roosevelt's administration to the Great Depression, the Social Security Act was signed into law on August 14, 1935, and first issued monthly retirement checks in January 1940. At that time, about 200,000 retirees received aggregate benefits valued at about $35 million. Since then, both the number of beneficiaries and the level of benefits has steadily grown. In 2004, more than 47 million beneficiaries received a total of about $493 billion through the Old Age, Survivor, and Disability Insurance programs (OASDI).

These benefits are funded by taxes on wage income. In an accounting sense, employers and employees equally share this funding by contributing 6.2 percent of taxable payroll each. Since employers focus on the total cost of labor, however, workers bear most of this combined 12.4 percent tax. For each worker, this tax applies to payroll beneath a ceiling that annually adjusts with the average wage index. That ceiling, which stood at $90,000 in 2005, increased to $94,200 for 2006.

Taxpayer Exposure to an Increasingly Large Social Security Burden

The overall cost of Social Security is substantial. The Office of Management and Budget (OMB) estimates that Social Security transfers amounted to 4.2 percent of GDP in 2005. During the coming decades, Social Security's share of GDP is expected to increase, reaching 6 percent in 2035.

In the short term, this increase will largely come from the retirement of baby boomers, which begins in 2008. It will persist in the long run, however, due to a combination of relatively low fertility rates and relatively high life expectancies. These factors will push the ratio of workers to retirees down from its current level of 3.3 to 1 to around 2 to 1 by the time that most baby boomers retire.

Since the benefits of those currently retired mostly come from taxes on those currently working, these developments will create considerable pressure to increase payroll taxes. Indeed, the Social Security Administration's actuaries estimate that, starting in 2017, the system's annual cost will exceed its total tax income (which includes taxes on payroll and Social Security benefits themselves).

From an accounting perspective, Social Security can still fully fund benefits at this point because the system has run surpluses since 1984, holding special Treasury bonds as IOUs. Although they are assets to the Trust Fund, however, these IOUs are equally debt to the Federal government, and thus an obligation that faces taxpayers.

The actuaries estimate that without legislative action, the Trust Fund's IOUs will run out by 2041, leaving a system that can fulfill only 74 percent of currently scheduled benefits. Even more, promised Social Security benefits from 2005 to 2080 are expected to exceed the sum of revenues and Trust Fund IOUs by $4 trillion in present value. Given these mounting costs, taxpayers and workers would be better off dealing with this problem now rather than later.

Social Security reform has been on the national radar for decades (see Box 3-1). Notably, former President Clinton convened an Advisory Council which, in 1996, released several recommendations. Two of the three plans supported by the Advisory Council involved some kind of voluntary personal retirement accounts (through publicly held individual accounts in one case and privately administered personal accounts in another), and the other plan also envisioned moving to a system of advance funding, albeit through government-directed investment in equities. Importantly, the longer it takes to initiate reforms, the greater any changes must be, because they will be shared by fewer generations.

Policy Reform: Progressive Indexing

Projections suggest that, under current law, the Social Security system will soon be unable to pay for itself. Many of the proposals to address this problem fall short of a productive and durable reform. Removing the cap on wages that are subject to the payroll tax, for example, would not only increase contributions to the system but also increase the system's promised benefits in the long term. Progressively reducing future benefit growth, on the other hand, may strike an attractive balance by closing roughly two-thirds of the system's long-range annual cash shortfalls while maintaining the system's capacity to act as a social safety net.

Initial benefits for new retirees are currently indexed to wage inflation rather than price inflation. Since wages typically increase at a faster rate than prices (reflecting gains in productivity), wage indexation results in increasingly large benefits in real dollar terms. Progressive indexing would decrease the rate of benefit growth for individuals whose lifetime earnings are the highest (less than the highest 1 percent of all wage earners) by linking their benefit growth to price increases. At the same time, it would maintain the current law's more generous benefit-growth rate for individuals whose lifetime earnings are relatively low. Benefits of retirees in the upper 70 percent of the

Box 3-1: Earlier Attempts to Shore Up Social Security

Congress has responded to developing problems with Social Security finances in the past. For example, both 1977 and 1983 saw the signing of significant amendments to improve the system's deteriorating financial condition.

Why were the system's finances deteriorating then, and why are they continuing to do so today? There are several answers. First, the 1972 amendments to Social Security effectively indexed benefit growth for those working at the time to both wage and price inflation, essentially providing two cost-of-living adjustments. This double-benefit indexation was amended in 1977 to establish the current method of wage indexation. But while wage indexation addressed the double-indexation issue, some experts warned that, coupled with demographic changes, it would still require future taxpayers to shoulder larger Social Security tax burdens than is required today.

Second, the economic projections following the amendments of 1972, 1977, and 1983 proved overly optimistic. From 1972 to 1976, for example, real wages grew by nearly 11 percent less than expected, resulting in lower than anticipated growth of the payroll income base on which Social Security taxes were collected. Similarly, from 1977 to 1981, real wages decreased by about 6.9 percent rather than increasing by 12.9 percent as projected. Assumptions made following the 1983 reforms were not as far off as those of 1972 and 1977, but are nonetheless responsible for some of the overstatement of Social Security's financial strength. Consequently, although the year for the exhaustion of the Trust Fund was forecast to be 2063 in 1983, it has been pushed forward and now stands at 2041.

Third, and perhaps most importantly, the 1983 reforms did not attain sustainable solvency. The 1983 reforms envisioned several decades of Social Security surpluses, followed by several decades of large and growing deficits. This meant that with the passage of time, Social Security would again become financially imbalanced. Even as early as the 1985 Social Security Trustees' report, it could be seen that the system was again heading out of long-term balance. This is one reason why a number of bipartisan commissions have since recommended that future Social Security reforms place the program on a sustainable, as opposed to merely a solvent, footing.

distribution would depend on a combination of price and wage increases. The system would be progressive because benefit growth would slow the most for those with higher earnings. This method of benefit growth would let future retirees enjoy benefits that are higher than those paid today while eventually ensuring that no person who works a full career would retire with a Social Security benefit below the poverty level.

Progressive indexing would slow the benefit-growth rate for high-income individuals in a manner that strongly pushes the system toward solvency. In addition, by maintaining a relatively fast rate of benefit growth for low-income individuals, progressive indexing would further protect retirement incomes from falling below the poverty level.

Policy Reform: Personal Accounts

The traditional Social Security system largely funds retirement benefits by transferring payroll taxes from current workers to beneficiaries. In addition to being subject to the risk of insolvency (which, as explained above, can be addressed in part through progressive indexing), this type of *pay-as-you-go* system runs the risk of future workers voting to cut back on their contributions. This risk may be considerable, as additional changes needed to restore solvency would leave future retirees with substantially smaller benefits than the current system's promises.

This problem comes in large part from a system that relies on future generations to fulfill promises made today. By letting individuals pre-fund their retirements, personal accounts allow current generations to rely in part on their own savings, rather than solely upon contributions that future generations may be unwilling or unable to make.

Because this issue is separate from that of solvency, personal accounts need not (and under the President's proposals, would not) adversely affect the system's long-term finances. If traditional benefits are offset by the amount that individuals could obtain by investing in low-risk assets, such a reform can be made approximately neutral with respect to the capacity to fulfill remaining traditional benefits. Such offsets are said to be roughly neutral on an actuarial basis because they leave (1) beneficiaries who remain wholly invested in government bonds with the same expected future benefit and (2) the Trust Fund with nearly the same expected long-term balance.

While they leave the long-term balance mostly unchanged, allocations to personal accounts do alter the timing of the system's future obligations. Their basic effect is to take some of the long-term obligation and shift it to an earlier time. Moving a portion of payroll taxes to personal accounts will take money off of the government ledger today, some of which is used to pay for current benefits and some of which has long been used to finance other Federal spending. At the same time, because voluntary personal retirement accounts will replace a portion of unfunded future benefits, they also reduce future strains on the system.

Shifting the future imbalance forward in time could increase transparency by making the system's impending shortfalls less of an abstraction. Financial markets tend to applaud such solutions to fiscal challenges and might do so again in this context by keeping interest rates at productive levels.

Pre-funding a portion of future benefits appears attractive in other dimensions as well. Every dollar of benefits funded today through personal accounts is a dollar of benefits that need not be paid by taxpayers in the future. Because rising benefit obligations would under current law lead to increased tax burdens over time, shifting forward the funding of some benefits could create a more equitable treatment of different generations.

In addition, redirecting assets to personal accounts increases the likelihood that real savings will be accumulated to meet tomorrow's retirement needs. If these assets are owned and controlled by individuals, they will be less available for the government to spend than if these assets are left on the Federal ledger. Finally, personal accounts would provide an opportunity for individuals to diversify their investment in Social Security, which may add to their retirement security.

Conclusion

This chapter's first section shows that today's generations are on track to have more retirement wealth than previous generations, though it is unclear whether these wealth gains have kept pace with rising preretirement incomes. Going forward, the relative security of retirement wealth may be compromised by fundamental problems with defined-benefit pensions and Social Security.

Both of these systems could be improved by more-effective funding rules and safeguards that protect against the opportunistic handling of retirement assets. Strengthening pension-contribution requirements, and watching more carefully how those contributions are managed, would go far to mitigate the growing risks to pensioners and taxpayers alike. Progressively targeting the rate of future benefit growth and expanding ownership over payroll contributions, likewise, would help strengthen Social Security for the future. In both cases, waiting to act allows the present problems to grow and increases the costs of adopting effective reforms.

CHAPTER 4

Improving Incentives in
Health Care Spending

Health care spending in the United States has increased rapidly over the
past several decades, rising 44 percent in real per capita terms in the past
ten years alone. Some of the reasons for this marked rise reflect higher-quality
health care, such as improved technological options for enhancing the health
and quality of life of the American people. However, other factors, such as
poorly functioning markets for health care, may have led to excessive
spending and inefficient patterns of medical care utilization. Furthermore,
whether this increased spending is of high value or not, it has put tremendous
pressures on individuals and the institutions that finance health care
spending. Family budgets are being strained as health care costs take up an
increasing share of incomes. Government health care expenditures have also
been increasing rapidly, burdening both Federal and state budgets. If not
curtailed, the increased costs to governments will eventually lead to large tax
increases, sharp cuts in nonhealth spending, or both.

This chapter reviews the causes and consequences of health care spending
growth and discusses how spending can be more efficient and of higher value
in the context of a consumer-driven, market-based system. The emerging
consumer-driven health care movement aims to empower consumers with
improved information and ability to make choices about their own health
care, which in turn can result in increased provider competition to better
serve patients' needs at lower costs. The key points of this chapter are:

- Growth in spending on health care has been much more rapid than general
  inflation, straining consumers, employers, and government budgets.
- Perverse tax and insurance incentives have led to inefficient levels and
  composition of spending on health care. Some increased spending has
  produced valuable health improvements, but in a better-functioning
  health care market these improvements could be attained at lower cost.
- Promoting a stronger role for consumers is a promising strategy for
  improving health care value and affordability.

The Growth in Health Care Spending

Spending in the health care sector has steadily grown from under 6 percent
of GDP in 1965 to 16 percent of GDP in 2004. If current trends continued,
health care spending would be projected to reach 19 percent of GDP by 2014

and 22 percent by 2025 (Chart 4-1). Since 1965, the government share of total health spending has risen from 25 percent to over 45 percent, mainly due to increased eligibility and generosity of Medicare and Medicaid. (Medicare is a Federal government program that pays for health care for senior citizens and those with certain disabilities. Medicaid, financed by both Federal and state governments, is focused on providing health care for the poor.) Medicare spending alone is projected to increase from 2.6 percent of GDP in 2006 to 4.3 percent by 2025. Among those without access to Medicare or Medicaid, most expenditures are financed by private health insurance (64 percent), provided mainly through employers (91 percent of those with private insurance). The rising costs of health care are reflected in premiums (employer plus employee share) for employer-provided insurance that in 2005 averaged almost $11,000 for a family (Chart 4-2), up from $6,700 in 1999 (in 2005 inflation-adjusted dollars). Per capita health care spending in the United States has risen from about $4,500 ten years ago to about $6,500 today (in 2005 dollars).

The United States today spends roughly twice as much per capita on health care as other industrialized countries, such as the other members of the Organization for Economic Cooperation and Development (OECD). This large difference in part reflects higher levels of per capita income and output

Chart 4-1 **National Health Expenditures as a Percentage of GDP**
National health expenditures have risen dramatically and are projected to continue rising.

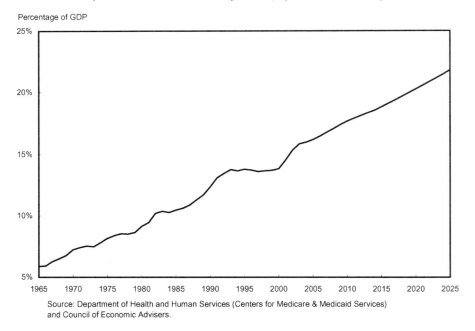

Source: Department of Health and Human Services (Centers for Medicare & Medicaid Services) and Council of Economic Advisers.

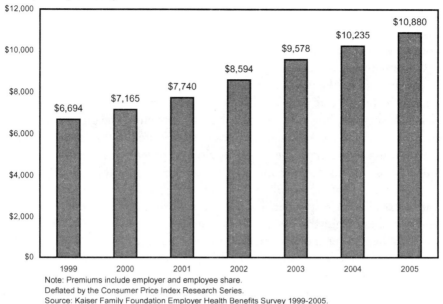

Chart 4-2 **Family Health Insurance Premiums 1999-2005**

Annual premium (2005 dollars)

Note: Premiums include employer and employee share.
Deflated by the Consumer Price Index Research Series.
Source: Kaiser Family Foundation Employer Health Benefits Survey 1999-2005.

in the United States, since richer countries tend to spend proportionately more on health care, but the United States spends a substantially larger share of GDP on health care than other wealthy countries do. For example, the United Kingdom spends about 8 percent of its GDP on health care, compared with the United States' 16 percent. The U.S. expenditure as a percent of GDP is more than six percentage points higher than the average in OECD countries. Rates of spending *growth*, however, are much more similar across countries. For example, from 1998 to 2003, average real health care spending increased 4.6 percent per year in the United States as compared to 4.5 percent in the OECD as a whole. This suggests that many of the underlying international spending differences stem from longer-term factors.

When looking at these statistics, it is also important to remember that buying more health care is not necessarily equivalent to buying more health. Health care is one of many different determinants of health status, and for many people marginal increases in health care consumption may be less cost-effective than marginal increases in spending on other determinants such as a healthier lifestyle (exercising, not smoking, eating a healthier diet). Evaluating the relative cost-effectiveness of spending on different health determinants can be challenging, however, in part because it is difficult to measure the quality of health services consumed.

Where Health Spending Has Grown

There have been significant increases over time in all major spending categories, including outpatient, acute inpatient, long-term care, and pharmaceuticals. Both personnel costs and goods costs have increased. Spending has grown for both privately and publicly financed and delivered care.

One might guess that the aging of the U.S. population would explain an important part of the increase in health care costs, especially since about one-quarter of health care in a given year is spent on those who die that year. Research suggests, however, that less than 10 percent of the growth in health spending over the last several decades can be attributed to this factor. Another contributing factor might be America's rising prosperity, because richer individuals and nations demand more health care, but again this factor can only account for a relatively small portion of the health care spending growth. Various studies have speculated about the contribution of other factors such as rising obesity, but there is as yet no consensus on the importance of these factors. There is general agreement, however, that the rapid growth in development and use of expensive new health care treatments accounts for a large share of overall health care spending growth over time.

A useful framework for understanding increases in medical spending breaks these spending increases into three components: (1) changes in the quantity demanded of existing health-related goods and services, (2) changes in the prices of those existing goods and services, and (3) the effects of technological advances that change the available set of health-related goods and services. The next part of this section looks at each of these three factors.

Quantity of Health Care Demanded

Do we demand higher volumes of health care today than in the past? While we clearly consume more of some types of care (based on higher incomes, changing medical needs, etc.), health care visits per capita have not increased. The biggest components of health care spending are physician and hospital services. Doctor visits per capita dropped somewhat from 1980 through the mid-1990s, and have increased only modestly since then. The number of hospital discharges per capita and the average hospital length-of-stay, however, have declined dramatically—they were 50-percent higher in 1980 than in 2000. Growth in spending within the United States does not seem to be explained by increased visits to the doctor or hospital.

Moreover, international differences in spending cannot be explained by differences in the quantity of physician and hospital visits. In fact, doctor visits and hospital nights per capita in the United States are lower than in many OECD countries. For example, in 2000 the United States had 0.7 hospital nights per capita, compared to 0.9 nights in the United Kingdom, 1.3 nights in Switzerland, and 1.9 nights in Germany. Service *intensity* in the

United States is very different, however, with U.S. hospital staffing levels at double the OECD median. Thus, while Americans have fewer health care contacts, they appear to receive more services at each contact. This difference explains in part why the average U.S. hospital night costs three times the OECD average.

Health Care Prices

The official medical consumer price index (medical CPI), which measures price increases for medical goods and services and is published by the Department of Labor's Bureau of Labor Statistics, indicates that health care prices over the last few decades have grown more rapidly than prices of other goods and services in the economy. From 2000 to 2004, the health care component of the CPI grew 19 percent compared to only 10 percent for the general CPI, indicating 9 percent real growth in health care prices. Thus of the 33 percent growth in total per capita health spending over this period, one-quarter apparently derived from increases in the prices of health care relative to other goods and services.

Why would health care prices rise so rapidly? One possible explanation for these recent price increases is that supplier consolidation has led to reduced competition among health care providers, enabling hospitals and physician groups to leverage market power to raise prices. For example, there were about 900 hospital consolidations during 1994-2000 (from a base of roughly 6,000 hospitals). Some of these mergers have appeared to result in monopolistic price increases, and even some major metropolitan areas have become dominated by just two or three hospital systems. It is not clear how important such trends will be in the future, however, in the face of vigorous antitrust enforcement.

Part of the apparent increase in relative prices may, however, be the illusory result of measurement problems. Standard price indices such as the medical CPI may overestimate price growth in health care if they do not adequately account for improvements in health care quality. Price indices are supposed to reflect price changes for a given product. However, because health care quality is constantly increasing, rising prices for a given health care visit may reflect improved quality, rather than just higher costs for a given level of care. For example, the coronary artery bypass graft that the average patient receives today may result in fewer complications and longer and higher quality of life afterward than would have been the case for a patient receiving the procedure 10 years ago—so the higher price paid for the procedure reflects in part the fact that the patient is receiving more "health," not just paying more for the same service.

That said, higher prices for medical services do appear to be an important part of the explanation for why the United States spends more on health care than other OECD countries do. For example, one study of Australia,

Denmark, France, Canada, Germany, and the United Kingdom found that physician wages in the United States are 77 percent higher than the average across those countries. This does not mean, however, that those countries provide a model that should be emulated: Heavy price regulation in some countries has led to long waiting lists for certain types of medical services. One recent survey found that over half of patients in Canada and the United Kingdom had to wait longer than a month for a specialist appointment, compared to less than a quarter of patients in the United States. Similarly, more than a third of patients had to wait longer than four months for elective surgeries in Canada and the United Kingdom, compared to fewer than 10 percent in the United States.

There is a common perception that drug prices are unduly higher in the United States than in other OECD countries, perhaps due to aggressive price negotiation by European governments, but recent research suggests that this may be misleading for several reasons. First, carefully accounting for manufacturer discounts to insurers in the United States shows price differences to be smaller than simple retail price comparisons would suggest (U.S. prices are discounted by about 8 percent on average). Second, U.S. consumers use a much higher proportion of generic drugs than do consumers in other countries (e.g., 58 percent of units in the United States versus 28 percent in France). When comparing average prices paid for each active ingredient (whether generic or name brand), rather than only prices for selected name brand drugs, the international price differences are further narrowed.

Furthermore, some experts suggest that wealthier countries such as the United States should pay a larger share of drug development costs than should less-wealthy countries, because of both equity and efficiency arguments. Thus, observing lower drug prices in developing countries than in the United States does not generate great controversy. Many people do not recognize, however, that the United States is also substantially richer than most other OECD countries. For example, per capita income in the United States is 22-percent higher than in the United Kingdom. After adjusting for differences in manufacturer discounts, use of generics, and per capita income, average drug prices are in fact higher in many other OECD countries. Research has found that U.S. drug prices relative to income are 7-percent lower in France, but 4-percent higher in Canada, 10-percent higher in Germany, and 25-percent higher in the United Kingdom. Thus, the United States' higher health care spending as a share of GDP does not appear to be explained by higher drug prices.

Technological Change

Research suggests that, over time, a major source of health care spending increases has been adoption of new, technologically intensive health care goods and services. For example, one study found that average spending per heart attack case in the United States increased in real terms from $12,000 in 1984 to about $22,000 in 1998, and that about half of this spending increase could be attributed to the adoption of more-sophisticated technologies. This does not mean that the higher spending is not of very high value: post-heart attack life expectancy over this same period increased from five years to six years, with 70 percent of that increase attributable to the adoption of better technology.

The United States appears to use some expensive technologies more intensively than do other countries. For example, the United States has more than 50-percent more MRI units per capita than do other OECD countries on average. The United States' more-intensive use of technology partly reflects its higher rate of innovation and earlier adoption of technology. For example, angioplasty was relatively rare outside the United States in 1990, with the U.S. utilization rate three times higher than the next-closest country; Germany finally reached the U.S. level by about 1998, while adoption in other countries continued to lag.

It is worth noting that the adoption of new technologies does not inevitably raise costs. New technologies regularly reduce costs in many other sectors of the economy, such as the semiconductor industry. In the U.S. health care industry, however, the combination of technological change along with muted consumer incentives to demand lower costs is responsible for a significant portion of rising health care spending.

First-Dollar Insurance Inhibits Consumer Cost-Consciousness

In most markets outside of health care, consumers decide what to purchase by comparing the price of a good or service against the benefit it brings them. By contrast, in the health care sector, consumers often do not learn the prices of goods and services consumed until bills are received weeks or months later, if ever. Instead, physicians are expected to make health care consumption choices for patients, despite the fact that physicians frequently lack the incentive to match the benefits of care with its costs, and may even lack information about the costs themselves. A major reason for this lack of consumer incentive is the fact that many health insurance policies provide close to "first-dollar coverage" of health care costs. That is, people with health insurance typically pay only a relatively small portion of the total cost—or in some cases, literally none of the cost—of the health care services they receive. This section reviews the causes and consequences of first-dollar insurance coverage.

Causes of First-Dollar Insurance Coverage

Unlike most other types of insurance, health insurance in the United States often includes first-dollar coverage of the cost of even routine, predictable services. By contrast, most other forms of insurance focus on protecting the insured from large and unexpected losses. If automobile insurance had the first-dollar coverage of even routine services that many health insurance policies offer, it would cover the costs of oil changes and new tires, rather than just protecting against unpredictable catastrophes such as automobile accidents.

Health insurance policies have this unusual first-dollar coverage feature in large part because the tax code makes it cheaper for people to purchase health care indirectly through insurance than directly through out-of-pocket payments (see Box 4-1). Another factor underlying first-dollar coverage is the increased use of managed care programs, which spread rapidly during the 1990s. Most managed care plans are characterized by minimal cost sharing, relying instead on gatekeepers to regulate use of resources. Interest in managed care programs has decreased recently, because of public backlash against the cost-containment measures used in these programs.

Box 4-1: Tax Preferences for Employer Health Insurance Premiums

Since the 1940s, the tax code has excluded employer payments for health insurance premiums from the portion of workers' compensation subject to taxation (both payroll and personal income taxes). The total value of the tax exclusion is quite large, reducing Federal taxes by over $200 billion in 2006 ($133 billion for the income tax exclusion and $80 billion for the payroll tax exclusion), which is equivalent to about 10 percent of actual Federal tax receipts. This exclusion of health insurance premiums from taxation was a by-product of wage-control legislation during World War II (which established a precedent for treating employee benefits differently from regular wages), and was not intentionally designed to promote health insurance coverage. But this tax treatment of employer-provided health insurance premiums has had important consequences for insurance markets.

First, it has caused the private insurance system to become predominantly employment-based. More than 91 percent of privately insured individuals under age 65 receive their health insurance through their employers. Except for the self-employed, those who purchase insurance on the individual market (that is, not through their employers) must do so with after-tax dollars. The self-employed receive an "above-the-line" income tax deduction for health insurance premiums (equivalent to the income-tax exclusion for employer insurance), though they still owe full payroll taxes on the income used to buy premiums. For someone in the

---

15-percent income tax bracket and subject to the 15.3-percent payroll tax, a policy with a $10,000 premium would cost roughly $7,000 if purchased through an employer, $8,500 if the person were self-employed, and the full $10,000 if the person were not self-employed and purchased the policy individually. This tax treatment has created a strong financial incentive for individuals to purchase health insurance through their employer, even if their first choice of insurance product is not offered by the employer. In addition, as an incentive to buy health insurance, this tax subsidy is larger for people in higher tax brackets (as shown in the chart), despite the fact that a given subsidy amount would reduce uninsurance much more among lower-income households.

Furthermore, the employer premium tax exclusion promotes low-deductible insurance coverage with minimal out-of-pocket cost sharing. In most cases, while insurance premiums are paid with pretax dollars, out-of-pocket health spending must be paid for with after-tax dollars. For example, $1,000 of health care services covered by full insurance costs the person with employer-provided insurance only about $700 in after-tax dollars (assuming a 15-percent income tax bracket and 15.3-percent payroll tax), whereas those same services would cost $1,000 if paid out-of-pocket. Because of the tax penalty for out-of-pocket spending relative to insurance premiums, there is a strong incentive for employers to provide and employees to select first-dollar coverage, even if they would have preferred higher deductibles and lower premiums in the absence of the tax provision. This has, in turn, diminished the role of consumers as guardians against wasteful spending and unduly high prices.

Annual Value of Employer-Provided Health Insurance Tax Exclusion by Income
The tax exclusion provides the greatest benefit to those in higher tax brackets.

Value of tax exclusion for $10,000 annual premium

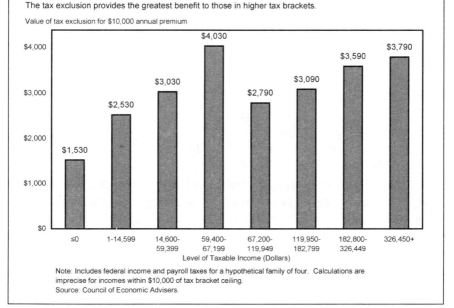

Note: Includes federal income and payroll taxes for a hypothetical family of four. Calculations are imprecise for incomes within $10,000 of tax bracket ceiling.
Source: Council of Economic Advisers.

Consequences of First-Dollar Insurance Coverage

The original purpose of health insurance, like other forms of insurance, was to protect individuals from catastrophic and unexpected costs by spreading risk across a larger population. However, as discussed, health insurance in the United States has now also become a vehicle for financing relatively low-cost, routine expenditures. This use of insurance as "prepaid medical care" has three important consequences: (1) It encourages consumers to overuse certain types of health care. (2) It gives little incentive for consumers to search for the lowest-price providers. (3) It distorts incentives for technological change. Rather than focusing research incentives on cost-effective technology, it induces adoption of technologies for which costs exceed incremental benefits, while undermining the development of cost-saving technologies. We discuss each of these points.

First, heavily insured individuals, being insulated from most health care costs, have the incentive to overconsume certain types of care, a phenomenon referred to as *moral hazard*. An allergy drug may have great value for patient A who has serious symptoms, but little value for patient B who has only mild symptoms. If the two patients faced the market price of $100/month, then A might decide the drug is worth the cost but B might forgo it, given its negligible benefit for him. With first-dollar insurance coverage, however, B might instead choose to continue taking the drug as long as the expected benefits to him were greater than zero. In this case, B's decision would inefficiently drive up health care spending at a loss to society, since the benefit of the drug would be less than the real cost.

Some would argue that such scenarios are rare because physicians should not prescribe the drug for person B if it would be wasteful or of little practical use in improving his health. But in fact physicians may not have enough information to fully evaluate the benefit to patients, and often have little incentive to limit inappropriate care to highly insured patients. Providing extra services increases their incomes and protects them from the charge that they did not take every action with conceivable benefit to the patient. Box 4-2 discusses the role of medical malpractice liability in increasing medical expenditures.

In order to quantify the moral hazard effects of first-dollar insurance coverage, the RAND Health Insurance Experiment randomized individuals into health insurance plans with different *co-insurance* levels. (Co-insurance refers to the percentage of health insurance spending above the deductible an individual must contribute.) A higher co-insurance level gives both the patient and the doctor greater incentive to avoid the use of drugs or procedures that are costly and have low expected benefit. The study found that changing the structure of health insurance does affect the behavior of patients and their

Box 4-2: Medical Liability Costs

Substantial costs in the U.S. health care system are associated with the medical liability system. This affects health care spending in several ways. First, the cost of malpractice damage awards, the legal costs of malpractice lawsuits, and the costs of underwriting malpractice insurance policies are passed on to providers through malpractice insurance premiums and then to patients through out-of-pocket payments and insurance premiums. Second, defensive medicine—ordering tests and procedures solely to guard against potential malpractice claims—may have an even bigger effect on health care spending than the direct costs associated with malpractice suits.

The President has called on Congress to pass liability reforms to make the system fairer and more predictable while reducing wasteful costs. The trend toward greater consumer decision making in health care may have complementary effects in reducing liability costs associated with defensive medicine. Consumers with first-dollar insurance coverage have little incentive to decline many of the tests and procedures suggested by physicians, even if they and their physicians understand that there may be very little health benefit from the increased spending. But as consumers pay for a greater portion of noncatastrophic care, they may decide to forgo expensive and unnecessary tests and procedures suggested by physicians primarily to avoid lawsuits rather than to improve patients' health.

doctors. Specifically, individuals with first-dollar coverage had 45-percent higher health expenditures than individuals who were randomly assigned insurance plans with 95-percent co-insurance up to a catastrophic out-of-pocket maximum level (the out-of-pocket maximum was about $3,500 in today's dollars). Importantly, the extra care received in the first-dollar coverage plans produced no discernible extra health benefits in the studied sample as a whole. There were, however, some health benefits for select subpopulations of low-income and chronically ill individuals, suggesting that care should be taken not to expose lower-income families to excessively high cost sharing relative to their income, and that certain preventive measures such as chronic-disease management are important to exempt from cost sharing. For most services consumed by the majority of the population, however, the RAND study showed that higher cost sharing can be a powerful tool to induce consumers to take responsibility for focusing their health care spending on only those products and services with the highest value.

A second consequence of first-dollar insurance coverage is that consumers are less sensitive to the prices of health care consumed, an outcome that dulls the competitive forces that keep prices down in most other markets. Many insurers attempt to reduce the range of choices available to enrollees through mechanisms such as selective contracting and preferred provider networks, but such practices are even more effective when the consumer is also price-sensitive. Imagine two hospitals that provide the same service, but hospital A charges $1,000 and is located in an older facility while hospital B charges $2,000 but is located in an updated facility with a wide array of amenities and equipment on site. Given these choices, a consumer facing the actual price may prefer hospital A, but in a world of first-dollar coverage, most people would choose hospital B, even if the extra amenities of hospital B provided only modest benefit. As a result of this structure of incentives, health care providers may compete for patients by providing greater convenience or amenities with little incentive to control costs. This lack of price sensitivity on the part of the consumers of health care is one of the major forces underlying the rapid growth of health care costs.

A third consequence of first-dollar insurance coverage is distorted incentives for technological development. One type of distortion is that new technologies may be developed and marketed even when they are of low incremental cost-effectiveness relative to other available options. For example, if a new drug is even slightly more effective than an existing drug, a person with first-dollar insurance coverage may demand the new drug even if it is priced well above existing satisfactory and effective alternatives. When consumers have dulled price incentives pharmaceutical companies will invest in bringing a new drug to market even if it provides little new value. In a world in which most consumers had high-deductible insurance and were sensitive to the full cost of drugs, the pharmaceutical company might choose not to spend the large amount of resources necessary to complete clinical trials and bring the drug to market if they knew its incremental improvement over existing drugs would be small.

Likewise, dulled price sensitivity on the part of consumers reduces the incentive to develop cost-reducing technologies. In many other sectors of the economy, such as computer memory chips, technological progress results in cheaper and more cost-effective products each year as producers look for more-efficient manufacturing processes and product innovations to keep them ahead of their competitors. In health care, this type of technological innovation is much rarer, since few consumers have the incentive to adopt a cheaper product, particularly if it has even slightly lower effectiveness. If more health care consumers were to become price sensitive, the health care sector would have the incentive to pursue more such cost-reducing technologies that could, over the long term, help reduce the rate at which health care spending is growing.

Some observers have expressed concern that changes to the current system might be harmful if they result in reduced innovation, but these observers have often failed to distinguish cost-effective from cost-ineffective innovations. Life expectancy at birth has increased from 70 to almost 78 years since 1962. In addition to living longer, we are also enjoying more years in better health and with fewer disabilities. While some of these health improvements have been due to lifestyle changes, some can clearly be traced to medical technologies, such as those that have reduced infant mortality, improved survival rates after heart attacks, improved treatment of depression and other mental illnesses, and improved the management of chronic illnesses. Research suggests that *on average* our spending on new medical technology has indeed been cost-beneficial. This indicates that, as a society, we would not want to return to the health spending levels of 1960, for example, if doing so also meant returning to the types of medical care available in 1960. But economic efficiency depends on each ("marginal") individual new technology being cost-beneficial, not just the average of all technologies. The fact that on average our investment in medical technology has paid off does not preclude the possibility that our system contains significant inefficiencies, and that some of the new technology may have contributed little compared to the amounts spent on it. If consumers were given the information they need about the actual costs and benefits of various treatments, as well as the incentives to compare those costs and benefits, it might be possible to eliminate some of that wasteful spending.

Consequences of Inefficient Health Care Spending

Rising health care spending is a burden to employers, consumers, and taxpayers. Employers who offer insurance complain that rising premiums strain their labor relations and threaten their balance sheets. Rising premiums make health insurance less affordable, contributing to the ranks of the uninsured. Those who are insured face rising out-of-pocket costs and lower cash wage growth. And taxpayers must finance the rapidly increasing costs of publicly provided health care for seniors, the disabled, and the poor.

Private Spending

As consumers spend more of their budgets on health care, they must spend less on other goods and services. Since 1980, for example, the share of consumer spending that has gone to medical care has increased from 10 percent to 17 percent, while the shares of spending on items such as food and clothing have decreased. Of the $7.5 trillion increase in personal income since 1980, $1.5 trillion has been devoted to health care. Similarly, of the $2.19 real increase in hourly compensation over the past five years, $0.54 (25 percent) has gone toward higher health insurance premium costs. Thus, take-home pay has grown more slowly than total compensation (including health insurance and other benefits) (Chart 4-3).

The costs of health care would be of less concern if most health care spending reflected optimal decisions by consumers weighing the costs and benefits of the services they buy. For example, the fact that consumer spending on DVDs increased 31 percent in 2004 alone has not alarmed anyone nor led to calls for government intervention. But spending on private health care is different, because health care is considered a "merit" good deserving of government support for those that cannot afford it, because of the government's extensive role in the health care market, and because of the forces that interfere with the efficient allocation of resources.

Employers have also been affected by increasing health care costs. In particular, firms that have promised generous health benefits to retirees have borne increasingly heavy costs. The economic consequences of this may include the need for restructuring of some of these firms, loss of expected benefits for some retirees, and potential costs to taxpayers if some of these retirees increase their reliance on public health insurance. Rising costs for current employees have also affected employer behaviors. Some employers have tried to reduce their insurance costs by hiring more part-time workers (who are generally

Chart 4-3 **Real Hourly Compensation of the Civilian Population**
Health insurance spending growth exerts downward pressure on wages.

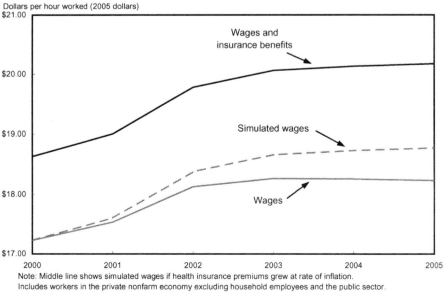

Note: Middle line shows simulated wages if health insurance premiums grew at rate of inflation.
Includes workers in the private nonfarm economy excluding household employees and the public sector.
Source: Department of Labor (Bureau of Labor Statistics).

ineligible for insurance benefits), asking employees to contribute more to premiums, reducing the generosity of the plans they offer, or discontinuing health insurance benefits altogether.

In the long run, however, it is not the employers but rather the workers who bear the burden of rising health insurance costs. Economists have shown that even though employers may make the bulk of the payments to cover the health insurance premiums of workers, these payments are treated just like wages or any other component of workers' total compensation. This total compensation depends on worker productivity and labor-market supply and demand. Rising insurance premiums may thus change the mix of workers' compensation by increasing health benefits and decreasing wages, but if they do not affect workers' productivity they will not lead firms in competitive markets to raise total compensation. Institutional factors such as minimum-wage laws and sluggish wage adjustment may mean that health insurance premiums affect employer profits in the short run, but in the long run most or all of increases in health insurance costs are shifted to employees in the form of wages that are lower than they otherwise would have been.

Public Spending

When per capita spending on health care rises rapidly, the pressures on government programs become particularly intense. First, if the standard of care received by enrollees in government programs is not to differ too radically from that of the general public, the costs of helping those already enrolled in the programs will rise as well. Second, rising insurance premiums may cause some people to drop private insurance and to rely instead on public insurance such as Medicaid or on safety-net providers (e.g., uncompensated hospital care) subsidized by taxpayers. Not only does rising uninsurance lead to higher government costs, but uninsured people often consume health care resources inefficiently—for example, by failing to obtain preventive care, delaying necessary care, or overusing emergency rooms relative to less-costly clinic settings.

The largest government programs that finance health care for those not otherwise insured are Medicare and Medicaid. These programs are becoming increasingly expensive to taxpayers. For example, according to projections, if current trends were to continue unchecked, Medicare costs would increase from the current share of 2.6 percent of GDP to 6.9 percent by 2050. Medicaid, jointly financed by the Federal and state governments, is also becoming an increasingly large share of budgets, with just the Federal portion of spending projected to increase from 1.5 percent of GDP today to 2.5 percent by 2050. The costs of these public programs are unsustainable under any reasonable projections. Closing the currently projected 75-year deficit in just the Hospital Insurance (HI) portion of Medicare would require tax increases of 107 percent or benefits reductions of 48 percent. Ultimately, the benefits paid by these programs must be significantly pared back, the taxes dedicated to their support must be increased, or major reforms must be enacted that slow the rate of growth in health care spending.

Strengthening the Role of Health Consumers Through Public Policy

This chapter has discussed the central role of first-dollar insurance coverage in dulling the incentives for consumers to shop carefully for cost-effective health care. By giving consumers both the incentives and the information needed to become better shoppers for health care, public policy can help control the growth in health care costs and improve the efficiency of the use of health care resources.

The President has proposed a wide-range of measures to help make health care more efficient and accessible, such as improving community health centers, reforming medical liability laws, creating Association Health Plans for small businesses, allowing insurance to be more portable and purchased more easily across state lines, and many other reforms. This section will focus specifically on proposals that help improve incentives for consumers.

An important policy advance has aimed to reduce the bias toward first-dollar insurance coverage by allowing more out-of-pocket health care expenditures to be paid with pretax dollars through the innovative mechanism of Health Savings Accounts (HSAs). Complementary initiatives to improve information available to consumers for making appropriate health care choices can help facilitate the movement toward HSA-based consumer-directed health care.

The potential benefits of reforms that slow spending growth could be great. Consider a scenario in which new policies successfully reduce future national health spending by one percentage point per year, through a combination of short-run quantity decreases, medium-term price decreases, and long-run increases in cost-reducing technological change. If spending were to grow by 6 percent per year, instead of by 7 percent per year as currently projected, by 2025 the expected health share of GDP would be reduced from 22 percent to 18 percent, a substantial difference.

Health Savings Accounts (HSAs)

HSAs are tax-favored accounts to which individuals can contribute funds they can then use to pay current and future out-of-pocket medical expenses. These accounts were signed into law by the President in 2003 and went into effect in 2004. HSAs represent a major improvement over previous tax-preferred medical spending accounts such as Flexible Spending Arrangements (which must be exhausted each year, a factor that limits their use) and Health Reimbursement Accounts (which are owned by employers, not consumers). In contrast, HSAs are owned by individual consumers regardless of employer, and unused account balances can be retained and grow from year-to-year without penalty. HSAs are designed to be used in conjunction with high-deductible health plans, defined as plans having minimum deductibles (currently $1,050 for individuals and $2,100 for families) with annual out-of-pocket limits (currently no more than $5,250 or $10,500 for individuals and families, respectively). Deductibles and out-of-pocket limits are indexed to adjust over time with inflation. Certain types of preventive care may be provided with first-dollar coverage if deemed appropriate by the insurer.

HSA enrollees with qualifying insurance plans may contribute annually up to the lesser of the plan deductible or $2,700 (individuals)/ $5,450 (family). These contributions are excluded from income taxes both at the time of deposit and at the time of "qualifying" withdrawal; the funds may be used to pay for out-of-pocket medical expenditures, rolled over indefinitely, or with-drawn after age 65 (in which case they are taxed as ordinary income if not used for health expenditures).

A key benefit of HSAs is that they lower the previous tax bias toward low-deductible or first-dollar health insurance relative to higher-deductible policies with higher out-of-pocket spending. To illustrate this point, consider a sample health insurance purchaser facing the choice of a low-, medium-, or high-deductible plan. Table 4-1 illustrates how this person's premiums depend on the plans' deductibles, according to actuarial estimates for a representative person. The premium for a $250 (low) deductible policy with a $2,000 out-of-pocket limit would be $4,000, but that premium could be lowered by $1,600 (or 40 percent) by moving to a catastrophic policy with a $2,500 (high) deductible and an out-of-pocket limit of $5,000. Suppose that this person had no health expenditures in the first year of coverage, but a $15,000 catastrophic event in the second year. How is her total two-year spending on health care under these plans affected by the tax code?

- *If there are no tax preferences:* If she buys the traditional (low deductible) plan, her spending is $4,000 in premiums in each year plus $2,000 out-of-pocket in year two, totaling $10,000. If she buys the catastrophic (high deductible) plan, her spending is $2,400 in premiums in each year plus $5,000 out-of-pocket in year two, totaling $9,800. Thus, she would be slightly better off financially under the catastrophic plan in the absence of tax preferences.
- *If insurance premiums (but not out-of-pocket spending) are tax-preferred:* Under the traditional plan, if she is in the 30-percent marginal tax

	Examples of Three Insurance Plans		
	Low Deductible	Medium Deductible	High Deductible
Premium..	$4,000	$3,500	$2,400
Cost Sharing			
Deductible..	$250	$1,000	$2,500
Coinsurance after Deductible.............................	20%	20%	20%
Out-of-Pocket Maximum....................................	$2,000	$3,000	$5,000

The premiums in this table represent the actuarial value of each plan for a representative enrollee.

bracket, she receives a $2,400 tax subsidy (over two years), but under the catastrophic plan she only receives a $1,440 tax subsidy. Thus, the tax subsidy makes her prefer the traditional plan where she might otherwise have preferred the catastrophic plan.

- *If tax-preferred HSAs are available:* If she contributes the maximum $2,500 to the HSA in both years, she would receive a new $1,500 tax subsidy by using the HSA to pay her out-of-pocket expenses in year two with tax-free dollars. This mitigates the previous tax-induced bias against catastrophic plans, again making her better off financially under the catastrophic policy.

This illustration of course simplifies many dimensions of the comparison between policies. For example, it ignores the fact that catastrophic events are rare, so that most people would be able to accumulate many more years of premium and HSA savings, further increasing the attractiveness of the HSA-qualified plans. In addition, the example ignores the moral hazard effect of reduced health care utilization in the catastrophic plan, as the patient now has increased incentive to shop carefully for health care.

Not all individuals will benefit equally from moving to a high-deductible policy. First, some poorly informed consumers may forgo recommended care, such as preventive services—care that they might have received under a traditional low-deductible policy. The HSA provision that allows plans to waive the deductible for preventive care is designed to mitigate this possibility. Second, some chronically ill individuals with persistently high spending may be relatively worse off, to the extent that high-deductible policies lead to less cross-subsidization from healthier people in their risk pool. This could be mitigated while preserving the beneficial effects of cost sharing, for example, through improved insurance benefits for the chronically ill, differential premium cross-subsidies in employer insurance, or targeted high-risk-pool subsidies in the individual market. Third, credit-constrained enrollees and those in lower tax brackets will benefit less from provisions allowing tax-free HSA contributions and accumulation. This is also true of the tax exclusion for employer health insurance premiums. These concerns must be balanced against the potential benefits of greater price sensitivity by health care consumers: As more consumers shift into high-deductible plans, there is greater potential for slowing price growth and long-run increases in cost-reducing technology, which could benefit even consumers in traditional insurance plans.

Since the inception of HSAs in 2004, the number of people enrolled in high-deductible HSA-qualified plans has increased rapidly. The new tax benefits that further lower health costs for high-deductible plans have made them attractive not only to the uninsured and small businesses, but to large firms as well. Although HSAs are new enough that comprehensive data are difficult to obtain, as of January 2006, at least 3 million people were covered by HSA-qualified plans sold by insurance company members of the industry group America's Health Insurance Plans (AHIP). Of the people covered by AHIP-related plans, about half purchased their plans in the individual market and 14 percent through small businesses.

Additional tax-code changes could make high-deductible HSA-qualified plans even more attractive and affordable, further strengthening incentives for more consumers to be well-informed, cost-conscious health care decision makers. The President's 2007 budget aims to expand HSAs through proposals that include:

- *Raising the HSA contribution limits up to the plan out-of-pocket maximum.* Current law allows contributions only up to the deductible level, which is often less than half of the out-of-pocket maximum. This change would further limit the tax-induced bias against out-of-pocket spending for medical care. It would also increase the attractiveness of HSA-qualified plans, in particular for the chronically ill who have a higher probability of out-of-pocket spending above their deductible.
- *Further reducing disparities in tax treatment of HSA contributions versus insurance premiums.* Currently, individual contributions to HSAs are excluded from income taxes but not payroll taxes (employer contributions are excluded from both). The President proposes to provide a new income tax credit equal to the payroll taxes paid on the HSA contribution amounts. This will further remove distortions that have encouraged first-dollar insurance coverage. When combined with the first new proposal discussed above, Americans with HSAs would be able to pay all of their out-of-pocket expenses with pretax earnings.
- *Equalizing tax preferences for purchasing HSA-qualified insurance in the employer and individual markets.* The President proposes to exclude from income taxes the value of HSA-qualified insurance premiums if

purchased on the individual market. In addition, taxpayers purchasing these policies on the individual market would receive a new income tax credit equal to the payroll taxes paid on the premium amounts. Thus, all taxpayers would receive the same tax treatment of HSA-qualified insurance premiums, even if working for one of the 40 percent of employers that do not offer health benefits.

- *Helping the chronically ill.* In addition to allowing all out-of-pocket expenses to be paid tax-free through an HSA, the President also proposes allowing employers to make larger HSA contributions for their chronically ill employees so that employers can make HSA-qualified plans equally attractive to all employees regardless of health status. Finally, the President proposes $500 million in annual grants to states to test innovative solutions to subsidize insurance for the chronically ill, in order to enhance the functioning of markets for individual insurance. For example, states could use the funds for risk-adjusted premium subsidy programs, or for creative enhancements of state high-risk pools such as funding HSA accounts for enrollees.

- *Enhancing affordability via a tax credit for low-income people purchasing HSA-qualified insurance in the individual market.* The credit would be worth up to $1,000 for one adult, $2,000 for two adults, or $3,000 for families (not exceeding 90 percent of the premium). It would phase out at incomes of $30,000 for individuals and $60,000 for families. The credit would be advanceable, paid directly by the government at the time of insurance purchase.

Informed Consumers Are Better Consumers

It is important to provide incentives for consumers to choose health care providers and services sensibly, but providing those incentives does not guarantee that consumers will in fact be able to make good choices. Consumers must also have access to the information they need to make good health care decisions. Key information includes:

- *Provider prices.* Few medical providers today advertise their prices in a way that allows for comparison shopping. Several insurers have taken an important step by beginning to make available schedules of physician fees to their enrollees. Hospital fees raise more-difficult issues, since prices negotiated between hospitals and insurers are frequently subject to confidentiality agreements, despite the fact that consumers eventually observe the prices on bills presented to them after the fact. Of even greater use to consumers would be information on "package prices" for complete treatments of medical bundles or episodes. For example, a knee replacement without unusual complications might have ten major components of care, each of which is now billed separately. A package price for the entire treatment would provide an estimated cost for the entire operation, hospitalization, and follow-up treatment. This information could be combined with revised billing procedures, which would allow patients to identify more easily the costs associated with the treatment they had received. The President strongly supports efforts to increase price transparency in the health care market. He has called for hospitals, physician groups, insurers, employers, and other health groups to cooperate in speeding the transition toward a market in which Americans can easily obtain user-friendly and comparable information on prices when shopping for health care.

- *Data on provider quality and value.* Price information by itself is not sufficient for good decision making in the absence of comparative quality data. There is growing interest in providing accurate and usable measures of the quality of care offered by individual health care providers such as hospitals and physician groups. Great progress has been made by researchers in improving the methodology for developing reliable measures, and insurers are now helping to improve the effective dissemination of such data. Measures that combine price and quality data into indicators of overall value are not yet as well developed, but would be another useful decision-making tool.

Better information would also be of use to providers of medical services, who would then be better able to help their patients make sound, cost-effective decisions. Examples include:

- *Practice guidelines.* One key barrier to more-efficient health care spending is the lack of a research base on the appropriate treatment in many medical situations. There is a clear role for government in this area. For example, the Agency for Health Research and Quality (AHRQ) is sponsoring comparative effectiveness research studies relating to medical practice, as authorized under the 2003 Medicare Modernization Act. Such research can produce high returns in terms of improved health care efficiency. Further work to translate such guidelines into educational materials for health care consumers would also greatly enhance the ability of consumers to make wise health care choices.

- *Cost-effectiveness studies.* If the usage of expensive but low-value technologies is to be reduced by the actions of better-informed consumers in consultation with their doctors, then more information is needed about the cost-effectiveness of various technologies and procedures, and about how cost-effectiveness depends on particular factors such as the patient's age and specific condition. Private insurers sponsor some such studies, but the private sector will tend to underinvest in this type of "public good" research. Government support for research in this area, such as the research being conducted by agencies such as AHRQ, has a strong economic justification.

Conclusion

As the United States grows richer and older and as new life-saving technologies develop, Americans are likely to continue to spend a rising share of their growing incomes on health. Indeed, our health care spending overall has returned good value, with Americans living longer and healthier lives. We could achieve this improved health at lower cost, however, by promoting a greater role for consumer decision making in health. Health Savings Accounts provide one tool for doing so, by leveling the playing field for people who prefer to save money by moving toward higher-deductible health insurance policies. As health researchers, the insurance industry, and government work to develop better consumer decision-making tools, more consumers will be able to benefit from moving to such plans. In the long run, the payoff to allocating health care resources toward higher-value and more cost-effective care would be great.

CHAPTER 5

The U.S. Tax System in International Perspective

All governments face two important decisions. They must choose the scope and scale of public goods and services to provide for their citizens, including national defense, public safety, education, law enforcement, and social insurance. They must also decide how to collect the funds to finance those public services, including what things to tax and at what rate to tax them. These tax policy decisions affect job creation, the allocation of resources, economic efficiency, economic growth, and ultimately the living standards of their citizens. In this chapter, we examine U.S. choices in the context of the varied choices of other countries around the world.

Recent calls for fundamental tax reform reflect long-standing public frustration with the complexity of the U.S. system and dissatisfaction with its economic effects. Last year's *Economic Report of the President* outlined the need for tax reform and evaluated several prototypes for reform. The President created a bipartisan Advisory Panel on Federal Tax Reform that spent the year evaluating the current tax system and recommended two options for reform. This chapter provides a broader context for evaluating these and other potential reforms.

This chapter makes three essential points:

- Every country makes fundamental choices about its tax system: what level of overall tax burden to impose, what to tax, and what tax rates to apply. These choices matter because they have important economic consequences that affect the living standards of their citizens.
- The United States has made different choices than other countries: We have a relatively low tax burden, and we finance more of that burden with a tax on personal income instead of consumption.
- When viewed in an international perspective, the U.S. system has been improved by some significant changes but could benefit greatly from others, particularly those focused on reforming the taxation of capital income.

Fundamental Choices in Tax Systems

The two fundamental questions that must be answered in designing a tax system to raise revenue for government expenditures are what to tax (the "base") and how much to tax it (the "rates"). Public discussion of tax policy often also focuses on the distributional consequences of these decisions, which are certainly important. However, economists point out that the answers to these two fundamental questions have equally important implications for the economic decisions made by individuals and small and large businesses, and thus for the overall performance of the economy. In this section we discuss these tax policy choices and their effects on economic decisions.

Designing a Tax System

Governments choose the size and scope of the public services they wish to provide and the corresponding level of spending required. At the same time, they choose how to finance that spending, through a combination of taxation and borrowing. The use of borrowing (deficits) to finance government spending has varied over time, and the optimal level depends on many factors. For example, economists have argued that it is reasonable to borrow to finance temporary increases in spending (e.g., during times of war or to provide aid after a disaster) or temporary declines in revenue (as in a recession). In any case, the cost of government borrowing must ultimately be financed by tax revenues, and so we focus here on the tax system.

Every tax system is defined by two factors: the tax base and the tax rate structure. The base defines what is subject to taxation and the rate determines what portion is taken in tax. We begin by considering two of the most common tax bases used: income and consumption.

A tax system with a pure income tax base is designed to tax all of the resources that increase a taxpayer's ability to consume, regardless of what that taxpayer actually does consume. Taxable income under this system includes all wage and salary income, interest income, and dividends, and also can include increases in wealth such as unrealized capital gains and noncash income such as the implicit rental value of owner-occupied housing. In short, under a pure income-based tax system, all income plus all increases in wealth can be subject to taxation.

A consumption-based tax system, in contrast, taxes only the share of income that is consumed, exempting the share that is saved. Examples of consumption-based tax systems, such as a national retail sales tax, a value-added tax, a consumption-based Flat Tax, or a consumed-income tax, were presented in Chapter 3 of the 2005 *Economic Report of the President*, which addressed "Options for Tax Reform."

The U.S. tax system is neither a pure income tax nor a pure consumption tax, but rather a hybrid of the two. Although nominally based on income, the U.S. system excludes significant portions of the return to savings from the tax base (e.g., interest earned on assets held in a 401(k) employment-based retirement plan or an Individual Retirement Account). The U.S. system also excludes other forms of income from the tax base, two key examples being the premiums paid by employers for employee health insurance and the implicit rental value of owner-occupied housing.

Another central aspect of designing a tax base is the treatment of international activity, both of foreigners acting within U.S. borders and of U.S. citizens and corporations conducting business abroad. Currently, the United States applies its income tax, in principle, on a *worldwide* basis, taxing all income earned by U.S. residents on their economic activity in the United States and the rest of the world, and allowing a limited credit for taxes paid to foreign governments. Taxing on a worldwide basis means the U.S. applies its tax to all economic activity in the country (regardless of the nationality of ownership) and to all activity of U.S. residents and U.S.-owned companies (regardless of the country in which that activity occurs). The United States could, alternatively, tax on a *territorial* basis, taxing all income earned within U.S. borders regardless of the nationality of the person or corporations earning the income, but not taxing income earned abroad. Territorial tax treatment would exclude from the tax base all foreign earnings of U.S. residents (both individuals and corporations). With increasing competition among the United States and other countries for economic activity, this choice also has important implications for economic growth and efficiency.

In addition to choosing the tax base, the tax authorities must also determine the tax rate structure. This choice has significant effects on both the efficiency and the equity of the tax system. Countries might choose one tax rate to apply to the entire tax base, or a progressive schedule of tax rates, with higher rates applying to those with greater resources. A key determinant of the effect of the tax system on the efficiency of the economy is the tax rate that is applied to the incremental use of resources—such as an additional dollar of income or an additional dollar of consumption. This *marginal tax* rate is important because it affects the taxpayers' incentives, and thus their economic behavior, inducing them to make decisions that are different from those they might have made in the absence of the tax. These "distortions" of behavior (relative to the no-tax benchmark) are the major channel through which the tax system affects the efficiency of the economy.

Taxes Distort Economic Decisions

Virtually all forms of taxation distort economic decision making because they change the cost of allocating resources to different uses. Those distortions have a real economic cost that goes beyond the burden of the tax being paid. The reduction in economic efficiency generated by the changes in economic behavior that a tax induces is called the *excess burden* of the tax. The excess burden imposed by a tax increases dramatically as the marginal tax rate increases. A standard demonstration in economics textbooks is that excess burden is proportional to the square of the tax rate, so that doubling the marginal tax rate roughly quadruples the excess burden of the tax. This relationship between marginal tax rates and economic efficiency is the reason that tax systems with broad bases and low rates are generally considered the most efficient way to raise revenue.

Of course, the tax rate specified in statute may not correspond with what businesses and individuals actually pay in taxes because of exemptions, deductions, and credits that reduce their tax burden. The *effective tax* rate that people pay (and that drives their behavior) may thus be lower than the *statutory rate*. Designing a tax system involves choosing the statutory tax rates, defining the tax base including any exemptions and deductions, and specifying tax credits. The combination of those choices determines the effective tax rate that people and firms pay, and that can alter their behavior and cause distortions in the economy. In the next section we discuss the distortions created by different tax systems.

Tax Systems and Economic Distortions

The complexities of modern tax systems can change many decisions made by individuals and businesses alike. For example, individuals choose how much they work, the forms of compensation they receive (such as wages or health insurance), how much they save, and whether they own or rent a home. Businesses must choose how many workers to hire, where to locate workers and capital assets around the world, the types of assets in which to invest, and the means of financing these assets (e.g., debt, equity, or retained earnings). Taxes can affect all of these decisions.

The choice between an income-based and a consumption-based tax system affects the labor market decisions of workers, the savings decisions of families, and the behavior of entrepreneurs. For example, a worker facing a marginal tax rate of 40 percent on income (who would thus take home only $6 for an additional $10 earned) may decide to work less than someone who faces a marginal tax rate of 20 percent (and would thus take home $8 for an additional $10 earned).

Relative to a consumption tax base, the use of an income tax base increases the costs to individuals of saving for the future, as detailed in Chapter 3 of the 2005 *Economic Report of the President*. A tax system with the property of *static efficiency* does not distort the choices that people make about how to allocate resources today (for example, it does not affect their decision about whether to consume apples or oranges). A system with the property of *dynamic efficiency* does not distort the choice of how to allocate resources between today and tomorrow (it does not affect the choice between consuming apples today and consuming apples in the future).

Consumption-based taxes are more likely to be dynamically efficient than income-based taxes. Someone earning a higher return on a savings account can expect to consume more in the future for each dollar saved, and is thus likely to save more. Taxing savings (as is done in a pure income-based system) makes future consumption relatively more costly, which leads people to save and invest less, with adverse consequences for economic growth.

Further distortions are introduced into the U.S. economy by the separate taxation of corporate income, rather than integration of taxation of corporate and personal income. Corporate profits are essentially taxed twice, first under the corporate income tax and again under the personal income tax when corporate profits are paid out as dividends. The result is a higher tax on income earned in the corporate sector than that earned elsewhere in the economy. For corporate income that is paid out as dividends, the combined tax rate can be remarkably high: as much as 35 percent at the corporate level and another 15 percent through the individual income tax, considering Federal taxes alone. Including state tax rates and accounting for deductibility, the Organization for Economic Cooperation and Development (OECD) estimates the U.S. combined tax rate can be as high as 50.8 percent. This double-taxation of corporate income creates both static and dynamic inefficiencies. It is also inconsistent with either a pure income tax base or a pure consumption tax base.

The U.S. tax code also makes it costlier for firms to make some kinds of investments than others, leading to additional distortions of economic decision making. For example, investment financed from prior earnings (equity) and investment financed from borrowing (debt) are taxed differently, various assets are subject to different depreciation rules, and dividend income received by shareholders is taxed differently from capital gains. There are also ways that U.S. firms can reduce their effective tax rate by deferring their tax payments. Each of these differences affects the choices that businesses make about where and how much to invest.

Finally, the U.S. application of a worldwide tax base affects firms' decisions about where to locate and where to make investments. Foreign-sourced income of U.S. companies is taxable, but the credits taxpayers receive for foreign taxes paid are not applied uniformly. There are limits to the amount of foreign tax credit a firm can claim, which can create incentives for firms to change their investment and business activity patterns across countries based on international tax rates. Under this worldwide system, U.S. firms operating in a foreign country may eventually be liable for not just that host country's taxes, but also for U.S. taxes under some circumstances. Competitors from countries taxing on a territorial basis are not subject to this U.S. tax, and therefore may have a competitive advantage, all else being equal.

More generally, the tax treatment of the foreign-source income of U.S. multinationals under the current worldwide system is widely thought to be one of the most complex aspects of U.S. taxation. This complexity itself imposes a burden on these companies, causing them to allocate substantial resources to tax planning and compliance. With globalization and the increasing importance of international capital flows, the distortions and complexity generated by the current U.S. system are increasingly costly to the U.S. economy.

U.S. Tax Policy in International Perspective

In this section we examine the choices the United States has made about the size of the national tax burden, the forms of taxation to employ, and the tax rates applied. We compare these choices to those made by other countries and show that the United States has a relatively low overall tax burden, and its choices about which tax sources to rely upon differ substantially. Recent reforms in other countries are highlighted.

International Comparison of Overall Tax Burdens

A common measure of the overall tax burden is the ratio of total taxes paid to all levels of government to the gross domestic product (GDP). This share represents the fraction of the total output of the economy that is taken in taxes in any given year, or the average tax rate. This measure of overall tax burden is particularly useful for international comparisons. First, it is unaffected by international differences in national versus subnational government responsibilities. Second, it adjusts for differences in the overall size of the countries' economies.

Among countries in the OECD, the United States has a relatively low total tax burden (including Federal, state, and local taxes). Total taxes in the United States at all levels of government amounted to 26.4 percent of GDP in 2002, substantially lower than the OECD average of 36.3 percent. This share is also below the European Union (EU) average of 40.6 percent.

Chart 5-1 uses OECD data from 2002 to illustrate the average tax rates (total taxes as a share of GDP) for the 15 largest countries of the OECD. Only Mexico, Korea, and Japan had total tax burdens smaller than that of the United States in 2002. OECD countries such as Sweden and Denmark, on the other hand, had tax burdens that were as much as 20 percentage points of GDP higher than that of the United States.

The United States faces a significant fiscal challenge in keeping the overall tax burden low in the future. Growth in Federal entitlement spending if not checked, threatens to require substantial increases in taxes, significantly altering the tax choices the United States has made in the past. Box 5-1 provides an overview of this fiscal challenge and its implications for tax policy.

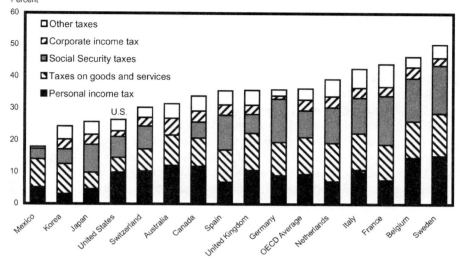

Chart 5-1 **Tax Revenues as a Percent of GDP for the OECD Countries in 2002**
The United States has a relatively small total tax burden and uses personal income taxes to collect a
larger share of total revenue than most other countries.

Note: The countries shown have the 15 largest economies in the OECD. Mexico's personal and corporate tax revenues
are combined, as they were not available separately.
Source: Organization for Economic Cooperation and Development.

International Comparison of Tax Bases and Rate Structures

Beyond different choices about the scope and size of government, the OECD countries have also made different choices about the tax systems used to raise funds. Almost all of the OECD countries use some mix of personal income, corporate income, payroll, sales, and other taxes (e.g., estate and excise taxes), but they differ significantly in their degree of reliance on each. Chart 5-1 illustrates the composition of each country's tax revenue sources: personal income taxes, taxes on goods and services (consumption taxes), social security taxes, corporate income taxes, and other taxes.

The United States relies more heavily on personal income taxation than other OECD countries do. Indeed, in 2002 the United States collected 37.7 percent of its total taxes through the personal income tax compared to an OECD average of 26.0 percent. Given this difference, one might then ask how other countries finance their spending. The primary alternative tax base is consumption. OECD countries collected an average of 31.9 percent of total revenues from taxes on goods and services, mainly through value-added taxes (VATs). A VAT is a tax applied to the gross receipts earned by sellers of products, but sellers receive a tax credit for taxes paid on the inputs they use, so the tax effectively applies only to the value that they themselves added in the

Box 5-1: Fiscal Challenges Ahead

U.S. Federal tax revenues and Federal expenditures have remained fairly stable as a share of national output (GDP) over the past four decades. Despite this overall stability, substantial changes have occurred in the composition of both revenues and expenditures. These expenditure trends in particular foreshadow a major fiscal challenge facing the United States.

Total Federal revenues have averaged 18.2 percent of GDP since the 1960s, with only modest variation around that average, although the composition of revenues has shifted toward payroll taxes and away from excise and corporate income taxes. As discussed in this chapter, the income tax base and rates have changed many times during this period, but the overall contribution of income taxes to total revenues has been fairly stable.

Total Federal outlays since the 1960s have also remained close to the long-run average of about 20.4 percent of GDP, despite many changes in the economy and the mix of government programs that have occurred since 1962. This stability masks important underlying trends, however, in the composition of expenditures. The share of GDP and of the government's budget allocated to spending on Medicare, Medicaid, and Social Security has risen steadily, while the share devoted to defense has fallen. If the growth of spending on these programs goes unchecked, there will soon be a major break in the generally stable fiscal situation that the United States has enjoyed for most of the postwar period.

The cost to the Federal government of these three entitlement programs is expected to rise from 8.0 percent of GDP today to about 15.6 percent of GDP in 2045. In 2005, all other spending programs of the Federal government, excluding interest payments on the national debt, amounted to 9.0 percent of GDP. With this growth, and other programs remaining constant as a share of GDP, in 2045 the Federal budget excluding interest on the debt will consume 24.6 percent of the GDP, compared to 17.0 percent today, with continuing increases beyond that date. Adding back interest on the national debt could make the share of GDP absorbed by the Federal budget even larger.

The implications of these trends are grave. If the major entitlement programs grow as forecast, future generations will be forced to choose between massive tax increases, near-elimination of all government programs outside of entitlements (including defense and essential services), or some combination.

making of the product. Only 17.6 percent of U.S. tax revenues came from taxes on goods and services in 2002, primarily through state and local sales and excise taxes. Recall, however, that the personal income tax is actually a hybrid income-consumption tax, so that some of the taxes collected through the U.S. income tax system, and those of other countries, might be thought of as taxes on consumption.

The United States has also made different choices about the marginal tax rate structure to impose on its tax base. Chart 5-2 shows the top marginal personal income and corporate income tax rates in various OECD countries, including the 15 largest OECD economies and Ireland. The black bars illustrate the personal rate and the gray bars illustrate the corporate rate. The chart shows the OECD's "all-in" definition of the top rate, which includes taxes collected by all levels of government and the employee portion of the social security tax. The top marginal personal income tax rate of 43 percent in the United States is comparable to that of several of the OECD countries such as the United Kingdom (41 percent), and slightly lower than those in France (47 percent) and Japan (48 percent), which matches the OECD average (48 percent), and significantly below the rates in Germany and the Scandinavian countries (all 55 percent or higher). At the same time, the United States has a combined (Federal and state) marginal corporate income tax rate of 39 percent, well above the OECD average of 30 percent, and second highest to that of Japan.

Chart 5-2 illustrates several important points. First, while the U.S. top individual income tax rate is comparable to those of other OECD countries, its top corporate rate is relatively high. Second, except for Mexico, each country's top personal rate is higher than its top corporate rate. Third, there is no clear correlation between the top personal and corporate tax rates. Ireland, for example, has a moderately high personal rate but a very low corporate rate, while Germany has high rates in both cases.

The United States has also chosen to tax on a worldwide basis, as discussed above, unlike some other countries. In 2003, 13 of 30 OECD countries taxed on a worldwide basis, including Japan, Korea, Mexico, and the United Kingdom. The majority of OECD countries (17 countries in 2003) tax on a territorial basis, including Canada, France, Germany, Ireland, Netherlands, Spain, and Sweden.

Finally, the United States has made different choices about the integration of personal and corporate income tax structures. The United States uses a *classical system*, which taxes corporate and personal income separately, based on the status of corporations as separate legal entities. This results in the double taxation of income earned in the corporate sector. Other countries using this system include Ireland, Sweden, and Switzerland. Alternatives to the classical system provide some form of dividend tax relief, thereby avoiding

Chart 5-2 Top Marginal Personal and Corporate Tax Rates for the OECD Countries in 2004

The United States has a relatively high top corporate tax rate and a moderately low personal income tax rate in comparison with other large economies in the OECD.

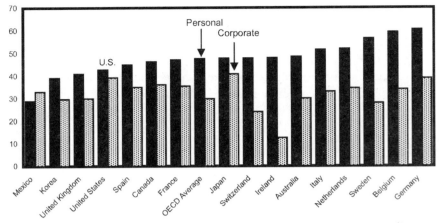

Note: The countries shown include the 15 largest OECD economies plus Ireland, which is interesting because of its relatively low corporate tax rate. The personal rates are the OECD's "all-in" (top marginal) tax rates, which are calculated as the additional central and subcentral government personal income tax, plus employee social security contribution, resulting from a unit increase in gross wage earnings. The corporate rates are the OECD's top combined central and subcentral government rates, with the deductibility of subcentral government taxes taken into account.
Source: Organization for Economic Cooperation and Development.

or reducing double taxation. Under the *imputation system*, shareholders are given a personal income tax credit for tax paid by the corporation on that portion of its profit. Countries using imputation systems (wholly or partially) include Australia, New Zealand, Norway, Canada, and the United Kingdom. Another alternative is the *dividend exclusion method*, under which a portion of dividends paid to individuals is excluded from tax at the individual level. Countries using this method include Germany, France, Finland, and Italy. A final method that can be used to avoid double taxation of dividend income is to apply a *two-rate system*. Under this approach, distributed corporate profits (paid out in dividends) and undistributed profits are taxed at two different rates with undistributed profits taxed at a higher rate. The extent to which this approach eliminates the double taxation of dividend income depends on the rates chosen.

Recent International Tax Reforms

We begin by reviewing several common trends in recent tax reforms that have been adopted by a diverse set of nations. We then examine the implications of these reforms for international tax competition and for reform of the U.S. system.

International Tax Reform Trends

According to the OECD, most countries making changes in their tax systems since 1999 have lowered personal and corporate income tax rates. Those rate reductions were often financed, at least in part, by base broadening. Within this overall pattern of lower personal and corporate income tax rates, there are four discernible trends.

One clear trend among OECD countries is *reducing the taxation of wage and salary income*. These taxes have been reduced through both rate reductions and increases in taxable income thresholds. The OECD average "all in" tax rate for a full-time production worker fell from 25.6 percent in 2000 to 24.8 percent in 2003. The corresponding marginal tax rate fell from 35.4 percent to 34.3 percent. Among G-8 countries since the year 2000, France, Germany, Japan, Russia, and the United States have all lowered personal income tax rates that apply to wage and salary income. Changes in the tax brackets and rate structures generally made these tax systems less progressive, although accompanying changes in exemptions, deductions, and credits complicate the distributional picture.

A second trend is *reducing the tax rates applied to corporate income*. The OECD average corporate income tax rate fell from 33.6 percent in 2000 to 30.8 percent in 2003. As in the case of wage and salary taxation, these rate reductions have typically been accompanied by base-broadening measures. Since 1999, the G-8 countries of France, Germany, Italy, and Japan all reduced their corporate tax rates.

A third trend is *reducing the taxation of capital income* (especially capital gains and dividends) under the personal income tax. Top marginal tax rates on dividend income (corporate plus personal) fell over the period 2000-2003 among OECD countries from 50.1 percent to 46.4 percent. Reforms in Italy, Japan, and the United States, in particular, all reduced the personal income tax rates applied to interest, dividends, or capital gains. Six of the G-8 countries have also altered their tax systems to better coordinate their personal and corporate income taxes. Several countries of the EU, including France, Germany, and Italy, applied partial dividend exclusions, and Russia lowered its dividend tax rate.

A fourth trend is the increasing popularity of *flat rate* income tax schedules. Since the mid-1990s, eight Eastern European countries, including Russia, have adopted income taxes with flat rate structures. The personal tax rates among these eight reform countries range from a low of 12 percent in Georgia to a high of 33 percent in Lithuania, and average 20.6 percent. On the corporate income side, the tax rates range from a low of 10 percent in Serbia to a high of 24 percent in both Estonia and Russia, and average 17.9 percent. Countries adopting these flat income tax structures tend to also apply value-added taxes at relatively high rates, typically 18%.

Evidence on International Tax Competition

Evaluating the U.S. tax system in relation to other national tax systems is particularly important in a world where nations compete for business and mobile capital (including physical, financial, and human capital) by making their tax systems more attractive. A recent review of evidence on international tax competition suggests a systematic change in the pattern of tax rate setting. From 1982 to 1999, there was a substantial increase in international capital mobility, reflected in the amount of foreign direct investment (purchase of buildings, machinery, and equipment) and other measures of the flow of international capital. At the same time, statutory corporate tax rates (tax rates established in the law) declined all around the world and corporate tax bases were broadened, resulting in little change in effective average rates. An exception to that general rule is that effective tax rates for foreign subsidiaries of U.S. firms located in small countries fell sharply between 1992 and 2000.

While the United States reduced its top combined corporate tax rate from 50 percent in 1982 to 39 percent in 2005, as measured by the Institute for Fiscal Studies, other countries have made even more significant reductions. The United States now has the second highest combined corporate income tax rate among OECD countries, behind only Japan. With international tax rates falling overall, and a convergence between rates applied by large and small countries, the United States risks becoming less competitive in attracting capital. As capital becomes more mobile, it is increasingly easy for companies to move their productive activities, including physical capital, export/import operations, research and development activities, and other forms of knowledge creation, around the world in response to tax incentives. (Chapter 7, The History and Future of International Trade, discusses the role of global engagement in firm performance.) In the current environment of international tax competition, the United States will be increasingly challenged as the destination of choice for internationally mobile capital and jobs.

U.S. Tax Reforms: Past, Present, and Future

Reform of the U.S. tax system can play a critical role in improving economic efficiency and the competitiveness of U.S. firms In this section, we examine past tax-reform efforts in the United States, starting with the Tax Reform Act of 1986 (TRA86), and project potential future reforms. We focus in particular on reform of the U.S. tax base and on the taxation of savings or the return to savings, such as interest, dividends, and capital gains.

Twenty Years of Tax Reform

The U.S tax code has many provisions that give preferential treatment to certain types of income. In some instances, these preferences may improve efficiency, such as incentives to increase retirement saving or investment in new equipment that offset distortions introduced by the income tax system. In other cases, tax preferences intentionally distort economic decisions in order to promote certain kinds of economic activity, such as the introduction of tax credits that subsidize advanced education, labor market participation, research and experimentation, or the employment of disadvantaged workers. These provisions narrow the tax base and result in higher marginal tax rates for at least some taxpayers. They also add complexity to the tax code. The President's Advisory Panel on Federal Tax Reform illustrated the trade-off between tax rates and the tax base in the current U.S. tax system. Their calculations suggest that with a broader tax base, tax rates in all tax brackets could be reduced by about a third. Multiple changes to the tax base in the last two decades reflect this tension.

The Effect of Recent Reforms on the Tax Base

We have ample evidence from the last two decades that tax policy is always evolving. The last comprehensive U.S. tax reform was the Tax Reform Act of 1986. That reform was revenue-neutral, broadening income tax bases and lowering marginal tax rates dramatically. TRA86 actually built on reductions in marginal tax rates that began in 1981 when the top rate was reduced from 70 percent to 50 percent. Under the base-broadening provisions of TRA86, marginal tax rates were reduced further, with the top rate cut to 28 percent. Rates applied to different types of income were also made more uniform. For example, one study estimated that effective capital tax rates (taking into account depreciation schedules and other tax provisions that differ across types of capital) prior to TRA86 ranged from a 45.6 percent tax on income from industrial buildings to a 3.3 percent subsidy of income from general industrial machinery. After TRA86 those effective tax rates converged to 37 percent and 38 percent, respectively. Leveling the playing field in this way reduces the distortions to investment across various forms of capital. While TRA86 made effective tax rates more similar across types of capital income, it also raised the overall cost of capital, which likely discouraged investment and reduced dynamic efficiency.

Since TRA86, there have been more than 100 different acts of Congress making nearly 15,000 changes to the tax code. These changes have altered both the individual and the corporate tax bases. Some changes have narrowed the tax base (such as the 1997 repeal of the Alternative Minimum Tax for small business and the 2001 increase in the standard deduction for joint filers), while others have broadened it (such as the 1990 and 1993 limits on itemized deductions and the 1993 expansion of the taxability of Social Security benefits). Other reforms have changed the tax rates applied to this base, such as the rate reductions enacted in 2001 and accelerated in 2003. The introduction and expansion of numerous tax credits, such as the Child, HOPE, Lifetime Learning, Welfare to Work, and Renewal Communities credits, have narrowed the base and introduced disparities in tax rates applied to different types of income.

Disparities in effective marginal tax rates on capital are once again quite large, varying with the method by which capital is financed and by the type of asset. A recent study finds that the effective tax rate on corporations ranges between a tax of 36.1 percent on equity-financed activity to a subsidy of 6.4 percent of debt-financed activity. Furthermore, that study finds that the effective marginal tax rate varies from a high of 36.9 percent to a low of 9.2 percent, depending on the asset type. The current piecemeal tax system is thus both complex and inefficient. In the following section, we examine potential reforms to address these issues.

Potential Reforms to the Tax System

The increasingly globalized business environment in which U.S. investors and firms operate makes the design of an efficient and competitive tax system particularly crucial. Two central issues in the current tax reform debate are the choice of tax base along the income-consumption spectrum and the coordination of personal and corporate tax rates. Recent U.S. tax reforms have lowered the tax rates on capital income. Comprehensive reform could uniformly lower the level of capital income taxation, and could thus reduce the distortions of the current tax system and support greater potential economic growth.

Comprehensive Business Taxation

One shortcoming of the U.S. tax system, discussed above, is the double taxation of corporate income, which subjects capital income to a high effective rate. Since 2003, the United States has taken steps to reduce this problem by applying a substantially lower (15 percent) individual tax rate to dividend and capital gains income, thereby implicitly applying a two-rate system. The President has recommended making permanent these lower tax rates on capital.

Over the years, several comprehensive reforms to integrate corporate and personal income taxes have been proposed. The Treasury Department developed a proposal for a Comprehensive Business Income Tax (CBIT) in the 1990s. The proposed system was designed to give equal tax treatment to corporate debt and equity, tax corporate and noncorporate businesses alike, and reduce the tax distortions between retained and distributed earnings. The CBIT still provides a relevant prototype for integration within the context of an income tax system. Alternatives have also been proposed that move away from reliance on an income tax by implementing a cash-flow business tax (see Box 5-2, for example).

Box 5-2: *Simple, Fair, and Pro-Growth: Proposals to Fix America's Tax System*

Recommendations of the President's Advisory Panel on Federal Tax Reform

The President's Advisory Panel on Federal Tax Reform was charged with evaluating the current Federal tax system and developing alternatives that achieved improvements in simplicity, fairness, and growth potential. They were asked to make at least one recommendation based on the current income tax system, to make their recommendations revenue-neutral, and to preserve incentives for charitable giving and home ownership. In addition, the panel chose to design their recommendations to preserve the current distribution of tax burden. Their 2005 report recommends two alternatives to the present income tax system: a Simplified Income Tax (SIT) and a Growth and Investment Tax (GIT). The SIT plan is a simplified version of the current income tax system. The GIT plan moves to a modified consumption tax that retains some income tax elements.

These two proposals have several features in common. They both have fewer tax brackets and lower top marginal tax rates for individuals and families than the current system. Both plans would repeal the Alternative Minimum Tax (AMT) for families and corporations. Both simplify the tax treatment of savings and lower the tax burden on productivity-enhancing investments by businesses. Either plan would be substantially simpler than the present tax system, and both plans maintain the present distribution of tax burden across income groups.

The two plans diverge primarily in their taxation of business and capital income, using different bases for business taxation. The SIT plan retains a simplified income tax applied to corporations, while the GIT plan would apply a cash-flow tax to all businesses (not just corporations). While they both lower the effective tax rate on capital income, they use different approaches to do so. The SIT plan excludes dividends paid to individuals from the individual income tax base and excludes 75 percent

---

Box 5-2 — *continued*

of corporate capital gains from U.S. companies, while the GIT plan applies a uniform 15 percent tax to interest, dividends, and capital gains at the individual level. The SIT plan adopts a simple accelerated depreciation method for investments, while the GIT plan would permit full expensing of investment. The plans also tax foreign income differently. The SIT plan taxes income on a territorial basis (with foreign-sourced income untaxed), while the GIT cash-flow tax is destination-based (with exports untaxed).

Either of these two recommendations represents a significant step forward in making the U.S. tax system simpler, fairer, and growth-enhancing, but each would involve substantial transition costs. They deserve serious consideration and more comprehensive analysis.

The President's Tax Reform Panel

The broader goals of any comprehensive tax reform should be the creation of a system that is simple, is fair, and promotes economic growth. The President's Tax Reform Panel sought to design revenue-neutral and distribution-neutral plans to achieve these goals. The panel proposed two prototypes for reform: a Simplified Income Tax (SIT) and a Growth and Investment Tax (GIT), summarized in Box 5-2. Both of these proposals fundamentally alter the tax bases for individuals and businesses as well as the treatment of capital income. Either of these reforms would represent a large change and involve important transition issues. While each plan embodies features that are attractive from the point of view of efficiency, fairness, and simplicity, comprehensive review of these plans and policy debate is needed before making such substantial changes to the tax system.

Conclusion

Every government faces choices about how to design its tax system in order to finance the services it provides for its citizens. Because virtually all forms of taxation distort economic decision making, each country faces the challenge of designing a tax system that raises needed revenue and achieves distributional and other goals while distorting economic decisions as little as possible. By taking into account the effects of tax rules on the economic behavior of individuals and firms, governments can provide a tax environment that fosters the most-efficient allocation of resources and the best economic performance possible.

The United States has chosen to impose an overall tax burden that is low relative to most other industrial countries and to rely most heavily on the personal income tax. Governments of other advanced economies rely less on personal income taxation and more on consumption taxes, such as value-added taxes, in order to finance a larger public sector. Given the U.S. reliance on the personal income tax, we face the continuing challenge of keeping the income tax base broad and the rates low in order to keep the economic burden of taxation as small as possible.

Global tax reforms have changed the tax landscape substantially in recent years. Other advanced economies have generally reduced taxes on wage and salary income, reduced taxes on capital income under the personal income tax (in particular, capital gains and dividends), and reduced taxes on corporate income. While our personal income tax rates are comparable to those of other countries, our corporate tax rate is now the second highest among OECD countries. These international differences could endanger the ability of the U.S. economy to attract capital in a world where capital is increasingly mobile. Any reform of the U.S. tax system should aim to improve the performance of the U.S. economy and to spread the burden of financing government spending simply and fairly.

CHAPTER 6

The U.S. Capital Account Surplus

The United States conducts a large number of trade and financial transactions with other countries. These transactions are recorded in the U.S. balance of payments accounts. The *balance of payments* consists of two subaccounts. One subaccount is the *current account*. The current account consists largely of the trade balance, which records U.S. imports and exports of goods and services. The second subaccount is the *capital and financial account* (hereafter called the capital account), which records U.S. net sales or purchases of assets—stocks, bonds, loans, foreign direct investment (FDI), and reserves—with other countries during the same time period.

In 2004 (the most recent calendar year for which data exist), the United States ran a *current account deficit* of $668 billion. This deficit meant the United States imported more goods and services than it exported. The counterpart to the U.S. current account deficit was a U.S. *capital account surplus.* This surplus meant that foreign investors purchased more U.S. assets than U.S. investors purchased in foreign assets, investing more in the United States than the United States invested abroad. By economic definition, a country's current and capital account balances must offset one another. Therefore, the U.S. current account deficit was matched by a capital account surplus of $668 billion (including $85 billion in net statistical discrepancies within the capital account, which are included in part to ensure the accounts sum to zero).

Because foreigners invested more in the United States than the United States invested abroad, the United States received *net foreign capital and financial inflows* (hereafter called net capital inflows). Countries like the United States that run capital account surpluses and current account deficits receive net foreign capital inflows. In contrast, countries that run capital account deficits and current account surpluses experience net foreign capital outflows.

Between 1980 and 2004, the United States ran a capital account surplus and a current account deficit in all but three years. More recently, net capital inflows to the United States have risen sharply (Chart 6-1). The $668 billion in net inflows received in 2004 was nearly $300 billion greater than the level of net inflows received only three years earlier. As a percent of U.S. Gross Domestic Product (GDP), net capital inflows rose from 1.5 percent in 1995 to 4.2 percent in 2000 to 5.7 percent in 2004. In 2005, U.S. net capital inflows are likely to have exceeded 6 percent of GDP and ranged from $700 to $800 billion in dollar terms.

Chart 6-1 Net Capital Inflows to the United States

Net U.S. inflows have risen in recent years in absolute terms and as a percent of GDP.

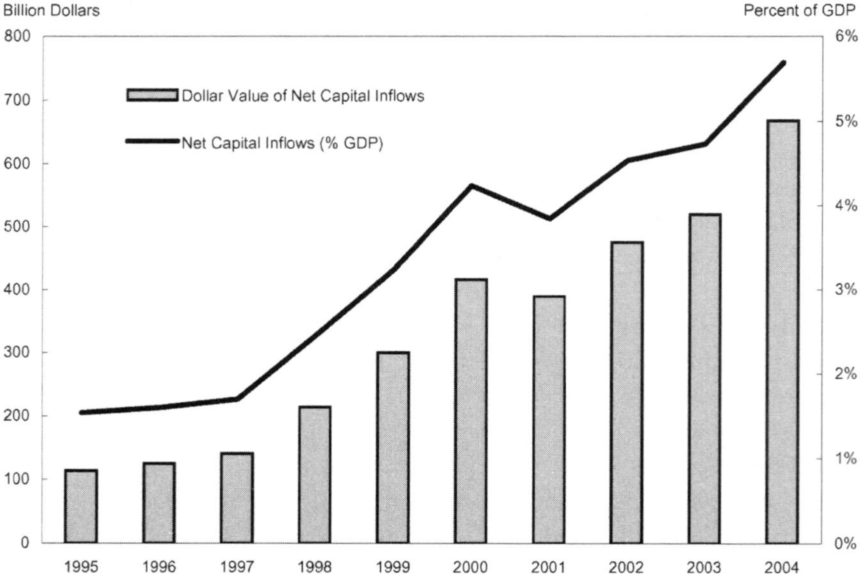

Note: Includes net inflows on the capital-financial accounts. Net statistical discrepancies in the financial account.
Source: Department of Commerce (Bureau of Economic Analysis).

Recent growth in U.S. net capital inflows has sparked debate about the causes of these inflows. As this chapter discusses, a variety of factors explain recent trends in U.S. capital inflows. One of these factors is the pattern of *national saving* (hereafter called domestic saving) and *domestic investment* in the United States and other countries. This perspective on foreign capital flows—linking domestic saving and investment balances—is consistent with, but somewhat different from, analyses that explain U.S. capital inflows by focusing narrowly and exclusively on the U.S. trade deficit. In a view that emphasizes trade flows, U.S. net capital inflows result directly from the excess of U.S. imports over U.S. exports. In contrast, a view that emphasizes domestic saving and investment balances highlights a wider range of factors within countries that can lead them to experience net capital inflows or outflows. Key points of this chapter are:

- The size and persistence of U.S. net capital inflows reflects a number of U.S. economic strengths (such as its high growth rate and globally competitive economy) as well as some shortcomings (such as its low rate of domestic saving).

- The recent rise in U.S. net capital inflows between 2002 and 2004 in part reflects global economic conditions (such as a large increase in crude oil prices) as well as policies (such as China's exchange rate policy) and weak growth in several other large economies (such as Germany) that led to greater net capital outflows from these countries.
- The United States is likely to remain a net foreign capital recipient for a long time. However, the magnitude of future U.S. net capital inflows is likely to moderate from levels observed in recent years.
- Encouraging greater global balance of capital flows would be helped by steps in several countries. The United States should raise its domestic saving rate. Europe and Japan should improve their growth performance and become more attractive investment destinations. Greater exchange rate flexibility in Asia, including China, and financial sector reforms could increase the role of domestic demand in promoting that region's future growth.

In addition, the chapter makes two broader points. First, global capital flows—the flow of saving and investment among countries—should be analyzed from a global perspective and not by considering U.S. economic policies alone. Global capital flows are *jointly* determined by the behavior of many countries. To understand why the United States receives large net capital inflows requires understanding why countries like Japan, Germany, China, and Russia experience large net capital outflows.

A second point is the need to distinguish between market-driven and policy-driven capital flows. For example, recent capital outflows from Germany have largely reflected market forces and private sector behavior. In contrast, China's recent net capital outflows largely reflect policy decisions. In the United States, capital inflows have reflected a combination of market forces and policy behavior. Separating market from policy-related sources of capital flows is important for understanding capital flow patterns and to consider how these flows may change in the future.

This chapter is structured in five parts. The first part explains the distinction between countries that are net capital importers (receiving net capital inflows) and countries that are net capital exporters (experiencing net capital outflows). One key theme is the link that exists between saving and investment balances *within* countries and capital flows *among* countries. The second part of the chapter examines recent trends in global capital flows. Next, the chapter examines four countries that were the world's largest net capital exporters in 2004—Japan, Germany, China, and Russia—to understand some of the factors driving their capital outflows. The chapter then examines recent U.S. capital inflows and their determinants. The final section discusses whether the United States can continue receiving net capital inflows indefinitely.

Global Capital Flows—Principles

Global capital flows reflect the matching of saving and investment opportunities in the global financial system. In any given period, countries can be classified as net capital exporters or net capital importers. Net capital exporters have supplies of domestic saving (which includes households, firms, and the government) that exceed domestic investment opportunities that are expected to be profitable. Because of their excess saving, these countries export some portion of their saving to other countries through net purchases of foreign assets—stocks, bonds, loans, FDI outflows, and reserves. In contrast, countries that are net capital importers have more domestic investment opportunities that are expected to be profitable than they can fund with their supply of domestic saving. These countries have excess demand for saving and import foreign saving through net sales of assets to foreign investors. Broadly speaking, therefore, global capital flows reflect the interaction between countries that are net capital importers and net capital exporters.

Stated differently, countries that are net capital exporters run *capital account deficits* and *current account surpluses*. Conversely, countries that are net capital importers run *capital account surpluses* and *current account deficits*. A country's capital account balance reflects its net sales or purchases of assets with other countries. Its current account balance reflects its net sales or purchases of goods and services with other countries along with net flows of income and transfer payments. The current account and capital account must exactly offset one another. This means the value of a current account surplus will be mirrored by the value of a capital account deficit, and a current account deficit will be mirrored by a capital account surplus of equal value.

Capital flows provide benefits to both groups of countries. For capital exporters, net outflows allow them to earn a higher return on their savings by investing abroad than they expect to earn by investing in their own countries. For capital importers, drawing on foreign savings allows domestic investment to be maintained at a higher level than would otherwise be possible given their level of domestic saving. Maintaining a high level of capital investment is critical for promoting future growth.

Changes in the rate of domestic saving or domestic investment will cause changes in a country's capital and current account balances. For example, a rise in domestic investment relative to saving will, all else equal, cause the capital account surplus to rise and the current account balance to fall. In this case, net capital inflows will increase (or, for countries already experiencing net capital outflows, net outflows will decrease). Conversely, an increase in domestic saving relative to investment will cause the capital account balance to decrease and the current account balance to increase. In that case, net foreign capital outflows will increase (or net capital inflows will decrease). Therefore, one way of assessing changes in current and capital account balances is to examine changes in domestic saving and investment rates (see Box 6-1).

Box 6-1: Analyzing the Current and Capital Account Balances

There are two ways to analyze the current account balance. The more widely used perspective measures a country's imports and exports of goods, services, net income flows, and net current transfer payments. Net capital flows, which are recorded in the capital account, reflect financing from foreigners needed to pay for net import purchases on the current account. By accounting necessity, the current account and capital account must sum to zero. Therefore, a current account deficit will be matched by a capital account surplus of equal magnitude.

The table below shows the U.S. current and capital accounts in 2004. The current account deficit of $668 billion was offset by an equivalent capital account surplus (including net statistical discrepancies, previously noted). Line items within the capital account specify the ways that foreigners invested in the United States. The largest net capital inflow component was portfolio investment ($763 billion in gross inflows and $103 billion in gross outflows, equaling $660 billion in net inflows). Because the United States has a floating exchange rate, changes in its official reserve assets were small. For countries with fixed exchange rates, changes in reserves are typically much larger because reserves are bought or sold through foreign exchange intervention that is undertaken to manage the value of their exchange rate.

Current Account (billion dollars)		Capital Account (billion dollars)	
Goods	- $665	Net capital transfers	- $2
Services	+ $48	Net foreign direct investment	- $145
Net income	+ $30	Net portfolio investment	+ $660
Net current transfers	- $81	Net banking and other flows	+ $67
Total	- *$668*	Net statistical discrepancies	+ $85
		Net change in official reserve assets	+ $3
		Total	+ *$668*

Source: Bureau of Economic Analysis, International Monetary Fund, International Financial Statistics

Another perspective on the current account compares domestic saving with domestic investment. When domestic investment exceeds domestic saving, a country has excess demand for saving that is met by drawing on other countries' saving. Foreign capital inflows may reflect expectations by foreign investors that they will realize a higher

---

return by investing in other countries than they will earn by investing in their own countries. In this case, capital inflows broadly reflect the attractiveness of investing in one economy relative to other economies.
    The table below shows U.S. domestic saving and domestic investment in 2004. Because domestic investment exceeded saving, a current account deficit and capital account surplus resulted. The total sums to the same amount regardless of whether the current account is looked at through trade flows or through saving and investment flows.

U.S. Savings and Investment—2004 (billion dollars)

Gross domestic saving	+ $1,572
Gross domestic investment	+ $2,301
Net other flows	+ $61
Total	$ 668

Source: Bureau of Economic Analysis

Global Capital Flows—Recent Patterns

What is the current pattern of net capital inflows and outflows across countries? How has this pattern changed in the past decade? Chart 6-2 shows the United States was the largest net capital recipient in 2004. Spain, Great Britain, Australia, and Turkey were also net capital recipients. Japan, Germany, China, Russia, and Saudi Arabia were the largest net capital exporters.

Between 1995 and 2004, global saving and investment patterns changed in a number of respects. Some of the more important changes were:

• *Declining concentration among net capital exporting countries.* Falling concentration means that a wider range of countries experienced net capital outflows. In 1995, the world's largest net capital exporter (Japan) accounted for 39 percent of global net capital outflows and the five largest net capital exporters accounted for 70 percent of net outflows. In 2000, the largest net capital exporter accounted for 24 percent of net outflows while the five largest net exporters accounted for 48 percent of net outflows. In 2004, the largest net exporter accounted for 20 percent of net outflows while the five largest net exporters accounted for 52 percent of net outflows.

• *Rising concentration among net capital importing countries.* Rising concentration means that a smaller number of countries received a larger

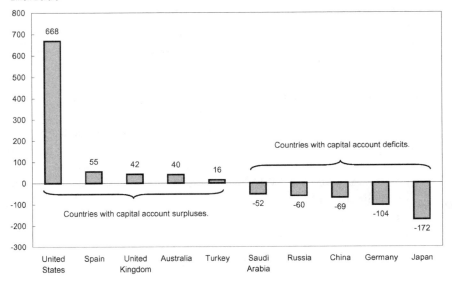

Chart 6-2 Largest Net Capital Importers and Exporters- 2004
The United States had the largest net capital inflows in dollar terms and Japan had the largest net capital outflows.
Billion Dollars

Note: Assumes net statistical discrepancies are in the capital and financial accounts.
Source: International Monetary Fund, *World Economic Outlook*, September 2005.

share of total net capital inflows. Most of this change reflected higher U.S. net capital inflows. The United States received 33 percent of global net capital inflows in 1995, 61 percent in 2000, and 70 percent in 2004. The five largest net capital recipients received 57 percent of global net capital inflows in 1995, 78 percent in 2000, and 86 percent in 2004.

- *A change in net capital flow positions for some large countries.* Germany experienced the largest change in its net capital flow position. In 1995 and 2000, Germany received $30 billion in net capital inflows but had $104 billion in net outflows in 2004. Saudi Arabia also went from small net capital inflows in 1995 ($5 billion) to large net capital outflows in 2004 ($52 billion).

- *A change in the regional composition of capital flows.* Developing Asian and Middle Eastern countries also became large net capital exporters. In 1995, developing Asian countries had net inflows of $42 billion, but had net outflows of $93 billion in 2004. China had $2 billion of net capital outflows in 1995, $21 billion of net outflows in 2000, and $69 billion in net outflows in 2004. Rising crude oil prices also caused many oil-producing countries to become large net capital exporters. Middle Eastern countries had net capital inflows of $1 billion in 1995 and $103 billion of net outflows in 2004.

- *Net capital outflows from developing countries.* In 1995, developing and emerging market countries as a whole received $84 billion in net capital inflows. In 2000, they experienced $91 billion in net outflows. In 2004, they experienced $367 billion in net outflows. While these countries remained net recipients of foreign direct investment (FDI) inflows, they became large net purchasers of foreign reserve assets. These purchases, made primarily by central banks, represent a capital outflow because domestic resources are being invested abroad rather than within these countries.

- *Rising global foreign reserve levels.* The value of global foreign reserves (held primarily by central banks) rose from roughly $1.5 trillion to $3.9 trillion between 1995 and 2004—a 160 percent increase in a period when the value of global GDP increased by roughly 40 percent. Global reserves increased by more than $1.3 trillion in 2002-04 alone. Three countries accounted for nearly 60 percent of this reserve increase—Japan, China, and South Korea.

Global Capital Exporters

To understand global capital flow patterns, we can examine in more detail saving and investment patterns in some of the largest capital importers and exporters. The world's four largest net capital exporters in 2004 were Japan, Germany, China, and Russia. In total, these countries exported more than $400 billion of domestic savings to other countries through their net purchases of foreign assets. Net capital outflows from these four countries represented 46 percent of outflows among all net capital exporting countries in 2004.

While these countries exported large amounts of their saving to other countries, they also differed in several respects. Recent capital outflows from Japan and Germany, for example, have been associated with weak growth while Russia and China have experienced rapid growth. Germany's capital outflows largely reflect private sector, market-driven behavior whereas China's outflows reflect policy behavior. Japan and Germany have run fiscal deficits while Russia has had a fiscal surplus. Japan and Germany have had falling rates of domestic investment while China has had a rising rate. What these countries have had in common, however, were supplies of domestic saving that exceeded their domestic investment.

Japan—Deflation and a Falling Investment Rate

With net capital outflows of $172 billion, Japan was the world's largest net capital exporter in 2004. Between 1995 and 2004, Japan was the world's largest net capital exporter every year, "pushing" more than $1.1 trillion in excess saving into the global financial system. Moreover, the level of Japan's net capital outflows increased each year from 2001 to 2004.

Recent growth in Japan's net capital outflows has resulted primarily from a falling domestic investment rate rather than a higher saving rate. Between 1995 and 2004, Japan's domestic saving rate fell from 30 percent to 28percent of GDP. During this same period, Japan's domestic investment rate fell from 28 percent to 24 percent of GDP. This widening gap between saving and investment—Japan's excess supply of saving—led to higher net capital outflows and a corresponding rise in its current account surplus. Japan's current account surplus rose from 2.1 percent of GDP in 1995 to 2.5 percent of GDP in 2000 to 3.7 percent of GDP in 2004.

Japan's investment rate has fallen for several reasons. A declining population and slowing growth in its labor force has reduced Japan's need for physical capital. Japan also arguably suffered from a large excess of capital investment in the late 1980s. This previous experience with overinvestment, growth in bad loans among Japan's banks, and the slow growth Japan has experienced since the early 1990s following the collapse of its "bubble economy" have made Japanese firms more cautious about undertaking new domestic investment. Deflationary pressures (a decline in the overall price level) have also weakened private investment since firms are often more reluctant to initiate new investment when future prices are expected to fall.

The key source of Japan's rising saving-investment imbalance has been its corporate sector. Between 1995 and 2004, Japan's corporate sector went from being a net borrower of funds (investing more than it saved) between 2 percent to 3 percent of GDP to a net lender of funds (saving more than it invested) equivalent to nearly 15 percent of GDP. During this same period, the rate of net saving in Japan's household sector fell by roughly 70 percent (from 10 percent to about 3 percent of GDP) while Japan's public sector was a large net borrower of funds. Therefore, rising net savings by Japanese firms explain much of the recent growth in Japan's net capital outflows.

After a long period of slow growth, Japan's economy showed some signs of improvement in 2005. Financial ratios among firms improved, and growth prospects appeared to improve. Japan's central bank forecast that deflation is likely to end in 2006. Business confidence strengthened and commercial bank lending began to resume. Japan's labor market also showed some signs of strength. The re-election of Prime Minister Koizumi strengthened prospects for future economic reform. To the extent Japan can achieve sustained growth, its future net capital outflows are likely to slow. Stronger growth in Japan will encourage a larger share of its savings to remain at home rather than being invested abroad.

Germany—Structural Rigidities and a Falling Investment Rate

With $103 billion in net capital outflows, Germany was the world's second largest net capital exporter in 2004. Between 1990 and 2000, Germany received total net foreign capital inflows of $175 billion. Between 2001 and 2004, in contrast, Germany experienced net capital outflows of more than $200 billion. Germany's rising net capital outflows have been mirrored by its rising current account surpluses. Between 2001 and 2004, Germany's current account surplus rose from 0.2 percent to 3.8 percent of GDP.

Like Japan, Germany's rising saving surpluses and net capital outflows have stemmed from a falling rate of domestic investment rather than a rising rate of domestic saving. At 21 percent of GDP, Germany's saving rate has been broadly stable over most of the past decade (though it did rise from 2003 to 2004). Domestic investment during this period, however, fell from 22 percent to 17 percent of GDP—the second lowest investment rate among G8 countries (the world's most advanced economies).

Why has Germany's investment rate declined? One factor has been structural rigidities in its economy that have slowed Germany's rate of growth and opportunities for profitable investment. These rigidities result in part from legal and microeconomic barriers that limit economic flexibility. Inflexibility can prolong periods of slow growth because an economy is less able to adjust effectively to changing conditions in its labor and product markets and achieve full levels of employment. According to the Organization for Economic Cooperation and Development (OECD), barriers to new business formation and investment are higher in Germany than the OECD average. A World Bank "employment rigidity index" scored Germany's labor market at 55 (scaled from 0-100, with higher scores implying greater rigidity) compared to 17 for Australia, 14 for Great Britain, and 3 for the United States. Germany's standardized unemployment rate is high (9.5 percent in 2005) and its long-term unemployment rate (measuring workers unemployed for a year or more) was more than 50 percent higher in 2004 than the average OECD rate.

Germany has taken some recent steps to reduce unemployment and accelerate its growth. Laws limiting temporary and part-time work have been relaxed. Passage of "Hartz IV" labor reforms in 2004 was aimed at reducing long-term unemployment by requiring unemployed workers to seek work more actively. Unit labor costs, which are one widely used indicator of competitiveness, have recently fallen relative to several other European countries. It is also hoped that Germany's new government, which took office in November 2005, may strengthen other growth incentives. Like Japan, stronger growth in Germany will encourage a larger share of its domestic savings to be used at home rather than invested abroad.

China—Exchange Rate Management and a Rising Saving Rate

With $69 billion in net outflows, China was the world's third largest net capital exporter in 2004. China's role as a net capital exporter may seem surprising given the large foreign investment inflows it experiences. While China does receive substantial foreign investment, it experiences even larger capital outflows due to foreign reserve accumulation by its central bank that results from its foreign exchange regime. As China's reserves have risen in recent years, its capital account balance has moved toward larger deficits and its current account toward larger surpluses. In 2004, China's current account surplus was equivalent to 4 percent of GDP (note that in December 2005, China increased the estimate of its 2004 GDP, which is likely to reduce the size of this current account surplus relative to GDP). Current projections indicate China's current account surplus is likely to have exceeded 6 percent of GDP in 2005.

China's reserves have increased due to its rising current account surpluses, net private capital inflows, and tightly managed pegged exchange rate system. China first adopted its currency peg in 1994, linking its currency (the renminbi) to the U.S. dollar at a rate of 8.3 renminbi-per-dollar. To maintain this peg, China's central bank has purchased large amounts of foreign currency assets in recent years to prevent its currency from appreciating. Even after modifying its exchange rate peg in July of 2005, however, (linking the renminbi to a basket of currencies rather than the U.S. dollar alone) China's foreign reserves have continued to rise. By the end of 2005, China's foreign reserve level exceeded $800 billion and may rise to $900-$1000 billion by the end of 2006. Between 2000 and 2005, China's foreign reserves increased by more than $600 billion.

In terms of its saving and investment balance, China's net capital outflows have resulted primarily from a rising saving rate. While China's rate of domestic investment has also been rising (projected 46 percent of GDP in 2005 prior to its GDP revision), its saving rate has risen even more rapidly. At roughly 52 percent of GDP, China's saving rate is the highest in the world.

Several factors contribute to China's high saving rate. China's "one child" policy, enacted to control its population growth, has contributed to its aging population by reducing the share of younger groups within its population. Because older workers typically earn and save more than younger workers, China's saving rate has increased as its workforce has aged. The absence of a strong social safety net (including adequate public pensions and health care) increases the need for precautionary household saving. The absence of well-developed financial markets and consumer credit mechanisms contribute to high saving by forcing many people in China to save large amounts of cash before making purchases rather than by taking consumer loans that can be repaid gradually. China's tightly managed exchange rate and foreign exchange intervention to limit currency appreciation also contribute indirectly to its high saving rate. Saving is encouraged, in effect, because consumption is discouraged by China's exchange rate policy. With a stronger currency, the global purchasing power of China's currency would rise, raising its income (in global terms) and consumption share, and thus reducing its rate of domestic saving.

Greater exchange rate flexibility would encourage China's productive resources to move toward domestic rather than export production. Greater financial development would help to raise consumption spending (and reduce saving) by providing credit mechanisms for purchases that are currently paid for with cash. A reduction in China's saving rate and greater reliance on domestic demand are essential for China to sustain its future growth. At roughly 45 percent of its GDP, China's domestic investment rate could create future risks for its economy (see Box 6-2).

Russia—Growth in "Petrodollars" and a Rising Saving Rate

With $60 billion in net outflows, Russia was the world's fourth largest capital exporter in 2004. Russia's net capital exports have been closely linked to higher export revenues resulting from rising oil and natural gas prices. Oil export revenues are sometimes referred to as "petrodollars." With oil sales accounting for over 40 percent of its exports, Russia's export revenues rose by more than 50 percent between 2002 and 2004 ($107 billion to $183 billion) while its current account surplus rose to more than 10 percent of GDP.

In terms of its domestic saving and investment balance, Russia's growing net capital outflows have resulted primarily from higher saving. Between 2002 and 2004, domestic saving rose from 29 percent to 31 percent of GDP. A higher saving rate has been reflected by rising fiscal surpluses. Between 2002 and 2004, Russia's fiscal surplus rose from 1 to 5 percent of GDP while its rate of net private sector saving declined from 8 to 5 percent of GDP.

Large petrodollar increases have also occurred in other oil producers. Chart 6-3 shows current account surplus levels among 12 of the world's largest oil exporters, whose combined current account surplus and net capital outflows rose by 134 percent between 2002 and 2004.

The United States and Net Capital Inflows

Overview

The United States received $668 billion in net foreign capital inflows in 2004 (including $85 billion in net statistical discrepancies recorded in its capital account). This capital account surplus was the counterpart to the U.S. current account deficit. This section examines four questions about the U.S.

Box 6-2: High Saving and Financial Sector Inefficiency

Can a country save too much? While a higher saving level might always seem beneficial, higher saving can create costs if those savings are poorly used. Excess saving can sometimes lead to overinvestment that reduces the quality and efficiency of new capital investment and can sometimes create problems in a country's banking system by increasing the share of non-performing loans (NPLs).

An NPL is a loan that cannot be fully repaid by a borrower. Higher NPL ratios imply that investment spending may be inefficient because loans are not being fully repaid. High NPLs can create a number of problems. One problem is that banks often become more cautious about new lending as NPL ratios rise. New loans are unlikely to be approved if previous loans are not being repaid. Slower bank lending, in turn, can slow economic growth more broadly.

Another more direct problem can result when NPL ratios become so high that banks themselves face bankruptcy due to widespread loan defaults and falling bank capital adequacy ratios. In this case, governments must sometimes recapitalize weak banks or pay off insured depositors of banks they close. The cost of closing U.S. savings and loan institutions that failed in the 1980s was $150 billion, or roughly 3 percent of GDP. In Chile, bank failures in the early 1980s cost more than 40 percent of GDP. Spain paid costs equivalent to nearly 20 percent of its GDP following a banking crisis in the late 1970s and early 1980s.

High saving rates can increase NPLs by encouraging banks to take imprudent risks. For example, lending standards may be reduced. Loans for weak borrowers that otherwise lack creditworthiness are more likely to be approved when saving is high and interest rates are low. If interest rates later rise, however, borrowers whose rates rise may not repay their loans, causing NPL ratios to rise. If in contrast interest rates that borrowers pay remain fixed, then banks can again suffer losses because they must pay higher rates to their depositors but cannot charge higher interest rates on loans to their current borrowers.

Japan arguably experienced a large capital overhang in the 1990s after a long period of high saving and investment as well as the emergence of its "bubble economy" in the late 1980s. Average saving and investment rates in Japan were roughly 35 percent of GDP in the 1970s and 30 percent of GDP in the 1980s. China, however, likely has even higher saving rates. Not surprisingly, China's NPL ratio is also believed to be high. While China's official statistics report NPLs are roughly 10 percent of outstanding loans, unofficial estimates suggest China's NPL ratio may be closer to 25 percent (by comparison, NPLs among U.S. banks are less than 1 percent).

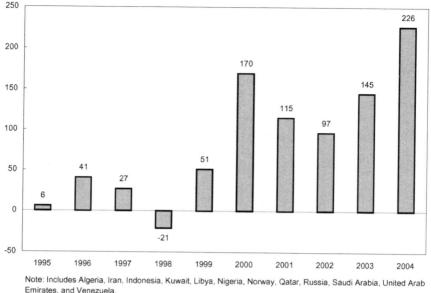

Chart 6-3 Current Account Balances of Oil-Producing Countries
Oil producers have experienced large recent increases in their current account surpluses.
Billion Dollars

Note: Includes Algeria, Iran, Indonesia, Kuwait, Libya, Nigeria, Norway, Qatar, Russia, Saudi Arabia, United Arab Emirates, and Venezuela.
Source: International Monetary Fund, *World Economic Outlook,* September 2005.

capital account: (1) How do U.S. capital inflows compare with other countries? (2) Has the U.S. share of global capital inflows changed? (3) Has the composition of U.S. capital inflows changed? (4) What factors encourage foreign capital flows into the United States?

Most of this section focuses on the final question. One conclusion is that a high rate of growth relative to many other advanced economies has contributed to U.S. net capital inflows. Among advanced economies, capital flow patterns in the past decade have tended to be positively correlated with growth performance. Countries with higher rates of growth have tended to run current account deficits (and received net capital inflows), while countries with lower growth rates have tended to run current account surpluses (and experience net capital outflows—Chart 6-4).

Net Capital Importers—International Comparisons

Since 1995, three countries have been consistent recipients of net capital inflows—the United States, Australia, and Great Britain. Average annual net capital flows to Australia have been largest (4.6 percent of GDP), second largest for the United States (3.3 percent of GDP), and third largest for Great Britain (1.6 percent of GDP). Spain also received average annual net capital inflows (2.5 percent of GDP) during this period. Australia has the longest

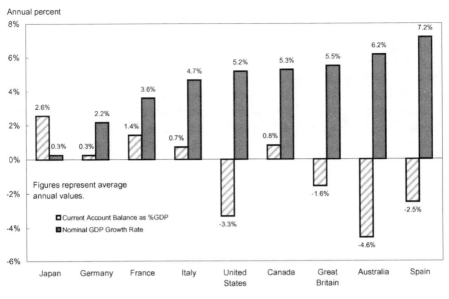

Source: International Monetary Fund, *World Economic Outlook*, September 2005.

record of capital account surpluses (and current account deficits), receiving net foreign capital inflows every year since 1974.

Between 2001 and 2004, net capital inflows increased for most of these countries. Spain's net inflows rose by 1.4 percent of GDP (to 5.3 percent of GDP). U.S. inflows rose by 1.9 percent of GDP (to 5.7 percent of GDP). Australia experienced the largest increase, where net inflows rose by 4.1 percent of GDP (to 6.4 percent of GDP). Net inflows to Great Britain slowed slightly (to 2.0 percent of GDP).

U.S. Share of Global Flows and the Asset Composition of U.S. Capital Inflows

The U.S. share of net global capital inflows has risen over the past decade. The United States received 33 percent of global net capital inflows in 1995, 62 percent in 2000, and 70 percent in 2004. The composition of net foreign capital inflows to the United States has varied. Between 1995 and 2004, foreign official sector holdings of U.S. assets averaged 14 percent of foreign asset holdings (ranging from a high of 16 percent to a low of 11 percent). Gross foreign direct investment (FDI) inflows to the United States, representing larger foreign equity purchases, averaged 26 percent of foreign holdings in this period (ranging from a high of 33 percent to a low of

22 percent). Foreign holdings of U.S. Treasury securities averaged 15 percent of foreign holdings (ranging from a high of 21 percent to a low of 11 percent).

Causes of U.S. Capital Inflows

What factors encourage large and persistent U.S. foreign capital inflows? Several factors, which reflect U.S. economic strengths, encourage these inflows. In particular, a high rate of U.S. growth encourages foreign capital to be "pushed" toward the United States. In contrast, one U.S. shortcoming that "pulls" foreign capital to the United States is its low rate of domestic saving.

Low and Declining U.S. Saving

At 13 percent of GDP, the U.S. domestic saving rate is the lowest among the advanced economy countries (Chart 6-5). Moreover, the U.S. domestic saving rate has declined in recent years. With a domestic investment rate equivalent to 20 percent of GDP, low U.S. saving requires the United States to draw on foreign saving to fund a part of its domestic investment. This excess U.S. demand for saving is reflected by the U.S. current account deficit.

Chart 6-5 Gross National Saving Rates - 1995-2004
The United States has had the lowest rate of national saving among advanced economies since 2002.
Percent of GDP

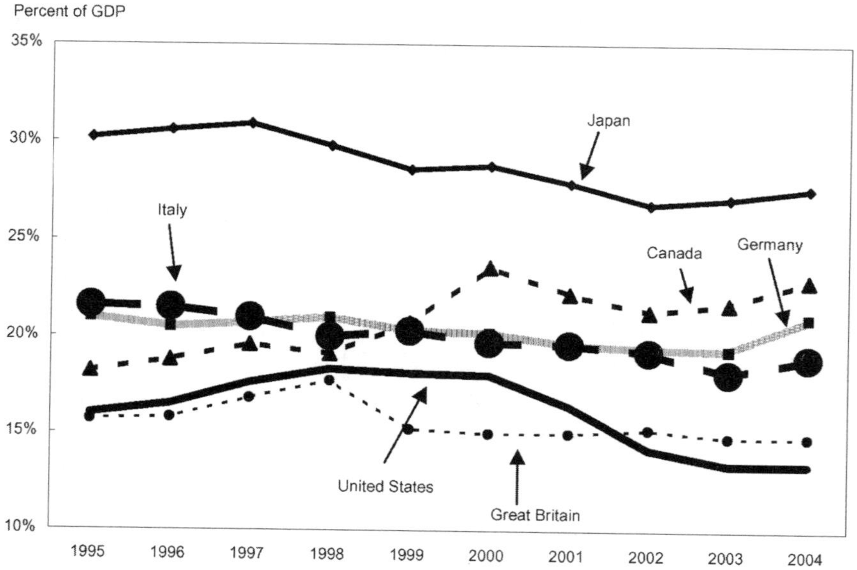

Source: International Monetary Fund, *World Economic Outlook*, September 2005.

When we disaggregate the decline in U.S. domestic saving into its three parts—personal saving, corporate saving, and public saving—we see the personal saving rate has declined from 3.4 percent of GDP in 1995 to 1.3 percent of GDP in 2004 (for more discussion, see Chapter 3 in this report on Saving for Retirement). This decline in personal saving is mirrored by a rise in personal consumption spending, whose share of GDP has risen from 67 percent to 70 percent of U.S. GDP. U.S. corporate saving has remained relatively stable at between 18 and 19 percent of GDP.

Public sector saving also declined. Between 2000 and 2004, the federal budget balance went from a surplus equivalent to 2.4 percent of GDP to a deficit equivalent to 3.6 percent of GDP. Fiscal deficits represent dissaving, or net borrowing, which requires the public sector to draw on domestic private sector resources (firms and households) and the foreign sector. While a growing fiscal deficit has contributed to U.S. demand for foreign saving, and thus affected the U.S. current account deficit, the extent to which it has done so is unclear (Box 6-3).

Box 6-3: The Link Between Fiscal and Trade Deficits

Most economists agree that fiscal deficits will, all else equal, lead to an increase in a country's trade and current account deficits. Fiscal deficits are a form of "dissaving," so fiscal deficits reduce the availability of domestic saving to fund investment. Unless this decline is matched by an equal decline in domestic investment, net demand for foreign saving will rise. Fiscal deficits will thus cause net capital inflows to increase.

However, the effect of fiscal deficits on trade and current account deficits may be considerably less than dollar-for-dollar. For example, one study by the Federal Reserve has estimated that each dollar change in the fiscal deficit leads to a change in the trade deficit of approximately 20 percent. This means that reducing the U.S. fiscal deficit by $100 billion would reduce the trade deficit by only $20 billion.

The relationship among fiscal deficits, the current account, and the capital account is complex because the current and capital accounts also depend on private sector behavior. In Japan and Germany, for example, recent current account surpluses and capital outflows have been associated with large fiscal deficits because private saving balances in those countries have been large and outweighed public sector dissaving.

Box 6-3 — *continued*

As the chart below indicates, U.S. fiscal and current account balances have sometimes moved in the same direction and other times in different directions. For example, between 1997 and 2000 the U.S. Federal public sector balance moved from a deficit of 0.3 percent of GDP to a surplus of 2.4 percent of GDP. During this same period, the current account deficit widened from 1.7 percent to 4.2 percent of GDP. In the early 1980s and early 1990s, the United States came close to current account balance even though the public sector ran large fiscal deficits because a large private sector saving surplus existed then.

U.S. Public Sector Balance, Private Sector Balance, and Current Account Balance
Trends in the U.S. public sector saving balance and private sector saving balance have often differed.
Percent of GDP

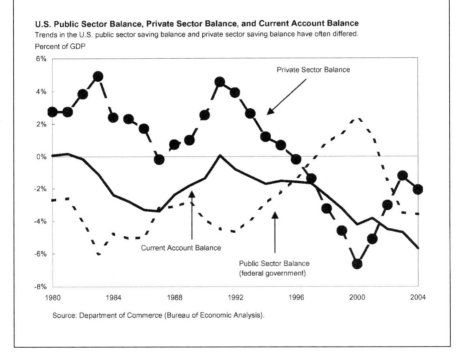

Source: Department of Commerce (Bureau of Economic Analysis).

High U.S. Economic and Productivity Growth

Other factors that attract foreign capital inflows to the United States reflect strengths of the U.S. economy. One factor is the high rate of U.S. growth. Between 1995 and 2004, annual real GDP growth in the United States averaged 3.2 percent compared to 1.1 percent in Japan, 1.4 percent in Germany, and 2.3 percent among Eurozone economies (the group of 12 European countries with a common currency). In the most recent years within this period, these growth differentials widened further.

Higher growth tends to attract foreign capital for two reasons. First, higher growth leads to a higher rate of import growth. All else equal, higher import growth will lead to a decline in a country's trade balance and increase its demand for foreign saving. Second, higher growth attracts foreign capital inflows because growth contributes to higher potential corporate earnings and investment returns.

High Productivity Growth

High U.S. growth and capital inflows are supported by high productivity growth. The broadest measure of productivity is *multi-factor productivity* (which broadly measures the efficiency with which capital and labor inputs are used). OECD data comparing multi-factor productivity across countries for the period 1995-2003 indicate that the United States and Australia had relatively high rates of productivity growth, Canada, Great Britain, and Germany had more modest rates of growth, while Japan had a low rate of productivity growth.

Favorable U.S. Business Climate and Global Competitiveness

A sound business climate can also support high growth and foreign capital inflows. A sound business climate can enhance efficiency by strengthening competition. It can reinforce profit maximizing incentives and effective corporate governance. A sound business climate can also encourage entrepreneurship by reducing the administrative burdens of new business formation. It can enhance the flexibility of industries through laws that facilitate rapid restructuring or liquidation of bankrupt firms. In addition, it can promote efficiency and specialization by reducing international trade barriers.

Several organizations compare business climates across countries. The World Bank publishes an annual "Doing Business" survey that compares legal frameworks and business practices. Countries are ranked in part by an "ease of doing business index." Results from the World Bank's most recent survey ranked New Zealand 1st, the United States 3rd, Australia 6th, Great Britain 9th, Japan 10th, Germany 19th, Spain 30th, Russia 79th, and China 91st. Another competitiveness survey is published by the World Economic Forum (WEF). In the WEF's most recent survey, the United States ranked second in overall competitiveness (Finland was first). The report ranked Japan 12th, Great Britain 13th, Germany 15th, China 49th, and Russia 75th.

Financial Market Size

The size of U.S. financial markets also attracts foreign capital by encouraging investors to hold dollar-denominated assets. Large and efficient financial markets reduce transaction costs and liquidity risk (the risk that assets cannot be sold at fair value on short notice) and increase the ability to diversify asset holdings. In 2004, U.S. financial markets comprised 32 percent of global financial markets compared to 26 percent for Eurozone countries and 15 percent for Japan. U.S. stock market capitalization represented 44 percent of global equity markets compared to 16 percent for Eurozone countries. U.S. bond markets represented 39 percent of global bond markets compared to 27 percent for Eurozone countries.

Global Role of the U.S. Dollar

Widespread use of the dollar in the global economy also contributes to U.S. capital inflows. The dollar's role can be seen in terms of the three classic functions of money. First, the dollar serves as a *medium of exchange*. Private firms in different countries use dollars to settle transactions. Second, the dollar serves as a *unit of account*. Globally traded goods like oil are denominated in dollars. Many global debt securities are also dollar-denominated. A number of countries also use the dollar either as their own currency or as an exchange rate peg to which their own currencies are tied. Third, the dollar is a *store of value*. Private firms hold dollars to help hedge financial risks. Central banks hold dollars as reserves to intervene in foreign exchange markets, meet foreign currency demand for debt servicing payments, or help maintain general financial confidence.

In recent years, the dollar's future role as a global reserve currency has been debated. Some have argued this role may diminish. One argument is that the dollar will face competition from the euro. However, recent estimates indicate the dollar's role as a reserve currency has been broadly stable over the past decade. In 1995, 59 percent of global reserve holdings consisted of dollar-denominated assets. In 1999, this figure rose to 71 percent and then declined to 66 percent in 2004.

U.S. Capital Flow Sustainability

In principle, the United States can continue to receive net capital inflows (and run current account deficits) indefinitely provided it uses these inflows in ways that promote its future growth and help the United States to remain an attractive destination for foreign investment. The key issue concerning U.S. foreign capital inflows is not their absolute level but the efficiency with which they are used. Provided capital inflows promote strong U.S. investment, productivity, and growth, they provide important benefits to the United States as well as to countries that are investing in the United States.

To evaluate the *sustainability* of these inflows, economists often evaluate a country's *external debt burden*. This debt burden can be seen in terms of a *stock* and a *flow* burden. One stock measure that is sometimes examined is a country's *net foreign asset position*. Net foreign assets measure the value of a country's foreign assets relative to the liabilities it owes to foreigners. When foreign assets exceed liabilities, a country is a *net foreign creditor*. When foreign liabilities exceed foreign assets, it is a *net foreign debtor*. Net capital inflows contribute to net foreign debt because some share of these inflows reflect foreign purchases of debt instruments. A rising level of net foreign debt may be a warning sign that debt could become unsustainable in the future.

U.S. current account deficits in recent years have caused its level of net foreign debt to rise from negative 4 percent of GDP in 1995 to negative 22 percent in 2004. Other countries vary in their net foreign asset or debt positions. For example, Japan is a net foreign creditor (foreign assets exceeding foreign liabilities) with net foreign assets equivalent to 38 percent of its GDP. In contrast, Australia is a net debtor with net foreign debt equivalent to 64 percent of its GDP. Great Britain's net foreign debt is equivalent to 13 percent of its GDP. While net foreign debt or asset positions can be a useful indicator, however, these figures must be interpreted cautiously since what constitutes an "excessive" amount of net foreign debt is far from clear.

One *flow measure* of the external debt burden is a country's *net foreign income*. Countries either receive or pay foreign income depending on their foreign asset and liability levels as well as the rate of return they earn and pay on these assets and liabilities. When a country receives more in interest, dividends, profit remittances, and royalties on its foreign assets than it pays on its foreign liabilities, it is a *net foreign income recipient*. When payments exceed receipts, a country makes *net foreign income payments*.

One striking feature of the U.S. balance of payments accounts is that the United States has continued to earn net foreign income despite its rising level of net foreign debt. For example, the United States earned $30 billion in net foreign income in 2004 despite a stock of net foreign debt equivalent to $2.5 trillion. By comparison, Japan received $86 billion in net foreign income payments in 2004 despite the fact that it held $1.8 trillion in net foreign assets. Between 1995 and 2004, the United States earned over $200 billion in net foreign income despite current account deficits that totaled more than $3 trillion during this period. Therefore, U.S. external debt has not appeared burdensome by this measure because its net foreign income flows have remained positive.

While U.S. capital inflows can continue indefinitely, recent levels of net inflows received are likely to moderate in the future. At more than 6 percent of GDP, U.S. net capital inflows are unusually high by historical standards. While no specific "critical value" exists beyond which a country can no longer necessarily receive net foreign capital inflows, recent growth in U.S. net inflows has attracted substantial attention. The key questions concern the rate and magnitude by which U.S. net inflows moderate in the future. In one scenario, U.S. net capital inflows might drop quickly. In another "soft landing" scenario, the adjustment process would occur in a more gradual manner. While a large share of U.S. net capital inflows reflects foreign private sector investment that believes a higher risk-adjusted return can be earned by investing in the United States than can be earned by investing elsewhere, some policy adjustments (see below) in the United States and abroad could nonetheless help to increase the likelihood of a soft landing.

Conclusion

This chapter has emphasized the interdependent nature of the global financial system. To understand U.S. net capital inflows, one must also understand factors that underlie net capital outflows from countries like Japan, Germany, China, and oil-producing and exporting countries like Russia. Global capital flows reflect a wide array of conditions in many countries rather than developments in the United States alone. In some instances, global capital flows reflect expectations among market participants who invest in countries where they expect to earn the highest level of risk-adjusted returns. In other instances, capital flows reflect policy decisions by central banks to manage their exchange rates.

In both instances, global capital flows provide important benefits for net capital importers as well as net capital exporters. Net capital importers like the United States benefit because they can maintain a level of domestic investment they would otherwise have to reduce given their levels of domestic saving. Net capital exporters benefit because they can earn higher returns on the saving they invest abroad than they expect to earn by investing in their own countries.

The interdependence of the global financial system implies that no one country can reduce its external imbalance through policy action on its own. Instead, reducing external imbalances requires action by several countries. Specifically, at least four steps may help to reduce these imbalances.

First, the United States must work to raise its domestic saving rate. Higher U.S. saving will reduce U.S. demand for other countries' savings. To increase saving, the United States should continue its efforts to reduce its fiscal deficit and raise its personal saving rate. Sections of the U.S. tax code that discourage saving should be reformed as appropriate. Health care, social security, and other entitlement programs will require reforms given their large projected impact on future public spending.

Second, China and other Asian countries should reduce their excess saving through policies and reforms that promote higher domestic demand. Financial systems can be reformed and modernized to help expand consumer credit and reduce the need for high levels of precautionary saving. Managed exchange rate regimes should be liberalized more fully. Greater exchange rate flexibility would provide China with a useful policy tool to help stabilize its business cycle. It would also help China to reorient its future growth away from net exports and toward higher domestic demand.

Third, Japan, Germany, and several other large countries should reduce their supplies of excess saving by promoting higher private domestic demand and improving their economic growth performance. Raising private domestic demand will require the implementation of further structural reforms in these countries that strengthen incentives for private consumption and private investment. In turn, higher consumption and investment will help to reduce their external surpluses. While structural reforms are often politically difficult to enact, they are essential if long-term growth performance in these countries is to improve.

Finally, oil producing and exporting countries could increase their domestic investment levels. At least some of this spending could be used to expand oil sector production that would reduce excess saving in these countries, enhance the future productive capacity of these economies, and help to ensure adequate future supplies of oil for the global economy.

CHAPTER 7

The History and Future of International Trade

For many decades, the United States has worked to break down trade barriers across the globe through a wide range of institutions and agreements. Both the United States and our trading partners have derived substantial benefits from greater global economic integration. Many American consumers, firms, and workers are better off because of these efforts.

While the economic research and performance of this time period show the benefits of trade outweigh the costs, trade liberalization has always brought anxieties. This has been the case both here in the United States and throughout the world. Temptations to retreat to economic isolationism often occur when trade agreements are negotiated and current negotiations are little different in this regard. Therefore, this chapter provides a retrospective on U.S. trade policy and an evaluation of the payoff from greater trade and investment liberalization that has been at the forefront of this country's international economic policy for the last 70 years.

The key points in this chapter are:

- Over the past 70 years, policymakers across political parties have consistently recognized the importance of unfettered international commerce to America's standard of living and economic growth, and have achieved major trade liberalization both here and abroad.
- The net payoff to America from these achievements has been substantial. Many American consumers, firms, and workers have benefited from increased trade.
- A number of barriers to trade, especially in services, remain, and the potential gains to the United States and other countries from further liberalization are still significant. To move beyond trade liberalization in goods, the United States is pursuing greater economic cooperation and more-open markets with our trading partners in order to stimulate economic growth.

A Retrospective on Trade

The country's historical influence in promoting global trade liberalization can be traced back to the early part of the twentieth century, and it spans both political parties. The early 1930s proved to be a critical turning point in the evolution of modern American trade policy and heralded the first major

American trade liberalization effort. In the decades following, the United States has spearheaded multinational, regional, and bilateral negotiations in the interest of advancing trade liberalization. This retrospective illustrates the undeniable progress toward trade liberalization in the United States. Revenues from tariffs (a tariff is a tax levied on imports coming into the United States) in the early 1900s accounted for about half of Federal revenues compared to less than 2 percent today. From the inception of this country until the Civil War, tariff revenues were a major source of government revenue. The addition of the sixteenth amendment to the U.S. Constitution in 1913 broadened the tax base by introducing the personal and corporate income tax. This change began the shift away from indirect taxation (import duties and excise taxes) toward direct taxation on personal and corporate incomes, thereby reducing this country's dependence on import duties as a form of revenue.

Before the 1930s, U.S. trade practices fluctuated between trade-promoting and trade-restricting policies. Prior to World War I, President Woodrow Wilson pursued an internationalist foreign policy that resulted in import tariff reductions through the Underwood Tariff Act of 1913. The economic depression and subsequent reversion to isolationism that followed the 1929 stock market crash led to a rejection of Wilsonian policies in favor of greater protectionism. The Tariff Act of 1930 (otherwise known as the Smoot-Hawley Tariff) significantly raised average duties on selected imports to an all-time high of 59 percent. Such protectionism was designed to reduce unemployment and increase domestic output. By reducing export markets, however, the heightened tariff and nontariff trade barriers (such as quotas or quantitative import restrictions) exacerbated the Great Depression. The collapse of world trade from 1929 to 1933—a decline of more than two-thirds in just four years—followed in the wake of protectionist policies as countries depreciated their currencies, raised tariffs, and imposed quotas. These isolationist policies contributed to a spiraling contraction of world trade and a collapse of domestic demand.

The historic Reciprocal Trade Agreements Act of 1934 marked a turning point in modern trade legislation. The 1934 Act departed significantly from previous protectionist policies, and it began the historic shift toward lower U.S. and foreign trade barriers and greater global economic engagement. Signed into law by President Franklin D. Roosevelt, the Act passed Congress with overwhelming support. The 1934 Act was the first of many steps over the twentieth century leading to America's relatively liberal trade stance today. Table 7-1 shows that key milestones in American trade history have been consistently achieved by a number of administrations.

The Trade Act of 1934 changed U.S. trade policy. The 1934 Act made trade a shared Congressional and Executive Branch responsibility, and instituted a so-called bargaining tariff. Up to that point, trade policy had been primarily

TABLE 7-1.— *Important Milestones in American Trade History*

Milestone (years of negotiation)	Year Signed into U.S. Law	Administrations involved
Reciprocal Trade Agreements Act of 1934	1934	Roosevelt
Kennedy Round (1962–1967)	1962	Kennedy, Johnson
Tokyo Round (1973–1979)	1979	Nixon, Ford, Carter
Uruguay Round Agreements Act (1986–1994)	1994	Reagan, G.H.W. Bush, Clinton
North American Free Trade Agreement (1990–1993)	1994	G.H.W. Bush, Clinton
Trade Act of 2002 and Renewal of Trade Promotion Authority (2001–2002)	2002	G.W. Bush

a product of the legislative exercise of its Constitutional authority over foreign commerce. This Constitutional authority left Congress open to the protectionist demands of specific industries and special interests. President Roosevelt and Secretary of State Cordell Hull recognized this vulnerability and worked with Congress to enact this reciprocal trade program to make lower tariffs more politically durable. With the enactment of the Trade Act of 1934, Congress suspended passage of product-specific trade laws and delegated specific tariff-setting to the Executive Branch. Doing so formally changed the way Congress handled trade issues by insulating elected representatives from the pressures that had led to protectionism in the past.

The 1934 law also instituted the so-called bargaining tariff. This concept linked tariff setting to international negotiations, whereby U.S. tariff cuts were extended in bilateral negotiations to countries that offered reciprocal tariff reductions benefiting U.S. exporters. In this way, the bargaining tariff helped to shift the balance of trade politics by engaging the interests of U.S. exporters. The system effectively allowed the United States to reduce its own trade barriers and to persuade the rest of the world to reciprocate. In the aftermath of World War II, policymakers correctly predicted that postwar trade expansion would help to usher in a remarkable era of world prosperity and contribute to conditions for a stable peace.

A commitment to the Wilsonian notion that prosperity and peace go hand in hand is at the core of postwar trade liberalization for both political parties in the United States. An extension of the reciprocal trade agreement, which Presidents Roosevelt and Truman both had recommended as a keystone of the country's postwar international economic policy, passed Congress with strong support in 1945. The enabling legislation put the Administration in a position to begin in earnest the process of dismantling global trade barriers. President Harry S. Truman signed the General Agreement on Tariffs and Trade (GATT) in 1947, bringing the United States into the multilateral trade regime by executive agreement. The GATT took effect in 1948 and served as a forum for trade negotiations whereby every signatory country could enjoy the concessions of every other signatory (otherwise known as most-favored-nation status). Membership in the GATT not only brought the United States into the multilateral trade regime but also provided a vehicle to rebuild the postwar economies of Europe and Japan. The lessons of Smoot-Hawley contributed to broad support for freer trade that was to become a critical component of U.S. international economic policy. This political consensus marked a shift toward a broadly accepted liberal market and free-trade philosophy that set the stage for the various multilateral negotiating rounds that were to follow.

The next major acknowledgment of the necessity of liberalizing trade came in the 1960s. President John F. Kennedy led the Trade Expansion Act of 1962, which was approved with substantial support in Congress. The Act authorized the U.S. government to negotiate tariff cuts of up to 50 percent, which persuaded other countries to actively participate in the Kennedy Round (1962–1967) of multilateral trade negotiations. Congressional support was partly due to the inclusion of legislation to assist workers affected by trade, also known as Trade Adjustment Assistance. At the time, the Kennedy Round signified the most ambitious series of trade negotiations ever attempted under the auspices of the GATT. The Round included negotiations on agriculture for the first time, and reduced barriers to exporters for developing countries.

The Tokyo Round (1973–1979) led to further tariff reductions and provided new disciplines on nontariff barriers. The Tokyo Round included "codes of conduct" that were designed to curtail the use of such barriers as instruments of protection. Launched under President Richard M. Nixon, continued by President Gerald R. Ford, and signed into law by President Jimmy Carter with the Trade Agreements Act of 1979, the Round demonstrated a strong, consistent bipartisan commitment toward freer trade.

As trade liberalization negotiations moved increasingly beyond tariff reductions in nonagricultural products, progress toward greater liberalization became more difficult for many countries. The Uruguay Round (1986–1994) launched under President Ronald Reagan nearly collapsed in 1990 over disagreements about lowering barriers on agricultural products. Following a redrafting of the agreement by GATT Director-General Arthur Dunkel, President George H.W. Bush spearheaded efforts to complete negotiations of the Uruguay Round, and in 1994 President Bill Clinton signed legislation implementing the final agreement. The Uruguay Round achieved the most fundamental reform of global trade rules since the creation of the GATT. The Round established the World Trade Organization (WTO), extended international trade rules beyond goods to include intellectual property rights and trade in services, and greatly improved procedures for countries to resolve disputes over international trade.

At present, the United States is actively engaged in the current Doha Development Round of multilateral trade negotiations that began in 2001. This round aims to liberalize agricultural trade, lower remaining barriers in nonagricultural goods trade, and reduce trade barriers in services. The Round focuses on increasing market access for developing countries as a means to encourage economic development. Progress has been slower than anticipated, but the eventual success of the previous Uruguay Round suggests that a favorable outcome from Doha will emerge.

In addition to multilateral trade liberalization, over the past two decades the United States has signed a number of bilateral and regional trade agreements. The protracted nature of multilateral negotiations has been one factor that has led the United States to aggressively pursue other avenues toward free trade outside of the major negotiating rounds. Under President Reagan, the United States signed its first bilateral free trade agreement (FTA) with Israel in 1985. The United States and Canada signed a bilateral FTA in 1988 after three years of negotiations. The Bush Administration initiated negotiations for the North American Free Trade Agreement (NAFTA) in 1991, which President Clinton signed into law in 1993 and went into effect the following year. In addition to trade, NAFTA explicitly recognized the benefits of investment liberalization and included provisions designed to extend national (i.e., nondiscriminatory) treatment, among other protections to investors.

The United States has recently embarked on a renewed series of bilateral and regional free trade agreements. The ability of the United States to negotiate trade-liberalizing agreements was strengthened significantly when the President signed the Trade Act of 2002 into law. That legislation provides the Executive Branch with the ability to negotiate international agreements that are subject to an up or down vote, but not amendment, by Congress. The President's leadership was vital in securing this important authority to pursue a full trade agenda including multilateral, regional, and bilateral trade agreements. The President has implemented bilateral FTAs with Jordan, Chile, Singapore, and Australia. The Administration also has concluded FTAs with an additional ten countries: Costa Rica, El Salvador, Guatemala, Honduras, Nicaragua, the Dominican Republic (the Central American-Dominican Republic FTA, or CAFTA-DR), Morocco, Bahrain, Oman, and Peru. The United States is currently engaged in negotiations with the United Arab Emirates, the five nations of the Southern African Customs Union (Botswana, Lesotho, Namibia, South Africa, and Swaziland), Thailand, Panama, Colombia, and Ecuador. The adoption of CAFTA-DR is the latest chapter in America's trade book, which demonstrates the country's ongoing commitment toward trade liberalization and economic development.

Decades of U.S. trade liberalization achieved on a number of fronts have had a dramatic impact on U.S. openness to trade. Chart 7-1 shows how average U.S. tariffs have fallen since 1930. The average tariff on dutiable goods approached 60 percent at the height of the Great Depression and has dropped to 4.6 percent. The current average U.S. tariff on all goods (both dutiable and nondutiable) is just 1.4 percent.

Trade expansion has reached an important juncture, and resistance both here and abroad to further trade and investment expansion could jeopardize increased domestic and international economic growth. The retrospective presented above illustrates America's historic achievements in trade liberalization, and, as the next section demonstrates, Americans, on average, have accrued immense gains along with our trading partners from this liberalization. The United States has a large stake in the current multilateral negotiations of the Doha Round. The gains from prior trade agreements provide grounds to stay the course on trade liberalization.

Chart 7-1 **Average U.S. Tariff on Dutiable Goods, 1930-2005**
Since 1934 the United States has moved consistently towards freer trade.

Average U.S. tariff, percent

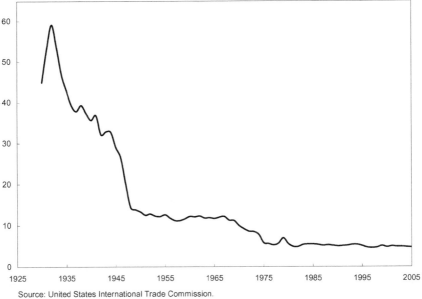

Source: United States International Trade Commission.

The Payoff to America from Global Economic Integration

Trade liberalization remains a controversial subject because competition invariably raises both anxieties and opportunities. Reducing obstacles to trade can help economies grow more rapidly and efficiently in the long run and create better, higher-paying jobs, while global competition can lead to hardships for others in the short run. (Impacts of international trade on labor markets are discussed in Box 7-2 later in the chapter.) The appropriate social and political response to these hardships is a critical issue. For instance, at the macro level, pro-growth government policies can help set the environment for economic growth and job creation. Constructive policies that help displaced workers train for and find new work and increase the portability of pension and health benefits can also ease adjustment.

The gains from trade liberalization are more widely dispersed than the losses and often not readily apparent. These gains are evident in lower consumer prices and the greater variety of products available to consumers. International commerce helps countries focus resources on strengths and forces firms to innovate and to set prices more competitively. Studies show that firms that are engaged in the international marketplace tend to exhibit higher rates of productivity growth and pay higher wages and benefits to their workers. An economy with higher overall productivity growth can support faster GDP growth without generating inflation. And higher productivity growth means higher sustainable living standards. Taken together, the net benefits from increased economic integration (greater trade and investment liberalization) historically have been positive for the United States.

Benefits to Consumers

Lower Prices

International trade fosters competition, which in turn restrains cost. There is now ample evidence across many countries that greater trade openness and the resulting exposure to foreign competition reduces the ability of a country's firms to charge high markups above production costs. Pressures for lower prices arise from the direct impact of cuts in trade barriers being passed through to cuts in prices. They also arise from the broader impact of raising market contestability.

At the detailed product level, many studies have linked lower prices and/or price-cost markups to measures of trade openness such as tariff rates. Chart 7-2 presents broader evidence of how trade helps lower prices. It presents indices of U.S. consumer prices and U.S. import prices since 1990. There is a clear difference between the two indices: Overall consumer prices, which include not just imported goods and services but largely nontraded goods and services, have risen much more than have import prices. The average annual growth in U.S. import prices for the period 1990–2004 was just 0.6 percent, compared to a 2.2-percent rise in overall consumer prices. In real terms, total U.S. imports grew threefold during this same period, from $553 billion to $1.5 trillion (in 2004 dollars).

In addition to the pro-competitive effects of trade, other important contributors to price restraint are technology advances and innovation. This has been especially true for consumer electronics and information technology (IT) products. For instance, in just the past eight years, consumer prices of color televisions are down 50 percent, and Americans today pay 60 percent less for camcorders and mobile phones. It can be difficult to empirically separate observed price declines into the relative contributions of trade, technological change, and other forces. But a simple approach to assessing the role of international trade in price changes is to compare price changes between more- and less-traded products. Consistent with the aggregate evidence in Chart 7-2, a clear divergence in price trends emerges when products are split in this way. Internationally traded products tend to experience lower inflation rates—even real price declines—while nontraded goods tend to exhibit price increases. Between 1997 and 2004, real prices fell for an array of highly traded goods, such as audio equipment (-26%), TV sets (-51%), toys (-34%), and clothing (-9%). In contrast, real prices rose for

Chart 7-2 **Consumer and Import Price Growth, 1990-2004**
Consumer price growth has outpaced import prices.

Index, 1990=100

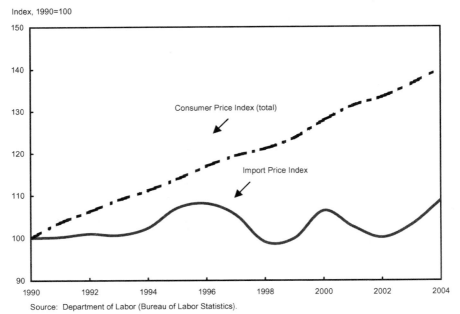

Source: Department of Labor (Bureau of Labor Statistics).

largely nontraded products, such as whole milk (+28%), butter (+23%), ice cream (+18%), peanut butter (+9%), and sugar and sweeteners (+9%).

Exactly which Americans most enjoy the benefits of lower prices depends on which products enjoy the largest cuts in trade barriers. Box 7-1 discusses the regressive nature of the current U.S. tariff schedule.

Box 7-1: The Regressive Nature of U.S. Tariffs

While the average tariff applied to U.S. imports is relatively low at 1.4 percent, there are peaks within the U.S. tariff schedule that fall most heavily on lower-income consumers. Studies have shown that, on balance, U.S. trade barriers are regressive because they disproportionately raise the relative price of goods consumed by lower-income Americans. Some of the most restrictive trade barriers persist on everyday consumer products such as textiles, apparel items, and footwear.

Tariffs disproportionately affect the poor in two ways. First, many tariffs are highest on products that represent higher shares of income expenditures for lower-income households. Staple consumer products such as shoes and clothing face import taxes over 30 percent, some of the highest tariffs in the U.S. tariff schedule. Footwear represents 1.3 percent of income expenditures for lower-income households (1.5 percent for single- parent households) compared to just 0.5 percent for higher-income households. Similarly, lower-income households (and single-parent households) spend roughly 6 percent of their disposable income on apparel, while upper-income households spend just 4 percent.

Second, within these high-tariff product categories, tariffs are often most pronounced on the cheapest products. That is, products that are more commonly purchased by lower-income consumers are subject to higher import taxes than are those commonly purchased by upper-income consumers. For example, lower-priced sneakers ($3–$6 per pair) are marked up with a 32-percent tariff, while higher-priced sneakers, such as $100 track shoes, are subject to a 20-percent tariff.

How did the structure of the U.S. tariff schedule become so regressive? The cause was not a concerted effort to maintain relatively high import taxes on cheaper products. Movement toward increased trade liberalization tends to occur more slowly in labor-intensive industries where greater liberalization may be viewed negatively. The situation may reflect a classic political-economy challenge to liberalizing trade. The beneficiaries of trade protection are often a much more concentrated, well-organized group of individuals or firms than the millions of households across the country that bear the costs. However, the current Doha Round of multilateral trade negotiations offers an opportunity to eliminate these tariffs and other trade barriers, provided other WTO members reciprocate.

Greater Product Variety

International trade also allows consumers to choose from a broader variety of goods and services. One study shows that that the number of imported product varieties has increased by a factor of four over the last three decades, reflecting an important source of gains from trade. Welfare gains from variety growth alone have been estimated to be a remarkable 2.8 percent of GDP, which translates into gains of over $4,000 for the average American family of four.

International trade allows year-round availability of seasonal and perishable food items such as fruits and vegetables. For example, U.S. consumers today enjoy grapes and peaches from Chile, limes and avocados from Mexico, mandarin oranges from China, and cashews from India, many during the off-season for U.S. production. Trade also provides U.S. consumers with greater variety and choice for agricultural products that the U.S. does not produce in large quantity. For example, Americans enjoy coffees from all over the world, including from Colombia, Costa Rica, Indonesia, Ethiopia, and Kenya.

Benefits to Firms and Their Workers

Firms can be linked to the global marketplace through many channels: exporting, importing, investing abroad, or receiving investment from foreign firms (foreign direct investment, or FDI). Stronger linkages to the global economy provide export opportunities for U.S. firms, allow firms to realize economies of scale, and provide the ability to establish and expand global production networks to lower prices and boost productivity. These opportunities can raise U.S. living standards by allocating national resources toward areas in which we have a comparative advantage and by raising firm productivity.

Firms exposed to global competition are exposed to the world's best practices in areas such as supply management, production processes, technology, and finance. Studies show that firms exposed to the world's best practices demonstrate higher productivity through many channels, such as learning from these best practices, and also creating new products and processes in response to this exposure. A number of U.S. industries have been compelled to adjust and innovate as a result of foreign competition via trade and FDI in the United States.

For instance, by the late 1970s, many Japanese carmakers were outperforming U.S. companies in overall assembly productivity, and U.S. imports of Japanese cars were rising sharply. America's leading automakers initially focused their response on trade protection. But competitive pressures from Japanese firms continued, in particular through foreign investment in the United States in the 1980s. This foreign investment established and expanded "transplant" production facilities in the United States that soon achieved productivity levels on par with Japanese plants. These transplants proved to be a major spur to stepped-up innovation and performance among American firms. In the steel industry, a combination of foreign competition and the growth of the highly productive mini-mill sector has compelled U.S. integrated-steel producers to improve their performance.

Various studies show that globally engaged firms have higher productivity growth and tend to innovate more than their purely domestic counterparts. For instance, evidence from the United Kingdom shows that from 1998 to 2000, just 18 percent of domestic firms reported either product or process innovations compared to 45 percent of globally engaged firms. In recent years in the United States, over 80 percent of total private-sector R&D spending has been accounted for by multinational companies (i.e., by the combination of U.S. parents of U.S.-headquartered multinationals and U.S. affiliates of foreign-headquartered multinationals). Sales per employee, one simple measure of productivity, is up to one-and-a-half times larger in exporting plants than in others. Value-added per employee, another measure of productivity, is up to one-and-a-third times larger in exporting plants than in others. Exporting plants adopt new technologies more frequently and intensively than nonexporting plants; they also report more significant benefits from doing so.

The different channels through which international trade and investment contribute to productivity growth are very important for long-run U.S. living standards. Since 1995, the United States has enjoyed an acceleration in labor-productivity growth. From 1973 to 1995, output per worker hour in the nonfarm business sector grew at 1.4 percent per year. From 1995 to 2004, this rate accelerated to 2.9 percent per year—with rates averaging over 3 percent since 2000. Productivity growth of just 1.4 percent per year means average living standards take 50 years to double. At the faster rate of 2.9 percent per year, living standards take just 24 years to double.

Many researchers have concluded that IT hardware has been at the core of this productivity acceleration, citing both faster productivity growth among IT-hardware firms and greater investment in IT hardware throughout the economy. It is important to note that these highly successful IT-producing U.S. firms are among the most globally engaged firms in the U.S. economy. Exports and imports in the IT sector represent over 70 percent of sector output, compared to an economy-wide average of 10 percent. In recent years, IT firms have grown stronger by expanding their global production networks through increased international investment and trade, with output that entails multiple production stages across multiple countries. Indeed, today the United States runs large trade *deficits* in core IT sectors such as computers and office products (see Chapter 10).

American workers, like firms, also benefit from stronger linkages to the global economy. Studies show that workers in U.S. multinationals receive wages and benefits up to 18 percent higher on average than their peers in purely domestic firms. International investment plays an important role, too. Evidence suggests that wage premiums are 19 percent and 13 percent for blue- and white-collar manufacturing workers, respectively, in foreign-owned multinational firms. For American workers in multinationals with foreign investment backing the wage premiums are 7 percent and 2.5 percent, respectively. The productivity advantages of globally engaged firms benefit American workers, insofar as high and rising labor productivity is the foundation for gains in real wages economy-wide.

Taking Stock of the Benefits of Trade to America

The decades of American efforts to advance trade liberalization described above have generated substantial gains for the country overall. On the consumption side, households have enjoyed lower product prices and greater product variety. On the production side, firms have more efficiently allocated resources by focusing on areas in which they have a comparative advantage. Those firms directly engaged in international commerce tend to be more innovative, more productive, and pay higher wages and benefits to their workers. Overall, there is substantial evidence that trade has contributed to high and rising living standards for the average American.

Having discussed the different ways through which freer trade benefits America, the bottom-line question is how much has America benefited in total from decades of trade liberalization? Studies have estimated that the annual payoff from U.S. trade and investment liberalization to date, including from the Tokyo Round, Kennedy Round, and Uruguay Round, NAFTA, and other FTAs, is over $5,000 per capita or $20,000 for an average American family of four. These gains arise through many channels: higher long-term levels of trade exposure in goods and services that come from trade and investment liberalization; increased product variety; more efficient allocation of resources; and better transportation and communication technology. Some economists have conjectured that trade liberalization alone has accounted for about half of these gains, which implies that the annual income gain from trade liberalization to date is over $10,000 for an average American family of four.

Box 7-2 includes a discussion of the impacts of international trade on labor markets. The effects of trade on the environment are discussed in Box 7-3.

Box 7-2: Trade and Labor

Job growth in America is driven largely by demographics—population growth and choices about labor-force participation—and by macroeconomic policies that affect, in particular, the business cycle. As the chart below shows, total employment has closely tracked the number of people in the labor force (employable people) since 1960, which in turn has closely tracked the overall U.S. population. Import competition has the potential to generate job losses where firms fail to adjust their operations to meet new competitors. International trade can also create better, higher-paying jobs in other industries. As discussed in the chapter, American jobs in globally-engaged firms (firms that are engaged in international trade or investment) are on average better and higher-paying than are jobs in purely domestic firms.

The dynamic U.S. economy creates and eliminates millions of jobs each year. The enormous turnover in the U.S. labor market is a reflection of the continuous stream of entry, exit, and resizing of firms in our ever-changing economy. On average over the past decade, the economy has had a net creation of nearly 2 million jobs each year. This net increase has been the result of approximately 17 million jobs created and 15 million jobs eliminated each year. International trade is one of the factors behind job turnover, along with changes in consumer tastes, domestic competition, productivity growth, and technological innovation. Survey data from the Bureau of Labor Statistics show in layoffs of 50 or more people between 1996 and 2004 less than 3 percent were attributable to import competition or overseas relocation. Moreover, studies have shown that the rate of job creation in globally engaged companies is faster than the overall private-sector rate, and that trade-related dislocations on average do not involve longer unemployment duration or lower re-employment earnings than do dislocations from other causes.

Any job loss involves hardship, and any job change can involve challenge. The President has outlined ways to help people gain new skills in fields where jobs are being created.

It is often asserted that international competition pressures American earnings. In today's economy, education is valued more than ever and is a key determinant of worker earnings. Since the late 1970s, the returns to education have been rising in the United States, despite the fact that the supply of educated workers has also grown rapidly,

Box 7-2 — *continued*

Labor Force and Employment, 1950-2004
Employment closely tracks the number of people in the labor force.

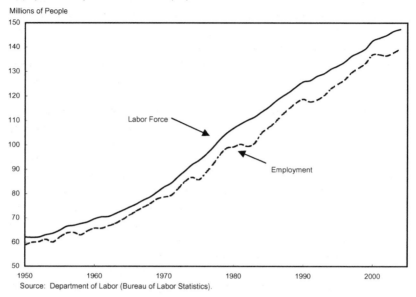

Source: Department of Labor (Bureau of Labor Statistics).

suggesting that the demand for skills and education has grown even faster than supply. There is now a large body of empirical research exploring the causes of rising wage inequality across skills. There is broad consensus that trade has marginally contributed to rising wage inequality by placing a higher premium on skills and education. This contribution has been small compared to other factors such as the advent of new technologies that demand higher levels of skill.

It is important that the United States help our workers thrive in a competitive world. The President has said he will not be satisfied until everyone who wants to work can find a job. At the macroeconomic level, monetary policy can aim to achieve maximum sustainable employment with low inflation—irrespective of the trade situation. At the microeconomic level, constructive policies can help students and workers, including displaced workers—regardless of the cause of displacement—train for and find good work in the 21st century. The President has proposed a number of measures to improve job training, including Community-based Job Training Grants and Career Advancement Accounts (for further discussion, see Chapter 2).

Box 7-3: Trade and the Environment

A nation's environmental policies are largely determined by domestic factors. The most direct mechanism through which trade liberalization could affect environmental quality is through changes in the composition of industries or the scale of industrial or agricultural output. Trade means greater specialization, potentially increasing the concentration of polluting industries in some countries (so-called pollution havens) and decreasing it in others. On the other hand, multinational corporations from industrialized countries that set up operations in lesser-developed countries often bring a higher level of environmental performance with them. There is little or no empirical evidence directly linking trade liberalization to environmental changes.

Trade can affect the environment indirectly as well, both positively and negatively. Increased trade can lead to higher incomes, and as incomes rise, the demand for improved environmental quality rises. Another indirect effect is the influence of trade on the rate of economic growth, which could either decrease pollution (due to the use of cleaner technologies through capital stock turnover fueled by economic growth) or increase pollution (due to increased consumption).

While it is widely recognized that international trade policy measures are usually not the best method for achieving environmental objectives, recognition of the importance of the issue has resulted in a number of significant policy and institutional responses, both nationally and multilaterally. For instance, the environmental side agreements of NAFTA established the North American Commission for Environmental Cooperation to undertake capacity-building projects and to put procedures in place that help to monitor each country's effective enforcement of environmental laws. Active participation by governments and institutions is a necessary component of the success of such efforts.

FTAs can provide a basis for enhanced bilateral cooperation on environmental issues. Environmental provisions in NAFTA and U.S. free trade agreements require each country to effectively enforce its own environmental laws, and strive to ensure that failure to enforce these laws does not affect trade or investment. These agreements are accompanied by separate environmental cooperation agreements or arrangements intended to take advantage of the closer economic ties and broadened environmental cooperation that goes beyond the trade sphere. Although some criticize trade agreements for a failure to do even more to advance environmental policy objectives, others acknowledge the significant benefits associated with the core obligations and cooperation mechanisms.

The Policy Scene Today:
Avenues to Further Liberalization

Trade liberalization to date has had substantial benefits. Still, barriers to international trade and investment remain and limit growth opportunities for many countries. With the United States accounting for just 5 percent of the world's population, 95 percent of the potential consumers of U.S. goods and services live outside our borders. The prospective gains from further liberalization, particularly in services (e.g., finance, insurance, information technology, and professional and business services), are substantial for the United States and our trading partners through greater efficiency of production and higher national incomes. The extent to which different countries experience gains depends on both the range of sectors that are liberalized and the extent of liberalization within each sector. The United States is pressing for freer trade, especially in services, through bilateral, regional, and multilateral agreements.

Prospective Gains from Further Liberalization

Prospective Gains for the United States

The prospective gains for the United States from further trade reform are substantial. One study suggests that global free trade in manufacturing and agriculture would generate annual economic gains of over $16 billion for the United States, or roughly $220 for the typical family of four. The gains from removing all remaining barriers to trade in services are substantially larger, amounting to about an additional $520 billion for the United States, or over $7,000 for the average American family of four. This is additional income each year that will not be available in the absence of trade reform. These income gains would be fully realized in about a decade from the date of liberalization. These large gains reflect the United States having a comparative advantage in services sectors and the high barriers to services trade in other countries, which are often investment restrictions that effectively block the main conduit for trade in services. These restrictions include limits on the number of service providers, minimum local-content requirements that limit the participation of foreign firms, nontransparent and burdensome standards and licensing procedures, and discriminatory access to distribution networks.

Prospective Gains for the Rest of the World

Further liberalization in trade would bring significant global economic gains, particularly for developing countries. One study reports that the reduction of all remaining barriers to trade in services would generate over

$1.5 trillion in income for the world. For full trade liberalization in agriculture and manufactured goods, the World Bank reports that reducing trade barriers would generate about $290 billion of additional income to the world economy each year once the full effects of liberalization are realized, about a decade out. The income gains are even higher at $460 billion with more generous assumptions of trade's effect on economic growth. Nearly half of those income gains would go to developing countries. Various studies find that at least half of the developing-country gains would be obtained from agriculture trade reform by industrialized countries (including the United States), including tariff reductions and the elimination of subsidies and domestic support programs. (Agricultural trade reform is discussed in detail in Chapter 8.)

Debt relief and foreign aid can help to reduce poverty, but trade is a more powerful tool. For instance, in 2004, industrialized countries spent over $78 billion on development assistance to poor countries and industrialized countries are currently considering debt relief of $56 billion. Even the conservative estimate of the $140 billion effect of trade liberalization to developing countries exceeds both assistance and debt relief combined. Studies show that reducing barriers to global trade has the potential to lift hundreds of millions out of poverty. Agriculture liberalization is particularly important since roughly 75 percent of the world's poor live in rural areas and farmers constitute the majority of the poor in developing countries.

The gains from integrating developing countries into the global economy are not one-sided. As developing countries increasingly participate in the global economy, industrialized countries benefit from increased export and investment opportunities in those markets. Over the past decade, U.S. export growth to developing countries exceeded the rate to industrialized countries. Yet tariffs and other trade barriers in developing countries remain high (Chart 7-3). Realizing these market opportunities and encouraging development in these countries requires further trade liberalization efforts while promoting transparency, good governance, and sound institutions, all necessary building blocks for economic growth.

Persuading developing countries to reduce trade barriers continues to be an important objective for the United States. As developing countries become more active participants in the global economy, they experience higher rates of economic growth and are better able to reduce poverty. Studies show that over the past two decades, developing countries that have been more open to free trade have experienced higher rates of economic growth. During the 1990s, per capita GDP in developing countries that liberalized more increased 5 percent compared to 1.4 percent growth in other developing countries. China's integration into the world economy is discussed in Box 7-4.

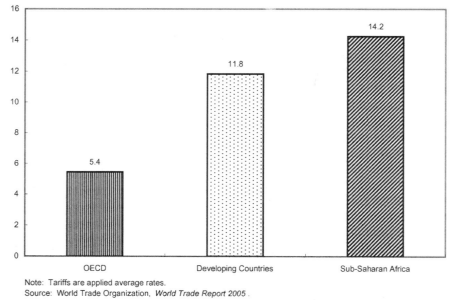

Chart 7-3 **Average Tariffs Across Countries**
Developed countries, on average, have lower tariffs than developing countries.

Percent

Note: Tariffs are applied average rates.
Source: World Trade Organization, *World Trade Report 2005*.

Box 7-4: U.S.-Asia Trade Relationship

The robust postwar economic performance of many Asian countries has driven the strong U.S.-Asia trade and economic relationship. In recent years Asian economies have experienced some of the world's highest growth rates and will continue to be key export markets for U.S. firms. Outside of South Asia, trade with the Pacific Rim region represents about 30 percent of U.S. trade with the world. The United States imports different items from the Asian region than it exports. The top imports from the Pacific Rim include electrical machinery, automobiles, toys, furniture, clothing, and footwear. The top U.S. exports to that region include aircraft, chemicals, plastics, agricultural products, automobiles, and pharmaceutical products.

U.S.-China Trade

Since 1995, U.S. trade with China has represented an increasing share of U.S. total trade, reflecting some substitution away from other Pacific Rim trading partners toward China. The United States imports different items from China than it exports to China. In 2004, top import items from China included a wide range of consumer goods, such as toys, sporting goods, apparel, and footwear. Top U.S. export items to China included a number of intermediate components and machinery,

Box 7-4 — *continued*

aircraft, soybeans, and cotton. Many imports from China now take the place of goods previously imported from other countries. China increasingly is a large and growing market for U.S. goods and services. As the chart below shows, since China's accession to the WTO, U.S. exports to China have risen faster than exports to the rest of the world.

Engaging China

The U.S.-Asia trade and economic relationship offers vast opportunities for citizens in all of these countries to prosper, however, China's integration into the global economy will not come without challenges. For instance, WTO membership has offered China new benefits, such as Permanent Normal Trade Relations with the United States and access to the WTO's rules-based dispute-settlement mechanism. China's WTO membership also brings new responsibilities, such as improving the protection of intellectual property, full compliance with trade agreements, and continued progress toward a flexible, market-based exchange-rate regime. China has made strides toward economic reform at all levels of government, but there are areas that require further progress. The United States will continue to work with China to assist its integration as a responsible stakeholder in the international economy and to ensure that bilateral economic relations are mutually beneficial.

U.S. Exports to China and the World
U.S. exports to China have been growing faster than to the rest of the world.

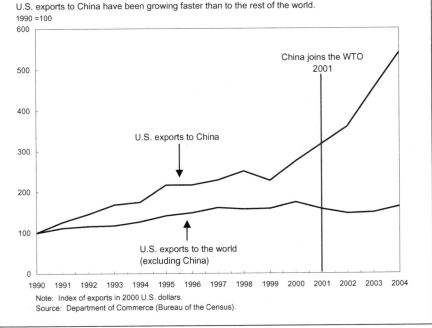

1990 =100

China joins the WTO 2001

U.S. exports to China

U.S. exports to the world (excluding China)

Note: Index of exports in 2000 U.S. dollars.
Source: Department of Commerce (Bureau of the Census).

Avenues for Further Liberalization

Countries are increasingly employing negotiations at the bilateral, regional, and multilateral levels to achieve further liberalization. These avenues are not mutually exclusive. The United States employs a multi-faceted approach, and in recent years has signed a number of bilateral and regional free trade agreements. These agreements set rules for trade, increase market access for firms, and strengthen the effective enforcement of intellectual property rights and environmental and labor laws. Other trading partners such as the European Union (EU) have pursued an even greater number of bilateral and regional agreements. The WTO nevertheless remains the most important forum for trade liberalization due to its global reach and the interdependence of the world economy.

The general consensus on the WTO among academics and practitioners is that the organization has facilitated increased trade and openness. By establishing a rules-based system, the organization provides a forum for all members to resolve trade disputes and offers a greater voice to developing countries in the establishment of global trade rules. These rules help to foster better business climates, particularly among developing countries, which can help to reduce corruption and attract more foreign direct investment. The United States fully supports the role of the WTO in promoting a rules-based global trading system, opening markets, and encouraging economic growth.

The 149 WTO members are currently engaged in the Doha Development Round of negotiations, which recognizes that global trade expansion can make a significant contribution to spurring economic growth and reducing global poverty. The Doha Round focuses on better integrating developing countries into the international trading system and enabling them to benefit from increased trade.

Moving Beyond Goods Trade Liberalization

To date, most trade liberalization has been in the form of reduction in barriers to goods trade. Using existing trade agreements and partnerships, trade and investment ties can be strengthened to include services and other nontariff measures that limit international commerce. This section discusses how the United States is pursuing deeper economic cooperation across North America and with the European Union.

Services Liberalization

From telecommunications and finance to health and education, services are the single largest sector in most industrialized and many developing countries. Not only do services provide the bulk of employment and income in many countries, but services provide critical input for the production of other goods and services. An in-depth look at financial services illustrates many of the key issues involved in liberalizing trade in services.

The unprecedented growth of global financial markets in recent years has given prominence to the issues associated with financial services liberalization. Liberalizing international trade in financial services can be a market-based means to strengthen financial systems. It is often an important catalyst in improving the quality of capital flows through exposure to foreign competition and in strengthening financial systems—particularly in developing and transitioning economies. Enhanced financial services trade can improve technology transfer and encourage better risk management across borders. Foreign competition challenges domestic firms to improve the quality of their financial services through broader opportunities for trade and portfolio diversification. This results in more consumer choice and competitive pricing.

Financial services liberalization for developing countries offers many possibilities for strengthening weak domestic financial systems through trade openness, competition, and sound regulation. Countries with fully open financial service sectors grow on average one percentage point faster than other countries. Foreign-backed financial institutions in developing countries often possess a greater ability to lend to those countries during economic downturns and thereby stabilize capital flows in times of crisis. Foreign banks that can extend credit to local businesses can be critical for stabilizing developing-country economies in the absence of more limited capacity of domestic financial intermediaries.

The General Agreement on Trade in Services (GATS) of the WTO is the most comprehensive framework to date that supports national programs of financial services liberalization within an international context. Insurance, banking, and financial services trade exists primarily in two forms: cross-border trade and commercial presence. In cross-border trade, domestic consumers purchase services from a foreign supplier abroad. In the case of commercial presence, a foreign supplier establishes itself in a country through direct investment.

U.S.-EU Economic Initiative

Trade and investment ties between Europe and the United States have been crucial in each region's economic growth for several decades. Trans-Atlantic trade is mostly free in terms of border taxes, with the exception of the agricultural sector. However, there remain a host of nontariff measures and regulatory divergences that hinder U.S.-EU trade and investment. In 2005, the United States and the European Union launched a trans-Atlantic economic initiative, which aims to promote regulatory cooperation and mutual recognition of standards, enhance trade in services, stimulate open and competitive capital markets, and promote innovation, among other economic-cooperation goals.

In order to enhance trade in services, the initiative calls for U.S. and European authorities to work with regulators and professional associations to identify sectors where the potential exists to achieve mutual recognition of professional qualifications. For instance, an agreement in architectural services might allow American architects to provide their services to European developers without having to navigate a complex and often nontransparent regulatory and licensing process. Underlying these goals to promote trans-Atlantic commerce is a commitment to greater cooperation beyond the reduction of traditional trade barriers.

Strengthening Economic Cooperation Across North America

NAFTA achieved important trade liberalization across the United States, Canada, and Mexico, and has laid the foundation for further economic cooperation in trade, investment, and other mutual interests such as immigration and security. Through the North American Security and Prosperity Partnership, the United States is working with the governments of Canada and Mexico to promote such economic cooperation. This "NAFTA-plus" initiative aims to eliminate nontariff barriers, streamline regulatory processes, expand duty-free treatment by liberalizing the rules of origin, and promote free and secure electronic commerce. Heightened security concerns since September 11, 2001, have resulted in greater port inspections, longer shipment times, and more-frequent delays. The imposition of security fees and increased inspections on NAFTA commerce can increase trade costs, adversely affecting businesses that have integrated their operations on a regional basis (such as the auto industry). This initiative also aims to harmonize safety standards for trade, streamline checkpoint operations, and make the movement of legitimate and low-risk traffic across North American borders more secure and efficient.

Conclusion

The expansion of international trade and investment over the past two decades has created an increasingly interdependent global economy. Achievements in trade liberalization have had substantial payoffs for the United States and our trading partners. With just 23 members (or "contracting parties") in 1948, the purview and membership of the GATT have grown dramatically. Today the WTO (the formal international organization of the GATT) has 149 members with many countries eager to join. While this increased engagement by countries in international commerce presents immense opportunities for U.S. consumers, workers, and firms, reaching consensus among all these countries on further reductions in trade barriers can be difficult. Like many other countries, the United States has pursued multilateral, regional, and bilateral agreements to achieve its goals. These avenues all lead to the same destination of more-open markets and greater economic growth. Existing trade partnerships and formal agreements can be platforms for further economic cooperation in areas such as services and investment. Recognizing the payoff to date and the prospective gains from further liberalization, the United States is committed to working with all countries to open markets and create favorable conditions for economic growth both here and abroad.

CHAPTER 8

The U.S. Agricultural Sector

In 2005, the Federal government spent approximately $20 billion on agricultural support payments in a sector forecast to produce approximately $270 billion of output in 2005. In addition, the United States maintains barriers to the import of some commodities, and these barriers raise the domestic prices of these commodities relative to world prices. To what extent do these payments and trade barriers serve a public purpose? Are they needed to maintain a healthy U.S. agricultural sector? Could alternative policies achieve this goal? This chapter addresses these and other questions.

Today's agricultural commodity support programs are rooted in the landmark New Deal legislation that followed the agricultural depression of the 1920s and 1930s. These programs were designed to sustain prices and incomes for producers of cotton, milk, wheat, rice, corn, sugar, tobacco, peanuts, and other crops, at a time when a large portion of the U.S. population was engaged in farming. Changing economic conditions and trends in agriculture since then suggest that many of the original motivations for farm programs no longer apply. For example, the increasing reliance of farm families on income earned from sources other than their farms and a shift toward market-oriented farm policies have made farms and commodity markets less vulnerable to adverse price changes than before. These changes imply that moving away from traditional commodity support programs today would have a much smaller impact on farm household income than in previous decades. Nonetheless, substantial government support of agriculture remains.

A more economically efficient farm policy would reflect contemporary economic conditions, environmental needs, and public values. Economic efficiency would be served by policies that are cost-effective and that give farmers greater opportunity to respond to market signals. Revising government policy to better meet these objectives would help unleash more of the innovative energy that has long characterized American agriculture. U.S. agriculture can successfully compete in a global marketplace that has been freed of domestic support and barriers to trade. The key findings of this chapter are:

- Most farmers do not benefit from commodity subsidies.
- Support to agriculture can be provided in many forms that are potentially less market-distorting than existing commodity subsidies.

The U.S. Farm Sector Has Evolved Dramatically Over Time

In the 1930s, farms accounted for a sizable share of U.S. employment and gross domestic product (GDP), but per capita farm income was only one-third the per capita income of the remaining population. Commodity programs were intended to reduce this disparity by sustaining farm household income, particularly in the face of adverse changes in agricultural prices. For instance, in the early 1930s farm household incomes were at the mercy of year-to-year fluctuations in farm prices. Commodity price support programs, which provided *price floors* (minimum prices) for agricultural producers, effectively insured them against adverse price swings. Proponents of these programs argued that they had macroeconomic benefits because they maintained rural purchasing power in times of general economic weakness. Many of today's basic Federal farm policies were established in the 1930s, and at the time, they were reasonably matched to this overall economic picture. Since that time, however, the U.S. agricultural industry has evolved dramatically.

As Table 8-1 shows, in the 1930s farm households accounted for 25 percent of the U.S. population and generated approximately 8 percent of GDP. Today they account for only 1 percent of the population (25 times lower than in 1930, as a percentage of total population) and generate approximately 1 percent of GDP. Over the same period, the rural share of the population has fallen far less (approximately two times lower than in 1930, as a percentage of total population), suggesting that rural areas are less dependent on farming's contribution to the rural economy. Our agricultural sector is still vital to our country, but due to both growth in other sectors of the economy and rapid gains in agricultural productivity that have lowered the prices of agricultural products, it has become a smaller share of the U.S. economy.

Astonishing progress in agricultural productivity growth likely explains much of the structural change in U.S. agriculture (Chart 8-1). Growth in agricultural total factor productivity averaged 2.1 percent annually between 1950 and 2002. In comparison, productivity growth in private nonfarm business over the same period averaged 1.2 percent annually. Technological progress and growth in farm productivity permit a smaller labor force to supply the agricultural needs of the country at ever lower cost. As a result, agriculture's contribution to total U.S. GDP has declined over time even though physical production has been rising (Chart 8-2).

TABLE 8-1.— *100 Years of Structural Change in U.S. Agriculture*

	1900	1930	1945	1970	2000
Number of farms (millions)	5.7	6.3	5.9	2.9	2.1
Average farm size (acres)	146	151	195	376	441
Average number of commodities produced per farm	5.1	4.5	4.6	2.7	1.3
Farm share of population (percent)	39	25	17	5	1
Rural share of population (percent)	60	44	36[b]	26	21
Farm share of workforce (percent)	41	22	16	4	2
Farm share of GDP (percent)	na	8	7	2	1[c]
Off-farm labor[a]	na	100 days	27%	54%	93%

na= not available.

[a]Off-farm labor measures the extent to which members of farm households work in other sectors besides farming. 1930, average number of days worked off-farm; 1945, percent of farmers working off-farm; 1970 and 2000, percent of farm households with off-farm income.

[b]Data for 1950.

[c]Data for 2002.

Sources: Department of Agriculture (Economic Research Service) and Department of Commerce (Bureau of Economic Analysis).

Chart 8-1 **Farm Sector Inputs, Output, and Total Factor Productivity**
Gains in farm productivity have driven increases in farm output and exceed nonfarm productivity gains.
Index, 1950 = 100

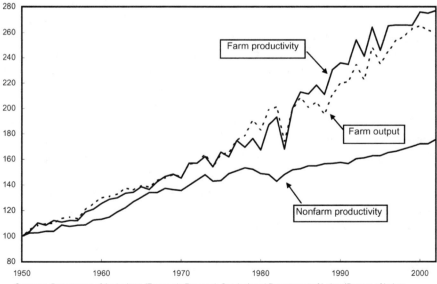

Sources: Department of Agriculture (Economic Research Service) and Department of Labor (Bureau of Labor Statistics).

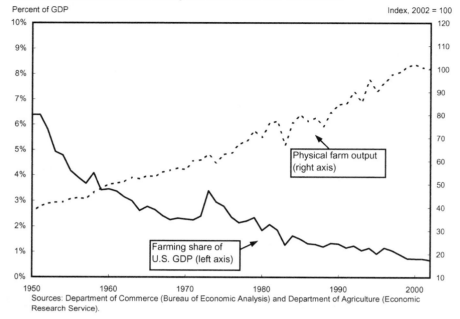

Chart 8-2 **Farming Output and Share of U.S. GDP**
Farm output has increased, while farming as a share of U.S. GDP has declined.

Percent of GDP   Index, 2002 = 100

Physical farm output (right axis)

Farming share of U.S. GDP (left axis)

Sources: Department of Commerce (Bureau of Economic Analysis) and Department of Agriculture (Economic Research Service).

The Average Farm Payment Recipient Is No Longer Poor

Fifty years ago, average household income for the farm population was approximately half that of the general population. Today, however, the average farm household tends to be better off than the average American household; in 2004, farm households earned about 35 percent more than the U.S. average household income.

While on average farm households earn more than other Americans, the relative contribution of farm income (income from farming activities, including crop, livestock, and other farm-related income, and government farm support payments) to total farm operator household income (income from all sources—farm and nonfarm—that is earned by a household that operates a farm) varies by farm size. Households operating the "rural residence farms" (Table 8-2 shows the farm size classifications) earn more than the U.S. average family income even though their net cash income from farming is negative (that is, the expenses from operating the farm exceed the gross revenues) on average. The income from these farms is unlikely to be sufficient to support a family, and households operating these farms receive their income from other sources. Households operating intermediate farms have on average positive net cash income from their farming operations, but most household income comes from sources other than farming. Households operating commercial farms have average household income over three times higher than the U.S. average family income in 2004, with most of their income coming from farming.

Production and Government Payments Are Concentrated on Large Farms

The structure of farming continues to move toward fewer, larger operations producing the bulk of farm commodities, complemented by a growing number of smaller farms earning most of their income from off-farm sources. As Table 8-3 shows, most farms in the United States are still small farms or "rural residence farms," but they produce only a small share of total agricultural output and receive only a small share of direct agricultural subsidy payments. Most production and government payments are now associated with intermediate and commercial farms, particularly the latter, which account for a relatively small percentage of the total number of U.S. farms but receive over half of direct payments.

TABLE 8-2.— *Farm Income and Farm Operator Household Income by the USDA Farm Size Classification, 2004*

Item	Rural residence farms	Intermediate farms	Commercial farms	All farms
Farm operator households (total number)	1,373,956	529,071	157,795	2,060,822
Average gross cash per farm income per farm operator household (dollars)ª	15,343	73,053	751,696	86,540
	Percent of average gross cash farm income per farm operator household by source			
Crop, livestock, and other farm-related income	*91.8*	*92.7*	*95.5*	*94.5*
Government payments	*8.2*	*7.3*	*4.5*	*5.5*
	Average per farm operator household (dollars)			
Total cash farm expenses	15,980	58,423	525,655	65,902
Net cash farm income	-638	14,630	226,041	20,638
Farm operator household incomeᵇ	75,316	64,789	191,115	81,480

Source: Department of Agriculture (Agricultural Resource Management Survey).

ªGross cash farm income is income from crop, livestock, and other farm-related income, including agricultural subsidy payments.

ᵇFarm operator household income is income from all sources, farm and nonfarm related, earned by the farm household.

Note: **Rural residence farms.** Small farms with agricultural sales less than $250,000—whose operators report they are retired or have a major occupation other than farming. Rural residence farms also include limited-resource farms, regardless of the occupation of their operator. (Limited-resource farms have sales less than $100,000 and are also operated by households with low household income during the two previous years.)

Intermediate farms. Small farms with sales less than $250,000—whose operators report farming as their major occupation. This category excludes farms classified as limited-resource farms, even if their operators report farming as their major occupation.

Commercial farms. These comprise farms with annual sales of $250,000 or more.

Item	Rural residence farms	Intermediate farms	Commercial farms
Farms (number)	1,429,953	502,771	188,095
Farms (percent of total farms)	67	24	9
Percent of total value of agricultural production...............	9	19	72
Percent of total direct government payments received	17	32	51

Source: Department of Agriculture (Agricultural Resource Management Survey).

[a]See bottom of Table 8-2 for the definitions of the USDA Farm Size Classifications, but with the inclusion of farms organized as nonfamily corporations or cooperatives, as well as farms operated by hired managers.

The United States is not the only country in which subsidy payments are concentrated among a relatively small portion of farms receiving commodity subsidy payments. Data on the distribution of payments by farm size are relatively hard to come by for most European Union (EU) countries. However, in 2001 in France, farms of approximately 500 acres or more represented 2 percent of farms and received 11 percent of direct payments for arable crops (grains and oilseeds), while small farms (25 to 50 acres) represented 19 percent of farms but received 7 percent of direct payments for arable crops. While the EU is currently in the process of converting most of its various forms of direct farm payments into "single farm payments" that will be largely independent of production, the direct farm payments will be based on payments historically received by a farm. Hence, it is likely that direct payments to European farmers will remain concentrated among a relatively small portion of farms.

Issues in Current U.S. Farm Policy

In the United States, producers of bulk commodities, such as cash grains (wheat, rice, and corn), cotton, oilseeds, and peanuts, and producers of several other minor crops are eligible for commodity support in various forms, including fixed direct payments, countercyclical payments, and marketing loan program benefits (whose particulars will be discussed in a later section). Dairy, sugar, and (until 2004) tobacco prices are also supported through production and import control programs.

Agricultural Production and Farm Program Benefits Are Increasingly Concentrated

Because of differences in farm size and types of commodities produced across farms, the distribution of government payments is unbalanced. Among the factors affecting the allocation of government payments are farm size (acreage), location, and types of commodities produced.

Less than half of the Nation's 2.1 million farms receive government payments—only 40 percent received government payments (including income support and conservation payments) in 2003. Direct government payments on crops eligible for commodity support reach only about 500,000 farms (around 25 percent of all farms). Even for farms that receive payments, government payments typically represent a small share of gross farm income (revenue from farming activities, including crop, livestock, and other farm-related income, and government farm support payments) and an even smaller share of farm operator household income. Government payments accounted for only about 5 percent of receipts for commercial farms (Table 8-2).

Most program payments go to larger farms, because program commodity production is concentrated on larger farms. While commercial farms received approximately half of government payments in 2003, they accounted for only 15.5 percent of farms receiving payments, and the average household income of their operator is almost three times higher than U.S. average household income. The largest of the commercial family farms (those with gross annual sales of $500,000 or more) received 27 percent of payments even though they account for 5.5 percent of farms receiving payments. Some of the largest farms in terms of value of production produce livestock or fruits and vegetables and thus may not receive any government program payments. As Charts 8-3 and 8-4 show, both production and program payments have become increasingly concentrated over time, with notable shifts toward larger farms even over the last decade.

Chart 8-3 **Value of Agricultural Production by Farm Size (1989 versus 2003)**
Agricultural production is shifting toward larger farms.

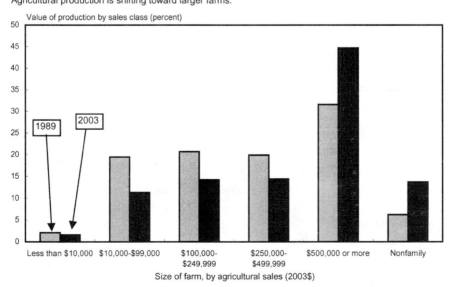

Note: Non family farms comprise those farms organized as nonfamily corporations or cooperatives, as well as farms operated by hired managers.
Source: Department of Agriculture (Economic Research Service).

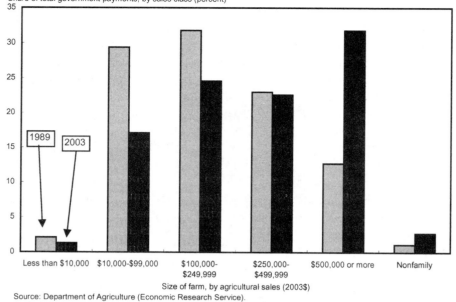

Share of total government payments, by sales class (percent)

Size of farm, by agricultural sales (2003$)

Source: Department of Agriculture (Economic Research Service).

The share of program participants is highest in regions where production of corn, oilseeds, wheat, rice, and cotton is concentrated. Cotton and rice farms reported the highest average payment level. In 2003, cash grain (wheat, rice, corn, barley, oats, and sorghum) and soybean farms received 49 percent of total payments even though they represented only 21 percent of the value of total agricultural commodity sales. Farms that receive no payments typically specialize in the production of nonprogram commodities such as meats, vegetables, fruits, and nursery products.

Farmers Today Have Many Options for Managing the Risks They Face

Farmers face many risks. The uncertainties of weather, crop yields, prices, government policies, global markets, and other factors can cause wide swings in farm income. Furthermore, farm income is more variable than income from off-farm activities.

Risk management involves choosing among many options for reducing the financial effects of such uncertainties. In addition to participating in government commodity programs that are available for certain commodities, farmers today have private options for managing risk that were not available when commodity price support programs were introduced. For instance, the growth of futures and options markets provides a market-based method for farmers to protect themselves against short-term price declines. Other private means to stabilize farm incomes include saving, borrowing, diversifying among different types of crops and livestock, contracting farm output with processors at assured prices, crop insurance and total revenue insurance, utilizing a wide range of farm management practices that reduce crop loss (e.g., irrigation, pesticide use), leasing out farmland, and taking advantage of expanded opportunities for earning nonfarm income.

The sources of income for farm households are increasingly diversified, which means many of them are less vulnerable to the volatilities of farm income. By 2000, 93 percent of farm households earned off-farm income, including off-farm wages, salaries, business income, investments, and Social Security. Off-farm work has played a key role in raising farm household income, which, as already noted, now exceeds the national average. Chart 8-5 shows the increasing importance of nonfarm income for farm households in the United States.

While farm household incomes have become more diversified, farm operations have become increasingly specialized: In 1900, a farm produced an average of about five commodities; by 2000, this average had fallen to about one per farm. This change reflects not only the production and marketing efficiencies gained by concentration on fewer commodities, but also the effects of farm

Chart 8-5 **Composition of U.S. Farm Household Income by Source (household average)**
The ratio of off-farm income to on-farm income has been rising over time.
Dollars (nominal)

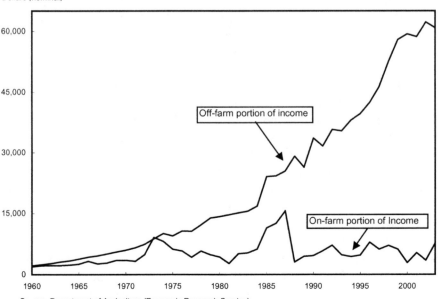

Source: Department of Agriculture (Economic Research Service).

price and income policies that have reduced the risk of depending on returns from only one crop or just a few crops. Farms would likely cope with decreases in commodity subsidies by increasing the number of different commodities they produce and by the other income stabilizing strategies already discussed.

Economic Costs of Commodity Support Programs

Despite the decreasing share of agriculture in U.S. GDP, the decreasing share of farm income in total farm household income, and despite the fact that the average farm household is no longer poor, U.S. farmers continue to receive billions of dollars in subsidy payments from U.S. taxpayers every year (Chart 8-6). Total payments to farmers from the Federal government were approximately $20 billion in 2005 and are projected to be approximately $21 billion in 2006. This constitutes about 6 percent of the U.S. Federal budget deficit for 2005 of $319 billion.

In addition, these subsidy payments can cause market distortions by stimulating more production than would occur without the subsidies. To the extent that payments are tied to production and prices, they send market signals to farmers that differ from those they would receive from a market operating free from government intervention. These distorted price signals lead to an economically inefficient allocation of resources both within the agricultural sector and across other sectors of the economy. The link between agricultural support payments and markets varies among programs. For instance, fixed direct payments (FDPs) are based on a farm's historic production and are fixed lump-sum payments. Countercyclical payments (CCPs) are based on historic production but the per acre payment varies with changes in the current market price. Marketing loan benefits (MLBs) are calculated based on current production and prices. Although there is some debate over the relative levels of the market distortions caused by these direct payments, FDPs are generally believed to be minimally market-distorting per dollar of expenditure, followed by CCPs, and finally MLBs, which are generally perceived to result in the most market distortion per dollar of expenditure.

While these domestic support policies increase costs to taxpayers, they are only part of the support that agriculture receives and these other forms of support can also cause market distortions. In particular, for some commodities, market price supports such as tariffs impose additional costs on U.S. consumers of commodities by raising their domestic prices relative to world prices and thus reducing consumer purchasing power. Such support is especially high as a percentage of the value of the commodity in the case of sugar. Because of the U.S. tariff rate quota system on sugar imports, the domestic price of sugar has been approximately double world sugar price over the last few years. An estimate by the OECD found that the cost of U.S. sugar policies to U.S. sugar consumers due to increased sugar prices was $1.5 billion in 2004.

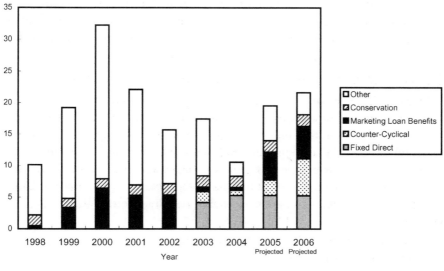

Chart 8-6 **Net Direct Payments to Farmers**

Billion Dollars

Legend:
- □ Other
- ▨ Conservation
- ■ Marketing Loan Benefits
- ▨ Counter-Cyclical
- ▨ Fixed Direct

Years: 1998, 1999, 2000, 2001, 2002, 2003, 2004, 2005 Projected, 2006 Projected

Year

Source: Department of Agriculture (Farm Services Agency).

In general, U.S. commodity support programs promote overproduction of commodities in the United States and hurt countries that could benefit from exporting these commodities to the United States. The existence of these U.S. programs in turn has prompted some U.S. trading partners to insist that we reduce these market-distorting programs in exchange for concessions important to United States trade in services and manufacturing. At the same time, as discussed in the next section, U.S. agriculture increasingly depends on the availability of foreign markets.

This section focused on distortions of market for land-based food resources. For an example of government policy that increases economic efficiency through market-based management of marine food resources, see Box 8-3 at the end of this chapter.

Trade Policy Issues

The potential economic gains from further trade liberalization in agriculture as well as in manufactured goods and in services are large (see Chapter 7, The History and Future of International Trade, for more information). Trade ministers are working at the World Trade Organization to resolve differences about how to reform various protections for agriculture, a key issue that must be addressed before negotiations in other areas can proceed. Areas of significant policy interest are the economic impacts of agricultural trade liberalization and the potential impact on the environment and the supply of amenities.

Trade Is Essential to the U.S. Agricultural Sector

Trade is important for all major sectors of the U.S. economy, and agriculture is no exception. The quantity of agricultural goods exported from the United States has grown dramatically over the last half century, and is approximately eight times higher today than in 1950. With the productivity of U.S. agriculture growing faster than domestic food and fiber demand, U.S. farmers and agricultural firms rely heavily on export markets to sustain prices and revenues. U.S. export revenues have accounted for 20-30 percent of U.S. farm income during the last 30 years and are projected to remain at this level.

Nonsubsidized Commodities Now Account for Most of U.S. Agricultural Exports

Historically, bulk commodities—wheat, rice, coarse grains, oilseeds, cotton, and tobacco—accounted for most of U.S. agricultural exports. Because of a cost advantage due to favorable land resources and capital-to-labor ratios, the United States is comparatively better at producing these crops than many other countries. The adoption of biotechnology and consolidation of farm operations have further boosted productivity. Stagnant import demand in some major markets, however, has resulted in a shift in U.S. exports of grains and oilseeds. Over the last decade, the share of U.S. bulk commodity exports shipped to developed countries dropped from 43 to 34 percent. Fast-growing developing countries are the prospective future markets for U.S. bulk crops and other farm exports. China, for example, is now the largest importer of U.S. soybeans, having surpassed the EU.

In the 1990s, U.S. exports of high-value products—meats, poultry, live animals, meals, oils, fruits, vegetables, and beverages—showed steady growth, while exports of bulk commodities tended to fluctuate more widely, particularly in response to changes in global supplies and prices (Chart 8-7). As population and incomes rose worldwide in the 1990s, U.S. exports of high-value products (HVPs) expanded in response to demand for greater diversification of diets. In fiscal 1991, HVP exports exceeded exports of bulk products for the first time (in terms of value). Notwithstanding that producers of HVPs receive little in the way of commodity subsidy payments compared to producers of bulk commodities, HVP exports have continued to exceed bulk exports, regardless of overall growth of U.S. agricultural trade.

Chart 8-7 **Value of U.S. Agricultural Exports of Bulk and High-Value Commodities**
High value commodities are now a greater share of U.S. agricultural exports.

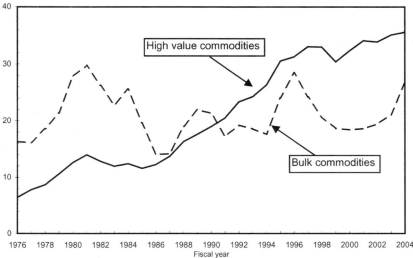

Note: Bulk commodities are wheat, rice, coarse grains, oilseeds, cotton, and tobacco. High-value products are meats, poultry, live animals, meals, oils, fruits, vegetables, and beverages.
Source: Department of Agriculture (Economic Research Service).

Trade Agreements Promote Reform of U.S. Commodity Support Programs

The November 2001 declaration of the World Trade Organization's (WTO) Fourth Ministerial Conference in Doha, Qatar, provides for negotiation on a range of subjects, including the reform of agricultural and trade policies among all 149 members. This 2001 declaration was further supported by the March 2005 ruling of the WTO Dispute Settlement Body against certain U.S. cotton program subsidies.

The United States has implemented free trade agreements with several countries, and has negotiated and is currently negotiating free trade agreements with various additional countries (see Chapter 7, The History and Future of International Trade, for further information); all of these agreements call for increases in market access, both for agriculture and for other goods and services. As an example of the impact of these types of agreements, the North American Free Trade Agreement (NAFTA), implemented in 1994, has spurred market integration among businesses and communities in Canada, Mexico, and the United States, with research showing that NAFTA boosted agricultural trade substantially above levels that would have occurred without the agreement. Trade negotiations provide an opportunity to remove market distortions and increase market access for U.S. exports including agricultural exports.

Benefits of Agricultural Trade Liberalization

At a global level, agricultural land and other resources are used most efficiently when farmers in each country face the same price signals. Prices are the market's way of indicating how much of each crop is produced, how it is produced, and where it should be produced in order to achieve the most efficient production patterns and the best, least-cost outcomes for consumers. Trade barriers, export subsidies, and domestic support programs distort the price signals that farmers receive and limit the potential economic gains that consumers and producers can obtain from trade. Trade liberalization that removes or at least lowers these distortions is motivated by the prospects of economic gains from trade (as in the example in Box 8-1 on New Zealand's experience with trade liberalization).

Empirical evidence suggests that global agricultural policy distortions impose substantial costs on the world economy. One study finds that agricultural tariffs, domestic subsidies, and export subsidies could leave world agricultural prices about 12 percent below levels otherwise expected in an intervention-free market. Because U.S. tariffs, domestic support, and export subsidies are relatively low compared to some other OECD countries, most of the benefits for the United States would come from our trade partners' policy reforms. A new study shows that global reform of agricultural and food trade policy would provide roughly 60 percent of the global gains from merchandise (agricultural and manufactured goods) trade reform—$180 billion of a total of approximately $290 billion (in 2001 dollars) by 2015. Even though agriculture is a relatively small portion of world output, agriculture is more protected than other sectors, which accounts for the significant contribution of agricultural trade liberalization to the benefits of total trade liberalization.

U.S. agriculture will continue to be competitive if global agriculture policy distortions are eliminated. According to the same study, with removal of all global agriculture policy distortions U.S. farm exports would increase by 12 percent in volume and the value of U.S. agricultural exports would continue to exceed the value of farm imports to the United States. With global agriculture and food reform, average annual agricultural production growth in the United States would continue to be positive.

Even though the net gains from removal of domestic supports would likely be positive, their removal would likely come with some costs. For example, a portion of domestic support payments are included in the value of farmland and other farm assets, thereby distorting their values. These asset values can decrease in sectors where the subsidies are reduced. However, if the market-distorting subsidies can be replaced by less-distorting payments—in particular, payments that are not closely tied to market prices or quantities, such as lump sum payments—the adverse impacts on farm asset values should be minimized.

Box 8-1: New Zealand's Abolition of Agricultural Subsidies

The farming sector in New Zealand now has negligible subsidies. Historically, assistance to New Zealand farmers was low until the 1970s, when it started to increase dramatically. The support policies of the seventies and early eighties shielded the rural economy from adopting efficient practices, increased transaction costs, and undermined the farm sector's capacity to adjust successfully to international market demands.

Within a broad package of reforms to New Zealand's economy in the 1980s, subsidies to agriculture were abolished in 1985. The reforms had an immediate and widespread effect on agriculture and the rural economy: farm incomes fell, farm input costs (particularly fertilizers) increased, farm profitability declined, the farm debt burden rose, and land values fell. Farmers' problems were compounded by low international prices for some agricultural products during the middle and late 1980s and increasing interest rates. The slower pace of reform for the manufacturing sector and the ensuing appreciation of the real exchange rate made the adjustment process of rural households more acute than the withdrawal of agricultural support would have caused on its own.

Within five years, however, the economy picked up, farm incomes had fully recovered and fears of a rural collapse never materialized. Rural population and farm households proved resourceful in adapting to the changes that swept the sector. Despite the early problems, few farmers were forced to leave their land. The rural economy and the agricultural sector as a whole have become more efficient, and competitive. Farmers have had to become more responsive to world price signals and have shown that they are able to explore and develop new niche markets. A research paper estimated that the annual rate of productivity growth was approximately 50 percent higher during 1985-1998, compared to that of 1972-1984. The level of producer support in New Zealand is now the lowest across member countries of the OECD, domestic and world prices are aligned, and government payments are only provided for pest control or relief against climate disasters. Even with low levels of government support, it is estimated that agriculture accounted for 7 percent of New Zealand's GDP over 2002-2004 compared to 8 percent over 1983-1985, and with a post-liberalization high of 9 percent in 2001. Agriculture accounted for 43 percent of New Zealand's total exports in 2004.

With the removal of global agriculture policy distortions, U.S. consumers would face higher prices for those commodities that currently receive domestic support, such as grains, because their production would fall. U.S. consumers would face lower prices for a few products, such as sugar, that are currently protected by border measures and that will face increased competition from imports.

The recent study estimates that nearly half of the global income gains of approximately $290 billion would go to developing countries. Global reform thus becomes an effective supplement to, and in some cases a substitute for, less-effective development aid. Several recent studies conclude that global agricultural trade reform would reduce rural poverty in developing economies, both because in the aggregate these countries have a strong comparative advantage in agriculture and because their agricultural sector is important for income generation.

Trade liberalization would be particularly beneficial for the poorest countries, with several studies finding the potential of trade liberalization for manufactured and agricultural goods to lift hundreds of millions of people out of poverty. Debt relief and foreign aid can also help to reduce poverty, but trade is a far more powerful tool. One study finds that the payoff from agricultural trade liberalization to developing countries alone would be $54 billion (in 2001 dollars) by 2015, roughly equal to the current debt relief proposal of $56 billion. Furthermore, development aid does not always trickle down to the underprivileged. Agricultural liberalization is particularly important because roughly 75 percent of the world's poor live in rural areas, and because farmers and other low-skilled workers constitute the vast majority of the poor in developing countries. An open global market for agricultural goods would lead to greater crop specialization, increased agricultural exports, and higher farm incomes in poor countries.

Alternatives to Commodity Subsidies

Support to agriculture can come in many forms, not all of which are equally market-distorting. For example, some countries (including the United States) offer fixed payments to farmers, irrespective of what they produce. *Decoupled payments* are lump-sum income transfers to farm operators that do not depend on current or future production, factor use, or commodity prices. From an economic perspective, the best way to provide agricultural support would focus on forms of support that interfere less with market forces while achieving the desired policy objectives.

The WTO's Uruguay Round Agreement on Agriculture encourages countries to "decouple" support from the production of specific commodities by creating a "green box" category for agricultural support. The main criterion for a support program's eligibility to be included in the green box is that the program is "not more than minimally trade-distorting." Unlike the WTO's categories for support that is more trade-distorting, the green box is not subject to spending limits. Note that the term "green box" refers to potential trade-distorting impacts and not to environmental issues, although environmental programs may be included in the green box.

Besides including lump sum payments not tied to present or future prices or output, the green box includes payments for "doing something," such as conserving the soil. For instance, support can be shifted from payments based on commodity output to agri-environmental programs such as the U.S. Environmental Quality Incentive Program, which has provisions to pay farmers to adopt environmentally benign management practices. Payments can also be made for activities that benefit the entire farm sector. For example, investments in public goods like infrastructure for rural development (e.g., roads), agricultural research, market promotion, extension and teaching, as well as collecting and diffusing agricultural statistics and market information, are also included in the green box. Government support for activities that boost agricultural productivity in the United States relative to that in other countries can help to increase competitiveness of U.S. agriculture in world markets. The exemption of these decoupled payments from WTO payment ceilings provides members of the WTO with the flexibility to transfer income to their agricultural producers, but in a manner presumed to have minimal potential to distort production and trade.

While green box payments are not currently constrained by global trade rules, many countries argue that some of them distort production and trade and that their use should be limited. A recent study of the U.S. experience with decoupled payments finds that these payments have improved the well-being of recipient farm households, enabling them to comfortably increase spending, savings, investments, and leisure but with minimal distortion of U.S. agricultural production and trade.

Environmental Aspects of Agricultural Subsidies

In the 1980s, agri-environmental programs began to play a larger role in Federal farm policies, in part due to greater concern about environmental damage from agricultural production. While U.S. agri-environmental policies have long addressed the negative externalities of agricultural production, agri-environmental policy in a number of developed country members of the WTO is increasingly giving attention to the positive by-products of agriculture. Major US agri-environmental programs can be categorized as either incentive programs or cross-compliance mechanisms (see Box 8-2).

Agri-environmental incentive programs can be further categorized as follows:

- *Land retirement programs* remove land from crop production. In exchange for voluntarily retiring land, producers receive rental or easement payments plus cost sharing and technical assistance to aid in the establishment of permanent cover on the land. Economic use of the land is limited under retirement programs (e.g., the Conservation Reserve Program and the Wetlands Reserve Program). The bulk of U.S. agri-environmental programs expenditures fall in this category.

Box 8-2: Policy Mechanisms for Addressing Agri-environmental Issues

The United States and many other developed countries utilize a combination of programs to address agri-environmental issues:

- *Voluntary incentive-based programs.* Agri-environmental incentives are payments made to the farmer for the adoption of environmentally sound practices or to retire environmentally sensitive land from production. The advantage of incentives is that they increase the likelihood that farmers will adopt the desired practices or retire land. The disadvantage of incentives is the cost to taxpayers. Incentives can also have the effect of expanding production, so even if the disamenities (negative by-products of agricultural production) produced by each farm (or on each field) decrease, more farms (or fields) may now produce disamenities. For example, a business that would be unprofitable when subject to a tax may be made profitable through the payment of an incentive or a subsidy. While a tax may drive a business out of a competitive industry, an incentive may increase entry and induce expansion in competitive outputs. Nonetheless, while economic theory may suggest that taxes are the most economically efficient instrument to reduce pollution, they have seldom been used in agri-environmental programs at the Federal level in the United States. Note too that assessing taxes on the level of agricultural pollution is difficult due to its *nonpoint source* nature (that is, the originating source(s) of agricultural pollution cannot be easily pinpointed).
- *Regulation.* Regulatory requirements or standards represent an involuntary or mandatory approach to improving agri-environmental performance. Unlike policy choices in which farmer participation is uncertain, regulations require that all farmers participate. This feature can be particularly important if the consequences of not changing practices are drastic or irreversible. On the other hand, regulatory requirements are a blunt tool and can be the least flexible of all policy instruments. This regulatory instrument requires that producers reach a specific environmental goal or adopt specific practices without regard for cost or environmental effectiveness, which may vary significantly across farms, but are seldom known by regulators. Consequently, regulation can be less flexible and less efficient than economic incentives. Regulatory requirements are used sparingly in both the United States and the EU.
- *Cross-compliance.* Cross-compliance requires a basic level of environmental compliance as a condition for farmer eligibility for other government programs that farmers may find economically desirable, such as producer payments. Technically, cross-compliance is a voluntary instrument, but in practice it may not strictly be perceived by

farmers as voluntary, particularly when the existing subsidy represents an important share of total farm income. Namely, it may be difficult for a farmer to forgo cross-compliance when the value of the existing subsidies exceeds the farmer's costs of adopting the mandated practices. An advantage of cross-compliance programs is that less government spending is required than with subsidies to address environmental problems. Disadvantages are that it will have a lesser impact on farms that are not traditional participants in commodity payment programs or in situations when program payments are lower than the costs to farmers of complying.

- *Working land conservation programs* support adoption and maintenance of land management and structural conservation practices on agricultural land, including crop and grazing land, and in some cases, forestland, in exchange for cost-shares or incentives (e.g., the Conservation Security Program and the Environmental Quality Incentive Program).
- *Agricultural land preservation programs* help retain land in agricultural production by purchasing the landowner's right to convert land to other uses (e.g., the Farm and Ranch Land Protection Program).

A requirement for agri-environment programs to be included in the WTO green box is that they have not more than "minimally" trade-distorting effects. With the exception of the Conservation Reserve Program (CRP) and other land retirement programs that likely reduce U.S. production, current U.S. cost-sharing, incentive payment, and technical assistance programs have a minimal effect on production, given that the focus of such programs is on environmental improvements rather than altering production. In contrast, the focus of complaints brought before the WTO to date on agricultural subsidy programs has been on programs that may have a tendency to increase production, not reduce it.

If new WTO negotiations produce an agreement to further reduce trade-distorting domestic support, countries may find it necessary to shift support from programs that are subject to reduction to programs that are exempt. This may include agri-environmental programs that qualify for inclusion in the WTO green box. Nonetheless, great care needs to be taken in designing programs to ensure that they indeed have only minimal trade-distorting effects (in particular, production-increasing impacts tend to be a source of international contention); there is no reason to assume that environmental programs will automatically fall in the WTO green box.

Conclusion

While the income of farm operator households is higher than the U.S. average, their household income is more variable than that of the average U.S. household because farm income is more variable than income from off-farm sources. Management of the risks faced by large commercial farms—who receive the biggest share of U.S. subsidy payments—may be best served by crop or revenue insurance and forward pricing through participation in futures and options markets. And if one of society's goals for agricultural subsidies is to support the nonmarket benefits of agriculture, then there are more efficient instruments than those that are coupled to commodity production.

If the intent of commodity support programs is to assist low-income households, then these programs are failing in this task today because the bulk of payments go to farm households with incomes above the U.S. nonfarm average. Furthermore, as world trade in agricultural products increases, food security for U.S. consumers becomes less dependent on domestic production and, consequently, on domestic commodity subsidies programs. Not only are domestic commodity policies—domestic support, market access, and export subsidies—not targeting vulnerable populations in the United States, these policies, as used by the United States and other countries, reduce farm income in poor countries.

Box 8-3: A Market-Based Approach to Reduce Overfishing

The Nation's marine fisheries are valuable resources, contributing $31.5 billion in value added to U.S. GDP, supporting 82 million recreational fishing trips, and providing 9.5 billion pounds of protein-rich food. Unfortunately, many of these fisheries suffer from overfishing, excessive harvest capacity, and low profitability. Limited Access Privileges (LAPs)—which give individual commercial or recreational fishermen, cooperatives, or communities the exclusive privilege of harvesting a share of the total allowable catch—are a market-based approach to addressing these challenges.

Under traditional management approaches, fishermen compete for a share of a common resource. This leads to a "race for fish" that results in short fishing seasons, higher harvesting costs, lower profits, overcapacity, poor product quality, and environmentally damaging fishing

---

Box 8-3 — *continued*

practices. Traditional approaches often mandate certain fishing gear, specify short fishing seasons, and impose other restrictions to limit overfishing. These restrictions are difficult to enforce, do not provide incentives for fishermen to reduce their catch, and impede the development of innovative technology and fishing practices.

LAP programs, which include individual fishing quotas (IFQs) as well as allocations to fishing cooperatives, communities, and potentially, recreational fishermen, do not suffer from these same problems. LAPs with transferable quotas provide fishermen with the incentive to harvest fish at minimal cost, thereby reducing fleet overcapacity and increasing profitability. Each fisherman in a LAP program cannot harvest more fish than his individual quota permits. This means that fishermen can adopt new fishing practices to reduce bycatch (i.e., unwanted or unintentional catch) without concern that they will lose target catch to competitors, and have a lot more choice about when to fish, allowing them to avoid hazardous weather and sea conditions and improve their profitability by fishing when prices are best.

LAPs have been implemented in eight U.S. fisheries since 1990. Commercial fishermen in these fisheries have seen increased profits, decreased harvesting costs, and a safer and more stable industry. For example, due to improved product quality under a LAP program, the Alaska pollock catcher/processor cooperative fleet harvest in 2001 yielded 49 percent more products per pound than in 1998, the last year of the "race for fish." IFQs in the Alaska halibut and sablefish fishery ended the race for fish and increased season length from less than 5 days to 245 days per year. Profits have increased due to lower operating costs and higher product prices, which have more than doubled because halibut now arrive to market fresh rather than frozen, thereby benefiting consumers. Harvesting costs in the mid-Atlantic surf clam and ocean quahog fishery have fallen by 46 percent since implementation of an IFQ system.

In September 2005, the President proposed legislation reauthorizing the Magnuson-Stevens Fishery Conservation and Management Act that would implement key elements of the President's 2004 Ocean Action Plan, including encouragement for fishery managers to use market-based management, such as LAPs. At the same time, the Administration pledged to work with regional fishery management councils to double the number of LAP programs by 2010, bringing at least eight new fisheries under market-based management. The Administration is also working with regional fishery managers to create guidelines for planning and implementation of future LAP programs.

CHAPTER 9

The U.S. Financial Services Sector

Everyday life tends to expose people to the financial services sector. For example, people make deposits at banks and obtain loans from them. Nevertheless, understanding what this sector does can be difficult. Why do individuals go to intermediaries like banks for mortgages, rather than skip intermediaries (and their costs) and deal directly with savers? And why do financial service firms ask for so much information before making a loan and, afterward, place so many restrictions on borrowers?

This chapter explores what financial services do for an economy, how financial development relates to economic performance, and how financial services can be effectively regulated. In particular, it develops the following conclusions.

- The financial services sector addresses informational problems that can otherwise keep financial capital from finding productive uses. Moreover, the U.S. financial services sector tends to deliver these services in a cost-effective manner.
- Financial services facilitate innovation and thus encourage the economic growth that is necessary to increase living standards over time. They might also bolster economic stability.
- Financial regulation should protect consumers and ensure the system's safety and soundness. Moving too far in the public regulation direction, however, can stifle the productivity and innovation that are necessary for the economy to enjoy fully the benefits of financial services. An effective financial regulatory system appropriately balances the costs and benefits of public regulation.

The Economic Roles of Financial Services

Financial services address information problems inherent in lending and investing. This section explains this and other benefits, and presents evidence that the United States enjoys a comparative advantage in producing financial services.

Financial Services Address Information Problems in Lending and Investing

Adverse Selection

In general, information problems can hinder efficient economic behavior. Consider an example from the used-car market. In this market, sellers are likely to have better information than do buyers about the cars being sold. A buyer might have general information about the quality of a certain model, but the seller likely enjoys additional information about the particular car that is being considered. In this and related cases, information is said to be distributed *asymmetrically* across the transaction's parties.

Economic theorists have shown that, absent a tool for reducing information asymmetries, only the worst-quality cars will be sold. In the case of the used-car market, given the general nature of the buyer's information, he or she may be willing to pay only the average price that the model under consideration tends to command. But sellers may then only offer cars that are below average in quality—i.e., "lemons." Indeed, a seller would incur a loss by selling an above-average car at a price based on the value of the average car. Consequently, high-quality cars might never make their way to the market.

This tendency for sellers of lemons to *adversely select* themselves creates difficulties in a number of markets, including those for financial capital. For example, just as a used car's owner has relatively good information about that car's quality, a manager likely has better information about his or her business projects than does an outside supplier of financial capital. This information asymmetry, in turn, can encourage "low-quality" projects to adversely select themselves into the financial market. As in the automobile example, relatively well-informed sellers (managers) may want to withhold highly valued assets (the right to share in the proceeds of a new project) if the general nature of available information lets buyers bid only an average price. An economy may thus forgo the very projects that are important for its performance.

Moral Hazard

The above discussion shows that, when information is asymmetric before a transaction takes place, the side with relatively good information can adversely select itself. The prospect of this strategic behavior can discourage the financing of otherwise valuable projects. But even if parties to a potential transaction can address this problem, information can still be asymmetric after a transaction takes place. This latter type of asymmetry is known as *moral hazard* and, left untreated, it too can hinder economic efficiency.

Like adverse selection, moral hazard is problematic for a number of markets. For example, because insurance customers have better information about their behavior than do insurers, an individual who buys insurance can subsequently take on too much risk. Here, an insured driver might enjoy the benefit of driving faster (e.g., the value of time saved) while passing at least some of the costs on to the insurance agency (e.g., the value of an expected claim).

A similar phenomenon plays out in more narrowly defined financial services. Indeed, just as insurance customers tend to have better information about their behavior than do insurance sellers, businesses and households tend to have better information about how they use loans than do lenders.

Lending contracts, like insurance contracts, may thus be plagued by moral hazard problems. A manager might, for example, pursue a project that is more risky than what was agreed upon when the loan was made. In doing so, the manager enjoys the benefit of projects that ultimately perform well, but passes the cost of poorly performing projects onto the firm's lenders. Absent an institution that would discourage managers from acting in this manner, suppliers of financial capital will be reluctant to offer financing. Again, the problem of asymmetric information can lower an economy's level of productive activity.

Financial Services Can Mitigate Adverse Selection and Moral Hazard

The above discussions show that information problems can impede the efficient use of financial capital. Because these problems can stand in the way of better outcomes for *both* demanders (i.e., businesses, households) and suppliers (i.e., savers) of financial capital, opportunities exist for a third party to reduce informational obstacles. Financial service providers frequently play this important intermediary role.

Financial service firms can, for example, build expertise in evaluating and monitoring borrowers. Understanding what is, and what is not, a productive project can check the problem of adverse selection. An effective monitoring program can then keep borrowers on task with agreed-upon projects and thus limit moral hazard problems.

Demanding collateral can help mitigate information problems in this regard. To see how, suppose that a low- and a high-quality applicant ask for a loan and notice that, while information about quality is important for deciding whether to grant a loan, low-quality applicants may not want to divulge that information. In terms of the above discussion, lenders are worried about low-quality individuals *adversely selecting* themselves into the pool of applicants.

Asking for collateral can address this problem by encouraging applicants to truthfully (rather than strategically) reveal this information. Here, high-quality applicants are more willing to post collateral because they are more confident that they will not lose it. In this manner, collateral requirements can induce applicants to truthfully separate themselves into distinctive types of borrowers (rather than strategically masquerade as more attractive types).

Likewise, asking for collateral can mitigate the problem of *moral hazard*. Recall from the above discussion that borrowers may find it attractive to opportunistically increase a project's risk. Collateral requirements can mitigate this problem by essentially exposing the borrower's own capital to such risk taking.

In each case, financial service firms reduce informational obstacles that can stand in the way of lending. A good project can benefit both the project's manager and lenders. But because managers tend to have better information about projects, both before and after the projects are underway, passive lenders will be reluctant to offer the requisite funding. By specializing in setting collateral requirements and evaluating and monitoring projects, financial service firms can play the important economic role of reducing such asymmetries.

Financial Services Reduce the Cost of Collecting Information

A well-developed financial system not only mitigates information asymmetries, it does so in an efficient manner. Notice from the above example that individual savers could, in principle, mitigate these asymmetries themselves. In doing so, however, they would unnecessarily reproduce the same information a number of times. The relatively high cost of collecting information in this manner would still leave an economy with considerable information asymmetries and thus prevent financial capital from being matched with its most productive uses.

A reputable car dealer illustrates this point. After carefully examining a car, a dealer might offer a guarantee. In that case, prospective buyers can take some confidence from the guarantee itself, as opposed to having to reproduce information about the same car through repeated examinations. In a competitive environment, the associated cost savings can make their way to consumers. By essentially delegating the process of information discovery to experts, savers can likewise benefit from having financial service firms examine prospective investments on their behalf. In both cases, intermediaries not only facilitate mutually beneficial trades by reducing information asymmetries, they produce these benefits in a relatively low-cost manner.

Other Benefits of Financial Services

Diversifying Investment Risks

In addition to being concerned with asymmetric information problems, individuals are concerned with the fundamental risks to which their savings are exposed. Indeed, independent of information problems, the return on investments can be very uncertain. This type of risk can also discourage financial capital from finding productive uses. Financial services can address this problem by economizing on the costs of investing in diversified pools of loans.

By saving at a bank, for example, individuals do not expose themselves to the risk of any one investment. Instead, they can participate in the return from a pool of investments, some of which will perform better at times than do others. On average, then, savers can reduce the volatility that they would otherwise face in an undiversified portfolio while maintaining a relatively high rate of return.

Transforming Long-Term Investments into Liquid Assets

Financial services can economize on the cost of providing liquid access to even long-term investments. Individuals tend to save because they want to expand their consumption opportunities in the future. But while investments in assets like long-term loans might be good at expanding these opportunities, they are typically not good at facilitating exchanges. It is much easier to buy groceries, for example, with currency than it is with a long-term loan. Absent a mechanism that can readily transform loans into more readily usable forms of money, savers will again be reluctant to invest in projects that could otherwise be mutually beneficial.

Financial firms provide savers with liquidity. Banks, coupled with Federal deposit insurance (discussed in the Policy section below), can fund long-term business projects while fulfilling the transaction demands of depositors. Absent such a service, savers may be reluctant to commit their capital for longer periods of time. But innovative projects frequently need long gestation periods to build themselves into productive endeavors. By giving savers ready access to the proceeds of even long-term investments, financial services again encourage capital to find its best uses.

Providing Cost-Effective Means of Payment

The financial sector also furthers economic well-being by economizing on the costs of producing payment services. The most widely used means of payment, cash, is a good way to make small purchases, but creates difficulties for larger transactions and those made from a distance. Financial services have found innovative ways to make life easier here.

Services like processing checks and conducting electronic funds transfers, to name a couple, can enhance the speed, safety, and convenience of transacting. In addition, means of payment like these can open up opportunities to better match consumers with the producers of goods and services that they demand. Finally, the potential to expand these already considerable benefits is large. By moving even further toward an electronic payment system, for example, the savings in postage costs alone could reach into the billions of dollars.

The United States Enjoys a Comparative Advantage in Financial Services

The U.S. financial services sector has been making increasing contributions to GDP over the past several decades. The growing importance of this sector to the U.S. economy owes, in part, to the U.S. global comparative advantage in the production of financial services.

Chart 9-1 shows how financial services, such as central banking, taking deposits, and making loans, have accounted for a growing share of U.S. nominal GDP. This contribution has increased steadily from about 2 percent in 1977 (the first year for which data are available) to about 4 percent in 2003 (the most recent year for which data are available).

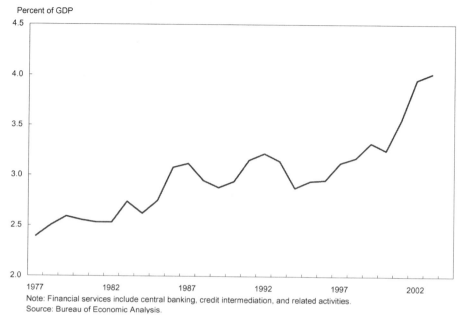

Chart 9-1 **Share of GDP from Financial Services**
The contribution of finance to GDP has risen about 68% since the late 1970s.

Percent of GDP

Note: Financial services include central banking, credit intermediation, and related activities.
Source: Bureau of Economic Analysis.

The growing importance of the financial services sector is consistent with U.S. workers having a global comparative advantage in the production of financial services. For example, financial firms open offices in other countries to serve foreigners (i.e., to export their services). Since 1997 (the first year for which these data are consistently available), exports of financial services have outpaced imports, with exports increasing by about $15 billion and imports increasing by only about $5 billion. In 2004, financial service exports totaled $27 billion while imports of financial services were only $11 billion.

Economic Growth and Stability

The above discussion highlights the potential for financial services to mitigate information asymmetries and economize on transactions costs. Recent research cites these attributes as important channels through which financial services can increase living standards and promote economic stability. This section elaborates on the general economic benefits that financial services can generate in this regard.

Financial Development and Economic Growth

Well-developed financial markets are important for economic growth. Equipped with a comparative advantage in reducing information asymmetries and transactions costs, financial service firms can productively identify and guide promising entrepreneurs, and thus pave the way for scarce resources to find innovative projects. Innovations, in turn, can help turn a fixed amount of resources into more output, and thus facilitate increases in living standards. This funneling of resources to productive projects can also encourage the replacement of outdated and inefficient technologies. Absent productive financial services, for example, individuals can pursue innovations only when they have enough resources to get their projects off the ground. "Idea-rich" but "capital-poor" innovators pose little threat to a market's incumbents, who can become complacent and set the stage for poor performance to entrench itself. By easing the way for newcomers to participate in the economy, financial services can hasten the replacement of bad ideas with growing opportunities. Box 9-1 discusses the role of financial intermediaries in the development and implementation of particularly innovative ideas.

Box 9-1: Venture Capital and Innovation

Venture capitalists raise funds, search for profitable investments, and then guide investments until sufficient proceeds can be returned to the original contributors. Working through this process, venture capitalists can be especially successful in identifying and guiding productive innovations. An influential study finds, for example, that a dollar of venture capital produces about three times more patents than does a dollar of corporate research and development (R&D). In addition, patents that ultimately emerge from venture capitalization tend to be of high quality.

The previous section of this chapter showed that asymmetric information can slow, or even preclude, mutually beneficial transactions from taking place. In this way, information problems can prevent financial capital from flowing to its most-productive enterprise. These problems can become even more difficult when the project that seeks funding is an innovative one. Indeed, the features of innovative projects tend to be intangible, and thus expand opportunities to strategically act on informational advantages. Without a mechanism for dealing with these advantages, an economy may thus forgo projects that would contribute most to its growth.

Venture capital firms are one such mechanism. Their expertise in identifying productive ideas and creating incentive structures that productively guide development therein lets them attract the type of long-term steady funding that is necessary to see innovations through from start to finish. This necessity for commitment creates risks that do not let other intermediaries succeed. Here, for example, even the most innovative borrowers may lack the credit or business track record that

---

would make them attractive prospects to conventional lenders. Venture capitalists overcome such obstacles by taking extraordinary measures to examine prospective projects and maintaining a hands-on approach after making an investment. One study indicates that by discovering worthy projects and shepherding them to fruition, venture capitalists are able to annually attract upward of $100 billion in funding, and channel this capital in a manner that accounts for about 14 percent of U.S. innovative activity.

Consistent with the argument that financial services encourage growth and discourage entrenchment, one study finds that industries that tend to lack their own funding (and thus rely heavily on external sources to finance projects) grow significantly faster when they are located in countries that have well-developed financial intermediaries (such as banks). In addition, studies show that countries that maintain well-developed financial systems tend to grow their economies at relatively high rates.

This relationship between financial development and economic performance also shows up in data from U.S. states. The relaxation of multi-state branch banking restrictions since the mid-1970s, for example, appears to have improved the quality of U.S. bank lending (as measured by a decline in nonperforming loans). Evidence suggests that the entrepreneurial sector responded to this enhanced development by leading state-level economies onto higher and more stable growth paths. Looking at data at the firm- and economy-levels, as well as across countries and U.S. states, researchers have thus found evidence to suggest that an economy's living standards and growth prospects depend to a considerable degree on its financial development.

Financial Services and Economic Stability

The above discussion suggests that economic growth increases with the development of financial markets and services. Fortunately, such long-term benefits need not compromise short-term stability. Indeed, financial development may contribute to a reduction in the volatility of economic activity.

The reduction in economic volatility over the past several decades is well documented. As indicated in Chart 9-2, the volatilities of real output and consumption growth (measured by their standard deviations over 20-quarter periods) have both trended down since 1950. This remarkable decline in aggregate volatility, coined "The Great Moderation," appears to have set the stage for a stable macroeconomic landscape that better avoids the inefficiencies that might emerge from increased economic uncertainty.

The evolution of the financial system may have played an important, though not exclusive, role in the Great Moderation. One change in the financial system that may have contributed to the Great Moderation was the removal of regulations that created volatility. Evidence suggests, for example, that Regulation Q, which limited the maximum interest that banks could pay on deposits until its repeal in 1980, depressed lending in high-interest-rate environments. As a result, banks may have created volatility by translating financial shocks into real ones.

The Great Moderation may also reflect the financial system's development of more sophisticated ways of managing and sharing risk. For example, banks now use *derivative securities* to insulate their balance sheets from interest-rate risk. Derivatives are contractual arrangements that specify payments between parties, where the payments are usually tied to some observable and verifiable measure (e.g., an interest rate or stock market index). Banks may also use derivatives to essentially purchase insurance against the defaults of large loans. In addition, banks have developed new methods for selling loans to investors through *securitizations,* the process of pooling loans and selling claims on these pools to dispersed investors.

Chart 9-2 **Long-Term Decline in Volatility of Macroeconomic Indicators**
The volatility of macroeconomic variables has declined over the past several decades.

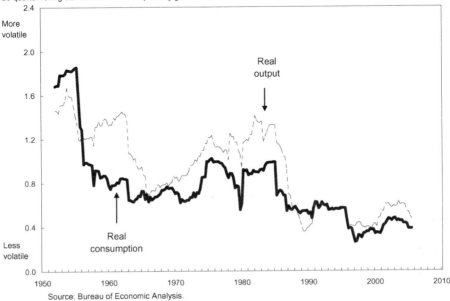

20-quarter rolling standard deviation of quarterly growth rates

Source: Bureau of Economic Analysis.

Further, innovations in consumer financial products offered by banks, such as cash-out-mortgage refinancing (COMR), may have helped to moderate economic fluctuations. This role was evident in 2001, the year of the most recent recession, when households reportedly extracted $83 billion of home equity, up from $26 billion in the prior year. In addition, the widespread distribution of consumer credit has almost certainly allowed many individuals to insulate themselves from short-term economic shocks.

Policy Issues

The financial services sector appears to favorably affect economic growth and may also reduce economic volatility. As the above discussions about financial mechanisms such as collateral and monitoring illustrate, private financiers do a lot to facilitate financial development. However, public policy plays a productive role. In particular, the desire to protect consumers and ensure the safety and soundness of the financial system has motivated policies in this area.

Consumer Protection

Policies protect consumers in a number of settings. The Food and Drug Administration (FDA), for example, requires producers to disclose certain nutritional content and other information about their products. In the financial services sector, the Truth-in-Lending Act also requires informational disclosures. The Act requires that consumers be made aware of information about the amount and rate of interest that they are paying on a loan.

A consumer-protection issue of current interest is identity theft. To conduct their operations and reduce the risks of lending, financial service firms rely heavily on the Nation's credit-reporting system to both assess risk and verify the identity of credit applicants. Identity thieves prey on this system by using another consumer's personal information to obtain credit in the consumer's name.

Identity theft is a considerable problem. In 2005, banks, credit card companies, retailers, and data brokers were involved in high-profile security breaches that affected up to 50 million account holders. The entity whose security is breached generally bears the costs of direct losses from identity theft. However, consumers bear significant indirect costs of verifying fraudulent charges and correcting the damage to their credit profiles.

The Administration has taken substantial steps to protect individuals from identity theft. In 2003, the President signed the Fair and Accurate Credit Transactions Act, which allows all Americans free access to review credit reports annually to ensure the security and accuracy of their credit reports and to protect against identity theft. In 2004, the President signed the Identity

Penalty Enhancement Act, which defined a new crime of "aggravated identity theft" and increased penalties for identity fraud. Congress may enact additional protective measures, and the Administration has recommended that it consider extending to brokers and other entities the consumer safeguards that govern the way financial institutions secure their databases. The Administration also supports narrowly tailored legislation requiring companies to notify consumers if the security of their information has been breached in a manner that creates a significant risk of identity theft. Enacting this legislation would result in uniform national rules for dealing with identity theft, rather than the current patchwork of inconsistent state and local regulations. Of course, some regulations can be overly burdensome if not carefully crafted (see Box 9-2 for additional discussion).

Box 9-2: Regulation Is Not Costless

While regulation can improve economic performance, it can also have the opposite effect if not carefully crafted. For instance, if consumer-protection laws for some transactions are unduly burdensome, financial service firms may stop engaging in those transactions altogether. Therefore, regulations must carefully assess the overall benefit to consumers to be sure the regulation's benefits outweigh its costs.

Excessive regulation can increase the cost of producing financial services. The now-repealed Glass-Steagall Act is illustrative. The Act prohibited banks from producing commercial and investment services under the same roof. This prohibition addressed the concern that a bank's investment arm (where banks sell financial securities, like stocks) could opportunistically sell low-quality investments, and then use the proceeds to shore up bad loans from its commercial arm (where banks take in deposits and turn out loans). However, by decreasing the scope of activities in which banks could engage, research has argued that it pushed out economical ways of producing financial services. The costs of regulation, in this case, could very well have outweighed the benefits.

Finally, regulation can work against the ability of financial services to encourage capital to find productive uses. As described in the previous section, research has found that historical restrictions on banks opening new branches in other states decreased the quality of loans. When banks make bad loans, financial capital may not find its most productive use. Consistent with this argument, state-level economies grew at faster and more stable rates after they relaxed bank branch restrictions.

Safety and Soundness

Another policy concern, the financial system's safety and soundness, has deep historical roots. Until the 1930s, the banking sector was largely unregulated. As such, it was susceptible to *bank runs,* whereby depositors raced to withdraw funds in anticipation that others would do so first. Bank runs are problematic because banks cannot quickly turn loans into cash in order to repay depositors. Indeed, faced with a deposit run, a bank may be forced to sell loans at a discount, which could leave depositors toward the end of the run with little or no money.

To address this problem, the Federal government began to insure deposits. Depositors have little reason to run on a bank when their funds are guaranteed by the government. However, given that this insurance can expose the U.S. taxpayer to potentially large losses, the Federal government has an obligation to ensure that banks operate in a safe and sound manner.

Federal banking agencies have sought to achieve safety and soundness through *supervision* and the setting of *capital requirements.* Agencies supervise banks much like banks would monitor their loan customers. Bank capital requirements dictate the amount of capital or liquid assets that banks must hold as a cushion against potential losses.

The Basel Accords

Capital requirements have found guidance over the past two decades from two international agreements known as the Basel Accords. These agreements were created under the auspices of the Basel Committee on Banking Supervision (which is organized and operated by the G-10 countries) within the larger Bank for International Settlements (BIS) located in Basel, Switzerland. The Basel Accords aim to produce general principles and guidelines rather than promulgate binding law.

Basel I was instituted in 1988, and Basel II was issued in June 2004 (but has not yet been implemented). Basel II was designed to improve upon its predecessor, Basel I, in the areas of risk management and capital adequacy. And while the Accords are intended for large international banks, a number of countries are using them to guide domestic banking industries.

In addition to protecting depositors, Basel I and II aim to mitigate global *systemic risk*: the risk that an event will trigger significant adverse effects on the economy through loss of economic value and confidence in the global financial system. Systemic risk is normally associated with spillover effects, in which the original shock spreads contagiously to other parts of the global financial system and disrupts output and employment. The adverse effects of systemic problems can arise from disruption of credit and capital flows. The failure of a major international bank due to inadequate capital financing provides one example of the type of "event" that could trigger adverse shocks.

Prior to Basel I, countries operated under very different regulatory capital regimes for their banks. Over time this arrangement raised competitiveness and financial soundness concerns, prompting banking supervisors in the industrialized countries to establish common approaches to defining regulatory capital and setting minimum regulatory capital requirements. Still, under Basel I, minimum capital requirements can lack sensitivity to the underlying riskiness of a bank's business activities. This encourages bank investments in higher-risk assets for which regulatory capital charges are too low, and fails to reward improvements in the bank's underwriting and risk-management processes. The lack of risk sensitivity also reduces the effectiveness of statutorily mandated, prompt corrective-action policies in the United States, which are tied to a bank's regulatory capital ratios. In recent years, financial innovations, such as securitization and credit derivatives, and the greater sophistication and complexity of risk-management techniques have rendered the current regulatory capital framework, and related bank-reporting and disclosure policies, increasingly outmoded for large, internationally active banking organizations.

On September 30, 2005, the four Federal banking regulators (the Board of Governors of the Federal Reserve System, the Office of the Comptroller of the Currency, the Federal Deposit Insurance Corporation, and the Office of Thrift Supervision) announced their intent to issue in 2006 a Notice of Proposed Rulemaking for the U.S. implementation of Basel II. The banking regulators plan to implement only the so-called "advanced" Basel II approaches, under which minimum capital requirements would be much more closely aligned with a bank's actual risk taking by linking these requirements to the bank's own internal risk assessments. This new framework introduces three "pillars" intended to make reported regulatory capital ratios better indicators of a bank's financial condition and to make a bank's risk taking more transparent to both supervisors and the general public. Pillar 1 sets a bank's minimum capital requirement based on capital formulas whose basic inputs are derived from the bank's internal risk-management systems. Pillar 2 establishes a process through which supervisors and senior bank management will review a bank's overall capital adequacy in relation to its business activities and plans. Last, Pillar 3 attempts to enhance transparency through requiring expanded public disclosures of a bank's risk positions. Under the plan announced by the banking agencies, qualified U.S. banks could begin transitioning to the advanced Basel II approaches in January 2009.

Within the United States, only a few banks are expected to apply this new framework. It will be mandatory only for the largest, internationally active U.S. banks under the belief that the advanced risk-measurement and management standards are most appropriate and cost-effective for these institutions. However, any U.S. bank may elect to adopt the new framework voluntarily.

To address potential competitiveness concerns that might arise from banks being subject to different capital standards, the Federal banking agencies also are considering possible modifications of the U.S. capital rules that would apply to those banks not adopting the advanced Basel II approaches. Broadly, such modifications would be designed to make the rules applicable to the vast majority of banks more risk sensitive, but without sacrificing overall simplicity of the current capital framework.

As discussed above, capital standards for large banks are motivated by the need to protect depositors and limit systemic risk. Concerns about systemic risk extend beyond the traditional banking sector to other sectors, such as government sponsored enterprises (GSEs).

Government Sponsored Enterprises (GSEs)

The Federal National Mortgage Association and the Federal Home Loan Mortgage Corporation, more popularly known as Fannie Mae and Freddie Mac, are two *government sponsored enterprises* (GSEs) that are organized by the Federal government for the purpose of supporting the secondary market for residential mortgages. The original congressional intent behind the formation of these institutions was to provide stability and liquidity in the mortgage market and to promote home ownership, particularly among low-income families, by reducing the costs of mortgages. (The government also pursues these objectives through the Federal Home Loan Bank (FHLB) system.)

Fannie and Freddie primarily run two businesses: mortgage securitization and portfolio management. In their securitization program, Fannie and Freddie buy home mortgages from banks and other mortgage loan originators, package them into pools, and sell claims on these pools to investors as *mortgage-backed securities* (MBS). To augment investor demand, Fannie and Freddie guarantee the interest and principal on the underlying mortgages. These securitization programs provide liquidity to mortgage markets by expanding the range of investors who hold mortgage assets. The portfolio-management function of Fannie and Freddie arises because they purchase and hold MBS on their balance sheets. The combined assets on the balance sheets of Freddie and Fannie rose from $132 billion (5.6 percent of the single-family home-mortgage market) at the end of 1990 to $1.38 trillion (23 percent of the home-mortgage market) by 2003.

The market perception that the U.S. government backs GSE-issued debt has facilitated the growth in Fannie and Freddie's portfolios. Although GSE debt is not guaranteed by the government, the balance of evidence suggests that most investors perceive that the Federal government would step in to prevent a GSE default. This perception allows GSEs to issue debt at an estimated 40 basis points (i.e., 0.40 percent) below the rates of their peer institutions. With access to relatively inexpensive funds, the GSEs can easily finance expansions of their portfolios.

The growth in GSE portfolios is accompanied by prepayment risk. Prepayment of mortgages is problematic because GSEs tend to raise funds at fixed interest rates, and prepayments tend to occur when interest rates fall. Raising funds at fixed interest rates implies that GSE debt issued to finance a purchase of mortgages is fixed until the debt matures. However, if interest rates fall and, as a result, prepayments occur, the GSEs must reinvest the funds from the prepayment in the now-lower interest-rate environment. Typical methods for hedging prepayment risk (without assuming additional credit risk) include the use of interest-rate swaps to turn fixed-rate debt obligations into floating-rate ones, and the buying of Treasury securities. Both methods generate income when interest rates fall, helping to offset the decline in income caused by prepayments.

While all mortgage investors may face prepayment risk, the size of the GSEs makes this risk of particular concern to financial markets and regulators. Given the large size of their portfolios, it might be very difficult for the GSEs to quickly adjust their portfolios if hedges turned out to be less than perfect. The sudden failure of one of these enormous providers of mortgage liquidity could severely diminish the liquidity of the mortgage market and create severe financial stress for holders of GSE securities. Prepayment risk is also compounded by the low level of GSE capital. The capital-to-asset ratios (measures of the financial cushion available to absorb portfolio losses without becoming insolvent) of Fannie and Freddie are roughly half the average capital-to-asset ratios at comparable financial institutions.

The Administration's policy proposals have attempted to minimize the systemic risks posed by GSEs, while preserving the benefits for low-income home owners and the liquidity that GSEs provide to mortgage markets. In particular, the Administration has proposed that the GSEs focus on the business of mortgage securitization. As a result, market liquidity will be enhanced for a wider range of mortgages, and the home owner and liquidity benefits associated with the GSEs will be maintained. Moreover, the resulting reduction in the sizes of the portfolios will make the portfolios easier to hedge, decreasing the likelihood of systemic problems with little adverse impact on the liquidity of the market. Indeed, at the behest of the Office of Federal Housing Enterprise Oversight (OFHEO), Fannie's portfolio has declined by $75 billion in the first half of 2005 without any noticeable effects on the MBS and home mortgage markets. Apparently, there was ample MBS demand from other investors, including banks and insurance companies.

The Administration has also recommended that regulators be allowed a free hand in setting minimum and critical capital levels for the GSEs, and that a clear and credible receivership process be established for the GSEs. This extension of regulatory authority should have little impact on the liquidity-generating activities of the GSEs (i.e., their securitization activities), but would help to mitigate the likelihood of systemic events.

Conclusion

Information tends to distribute itself asymmetrically—e.g., borrowers tend to have better information about how they will use funds than do lenders. The potential to exploit such advantages can stand in the way of mutually beneficial transactions. Financial services are important for economic performance because they can check this potential in an efficient manner. While they do not make tangible goods, these organizations can play an integral role in expanding economic possibilities.

Public policy can improve upon unregulated outcomes, but must do so in a cost-effective manner. Moving too far on deregulation could compromise consumer protection and system soundness. But moving too far on public regulation can weaken economic performance. A well-developed financial system is thus one that balances the costs and benefits of public regulation. Systems like that in the United States appear to have found this balance, and thus tend to support strong economies.

CHAPTER 10

The Role of Intellectual Property in the Economy

Certainly an inventor ought to be allowed a right to the benefit of his invention for some certain time. It is equally certain it ought not to be perpetual; for to embarrass society with monopolies for every utensil existing, and in all the details of life, would be more injurious to them than had the supposed inventors never existed... How long the term should be is the difficult question.

—Thomas Jefferson, 1807

The founders of this country believed that *intellectual property* was so important that one of the specific grants of power to Congress under Article I, Section 8 of the Constitution was the power "To promote the Progress of Science and the useful Arts, by securing for limited Times to Authors and Inventors the exclusive Right to their respective Writings and Discoveries." This grant gives Congress the power to define and to protect intellectual property through measures such as the issuance of patents and copyrights.

Other powers granted to Congress by Article I, Section 8 of the Constitution include taxation, regulating interstate commerce, coining money, borrowing, and naturalization. (For more on the early history of intellectual property rights in the U.S. see Box 10-1.)

Economic research over the past two centuries confirms the Founders' wisdom regarding the importance of intellectual property. This chapter examines how intellectual property differs from other, more tangible, forms of property, the justification for having a formal system for its protection, and its role in economic growth. The chapter also looks at certain policy challenges in ensuring that intellectual property protection continues to promote U.S. economic growth and development. The key points of this chapter are:

- Intellectual property rights create incentives for individuals and firms to invest in research and development, and to commercialize inventions and other creations by allowing individuals and firms to profit from their creative activities.
- Well-defined and enforced intellectual property rights are an important element of the American economy and can contribute to the economic growth of all countries.

- The Administration continues to vigorously enforce the laws that protect the rights of American intellectual property owners.

Knowledge Is Different from Other Types of Goods

Economists generally recognize that intellectual property (such as knowing how to make bread) differs from physical property (such as a loaf of bread) in two basic attributes:

1. Can more than one person use the good at a time? Physical property, like a slice of bread, can be effectively used for only one purpose at a time, and that use precludes other uses. For instance, a slice of bread used to make a ham sandwich for one person cannot be used to make a grilled cheese sandwich or a ham sandwich for another person. This makes bread a good that is *rival in consumption*, which means that one use or one person's use of the product partially or wholly prevents another use or another person from using it.

2. Can other people be effectively prevented from using the good? The owner of physical property, such as a slice of bread, can prevent others from using that slice with relative ease. This makes physical goods like bread *excludable*, which means that others can readily be prevented from using the good.

Something that could be intellectual property, such as bread-making knowledge, differs from physical property in both of these attributes. Unlike a slice of bread, any person can use bread-making knowledge without diminishing the practical usefulness of that knowledge to anyone else. This makes bread-making knowledge, like all knowledge, a good that is *nonrival in consumption*.

In addition, it is very difficult to exclude others from using knowledge such as the knowledge of bread-making once it is created and publicized. If someone wanted to reap the economic rewards for his creation of such knowledge, his only option may be to not disclose the information at all. Even this approach may not be sufficient if others take active measures, such as *reverse engineering*, to learn how the knowledge was used to produce a product. Once others learn such knowledge, the person who developed it will be unable to prevent others from using it. Under the rules that apply to physical property, this makes knowledge a *nonexcludable* good.

Most knowledge also differs from physical goods in that the costs of developing knowledge are upfront, fixed costs that do not vary with the number of times the knowledge is used. Once it is produced, knowledge can be replicated repeatedly at effectively no cost. For a firm to have an incentive to create new forms of knowledge, such as a formula for a new drug or a software program, it must be able to recoup its initial costs of development. It may not be able to do this if the knowledge becomes publicly available and competition forces prices down to the level at which they reimburse the seller only for the material costs of the products produced using this knowledge.

Treating Knowledge as Intellectual Property

Because knowledge is nonrival in consumption and nonexcludable, any person who incurs the fixed cost of developing a new or better product or process will soon find that others, including competitors, are using that knowledge. Competition could drive the price of the product down to the cost of the physical inputs used to make one unit of the product. The innovator would receive little or no financial return for paying the cost and undertaking the risk involved in developing such knowledge. Without the potential to profit from such innovation, most individuals will be unwilling to incur the fixed costs and financial risks associated with creating new knowledge.

This is not to say that there is no innovation without the potential for profit. Some innovations might occur as a by-product of the normal production process. Other innovators might still invest in research and development but try to prevent the use of their discoveries by keeping them secret. For many types of innovations this is likely to be costly and ineffective. However, if innovators cannot control the knowledge they have developed, they are significantly less likely to invest in developing such new knowledge.

An intellectual property system creates an incentive to develop certain types of knowledge by granting exclusive rights, enforceable through government action and a well-functioning legal system, to use that knowledge. These exclusive rights enable individuals to profit from their inventions by excluding others from using the innovation. Most intellectual property systems offer innovators an exchange. The innovator is given the right to exclude others— for a limited time—from the use of the innovation, but must provide the public with the complete details of the innovation. This public disclosure furthers the development of the knowledge base by enabling others to build on the knowledge embodied in the intellectual property and avoids the duplication of research efforts.

The Social Costs of an Intellectual Property System

Social costs could arise from making intellectual property protection too strong. These costs go beyond the obvious bureaucratic costs of intellectual property systems. Economics tends to focus on two of these social costs: the potential for creating monopoly power and the restrictions on exploiting useful technologies.

Box 10-1: Intellectual Property in the Early American Republic

While the phrase "intellectual property" is the product of more modern times, the concept in American thought harkens back to the Constitution. The gradual recognition of intellectual property rights in early America predates the Constitutional Convention, where it was formalized in the Constitution. By 1787, every state but one had passed copyright laws and many had already begun granting patents to inventors. Two delegates to the Constitutional Convention of 1787, James Madison and Charles Pinckney, were ardent advocates of assigning copyrights and patents to promote and protect the rights of the authors and innovators. The Framers of the Constitution assented to giving Congress its mandate in Article I, Section 8 to "promote the Progress of Science and useful Arts."

This is not surprising. The founders, among them Jefferson and Franklin, were deeply influenced by the British common law system and the preeminence of scientific achievements throughout the Age of Enlightenment. Copyright and patent rights in early America, while distinguishable from their English predecessors, were justified on the same basic premise that defense of property rights precipitated economic growth. George Washington noted in his first inaugural address that the ownership of intellectual property is a necessary means of encouraging "exertions of skill and genius" to foster technological development.

Article I, Section 8 (Clause 8) provided the necessary authorization for Congress to extend intellectual property rights in the form of the patent statutes of 1790, 1793, 1800, 1836, and 1839 that were in effect until the Civil War period. Manufacturing productivity at the firm level in early nineteenth-century America has been documented to have varied directly with the level of patent protections afforded to inventors. Spurred by their belief in individual enterprise and the maximization of social returns through private protections, the early policymakers of the American Republic were prescient in their recognition of the importance of intellectual property rights in a market economy.

As Thomas Jefferson noted in the passage quoted at the start of this chapter, the power to exclude, depending on its length, has the potential to create monopoly power. Modern economic analysis supports this conclusion. The holder of intellectual property has a monopoly over the use of that intellectual property, but this control may not result in monopoly power in any meaningful sense. The potential for monopoly power is related to the breadth and length of the power to exclude others from making use of the intellectual property. If this power is narrow or for a short duration, others can enter the market and compete in a timely manner, and the innovator will have little or no market power. Overly long or broad grants of exclusivity potentially limit the ability of others to compete and create a greater possibility of market power.

Economic research over the past two decades suggests that another social cost of an intellectual property system is that the power to exclude may deter others from advancing the state of knowledge by building on protected intellectual property since permission to use the property may be too expensive or may not be granted. Finally, the expiration of intellectual property protection after a specific time period may also spur firms to continue to innovate to ensure continued market success.

Intellectual Property Rights Basics

Intellectual property protection allows individuals to profit from their innovative or creative activities thereby creating an incentive to innovate and promote technological progress. Balanced against this benefit are the potential costs of giving the innovator monopoly power and limiting the ability of subsequent innovators to build on that invention. In crafting the existing intellectual property laws, Congress and the states have considered these associated costs and benefits and have granted differing levels of protection for four basic types of intellectual property: patents, copyrights, trademarks, and trade secrets. In recognition of the potential social costs of intellectual property protection for some kinds of knowledge, Congress has refused to allow individuals to claim intellectual property protection for certain types of knowledge.

The boundary between what can and cannot be protected is sometimes difficult to define. However, it is generally understood that intellectual property rights cannot protect things like intellectual concepts, mental processes, and basic laws of nature. While many justifications have been offered for these exclusions, one possible explanation, consistent with an economic understanding of the social costs of intellectual property, is that allowing ownership of any of these types of knowledge will create broad restrictions on innovators and will slow technical progress. To prevent stifling of innovation, intellectual property rights are granted only after fulfilling specific legislatively defined criteria and protect only a *particular* implementation, expression, or representation of an idea.

Patents: Protecting a Particular Implementation of an Idea

Thomas Jefferson wrote the original statute defining what may be patented. The language was brief and has changed little since the passage of the original patent act. "[A]ny new and useful process, machine, manufacture, or composition of matter, or any new and useful improvement thereof" may be patented. Patents protect what is normally called an invention but not the idea the machine or process is implementing.

The Constitution grants Congress the power to establish the requirements an inventor must satisfy before a patent is granted. Under current law, Congress requires that an inventor submit plans describing the invention to the United States Patent and Trademark Office (USPTO). To be granted a patent, the invention or innovation must satisfy a patent examiner under a "preponderance of the evidence standard" that the invention is useful, novel, and nonobvious. Once a patent is granted, its holder can exclude others from making, selling, or using the patented invention or substantially similar inventions for up to a Congressionally mandated 20 years after the patent application was initially filed. (A subset of patents called "design patents," which protect an ornamental design of a product, provide patent protection for only 14 years.) The scope of this right to exclude depends on the legitimate breadth of the patent's claims. In general, the more novel and innovative a patented product is, the broader are its claims and its protection.

Copyrights: Protecting the Expression of an Idea

Copyrights protect a particular expression of an idea and are generally associated with a variety of creative works including books, music, movies, magazines, paintings, sculptures, and any other expressive work. The key factor for obtaining a copyright is originality, and only a minimal amount of that is necessary. Registering a work with the Copyright Office in the Library of Congress provides some important litigation benefits—including the ability to obtain monetary damages when suing for infringement—but such registration is not necessary. A copyright exists the moment an expressive work is created and, except for work for hire, becomes the property of the author creating the work.

A copyright entitles the holder to exclude others from performing, publishing, or otherwise copying the work. It also entitles the holder to exclude others from producing "derivative works," such as a movie adaptation of a book or its translation into a foreign language. Copyright protection generally lasts the life of the author plus 70 years. In the case of work for hire or anonymous works, copyright lasts 95 years from publication or 120 years from creation, whichever is shorter.

Trademarks: Protecting the Symbol of an Idea, Product, or Service

Trademarks can be words, phrases, designs, colors, sounds, or any combination of these that are used to distinguish the products or services of one entity from those of another. Trademarks reduce consumer search costs because they make it easier for consumers to identify and find products and services. Trademarks also protect consumers by providing an assurance of quality or attributes that can be expected with the trademarked product. Because the key function of a trademark is to uniquely identify a company, a product, or a service, the qualifying factor for a trademark is distinctiveness. Generic terms for a product and, in some cases, even descriptive terms cannot be a trademark.

Trademarks do not have to be registered with the USPTO but such registration provides the benefit of a legal presumption of nationwide ownership and exclusive right to use the mark for the goods or services identified in the registration. However, a trademark only becomes intellectual property when it is used in commerce to identify a product, service, or company. Trademarks give the holder the ability to exclude others from using that mark to identify any similar product and, in some cases, exclude others from using their mark if that use dilutes or weakens consumer association of the product or service with that mark. Validity of the trademark lasts as long as the trademark continues to identify the product or the company, which in some cases may be for centuries. The oldest U.S. registered trademark still in use today is for Samson Rope and was registered in 1884. However, trademark protection may be lost if the mark becomes associated with a product generically rather than a particular brand as occurred with the term "escalator," which was once a trademark for escalators sold by the Otis Elevator company.

Trade Secrets: Limited Protection for Knowledge Kept Secret

Trade secrets consist of any information possessed by a firm that the firm takes reasonable measures to keep secret, is legitimately kept secret, and has commercial value because it is secret. This information may include information that could be protected as other forms of intellectual property but also includes knowledge that cannot be so protected, including customer lists, contracts, and other information whose value is diminished if it becomes publicly available.

Trade secrets are not formally protected in the way other intellectual property is protected. Protection is provided under sta :, rather than Federal, law. For example, protection occurs through the enfc cement of the firm's confidentiality provisions in contracts and the use of th legal system to block those who have improperly or illegally obtained a firm's trade secrets from using or disclosing them. In general, however, a firm has no legal recourse to prevent others from using its trade secrets if they become publicly available. Trade-secret protection lasts only as long as the firm can maintain secrecy. One of the most successful trade secrets in this regard is the formula for Coca-Cola.

Intellectual Property, the American Economy, and Economic Growth

Intellectual property played an important role in the growth of the American economy from a primarily agrarian society through an industrial economy to the current information age. One researcher notes that even in the early part of the nineteenth century, the American patent system granted effective intellectual property rights that led to the development and diffusion of new technologies that fueled economic growth and prosperity. Today intellectual property protection plays an important role in many industries in which the United States has a comparative advantage and contributes to the size, growth, and exports of the American economy.

Intellectual Property and the American Economy

Industries such as chemicals, pharmaceuticals, information technology, and transportation are highly dependent on patent protection to provide the incentives to innovate. Some industries, such as software, entertainment, publishing, broadcasting, and other broadly defined communication industries, are highly dependent on copyright protection to ensure that the creators of such content are fully compensated for their efforts and continue to have the incentive to create such works. The combination of these patent and copyright-dependent industries and any such support industries that are necessary for these industries to function can be grouped together as intellectual property industries. Chart 10-1 shows the total economic activity generated by this group of industries. In 2003, these industries represented approximately 17.3 percent of total U.S. economic activity and approximately one-fifth of private economic activity. Their combined activity exceeds the total economic activity of all levels of government in the United States.

The estimate in Chart 10-1 represents the income generated in intellectual property industries. Equally important is the stock of intellectual property assets that generates these returns. Intellectual property is one of many intangible assets a firm may hold. Other intangible assets include brand value, organizational efficiencies, and firm-specific human capital. It has been estimated that approximately 70 percent of the value of publicly traded companies comes from intangible assets.

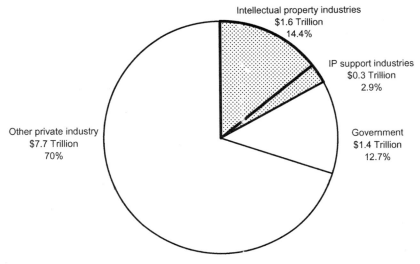

Chart 10-1 Intellectual Property Industries' Share of 2003 Gross Domestic Product
In 2003, intellectual property and IP support industries represented 17.3% of total value added.

Intellectual property industries
$1.6 Trillion
14.4%

IP support industries
$0.3 Trillion
2.9%

Other private industry
$7.7 Trillion
70%

Government
$1.4 Trillion
12.7%

Note: 2003 GDP equals $11 trillion.
Source: "Engines of Growth: Economic Contributions of the U.S. Intellectual Property Industries" (2005) by Stephen E. Siwek.

Chart 10-2 shows the total asset value o ˙U.S. publicly traded firms broken out by the value of tangible assets, the va ᴉe that can be inferred for various types of intellectual property, and the value of other intangible assets. Intellectual property accounts for approximately 33 percent of the value of U.S. corporations—with software and other copyright-protected materials representing nearly two-fifths of this value, patents representing one-third, and trade secrets representing the rest. In all, U.S. intellectual property may be worth more than $5 trillion.

The one type of intellectual property excluded from the estimate in Chart 10-2 is trademarks. While there is no doubt that trademarks represent an important element of any firm's assets, it is difficult to separate the value of a trademark from the value of the rest of the value of branding. However, the sources used to create Chart 10-2 also suggest that the combined value of branding and trademarks represents approximately 14 percent of the total value of publicly traded U.S. firms. In some instances, this value may be a company's most important asset.

Other studies have indicated that intellectual property-related industries tend to grow at approximately twice the rate of the economy as a whole and are an important contributing factor not or ly to the productivity growth of the intellectual property-related sectors of the economy but also to the growth of all sectors of the economy. These industries also represent a growing share

Chart 10-2 **Share of Assets in Current Market Value of Public U.S. Corporations**
Intellectual property assets represent approximately one-third of the value of American corporations.

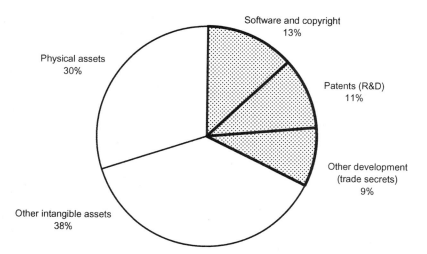

Software and copyright
13%

Physical assets
30%

Patents (R&D)
11%

Other development
(trade secrets)
9%

Other intangible assets
38%

Note: Total value of publicly traded U.S. corporations on 09/06/2005 was $15.2 trillion.
Sources: Council of Economic Advisers' calculation based on "The Economic Value of Intellectual Property " by Shapiro and Hassett (USA for Innovation) and "Measuring Capital and Technology: An Expanded Framework," Table 3 by Corrado, Hulten and Sichel (Finance & Economics Discussion Series 2004-65, Federal Reserve Board).

of exports. Chart 10-3 shows the annual growth rates for the exports from U.S. copyright-based industries from 1991 to 2002. In all but one of those years (1995), exports from copyright industries grew at a faster rate than total exports. Indeed, on average, U.S. copyright exports grew faster by approximately six percentage points than total exports and have become an increasing share of our total exports.

This analysis, however, obscures an important point about the role of intellectual property in the economy and undervalues its contribution. There are many industries that are not counted among the intellectual property industries but generate innovations and rely on patent and other intellectual property protection to create incentives for innovation and growth. More importantly, many innovations from the past have led to significant productivity advances in industries such as medicines, textiles, railroads, steel manufacture, and farm equipment. The capital value of these innovations was dissipated as the intellectual property protecting these innovations expired and the innovative knowledge and information entered the public domain. Even after these innovations become public knowledge, however, the country still benefits from the productivity gains the innovations produced. Any complete consideration of the overall importance of intellectual property to the American economy should include the value of these advances. Such a consideration is beyond the scope of this chapter but would suggest that the

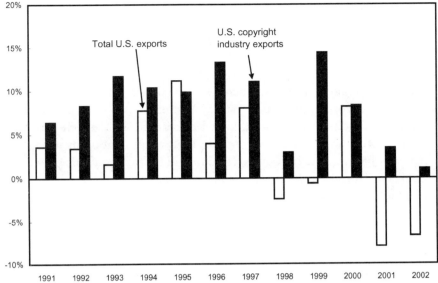

Chart 10-3 **Growth Rate of U.S. Exports**
Since 1991, the growth rate of copyright industries has exceeded the growth rate of overall exports.

Growth rate

Total U.S. exports

U.S. copyright
industry exports

Sources: International Monetary Fund, Bureau of Labor Statistics, and *Copyright Industries in the U.S. 1998, 2004.*

estimates discussed above underestimate the importance of intellectual property to the American economy.

Intellectual Property Protection and Economic Growth

The protection of intellectual property rights plays an important role in inducing technological change and facilitating economic growth. Intellectual property protection does not directly lead to growth, but it helps create an incentive structure that encourages research and development, which in turn leads to increased innovation. Increased innovation generates greater rates of economic growth.

The link between improved intellectual property protection and increased innovation can be seen at the firm level for companies in developing and developed countries. One study showed that 80 percent of 377 firms surveyed in Brazil would invest more in internal research if more legal protection, such as improved intellectual property-right protection, were available. A similar study of U.S. firms showed that the availability of patent protection in the United States was a critical factor in research and development decisions. Using a random sample of 100 U.S. manufacturing firms, this study found that had it not been for the availability of patents, 60 percent of the inventions in the pharmaceutical industry and nearly 40 percent of the inventions in the chemical industry would not have been developed.

A number of other recent economic studies have shown a more direct link between greater intellectual property protection and capital investment. One study of the relationship between patent protection and investment in research and development found that countries with the lowest level of patent protection invested less than one-third of 1 percent of their GNP in research and development while countries with the highest level of protection invested six times as much. Likewise, another study suggests that increasing intellectual property protection increases capital and research investment. As intellectual property protection makes investment in research and development more attractive, the supply of knowledge is increased, lowering the cost of innovation. The increase in innovation leads to an increase in the rate at which new products are introduced, resulting in greater economic growth.

Intellectual property protection alone does not drive economic growth. There must be an existing research base in the country, a relatively unconstrained trade regime, a stable macroeconomic environment, the rule of law, and well-functioning institutions that grant, monitor, and enforce the intellectual property rights.

Intellectual Property Policy Challenges

Technological and economic change sometimes expose weaknesses in existing intellectual property laws and necessitate modifications of those laws to ensure their continued effectiveness in protecting intellectual property and ensuring economic growth. The Administration has continually reviewed and implemented policies to improve the intellectual property laws to ensure the efficiency of the patent review process, to protect the intellectual property of American firms engaged in international trade, and to prevent potentially dangerous counterfeit products from entering U.S. and foreign markets.

Ensuring the Integrity of the Patent Process

As noted earlier, patents have broader protection than copyrights or trademarks and, of these three, patents have the only formal review process prior to being granted. The effectiveness of the patent system in fostering technical progress and economic growth is tied to the efficiency of this review process. Patents granted in error may create market power without any offsetting benefit of inducing innovation. If a patent increases the cost of using existing technology, it may deter innovation or simply cause a firm to use a less-efficient technology. In 2004, the USPTO issued 187,170 patents. Occasionally a very small percentage of patents are challenged or overturned, and it is this particular process within the patent system that is examined below.

Challenging a patent's validity can be costly and time-consuming. Estimates suggest that median litigation costs average $4 million each for the plaintiff and defendant when more than $25 million is at stake in a patent suit. Research has found that on average it takes approximately three and a half years to challenge a patent through litigation and that the typical patent challenge is initiated after the patent has been in force for approximately eight and half years. An unwarranted patent could be in force for more than twelve years of a twenty-year term before the legal system would find it to be invalid.

Challenging a patent's validity can also be financially risky. Generally a firm cannot sue to have a patent invalidated. It must first infringe on that patent, wait for the patent holder to sue, and then claim patent invalidity as a defense to infringement. Firms that do this incur a great financial risk because intentional infringement of a patent may result in triple damages. Patents are presumed to be valid and an accused infringer must prove it is invalid by "clear and convincing evidence" to overturn this presumption. This is greater than the burden that a patent application must satisfy before a patent is issued. Despite the hurdles faced by a firm challenging the validity of a patent, researchers have found that 46 percent of the fully litigated patent challenges between 1989 and 1996 ultimately resulted in the patent being judged to be invalid.

In recent years, businesses and commentators have noted substantial increases in the number of patent applications received by the USPTO. This trend, combined with an increased availability of patents in areas such as business methods, has led some to question whether wrongly issued patents might affect the competitiveness of the U.S. economy. Patent policy can foster innovation, but must also be balanced with the consumer protection provided by competition in the marketplace.

Because of increased interest in how best to balance patent and competition interests, in 2002, the Federal Trade Commission (FTC), together with the Antitrust Division of the Department of Justice (DOJ), held extensive hearings with testimony and written comments from investors, entrepreneurs, antitrust organizations, and scholars. While hearing participants praised many aspects of the current patent system, many participants expressed concerns about poor patent quality and legal standards that may inadvertently create market power and reduce innovation.

In 2003, the FTC issued a report based on the information gained in the hearings conducted in the prior year. This report contained several recommendations to alleviate the problems discussed above. Two of these recommendations were also supported by a subsequent report issued by the National Academy of Sciences.

The first recommendation was to create an administrative post-grant appeal procedure that would allow firms to challenge the validity of a questionable patent within a limited period after it has been issued. This procedure could significantly shorten the time period in which a wrongly issued patent is in force and reduce the risk of some patent challenges. The second recommendation was to reduce the firm's risk of triple damages in cases in which firms infringe a patent with knowledge of that patent. This change would encourage firms to read their competitors' patents more frequently, to develop noninfringing business plans, and to reduce wasteful duplication of effort.

Intellectual Property and International Trade

As intellectual property became a more important element of international trade starting in the 1980s, differences in the level of protection for intellectual property across various countries started to lead to an increasing number of trade disputes about the use and alleged misuse of the intellectual property belonging to others. These trade frictions had the potential to disrupt the benefits of increased worldwide trade. In the Uruguay Round of trade negotiations from 1986 to 1994, the members of the World Trade Organization (WTO) negotiated an agreement to introduce more order and predictability into the international protection of intellectual property rights. The WTO Agreement on Trade-Related Aspects of Intellectual Property Rights (TRIPs) is the first comprehensive and enforceable global set of rules covering intellectual property rights.

The TRIPs Agreement helps alleviate trade frictions by reducing nontariff trade barriers related to differing intellectual property protection regimes and by setting minimum intellectual property rights standards for all WTO members. The agreement established transparency standards that require all members to publish laws, regulations, judicial decisions, and administrative findings that affect the treatment of intellectual property. The agreement also requires nondiscrimination between nationals and non-nationals and for the first time applies the Most-Favored Nations (MFN) obligation (prohibiting discrimination across trading partners) to international intellectual property rights.

The TRIPs Agreement took effect in 1995, but only industrialized countries had to ensure that their laws and practices conformed to it by January 1, 1996. Developing countries and transition economies were given five years, until 2000, and the least-developed countries were given 11 years, until 2006 to comply. The 2006 deadline applicable to least-developed countries was recently extended to 2016 for pharmaceutical patents and July 2013 for other obligations. Questions remain, however, about the extent to which some developing countries are in compliance with their TRIPs obligations, and many least-developed countries are unlikely to be in full compliance by July 2013. In addition, many developed countries have implemented a variety of cost-containment efforts that greatly reduce the value of intellectual property. Thus, an apparent strong patent protection stance may, in fact, not be a completely accurate representation, at least across all industries. Consequently, the level of intellectual property-rights protection varies across countries.

Developing Countries Tend to Have Weaker Intellectual Property Regimes

Economists have developed a number of indices to determine the strength of various countries' intellectual property protection regimes. While the results of the research using these indices are not uniform, they suggest that the level of intellectual property protection increases with a country's real gross domestic product per capita. Economists have offered some explanations for this relationship. Rising income increases the demand for higher-quality, differentiated products. This increase in demand leads to growing preferences for the protection of intellectual property, such as patents, copyrights, and trademarks, which provide an innovator with certain protections when producing such products.

Countries with lower per capita gross domestic product may prefer intellectual property regimes with little or weak intellectual property protection because they believe it allows free access to information that would otherwise have to be paid for. These countries may also believe that lack of intellectual property protection allows them to access technological development through imitation and domestic efforts to build upon the existing stock of worldwide knowledge. However, the lack of intellectual property protection may slow development in these countries by inhibiting the development of domestic innovative and creative industries that generate much of the economic growth in more-developed countries. Furthermore, the ubiquity of counterfeit products that is generally associated with weak intellectual property protection may have health and safety implications because it is difficult for consumers to be certain of the origin and efficiency of medicines, machine parts, and other critical products.

Countries like the United States, with greater levels of intellectual property protection and with comparative advantages in knowledge-intensive goods and services, place a high priority on intellectual property-rights protection. Most indices of the strength of intellectual property protection tend to show that the United States is among the countries with the highest level of protection. More objective measures also suggest that the United States has a comparative advantage in knowledge-intensive goods. The United States holds one of the highest shares of global patents and has a trade surplus in intellectual property-dependent services and in royalties and license fees.

Economic Costs of Intellectual Property Theft in Foreign Markets

Theft in foreign markets of intellectual property belonging to American companies is significant. In China alone, industry estimates suggest that in 2003 and 2004 the piracy rate was 90 percent or more, which means that at least 90 percent of the existing copies of a particular work (such as CDs and DVDs) in China were produced without the copyright holder's permission. Industry estimates show that the piracy rates in Latin America were more than

60 percent and the global software piracy rate was approximately 35 percent. Some of these pirated copies are exported to the United States. Piracy is an especially serious problem for American companies because of the strong comparative advantage they hold in intellectual property-related goods.

Turning these estimates of piracy rates into estimates of lost revenues involves consideration of two factors: (1) how many copies would have been sold by legitimate producers in the absence of the pirated copies, and (2) the price that would have been charged for those copies. Without the competition from pirated copies, the legitimate holder of the copyright might have been able to sell the product for a higher price and earn higher revenues. In addition, because pirated products are generally sold at a much lower price than what a legitimate producer charges, fewer copies might have been sold if consumers had to pay the higher prices for the legitimate copies. Many estimates assume that sales of intellectual property-protected goods would correspond to the current sales of the infringing goods. Under this assumption, industry estimates suggest that in 2004 software piracy alone cost U.S. developers at least $6.6 billion.

Preventing Global Intellectual Property Piracy

The Administration is strongly committed to addressing the issues of piracy (unauthorized copies of copyrighted materials) and counterfeiting (unauthorized reproduction of trademarked or patented goods) without sacrificing the benefits to be gained through trade and specialization. To accomplish these goals, the White House initiated the Strategy Targeting Organized Piracy (STOP!) in October 2004. The STOP! initiative brings together nine federal agencies, including the Office of the U.S. Trade Representative, the Department of Commerce, the Department of Justice, the Department of Homeland Security, and the State Department. Under STOP!, these agencies and departments have and continue to develop new tools to help U.S. businesses better protect their intellectual property, increase efforts to seize counterfeit goods at our borders, pursue criminal enterprises involved in piracy and counterfeiting, and aggressively engage our trading partners to join our efforts. Through STOP!, new forms of federal assistance are being provided to U.S. companies, increased law enforcement resources are being provided, and the Administration has developed an international law enforcement network to increase criminal enforcement abroad.

Domestically, the Department of Justice has created a Task Force on Intellectual Property and increased from 5 to 18 the number of Computer Hacking and Intellectual Property Units in U.S. Attorneys' Offices across the country. This increased to 229 (one in each Federal district) the number of specially trained prosecutors available to focus on intellectual property and high-tech crimes.

Internationally, the United States has conducted several hundred intellectual property rights enforcement and technical assistance projects around the world. The Administration has established a "Global Intellectual Property Rights Academy," located within the USPTO, to consolidate and expand intellectual property training programs for foreign judges, enforcement officials, and relevant administrators. These programs are designed to foster respect for intellectual property, encourage governmental and rights holders' efforts to combat infringement, and promote best practices in the enforcement of intellectual property rights. The Administration is also expanding its intellectual property attaché program at our embassies in China, India, Brazil, and Russia. These attachés will assist American businesses, advocate U.S. intellectual property policy, and conduct intellectual property rights training. STOP! objectives have also been endorsed in numerous multilateral forums including the G-8, Organization for Economic Cooperation and Development, the U.S.-EU summit, and Asia-Pacific Economic Cooperation sphere.

The Administration also created a new senior-level office of the Coordinator for International Intellectual Property Enforcement. This office will coordinate the strategies of the Federal Government to use its capabilities and resources to provide an internationally secure and predictable environment for American intellectual property.

Technological Change and Intellectual Property Reform

As technology has advanced, it has become cheaper for legitimate producers to produce many types of intellectual property-related products, including medicines, CDs, DVDs, automotive and airplane parts, and other products. Technology also holds the promise for new, more efficient means of distribution of intellectual property-related products, including digital music and video content. Producers of these products have a great opportunity to take advantage of changing technologies and a great challenge to limit the use of these technologies to legitimate producers of these products. Based on current distribution preferences, intellectual property holders have lost some control over the distribution of their products.

There are many manifestations of this loss in control. For instance, some peer-to-peer networks provided technology that enabled individuals to freely download copyrighted music from the computers of other individuals on these networks. Moreover, current technology can less expensively and more faithfully reproduce some intellectual property-protected materials than previous technologies could. These illegal copies are difficult to detect. In the United States and internationally, this has resulted in a significant increase in the production and sale of counterfeit products. These counterfeit copies may directly harm consumers through the sale of fake medicines and defective products, such as batteries, automobile parts, and airplane parts. Furthermore, in the long run, counterfeiting harms all consumers by reducing the profitability of and the incentive to produce new and interesting innovative products and creative works.

Box 10-2: The Free Software Licensing Movement

In the early stages of computing, a number of software developers wanted to put their work in the public domain, but also wanted to prevent individuals who modified the software from limiting its accessibility. This resulted in the development of free software licensing, sometimes called open source, wherein software is licensed for free use and modification but requires that any subsequent modifications also remain available for free use and modification by others. Many of the developers of free, or open-source, software are individuals in academic environments where open and cooperative development projects are especially important. Others are hobbyists or companies that are in the business of providing computing support services to third parties.

General Public Licenses (GPLs) and other free software licenses differ from traditional commercial licenses by granting to their users the freedom to run, study, improve, and redistribute copies of the program. A GPL uses traditional copyright law to ensure that these freedoms are retained in derivative works by requiring those works to also be licensed under GPL terms. Many advocates of these types of licenses believe that they increase network benefits by creating a pool of commonly accessible work and requiring any improvements made to the original software code to be contributed to that pool. These advocates believe that by having an unlimited number of developers viewing the source code and working to modify and improve it, the quality and testing of software are improved.

GPL licensees are permitted to charge for copying or distribution of their works. Further, nothing prevents software from being licensed under both GPL and traditional licensing. Dual-licensing was developed to respond to consumers of free software who were unwilling or unable to accept the reciprocity requirements of an open-source license and were willing to pay to avoid them. Open-source licensing such as GPL licenses is just another business model of software development that has been embraced by such companies as Sun Microsystems, Intel Corporation, and IBM.

Traditional and open-source development models currently compete in the market. Different developers are motivated by different aims and have different target customers. A system that neither favors nor discourages either licensing model would best serve a market consisting of diverse customers and developers. Competition on a level playing field would ensure that the better licensing system becomes the most successful. If each system has different advantages, it is likely that both systems will survive and find success.

In November 2005, the Administration forwarded proposed legislation to Congress that would implement some of the changes necessary to respond to these technical developments. The Intellectual Property Protection Act of 2005 would strengthen intellectual property protection, toughen penalties, and increase the range of investigative tools in both criminal and civil intellectual property-law enforcement.

In the past, it might not have been necessary to sanction criminally certain types of actions because they had little impact on the level of the counterfeiting of intellectual property. For instance, while there are criminal sanctions for selling a counterfeit good, there are no criminal sanctions against giving it away. It has only recently become profitable for a company that engages in, or contributes to, infringement to give a counterfeit product away and profit from the sale of auxiliary products and services. Technically, these actions are not criminal violations, but they still diminish the value of the intellectual property to its owner. The Administration's proposed legislation provides for criminal sanctions for distributing any infringing materials for the purpose of commercial advantage, including the selling of complementary products.

Because the production of a large number of copies is now cheap and easy, it is much easier for a counterfeiter to flood the market with illegal copies. Because current intellectual property law was designed when such an action was not easily accomplished, merely possessing a large number of infringing products with the intent to sell does not necessarily constitute a crime. Only the sale of the good itself is a criminal violation. Infringers are now capable of flooding the market and imposing significant financial harm on the intellectual property holder before criminal sanctions can be applied to limit the damage from this activity. The Administration's proposed legislation modifies the law to criminalize the possession of infringing materials with the intent to sell and will help stop the sale of counterfeits before they have an injurious impact on intellectual property holders.

Conclusion

Well-defined and well-enforced intellectual property rights are an important component of the U.S. economy and an important element in fostering continued economic growth. Intellectual property differs from other more tangible property in at least two key characteristics: it is nonrival in consumption and nonexcludable. An intellectual property system creates an incentive to innovate by rewarding the developers of new inventions with the right to exclude others from using that innovation for a limited period of time. In this way, inventors can benefit financially from their innovation. Economic research supports the conclusion of the American founders that a well-defined intellectual property system rewards innovation and fosters economic growth. By continually adapting to economic and technical change, the American intellectual property law system will continue to foster economic growth in the United States and throughout the world.

CHAPTER 11

Recent Developments in Energy

Energy is essential to the U.S. economy. It provides light and heat for our homes and businesses, brings our computers and appliances to life, and powers life-saving medical devices. It propels the automobiles, buses, and trains that carry us to home, work, and school, and the aircraft that fly us from city to city. It fuels the tractors that harvest our food, the machines we use to turn raw materials into final products, and the trucks, trains, and ships that carry these goods across our Nation and around the world. All told, the United States spent about $870 billion on energy in 2004, an amount equivalent to 7.4 percent of GDP, and was on pace to spend an estimated $1.1 trillion on energy in 2005, or about 8.6 percent of GDP.

Over the past several decades, the U.S. economy has seen a steady decline in its energy intensity—that is, the ratio of total physical units of energy consumed per dollar of real GDP. Nonetheless, households and businesses remain keenly aware of the prices they pay for energy products and the impact of rising energy prices on their budgets and bottom lines. When prices change gradually, households and businesses have time to adapt their energy consumption levels, fuel choices, and purchases of energy-using products to new price levels. Sometimes, however, disruptions to our energy production and distribution infrastructure, such as those caused by the recent hurricanes Katrina and Rita, result in temporary but sharp price increases to which households and businesses cannot adjust quickly.

This chapter discusses energy markets—systems that connect consumers and suppliers of energy products, where prices are determined by what buyers will pay and what sellers will accept. The chapter reviews recent developments in energy markets for crude oil, refined petroleum products, and natural gas, as well as recent developments in the electricity-generation sector. It considers these developments in the context of historical experience, and offers an economic perspective on energy market, policy, and technological innovations that benefit the Nation.

The key points in this chapter are:

- Crude oil prices have risen steadily over the past several years due to growing world demand, leading to rising prices for gasoline and other refined petroleum products and stimulating further development of alternative energy sources. Recent price increases have occurred more gradually than in the past.
- Disruptions to energy supply and distribution networks can lead to sharp short-term price increases. Recent hurricanes Katrina and Rita

231

demonstrate that competitive markets connecting energy producers, distributors, and consumers play a central role in encouraging conservation and allocating scarce energy resources, especially during times of natural disaster or national emergency.

- The continued expansion of natural gas and other energy markets through regional and global trade can improve our economic security by increasing access to low-cost energy resources and mitigating the impacts of local energy shortages and price increases. Innovative market instruments designed to insure against market volatility can also help lessen these impacts.

- Absent policy, individual energy market participants may not have an incentive to tackle certain problems associated with their energy production and consumption. Carefully targeted policies that reduce U.S. vulnerability to energy disruptions, encourage energy efficiency, and protect the environment can therefore be beneficial supplements to markets. These policies can be made more effective and less costly when designed based on economic incentives.

The first section below provides an overview of U.S. energy sources and uses. The second section discusses the world market for crude oil. The third section examines markets for refined petroleum products, including the impact of crude oil prices on refined product prices. The fourth section considers the expansion of natural gas markets from limited geographic regions to a more global level. The fifth section describes challenges and recent changes in the electricity-generation sector, and the final section concludes with a look toward the future.

Energy Sources and Uses

One British thermal unit (Btu) is the amount of energy required to raise the temperature of one pound of water one degree Fahrenheit. The United States used approximately 100 quadrillion Btu of energy in 2004 (see Table 11-1)—the energy equivalent of about 17 billion barrels of oil or 60 barrels of oil per person. Eighty-six percent of this energy came from fossil fuels, including 40 percent from petroleum, 23 percent from coal, and 23 percent from natural gas. The remaining 14 percent of this energy came from nuclear and renewable sources, such as hydroelectric power, wind, biomass (e.g., wood and agricultural crops), and solar energy.

On the consumption side, 39 percent of total U.S. energy use in 2004 passed through the electricity-generation sector. Roughly one-third of electricity-sector energy input was converted into electricity and delivered to end-use customers. The remaining two-thirds was lost due to inefficiencies in the production and transmission of electricity. Of the 73 quadrillion Btu of energy delivered to

TABLE 11-1.— *Energy Sources and Uses, 2004*
[Quadrillion BTU]

Energy sources	Energy Uses						
	End-use sectors					Electricity sector	All sectors
	Transport	Industrial	Residential	Commercial	All end-use		
Total primary......................	27.7	22.1	7.0	4.1	60.9	38.9	99.7
Petroleum	26.7	9.6	1.6	0.8	38.6	1.2	39.8
Natural gas..................	0.7	8.7	5.0	3.1	17.5	5.5	23.0
Coal............................	0.0	2.2	0.0	0.1	2.3	20.3	22.5
Nuclear	0.0	0.0	0.0	0.0	0.0	8.2	8.2
Renewable	0.3	1.7	0.4	0.1	2.5	3.6	6.1
Electricity retail sales.........	0.0	3.5	4.4	4.2	12.1		
Total end-use	27.7	25.6	11.4	8.3	73.0		

Note: Because total primary energy consumption in 2004 was almost exactly 100 quadrillion Btu, numbers in the table can also be interpreted approximately as the percent of total primary energy consumption coming from various sectors and going to various uses. Total end-use energy consumption of 73 quadrillion Btu is less than total primary energy consumption due to electricity-sector energy losses.

Source: Department of Energy (Energy Information Administration).

end-use customers, 38 percent went to the transportation sector (to power vehicles used to transport people and goods), 35 percent went to industry (for manufacturing, agriculture, mining, and construction), 16 percent was used in residences, and 11 percent was used by the commercial sector (in business, government, schools, and other public and private organizations).

Crude Oil

U.S. crude oil consumption in 2004 was 15.5 million barrels per day, approximately 65 percent of which was imported. Crude oil is used to produce a wide array of petroleum products, including gasoline, diesel and jet fuels, heating oil, lubricants, asphalt, plastics, and many other products used for their energy or chemical content. Not surprisingly, crude oil markets are monitored closely by consumers, businesses, and governments, because the prices of petroleum-based products depend heavily on the price of crude oil.

A Global Market in Crude Oil

Crude oil can be transported long distances cheaply. Transportation costs average roughly $2 per barrel for crude oil imported into the United States. As a result, oil prices generally are determined by the balancing of supply and demand at the global level, where prices are roughly uniform for a given grade of oil. U.S. refiners, and ultimately U.S. consumers, realize great benefit from having the option of purchasing crude oil from both nearby sources, such as Texas or Oklahoma, and from sources halfway around the globe, such as Russia or the Middle East.

The international crude oil market is very active. Out of a total global crude oil production of 67 million barrels per day in 2002, roughly 60 percent was traded internationally. However, crude oil is produced in large quantities for export in a relatively limited number of locations around the world. In the first nine months of 2005, the top ten oil-producing countries accounted for over 50 percent of global production, and nearly 30 percent of global production originated in the Persian Gulf. Although the United States was the world's third-largest oil producer in 2004, trailing only Saudi Arabia and Russia, the United States ranks eleventh in total proven oil reserves, with just 2 percent of total proven world reserves (Chart 11-1).

Crude Oil Prices

Crude oil prices generally change gradually in response to slowly evolving domestic and international trends in oil demand and supply, though prices have spiked sharply on a limited number of occasions. Some of these spikes were short-lived, while others persisted for several years.

Recent Price Rises

Because crude oil is traded in a global market, long-term trends in demand by other consuming nations and unexpected events in other countries affect the world market price that U.S. refiners pay and the price that domestic oil

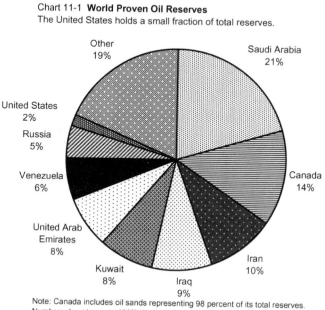

Chart 11-1 **World Proven Oil Reserves**
The United States holds a small fraction of total reserves.

Other 19%
Saudi Arabia 21%
United States 2%
Russia 5%
Venezuela 6%
Canada 14%
United Arab Emirates 8%
Kuwait 8%
Iraq 9%
Iran 10%

Note: Canada includes oil sands representing 98 percent of its total reserves.
Numbers do not sum to 100% due to independent rounding.
Sources: Department of Energy (Energy Information Administration), PennWell Corporation (Oil & Gas Journal).

producers receive. Due to robust economic growth in the United States, China, and other high-growth countries in Asia, world consumption of petroleum products grew strongly over the past several years.

On the supply side, industrial countries have exhausted most low-cost opportunities for profitable domestic exploration and development, and international energy companies often face considerable risk when making investments for exploration, development, and production in less-developed countries. Some countries, particularly those with national oil companies, prohibit or restrict foreign investment. Consequently, new production capacity has been slow to emerge. World crude oil production in 2005 stood at about 74 million barrels per day, while the Department of Energy estimates that current world oil production capacity is only 1-1.5 million barrels per day higher—the lowest level of world spare capacity in more than three decades. Most of this spare capacity is in Saudi Arabia. As a result of this tight market, crude oil prices have increased roughly threefold since the beginning of 2002.

Past Oil Price Spikes

Although high, the current price of West Texas Intermediate (WTI) crude oil (a common pricing benchmark) is lower than the historic peak of over $87 per barrel (in 2005 dollars) reached in 1980. Oil prices more than doubled from the last quarter of 1973 to the first quarter of 1974 as a result of the Arab Oil Embargo. Oil prices more than doubled again from mid-1979 to mid-1980 following the 1979 Iranian Revolution. Prices fell gradually from this point until 1985-1986, and then they fell rapidly after Saudi Arabia and other oil-exporting countries increased production. A short-lived shock in 1990 was associated with the Persian Gulf War. The recent increase in crude oil prices, which has come largely through a surge in world oil demand, has occurred much more gradually than past price spikes, which resulted from abrupt reductions in production in oil-exporting countries.

The Strategic Petroleum Reserve

Sudden oil supply shocks are potentially damaging to the U.S. economy. The Strategic Petroleum Reserve (SPR) provides the United States with an insurance policy should a severe energy supply disruption occur. These Federally owned crude oil stocks, which totaled 684 million barrels in late 2005, are sufficient to cover about 68 days of U.S. crude oil imports or 44 days of total U.S. crude oil consumption. The President of the United States has authorized an emergency drawdown of the SPR on two occasions: once during Operation Desert Storm in 1991, and a second time in September 2005 following Hurricane Katrina, which temporarily shut down crude oil production facilities in the Gulf of Mexico (See Box 11-2). The Secretary of Energy has also approved a number of short-term loans of SPR oil to help companies address short-term disruptions to their operations, including after hurricanes Lili in 2002, Ivan in 2004, and Katrina in 2005. The Administration recognizes the critical importance of the SPR, and has increased SPR stocks by about 25 percent since January 2001.

Future Price Expectations and Incentives for Nonconventional Fuels

Although world oil production capacity is expected to increase, world demand is expected to increase as well, and we are likely to face tight crude oil markets for a number of years. Prices on contracts for future deliveries of crude oil (called crude oil *futures*) indicate that market participants expect oil prices to remain elevated at or near current levels through at least the end of 2006. Box 11-1 looks at the development of energy futures markets, which can help energy suppliers and users manage the risks associated with market fluctuations, and which can help facilitate investment in new conventional and alternative sources of energy.

In the longer term, an expectation of high future petroleum prices serves as a signal to potential developers of alternative fuels and producers of petroleum from nonconventional sources that investment in exploration, research, development, production, and marketing of such alternatives is likely to be profitable. Chart 11-2 presents cost estimates for commercial production of potential alternative fuels and nonconventional petroleum sources. Commercial production of some of these alternatives has already begun. For other alternatives, such as coal-to-liquids and oil shale, the technologies needed for production are not yet mature, and their production cost estimates do not include research, development, and initial demonstration costs. In all cases, the production cost estimates reflect expenditures on variable inputs (e.g., raw materials and labor), as well as capital costs for production facilities. These production costs vary widely.

Although oil prices have risen to more than $60 per barrel in recent months, they have averaged as low as $25 per barrel within the last five years. Having experienced past volatility in oil prices, oil companies report using a working assumption of $15-$30 per barrel for the future price of oil when making long-term investment planning decisions. Only a handful of alternative fuels and nonconventional sources of petroleum are profitable at these prices, including petroleum from Canadian oil sands and ethanol (when subsidized at current levels). Canada's petroleum industry reports that production of crude oil from oil sands is currently at 1 million barrels per day and is expected to approach 2.7 million barrels per day by 2015.

Ethanol—an alcohol fuel made from the sugars found in corn and other crops—can be burned by most automobile engines in the United States when blended with gasoline. U.S. ethanol production, which is supported by

Box 11-1: Energy Futures Markets

A futures contract is a legal agreement to buy or sell a particular, precisely defined commodity at a specified price and location at a specified date in the future. Trading in energy futures allows suppliers or consumers of energy to lock in a specific price at which they can sell or purchase energy products, thereby reducing or eliminating price risk. This can aid in investment planning for energy production.

The market for crude oil futures in organized exchanges, such as the New York Mercantile Exchange (NYMEX) and the International Petroleum Exchange in London, is well developed and increasing in size. For example, the quantity of oil committed under NYMEX futures contracts with maturities of three months or less increased from a value equal to 30 percent of U.S. oil production in 1997 to 80 percent in mid-2005. The expansion of markets for contracts with longer maturities is even more striking, with the quantity of oil committed under NYMEX futures contracts with six-year maturities growing from less than 1 percent of U.S. production in 1997 to 9 percent in 2005.

Although there is very little trading in crude oil futures with longer maturities, futures contracts for horizons of longer than six years can be arranged privately with the assistance of investment banks or other financial intermediaries in so-called over-the-counter transactions.

Energy futures are examples of financial instruments known as derivatives, which firms use to manage risks associated with market fluctuations. Weather derivatives also have been used by firms in recent years in order to manage risks associated with fluctuations in temperature and precipitation, which can have a significant effect on energy markets.

various Federal subsidies, currently stands at about 250,000 barrels per day. Ethanol production is expected to increase substantially in response to a mandate included in the Energy Policy Act of 2005 that gasoline sold in the United States contain at least 7.5 billion gallons of renewable fuels in 2012 (about half-a-million barrels per day).

Private-sector development of nonconventional fuels, such as coal-to-liquids or oil shale, may accelerate if high oil prices are sustained over the long term. For the time being, however, these alternatives are in a developmental stage and their future commercial success will depend on future energy prices, technological advances, and environmental and other regulatory requirements.

High energy prices also provide incentives for expanded domestic production of conventional oil and gas. The Administration supports greater access to oil and natural gas resources in Federal waters off shore states that support such

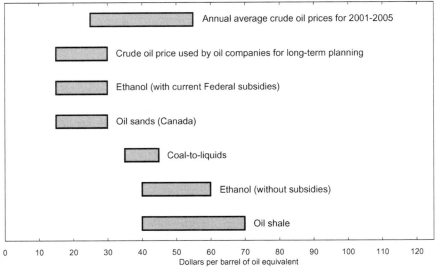

Note: Annual average oil prices are for West Texas Intermediate crude. Oil shale and coal-to-liquids are not currently commercial in the United States; cost estimates are for a mature industry and do not include research, development, and initial demonstration.
Sources: Wall Street Journal, Department of Energy, Department of Agriculture, Council of Economic Advisers.

development and supports opening a small portion of the Arctic National Wildlife Refuge (ANWR) in Alaska for environmentally responsible oil and gas exploration. According to estimates by the U.S. Geological Survey (USGS), the 1.5-million-acre coastal plain of ANWR and adjacent Native lands and state offshore waters hold between 5.7 and 16 billion barrels of technically recoverable reserves, with a mean estimate of 10.4 billion barrels—enough to supply 1 million barrels per day for over 28 years.

Gasoline and Other Refined Products

The United States derives approximately 40 percent of the energy it uses from petroleum, making petroleum the single largest source of energy for our Nation. Refined petroleum products, such as gasoline, diesel, and jet fuel, provide 96 percent of the energy used in the U.S. transportation sector, and are also important for the industrial sector, which gets 37 percent of its energy from petroleum. The residential sector gets 14 percent of its energy from refined petroleum products (mainly home heating oil), while petroleum supplies 10 percent of the energy used in the commercial sector.

Gasoline Prices

The prices that consumers and other end users pay for gasoline depend heavily on the prices that petroleum refiners pay for crude oil. During the first eleven months of 2005, the cost of crude oil accounted for about 53 percent of the retail price of gasoline (the most recent available data from the Department of Energy). Refining costs and profits accounted for 20 percent, Federal and state taxes another 20 percent, and distribution and marketing about 8 percent of the retail price of gasoline.

Crude oil price changes are passed directly through to consumers in the form of changing prices for gasoline and other refined products, at the rate of about 2.4 cents per gallon of refined product for every $1 per barrel change in the price of crude oil. According to Department of Energy data, rising crude oil prices explain roughly two-thirds of the increase in average gasoline prices between 2000 and 2005.

In addition to crude oil prices, other factors have a lesser but sometimes pronounced effect on the price that consumers pay for gasoline. Refinery or pipeline shutdowns caused by damaging weather, such as hurricanes Katrina and Rita, can impede the ability of refiners to produce or distribute refined petroleum products, leading to short-term local or regional spikes in the price of gasoline and other refined products that do not coincide with spikes in the price of crude oil (Box 11-2).

Box 11-2: The Effects of Hurricanes Katrina and Rita on Energy Supplies

In late August 2005 the states of Alabama, Louisiana, and Mississippi were struck by Hurricane Katrina, a powerful storm that disrupted, damaged, or destroyed portions of our Nation's energy infrastructure. Hurricane Rita followed almost exactly one month later, while recovery from Katrina was still underway. The impact of these disruptions on prices for crude oil, gasoline, other refined petroleum products, and natural gas varied substantially, and the divergent impacts help illustrate key differences in markets for these energy sources (see Chapter 1 for a discussion of the effects on the economy generally).

Due to evacuations and subsequent damage of oil rigs and platforms, virtually all of Gulf-region oil production—about 28 percent of total U.S. production—was shut down. Because there is a robust world market for crude oil, however, the effect on world prices and the prices that U.S. refiners pay for crude oil was relatively small. The Administration approved several temporary loans of oil from the Strategic Petroleum Reserve (SPR) to help refineries offset short-term physical supply

---

Box 11-2 — *continued*

disruptions. The President also authorized the emergency sale of up to an additional 30 million barrels of crude oil from the SPR. These actions also helped to moderate any impact the production shut-downs had on U.S. oil supplies.

About two dozen Gulf region refineries were also shut down by flooding and electricity outages associated with the hurricanes, so that following Hurricane Rita more than half of Gulf region refining capacity and roughly one-quarter of total U.S. refining capacity were shut down. Katrina initially led to a shutdown of the Colonial and Plantation pipelines, which deliver most of the refined petroleum products consumed on the East Coast, as well as the Capline pipeline, which delivers crude oil from the Gulf region to pipeline systems serving refineries in the Midwest. After the storm passed and safety assessments revealed no damage, these pipelines began operation substantially below capacity due to electricity outages and product shortages. Hurricane Rita subsequently led to shutdowns in several other pipelines. As a result of these shutdowns of refineries and pipelines, gasoline and refined product price increases were particularly pronounced in regions served by these refineries and pipelines—namely, the East Coast, Midwest, and Gulf regions. The effects on West Coast refined product prices were less pronounced.

The International Energy Agency (IEA) of the Organisation for Economic Cooperation and Development responded by coordinating the release of IEA members' reserve stocks of petroleum. The United States made SPR crude oil available, while other IEA countries primarily offered refined petroleum products. These and other imports of refined petroleum products helped ease the impact of the hurricanes on gasoline and refined product prices, and prices declined further as petroleum refineries and pipelines came back on line.

Offshore natural gas production faced similar disruptions, with shutdowns of up to about 85 percent of Gulf daily natural gas production or 16 percent of total U.S. production. Onshore natural gas processing facilities and gathering lines were also damaged, further disrupting natural gas markets. Unlike crude oil prices, however, natural gas prices rose by over half as a result of the hurricane-related supply disruptions, due to the regional isolation of U.S. natural gas markets.

By the end of 2005, less than 10 percent of U.S. oil production capacity, less than 5 percent of U.S. refining capacity, and less than 5 percent of U.S. natural gas production capacity remained off-line, and further recovery was expected. Prices for crude oil, gasoline, and natural gas had returned to pre-Katrina levels, although natural gas prices were still experiencing volatility.

Another related factor is that surplus refining capacity has declined substantially during the last 25 years. In the early 1980s, U.S. petroleum refiners were producing at only about 70 percent of their total potential production capacity. In contrast, total refiner output has been over 90 percent of capacity for the last decade. Several factors explain this trend. First, many small, inefficient refineries exited the industry in the early 1980s following the removal of poorly conceived Federal petroleum price and allocation controls that had favored such refineries. Without these controls, inefficient refineries were no longer profitable, and total U.S. refining capacity fell by 19 percent from roughly 19 million barrels per day at its peak in 1981 to about 15 million barrels per day in 1994. Second, low profitability in the refining sector during the early to mid 1990s did not provide the necessary incentive to expand total refining capacity. Finally, local concerns about environmental quality have made it increasingly difficult to site new heavy industrial facilities, including refineries. Constraints on the expansion of refining capacity to keep pace with growing demand can lead to higher prices for refined products in the long run.

Refinery profitability increased in the late 1990s, however. As a result, domestic refining capacity rose 12 percent from 1994 to 17 million barrels per day in 2004. This increase in capacity has come exclusively through the expansion of existing refineries, as no new refinery has been built in the United States since 1976. In response to more-stringent clean-air regulations over the last two decades, much of the recent investment in refining has been directed toward increased capacity for producing cleaner fuels, even while using heavier crude oils with higher sulfur contents. Rising refinery costs and profits explain roughly one-quarter of the increase in average gasoline prices between 2000 and 2005.

Short-Run Impacts of High Gasoline Prices

When gasoline prices increase unexpectedly, households and businesses are not able to cut their gasoline consumption quickly enough to fully offset the higher costs. In the short term, then, gasoline price increases cut into household budgets and increase business costs. Price increases can have a substantial impact over the longer term, as well. Mirroring year-to-year changes in gasoline prices, household gasoline expenditures have increased recently after declining for several years from a peak of about 6 percent of mean household income in 1981 (Chart 11-3). Fuel-intensive transportation industries, such as airlines and trucking, also face substantially higher costs when prices of refined petroleum products increase.

When such price increases occur in response to a natural disaster or a failure of energy supply infrastructure, sellers are often accused of "price gouging." Following hurricanes Katrina and Rita, which caused energy supply disruptions and price spikes, the Administration remained vigilant to pursue and

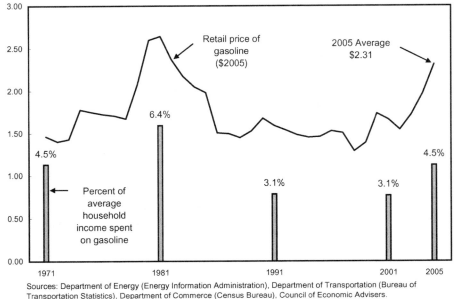

Sources: Department of Energy (Energy Information Administration), Department of Transportation (Bureau of Transportation Statistics), Department of Commerce (Census Bureau), Council of Economic Advisers.

investigate reports of illegal pricing practices, while recognizing that competitive markets are the most effective means for delivering energy supplies to areas of greatest need. Rising prices encourage consumers to conserve fuel and provide domestic producers and importers with incentives to increase supply. If prices are controlled artificially and not allowed to increase, however, consumers will demand more than suppliers are willing to deliver, leading to nonprice rationing (e.g., long lines) and potentially exacerbating the shortage. At least 28 states currently have statutes that address potential market manipulation in the aftermath of a disaster, and a number of these states have initiated investigations of anticompetitive behavior. The Federal Trade Commission has also launched an investigation to scrutinize the refining industry for evidence of unlawful and anticompetitive behavior.

Refining Capacity and Trade

Efficiency improvements and restructuring in the refining industry have led to lower operating costs per barrel. Excluding oil and other energy inputs, refinery operating costs fell roughly 20 percent between the early 1980s and 2003. These cost reductions tend to reduce the price of gasoline for consumers. Lower surplus capacity may, however, increase the sensitivity of gasoline prices to temporary disruptions in production at particular refineries. When production at one refinery is disrupted, it is difficult for other refineries to compensate by ramping up production. As a result, we are more likely to see short-term spikes in the price of gasoline.

Although U.S. refining capacity and utilization have increased since the early 1990s, these increases in production have not kept pace with U.S. demand for gasoline and other refined products. As a consequence, U.S. imports of refined petroleum products, including gasoline, have grown from 11 percent of total refined product consumption in 1993 to 15 percent in 2004.

Demand for various types of petroleum products within a country and the configuration of its domestic refining capacity drive much of this international trade. For instance, Europe has moved toward consuming more diesel fuel relative to gasoline. According to industry sources, diesel-powered vehicles increased from roughly 30 percent of European new car sales in 2000 to 40 percent in 2005. This has resulted in an excess supply of gasoline at European refineries, which Europe now exports to the United States. At the same time, Europe imports diesel fuel from the United States and other countries. Likewise, other countries have differences between domestic consumption patterns and production capacity. These patterns have resulted in the United States exporting certain refined petroleum products to North America, South America, and Europe, while importing other refined products from these same countries, as well as from the Middle East and the Caribbean.

Transport costs for refined petroleum products are sufficiently low that international trading can moderate the effects of regional price spikes. For example, when supplies of gasoline and other refined petroleum products ran short in the United States following Hurricane Katrina, and prices began to rise quickly, importers responded to this price incentive by delivering significantly more product to the United States.

Price-Induced Substitution and Technological Change

In the long run, households and businesses respond to higher fuel prices by cutting consumption, purchasing products that are more efficient, and switching to alternative energy sources. Higher energy prices also encourage entrepreneurs to invest in the research and development of new energy-conserving technologies and alternative fuels, further expanding the opportunities available to households and businesses to reduce energy use and switch to low-cost energy sources.

The energy intensity of the U.S. economy—that is, the ratio of total Btu of energy consumed per dollar of real GDP—has declined substantially over the past several decades (Chart 11-4). And, as one might expect, energy intensity declined most rapidly from the mid-1970s though the mid-1980s, when energy prices were at their highest in real terms. Reductions in overall energy intensity result from both shifts in economic activity toward less energy-intensive sectors, as well as from energy efficiency improvements within particular sectors. Recent research suggests that energy efficiency improvements account for roughly one-third of the reduction in energy intensity between 1985 and 2002, after controlling for shifts in economic activity between different sectors.

Although reductions in energy consumption are made primarily in response to changes in market conditions, government policy may also play a role in facilitating improvements in energy efficiency. This role has included supporting the development of new technologies, encouraging investment in improved efficiency, and in some areas, mandating efficiency improvements to new appliances, equipment, buildings, and vehicles. For example, on-road fuel efficiency for new cars and light trucks (e.g., minivans, pickup trucks, and SUVs) increased from an average of 13 miles per gallon in 1975 to 21 miles per gallon in 2005. This rise is due in part to higher fuel prices, technological improvements, and Corporate Average Fuel Economy (CAFE) standards, which mandate fuel efficiency in passenger cars and light trucks (Box 11-3). The benefits of any such government policy must be weighed carefully against the costs to U.S. taxpayers, consumers, workers, and businesses. The Administration recently proposed new CAFE standards for light trucks in model years 2008-2011 based on a careful accounting of these benefits and costs.

Chart 11-4 **U.S. Energy Intensity**
Energy intensity decreased most rapidly during periods of high energy prices.

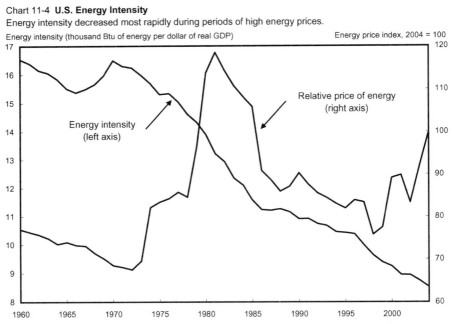

Sources: Department of Energy (Energy Information Administration), Department of Commerce (Bureau of Economic Analysis).

Box 11-3: Automobile Fuel Economy Standards

For three decades, Corporate Average Fuel Economy (CAFE) standards have mandated separate average fuel economy targets for passenger cars and light trucks sold in the United States, and each domestic and foreign manufacturer must meet these same targets in every model year. Congress has established a default level of 27.5 miles per gallon for passenger cars, and passenger car standards have remained at this default level since 1990. The Department of Transportation (DOT) sets CAFE standards for light trucks for each model year, and the Administration raised those standards from 20.7 miles per gallon in 2004 to 22.2 miles per gallon by model year 2007.

There are concerns that the structure of current CAFE standards encourages manufacturers to build minivans, SUVs, and other light trucks instead of cars, because the fuel economy standard for light trucks is lower than the standard for cars. This could lead to an overall decrease in average fuel economy. There are also concerns that manufacturers might meet higher CAFE targets primarily by reducing vehicle size and weight, rather than by applying fuel-saving technologies, and that these size and weight reductions could have a negative impact on the safety of vehicle occupants.

Motivated by these concerns, DOT has proposed a new CAFE rule for light trucks for model years 2008-2011 (to be finalized by April 2006) that incorporates two notable reforms. First, DOT has proposed that CAFE standards for light trucks depend on vehicle size, whereby smaller light trucks will face higher fuel economy standards than larger light trucks. Size-dependent CAFE standards will reduce the incentive to build light trucks instead of cars, discourage manufacturers from achieving CAFE standards only by selling smaller vehicles, encourage greater fuel savings in small light trucks, and spread the burden of achieving CAFE standards more evenly across manufacturers. Second, proposed standards for 2011 would be set using a new economic model developed by DOT that sets CAFE standards to maximize economic benefits minus costs—a milestone in the use of benefit-cost analysis in the rule-making process. The model takes into account the impact of mandated fuel economy improvements on vehicle costs, the value of fuel savings, environmental benefits and costs, and other factors. The proposed rule will save an estimated 10 billion gallons of fuel over the lifetime of the light trucks affected by the rule.

The Administration has requested authority from Congress to implement further reforms to the CAFE system, including utilization of market-based incentives, such as trading of fuel economy credits, to obtain fuel savings at the lowest possible cost to consumers. The Energy Policy Act of 2005 signed by the President calls for a report on CAFE reform ideas to be delivered to Congress within one year.

Reform of the New Source Review Program

Unfortunately, government mandates sometimes lead unintentionally to outcomes that are contrary to their environmental goals. An example of this is the New Source Review (NSR) component of the 1977 Clean Air Act Amendment. NSR requires that new refineries, electric generating units, and other industrial sources of air emissions apply the best-available air emissions control technology. Existing facilities that undertake significant modifications are also required to apply the best-available technology. NSR requirements were designed to ensure that new emissions sources are appropriately controlled so that the local air quality is not compromised. Unfortunately, NSR has led over time to sources seeking to avoid its requirements because the permitting process was complicated, potentially expensive, and time-consuming, especially for sources modifying their facilities. This can provide an incentive for existing sources of emissions to continue their business operations for longer than would have been the case under normal market conditions without the regulation. It also provides an incentive for existing plants to forgo modifications.

New production sources tend to be less polluting than old ones even in the absence of regulations, so extending the business operations of older plants without making modifications could result in higher emissions. Applying different regulations for "routine" versus "major" modifications also leads to ambiguity, litigation delays, and uncertainty in business planning, all of which can harm the economy and may impede environmental improvements. The Administration recently addressed this problem by establishing clear rules that remove disincentives for facilities to modify and undertake routine equipment replacement activities that could improve the safety, reliability, and efficiency of the plants. The Administration also established rules that provide facilities with greater flexibility to modernize their operations without increasing air pollution, encourage the installation of state-of-the-art pollution controls, and base NSR requirements more accurately on actual facility emissions levels. These changes will help to address the extreme demands being placed on our Nation's energy supply infrastructure by assuring that the NSR program provides greater regulatory certainty and flexibility for business investment decisions, while protecting the environment.

Natural Gas

Nearly a quarter of U.S. energy consumption is supplied by natural gas. Natural gas has numerous uses in homes, industry, commerce, electricity production, and transportation and is a vital component of fertilizer and chemical production. The United States consumed 61 billion cubic feet of natural gas per day in 2004: 38 percent in industry (roughly one-tenth of which was used as a feedstock), 24 percent in electricity generation, 22 percent by households, 13 percent in the commercial sector, and the remaining 3 percent in transportation. U.S. natural gas consumption is projected to grow to 74 billion cubic feet per day by 2025.

Natural gas is produced from underground reservoirs that are sometimes associated with crude oil; much smaller amounts are generated from landfills, coal mines, and other sources. Domestic onshore production totaled about 42 billion cubic feet per day in 2004, while offshore production totaled 12 billion cubic feet per day. Total domestic production of 54 billion cubic feet per day is enough to heat about 300 million typical Midwestern homes for one year. After extraction, natural gas is processed to remove impurities (e.g., heavier hydrocarbons) and distributed via pipelines to retailers and eventually to end-use consumers in all sectors of the economy.

Regionalized Natural Gas Markets

Unlike crude oil, which trades on a global market at roughly uniform world prices, the current natural gas marketplace is highly regionalized. As a point of comparison, about 60 percent of global crude oil production was traded internationally in 2002, whereas only 28 percent of global natural gas production was traded. These differences stem from relatively high shipping costs for natural gas and a less-developed infrastructure for natural gas trade. International trade in natural gas occurs mainly within the regions of North America, Western Europe/Russia, and Asia-Pacific/Japan, each with its own unique pricing system and other market characteristics.

In North America, pipelines move natural gas between the United States, Canada, and Mexico with subregions of the continent supplying the majority of their own consumption needs. U.S. net imports of natural gas were 9.3 billion cubic feet per day in 2004, representing 15 percent of total U.S. natural gas consumption. Most imports came by gas pipeline from Canada. Only a relatively small amount was imported from beyond North America, as liquefied natural gas (LNG) from Trinidad, Algeria, and other countries. The United States also exports small amounts of natural gas to Canada and Mexico by pipeline and to Japan as LNG from Alaska.

Natural Gas Prices

Wholesale natural gas prices at Henry Hub on the Louisiana Gulf coast (a common natural gas pricing benchmark) averaged around $2-$3 per million Btu from 1994 through the middle of 2000. One million Btu of natural gas is equal to about one thousand cubic feet of natural gas. Prices then spiked to a peak of $10.50 per million Btu in December of 2000 in response to an unusually cold winter before falling back to their previous low levels. Prices have increased substantially since then from roughly $3 per million Btu in early 2002 to over $10 per million Btu in November 2005. Prices rose roughly in tandem with crude oil prices due to the presence of close substitution possibilities between natural gas and oil in power production and heating, though there have been some bumps along the way. Prices spiked to a peak of $19 per million Btu in February 2003 in response to another unusually cold winter, rose as high as $15 per million Btu in September 2005 following hurricanes Katrina and Rita, and increased to over $15 again in December 2005 with the onset of cold temperatures.

Volatility in Natural Gas Prices

Regionalization reduces the frequency and extent to which natural gas price spikes in other regions affect U.S. natural gas prices. However, the absence of a robust international market for natural gas also makes the United States more susceptible to price shocks within our own region. Disruptions to supply or increases in demand may necessitate large price changes to reestablish equilibrium between regional supply and demand. Opportunities for the import of natural gas from other regions would dull these sharp price spikes, although localized price spikes in some regions will likely never be eliminated completely due to limitations in the natural gas distribution infrastructure.

Volatility in natural gas prices in the United States is often related to extreme and unexpected weather events. In the summer months, for example, periods of extreme heat drive up demand for electricity to power air conditioners, leading to increased demand for natural gas for electricity production. Droughts and periods of low rainfall deplete resources for hydroelectric power generation and may require increased use of natural gas for replacement electricity generation. In the winter, periods of extreme cold drive up demand for natural gas for heating. Hurricanes, floods, and other severe weather events may shut down natural gas production and processing facilities and pipeline distribution networks, leading to supply disruptions.

Liquefied Natural Gas

Liquefied natural gas (LNG)—natural gas in liquid form—is expanding natural gas markets to a more global level, which in the future holds potential to moderate some of this price volatility. LNG is created by cooling natural gas to minus 260 degrees Fahrenheit, at which point it turns into a liquid, significantly reducing its volume. Specially manufactured double-hulled ships are then able to transport LNG over long distances at lower cost than pipeline transport of natural gas. Upon reaching port, LNG is pumped into a receiving terminal where it is converted back into gas (regasified) and then distributed to consumers via pipeline.

Although some inter-regional movement of natural gas does occur, three key factors have limited the development of a full-scale international market. First, natural gas resources are widely distributed internationally, which at least until recently, has limited the need of many countries to import natural gas from distant sources. Second, it is still costly to transport natural gas as LNG over long distances, which means that regional price differentials need to be large before international trade is cost-effective. Finally, natural gas price differentials are now high enough to justify long-distance shipping of LNG, but the infrastructure for liquefying natural gas into LNG is not well developed in many countries with natural gas supplies.

Although the United States has been able to maintain a high level of natural gas production, North America holds only 4 percent of proven world reserves, including 3 percent of world reserves in the United States and 1 percent in Canada (Chart 11-5). Assuming U.S. demand continues to increase, the need for imports from sources outside the region will grow. At present, it appears that LNG is the best means for importing natural gas from beyond North America, and current Department of Energy projections are that LNG imports from various regions will increase from about 3 percent of U.S. natural gas consumption in 2004 to 15 percent by 2025.

Chart 11-5 **World Proven Natural Gas Reserves**
The United States holds a small fraction of total reserves.

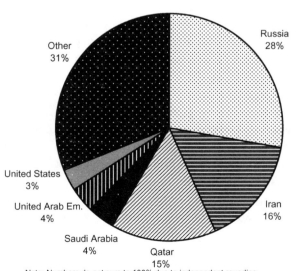

Other
31%

Russia
28%

United States
3%

United Arab Em.
4%

Iran
16%

Saudi Arabia
4%

Qatar
15%

Note: Numbers do not sum to 100% due to independent rounding.
Sources: Department of Energy (Energy Information Administration), PennWell Corporation (Oil & Gas Journal).

LNG Conversion and Transport Costs

A truly global market for natural gas will require transporting natural gas over long distances, and LNG is superior to pipeline transport in this regard. Currently, pipeline transport is less expensive than LNG for distances up to about 1,300 miles in the case of offshore pipelines and up to about 2,400 miles in the case of onshore pipelines. Beyond these distances, LNG transport in tankers is less expensive.

In addition to the cost of extracting and processing natural gas at the supply source, LNG must be liquefied, transported via special tanker, and then turned back into gas upon arrival. The costs associated with liquefying LNG have decreased between 35 percent and 50 percent over the past ten years, while transport and regasification costs have also fallen. These costs are still high enough, however, that U.S. natural gas prices need to exceed wellhead prices in LNG-supplying countries by at least $1.50 to $3 per million Btu— roughly $9 to $17 per barrel of oil equivalent—before LNG transport is cost-effective. As these costs continue to fall, the international marketability of LNG will grow.

U.S. LNG Terminal Capacity

Total LNG import costs are about $2-$4 per million Btu, which is far below current domestic natural gas prices. Given sufficient LNG infrastructure capacity, therefore, domestic prices eventually could be reduced through increased imports. Over 150 LNG tankers were in operation in 2003, and another 50 are under construction. Currently, there are five existing LNG import terminals in the continental United States (four onshore and one offshore), and these facilities operated at about 40 percent of capacity in 2005. About a dozen additional terminals have been approved, and about 20 others have been proposed. The recent Energy Policy Act of 2005 signed by the President took steps to remove unnecessary impediments to siting LNG termi- nals by clarifying the role of the Federal Energy Regulatory Commission (FERC) as the lead agency for coordinating authorization of onshore LNG terminals and LNG terminals in state waters. Federal approval of projects will continue to be conditional on state approval under various environmental laws.

With ample capacity in both shipping and receiving, the current bottleneck in LNG imports to the United States is an insufficient supply of overseas facil- ities for liquefying LNG. As long as capacity for liquefying LNG is in short supply abroad, there will be great competition in international markets for LNG cargoes, as is already happening among the major importers of LNG, including the United States, Japan, Spain, and other countries. Not surpris- ingly, high natural gas prices in these and other countries have led to an expansion of capacity to liquefy LNG abroad. Qatar, which has 15 percent of proven world natural gas reserves, recently began exporting LNG. The

12 nations that currently export LNG hold more than one-quarter of proven world reserves, and some of the world's largest natural gas exporters are in the process of constructing plants to develop LNG export capacity, including Russia and Norway.

Future Prospects for an International LNG Market

Currently, LNG markets are undergoing a substantial evolution, with demand growing and strong future growth expected. Between 1993 and 2003, international LNG trade grew at an average annual rate of 7 percent, and global LNG capacity is expected to grow by more than one-third between 2003 and 2007. Although international trade in LNG is expanding, the market has not yet evolved to the point where it can respond fully to price spikes in North America and other regional markets. The market for prompt delivery of LNG "spot cargoes," although growing, is still less than 10 percent of world LNG trade, with most LNG cargoes delivered under long-term contracts.

Prospects for Domestic Production of Natural Gas

The emergence of international natural gas markets does not eliminate the need to develop domestic production. Greater domestic natural gas production holds promise both in Alaska and on the outer continental shelf (OCS)—Federally controlled offshore areas within the 200-mile exclusive economic zone of the United States but beyond the 3-mile zone under state jurisdiction—as well as other areas. A difficulty in Alaskan production has been the lack of infrastructure to transport remote natural gas resources to market, which would be solved by development of the Alaska natural gas pipeline to the lower 48 states. The Alaska Natural Gas Pipeline Act signed by the President in October 2004 established an expedited Federal approval process for construction of the pipeline, and FERC has been working with state, Federal, and Canadian agencies to establish a framework for coordinating permitting activities.

The OCS has vast additional natural gas resources. Proven Federal offshore reserves as of 2003 were about 23 trillion cubic feet—12 percent of total U.S. proven reserves of 189 trillion cubic feet. The Department of Interior estimates the OCS also contains 400 trillion cubic feet of undiscovered, technically recoverable natural gas. About 20 percent of this natural gas—80 trillion cubic feet—is currently subject to Federal offshore leasing moratoria. The Administration supports greater access to natural gas and oil resources in Federal waters off shore of states that support such development. This would open up substantial additional natural gas supplies for the Nation.

Electricity

Although 39 percent of total U.S. energy consumption in 2004 passed through the electricity-generation sector, only about one-third of electricity-sector energy input was converted into electricity and passed on to end-use customers (Table 11-1). The remaining two-thirds was lost due to inefficiencies in the production and transmission of electricity. Some of these losses could be avoided through further efficiency improvements, though most are unavoidable due to the physics of electricity production and transmission. Retail electricity consumption is divided roughly equally among the residential, commercial, and industrial sectors. The residential sector consumed 36 percent of this electricity for lighting, heating, air conditioning, and powering household appliances, while 35 percent went to the commercial sector for similar uses. Industry consumed 29 percent, and less than 1 percent went to the transportation sector to power electric rail transport.

Electricity-Generation Technologies

A range of energy sources and technologies are used to produce electricity. A total of 71 percent of generated electricity comes from fossil fuels, including 50 percent from coal, 18 percent from natural gas, and 3 percent from petroleum. Nuclear power provides about 20 percent of electricity, while hydroelectric power provides 7 percent, and other renewable sources, such as wind, biomass, and solar, provide a combined 2 percent.

With the exception of solar power and diesel-powered internal combustion engines, all electricity is generated by the turning of turbines that drive electric generators. Falling water drives the turbines in a hydroelectric plant, and wind turns the turbine of a windmill. Natural gas plants use a combustion process like that in a jet aircraft engine to generate a high-speed stream of combustion gases, which is used to drive a natural gas turbine. In natural-gas-combined-cycle plants, exhaust gases exiting the gas turbine are used to heat water, which generates high-pressure steam that drives a second turbine. Nuclear and conventional coal plants generate high-pressure steam to drive turbines by heating water using the energy released by nuclear reactions and coal combustion, respectively. Advanced coal-fired generating plants use various alternative technologies to enhance efficiency and cut emissions. Combined heat and power plants can very efficiently generate steam or hot water for heating and production processes, as well as for electricity.

The Real-Time Challenge of Electricity Markets

Most fuels, such as gasoline, home heating oil, or natural gas, can be manufactured and then stored for later distribution and use. Unlike these energy sources, however, the generation and consumption of electricity must match exactly in real time. Although it is possible to store electricity in batteries, storing electricity on a large scale is too costly. If generation fails to provide the energy needed to satisfy demand, the electricity production and distribution network can become unstable, leading to outages or system failures. Shutdowns of generating plants in one location can therefore affect the entire network, as was the case in August 2003, when a plant shutdown in Ohio triggered cascading failures that ultimately forced the shutdown of at least 265 power plants. These shutdowns left an estimated 50 million people in the United States and Canada without power and led to economic losses of $4-$10 billion in the United States and noticeable downturns in Canadian hours worked, manufacturing shipments, and economic output. The Federal government took a number of actions after the blackout to diminish the risk that a similar disruption would occur in the future.

The demand for electricity fluctuates with the seasons and during the course of each day. For example, the hot summer months bring increased demand for electricity to power air conditioners, and electricity demand peaks each afternoon and drops to its lowest level late at night. Because the production and use of electricity must match in real time, electricity generation fluctuates one-for-one with these seasonal and daily consumption patterns. Electricity-generating capacity is tuned to match these fluctuations. Plants that have low operating costs or that are difficult to turn on and off, such as nuclear and coal-fired steam plants, provide the "baseload" power that is used all day every day. Plants that have higher operating costs or that can be started up quickly, such as natural gas turbine plants, start up incrementally as electricity demand increases and peaks, with some units remaining idle for much of the day or even much of the year. Hydroelectric plants, which have low operating costs and can be started quickly, are suitable for both baseload and peak electricity production.

These fluctuations can have impacts in other energy markets. Reduced hydroelectric power due to low rainfall and falling reservoir levels can increase demand for electricity from natural gas. Likewise, particularly hot summers increase electricity demand to power air conditioners, increasing demand for natural gas as gas-powered generators come on line. If the weather is drier or the summer is hotter than marketers of natural gas anticipate, stored levels of natural gas will be low relative to unexpectedly high demand, and natural gas prices will increase.

Real-Time Pricing and Other Reforms

Because electricity-generating units are dispatched incrementally in order of increasing operating cost, the marginal cost of producing electricity—that is, the additional cost of producing one additional unit of electricity—is highest during periods of peak production and lowest during periods of low production. In practice, however, most retail customers pay a fixed seasonal rate for the electricity they use and thus have no incentive to reduce their consumption of electricity during the times of day when it is most costly to produce. As a result, electricity producers must invest in generating units that remain idle most of the time, and the capital costs of these units are passed on to consumers in the form of higher average prices. Constraints in the electricity transmission system, which limit the extent to which electricity can be directed to areas of high demand or low supply, can also lead to high electricity prices in some regions.

The recent Energy Policy Act of 2005 signed by the President addresses the issue of inefficient pricing by requiring electric utilities and competitive retailers to offer customers time-based rates by February 2007. By ensuring that electricity suppliers offer their customers rates that better reflect the cost of electricity generation, these provisions will encourage consumers and businesses to conserve electricity during times of peak demand. This will reduce the need for excess generating capacity that remains idle most of the time and will, as a result, lower average electricity bills for retail customers. The Act also establishes energy-efficiency standards for household products and Federal buildings, which will reduce consumption of energy.

Environmental Protection

Combustion of fossil fuels, coal in particular, generates sulfur oxides and nitrogen oxides, which contribute to poor air quality if not controlled. Currently, emissions of sulfur and nitrogen oxides from electric utilities are regulated under the 1990 amendments to the Clean Air Act, which established a cap-and-trade system of tradable permits that holds total annual emissions to a mandated level at low cost. See Box 11-4, which includes a discussion of the Clean Air Interstate Rule and the President's Clear Skies proposal, which calls for a further 70 percent reduction in air emissions.

Fossil fuel combustion also generates emissions of carbon dioxide and other greenhouse gases, which contribute to the warming of the Earth's surface. The Administration is supporting the development of various technologies that will improve power plant efficiency, while greatly reducing air pollution and greenhouse gas emissions. For example, the Department of Energy is supporting research and development of technologies that turn coal into a highly enriched hydrogen gas, which can be burned much more cleanly than burning coal directly or can be used as an industrial feedstock. These technologies also provide opportunities to remove and sequester emissions of carbon dioxide and air pollutants prior to combustion. In February 2003 the President announced FutureGen, a government-industry partnership to build a prototype fossil fuel power plant that will demonstrate these technologies.

Box 11-4: Cap-and-Trade Programs for Air Pollution

Title IV of the 1990 Clean Air Act Amendments established a national cap-and-trade system for sulfur dioxide (SO2) emissions. SO2 emissions, which are generated by the burning of fossil fuels—such as coal in an electric power plant—can lead to health concerns and are a component of acid rain. Title IV's program caps total allowable SO2 emissions from power plants nationwide and requires that each facility own a permit for every unit of SO2 it emits. The Environmental Protection Agency (EPA) monitors and enforces this cap rigorously.

Under the Title IV program, SO2 permits can be bought and sold by emitting facilities. Trading allows facilities with high pollution-reduction costs to purchase permits from facilities with low reduction costs, thereby allowing the power industry to achieve mandated emissions reductions in a cost-effective manner. The program does not tell power producers how to reduce pollution, but rather they are free to choose the most cost-effective method for achieving reductions.

The SO2 trading program has been very successful at reducing emissions at a lower cost than direct plant-level emissions standards. The compliance has been nearly 100 percent, and research shows the trading program saves U.S. power producers hundreds of millions of dollars per year relative to direct plant-level standards. Thus, cap-and-trade programs promote clean air while reducing the cost impact on energy consumers. A similar regional cap-and-trade program exists in the eastern United States to control nitrogen oxide emissions, which contribute to regional ozone and smog problems.

In 2002, the President proposed "Clear Skies" legislation, which would expand the Clean Air Act Title IV cap-and-trade approach for SO2 to also include nitrogen oxide and mercury, reducing these emissions to roughly 70 percent below 2000 levels by 2018. As Congress has not yet enacted Clear Skies, the EPA has sought to achieve much of the benefits of the Clear Skies legislation by issuing the Clean Air Interstate Rule (CAIR) and the Clean Air Mercury Rule (CAMR) in March 2005. CAIR requires 28 states in the eastern half of the country to regulate power plant emissions of SO2 and nitrogen oxides and encourages them to do this within the framework of an interstate cap-and-trade system. When fully implemented, CAIR will reduce power-plant SO2 emissions in these states by over 70 percent and nitrogen oxide emissions by over 60 percent from 2003 levels. CAMR is the first-ever regulatory action to reduce mercury emissions from coal-fired power plants and includes a cap-and-trade approach as a way of achieving nearly 70-percent reductions in mercury emissions.

The Administration is also supporting further development of renewable sources of electricity, such as wind, solar energy, and biomass (e.g., wood and agricultural crops), which generate little or zero net greenhouse gas emissions. Finally, the Administration is supporting the development of nuclear power, which does not generate air pollution or greenhouse gases. The Nuclear Power 2010 program is a cost-shared government-industry partnership to identify sites for new nuclear power plants, improve nuclear technologies, and demonstrate untested regulatory processes. The Generation IV nuclear power program supports the development of future technologies with reduced capital costs, enhanced safety, minimal waste, and reduced risk of weapons materials proliferation.

Electricity Markets in Transition

The electric power industry has gone through a transition over the past several decades, evolving from a highly regulated, monopolistic industry to a less regulated, more competitive industry. Traditionally, electric utilities owned and operated electricity-generating units, transmission lines, and distribution systems, and were the sole providers of electricity to a specific geographic area. Federal legislation and rule-making activities during the last decade, however, have opened up access to transmission lines and encouraged greater wholesale trade of electricity between generators and retailers. The market changes vary from state to state and are dynamic, with continual adjustments being made as problems emerge. Some states continue to operate under a traditional, integrated market structure, others are striving to encourage greater competition among generating companies, and some even have opened up competition between electricity retailers.

Recent Electricity Market Policy Reforms

Successful operation of the electric power system requires coordination among system participants. Competition can lead to better products and lower costs for consumers. Ensuring the benefits of competition and reliability are therefore key components of successful reform. Provisions in the Energy Policy Act of 2005 signed by the President promote competition and investment in transmission infrastructure by providing for reasonably priced access to transmission grids, while providing for the establishment of mandatory reliability rules for the electric system. In order to further reduce costs and increase reliability, the Act repealed the Public Utility Holding Company Act (PUHCA), which restricted the ability of regulated utilities to invest in electricity infrastructure, and amended the Public Utility Regulatory Policies Act (PURPA) to allow utilities greater flexibility to purchase wholesale electricity from producers with lower costs. The Energy Policy Act of 2005 improves market competition by promoting the dissemination of information about the availability and prices of wholesale electricity and transmission services. The Act also protects consumers by banning market manipulation, unauthorized disclosure of consumer information, and unfair trade practices, such as changing the electricity service providers chosen by consumers without their consent.

Conclusion

Today, most of our energy comes from petroleum, coal, and other fossil fuels. There are constraints on supplies of these resources in the short term. Increased scarcity and rising prices over time will encourage conservation, increase incentives for exploration, and stimulate the development of new, energy-efficient technologies and alternative energy sources. In the near term, unexpected disruptions to energy supply and distribution networks may continue to impact consumers and businesses. The recent hurricanes Katrina and Rita demonstrated that competitive markets play a central role in allocating scarce energy resources, especially during times of natural disaster or national emergency. The continued expansion of energy markets through regional and global trade can further increase our resilience to energy supply disruptions. Finally, individual energy market participants do not always have an incentive to tackle problems associated with the production and consumption of energy, such as environmental damage or the potentially damaging effects of energy price spikes on the U.S. economy. Policies that reduce U.S. vulnerability to supply disruptions, encourage energy efficiency, and protect the environment can therefore be beneficial supplements to markets. Policymakers can design these policies to be more effective and less costly by harnessing the power of economic incentives and aiming to minimize distortion of normal market forces.

Appendix A
REPORT TO THE PRESIDENT ON THE ACTIVITIES OF THE COUNCIL OF ECONOMIC ADVISERS DURING 2005

LETTER OF TRANSMITTAL

COUNCIL OF ECONOMIC ADVISERS,
Washington, D.C., December 30, 2005.

MR. PRESIDENT:

The Council of Economic Advisers submits this report on its activities during the calendar year 2005 in accordance with the requirements of the Congress, as set forth in section 10(d) of the Employment Act of 1946 as amended by the Full Employment and Balanced Growth Act of 1978.

Sincerely,

Ben S. Bernanke, *Chairman*
Katherine Baicker, *Member*
Matthew J. Slaughter, *Member*

Council Members and Their Dates of Service

Name	Position	Oath of office date	Separation date
Edwin G. Nourse	Chairman	August 9, 1946	November 1, 1949.
Leon H. Keyserling	Vice Chairman	August 9, 1946	
	Acting Chairman	November 2, 1949	
	Chairman	May 10, 1950	January 20, 1953.
John D. Clark	Member	August 9, 1946	
	Vice Chairman	May 10, 1950	February 11, 1953.
Roy Blough	Member	June 29, 1950	August 20, 1952.
Robert C. Turner	Member	September 8, 1952	January 20, 1953.
Arthur F. Burns	Chairman	March 19, 1953	December 1, 1956.
Neil H. Jacoby	Member	September 15, 1953	February 9, 1955.
Walter W. Stewart	Member	December 2, 1953	April 29, 1955.
Raymond J. Saulnier	Member	April 4, 1955	
	Chairman	December 3, 1956	January 20, 1961.
Joseph S. Davis	Member	May 2, 1955	October 31, 1958.
Paul W. McCracken	Member	December 3, 1956	January 31, 1959.
Karl Brandt	Member	November 1, 1958	January 20, 1961.
Henry C. Wallich	Member	May 7, 1959	January 20, 1961.
Walter W. Heller	Chairman	January 29, 1961	November 15, 1964.
James Tobin	Member	January 29, 1961	July 31, 1962.
Kermit Gordon	Member	January 29, 1961	December 27, 1962.
Gardner Ackley	Member	August 3, 1962	
	Chairman	November 16, 1964	February 15, 1968.
John P. Lewis	Member	May 17, 1963	August 31, 1964.
Otto Eckstein	Member	September 2, 1964	February 1, 1966.
Arthur M. Okun	Member	November 16, 1964	
	Chairman	February 15, 1968	January 20, 1969.
James S. Duesenberry	Member	February 2, 1966	June 30, 1968.
Merton J. Peck	Member	February 15, 1968	January 20, 1969.
Warren L. Smith	Member	July 1, 1968	January 20, 1969.
Paul W. McCracken	Chairman	February 4, 1969	December 31, 1971.
Hendrik S. Houthakker	Member	February 4, 1969	July 15, 1971.
Herbert Stein	Member	February 4, 1969	
	Chairman	January 1, 1972	August 31, 1974.
Ezra Solomon	Member	September 9, 1971	March 26, 1973.
Marina v.N. Whitman	Member	March 13, 1972	August 15, 1973.
Gary L. Seevers	Member	July 23, 1973	April 15, 1975.
William J. Fellner	Member	October 31, 1973	February 25, 1975.
Alan Greenspan	Chairman	September 4, 1974	January 20, 1977.
Paul W. MacAvoy	Member	June 13, 1975	November 15, 1976.
Burton G. Malkiel	Member	July 22, 1975	January 20, 1977.

Council Members and Their Dates of Service

Name	Position	Oath of office date	Separation date
Charles L. Schultze	Chairman	January 22, 1977	January 20, 1981.
William D. Nordhaus	Member	March 18, 1977	February 4, 1979.
Lyle E. Gramley	Member	March 18, 1977	May 27, 1980.
George C. Eads	Member	June 6, 1979	January 20, 1981.
Stephen M. Goldfeld	Member	August 20, 1980	January 20, 1981.
Murray L. Weidenbaum	Chairman	February 27, 1981	August 25, 1982.
William A. Niskanen	Member	June 12, 1981	March 30, 1985.
Jerry L. Jordan	Member	July 14, 1981	July 31, 1982.
Martin Feldstein	Chairman	October 14, 1982	July 10, 1984.
William Poole	Member	December 10, 1982	January 20, 1985.
Beryl W. Sprinkel	Chairman	April 18, 1985	January 20, 1989.
Thomas Gale Moore	Member	July 1, 1985	May 1, 1989.
Michael L. Mussa	Member	August 18, 1986	September 19, 1988.
Michael J. Boskin	Chairman	February 2, 1989	January 12, 1993.
John B. Taylor	Member	June 9, 1989	August 2, 1991.
Richard L. Schmalensee	Member	October 3, 1989	June 21, 1991.
David F. Bradford	Member	November 13, 1991	January 20, 1993.
Paul Wonnacott	Member	November 13, 1991	January 20, 1993.
Laura D'Andrea Tyson	Chair	February 5, 1993	April 22, 1995.
Alan S. Blinder	Member	July 27, 1993	June 26, 1994.
Joseph E. Stiglitz	Member	July 27, 1993	
	Chairman	June 28, 1995	February 10, 1997.
Martin N. Baily	Member	June 30, 1995	August 30, 1996.
Alicia H. Munnell	Member	January 29, 1996	August 1, 1997.
Janet L. Yellen	Chair	February 18, 1997	August 3, 1999.
Jeffrey A. Frankel	Member	April 23, 1997	March 2, 1999.
Rebecca M. Blank	Member	October 22, 1998	July 9, 1999.
Martin N. Baily	Chairman	August 12, 1999	January 19, 2001.
Robert Z. Lawrence	Member	August 12, 1999	January 12, 2001.
Kathryn L. Shaw	Member	May 31, 2000	January 19, 2001.
R. Glenn Hubbard	Chairman	May 11, 2001	February 28, 2003.
Mark B. McClellan	Member	July 25, 2001	November 13, 2002.
Randall S. Kroszner	Member	November 30, 2001	July 1, 2003.
N. Gregory Mankiw	Chairman	May 29, 2003	February 18, 2005.
Kristin J. Forbes	Member	November 21, 2003	June 3, 2005.
Harvey S. Rosen	Member	November 21, 2003	
	Chairman	February 23, 2005	June 10, 2005.
Ben S. Bernanke	Chairman	June 21, 2005	
Katherine Baicker	Member	November 18, 2005	
Matthew J. Slaughter	Member	November 18, 2005	

Report to the President on the Activities of the Council of Economic Advisers During 2005

The Council of Economic Advisers was established by the Employment Act of 1946 to provide the President with objective economic analysis and advice on the development and implementation of a wide range of domestic and international economic policy issues.

The Chairman of the Council

Ben S. Bernanke was appointed by the President on June 21, 2005 as Chairman of the President's Council of Economic Advisers. Dr. Bernanke succeeded Harvey S. Rosen, who returned to Princeton University, where he is the John L. Weinberg Professor of Economics and Business Policy. Dr. Rosen succeeded N. Gregory Mankiw, who returned to Harvard University, where he is the Robert M. Beren Professor of Economics.

Prior to his appointment to the Council, Dr. Bernanke served as a Member of the Board of Governors of the Federal Reserve System. Before becoming a Member of the Board, Dr. Bernanke was the Howard Harrison and Gabrielle Snyder Beck Professor of Economics and Public Affairs and Chair of the Economics Department at Princeton University (1996-2002). Dr. Bernanke had served as a Professor of Economics and Public Affairs at Princeton since 1985.

Dr. Bernanke was nominated by the President on October 24, 2005 to be Chairman of the Federal Reserve System for a term to begin on February 1, 2006. Dr. Bernanke subsequently recused himself from the development of the Administration's economic forecast for the fiscal year 2007 budget.

The Chairman of the Council is responsible for communicating the Council's views on economic matters directly to the President through personal discussions and written reports. He represents the Council at Cabinet meetings, meetings of the National Economic Council, daily White House senior staff meetings, budget team meetings with the President, and other formal and informal meetings with the President. He also travels within the United States and overseas to present the Administration's views on the economy. The Chairman is the Council's chief public spokesperson. He directs the work of the Council and exercises ultimate responsibility for the work of the professional staff.

The Members of the Council

Katherine Baicker was appointed by the President as a Member of the Council of Economic Advisers on November 8, 2005. She succeeds Dr. Rosen, who had served as a Member prior to being appointed Chairman. Dr. Baicker is on leave from the University of California in Los Angeles, where she is an Associate Professor in the Department of Public Policy. At the Council Dr. Baicker's responsibilities include work on public finance, labor, and health issues.

Matthew J. Slaughter was appointed by the President as a Member of the Council of Economic Advisers on November 8, 2005. He succeeds Kristin J. Forbes, who returned to the Massachusetts Institute of Technology Sloan School of Management where she is the Mitsubishi Career Development Chair of International Management and Associate Professor of International Management in the Applied Economics Group. Dr. Slaughter is on leave from the Tuck School of Business at Dartmouth College where he is an Associate Professor of Business Administration. At the Council Dr. Slaughter's responsibilities include work on international finance and trade, and industrial organization issues.

Macroeconomic Policies

As is its tradition, the Council devoted much time during 2005 to assisting the President in formulating economic policy objectives and designing programs to implement them. In this regard the Chairman kept the President informed, on a continuing basis, of important macroeconomic developments and other major policy issues through regular macroeconomic briefings. The Council prepares for the President, the Vice President, and the White House senior staff regular memoranda that report key economic data and analyze current economic events.

The Council, the Department of the Treasury, and the Office of Management and Budget (OMB)—the Administration's economic "troika"—are responsible for producing the economic forecasts that underlie the Administration's budget proposals. The Council, under the leadership of the Chairman and the Chief Economist, initiates the forecasting process twice each year. In preparing these forecasts, the Council consults with a variety of outside sources, including leading private sector forecasters.

In 2005, the Council took part in discussions on a range of macroeconomic issues. An important concern in the second half of the year was providing analysis related to hurricanes Katrina and Rita. The Council works closely with the Treasury, the Federal Reserve, and other government agencies in providing analyses to the Administration on these topics of concern. It also works closely with the National Economic Council, the Office of Management and Budget, and other offices within the Executive Office of the President in assessing the economy and economic policy proposals.

International Economic Policies

The Council was involved in a range of international trade issues, including discussions on trade liberalization at the global, regional, and bilateral levels. This involvement included extensive analysis of alternative liberalization scenarios, participation in deliberations concerning trade policy in a number of industries, and analysis related to U.S. economic interaction with China. In international finance, the Council provided extensive analysis of the implications of changes in the U.S. external position and developments in foreign-exchange markets. The Council participated in discussions concerning international financial relations with both advanced and emerging market economies. Council members regularly met with representatives of the Council's counterpart agencies in foreign countries, as well as with foreign-trade ministers, other government officials, and members of the private sector. In recent months, meetings have been held with the ministers of finance from countries including Great Britain, Japan, and India as well as officials from the European Commission and international financial institutions such as the International Monetary Fund.

Council staff were part of the U.S delegation that participated in Joint Economic Committee discussions in Beijing, focused on banking reform and capital market development in China. In addition, the Council participated in discussions with Chinese officials in the U.S.-China Joint Commission on Commerce and Trade. The Council participated in the development of U.S. proposals for providing additional debt relief to the world's poorest countries (Highly Indebted Poor Countries, or HIPCs) that were agreed to at the G-8 Summit held at Gleneagles, Scotland, and prepared analyses for the summits involving the countries of the Asia Pacific Economic Cooperation (APEC). The Council is also a leading participant in the Organization for Economic Cooperation and Development (OECD), the principal forum for economic cooperation among the high-income industrial countries. The Chairman heads the U.S. delegation to the semiannual meetings of the OECD's Economic Policy Committee (EPC) and serves as the EPC Chairman. Dr. Rosen, Dr. Forbes, and Dr. Slaughter participated in meetings of the Economic Policy Committee, as well as meetings of the OECD's Working Party 3 on macroeconomic policy and coordination. Council staff participated in additional OECD meetings.

Microeconomic Policies

A wide variety of microeconomic issues received Council attention during 2005. The Council actively participated in the Cabinet-level National Economic Council, dealing with such diverse issues as health care policy, energy policy, environment, Social Security, tax policy, immigration, education reform, asbestos litigation, and financial markets and institutions. The Council was particularly active in the area of health care policy, conducting analyses of the sources and impact of rising health care costs, the use of health savings accounts, and a number of issues related to the Medicare and Medicaid programs. The Council also participated in discussions related to market-based health care reforms and the tax treatment of health care spending. Energy policy was also an important focus of the Council, with analysis on the impact of hurricanes Katrina and Rita on energy markets, increasing world demand for oil, and the impact of various policy proposals regarding both energy efficiency and energy supply.

The Staff of the Council of Economic Advisers

The professional staff of the Council consists of the Chief of Staff, the Chief Economist, the Director of Macroeconomic Forecasting and Statistics, nine senior economists, four staff economists, and five research assistants. The professional staff and their areas of concentration at the end of 2005 were:

Chief of Staff
Gary D. Blank

Chief Economist
H. Keith Hall

Director
of
Macroeconomic Forecasting and Statistics
Steven N. Braun

Senior Economists

John E. Anderson............................ Public Finance
William D. Block............................. International Finance and Development
Joseph C. Cooper............................ Agriculture and Natural Resources
Daniel M. Covitz .... Macroeconomics and Finance
William H. Dow............................. Health
Wayne R. Dunham .... Regulation, Technology, and
.... Transportation
Dino D. Falaschetti........................ Regulation and Finance
Christine A. McDaniel.................... International Trade
Richard G. Newell .... Energy and Environment

Economist
Rebecca J. Kalmus .... Labor

Staff Economists

Faisal Z. Ahmed............................ International Finance and Trade,
.... and Macroeconomics
Soren T. Anderson .... Regulation
Andrew R. Hanson .... Public Finance

Research Assistants

Jeffrey P. Clemens .... Public Finance and Regulation
Sarena F. Goodman...................... Macroeconomics and Labor
Dagmara K. Tchalakov .... International Trade and Finance
Diana C. Wielocha .... Macroeconomics, Finance,
                                           and Regulation
Jonathan A. Wolfson..................... Health and Regulation

Statistical Office

The Statistical Office maintains and updates the Council's statistical information, oversees the publication of the monthly *Economic Indicators* and the statistical appendix to the *Economic Report of the President*, and verifies statistics in Presidential and Council memoranda, testimony, and speeches.

Linda A. Reilly............................. Program Analyst (Statistical)
Brian A. Amorosi.......................... Program Analyst (Statistical)
Dagmara A. Mocala .... Research Assistant

Catherine Furlong retired from Federal service on September 2, 2005. She had worked in the CEA Statistical Office for 54 years, and had been its Senior Statistician since 1977. A retirement ceremony was held on September 30, where she was honored in comments by present and former Council Chairmen, Ben Bernanke, Alan Greenspan, and Charles Schultz. Chairman Raymond Saulinier was also in attendance. Her untiring dedication to accuracy, detail and the reputation of the Council will indeed be missed. All future Councils will benefit from that wisdom.

Administrative Office

The Administrative Office provides general support for the Council's activities. This includes financial management, human resource management, and travel, facility, security, information, and telecommunications management support.

Rosemary M. Rogers .... Administrative Officer

Office of the Chairman

Alice H. Williams .... Executive Assistant to the Chairman
Sandra F. Daigle........................... Executive Assistant to the Chairman
                                           and Assistant to the Chief of Staff

Lisa D. Branch.............................. Executive Assistant to Dr. Slaughter
Mary E. Jones .... Executive Assistant to Dr. Baicker

Staff Support
Sharon K. Thomas........................ Administrative Support Assistant

Jane Tufts and Barbara Pendergast provided editorial assistance in the preparation of the 2006 Economic Report of the President.

Student Interns during the year were: Matthew B. Adler, Taylor W. Buley, Sean D. Clifford, Andrew M. Dietrich, Alan Y. Gu, Brett W. Hollenbeck, Rebecca L. Homkes, Thomas R. Johnson, Aaron W. Kletzing, Edwin H. Lee, Stephanie Mak, Andrew Park, Sean X. Qin, Elizabeth M. Schultz, Brian C. Tucci, and Joseph S. Vavra.

Fellows during the year were: Courtney Biesecker, Kenneth Gillingham, and Neal Rappaport.

Departures

Phillip P. Swagel left the Council as Chief of Staff in February of 2005 to join the American Enterprise Institute as a resident scholar.

Donald B. Marron left the Council as Chief Economist in October of 2005 to join the Congressional Budget Office where he is currently the Acting Director.

The Council's senior economists, in most cases, are on leave of absence from faculty positions at academic institutions or from other government agencies or research institutions. Their tenure with the Council is usually limited to one or two years. Some of the senior economists who resigned during the year returned to their previous affiliations. They are: Raymond R. Geddes (Cornell University), Pia M. Orrenius (Federal Reserve Bank of Dallas), John C. Driscoll (Federal Reserve Board), Joshua S. Graff Zivin (Columbia University), Gerald Auten (Department of the Treasury), Alexander Raskovich (Department of Justice), Philip Levy (State Department)

Staff economists are generally graduate students who spend one year with the Council and then return to complete their dissertations. Those who departed the Council in 2005 are: Maria Damon, Peter R. Kingston, Anne Berry, and Carol Cohen.

Those who served as research assistants at the Council and resigned during 2005 were: Namita K. Kalyan, Therese C. Scharlemann, Derek A. Haas, James Soldano, and Daniel Ramsey.

Brenda Compton, Finance Manager, accepted a position with the Census Bureau.

Satiah Pee, Information Management Assistant accepted a position with the Discovery Channel.

Public Information

The Council's annual *Economic Report of the President* is an important vehicle for presenting the Administration's domestic and international economic policies. It is available on the Internet at www.gpoaccess.gov/eop. The Council also has responsibility for compiling the monthly *Economic Indicators*. The Internet address for the *Economic Indicators* is www.gpoaccess.gov/indicators. The Council's home page is located at www.whitehouse.gov/cea.

Appendix B
STATISTICAL TABLES RELATING TO INCOME, EMPLOYMENT, AND PRODUCTION

CONTENTS

Page

NATIONAL INCOME OR EXPENDITURE:

TABLE B–1.—*Gross domestic product, 1959–2005*

[Billions of dollars, except as noted; quarterly data at seasonally adjusted annual rates]

Year or quarter	Gross domestic product	Personal consumption expenditures				Gross private domestic investment							Change in private inventories
		Total	Durable goods	Non-durable goods	Serv-ices	Total	Fixed investment						
							Total	Nonresidential				Resi-dential	
								Total	Total	Struc-tures	Equip-ment and soft-ware		
1959	506.6	317.6	42.7	148.5	126.5	78.5	74.6	46.5	18.1	28.4	28.1	3.9
1960	526.4	331.7	43.3	152.8	135.6	78.9	75.7	49.4	19.6	29.8	26.3	3.2
1961	544.7	342.1	41.8	156.6	143.8	78.2	75.2	48.8	19.7	29.1	26.4	3.0
1962	585.6	363.3	46.9	162.8	153.6	88.1	82.0	53.1	20.8	32.3	29.0	6.1
1963	617.7	382.7	51.6	168.2	162.9	93.8	88.1	56.0	21.2	34.8	32.1	5.6
1964	663.6	411.4	56.7	178.6	176.1	102.1	97.2	63.0	23.7	39.2	34.3	4.8
1965	719.1	443.8	63.3	191.5	189.0	118.2	109.0	74.8	28.3	46.5	34.2	9.2
1966	787.8	480.9	68.3	208.7	203.8	131.3	117.7	85.4	31.3	54.0	32.3	13.6
1967	832.6	507.8	70.4	217.1	220.3	128.6	118.7	86.4	31.5	54.9	32.4	9.9
1968	910.0	558.0	80.8	235.7	241.6	141.2	132.1	93.4	33.6	59.9	38.7	9.1
1969	984.6	605.2	85.9	253.1	266.1	156.4	147.3	104.7	37.7	67.0	42.6	9.2
1970	1,038.5	648.5	85.0	272.0	291.5	152.4	150.4	109.0	40.3	68.7	41.4	2.0
1971	1,127.1	701.9	96.9	285.5	319.5	178.2	169.9	114.1	42.7	71.5	55.8	8.3
1972	1,238.3	770.6	110.4	308.0	352.2	207.6	198.5	128.8	47.2	81.7	69.7	9.1
1973	1,382.7	852.4	123.5	343.1	385.8	244.5	228.6	153.3	55.0	98.3	75.3	15.9
1974	1,500.0	933.4	122.3	384.5	426.6	249.4	235.4	169.5	61.2	108.2	66.0	14.0
1975	1,638.3	1,034.4	133.5	420.7	480.2	230.2	236.5	173.7	61.4	112.4	62.7	–6.3
1976	1,825.3	1,151.9	158.9	458.3	534.7	292.0	274.8	192.4	65.9	126.4	82.5	17.1
1977	2,030.9	1,278.6	181.2	497.1	600.2	361.3	339.0	228.7	74.6	154.1	110.3	22.3
1978	2,294.7	1,428.5	201.7	550.2	676.6	438.0	412.2	280.6	93.6	187.0	131.6	25.8
1979	2,563.3	1,592.2	214.4	624.5	753.3	492.9	474.9	333.9	117.7	216.2	141.0	18.0
1980	2,789.5	1,757.1	214.2	696.1	846.9	479.3	485.6	362.4	136.2	226.2	123.2	–6.3
1981	3,128.4	1,941.1	231.3	758.9	950.8	572.4	542.6	420.0	167.3	252.7	122.6	29.8
1982	3,255.0	2,077.3	240.2	787.6	1,049.4	517.2	532.1	426.5	177.6	248.9	105.7	–14.9
1983	3,536.7	2,290.6	280.8	831.2	1,178.6	564.3	570.1	417.2	154.3	262.9	152.9	–5.8
1984	3,933.2	2,503.3	326.5	884.6	1,292.2	735.6	670.2	489.6	177.4	312.2	180.6	65.4
1985	4,220.3	2,720.3	363.5	928.7	1,428.1	736.2	714.4	526.2	194.5	331.7	188.2	21.8
1986	4,462.8	2,899.7	403.0	958.4	1,538.3	746.5	739.9	519.8	176.5	343.3	220.1	6.6
1987	4,739.5	3,100.2	421.7	1,015.3	1,663.3	785.0	757.8	524.1	174.2	349.9	233.7	27.1
1988	5,103.8	3,353.6	453.6	1,083.5	1,816.5	821.6	803.1	563.8	182.8	381.0	239.3	18.5
1989	5,484.4	3,598.5	471.8	1,166.7	1,960.0	874.9	847.3	607.7	193.7	414.0	239.5	27.7
1990	5,803.1	3,839.9	474.2	1,249.9	2,115.9	861.0	846.4	622.4	202.9	419.5	224.0	14.5
1991	5,995.9	3,986.1	453.9	1,284.8	2,247.4	802.9	803.3	598.2	183.6	414.6	205.1	–.4
1992	6,337.7	4,235.3	483.6	1,330.5	2,421.2	864.8	848.5	612.1	172.6	439.6	236.3	16.3
1993	6,657.4	4,477.9	526.7	1,379.4	2,571.8	953.4	932.5	666.6	177.2	489.4	266.0	20.8
1994	7,072.2	4,743.3	582.2	1,437.2	2,723.9	1,097.1	1,033.3	731.4	186.8	544.6	301.9	63.8
1995	7,397.7	4,975.8	611.6	1,485.1	2,879.1	1,144.0	1,112.9	810.0	207.3	602.8	302.8	31.1
1996	7,816.9	5,256.8	652.6	1,555.5	3,048.7	1,240.3	1,209.5	875.4	224.6	650.8	334.1	30.8
1997	8,304.3	5,547.4	692.7	1,619.0	3,235.8	1,389.8	1,317.8	968.7	250.3	718.3	349.1	72.0
1998	8,747.0	5,879.5	750.2	1,683.6	3,445.7	1,509.1	1,438.4	1,052.6	275.2	777.3	385.8	70.8
1999	9,268.4	6,282.5	817.6	1,804.8	3,660.0	1,625.7	1,558.8	1,133.9	282.2	851.7	424.9	66.9
2000	9,817.0	6,739.4	863.3	1,947.2	3,928.8	1,735.5	1,679.0	1,232.1	313.2	918.9	446.9	56.5
2001	10,128.0	7,055.0	883.7	2,017.1	4,154.3	1,614.3	1,646.1	1,176.8	322.6	854.2	469.3	–31.7
2002	10,469.6	7,350.7	923.9	2,079.6	4,347.2	1,582.1	1,570.2	1,066.3	279.2	787.1	503.9	11.9
2003	10,971.2	7,709.9	950.1	2,189.0	4,570.8	1,670.4	1,654.9	1,082.4	276.9	805.6	572.5	15.4
2004	11,734.3	8,214.3	987.8	2,368.3	4,858.2	1,928.1	1,872.6	1,198.8	298.4	900.4	673.8	55.4
2005 *P*	12,479.4	8,745.9	1,025.7	2,564.3	5,155.9	2,099.5	2,084.3	1,328.3	334.5	993.8	756.0	15.2
2002: I	10,333.3	7,230.3	915.2	2,044.9	4,270.2	1,564.1	1,572.4	1,085.2	292.2	793.0	487.2	–8.3
II	10,426.6	7,323.0	918.9	2,078.9	4,325.2	1,571.4	1,568.8	1,067.8	280.9	787.0	501.0	2.6
III	10,527.4	7,396.6	940.1	2,085.1	4,371.4	1,592.9	1,566.8	1,061.4	272.1	789.3	505.4	26.0
IV	10,591.1	7,453.1	921.5	2,109.7	4,421.8	1,600.1	1,572.8	1,050.7	271.7	779.0	522.1	27.3
2003: I	10,717.0	7,555.2	919.7	2,156.0	4,479.5	1,610.0	1,588.2	1,048.2	268.4	779.8	540.0	21.8
II	10,844.6	7,635.3	942.2	2,153.1	4,540.0	1,619.3	1,619.7	1,066.8	277.1	789.7	552.9	–.4
III	11,087.4	7,782.4	974.7	2,213.5	4,594.2	1,694.2	1,683.7	1,098.8	279.0	819.8	584.9	10.6
IV	11,236.0	7,866.6	963.6	2,233.6	4,669.5	1,757.9	1,728.2	1,116.0	283.0	833.0	612.2	29.8
2004: I	11,457.1	8,032.3	974.2	2,302.7	4,755.4	1,818.2	1,772.7	1,140.7	285.3	855.3	632.0	45.5
II	11,666.1	8,145.6	974.6	2,355.2	4,815.9	1,928.5	1,856.6	1,182.7	296.3	886.5	673.9	71.9
III	11,818.8	8,263.2	993.8	2,378.4	4,891.0	1,961.2	1,908.7	1,219.0	302.1	916.9	689.7	52.5
IV	11,995.2	8,416.1	1,008.6	2,437.1	4,970.4	2,004.5	1,952.6	1,252.9	309.8	943.1	699.7	51.9
2005: I	12,198.8	8,535.8	1,017.3	2,476.6	5,041.8	2,058.5	1,998.7	1,280.1	315.9	964.3	718.5	59.9
II	12,378.0	8,677.0	1,035.5	2,533.7	5,107.8	2,054.4	2,058.5	1,313.5	325.6	987.9	745.0	–4.2
III	12,605.7	8,844.0	1,050.9	2,604.6	5,188.3	2,099.5	2,119.2	1,348.9	340.2	1,008.7	770.3	–19.7
IV *P*	12,735.3	8,926.9	999.0	2,642.0	5,285.9	2,185.7	2,160.9	1,370.6	356.3	1,014.3	790.3	24.8

See next page for continuation of table.

[Billions of dollars, except as noted; quarterly data at seasonally adjusted annual rates]

Year or quarter	Net exports of goods and services			Government consumption expenditures and gross investment					Final sales of domestic product	Gross domestic purchases [1]	Addendum: Gross national product [2]	Percent change from preceding period	
	Net exports	Exports	Imports	Total	Federal			State and local				Gross domestic product	Gross domestic purchases [1]
					Total	National defense	Non-defense						
1959	0.4	22.7	22.3	110.0	65.4	53.8	11.5	44.7	502.7	506.2	509.3	8.4	8.5
1960	4.2	27.0	22.8	111.6	64.1	53.4	10.7	47.5	523.2	522.2	529.5	3.9	3.2
1961	4.9	27.6	22.7	119.5	67.9	56.5	11.4	51.6	541.7	539.8	548.2	3.5	3.4
1962	4.1	29.1	25.0	130.1	75.3	61.1	14.2	54.9	579.5	581.5	589.7	7.5	7.7
1963	4.9	31.1	26.1	136.4	76.9	61.0	15.9	59.5	612.1	612.8	622.2	5.5	5.4
1964	6.9	35.0	28.1	143.2	78.5	60.3	18.2	64.8	658.8	656.7	668.5	7.4	7.2
1965	5.6	37.1	31.5	151.5	80.4	60.6	19.8	71.0	709.9	713.5	724.4	8.4	8.6
1966	3.9	40.9	37.1	171.8	92.5	71.7	20.8	79.2	774.2	783.9	792.9	9.5	9.9
1967	3.6	43.5	39.9	192.7	104.8	83.5	21.3	87.9	822.7	829.0	838.0	5.7	5.8
1968	1.4	47.9	46.6	209.4	111.4	89.3	22.1	98.0	900.9	908.6	916.1	9.3	9.6
1969	1.4	51.9	50.5	221.5	113.4	89.5	23.8	108.2	975.4	983.2	990.7	8.2	8.2
1970	4.0	59.7	55.8	233.8	113.5	87.6	25.8	120.3	1,036.5	1,034.6	1,044.9	5.5	5.2
1971	.6	63.0	62.3	246.5	113.7	84.6	29.1	132.8	1,118.9	1,126.5	1,134.7	8.5	8.9
1972	-3.4	70.8	74.2	263.5	119.7	87.0	32.7	143.8	1,229.2	1,241.7	1,246.8	9.9	10.2
1973	4.1	95.3	91.2	281.7	122.5	88.2	34.3	159.2	1,366.8	1,378.6	1,395.3	11.7	11.0
1974	-.8	126.7	127.5	317.9	134.6	95.6	39.0	183.4	1,486.0	1,500.8	1,515.5	8.5	8.9
1975	16.0	138.7	122.7	357.7	149.1	103.9	45.1	208.7	1,644.6	1,622.4	1,651.3	9.2	8.1
1976	-1.6	149.5	151.1	383.0	159.7	111.1	48.6	223.3	1,808.2	1,826.9	1,842.1	11.4	12.6
1977	-23.1	159.4	182.4	414.1	175.4	120.9	54.5	238.7	2,008.6	2,054.0	2,051.2	11.3	12.4
1978	-25.4	186.9	212.3	453.6	190.9	130.5	60.4	262.6	2,268.9	2,320.1	2,316.3	13.0	13.0
1979	-22.5	230.1	252.7	500.8	210.6	145.2	65.4	290.2	2,545.3	2,585.9	2,595.3	11.7	11.5
1980	-13.1	280.8	293.8	566.2	243.8	168.0	75.8	322.4	2,795.8	2,802.6	2,823.7	8.8	8.4
1981	-12.5	305.2	317.8	627.5	280.2	196.3	84.0	347.3	3,098.6	3,141.0	3,161.4	12.2	12.1
1982	-20.0	283.2	303.2	680.5	310.8	225.9	84.9	369.7	3,269.9	3,275.0	3,291.5	4.0	4.3
1983	-51.7	277.0	328.6	733.5	342.9	250.7	92.3	390.5	3,542.4	3,588.3	3,573.8	8.7	9.6
1984	-102.7	302.4	405.1	797.0	374.4	281.6	92.8	422.6	3,867.8	4,035.9	3,969.5	11.2	12.5
1985	-115.2	302.0	417.2	879.0	412.8	311.2	101.6	466.2	4,198.4	4,335.5	4,246.8	7.3	7.4
1986	-132.7	320.5	453.3	949.3	438.6	330.9	107.8	510.7	4,456.3	4,595.6	4,480.6	5.7	6.0
1987	-145.2	363.9	509.1	999.5	460.1	350.0	110.0	539.4	4,712.3	4,884.7	4,757.4	6.2	6.3
1988	-110.4	444.1	554.5	1,039.0	462.3	354.9	107.4	576.7	5,085.3	5,214.2	5,127.4	7.7	6.7
1989	-88.2	503.3	591.5	1,099.1	482.2	362.2	120.0	616.9	5,456.7	5,572.5	5,510.6	7.5	6.9
1990	-78.0	552.4	630.3	1,180.2	508.3	374.0	134.3	671.9	5,788.5	5,881.1	5,837.9	5.8	5.5
1991	-27.5	596.8	624.3	1,234.4	527.7	383.2	144.5	706.7	5,996.3	6,023.4	6,026.3	3.3	2.4
1992	-33.2	635.3	668.6	1,271.0	533.9	376.9	157.0	737.0	6,321.4	6,371.0	6,367.4	5.7	5.8
1993	-65.0	655.8	720.9	1,291.2	525.2	362.9	162.4	766.0	6,636.6	6,722.4	6,689.3	5.0	5.5
1994	-93.6	720.9	814.5	1,325.5	519.1	353.7	165.5	806.3	7,008.4	7,165.8	7,098.4	6.2	6.6
1995	-91.4	812.2	903.6	1,369.2	519.2	348.7	170.5	850.0	7,366.5	7,489.0	7,433.4	4.6	4.5
1996	-96.2	868.6	964.8	1,416.0	527.4	354.6	172.8	888.6	7,786.1	7,913.1	7,851.9	5.7	5.7
1997	-101.6	955.3	1,056.9	1,468.7	530.9	349.6	181.3	937.8	8,232.3	8,405.9	8,337.3	6.2	6.2
1998	-159.9	955.9	1,115.9	1,518.3	530.4	345.7	184.7	987.9	8,676.2	8,906.9	8,768.3	5.3	6.0
1999	-260.5	991.2	1,251.7	1,620.8	555.8	360.6	195.2	1,065.0	9,201.5	9,528.9	9,302.2	6.0	7.0
2000	-379.5	1,096.3	1,475.8	1,721.6	578.8	370.3	208.5	1,142.8	9,760.5	10,194.4	9,855.9	5.9	7.0
2001	-367.0	1,032.8	1,399.8	1,825.6	612.9	392.6	220.3	1,212.8	10,159.7	10,495.0	10,171.6	3.2	2.9
2002	-424.4	1,005.9	1,430.3	1,961.1	679.7	437.1	242.5	1,281.5	10,457.7	10,894.0	10,500.2	3.4	3.8
2003	-500.9	1,045.6	1,546.5	2,091.9	754.8	496.7	258.2	1,337.1	10,955.8	11,472.1	11,039.3	4.8	5.3
2004	-624.0	1,173.8	1,797.8	2,215.9	827.6	552.7	274.9	1,388.3	11,678.9	12,358.3	11,788.0	7.0	7.7
2005 P	-725.7	1,299.2	2,024.9	2,359.7	874.8	585.3	289.5	1,484.9	12,464.2	13,205.2	....	6.4	6.9
2002: I	-373.1	976.4	1,349.5	1,912.0	654.9	418.2	236.6	1,257.2	10,341.6	10,706.4	10,359.5	4.3	4.9
II	-416.1	1,008.2	1,424.3	1,948.3	675.2	431.1	244.1	1,273.1	10,424.0	10,842.7	10,443.3	3.7	5.2
III	-433.8	1,022.9	1,456.7	1,971.8	682.0	438.0	243.9	1,289.8	10,501.4	10,961.2	10,557.0	3.9	4.4
IV	-474.6	1,016.2	1,490.8	2,012.5	706.6	461.1	245.5	1,305.9	10,563.9	11,065.7	10,641.1	2.4	3.9
2003: I	-502.6	1,018.8	1,521.4	2,054.4	724.0	467.2	256.8	1,330.4	10,695.2	11,219.6	10,761.9	4.8	5.7
II	-500.6	1,016.1	1,516.6	2,090.5	763.4	507.2	256.3	1,327.1	10,845.0	11,345.2	10,911.4	4.8	4.6
III	-495.3	1,046.6	1,541.9	2,106.2	761.8	500.3	261.5	1,344.4	11,076.9	11,582.8	11,154.8	9.3	8.6
IV	-505.0	1,101.1	1,606.1	2,116.5	770.0	512.0	258.0	1,346.5	11,206.2	11,741.1	11,329.2	5.5	5.6
2004: I	-559.6	1,130.8	1,690.3	2,166.2	808.3	538.7	269.6	1,357.9	11,411.6	12,016.7	11,540.1	8.1	9.7
II	-613.1	1,163.3	1,776.4	2,205.0	824.6	547.2	277.4	1,380.4	11,594.2	12,279.1	11,712.8	7.5	9.0
III	-638.0	1,183.8	1,821.8	2,232.5	836.5	562.9	273.6	1,395.9	11,766.3	12,456.8	11,867.3	5.3	5.9
IV	-685.4	1,217.1	1,902.5	2,260.0	840.8	562.0	278.8	1,419.1	11,943.3	12,680.6	12,032.0	6.1	7.4
2005: I	-697.5	1,253.2	1,950.6	2,302.0	860.2	575.3	285.0	1,441.7	12,138.9	12,896.3	12,238.2	7.0	7.0
II	-691.0	1,297.1	1,988.1	2,337.6	869.8	582.5	287.3	1,467.7	12,382.1	13,069.0	12,413.5	6.0	5.5
III	-730.4	1,314.6	2,045.1	2,392.7	892.2	601.7	290.5	1,500.4	12,625.4	13,336.1	12,650.0	7.6	8.4
IV P	-784.1	1,331.8	2,115.8	2,406.8	876.9	581.6	295.3	1,529.9	12,710.5	13,519.3	....	4.2	5.6

[1] Gross domestic product (GDP) less exports of goods and services plus imports of goods and services.
[2] GDP plus net income receipts from rest of the world.
Source: Department of Commerce, Bureau of Economic Analysis.

TABLE B–2.—*Real gross domestic product, 1959–2005*

[Billions of chained (2000) dollars, except as noted; quarterly data at seasonally adjusted annual rates]

Year or quarter	Gross domestic product	Personal consumption expenditures				Gross private domestic investment						
		Total	Durable goods	Non-durable goods	Services	Total	Fixed investment				Residential	Change in private inventories
							Total	Nonresidential				
								Total	Structures	Equipment and software		
1959	2,441.3	1,554.6	....	....	....	266.7	....	....	....	....	....	....
1960	2,501.8	1,597.4	....	....	....	266.6	....	....	....	....	....	....
1961	2,560.0	1,630.3	....	....	....	264.9	....	....	....	....	....	....
1962	2,715.2	1,711.1	....	....	....	298.4	....	....	....	....	....	....
1963	2,834.0	1,781.6	....	....	....	318.5	....	....	....	....	....	....
1964	2,998.6	1,888.4	....	....	....	344.7	....	....	....	....	....	....
1965	3,191.1	2,007.7	....	....	....	393.1	....	....	....	....	....	....
1966	3,399.1	2,121.8	....	....	....	427.7	....	....	....	....	....	....
1967	3,484.6	2,185.0	....	....	....	408.1	....	....	....	....	....	....
1968	3,652.7	2,310.5	....	....	....	431.9	....	....	....	....	....	....
1969	3,765.4	2,396.4	....	....	....	457.1	....	....	....	....	....	....
1970	3,771.9	2,451.9	....	....	....	427.1	....	....	....	....	....	....
1971	3,898.6	2,545.5	....	....	....	475.7	....	....	....	....	....	....
1972	4,105.0	2,701.3	....	....	....	532.1	....	....	....	....	....	....
1973	4,341.5	2,833.8	....	....	....	594.4	....	....	....	....	....	....
1974	4,319.6	2,812.3	....	....	....	550.6	....	....	....	....	....	....
1975	4,311.2	2,876.9	....	....	....	453.1	....	....	....	....	....	....
1976	4,540.9	3,035.5	....	....	....	544.7	....	....	....	....	....	....
1977	4,750.5	3,164.1	....	....	....	627.0	....	....	....	....	....	....
1978	5,015.0	3,303.1	....	....	....	702.6	....	....	....	....	....	....
1979	5,173.4	3,383.4	....	....	....	725.0	....	....	....	....	....	....
1980	5,161.7	3,374.1	....	....	....	645.3	....	....	....	....	....	....
1981	5,291.7	3,422.2	....	....	....	704.9	....	....	....	....	....	....
1982	5,189.3	3,470.3	....	....	....	606.0	....	....	....	....	....	....
1983	5,423.8	3,668.6	....	....	....	662.5	....	....	....	....	....	....
1984	5,813.6	3,863.3	....	....	....	857.7	....	....	....	....	....	....
1985	6,053.7	4,064.0	....	....	....	849.7	....	....	....	....	....	....
1986	6,263.6	4,228.9	....	....	....	843.9	....	....	....	....	....	....
1987	6,475.1	4,369.8	....	....	....	870.0	....	....	....	....	....	....
1988	6,742.7	4,546.9	....	....	....	890.5	....	....	....	....	....	....
1989	6,981.4	4,675.0	....	....	....	926.2	....	....	....	....	....	....
1990	7,112.5	4,770.3	453.5	1,484.0	2,851.7	895.1	886.6	595.1	275.2	355.0	298.9	15.4
1991	7,100.5	4,778.4	427.9	1,480.5	2,900.0	822.2	829.1	563.2	244.6	345.9	270.2	−.5
1992	7,336.6	4,934.8	453.0	1,510.1	3,000.8	889.0	878.3	581.3	229.9	371.1	307.6	16.5
1993	7,532.7	5,099.8	488.4	1,550.4	3,085.7	968.3	953.5	631.9	228.3	417.4	332.7	20.6
1994	7,835.5	5,290.7	529.4	1,603.9	3,176.6	1,099.6	1,042.3	689.9	232.3	467.2	364.8	63.6
1995	8,031.7	5,433.5	552.6	1,638.6	3,259.9	1,134.0	1,109.6	762.5	247.1	523.1	353.1	29.9
1996	8,328.9	5,619.4	595.9	1,680.4	3,356.0	1,234.3	1,209.2	833.6	261.1	578.7	381.3	28.7
1997	8,703.5	5,831.8	646.9	1,725.3	3,468.0	1,387.7	1,320.6	934.2	280.1	658.3	388.6	71.2
1998	9,066.9	6,125.8	720.3	1,794.4	3,615.0	1,524.1	1,455.0	1,037.8	294.5	745.6	418.3	72.6
1999	9,470.3	6,438.6	804.6	1,876.6	3,758.0	1,642.6	1,576.3	1,133.3	293.2	840.2	443.6	68.9
2000	9,817.0	6,739.4	863.3	1,947.2	3,928.8	1,735.5	1,679.0	1,232.1	313.2	918.9	446.9	56.5
2001	9,890.7	6,910.4	900.7	1,986.7	4,023.2	1,598.4	1,629.4	1,180.5	306.1	874.2	448.5	−31.7
2002	10,048.8	7,099.3	964.8	2,037.1	4,100.4	1,557.1	1,544.6	1,071.5	253.8	820.2	469.9	12.5
2003	10,320.6	7,306.6	1,028.5	2,101.8	4,183.9	1,617.4	1,600.0	1,085.0	243.1	846.8	509.4	15.5
2004	10,755.7	7,588.6	1,089.9	2,200.4	4,310.9	1,809.8	1,755.1	1,186.7	248.4	947.6	561.8	52.0
2005 ᴾ	11,131.1	7,858.1	1,137.7	2,298.0	4,438.0	1,915.6	1,896.1	1,287.6	253.1	1,049.8	602.1	17.2
2002: I	9,977.3	7,042.2	948.4	2,026.8	4,069.4	1,541.7	1,551.5	1,090.3	270.3	820.9	459.0	−10.2
II	10,031.6	7,083.5	956.9	2,033.4	4,095.7	1,549.0	1,545.9	1,073.3	256.4	819.0	469.5	2.6
III	10,090.7	7,123.2	983.4	2,035.0	4,109.0	1,570.9	1,543.2	1,068.0	245.8	825.7	471.8	28.0
IV	10,095.8	7,148.2	970.4	2,053.1	4,127.4	1,567.0	1,537.8	1,054.5	242.5	815.4	479.3	29.5
2003: I	10,138.6	7,192.2	979.1	2,069.5	4,146.5	1,565.3	1,540.9	1,051.6	237.3	818.7	484.8	24.0
II	10,230.4	7,256.8	1,014.0	2,079.1	4,169.7	1,575.8	1,573.7	1,072.9	244.8	832.0	496.0	−.4
III	10,410.9	7,360.7	1,061.0	2,121.2	4,190.2	1,640.6	1,629.0	1,101.8	244.7	862.4	521.2	9.3
IV	10,502.6	7,416.4	1,060.0	2,137.3	4,229.4	1,687.9	1,656.3	1,113.7	245.5	874.0	535.7	29.0
2004: I	10,612.5	7,501.4	1,071.6	2,171.9	4,269.0	1,729.1	1,684.4	1,135.1	243.4	899.1	542.4	41.9
II	10,704.1	7,536.6	1,072.5	2,186.1	4,288.6	1,813.0	1,744.5	1,171.6	248.5	931.4	565.1	65.6
III	10,808.9	7,617.5	1,100.4	2,206.9	4,324.0	1,833.4	1,780.2	1,204.8	249.4	965.6	568.8	50.4
IV	10,897.1	7,698.8	1,115.1	2,236.5	4,362.0	1,863.9	1,811.3	1,235.1	252.3	994.2	571.0	50.1
2005: I	10,999.3	7,764.9	1,122.3	2,265.6	4,392.0	1,902.9	1,842.0	1,252.2	251.0	1,014.2	584.1	58.2
II	11,089.2	7,829.5	1,143.9	2,285.9	4,417.6	1,885.0	1,884.7	1,279.0	252.7	1,040.9	599.3	−1.7
III	11,202.3	7,907.9	1,169.7	2,305.8	4,453.5	1,909.4	1,921.5	1,305.2	254.1	1,067.5	610.0	−13.3
IV ᴾ	11,233.5	7,930.2	1,114.7	2,334.7	4,489.1	1,965.1	1,935.9	1,314.2	254.5	1,076.8	615.2	25.7

See next page for continuation of table.

282

[Billions of chained (2000) dollars, except as noted; quarterly data at seasonally adjusted annual rates]

Year or quarter	Net exports of goods and services			Government consumption expenditures and gross investment					Final sales of domestic product	Gross domestic purchases [1]	Addendum: Gross national product [2]	Percent change from preceding period	
	Net exports	Exports	Imports	Total	Federal			State and local				Gross domestic product	Gross domestic purchases [1]
					Total	National defense	Non-defense						
1959	....	77.2	101.9	714.3	....	....	....	....	2,442.7	2,485.9	2,457.4	7.1	7.1
1960	....	90.6	103.3	715.4	....	....	....	....	2,506.8	2,529.6	2,519.4	2.5	1.8
1961	....	91.1	102.6	751.3	....	....	....	....	2,566.8	2,587.6	2,579.3	2.3	2.3
1962	....	95.7	114.3	797.6	....	....	....	....	2,708.5	2,751.4	2,736.9	6.1	6.3
1963	....	102.5	117.3	818.1	....	....	....	....	2,830.3	2,866.0	2,857.2	4.4	4.2
1964	....	114.6	123.6	836.1	....	....	....	....	2,999.9	3,023.2	3,023.6	5.8	5.5
1965	....	117.8	136.7	861.3	....	....	....	....	3,173.8	3,228.6	3,217.3	6.4	6.8
1966	....	126.0	157.1	937.1	....	....	....	....	3,364.8	3,450.3	3,423.7	6.5	6.9
1967	....	128.9	168.5	1,008.9	....	....	....	....	3,467.6	3,545.1	3,510.1	2.5	2.7
1968	....	139.0	193.6	1,040.5	....	....	....	....	3,640.3	3,727.5	3,680.0	4.8	5.1
1969	....	145.7	204.6	1,038.0	....	....	....	....	3,753.7	3,844.1	3,792.0	3.1	3.1
1970	....	161.4	213.4	1,012.9	....	....	....	....	3,787.7	3,837.4	3,798.2	.2	−.2
1971	....	164.1	224.7	990.8	....	....	....	....	3,893.4	3,974.2	3,927.8	3.4	3.6
1972	....	176.5	250.0	983.5	....	....	....	....	4,098.6	4,192.8	4,136.2	5.3	5.5
1973	....	209.7	261.6	980.0	....	....	....	....	4,315.9	4,399.1	4,383.6	5.8	4.9
1974	....	226.3	255.7	1,004.7	....	....	....	....	4,305.5	4,343.8	4,367.5	−.5	−1.3
1975	....	224.9	227.3	1,027.4	....	....	....	....	4,352.5	4,297.0	4,348.4	−.2	−1.1
1976	....	234.7	271.7	1,031.9	....	....	....	....	4,522.3	4,575.0	4,585.3	5.3	6.5
1977	....	240.3	301.4	1,043.3	....	....	....	....	4,721.6	4,818.5	4,800.3	4.6	5.3
1978	....	265.7	327.6	1,074.0	....	....	....	....	4,981.6	5,081.5	5,064.4	5.6	5.5
1979	....	292.0	333.0	1,094.1	....	....	....	....	5,161.2	5,206.8	5,240.1	3.2	2.5
1980	....	323.5	310.9	1,115.4	....	....	....	....	5,196.7	5,108.9	5,227.6	−.2	−1.9
1981	....	327.4	319.1	1,125.6	....	....	....	....	5,265.1	5,244.7	5,349.7	2.5	2.7
1982	....	302.4	315.0	1,145.4	....	....	....	....	5,233.4	5,175.1	5,249.7	−1.9	−1.3
1983	....	294.6	354.8	1,187.3	....	....	....	....	5,454.0	5,477.6	5,482.5	4.5	5.8
1984	....	318.7	441.1	1,227.0	....	....	....	....	5,739.2	5,951.6	5,869.3	7.2	8.7
1985	....	328.3	469.8	1,312.5	....	....	....	....	6,042.1	6,215.8	6,093.4	4.1	4.4
1986	....	353.7	510.0	1,392.5	....	....	....	....	6,271.8	6,443.6	6,290.6	3.5	3.7
1987	....	391.8	540.2	1,426.7	....	....	....	....	6,457.2	6,644.1	6,500.9	3.4	3.1
1988	....	454.6	561.4	1,445.1	....	....	....	....	6,734.5	6,857.9	6,775.2	4.1	3.2
1989	....	506.8	586.0	1,482.5	....	....	....	....	6,962.2	7,060.8	7,015.4	3.5	3.0
1990	−54.7	552.5	607.1	1,530.0	659.1	479.4	178.6	868.4	7,108.5	7,161.6	7,155.2	1.9	1.4
1991	−14.6	589.1	603.7	1,547.2	658.0	474.2	182.8	886.8	7,115.0	7,101.2	7,136.8	−.2	−.8
1992	−15.9	629.7	645.6	1,555.3	646.6	450.7	195.4	906.5	7,331.1	7,338.9	7,371.8	3.3	3.3
1993	−52.1	650.0	702.1	1,541.1	619.6	425.3	194.1	919.5	7,522.3	7,577.2	7,568.6	2.7	3.2
1994	−79.4	706.5	785.9	1,541.3	596.4	404.6	191.7	943.3	7,777.8	7,911.3	7,864.2	4.0	4.4
1995	−71.0	778.2	849.1	1,549.7	580.3	389.2	191.0	968.3	8,010.2	8,098.4	8,069.8	2.5	2.4
1996	−79.6	843.4	923.0	1,564.9	573.5	383.8	189.6	990.5	8,306.5	8,405.7	8,365.3	3.7	3.8
1997	−104.6	943.7	1,048.3	1,594.0	567.6	373.0	194.5	1,025.9	8,636.6	8,807.6	8,737.5	4.5	4.8
1998	−203.7	966.5	1,170.3	1,624.4	561.2	365.3¹	195.9	1,063.0	8,997.6	9,272.5	9,088.7	4.2	5.3
1999	−296.2	1,008.2	1,304.4	1,686.9	573.7	372.2	201.5	1,113.2	9,404.0	9,767.7	9,504.7	4.5	5.3
2000	−379.5	1,096.3	1,475.8	1,721.6	578.8	370.3	208.5	1,142.8	9,760.5	10,196.4	9,855.9	3.7	4.4
2001	−399.1	1,036.7	1,435.8	1,780.3	601.4	384.9	216.5	1,179.0	9,920.9	10,290.1	9,933.6	.8	.9
2002	−471.3	1,013.3	1,484.6	1,858.8	643.4	413.2	230.2	1,215.4	10,036.5	10,517.7	10,079.0	1.6	2.2
2003	−521.4	1,031.2	1,552.6	1,911.1	687.8	449.7	238.0	1,223.3	10,303.6	10,837.3	10,385.2	2.7	3.0
2004	−601.3	1,117.9	1,719.2	1,952.3	723.7	481.3	242.2	1,228.4	10,702.4	11,348.7	10,805.7	4.2	4.7
2005 ᴾ	−631.9	1,193.3	1,825.2	1,985.1	738.4	492.2	246.0	1,246.5	11,112.2	11,754.1	....	3.5	3.6
2002: I	−441.3	992.8	1,434.0	1,832.0	623.2	399.2	224.0	1,208.9	9,986.8	10,418.0	10,004.1	2.7	3.6
II	−458.9	1,018.0	1,476.9	1,853.4	641.7	410.2	231.5	1,211.8	10,028.4	10,488.5	10,048.6	2.2	2.7
III	−472.2	1,025.2	1,497.4	1,863.9	646.5	414.4	232.2	1,217.5	10,063.5	10,560.4	10,119.7	2.4	2.8
IV	−513.0	1,017.2	1,530.2	1,885.8	662.3	428.9	233.4	1,223.6	10,067.3	10,604.1	10,143.8	.2	1.7
2003: I	−510.7	1,009.7	1,520.4	1,884.4	662.8	425.0	237.9	1,221.6	10,114.7	10,644.7	10,182.0	1.7	1.5
II	−528.4	1,004.5	1,532.9	1,917.5	696.8	460.1	236.4	1,220.7	10,228.2	10,753.8	10,294.1	3.7	4.2
III	−516.2	1,032.2	1,548.4	1,920.1	693.2	452.5	240.6	1,226.8	10,399.5	10,923.1	10,474.7	7.2	6.5
IV	−530.2	1,078.4	1,608.6	1,922.6	698.5	461.2	237.0	1,224.1	10,471.8	11,027.6	10,590.0	3.6	3.9
2004: I	−563.0	1,091.8	1,654.8	1,938.4	716.5	476.4	239.9	1,221.8	10,568.9	11,168.8	10,689.5	4.3	5.2
II	−601.7	1,110.2	1,711.9	1,949.5	722.2	477.4	244.6	1,227.1	10,637.4	11,297.4	10,747.7	3.5	4.7
III	−606.5	1,125.0	1,731.5	1,958.4	728.6	487.7	240.6	1,229.6	10,757.1	11,407.0	10,854.1	4.0	3.9
IV	−634.1	1,144.5	1,778.6	1,962.8	727.6	483.7	243.6	1,235.0	10,846.0	11,522.0	10,931.8	3.3	4.1
2005: I	−645.4	1,165.3	1,810.7	1,971.9	731.8	487.3	244.3	1,239.8	10,940.3	11,635.4	11,036.3	3.8	4.0
II	−614.2	1,195.4	1,809.6	1,984.1	736.1	491.7	244.2	1,247.8	11,089.2	11,694.8	11,122.5	3.3	2.1
III	−617.5	1,202.7	1,820.2	1,998.1	749.5	503.6	245.6	1,248.5	11,214.4	11,811.2	11,243.2	4.1	4.0
IV ᴾ	−650.3	1,209.8	1,860.1	1,986.2	736.1	486.2	249.7	1,249.8	11,205.0	11,875.1	....	1.1	2.2

[1] Gross domestic product (GDP) less exports of goods and services plus imports of goods and services.
[2] GDP plus net income receipts from rest of the world.

Source: Department of Commerce, Bureau of Economic Analysis.

TABLE B–3.—*Quantity and price indexes for gross domestic product, and percent changes, 1959–2005*

[Quarterly data are seasonally adjusted]

Year or quarter	Gross domestic product (GDP)						
	Index numbers, 2000=100			Percent change from preceding period [1]			
	Real GDP (chain-type quantity index)	GDP chain-type price index	GDP implicit price deflator	GDP (current dollars)	Real GDP (chain-type quantity index)	GDP chain-type price index	GDP implicit price deflator
1959	24.868	20.754	20.751	8.4	7.1	1.2	1.2
1960	25.484	21.044	21.041	3.9	2.5	1.4	1.4
1961	26.077	21.281	21.278	3.5	2.3	1.1	1.1
1962	27.658	21.572	21.569	7.5	6.1	1.4	1.4
1963	28.868	21.801	21.798	5.5	4.4	1.1	1.1
1964	30.545	22.134	22.131	7.4	5.8	1.5	1.5
1965	32.506	22.538	22.535	8.4	6.4	1.8	1.8
1966	34.625	23.180	23.176	9.5	6.5	2.8	2.8
1967	35.496	23.897	23.893	5.7	2.5	3.1	3.1
1968	37.208	24.916	24.913	9.3	4.8	4.3	4.3
1969	38.356	26.153	26.149	8.2	3.1	5.0	5.0
1970	38.422	27.538	27.534	5.5	.2	5.3	5.3
1971	39.713	28.916	28.911	8.5	3.4	5.0	5.0
1972	41.815	30.171	30.166	9.9	5.3	4.3	4.3
1973	44.224	31.854	31.849	11.7	5.8	5.6	5.6
1974	44.001	34.721	34.725	8.5	−.5	9.0	9.0
1975	43.916	38.007	38.002	9.2	−.2	9.5	9.4
1976	46.256	40.202	40.196	11.4	5.3	5.8	5.8
1977	48.391	42.758	42.752	11.3	4.6	6.4	6.4
1978	51.085	45.762	45.757	13.0	5.6	7.0	7.0
1979	52.699	49.553	49.548	11.7	3.2	8.3	8.3
1980	52.579	54.062	54.043	8.8	−.2	9.1	9.1
1981	53.904	59.128	59.119	12.2	2.5	9.4	9.4
1982	52.860	62.738	62.726	4.0	−1.9	6.1	6.1
1983	55.249	65.214	65.207	8.7	4.5	3.9	4.0
1984	59.220	67.664	67.655	11.2	7.2	3.8	3.8
1985	61.666	69.724	69.713	7.3	4.1	3.0	3.0
1986	63.804	71.269	71.250	5.7	3.5	2.2	2.2
1987	65.958	73.204	73.196	6.2	3.4	2.7	2.7
1988	68.684	75.706	75.694	7.7	4.1	3.4	3.4
1989	71.116	78.569	78.556	7.5	3.5	3.8	3.8
1990	72.451	81.614	81.590	5.8	1.9	3.9	3.9
1991	72.329	84.457	84.444	3.3	−.2	3.5	3.5
1992	74.734	86.402	86.385	5.7	3.3	2.3	2.3
1993	76.731	88.390	88.381	5.0	2.7	2.3	2.3
1994	79.816	90.265	90.259	6.2	4.0	2.1	2.1
1995	81.814	92.115	92.106	4.6	2.5	2.0	2.0
1996	84.842	93.859	93.852	5.7	3.7	1.9	1.9
1997	88.658	95.415	95.414	6.2	4.5	1.7	1.7
1998	92.359	96.475	96.472	5.3	4.2	1.1	1.1
1999	96.469	97.868	97.868	6.0	4.5	1.4	1.4
2000	100.000	100.000	100.000	5.9	3.7	2.2	2.2
2001	100.751	102.402	102.399	3.2	.8	2.4	2.4
2002	102.362	104.193	104.187	3.4	1.6	1.7	1.7
2003	105.130	106.310	106.305	4.8	2.7	2.0	2.0
2004	109.562	109.102	109.099	7.0	4.2	2.6	2.6
2005 ᵖ	113.386	112.144	112.113	6.4	3.5	2.8	2.8
2002: I	101.633	103.553	103.568	4.3	2.7	1.7	1.5
II	102.186	103.944	103.938	3.7	2.2	1.5	1.4
III	102.788	104.347	104.328	3.9	2.4	1.6	1.5
IV	102.840	104.926	104.907	2.4	.2	2.2	2.2
2003: I	103.276	105.724	105.705	4.8	1.7	3.1	3.1
II	104.211	106.019	106.004	4.8	3.7	1.1	1.1
III	106.050	106.500	106.498	9.3	7.2	1.8	1.9
IV	106.984	106.996	106.983	5.5	3.6	1.9	1.8
2004: I	108.104	107.951	107.958	8.1	4.3	3.6	3.7
II	109.037	108.976	108.987	7.5	3.5	3.9	3.9
III	110.104	109.371	109.343	5.3	4.0	1.5	1.3
IV	111.003	110.111	110.077	6.1	3.3	2.7	2.7
2005: I	112.044	110.950	110.905	7.0	3.8	3.1	3.0
II	112.959	111.655	111.622	6.0	3.3	2.6	2.6
III	114.112	112.567	112.527	7.6	4.1	3.3	3.3
IV ᵖ	114.429	113.407	113.369	4.2	1.1	3.0	3.0

[1] Quarterly percent changes are at annual rates.

Source: Department of Commerce, Bureau of Economic Analysis.

TABLE B–4.—*Percent changes in real gross domestic product, 1959–2005*

[Percent change from preceding period; quarterly data at seasonally adjusted annual rates]

Year or quarter	Gross domestic product	Personal consumption expenditures				Gross private domestic investment				Exports and imports of goods and services		Government consumption expenditures and gross investment		
						Nonresidential fixed								
		Total	Durable goods	Nondurable goods	Services	Total	Structures	Equipment and software	Residential fixed	Exports	Imports	Total	Federal	State and local
1959	7.1	5.6	12.1	4.1	5.3	8.0	2.4	11.9	25.4	10.3	10.5	3.4	3.1	3.8
1960	2.5	2.8	2.0	1.5	4.5	5.7	7.9	4.2	-7.1	17.4	1.3	.2	-2.7	4.4
1961	2.3	2.1	-3.8	1.8	4.2	-.6	1.4	-1.9	.3	.5	-.7	5.0	4.2	6.2
1962	6.1	5.0	11.7	3.1	5.0	8.7	4.5	11.6	9.6	5.1	11.3	6.2	8.5	3.1
1963	4.4	4.1	9.7	2.1	4.6	5.6	1.1	8.4	11.8	7.1	2.7	2.6	.1	6.0
1964	5.8	6.0	9.3	4.9	6.1	11.9	10.4	12.8	5.8	11.8	5.3	2.2	-1.3	6.8
1965	6.4	6.3	12.7	5.3	5.3	17.4	15.9	18.3	-2.9	2.8	10.6	3.0	.0	6.7
1966	6.5	5.7	8.4	5.5	5.0	12.5	6.8	16.0	-8.9	6.9	14.9	8.8	11.0	6.3
1967	2.5	3.0	1.6	1.6	4.9	-1.4	-2.5	-.7	-3.1	2.3	7.3	7.7	9.9	5.0
1968	4.8	5.7	11.0	4.6	5.2	4.5	1.5	6.2	13.6	7.9	14.9	3.1	.8	5.9
1969	3.1	3.7	3.5	2.7	4.8	7.6	5.4	8.8	3.0	4.8	5.7	-.2	-3.4	3.4
1970	.2	2.3	-3.2	2.4	4.0	-.5	.3	-1.0	-6.0	10.7	4.3	-2.4	-7.4	2.8
1971	3.4	3.8	10.0	1.8	3.9	.0	-1.6	1.0	27.4	1.7	5.3	-2.2	-7.7	3.1
1972	5.3	6.1	12.7	4.4	5.7	9.2	3.1	12.9	17.8	7.5	11.3	-.7	-4.1	2.2
1973	5.8	4.9	10.3	3.3	4.7	14.6	8.2	18.3	-.6	18.9	4.6	-.4	-4.2	2.8
1974	-.5	-.8	-6.9	-2.0	2.3	.8	-2.1	2.6	-20.6	7.9	-2.3	2.5	.9	3.8
1975	-.2	2.3	.0	1.5	3.7	-9.9	-10.5	-9.5	-13.0	-.6	-11.1	2.3	.3	3.7
1976	5.3	5.5	12.8	4.9	4.1	4.9	2.4	6.2	23.6	4.4	19.5	.4	.0	.7
1977	4.6	4.2	9.3	2.4	4.3	11.3	4.1	15.1	21.5	2.4	10.9	1.1	2.1	.4
1978	5.6	4.4	5.3	3.7	4.7	15.0	14.4	15.2	6.3	10.5	8.7	2.9	2.5	3.3
1979	3.2	2.4	-.3	2.7	3.1	10.1	12.7	8.7	-3.7	9.9	1.7	1.9	2.4	1.5
1980	-.2	-.3	-7.8	-.2	1.8	-.3	5.8	-3.6	-21.2	10.8	-6.6	2.0	4.7	-.1
1981	2.5	1.4	1.2	1.2	1.7	5.7	8.0	4.3	-8.0	1.2	2.6	.9	4.8	-2.0
1982	-1.9	1.4	-.1	1.0	2.1	-3.8	-1.7	-5.2	-18.2	-7.6	-1.3	1.8	3.9	.1
1983	4.5	5.7	14.6	3.3	5.5	-1.3	-10.8	5.4	41.4	-2.6	12.6	3.7	6.6	1.2
1984	7.2	5.3	14.6	4.0	4.1	17.7	14.0	19.8	14.8	8.2	24.3	3.3	3.1	3.6
1985	4.1	5.2	10.1	2.7	5.6	6.6	7.1	6.4	1.6	3.0	6.5	7.0	7.8	6.2
1986	3.5	4.1	9.7	3.6	2.9	-2.9	-11.0	1.9	12.3	7.7	8.6	6.1	5.7	6.4
1987	3.4	3.3	1.7	2.4	4.3	-.1	-2.9	1.4	2.0	10.8	5.9	2.5	3.6	1.5
1988	4.1	4.1	6.0	3.3	4.0	5.2	.6	7.5	-1.0	16.0	3.9	1.3	-1.6	3.7
1989	3.5	2.8	2.2	2.8	3.0	5.6	2.0	7.3	-3.0	11.5	4.4	2.6	1.5	3.4
1990	1.9	2.0	-.3	1.6	2.9	.5	1.5	.0	-8.6	9.0	3.6	3.2	2.0	4.1
1991	-.2	.2	-5.6	-.2	1.7	-5.4	-11.1	-2.6	-9.6	6.6	-.6	1.1	-.2	2.1
1992	3.3	3.3	5.9	2.0	3.5	3.2	-6.0	7.3	13.8	6.9	7.0	.5	-1.7	2.2
1993	2.7	3.3	7.8	2.7	2.8	8.7	-.7	12.5	8.2	3.2	8.8	-.9	-4.2	1.4
1994	4.0	3.7	8.4	3.5	2.9	9.2	1.8	11.9	9.6	8.7	11.9	.0	-3.7	2.6
1995	2.5	2.7	4.4	2.2	2.6	10.5	6.4	12.0	-3.2	10.1	8.0	.5	-2.7	2.6
1996	3.7	3.4	7.8	2.6	2.9	9.3	5.6	10.6	8.0	8.4	8.7	1.0	-1.2	2.3
1997	4.5	3.8	8.6	2.7	3.3	12.1	7.3	13.8	1.9	11.9	13.6	1.9	-1.0	3.6
1998	4.2	5.0	11.3	4.0	4.2	11.1	5.1	13.3	7.6	2.4	11.6	1.9	-1.1	3.6
1999	4.5	5.1	11.7	4.6	4.0	9.2	-.4	12.7	6.0	4.3	11.5	3.9	2.2	4.7
2000	3.7	4.7	7.3	3.8	4.5	8.7	6.8	9.4	.8	8.7	13.1	2.1	.9	2.7
2001	.8	2.5	4.3	2.0	2.4	-4.2	-2.3	-4.9	.4	-5.4	-2.7	3.4	3.9	3.2
2002	1.6	2.7	7.1	2.5	1.9	-9.2	-17.1	-6.2	4.8	-2.3	3.4	4.4	7.0	3.1
2003	2.7	2.9	6.6	3.2	2.0	1.3	-4.2	3.2	8.4	1.8	4.6	2.8	6.9	.6
2004	4.2	3.9	6.0	4.7	3.0	9.4	2.2	11.9	10.3	8.4	10.7	2.2	5.2	.4
2005 ᴾ	3.5	3.6	4.4	4.4	2.9	8.5	1.9	10.8	7.2	6.7	6.2	1.7	2.0	1.5
2002: I	2.7	1.4	-4.2	3.3	1.8	-12.8	-19.0	-10.4	10.4	5.2	11.7	4.3	5.9	3.5
II	2.2	2.4	3.6	1.3	2.6	-6.1	-19.0	-.9	9.5	10.6	12.5	4.8	12.5	1.0
III	2.4	2.3	11.5	.3	1.3	-2.0	-15.5	3.3	2.0	2.9	5.7	2.3	3.0	1.9
IV	.2	1.4	-5.2	3.6	1.8	-5.0	-5.3	-4.9	6.4	-3.1	9.0	4.8	10.2	2.0
2003: I	1.7	2.5	3.6	3.2	1.9	-1.1	-8.4	1.6	4.7	-2.9	-2.5	-.3	.3	-.6
II	3.7	3.6	15.1	1.9	2.3	8.4	13.3	6.7	9.6	-2.1	3.3	7.2	22.1	-.3
III	7.2	5.8	19.8	8.3	2.0	11.2	-.1	15.4	21.9	11.5	4.1	.5	-2.0	2.0
IV	3.6	3.1	-.3	3.1	3.8	4.4	1.3	5.5	11.5	19.1	16.5	.5	3.1	-.9
2004: I	4.3	4.7	4.4	6.6	3.8	7.9	-3.5	12.0	5.2	5.0	12.0	3.3	10.7	-.7
II	3.5	1.9	.4	2.6	1.8	13.5	8.8	15.2	17.8	6.9	14.5	2.3	3.2	1.8
III	4.0	4.4	10.8	3.9	3.4	11.8	1.4	15.5	2.6	5.5	4.7	1.8	3.6	.8
IV	3.3	4.3	5.5	5.5	3.6	10.4	4.7	12.4	1.6	7.1	11.3	.9	-.6	1.8
2005: I	3.8	3.5	2.6	5.3	2.8	5.7	-2.0	8.3	9.5	7.5	7.4	1.9	2.4	1.6
II	3.3	3.4	7.9	3.6	2.3	8.8	2.7	10.9	10.8	10.7	-.3	2.5	2.4	2.6
III	4.1	4.1	9.3	3.5	3.3	8.5	2.2	10.6	7.3	2.5	2.4	2.9	7.4	.2
IV ᴾ	1.1	1.1	-17.5	5.1	3.2	2.8	.7	3.5	3.5	2.4	9.1	-2.4	-7.0	.4

Note.—Percent changes based on unrounded data.

Source: Department of Commerce, Bureau of Economic Analysis.

[Percentage points, except as noted; quarterly data at seasonally adjusted annual rates]

Year or quarter	Gross domestic product (percent change)	Personal consumption expenditures				Gross private domestic investment							Change in private inventories
		Total	Durable goods	Non-durable goods	Services	Total	Fixed investment					Residential	
							Total	Nonresidential					
								Total	Structures	Equipment and software			
1959	7.1	3.55	0.97	1.25	1.33	2.80	1.94	0.73	0.09	0.64	1.21	0.86
1960	2.5	1.73	.17	.44	1.12	.00	.13	.52	.28	.24	−.39	−.13
1961	2.3	1.30	−.31	.53	1.08	−.10	−.04	−.06	.05	−.11	.01	−.05
1962	6.1	3.11	.89	.90	1.31	1.81	1.24	.78	.16	.61	.46	.57
1963	4.4	2.56	.77	.59	1.20	1.00	1.08	.50	.04	.46	.58	−.08
1964	5.8	3.71	.77	1.33	1.61	1.25	1.37	1.07	.36	.71	.30	−.13
1965	6.4	3.91	1.07	1.43	1.42	2.16	1.50	1.65	.57	1.07	−.15	.66
1966	6.5	3.50	.73	1.46	1.31	1.44	.87	1.29	.27	1.02	−.43	.58
1967	2.5	1.81	.13	.42	1.26	−.76	−.28	−.15	−.10	−.05	−.13	−.49
1968	4.8	3.50	.93	1.19	1.38	.90	1.00	.46	.06	.41	.53	−.10
1969	3.1	2.27	.31	.69	1.28	.90	.90	.78	.20	.58	.13	.00
1970	.2	1.42	−.28	.61	1.08	−1.04	−.31	−.06	.01	−.07	−.26	−.73
1971	3.4	2.38	.81	.47	1.09	1.67	1.10	.00	−.06	.07	1.10	.58
1972	5.3	3.80	1.07	1.11	1.61	1.87	1.81	.92	.12	.81	.89	.06
1973	5.8	3.05	.90	.82	1.33	1.96	1.46	1.50	.31	1.19	−.04	.50
1974	−.5	−.47	−.61	−.51	.65	−1.30	−1.04	.09	−.09	.18	−1.13	−.27
1975	−.2	1.42	.00	.37	1.05	−2.98	−1.71	−1.14	−.43	−.70	−.57	−1.27
1976	5.3	3.48	1.04	1.24	1.19	2.84	1.42	.52	.09	.43	.90	1.41
1977	4.6	2.68	.80	.60	1.27	2.43	2.18	1.19	.15	1.04	.99	.25
1978	5.6	2.76	.47	.91	1.38	2.16	2.04	1.69	.54	1.15	.35	.12
1979	3.2	1.52	−.03	.65	.90	.61	1.02	1.23	.52	.71	−.21	−.41
1980	−.2	−.17	−.65	−.04	.52	−2.12	−1.21	−.04	.27	−.30	−1.17	−.91
1981	2.5	.90	.09	.29	.51	1.59	.39	.74	.40	.34	−.35	1.20
1982	−1.9	.87	.00	.23	.65	−2.55	−1.22	−.51	−.09	−.42	−.71	−1.34
1983	4.5	3.65	1.07	.80	1.79	1.45	1.17	−.16	−.57	.41	1.33	.29
1984	7.2	3.44	1.15	.93	1.36	4.63	2.68	2.05	.60	1.44	.64	1.95
1985	4.1	3.31	.83	.61	1.87	−.17	.89	.82	.32	.50	.07	−1.06
1986	3.5	2.62	.83	.78	1.01	−.12	.20	−.36	−.50	.15	.55	−.32
1987	3.4	2.17	.16	.52	1.50	.51	.09	−.01	−.11	.10	.10	.42
1988	4.1	2.66	.53	.70	1.43	.39	.52	.57	.02	.55	−.05	−.14
1989	3.5	1.86	.19	.59	1.07	.64	.47	.61	.07	.54	−.14	.17
1990	1.9	1.34	−.02	.33	1.03	−.53	−.32	.05	.05	.00	−.37	−.21
1991	−.2	.11	−.46	−.05	.62	−1.20	−.94	−.57	−.39	−.18	−.37	−.26
1992	3.3	2.18	.44	.43	1.31	1.07	.79	.32	−.18	.50	.47	.29
1993	2.7	2.23	.59	.56	1.09	1.21	1.14	.83	−.02	.85	.31	.07
1994	4.0	2.52	.66	.71	1.14	1.93	1.30	.91	.05	.87	.39	.63
1995	2.5	1.81	.36	.44	1.01	.48	.94	1.08	.17	.91	−.14	−.46
1996	3.7	2.31	.64	.51	1.15	1.35	1.34	1.01	.16	.85	.33	.02
1997	4.5	2.54	.70	.53	1.31	1.95	1.42	1.33	.21	1.12	.08	.54
1998	4.2	3.36	.93	.78	1.66	1.63	1.60	1.28	.16	1.12	.32	.03
1999	4.5	3.44	.99	.89	1.56	1.33	1.36	1.09	−.01	1.11	.27	−.03
2000	3.7	3.17	.63	.74	1.80	.99	1.09	1.06	.21	.85	.03	−.10
2001	.8	1.74	.37	.40	.97	−1.39	−.50	−.52	−.07	−.44	.02	−.88
2002	1.6	1.90	.61	.50	.79	−.41	−.84	−1.06	−.55	−.51	.22	.43
2003	2.7	2.05	.57	.63	.85	.58	.54	.13	−.11	.24	.41	.05
2004	4.2	2.71	.51	.94	1.27	1.82	1.47	.92	.06	.86	.55	.35
2005 ᴾ	3.5	2.49	.37	.90	1.22	.96	1.28	.87	.05	.82	.42	−.32
2002: I	2.7	1.01	−.39	.65	.75	1.92	−1.04	−1.50	−.60	−.90	.46	2.95
II	2.2	1.64	.31	.26	1.07	.30	−.23	−.66	−.58	−.09	.43	.53
III	2.4	1.57	.98	.06	.54	.87	−.12	−.21	−.44	.23	.09	.98
IV	.2	.97	−.47	.70	.74	−.14	−.21	−.52	−.14	−.38	.30	.08
2003: I	1.7	1.70	.31	.63	.76	−.03	.13	−.10	−.22	.12	.23	−.16
II	3.7	2.55	1.23	.37	.94	.42	1.26	.79	.32	.47	.47	−.84
III	7.2	4.13	1.64	1.65	.84	2.53	2.15	1.08	.00	1.09	1.07	.38
IV	3.6	2.15	−.03	.61	1.57	1.78	1.03	.43	.03	.40	.59	.75
2004: I	4.3	3.27	.38	1.31	1.58	1.52	1.04	.76	−.09	.85	.28	.48
II	3.5	1.33	.03	.53	.77	3.10	2.22	1.29	.22	1.07	.93	.87
III	4.0	3.05	.88	.78	1.39	.75	1.31	1.15	.04	1.12	.15	−.56
IV	3.3	3.01	.45	1.09	1.47	1.11	1.13	1.04	.12	.92	.09	−.03
2005: I	3.8	2.44	.22	1.07	1.15	1.42	1.12	.58	−.05	.64	.54	.29
II	3.3	2.35	.64	.74	.97	−.63	1.51	.90	.07	.83	.62	−2.14
III	4.1	2.85	.76	.73	1.36	.87	1.31	.88	.06	.82	.43	−.43
IV ᴾ	1.1	.79	−1.56	1.04	1.32	1.95	.51	.30	.02	.28	.21	1.45

See next page for continuation of table.

TABLE B–5.—*Contributions to percent change in real gross domestic product, 1959–2005*—Continued

[Percentage points, except as noted; quarterly data at seasonally adjusted annual rates]

| Year or quarter | Net exports of goods and services | | | | | | | Government consumption expenditures and gross investment | | | | |
| | Net exports | Exports | | | Imports | | | Total | Federal | | | State and local |
		Total	Goods	Services	Total	Goods	Services		Total	National defense	Non-defense	
1959	0.00	0.45	−0.02	0.48	−0.45	−0.48	0.03	0.76	0.42	−0.23	0.65	0.34
1960	.72	.78	.76	.02	−.06	.05	−.11	.03	−.35	−.17	−.18	.39
1961	.06	.03	.02	.01	.03	.00	.02	1.07	.51	.45	.06	.56
1962	−.21	.25	.17	.08	−.47	−.40	−.07	1.36	1.07	.63	.44	.29
1963	.24	.35	.29	.06	−.12	−.12	.00	.58	.01	−.25	.26	.57
1964	.36	.59	.52	.07	−.23	−.19	−.04	.49	−.17	−.40	.23	.65
1965	−.30	.15	.02	.13	−.45	−.41	−.04	.65	.00	−.19	.19	.66
1966	−.29	.36	.27	.09	−.65	−.49	−.16	1.87	1.24	1.21	.03	.63
1967	−.22	.12	.02	.10	−.34	−.17	−.16	1.68	1.17	1.19	−.02	.51
1968	−.30	.41	.30	.10	−.70	−.68	−.03	.73	.10	.16	−.06	.63
1969	−.04	.25	.20	.05	−.29	−.20	−.09	−.06	−.42	−.49	.06	.37
1970	.34	.56	.44	.12	−.22	−.15	−.07	−.55	−.86	−.83	−.03	.31
1971	−.19	.10	−.02	.11	−.29	−.33	.04	−.50	−.85	−.97	.12	.36
1972	−.21	.42	.43	−.01	−.63	−.57	−.06	−.16	−.42	−.61	.18	.26
1973	.82	1.12	1.01	.11	−.29	−.34	.05	−.08	−.41	−.39	−.02	.33
1974	.75	.58	.46	.12	.18	.17	.00	.52	.08	−.05	.13	.44
1975	.89	−.05	−.16	.10	.94	.87	.07	.48	.03	−.06	.09	.45
1976	−1.08	.37	.31	.05	−1.45	−1.35	−.10	.10	.00	−.02	.03	.09
1977	−.72	.20	.08	.11	−.92	−.84	−.07	.23	.19	.07	.12	.04
1978	.05	.82	.68	.15	−.78	−.67	−.11	.60	.22	.05	.16	.38
1979	.66	.82	.77	.06	−.16	−.14	−.02	.37	.20	.17	.03	.17
1980	1.68	.97	.86	.11	.71	.67	.04	.38	.39	.25	.14	−.01
1981	−.15	.12	−.09	.21	−.27	−.18	−.09	.19	.42	.38	.04	−.23
1982	−.60	−.73	−.67	−.06	.12	.20	−.08	.35	.35	.48	−.13	.01
1983	−1.35	−.22	−.19	−.03	−1.13	−1.00	−.13	.77	.63	.50	.13	.13
1984	−1.58	.63	.46	.17	−2.21	−1.83	−.39	.70	.30	.35	−.05	.40
1985	−.42	.23	.20	.02	−.65	−.52	−.13	1.41	.74	.60	.14	.67
1986	−.30	.54	.26	.28	−.84	−.82	−.02	1.27	.55	.47	.08	.71
1987	.17	.78	.56	.21	−.61	−.39	−.22	.52	.36	.35	.01	.17
1988	.82	1.24	1.04	.20	−.42	−.36	−.07	.27	−.15	−.03	−.12	.42
1989	.52	.99	.75	.24	−.47	−.38	−.10	.52	.14	−.03	.17	.39
1990	.43	.81	.56	.26	−.39	−.26	−.13	.64	.18	.00	.18	.46
1991	.69	.63	.46	.16	.06	.01	.05	.23	−.02	−.07	.06	.24
1992	−.04	.68	.52	.16	−.72	−.77	.05	.11	−.15	−.32	.17	.26
1993	−.59	.32	.23	.09	−.91	−.85	−.06	−.18	−.35	−.33	−.02	.17
1994	−.43	.85	.67	.18	−1.29	−1.18	−.11	.00	−.30	−.27	−.03	.30
1995	.11	1.04	.85	.19	−.93	−.87	−.06	.10	−.20	−.19	−.01	.30
1996	−.14	.91	.68	.22	−1.05	−.94	−.11	.18	−.08	−.07	−.02	.26
1997	−.34	1.30	1.11	.19	−1.64	−1.45	−.19	.34	−.07	−.13	.06	.41
1998	−1.16	.27	.18	.09	−1.43	−1.20	−.23	.34	−.07	−.09	.02	.41
1999	−.99	.47	.29	.18	−1.46	−1.31	−.15	.67	.14	.08	.06	.54
2000	−.86	.93	.84	.09	−1.79	−1.55	−.25	.36	.05	−.02	.07	.31
2001	−.20	−.60	−.48	−.12	.40	.39	.01	.60	.23	.15	.08	.37
2002	−.69	−.23	−.28	.06	−.46	−.41	−.05	.80	.43	.29	.14	.37
2003	−.46	.17	.12	.05	−.63	−.56	−.07	.53	.45	.37	.08	.08
2004	−.73	.80	.59	.22	−1.53	−1.30	−.23	.41	.36	.32	.04	.05
2005 *P*	−.28	.68	.49	.18	−.96	−.86	−.09	.32	.14	.11	.04	.18
2002: I	−.97	.47	−.11	.59	−1.44	−.95	−.48	.79	.36	.14	.22	.43
II	−.62	.96	.88	.08	−1.58	−1.65	.07	.88	.76	.45	.31	.12
III	−.49	.27	.14	.13	−.76	−.72	−.04	.43	.20	.17	.03	.23
IV	−1.52	−.31	−.64	.33	−1.21	−.90	−.31	.89	.64	.59	.05	.25
2003: I	.08	−.29	.09	−.38	.37	.32	.05	−.05	.03	−.15	.18	−.08
II	−.66	−.20	.00	−.20	−.46	−.71	.26	1.37	1.40	1.46	−.06	−.04
III	.48	1.04	.58	.46	−.56	−1.00	−.46	.11	−.14	−.31	.17	.25
IV	−.47	1.69	1.05	.64	−2.16	−1.91	−.25	.10	.21	.35	−.14	−.11
2004: I	−1.16	.49	.50	−.01	−1.65	−1.41	−.23	.62	.71	.60	.11	−.09
II	−1.37	.67	.53	.14	−2.03	−1.71	−.32	.43	.22	.04	.19	.21
III	−.17	.53	.55	−.02	−.70	−.59	−.11	.35	.25	.41	−.16	.10
IV	−.98	.70	.25	.44	−1.68	−1.60	−.08	.17	−.04	−.16	.12	.21
2005: I	−.40	.74	.37	.37	−1.14	−1.05	−.10	.35	.17	.14	.03	.19
II	1.11	1.07	1.08	−.01	.04	.15	−.11	.47	.17	.17	−.01	.31
III	−.12	.26	.23	.03	−.38	−.46	.09	.54	.52	.46	.06	.03
IV *P*	−1.18	.25	.27	−.03	−1.42	−1.32	−.11	−.45	−.50	−.66	.15	.05

Source: Department of Commerce, Bureau of Economic Analysis.

TABLE B–6.—*Chain-type quantity indexes for gross domestic product, 1959–2005*

[Index numbers, 2000=100; quarterly data seasonally adjusted]

Year or quarter	Gross domestic product	Personal consumption expenditures				Gross private domestic investment					
							Fixed investment				
								Nonresidential			
		Total	Durable goods	Non-durable goods	Services	Total	Total	Total	Structures	Equipment and software	Residential
1959	24.868	23.067	10.822	33.491	20.794	15.367	15.736	10.760	36.530	6.065	37.820
1960	25.484	23.702	11.041	33.994	21.720	15.362	15.870	11.371	39.433	6.322	35.129
1961	26.077	24.191	10.622	34.621	22.626	15.261	15.820	11.299	39.966	6.200	35.227
1962	27.658	25.389	11.865	35.710	23.747	17.197	17.248	12.284	41.775	6.917	38.604
1963	28.868	26.436	13.017	36.463	24.830	18.351	18.584	12.966	42.239	7.500	43.154
1964	30.545	28.020	14.222	38.248	26.345	19.863	20.378	14.504	46.626	8.457	45.662
1965	32.506	29.791	16.025	40.277	27.749	22.650	22.459	17.031	54.058	10.007	44.329
1966	34.625	31.484	17.377	42.487	29.129	24.644	23.745	19.160	57.751	11.609	40.362
1967	35.496	32.422	17.648	43.157	30.552	23.517	23.306	18.900	56.284	11.532	39.092
1968	37.208	34.284	19.594	45.126	32.148	24.887	24.935	19.746	57.102	12.250	44.421
1969	38.356	35.558	20.289	46.326	33.691	26.338	26.486	21.246	60.189	13.334	45.733
1970	38.422	36.381	19.631	47.436	35.038	24.608	25.931	21.134	60.364	13.201	42.998
1971	39.713	37.770	21.593	48.294	36.400	27.413	27.894	21.135	59.370	13.332	54.789
1972	41.815	40.082	24.336	50.422	38.469	30.658	31.246	23.072	61.201	15.052	64.526
1973	44.224	42.048	26.849	52.068	40.274	34.249	34.101	26.429	66.200	17.812	64.112
1974	44.001	41.729	25.001	51.020	41.216	31.729	31.971	26.653	64.785	18.268	50.877
1975	43.916	42.688	24.996	51.771	42.743	26.111	28.541	24.022	57.984	16.529	44.271
1976	46.256	45.041	28.187	54.301	44.475	31.387	31.356	25.200	59.390	17.562	54.698
1977	48.391	46.950	30.809	55.609	46.392	36.130	35.863	28.649	61.841	20.208	66.440
1978	51.085	49.012	32.435	57.687	48.558	40.486	40.205	32.243	70.769	23.284	70.623
1979	52.699	50.204	32.325	59.226	50.044	41.776	42.473	35.489	79.731	25.318	68.032
1980	52.579	50.065	29.788	59.137	50.921	37.182	39.708	35.388	84.350	24.407	53.636
1981	53.904	50.779	30.149	59.839	51.773	40.615	40.591	37.398	91.074	25.445	49.336
1982	52.860	51.493	30.128	60.409	52.865	34.918	37.737	35.981	89.528	24.122	40.378
1983	55.249	54.436	34.535	62.417	55.760	38.172	40.491	35.518	79.865	25.420	57.093
1984	59.220	57.325	39.577	64.898	58.026	49.420	47.331	41.788	91.016	30.462	65.566
1985	61.666	60.303	43.577	66.665	61.303	48.963	49.823	44.561	97.502	32.397	66.604
1986	63.804	62.749	47.785	69.060	63.111	48.629	50.403	43.287	86.817	33.011	74.776
1987	65.958	64.840	48.616	70.715	65.843	50.130	50.682	43.259	84.340	33.463	76.269
1988	68.684	67.468	51.549	73.016	68.506	51.309	52.352	45.520	84.885	35.987	75.496
1989	71.116	69.369	52.686	75.044	70.555	53.269	53.928	48.063	86.583	38.624	73.204
1990	72.451	70.782	52.532	76.209	72.583	51.574	52.803	48.302	87.867	38.636	66.887
1991	72.329	70.903	49.564	76.033	73.812	47.378	49.379	45.712	78.091	37.643	60.460
1992	74.734	73.224	52.470	77.553	76.379	51.223	52.312	47.179	73.423	40.387	68.825
1993	76.731	75.672	56.577	79.619	78.540	55.795	56.788	51.287	72.891	45.428	74.446
1994	79.816	78.504	61.321	82.369	80.854	63.359	62.079	55.999	74.180	50.846	81.621
1995	81.814	80.623	64.011	84.152	82.973	65.340	66.090	61.885	78.903	56.930	79.005
1996	84.842	83.382	69.025	86.300	85.420	71.123	72.018	67.661	83.354	62.981	85.331
1997	88.658	86.533	74.935	88.605	88.270	79.061	78.657	75.820	89.432	71.641	86.947
1998	92.359	90.896	83.432	92.154	92.011	87.821	86.657	84.232	94.019	81.137	93.597
1999	96.469	95.537	93.192	94.373	95.652	94.647	93.884	91.980	93.619	91.437	99.254
2000	100.000	100.000	100.000	100.000	100.000	100.000	100.000	100.000	100.000	100.000	100.000
2001	100.751	102.537	104.327	102.027	102.403	92.103	97.047	95.817	97.737	95.136	100.357
2002	102.362	105.340	111.752	104.614	104.366	89.724	91.997	86.969	81.029	89.265	105.149
2003	105.130	108.416	119.134	107.938	106.493	93.195	95.297	88.063	77.621	92.154	113.989
2004	109.562	112.601	126.245	113.000	109.725	104.286	104.534	96.314	79.314	103.126	125.714
2005 ᴾ	113.386	116.600	131.777	118.014	112.960	110.379	112.929	104.510	80.802	114.250	134.732
2002: I	101.633	104.494	109.858	104.085	103.579	88.835	92.405	88.489	86.299	89.335	102.707
II	102.186	105.106	110.840	104.426	104.247	89.255	92.076	87.111	81.879	89.130	105.066
III	102.788	105.695	113.908	104.507	104.585	90.517	91.914	86.687	78.500	89.855	105.582
IV	102.840	106.066	112.404	105.439	105.055	90.290	91.593	85.584	77.438	88.739	107.242
2003: I	103.276	106.719	113.407	106.282	105.539	90.194	91.779	85.353	75.763	89.097	108.474
II	104.211	107.678	117.456	106.775	106.131	90.798	93.732	87.082	78.173	90.549	110.998
III	106.050	109.219	122.891	108.934	106.652	94.533	97.023	89.423	78.146	93.512	116.631
IV	106.984	110.046	122.784	109.762	107.649	97.257	98.652	90.394	78.400	95.117	119.861
2004: I	108.104	111.307	124.119	111.540	108.657	99.632	100.323	92.126	77.704	97.851	121.251
II	109.037	111.829	124.231	112.267	109.156	104.469	103.905	95.095	79.361	101.364	126.441
III	110.104	113.030	127.463	113.337	110.059	105.644	106.027	97.790	79.635	105.087	127.267
IV	111.003	114.236	129.166	114.857	111.027	107.398	107.880	100.246	80.554	108.201	127.772
2005: I	112.044	115.217	129.999	116.351	111.789	109.645	109.722	101.633	80.145	110.376	130.695
II	112.959	116.176	132.499	117.392	112.440	108.615	112.252	103.806	80.680	113.274	134.100
III	114.112	117.338	135.492	118.413	113.353	110.023	114.443	105.935	81.123	116.170	136.484
IV ᴾ	114.429	117.670	129.119	119.900	114.260	113.234	115.300	106.665	81.259	117.180	137.648

See next page for continuation of table.

[Index numbers, 2000=100; quarterly data seasonally adjusted]

Year or quarter	Exports of goods and services			Imports of goods and services			Government consumption expenditures and gross investment				
								Federal			State and local
	Total	Goods	Services	Total	Goods	Services	Total	Total	National defense	Non-defense	
1959	7.043	6.198	9.641	6.908	5.403	15.462	41.489	68.666	89.447	33.305	26.999
1960	8.266	7.651	9.797	7.000	5.314	16.669	41.553	66.779	87.977	30.672	28.182
1961	8.309	7.689	9.857	6.953	5.307	16.385	43.639	69.564	91.851	31.599	29.918
1962	8.729	8.031	10.535	7.742	6.092	17.150	46.329	75.492	97.412	38.144	30.839
1963	9.353	8.662	11.070	7.951	6.339	17.137	47.522	75.540	95.085	42.217	32.696
1964	10.454	9.849	11.733	8.374	6.757	17.579	48.563	74.530	91.304	45.880	34.913
1965	10.747	9.901	12.926	9.265	7.714	18.096	50.028	74.508	89.403	48.995	37.252
1966	11.492	10.589	13.814	10.642	8.930	20.395	54.430	82.737	102.205	49.501	39.590
1967	11.757	10.638	14.905	11.417	9.400	22.887	58.604	90.960	115.571	49.059	41.589
1968	12.681	11.481	16.049	13.118	11.342	23.298	60.436	91.681	117.416	47.912	44.048
1969	13.294	12.082	16.646	13.866	11.963	24.767	60.290	88.525	111.604	49.186	45.534
1970	14.723	13.460	18.128	14.457	12.432	26.059	58.833	81.997	101.477	48.674	46.797
1971	14.973	13.408	19.527	15.229	13.474	25.317	57.553	75.686	89.980	50.961	48.232
1972	16.096	14.849	19.404	16.943	15.307	26.390	57.128	72.574	82.921	54.551	49.291
1973	19.131	18.259	20.775	17.729	16.388	25.500	56.926	69.519	78.322	54.213	50.694
1974	20.643	19.709	22.396	17.327	15.932	25.472	58.360	70.134	77.714	57.023	52.603
1975	20.512	19.252	23.773	15.402	13.924	24.367	59.675	70.360	76.977	58.965	54.536
1976	21.408	20.165	24.476	18.413	17.073	26.049	59.940	70.388	76.706	59.523	54.937
1977	21.923	20.429	26.055	20.426	19.153	27.347	60.598	71.880	77.597	62.089	55.137
1978	24.234	22.712	28.234	22.196	20.871	29.297	62.383	73.681	78.259	65.947	56.938
1979	26.637	25.396	29.103	22.565	21.229	29.700	63.549	75.465	80.648	66.640	57.775
1980	29.506	28.422	30.919	21.066	19.653	29.037	64.790	79.043	84.160	70.373	57.736
1981	29.868	28.114	34.211	21.620	20.058	30.711	65.381	82.818	89.486	71.310	56.577
1982	27.586	25.573	33.263	21.348	19.554	32.346	66.530	86.018	96.244	67.888	56.607
1983	26.875	24.838	32.710	24.041	22.210	34.958	68.964	91.726	103.158	71.398	57.268
1984	29.068	26.801	35.627	29.893	27.584	43.724	71.273	94.550	108.186	70.035	59.322
1985	29.951	27.790	36.051	31.833	29.310	47.050	76.240	101.957	117.355	74.169	63.003
1986	32.259	29.217	41.325	34.561	32.314	47.638	80.885	107.754	124.871	76.764	67.064
1987	35.742	32.456	45.502	36.602	33.812	53.205	82.873	111.674	130.779	76.984	68.041
1988	41.469	38.572	49.616	38.039	35.181	55.010	83.940	109.898	130.161	73.037	70.582
1989	46.233	43.172	54.723	39.706	36.686	57.678	86.110	111.594	129.518	79.075	72.994
1990	50.394	46.810	60.480	41.139	37.770	61.430	88.869	113.873	129.472	85.651	75.991
1991	53.736	50.042	64.082	40.905	37.741	59.849	89.872	113.679	128.050	87.700	77.600
1992	57.439	53.785	67.590	43.748	41.263	58.321	90.342	111.713	121.708	93.749	79.318
1993	59.291	55.534	69.726	47.516	45.423	60.026	89.513	107.056	114.860	93.087	80.459
1994	64.447	60.937	74.097	53.256	51.466	63.421	89.525	103.050	109.259	91.957	82.543
1995	70.982	68.070	78.793	57.539	56.104	65.492	90.015	100.254	105.093	91.613	84.728
1996	76.930	74.086	84.483	62.544	61.337	69.094	90.896	99.091	103.648	90.955	86.668
1997	86.082	84.717	89.509	71.037	70.172	75.600	92.588	98.066	100.733	93.320	89.770
1998	88.164	86.614	92.077	79.299	78.364	84.222	94.354	96.970	98.650	93.985	93.014
1999	91.969	89.907	97.207	88.391	88.078	90.038	97.987	99.122	100.515	96.646	97.409
2000	100.000	100.000	100.000	100.000	100.000	100.000	100.000	100.000	100.000	100.000	100.000
2001	94.565	93.871	96.302	97.291	96.833	99.706	103.412	103.908	103.936	103.859	103.162
2002	92.430	90.143	98.104	100.601	100.377	101.824	107.969	111.169	111.578	110.441	106.354
2003	94.064	91.763	99.776	105.205	105.288	104.921	111.009	118.839	121.447	114.159	107.042
2004	101.970	99.899	107.119	116.495	116.830	114.991	113.398	125.038	129.970	116.166	107.487
2005 P	108.850	106.963	113.569	123.676	124.643	119.070	115.305	127.575	132.915	117.976	109.071
2002: I	90.557	88.206	96.393	97.172	96.360	101.358	106.411	107.667	107.801	107.428	105.782
II	92.858	91.181	97.034	100.078	99.998	100.577	107.658	110.873	110.780	111.040	106.033
III	93.520	91.670	98.120	101.467	101.580	100.995	108.266	111.700	111.897	111.358	106.532
IV	92.784	89.517	100.870	103.688	103.552	104.367	109.539	114.438	115.835	111.938	107.067
2003: I	92.103	89.842	97.714	103.023	102.892	103.800	109.454	114.521	114.772	114.102	106.895
II	91.624	89.843	96.058	103.872	104.476	101.044	111.378	120.383	124.259	113.414	106.814
III	94.159	91.830	99.938	104.923	104.711	106.053	111.528	119.770	122.200	115.415	107.351
IV	98.373	95.538	105.396	109.003	109.073	108.787	111.675	120.680	124.558	113.704	107.109
2004: I	99.591	97.292	105.303	112.134	112.311	111.401	112.595	123.791	128.643	115.064	106.911
II	101.269	99.153	106.532	115.999	116.225	115.027	113.236	124.774	128.908	117.336	107.377
III	102.622	101.120	106.368	117.328	117.563	116.317	113.753	125.881	131.709	115.399	107.592
IV	104.398	102.031	110.275	120.518	121.221	117.217	114.008	125.704	130.621	116.865	108.069
2005: I	106.295	103.356	113.578	122.698	123.629	118.292	114.537	126.446	131.595	117.188	108.697
II	109.037	107.266	113.466	122.620	123.276	119.561	115.248	127.188	132.791	117.120	109.183
III	109.710	108.104	113.738	123.340	124.335	118.596	116.063	129.491	135.990	117.814	109.246
IV P	110.357	109.124	113.493	126.044	127.332	119.830	115.372	127.174	131.286	119.782	109.365

Source: Department of Commerce, Bureau of Economic Analysis.

TABLE B–7.—*Chain-type price indexes for gross domestic product, 1959–2005*

[Index numbers, 2000=100, except as noted; quarterly data seasonally adjusted]

Year or quarter	Gross domestic product	Personal consumption expenditures				Gross private domestic investment						
							Fixed investment					
								Nonresidential				
		Total	Durable goods	Non-durable goods	Services	Total	Total	Total	Structures	Equipment and software	Residential
1959	20.754	20.432	45.662	22.765	15.485	29.474	28.262	35.114	15.923	50.882	16.630
1960	21.044	20.767	45.444	23.089	15.887	29.619	28.414	35.275	15.904	51.305	16.743
1961	21.281	20.985	45.551	23.227	16.173	29.538	28.325	35.076	15.810	51.025	16.769
1962	21.572	21.232	45.755	23.412	16.466	29.558	28.346	35.087	15.941	50.774	16.795
1963	21.801	21.479	45.915	23.683	16.701	29.467	28.267	35.088	16.085	50.495	16.663
1964	22.134	21.786	46.142	23.986	17.016	29.634	28.440	35.268	16.316	50.474	16.796
1965	22.538	22.103	45.721	24.423	17.334	30.107	28.926	35.672	16.791	50.520	17.272
1966	23.180	22.662	45.517	25.232	17.810	30.726	29.536	36.206	17.398	50.654	17.899
1967	23.897	23.237	46.228	25.830	18.349	31.538	30.364	37.129	17.943	51.776	18.521
1968	24.916	24.151	47.749	26.820	19.128	32.714	31.582	38.431	18.835	53.167	19.504
1969	26.153	25.255	49.067	28.062	20.106	34.264	33.140	40.018	20.074	54.645	20.853
1970	27.538	26.448	50.148	29.446	21.175	35.713	34.565	41.908	21.390	56.657	21.526
1971	28.916	27.574	51.975	30.359	22.340	37.493	36.306	43.880	23.040	58.340	22.775
1972	30.171	28.528	52.531	31.373	23.304	39.062	37.865	45.367	24.704	59.044	24.158
1973	31.854	30.081	53.301	33.838	24.381	41.172	39.958	47.115	26.619	60.047	26.297
1974	34.721	33.191	56.676	38.702	26.345	45.263	43.890	51.658	30.295	64.474	29.011
1975	38.000	35.955	61.844	41.735	28.595	50.847	49.384	58.763	33.911	74.001	31.706
1976	40.202	37.948	65.278	43.346	30.603	53.654	52.244	62.018	35.571	78.355	33.743
1977	42.758	40.410	68.129	45.911	32.933	57.677	56.342	66.258	38.651	83.011	37.147
1978	45.762	43.248	72.038	48.985	35.464	62.381	61.101	70.695	42.382	87.391	41.696
1979	49.553	47.059	76.830	54.148	38.316	68.027	66.642	76.440	47.313	92.932	46.374
1980	54.062	52.078	83.277	60.449	42.332	74.424	72.887	83.198	51.740	100.868	51.394
1981	59.128	56.720	88.879	65.130	46.746	81.278	79.670	91.245	58.880	108.077	55.587
1982	62.738	59.859	92.358	66.955	50.528	85.455	84.047	96.295	63.566	112.293	58.564
1983	65.214	62.436	94.181	68.386	53.799	85.237	83.912	95.432	61.939	112.530	59.908
1984	67.664	64.795	95.550	70.004	56.680	85.845	84.399	95.195	62.468	111.547	61.630
1985	69.724	66.936	96.620	71.543	59.295	86.720	85.457	95.936	63.940	111.413	63.219
1986	71.269	68.569	97.685	71.273	62.040	88.599	87.501	97.566	65.168	113.178	65.868
1987	73.204	70.947	100.465	73.731	64.299	90.289	89.118	98.435	66.199	113.796	68.561
1988	75.706	73.755	101.921	76.206	67.493	92.354	91.431	100.625	69.016	115.216	70.928
1989	78.569	76.972	103.717	79.842	70.708	94.559	93.641	102.731	71.707	116.657	73.211
1990	81.614	80.498	104.561	84.226	74.197	96.379	95.542	104.695	74.015	118.168	74.930
1991	84.457	83.419	106.080	86.779	77.497	97.749	96.960	106.314	75.355	119.854	75.912
1992	86.402	85.824	106.756	88.105	80.684	97.395	96.670	105.411	75.330	118.444	76.836
1993	88.390	87.804	107.840	88.973	83.345	98.521	97.805	105.487	77.602	117.243	79.941
1994	90.265	89.654	109.978	89.605	85.748	99.813	99.133	106.008	80.388	116.572	82.754
1995	92.115	91.577	110.672	90.629	88.320	100.941	100.292	106.239	83.879	115.224	85.769
1996	93.859	93.547	109.507	92.567	90.844	100.520	100.028	105.011	86.045	112.451	87.610
1997	95.415	95.124	107.068	93.835	93.305	100.157	99.785	103.696	89.381	109.120	89.843
1998	96.475	95.978	104.152	93.821	95.319	99.035	98.861	101.421	93.474	104.259	92.239
1999	97.868	97.575	101.626	96.173	97.393	98.972	98.888	100.057	96.257	101.366	95.780
2000	100.000	100.000	100.000	100.000	100.000	100.000	100.000	100.000	100.000	100.000	100.000
2001	102.402	102.094	98.114	101.531	103.257	101.013	101.023	99.683	105.403	97.708	104.633
2002	104.193	103.542	95.766	102.089	106.018	101.640	101.660	99.513	110.030	95.956	107.240
2003	106.310	105.520	92.372	104.151	109.246	103.311	103.432	99.764	113.889	95.133	112.379
2004	109.102	108.246	90.631	107.634	112.695	106.555	106.697	101.025	120.124	95.022	119.935
2005 ᴾ	112.144	111.298	90.159	111.585	116.176	109.796	109.937	103.155	132.176	94.666	125.568
2002: I	103.553	102.673	96.496	100.895	104.937	101.347	101.348	99.542	108.065	96.607	106.151
II	103.944	103.385	96.029	102.238	105.608	101.472	101.480	99.485	109.455	96.087	106.720
III	104.347	103.841	95.594	102.464	106.390	101.512	101.532	99.380	110.612	95.598	107.130
IV	104.926	104.268	94.946	102.760	107.137	102.229	102.279	99.645	111.988	95.534	108.960
2003: I	105.724	105.051	93.906	104.179	108.036	102.954	103.071	99.676	113.093	95.251	111.420
II	106.019	105.220	92.879	103.560	108.887	102.831	102.933	99.436	113.182	94.916	111.508
III	106.500	105.734	91.833	104.356	109.647	103.255	103.370	99.733	113.996	95.061	112.261
IV	106.996	106.076	90.868	104.509	110.414	104.202	104.354	100.211	115.287	95.304	114.330
2004: I	107.951	107.084	90.898	106.031	111.402	105.086	105.263	100.502	117.279	95.121	116.561
II	108.976	108.089	90.866	107.744	112.303	106.280	106.448	100.958	119.230	95.168	119.294
III	109.371	108.484	90.310	107.781	113.120	107.120	107.248	101.185	121.159	94.945	121.228
IV	106.996	106.076	90.868	104.509	110.414	104.202	104.354	100.211	115.287	95.304	114.330
2005: I	110.950	109.936	90.648	109.327	114.803	108.427	108.522	102.244	125.876	95.067	123.062
II	111.655	110.832	90.527	110.854	115.633	109.164	109.254	102.715	128.886	94.910	124.359
III	112.567	111.846	89.839	112.985	116.508	110.169	110.318	103.358	133.914	94.491	126.335
IV ᴾ	113.407	112.576	89.621	113.176	117.758	111.424	111.653	104.304	140.027	94.197	128.516

See next page for continuation of table.

TABLE B-7.—*Chain-type price indexes for gross domestic product, 1959–2005*—Continued

[Index numbers, 2000=100, except as noted; quarterly data seasonally adjusted]

Year or quarter	Exports	Imports	Gov. Total	Federal Total	National defense	Non-defense	State and local	Final sales of domestic product	GDP purchases Total	GDP purchases Less food and energy	Pct chg Gross domestic product	Pct chg GDP purchases Total	Pct chg GDP purchases Less food and energy
1959	29.433	21.901	15.404	16.450	16.257	16.591	14.475	20.581	20.365		1.2	1.2	
1960	29.846	22.110	15.597	16.590	16.383	16.798	14.738	20.872	20.646		1.4	1.4	
1961	30.300	22.110	15.909	16.871	16.619	17.296	15.093	21.108	20.865		1.1	1.1	
1962	30.375	21.849	16.314	17.228	16.940	17.808	15.564	21.398	21.139		1.4	1.3	
1963	30.307	22.273	16.669	17.597	17.320	18.116	15.911	21.629	21.385		1.1	1.2	
1964	30.556	22.743	17.132	18.191	17.822	19.036	16.234	21.963	21.725		1.5	1.6	
1965	31.529	23.059	17.588	18.658	18.314	19.408	16.685	22.368	22.102		1.8	1.7	
1966	32.481	23.596	18.330	19.330	18.950	20.190	17.507	23.010	22.724		2.8	2.8	
1967	33.725	23.688	19.099	19.913	19.518	20.815	18.488	23.729	23.389		3.1	2.9	
1968	34.461	24.048	20.128	20.995	20.539	22.116	19.475	24.752	24.380		4.3	4.2	
1969	35.627	24.675	21.341	22.130	21.664	23.251	20.780	25.988	25.580		5.0	4.9	
1970	36.993	26.135	23.079	23.915	23.321	25.478	22.488	27.369	26.964		5.3	5.4	
1971	38.358	27.739	24.875	25.957	25.387	27.400	24.087	28.741	28.351		5.0	5.1	
1972	40.146	29.682	26.788	28.495	28.319	28.780	25.524	29.994	29.619		4.3	4.5	
1973	45.425	34.841	28.743	30.449	30.396	30.394	27.477	31.673	31.343		5.6	5.8	
1974	55.965	49.847	31.646	33.162	33.217	32.819	30.500	34.517	34.546		9.0	10.2	
1975	61.682	53.997	34.824	36.615	36.460	36.746	33.481	37.789	37.761		9.5	9.3	
1976	63.707	55.622	37.118	39.217	39.117	39.209	35.563	39.987	39.938		5.8	5.8	
1977	66.302	60.523	39.694	42.180	42.079	42.152	37.872	42.546	42.634		6.4	6.8	
1978	70.342	64.798	42.235	44.785	45.035	43.983	40.359	45.551	45.663		7.0	7.1	
1979	78.808	75.879	45.775	48.231	48.628	47.099	43.944	49.322	49.669		8.3	8.8	
1980	86.801	94.513	50.761	53.299	53.908	51.683	48.858	53.806	54.876		9.1	10.5	
1981	93.217	99.594	55.752	58.476	59.229	56.516	53.709	58.859	59.896		9.4	9.1	
1982	93.645	96.235	59.414	62.446	63.392	60.020	57.140	62.489	63.296	62.221	6.1	5.7	
1983	94.015	92.629	61.778	64.612	65.617	62.038	59.666	64.739	65.515	64.685	3.9	3.5	4.0
1984	94.887	91.829	64.955	68.426	70.290	63.577	62.336	67.399	67.822	67.106	3.8	3.5	3.7
1985	91.983	88.813	66.970	69.974	71.621	65.740	64.739	69.361	69.760	69.232	3.0	2.9	3.2
1986	90.639	88.871	68.175	70.352	71.554	67.395	66.624	71.060	71.338	71.474	2.2	2.3	3.2
1987	92.874	94.251	70.056	71.200	72.281	68.616	69.361	72.985	73.527	73.716	2.7	3.1	3.1
1988	95.687	98.774	71.899	72.704	73.631	70.609	71.485	75.519	76.043	76.429	3.4	3.4	3.7
1989	99.310	100.944	74.139	74.677	75.528	72.826	73.940	78.383	78.934	79.151	3.8	3.8	3.6
1990	99.982	103.826	77.139	77.142	78.010	75.260	77.357	81.440	82.144	82.109	3.9	4.1	3.7
1991	101.313	103.420	79.787	80.232	80.821	79.100	79.681	84.286	84.836	84.942	3.5	3.3	3.5
1992	100.892	103.552	81.719	82.602	83.628	80.411	81.300	86.237	86.828	87.169	2.3	2.3	2.6
1993	100.898	102.671	83.789	84.788	85.313	83.728	83.294	88.226	88.730	89.211	2.3	2.2	2.3
1994	102.033	103.634	86.002	87.061	87.412	86.375	85.472	90.108	90.583	91.213	2.1	2.1	2.2
1995	104.376	106.412	88.358	89.503	89.598	89.351	87.778	91.965	92.483	93.176	2.0	2.1	2.2
1996	102.988	104.529	90.491	91.982	92.379	91.216	89.709	93.736	94.145	94.616	1.9	1.8	1.5
1997	101.232	100.816	92.139	93.533	93.716	93.192	91.414	95.320	95.440	95.865	1.7	1.4	1.3
1998	98.905	95.353	93.469	94.511	94.643	94.268	92.934	96.240	96.060	96.797	1.1	.6	1.0
1999	98.313	95.960	96.079	96.884	96.886	96.880	95.667	97.847	97.556	98.165	1.4	1.6	1.4
2000	100.000	100.000	100.000	100.000	100.000	100.000	100.000	100.000	100.000	100.000	2.2	2.5	1.9
2001	99.624	97.497	102.544	101.907	102.002	101.739	102.868	102.606	101.994	101.882	2.4	2.0	1.9
2002	99.273	96.341	105.507	105.631	105.792	105.345	105.435	104.197	103.583	103.796	1.7	1.6	1.9
2003	101.398	99.610	109.460	109.740	110.434	108.473	109.303	106.330	105.863	105.640	2.0	2.2	1.8
2004	104.999	104.571	113.505	114.354	114.840	113.498	113.022	109.124	108.899	108.224	2.6	2.9	2.4
2005 P	108.879	110.982	118.874	118.478	118.915	117.724	119.131	112.166	112.377	110.954	2.8	3.2	2.5
2002: I	98.360	94.146	104.378	105.098	104.784	105.665	103.997	103.554	102.755	103.150	1.7	1.5	1.8
II	99.048	96.474	105.126	105.231	105.112	105.449	105.064	103.946	103.385	103.579	1.5	2.5	1.7
III	99.772	97.304	105.795	105.502	105.744	105.073	105.943	104.352	103.816	103.990	1.6	1.7	1.6
IV	99.911	97.441	106.728	106.696	107.529	105.193	106.734	104.936	104.374	104.465	2.2	2.2	1.8
2003: I	100.909	100.069	109.030	109.238	109.939	107.966	108.909	105.743	105.418	105.115	3.1	4.1	2.5
II	101.165	98.938	109.026	109.579	110.229	108.396	108.714	106.036	105.513	105.367	1.1	.4	1.0
III	101.401	99.580	109.580	109.695	110.573	108.676	109.582	106.340	106.040	105.806	1.8	2.0	1.7
IV	102.116	99.853	110.087	110.241	110.995	108.853	110.005	107.021	106.483	106.270	1.9	1.7	1.8
2004: I	103.584	102.177	111.755	112.825	113.091	112.402	111.141	107.980	107.586	107.164	3.6	4.2	3.4
II	104.803	103.812	113.114	114.191	114.641	113.408	112.496	109.003	108.683	108.011	3.9	4.1	3.2
III	105.242	105.269	114.003	114.825	115.429	113.734	113.536	109.389	109.235	108.541	1.5	2.0	2.0
IV	106.366	107.026	115.148	115.575	116.198	114.447	114.914	110.124	110.092	109.181	2.7	3.2	2.4
2005: I	107.559	107.783	116.747	117.550	118.060	116.647	116.291	110.963	110.883	109.990	3.1	2.9	3.0
II	108.534	109.925	117.820	118.168	118.471	117.681	117.635	111.667	111.785	110.561	2.6	3.3	2.1
III	109.323	112.413	119.751	119.056	119.493	118.298	120.186	112.589	112.953	111.236	3.3	4.2	2.5
IV P	110.098	113.807	121.178	119.140	119.634	118.270	122.411	113.443	113.886	112.027	3.0	3.3	2.9

[1] Gross domestic product (GDP) less exports of goods and services plus imports of goods and services.

[2] Quarterly percent changes are at annual rates.

Source: Department of Commerce, Bureau of Economic Analysis.

TABLE B–8.—*Gross domestic product by major type of product, 1959–2005*

[Billions of dollars; quarterly data at seasonally adjusted annual rates]

Year or quarter	Gross domestic product	Final sales of domestic product	Change in private inventories	Goods Total: Total	Goods Total: Final sales	Goods Total: Change in private inventories	Durable goods: Final sales	Durable goods: Change in private inventories[1]	Nondurable goods: Final sales	Nondurable goods: Change in private inventories[1]	Services[2]	Structures
1959	506.6	502.7	3.9	237.6	233.6	3.9	86.3	2.9	147.3	1.1	206.5	62.5
1960	526.4	523.2	3.2	246.6	243.4	3.2	90.2	1.7	153.2	1.6	217.9	61.9
1961	544.7	541.7	3.0	250.1	247.2	3.0	90.2	−.1	157.0	3.0	231.0	63.6
1962	585.6	579.5	6.1	268.1	262.0	6.1	99.4	3.4	162.6	2.7	249.7	67.8
1963	617.7	612.1	5.6	280.1	274.5	5.6	106.0	2.6	168.5	3.0	265.0	72.7
1964	663.6	658.8	4.8	300.9	296.0	4.8	116.4	3.8	179.7	1.0	284.3	78.4
1965	719.1	709.9	9.2	329.4	320.2	9.2	128.4	6.2	191.8	3.0	305.0	84.7
1966	787.8	774.2	13.6	364.5	350.9	13.6	142.0	10.0	208.9	3.6	335.3	88.0
1967	832.6	822.7	9.9	373.9	364.0	9.9	146.4	4.8	217.6	5.0	369.1	89.6
1968	910.0	900.9	9.1	402.6	393.6	9.1	158.7	4.5	234.8	4.5	407.4	100.0
1969	984.6	975.4	9.2	432.0	422.8	9.2	171.1	6.0	251.7	3.2	444.4	108.3
1970	1,038.5	1,036.5	2.0	446.9	444.9	2.0	173.6	−.2	271.3	2.2	481.9	109.7
1971	1,127.1	1,118.9	8.3	472.9	464.7	8.3	181.1	2.9	283.6	5.3	525.8	128.4
1972	1,238.3	1,229.2	9.1	516.6	507.5	9.1	202.4	6.4	305.1	2.7	574.8	146.9
1973	1,382.7	1,366.8	15.9	597.1	581.2	15.9	236.6	13.0	344.6	2.9	622.7	162.9
1974	1,500.0	1,486.0	14.0	643.3	629.3	14.0	254.5	10.9	374.8	3.1	691.0	165.6
1975	1,638.3	1,644.6	−6.3	691.4	697.7	−6.3	284.5	−7.5	413.2	1.2	780.2	166.7
1976	1,825.3	1,808.2	17.1	777.5	760.4	17.1	321.2	10.8	439.2	6.3	856.6	191.2
1977	2,030.9	2,008.6	22.3	851.5	829.1	22.3	363.8	9.5	465.3	12.8	952.7	226.8
1978	2,294.7	2,268.9	25.8	961.0	935.2	25.8	413.2	18.2	522.0	7.6	1,059.7	273.9
1979	2,563.3	2,545.3	18.0	1,078.1	1,060.1	18.0	472.0	12.8	588.1	5.2	1,171.9	313.3
1980	2,789.5	2,795.8	−6.3	1,145.7	1,152.0	−6.3	500.1	−2.3	651.9	−4.0	1,322.5	321.3
1981	3,128.4	3,098.6	29.8	1,288.2	1,258.3	29.8	542.2	7.3	716.1	22.5	1,487.7	352.6
1982	3,255.0	3,269.9	−14.9	1,277.3	1,292.2	−14.9	539.7	−16.0	752.5	1.1	1,633.2	344.5
1983	3,536.7	3,542.4	−5.8	1,365.0	1,370.8	−5.8	578.1	2.5	792.7	−8.2	1,802.9	368.7
1984	3,933.2	3,867.8	65.4	1,549.6	1,484.2	65.4	650.2	41.4	834.0	24.0	1,957.8	425.8
1985	4,220.3	4,198.4	21.8	1,607.4	1,585.6	21.8	711.0	4.4	874.6	17.4	2,154.1	458.7
1986	4,462.8	4,456.3	6.6	1,657.0	1,650.5	6.6	739.9	−1.9	910.6	8.4	2,325.7	480.1
1987	4,739.5	4,712.3	27.1	1,751.3	1,724.2	27.1	764.9	22.9	959.3	4.2	2,490.5	497.6
1988	5,103.8	5,085.3	18.5	1,903.4	1,884.9	18.5	841.8	22.7	1,043.1	−4.3	2,685.3	515.0
1989	5,484.4	5,456.7	27.7	2,066.6	2,038.9	27.7	917.1	20.0	1,121.9	7.7	2,888.7	529.0
1990	5,803.1	5,788.5	14.5	2,155.8	2,141.3	14.5	950.2	7.7	1,191.1	6.8	3,113.7	533.5
1991	5,995.9	5,996.3	−.4	2,184.7	2,185.1	−.4	944.1	−13.6	1,241.0	13.2	3,311.3	499.9
1992	6,337.7	6,321.4	16.3	2,282.3	2,266.0	16.3	986.1	−3.0	1,279.8	19.3	3,532.7	522.7
1993	6,657.4	6,636.6	20.8	2,387.8	2,367.0	20.8	1,047.9	17.1	1,319.1	3.7	3,711.7	557.8
1994	7,072.2	7,008.4	63.8	2,563.8	2,500.0	63.8	1,125.0	35.7	1,375.0	28.1	3,901.2	607.3
1995	7,397.7	7,366.5	31.1	2,661.1	2,630.0	31.1	1,202.2	33.6	1,427.8	−2.4	4,098.4	638.1
1996	7,816.9	7,786.1	30.8	2,807.0	2,776.3	30.8	1,298.0	19.1	1,478.3	11.7	4,312.7	697.1
1997	8,304.3	8,232.3	72.0	3,007.7	2,935.7	72.0	1,409.1	39.9	1,526.6	32.1	4,548.4	748.2
1998	8,747.0	8,676.2	70.8	3,143.4	3,072.6	70.8	1,487.8	42.8	1,584.8	28.0	4,789.8	813.8
1999	9,268.4	9,201.5	66.9	3,311.3	3,244.4	66.9	1,576.5	40.0	1,667.9	26.9	5,081.8	875.3
2000	9,817.0	9,760.5	56.5	3,449.3	3,392.8	56.5	1,653.3	36.1	1,739.5	20.4	5,425.6	942.1
2001	10,128.0	10,159.7	−31.7	3,412.6	3,444.3	−31.7	1,630.3	−41.8	1,814.0	10.0	5,725.6	989.8
2002	10,469.6	10,457.7	11.9	3,442.4	3,430.5	11.9	1,559.9	15.1	1,870.7	−3.2	6,031.4	995.8
2003	10,971.2	10,955.8	15.4	3,536.7	3,521.2	15.4	1,586.7	12.4	1,934.6	3.0	6,366.1	1,068.4
2004	11,734.3	11,678.9	55.4	3,783.0	3,727.6	55.4	1,668.3	37.4	2,059.4	18.0	6,755.4	1,195.8
2005 ᴾ	12,479.4	12,464.2	15.2	3,962.1	3,946.9	15.2	1,782.0	18.9	2,164.9	−3.7	7,184.6	1,332.7
2002: I	10,333.3	10,341.6	−8.3	3,434.1	3,442.4	−8.3	1,570.7	−4.7	1,871.7	−3.7	5,908.8	990.4
II	10,426.6	10,424.0	2.6	3,437.0	3,434.4	2.6	1,560.7	6.7	1,873.7	−4.1	5,997.9	991.8
III	10,527.4	10,501.4	26.0	3,473.1	3,447.1	26.0	1,578.2	15.8	1,868.8	10.2	6,064.0	990.3
IV	10,591.1	10,563.9	27.3	3,425.4	3,398.2	27.3	1,529.7	42.6	1,868.4	−15.4	6,155.0	1,010.6
2003: I	10,717.0	10,695.2	21.8	3,448.2	3,426.4	21.8	1,534.4	20.3	1,892.0	1.5	6,243.4	1,025.4
II	10,884.6	10,845.0	−.4	3,466.9	3,467.3	−.4	1,565.0	.0	1,902.2	−.4	6,330.5	1,047.2
III	11,087.4	11,076.9	10.6	3,603.1	3,592.6	10.6	1,631.4	−4.8	1,961.2	15.4	6,396.8	1,087.5
IV	11,236.0	11,206.2	29.8	3,628.5	3,598.7	29.8	1,615.9	34.2	1,982.8	−4.5	6,493.9	1,113.7
2004: I	11,457.1	11,411.6	45.5	3,705.8	3,660.3	45.5	1,639.3	42.1	2,021.0	3.5	6,617.3	1,133.9
II	11,666.1	11,594.2	71.9	3,771.5	3,699.7	71.9	1,640.9	51.0	2,058.8	20.9	6,699.7	1,194.8
III	11,818.8	11,766.3	52.5	3,804.0	3,751.5	52.5	1,683.8	26.9	2,067.7	25.6	6,797.9	1,216.9
IV	11,995.2	11,943.3	51.9	3,850.8	3,799.0	51.9	1,709.0	29.9	2,090.0	22.0	6,906.7	1,237.7
2005: I	12,198.8	12,138.9	59.9	3,906.3	3,846.4	59.9	1,723.9	35.0	2,122.5	24.9	7,025.1	1,267.4
II	12,378.0	12,382.1	−4.2	3,954.4	3,958.5	−4.2	1,786.6	−7.3	2,171.9	3.1	7,112.4	1,311.2
III	12,605.7	12,625.4	−19.7	4,001.3	4,021.0	−19.7	1,827.6	5.6	2,193.4	−25.3	7,250.2	1,354.1
IV ᴾ	12,735.3	12,710.5	24.8	3,986.3	3,961.5	24.8	1,789.8	42.2	2,171.8	−17.4	7,350.8	1,398.1

[1] Estimates for durable and nondurable goods for 1996 and earlier periods are based on the Standard Industrial Classification (SIC); later estimates are based on the North American Industry Classification System (NAICS).

[2] Includes government consumption expenditures, which are for services (such as education and national defense) produced by government. In current dollars, these services are valued at their cost of production.

Source: Department of Commerce, Bureau of Economic Analysis.

TABLE B–9.—*Real gross domestic product by major type of product, 1959–2005*

[Billions of chained (2000) dollars; quarterly data at seasonally adjusted annual rates]

Year or quarter	Gross domestic product	Final sales of domestic product	Change in private inventories	Goods Total — Total	Goods Total — Final sales	Goods Total — Change in private inventories	Durable goods — Final sales	Durable goods — Change in private inventories[1]	Nondurable goods — Final sales	Nondurable goods — Change in private inventories[1]	Services[2]	Structures
1959	2,441.3	2,442.7	12.3	700.7							1,391.1	392.8
1960	2,501.8	2,506.8	10.4	721.1							1,433.0	389.1
1961	2,560.0	2,566.8	9.4	726.7							1,489.4	399.9
1962	2,715.2	2,708.5	19.5	773.8							1,574.3	422.8
1963	2,834.0	2,830.3	18.0	803.4							1,642.4	451.3
1964	2,998.6	2,999.9	15.4	856.4							1,720.1	481.7
1965	3,191.1	3,173.8	29.3	927.3							1,803.6	505.8
1966	3,399.1	3,364.8	42.1	1,005.2							1,916.7	506.4
1967	3,484.6	3,467.6	30.3	1,006.4							2,034.8	499.0
1968	3,652.7	3,640.3	27.4	1,047.9							2,140.4	529.7
1969	3,765.4	3,753.7	27.0	1,082.2							2,212.2	536.5
1970	3,771.9	3,787.7	5.0	1,076.3							2,255.4	513.4
1971	3,898.6	3,893.4	22.3	1,105.7							2,313.6	561.0
1972	4,105.0	4,098.6	23.1	1,180.5							2,393.7	602.7
1973	4,341.5	4,315.9	35.0	1,299.5							2,461.3	615.6
1974	4,319.6	4,305.5	25.9	1,288.1							2,522.8	551.8
1975	4,311.2	4,352.5	−11.3	1,263.7							2,612.1	501.7
1976	4,540.9	4,522.3	30.7	1,359.8							2,676.9	548.7
1977	4,750.5	4,721.6	38.5	1,423.2							2,770.5	600.6
1978	5,015.0	4,981.6	41.1	1,515.6							2,874.9	658.3
1979	5,173.4	5,161.2	25.1	1,577.9							2,943.3	677.0
1980	5,161.7	5,196.7	−8.0	1,567.1							3,004.2	627.8
1981	5,291.7	5,265.1	34.9	1,634.5							3,062.5	619.2
1982	5,189.3	5,233.4	−17.5	1,559.7							3,120.0	566.1
1983	5,423.8	5,454.0	−6.4	1,625.4							3,251.0	607.1
1984	5,813.6	5,739.2	71.3	1,810.9							3,341.1	689.2
1985	6,053.7	6,042.1	23.7	1,851.3							3,520.8	725.1
1986	6,263.6	6,271.8	8.3	1,906.0							3,671.0	735.9
1987	6,475.1	6,457.2	30.3	1,984.9							3,797.3	739.2
1988	6,742.7	6,734.5	20.3	2,108.9							3,930.9	737.9
1989	6,981.4	6,962.2	28.3	2,223.3							4,049.5	732.8
1990	7,112.5	7,108.5	15.4	2,252.7	2,244.3	15.4	872.8	7.2	1,402.1	3.5	4,170.0	718.3
1991	7,100.5	7,115.0	−.5	2,221.5	2,228.9	−.5	852.7	−13.6	1,410.3	6.1	4,251.2	662.8
1992	7,336.6	7,331.1	16.5	2,307.8	2,297.7	16.5	894.7	−3.0	1,434.3	8.7	4,373.7	688.3
1993	7,532.7	7,522.3	20.6	2,394.8	2,380.3	20.6	949.8	16.4	1,457.7	1.5	4,457.5	709.3
1994	7,835.5	7,777.8	63.6	2,550.6	2,493.9	63.6	1,016.4	33.4	1,501.4	12.6	4,558.3	746.0
1995	8,031.7	8,010.2	29.9	2,639.0	2,614.9	29.9	1,096.9	31.0	1,536.9	−1.2	4,654.7	753.5
1996	8,328.9	8,306.5	28.7	2,772.4	2,747.4	28.7	1,193.8	17.8	1,566.5	4.5	4,765.6	803.1
1997	8,703.5	8,636.6	71.2	2,971.3	2,904.6	71.2	1,317.4	38.5	1,593.4	32.4	4,901.1	835.7
1998	9,066.9	8,997.6	72.6	3,132.7	3,063.7	72.6	1,431.8	42.4	1,634.2	29.8	5,057.5	879.1
1999	9,470.3	9,404.0	68.9	3,312.6	3,246.4	68.9	1,554.3	40.4	1,692.6	28.1	5,245.1	913.0
2000	9,817.0	9,760.5	56.5	3,449.3	3,392.8	56.5	1,653.3	36.1	1,739.5	20.4	5,425.6	942.1
2001	9,890.7	9,920.9	−31.7	3,390.9	3,421.9	−31.7	1,655.6	−42.4	1,766.1	10.3	5,553.2	945.6
2002	10,048.8	10,036.5	12.5	3,432.5	3,419.7	12.5	1,610.8	15.5	1,806.3	−2.8	5,693.4	922.1
2003	10,320.6	10,303.6	15.5	3,549.0	3,531.2	15.5	1,680.7	12.6	1,849.3	3.3	5,820.7	951.6
2004	10,755.7	10,702.4	52.0	3,778.2	3,721.3	52.0	1,797.7	36.5	1,925.3	16.4	5,979.6	1,006.1
2005 ᵖ	11,131.1	11,112.2	17.2	3,950.7	3,932.0	17.2	1,929.4	18.0	2,008.6	.5	6,139.0	1,054.1
2002: I	9,977.3	9,986.8	−10.2	3,413.1	3,422.7	−10.2	1,609.4	−4.6	1,810.7	−5.7	5,635.1	928.7
II	10,031.6	10,028.4	2.6	3,425.5	3,422.3	2.6	1,609.2	6.8	1,810.3	−4.2	5,683.1	922.3
III	10,090.7	10,063.5	28.9	3,468.8	3,440.7	28.0	1,635.4	16.1	1,803.7	11.9	5,707.2	915.3
IV	10,095.8	10,067.3	29.5	3,422.8	3,393.2	29.5	1,589.3	43.6	1,800.5	−13.1	5,748.2	922.2
2003: I	10,138.6	10,114.7	24.0	3,458.9	3,434.1	24.0	1,605.8	21.6	1,824.6	2.9	5,758.2	920.2
II	10,230.4	10,228.2	−.4	3,478.4	3,476.6	−.4	1,651.3	−1.0	1,823.7	.5	5,810.7	938.6
III	10,410.9	10,399.5	9.3	3,616.3	3,604.4	9.3	1,735.8	−4.9	1,869.2	13.6	5,829.4	968.9
IV	10,502.6	10,471.8	29.0	3,642.5	3,609.9	29.0	1,729.8	34.6	1,879.7	−4.0	5,884.4	978.8
2004: I	10,612.5	10,568.9	41.9	3,706.5	3,660.0	41.9	1,760.3	41.9	1,900.3	1.8	5,932.1	980.1
II	10,704.1	10,637.4	65.6	3,749.6	3,678.2	65.6	1,765.1	50.0	1,913.1	17.2	5,950.1	1,010.9
III	10,808.9	10,757.1	50.4	3,809.9	3,754.7	50.4	1,820.5	25.8	1,936.8	24.7	5,994.6	1,014.0
IV	10,897.1	10,846.0	50.1	3,846.6	3,792.2	50.1	1,844.8	28.4	1,950.9	22.0	6,041.5	1,019.5
2005: I	10,999.3	10,940.3	58.2	3,888.0	3,824.9	58.2	1,858.8	33.4	1,969.3	25.3	6,089.9	1,032.5
II	11,089.2	11,089.2	−1.7	3,935.3	3,937.5	−1.7	1,929.6	−6.9	2,013.5	4.6	6,112.8	1,053.4
III	11,202.3	11,214.4	−13.3	3,986.8	4,002.6	−13.3	1,981.7	5.6	2,029.5	−17.4	6,167.8	1,062.0
IVᵖ	11,233.5	11,205.0	25.7	3,992.9	3,962.9	25.7	1,947.3	39.9	2,022.0	−10.5	6,185.4	1,068.4

[1] Estimates for durable and nondurable goods for 1996 and earlier periods are based on the Standard Industrial Classification (SIC); later estimates are based on the North American Industry Classification System (NAICS).
[2] Includes government consumption expenditures, which are for services (such as education and national defense) produced by government. In current dollars, these services are valued at their cost of production.

Source: Department of Commerce, Bureau of Economic Analysis.

TABLE B–10.—*Gross value added by sector, 1959–2005*

[Billions of dollars; quarterly data at seasonally adjusted annual rates]

Year or quarter	Gross domestic product	Business [1]			Households and institutions			General government [3]			Addendum: Gross housing value added
		Total	Non-farm [1]	Farm	Total	House-holds	Non-profit institutions serving households [2]	Total	Federal	State and local	
1959	506.6	408.2	390.9	17.3	40.1	29.8	10.3	58.3	31.9	26.5	36.9
1960	526.4	420.4	402.3	18.2	43.9	32.3	11.7	62.0	33.1	28.9	39.9
1961	544.7	432.0	413.7	18.3	46.7	34.3	12.4	66.0	34.4	31.6	42.8
1962	585.6	464.5	446.1	18.4	50.4	36.7	13.6	70.7	36.5	34.2	46.0
1963	617.7	488.7	470.2	18.5	53.6	38.8	14.8	75.5	38.4	37.1	48.9
1964	663.6	525.6	508.2	17.3	56.9	40.8	16.1	81.1	40.7	40.4	51.6
1965	719.1	571.4	551.5	19.9	61.0	43.3	17.7	86.7	42.4	44.2	54.9
1966	787.8	625.1	604.3	20.8	65.8	45.9	19.9	96.9	47.3	49.6	58.2
1967	832.6	654.5	634.4	20.1	70.9	48.8	22.1	107.2	51.7	55.5	62.1
1968	910.0	714.5	694.0	20.5	76.5	51.6	25.0	119.0	56.4	62.5	65.9
1969	984.6	770.3	747.5	22.8	84.3	55.6	28.7	130.0	60.0	70.0	71.3
1970	1,038.5	803.6	779.9	23.7	91.4	59.4	32.0	143.6	64.1	79.5	76.7
1971	1,127.1	869.9	844.5	25.4	100.9	65.1	35.7	156.4	67.8	88.6	83.9
1972	1,238.3	959.0	929.4	29.7	109.9	70.3	39.5	169.4	71.6	97.9	91.1
1973	1,382.7	1,079.4	1,032.7	46.8	120.0	76.0	44.0	183.3	74.0	109.3	98.3
1974	1,500.0	1,166.9	1,122.6	44.2	131.7	82.5	49.2	201.4	79.6	121.8	106.8
1975	1,638.3	1,268.5	1,222.8	45.6	145.4	90.3	55.1	224.5	87.3	137.1	117.2
1976	1,825.3	1,423.7	1,380.7	43.0	158.1	98.1	60.0	243.5	93.8	149.7	126.6
1977	2,030.9	1,593.5	1,549.9	43.5	172.8	107.3	65.6	264.6	102.1	162.6	140.3
1978	2,294.7	1,813.4	1,762.7	50.7	193.8	120.4	73.4	287.5	109.7	177.8	155.2
1979	2,563.3	2,032.9	1,972.8	60.1	217.4	135.0	82.5	313.0	117.6	195.4	172.5
1980	2,789.5	2,191.1	2,139.7	51.4	249.9	155.5	94.4	348.6	131.3	217.3	199.4
1981	3,128.4	2,459.4	2,394.5	65.0	283.7	176.8	106.9	385.3	147.4	237.9	228.4
1982	3,255.0	2,520.7	2,460.3	60.4	315.3	195.7	119.6	419.0	161.3	257.7	255.4
1983	3,536.7	2,747.2	2,702.3	44.9	344.0	211.7	132.4	445.4	171.3	274.1	277.4
1984	3,933.2	3,071.8	3,007.7	64.2	376.2	230.2	146.0	485.2	192.1	293.1	301.1
1985	4,220.3	3,290.8	3,227.4	63.4	406.0	249.6	156.4	523.5	205.1	318.4	332.9
1986	4,462.8	3,468.8	3,409.4	59.4	438.0	267.4	170.6	556.1	212.6	343.5	359.5
1987	4,739.5	3,669.9	3,608.4	61.6	478.4	287.6	190.8	591.2	223.4	367.8	385.5
1988	5,103.8	3,948.6	3,887.2	61.3	525.1	312.8	212.4	630.1	234.9	395.2	415.5
1989	5,484.4	4,243.2	4,169.7	73.6	569.6	337.0	232.6	671.5	246.6	424.9	443.8
1990	5,803.1	4,462.6	4,386.0	76.6	618.9	362.9	256.0	721.6	258.9	462.6	478.1
1991	5,995.9	4,569.3	4,499.5	69.9	660.7	383.4	277.3	765.9	275.0	490.9	508.5
1992	6,337.7	4,840.4	4,761.7	78.7	697.9	397.2	300.7	799.4	282.1	517.3	531.0
1993	6,657.4	5,096.2	5,025.6	70.6	732.0	413.7	318.3	829.3	286.3	543.0	549.1
1994	7,072.2	5,444.0	5,362.4	81.6	771.3	439.5	331.7	857.0	286.2	570.7	582.0
1995	7,397.7	5,700.6	5,632.0	68.5	815.5	463.3	352.1	881.6	284.7	596.9	613.3
1996	7,816.9	6,056.7	5,966.0	90.7	852.2	484.7	367.5	908.0	288.6	619.3	638.0
1997	8,304.3	6,471.9	6,383.8	88.1	895.8	509.6	386.2	936.7	290.9	645.8	667.7
1998	8,747.0	6,827.1	6,748.2	78.9	949.7	538.0	411.7	970.3	293.1	677.2	700.2
1999	9,268.4	7,243.4	7,174.7	68.8	1,012.3	576.4	435.9	1,012.7	300.9	711.8	747.8
2000	9,817.0	7,666.7	7,595.1	71.5	1,080.7	615.6	465.1	1,069.6	315.4	754.2	794.3
2001	10,128.0	7,841.2	7,768.0	73.1	1,160.4	662.0	498.4	1,126.4	325.7	800.8	849.8
2002	10,469.6	8,040.5	7,969.7	70.8	1,227.3	687.7	539.6	1,201.8	352.9	848.9	876.7
2003	10,971.2	8,427.8	8,339.8	88.0	1,267.1	696.9	570.3	1,276.3	382.6	893.7	875.5
2004	11,734.3	9,041.2	8,928.9	112.2	1,353.5	751.3	602.2	1,339.7	408.2	931.4	933.1
2005 ᴾ	12,479.4	9,640.7	9,554.6	86.1	1,436.0	789.7	646.4	1,402.7	424.1	978.5	972.1
2002: I	10,333.3	7,938.3	7,871.8	66.5	1,213.4	688.7	524.6	1,181.6	349.4	832.2	882.5
II	10,426.6	7,999.1	7,937.7	61.4	1,233.0	696.5	536.4	1,194.5	351.1	843.5	889.2
III	10,527.4	8,090.4	8,017.6	72.9	1,230.5	684.3	546.2	1,206.4	351.8	854.6	871.5
IV	10,591.1	8,134.2	8,051.6	82.6	1,232.3	681.0	551.3	1,224.7	359.2	865.5	863.8
2003: I	10,717.0	8,206.6	8,130.1	76.4	1,252.2	692.6	559.6	1,258.2	377.4	880.9	875.7
II	10,844.6	8,318.0	8,232.4	85.6	1,255.0	687.9	567.2	1,271.5	383.1	888.4	866.8
III	11,087.4	8,548.6	8,460.7	87.9	1,255.3	682.2	573.1	1,283.5	384.4	899.1	854.7
IV	11,236.0	8,638.1	8,536.0	102.1	1,306.0	724.8	581.2	1,291.9	385.4	906.5	904.7
2004: I	11,457.1	8,822.4	8,699.6	122.8	1,316.4	731.6	584.8	1,318.2	403.3	914.9	912.7
II	11,666.1	8,993.2	8,868.4	124.9	1,339.8	744.9	594.9	1,333.1	407.2	925.9	926.0
III	11,818.8	9,106.5	9,001.9	104.6	1,366.0	758.7	607.3	1,346.3	409.4	936.9	941.0
IV	11,995.2	9,242.5	9,145.9	96.6	1,391.7	770.0	621.6	1,361.0	413.1	948.0	952.9
2005: I	12,198.8	9,405.3	9,312.5	92.8	1,411.4	777.8	633.5	1,382.1	422.8	959.4	960.9
II	12,378.0	9,559.9	9,475.2	84.7	1,424.7	783.4	641.3	1,393.4	423.1	970.2	965.5
III	12,605.7	9,748.3	9,665.8	82.5	1,445.9	793.0	653.0	1,411.4	424.6	986.8	975.1
IV ᴾ	12,735.3	9,849.5	9,765.0	84.5	1,462.1	804.4	657.7	1,423.7	426.0	997.7	987.0

[1] Gross domestic business product equals gross domestic product excluding gross value added of households and institutions and of general government. Nonfarm product equals gross domestic business value added excluding gross farm value added.

[2] Equals compensation of employees of nonprofit institutions, the rental value of nonresidential fixed assets owned and used by nonprofit institutions serving households, and rental income of persons for tenant-occupied housing owned by nonprofit institutions.

[3] Equals compensation of general government employees plus general government consumption of fixed capital.

Source: Department of Commerce, Bureau of Economic Analysis.

TABLE B–11.—*Real gross value added by sector, 1959–2005*

[Billions of chained (2000) dollars; quarterly data at seasonally adjusted annual rates]

Year or quarter	Gross domestic product	Business [1]			Households and institutions			General government [3]			Adden-dum: Gross housing value added
		Total	Non-farm [1]	Farm	Total	House-holds	Non-profit institu-tions serving house-holds [2]	Total	Federal	State and local	
1959	2,441.3	1,716.0	1,684.1	21.2	261.7	161.6	97.8	514.5	279.4	236.7	195.0
1960	2,501.8	1,748.8	1,713.5	22.4	279.6	171.4	106.6	532.2	284.6	249.3	207.3
1961	2,560.0	1,782.8	1,747.8	22.6	291.5	179.6	109.6	550.9	290.5	262.1	219.2
1962	2,715.2	1,897.7	1,867.0	22.1	307.7	189.8	115.4	572.5	302.5	271.8	232.8
1963	2,834.0	1,985.4	1,954.3	22.8	320.4	197.7	120.0	589.5	305.2	285.9	244.3
1964	2,998.6	2,111.7	2,086.0	22.1	333.7	205.7	125.4	609.7	308.2	303.1	255.4
1965	3,191.1	2,260.6	2,233.5	23.5	350.2	215.2	132.6	630.3	310.4	321.5	268.9
1966	3,399.1	2,413.6	2,393.2	22.7	366.3	224.0	140.2	669.7	330.7	340.6	281.0
1967	3,484.6	2,459.5	2,434.1	24.5	381.6	233.1	146.5	705.2	352.2	354.9	294.0
1968	3,652.7	2,581.7	2,561.5	23.6	400.4	239.3	161.0	732.7	358.1	376.2	304.6
1969	3,765.4	2,660.3	2,639.1	24.5	417.8	249.1	168.8	751.3	359.0	393.4	318.7
1970	3,771.9	2,659.3	2,636.0	25.1	425.0	254.7	170.0	754.1	343.6	410.8	328.9
1971	3,898.6	2,761.5	2,736.2	26.4	443.0	266.5	176.1	755.3	327.8	427.5	343.8
1972	4,105.0	2,939.8	2,918.4	26.4	460.7	277.7	182.4	753.8	311.8	442.3	360.1
1973	4,341.5	3,145.0	3,131.5	26.2	476.3	287.5	188.2	757.2	300.1	457.8	373.0
1974	4,319.6	3,101.3	3,089.1	25.6	493.9	299.9	193.1	772.6	299.2	474.4	390.7
1975	4,311.2	3,071.2	3,037.5	30.5	513.7	308.0	205.2	785.1	297.5	488.9	402.7
1976	4,540.9	3,272.9	3,249.1	29.1	521.5	313.3	207.5	791.8	297.9	495.3	408.3
1977	4,750.5	3,456.2	3,431.1	30.7	528.3	316.2	211.6	800.1	298.8	502.9	418.3
1978	5,015.0	3,673.3	3,656.8	29.6	552.4	335.1	216.3	815.5	302.5	514.6	436.8
1979	5,173.4	3,796.7	3,774.2	32.2	576.7	350.4	225.3	824.2	302.3	523.7	453.9
1980	5,161.7	3,756.1	3,736.1	31.1	606.9	372.9	232.8	836.0	307.0	530.8	481.9
1981	5,291.7	3,859.5	3,814.7	41.0	626.5	384.7	240.5	840.6	311.7	530.6	501.0
1982	5,189.3	3,743.1	3,691.9	43.1	647.2	391.8	254.4	849.2	316.8	534.0	514.7
1983	5,423.8	3,944.3	3,932.8	26.9	665.9	399.4	265.7	854.6	324.2	531.8	526.2
1984	5,813.6	4,286.3	4,254.3	37.2	687.8	413.3	273.6	865.2	331.5	535.0	543.0
1985	6,053.7	4,484.5	4,434.2	46.7	700.1	423.2	275.9	890.0	341.0	550.3	564.4
1986	6,263.6	4,652.0	4,606.2	44.9	718.5	428.7	289.1	911.9	347.0	566.3	574.9
1987	6,475.1	4,815.5	4,769.8	45.5	745.7	440.3	304.8	931.8	356.1	577.2	588.8
1988	6,742.7	5,023.0	4,987.7	40.9	780.6	457.1	323.1	956.0	360.5	596.9	606.2
1989	6,981.4	5,206.6	5,162.3	46.4	812.3	471.5	340.6	978.8	364.9	615.3	620.3
1990	7,112.5	5,287.0	5,237.9	49.3	841.2	483.2	357.9	1,003.9	371.6	633.6	635.7
1991	7,100.5	5,245.4	5,194.7	50.0	865.3	497.8	367.5	1,014.3	373.8	641.7	657.2
1992	7,336.6	5,456.5	5,395.2	57.5	882.6	502.6	379.9	1,017.7	366.0	652.6	666.2
1993	7,532.7	5,625.9	5,576.0	50.6	904.8	507.9	396.9	1,019.8	358.9	661.6	669.9
1994	7,835.5	5,905.3	5,841.4	60.9	923.1	524.7	398.4	1,019.9	347.2	673.1	690.8
1995	8,031.7	6,076.8	6,030.2	49.6	945.1	534.3	410.8	1,020.6	334.1	686.5	705.7
1996	8,328.9	6,356.0	6,300.4	56.1	957.8	540.8	417.0	1,022.1	325.0	697.2	712.1
1997	8,703.5	6,693.8	6,627.2	64.4	983.5	554.0	429.5	1,030.0	318.8	711.2	726.5
1998	9,066.9	7,017.1	6,955.3	61.6	1,010.4	563.8	446.9	1,041.0	315.2	725.8	735.5
1999	9,470.3	7,376.8	7,314.2	62.9	1,042.3	590.7	451.6	1,051.4	312.7	738.7	767.2
2000	9,817.0	7,666.7	7,595.1	71.5	1,080.7	615.6	465.1	1,069.6	315.4	754.2	794.3
2001	9,890.7	7,691.0	7,625.7	65.6	1,110.0	634.8	475.1	1,089.3	317.0	772.3	815.1
2002	10,048.8	7,806.9	7,736.9	70.1	1,130.9	634.2	496.6	1,110.4	323.3	787.1	809.0
2003	10,320.6	8,070.6	7,994.6	76.0	1,126.3	625.9	500.3	1,126.3	331.8	794.4	786.5
2004	10,755.7	8,454.4	8,379.5	75.9	1,172.0	666.5	506.0	1,135.7	334.9	800.7	827.8
2005ᵖ	11,131.1	8,790.7	8,726.4	69.1	1,204.0	690.1	514.8	1,146.8	336.7	810.1	852.4
2002: I	9,977.3	7,740.7	7,686.5	54.5	1,131.4	642.1	489.4	1,104.2	320.4	783.7	823.2
II	10,031.6	7,780.4	7,712.9	67.4	1,141.0	645.3	495.7	1,108.9	322.5	786.3	824.0
III	10,090.7	7,848.8	7,772.7	76.3	1,129.1	628.8	500.2	1,112.6	324.6	788.0	801.0
IV	10,095.8	7,857.6	7,775.5	82.1	1,122.1	620.8	501.2	1,116.0	325.7	790.4	787.7
2003: I	10,138.6	7,891.8	7,814.2	77.1	1,124.3	623.6	500.6	1,122.4	329.7	792.6	789.6
II	10,230.4	7,982.5	7,903.8	81.9	1,119.5	619.8	499.5	1,126.1	332.4	793.6	781.3
III	10,410.9	8,176.1	8,102.4	73.7	1,112.5	612.8	499.4	1,127.4	332.6	794.7	767.4
IV	10,502.6	8,228.3	8,157.9	71.2	1,149.1	647.6	501.7	1,129.1	332.5	796.5	807.9
2004: I	10,612.5	8,328.2	8,241.6	83.6	1,157.9	654.5	503.7	1,131.5	334.1	797.3	814.2
II	10,704.1	8,410.5	8,335.3	76.0	1,166.9	662.0	505.3	1,132.7	333.7	799.0	821.9
III	10,808.9	8,501.7	8,430.2	73.8	1,177.6	671.1	507.0	1,136.6	335.0	801.5	832.6
IV	10,897.1	8,577.2	8,510.7	70.4	1,185.4	678.5	507.9	1,142.0	337.0	804.9	842.4
2005: I	10,999.3	8,669.6	8,601.7	71.6	1,194.5	683.8	511.4	1,143.9	337.4	806.4	847.1
II	11,089.2	8,754.8	8,694.8	65.3	1,199.9	686.5	514.2	1,144.6	336.5	808.1	849.4
III	11,202.3	8,857.8	8,794.3	68.5	1,208.1	691.5	517.4	1,148.0	336.1	812.0	853.4
IVᵖ	11,233.5	8,880.8	8,814.6	70.9	1,213.7	698.5	516.3	1,150.5	336.8	813.7	859.5

[1] Gross domestic business product equals gross domestic product excluding gross value added of households and institutions and of general government. Nonfarm product equals gross domestic business value added excluding gross farm value added.

[2] Equals compensation of employees of nonprofit institutions, the rental value of nonresidential fixed assets owned and used by nonprofit institutions serving households, and rental income of persons for tenant-occupied housing owned by nonprofit institutions.

[3] Equals compensation of general government employees plus general government consumption of fixed capital.

Source: Department of Commerce, Bureau of Economic Analysis.

TABLE B–12.—*Gross domestic product (GDP) by industry, value added, in current dollars and as a percentage of GDP, 1974–2004*

[Billions of dollars; except as noted]

Year	Gross domestic product	Total private industries	Agriculture, forestry, fishing, and hunting	Mining	Construction	Manufacturing Total manufacturing	Durable goods	Nondurable goods	Utilities	Wholesale trade	Retail trade
						Value added					
1974	1,500.0	1,277.3	50.1	29.3	74.0	318.2	192.5	125.7	29.2	104.7	113.4
1975	1,638.3	1,391.5	51.4	33.8	74.8	337.1	198.5	138.6	37.1	114.6	127.3
1976	1,825.3	1,556.2	50.2	37.5	85.5	386.7	230.2	156.5	41.5	122.7	144.0
1977	2,030.9	1,739.4	51.3	43.4	94.2	438.6	265.0	173.6	45.9	134.9	158.5
1978	2,294.7	1,977.0	59.8	49.5	111.5	489.9	303.4	186.5	50.4	153.4	177.6
1979	2,563.3	2,217.7	70.6	58.4	127.0	543.8	331.1	212.7	51.9	175.8	193.2
1980	2,789.5	2,405.8	62.0	91.3	130.3	556.6	333.9	222.7	60.0	188.7	200.9
1981	3,128.4	2,702.5	75.4	122.9	131.8	616.5	370.4	246.1	70.7	208.3	221.0
1982	3,255.0	2,792.6	71.3	120.0	128.8	603.2	353.4	249.8	81.7	207.9	229.9
1983	3,536.7	3,043.5	57.1	103.1	139.8	653.1	379.3	273.8	91.6	222.9	261.6
1984	3,933.2	3,395.1	77.1	107.2	164.4	724.0	443.5	280.5	102.3	249.4	293.6
1985	4,220.3	3,637.0	77.1	105.4	184.6	740.3	449.2	291.1	109.2	268.3	318.7
1986	4,462.8	3,842.9	74.2	68.9	207.7	766.0	459.3	306.7	114.4	278.5	336.6
1987	4,739.5	4,080.4	79.8	71.5	218.2	811.3	483.8	327.5	123.0	285.3	349.9
1988	5,103.8	4,399.1	80.2	71.4	232.7	876.9	519.0	357.9	122.8	318.1	366.0
1989	5,484.4	4,732.3	92.8	76.0	244.8	927.3	543.2	384.1	135.9	337.4	389.0
1990	5,803.1	4,997.8	96.7	84.9	248.5	947.4	542.7	404.7	142.9	347.7	398.8
1991	5,995.9	5,138.7	89.2	76.0	230.2	957.5	540.9	416.6	152.5	360.5	405.5
1992	6,337.7	5,440.4	99.6	71.3	232.5	996.7	562.8	433.8	157.4	378.9	430.0
1993	6,657.4	5,729.3	93.1	72.1	248.3	1,039.9	593.1	446.8	165.3	401.2	458.0
1994	7,072.2	6,110.5	105.6	73.6	274.4	1,118.8	647.7	471.1	174.6	442.7	493.3
1995	7,397.7	6,407.2	93.1	74.1	287.0	1,177.3	677.2	500.0	181.5	457.0	514.9
1996	7,816.9	6,795.2	113.8	87.5	311.7	1,209.4	706.5	502.9	183.3	489.1	543.8
1997	8,304.3	7,247.5	110.7	92.6	337.6	1,279.8	755.5	524.3	179.6	521.2	574.2
1998	8,747.0	7,652.5	102.4	74.8	374.4	1,343.9	806.9	537.0	180.8	542.9	598.6
1999	9,268.4	8,127.2	93.8	85.4	406.6	1,373.1	820.4	552.7	185.4	577.7	635.5
2000	9,817.0	8,614.3	98.0	121.3	435.9	1,426.2	865.3	560.9	189.3	591.7	662.4
2001	10,128.0	8,869.7	97.9	118.7	469.5	1,341.3	778.9	562.5	202.3	607.1	691.6
2002	10,469.6	9,131.2	95.4	106.5	482.3	1,352.6	774.8	577.9	207.3	615.4	719.6
2003	10,971.2	9,556.8	114.2	142.3	501.0	1,369.2	785.5	583.7	222.6	633.0	751.0
2004	11,734.3	10,251.0	141.6	171.9	549.5	1,420.1	824.1	596.1	235.3	694.7	790.4
	Percent					**Industry value added as a percentage of GDP (percent)**					
1974	100.0	85.2	3.3	2.0	4.9	21.2	12.8	8.4	1.9	7.0	7.6
1975	100.0	84.9	3.1	2.1	4.6	20.6	12.1	8.5	2.3	7.0	7.8
1976	100.0	85.3	2.7	2.1	4.7	21.2	12.6	8.6	2.3	6.7	7.9
1977	100.0	85.6	2.5	2.1	4.6	21.6	13.1	8.5	2.3	6.6	7.8
1978	100.0	86.2	2.6	2.2	4.9	21.3	13.2	8.1	2.2	6.7	7.7
1979	100.0	86.5	2.8	2.3	5.0	21.2	12.9	8.3	2.0	6.9	7.5
1980	100.0	86.2	2.2	3.3	4.7	20.0	12.0	8.0	2.2	6.8	7.2
1981	100.0	86.4	2.4	3.9	4.2	19.7	11.8	7.9	2.3	6.7	7.1
1982	100.0	85.8	2.2	3.7	4.0	18.5	10.9	7.7	2.5	6.4	7.1
1983	100.0	86.1	1.6	2.9	4.0	18.5	10.7	7.7	2.6	6.3	7.4
1984	100.0	86.3	2.0	2.7	4.2	18.4	11.3	7.1	2.6	6.3	7.5
1985	100.0	86.2	1.8	2.5	4.4	17.5	10.6	6.9	2.6	6.4	7.6
1986	100.0	86.1	1.7	1.5	4.7	17.2	10.3	6.9	2.6	6.2	7.5
1987	100.0	86.1	1.7	1.5	4.6	17.1	10.2	6.9	2.6	6.0	7.4
1988	100.0	86.2	1.6	1.4	4.6	17.2	10.2	7.0	2.4	6.2	7.2
1989	100.0	86.3	1.7	1.4	4.5	16.9	9.9	7.0	2.5	6.2	7.1
1990	100.0	86.1	1.7	1.5	4.3	16.3	9.4	7.0	2.5	6.0	6.9
1991	100.0	85.7	1.5	1.3	3.8	16.0	9.0	6.9	2.5	6.0	6.8
1992	100.0	85.8	1.6	1.1	3.7	15.7	8.9	6.8	2.5	6.0	6.8
1993	100.0	86.1	1.4	1.1	3.7	15.6	8.9	6.7	2.5	6.0	6.9
1994	100.0	86.4	1.5	1.0	3.9	15.8	9.2	6.7	2.5	6.3	7.0
1995	100.0	86.6	1.3	1.0	3.9	15.9	9.2	6.8	2.5	6.2	7.0
1996	100.0	86.9	1.5	1.1	4.0	15.5	9.0	6.4	2.3	6.3	7.0
1997	100.0	87.3	1.3	1.1	4.1	15.4	9.1	6.3	2.2	6.3	6.9
1998	100.0	87.5	1.2	.9	4.3	15.4	9.2	6.1	2.1	6.2	6.8
1999	100.0	87.7	1.0	.9	4.4	14.8	8.9	6.0	2.0	6.2	6.9
2000	100.0	87.7	1.0	1.2	4.4	14.5	8.8	5.7	1.9	6.0	6.7
2001	100.0	87.6	1.0	1.2	4.6	13.2	7.7	5.6	2.0	6.0	6.8
2002	100.0	87.2	.9	1.0	4.6	12.9	7.4	5.5	2.0	5.9	6.9
2003	100.0	87.1	~1.0	1.3	4.6	12.5	7.2	5.3	2.0	5.8	6.8
2004	100.0	87.4	1.2	1.5	4.7	12.1	7.0	5.1	2.0	5.9	6.7

[1] Consists of agriculture, forestry, fishing, and hunting; mining; construction; and manufacturing.

[2] Consists of utilities; wholesale trade; retail trade; transportation and warehousing; information; finance, insurance, real estate, rental, and leasing; professional and business services; educational services, health care, and social assistance; arts, entertainment, recreation, accommodation, and food services; and other services, except government.

Note.—Value added is the contribution of each private industry and of government to gross domestic product. Value added is equal to an industry's gross output minus its intermediate inputs. Current-dollar value added is calculated as the sum of distributions by an industry to its labor and capital which are derived from the components of gross domestic income.

See next page for continuation of table.

TABLE B–12.—*Gross domestic product (GDP) by industry, value added, in current dollars and as a percentage of GDP, 1974–2004*—Continued

[Billions of dollars; except as noted]

Year	Private industries—continued								Government	Private goods-producing industries [1]	Private services-producing industries [2]
	Transportation and warehousing	Information	Finance, insurance, real estate, rental, and leasing	Professional and business services	Educational services, health care, and social assistance	Arts, entertainment, recreation, accommodation, and food services	Other services, except government				
						Value added					
1974	58.5	50.9	223.3	84.6	64.3	40.9	35.8	222.6	471.7	805.6
1975	59.4	56.5	248.2	92.9	74.2	45.7	38.4	246.9	497.2	894.3
1976	68.8	63.5	272.1	105.1	84.0	51.9	42.8	269.1	559.8	996.4
1977	76.2	71.1	304.0	122.7	93.8	58.8	46.1	291.5	627.5	1,111.9
1978	86.7	81.4	347.4	141.9	106.4	67.9	53.2	317.7	710.6	1,266.4
1979	96.6	90.3	390.3	164.0	120.5	77.1	58.2	345.7	799.7	1,417.9
1980	102.3	99.0	442.4	186.3	139.7	83.5	62.6	383.7	840.2	1,565.6
1981	109.9	112.7	498.4	213.2	159.9	93.5	68.5	425.9	946.6	1,755.9
1982	105.9	123.6	539.9	230.9	177.9	100.9	70.7	462.4	923.3	1,869.3
1983	117.8	140.0	604.6	262.5	198.3	112.0	79.2	493.1	953.1	2,090.5
1984	131.4	147.1	670.2	303.8	214.1	121.2	89.3	538.1	1,072.7	2,322.3
1985	136.3	162.9	729.7	340.8	231.3	134.3	98.0	583.3	1,107.4	2,529.5
1986	145.6	173.1	795.1	378.8	252.0	144.9	107.2	620.0	1,116.7	2,726.1
1987	151.1	185.0	840.3	414.1	286.5	152.1	112.3	659.1	1,180.8	2,899.5
1988	161.1	194.0	910.1	466.3	309.1	165.9	124.4	704.7	1,261.3	3,137.8
1989	164.1	210.4	975.4	518.0	347.0	180.2	133.9	752.0	1,341.0	3,391.4
1990	169.4	225.1	1,042.1	569.8	386.7	195.2	142.6	805.3	1,377.4	3,620.4
1991	178.2	235.2	1,103.6	579.3	424.8	202.2	144.2	857.2	1,352.8	3,785.9
1992	186.6	250.9	1,177.4	626.7	463.5	216.2	153.0	897.3	1,400.0	4,040.5
1993	201.0	272.6	1,241.5	659.1	488.0	225.5	163.7	928.1	1,453.4	4,275.9
1994	218.0	294.0	1,297.8	698.4	511.1	235.0	173.2	961.8	1,572.4	4,538.0
1995	226.3	307.6	1,383.0	743.1	533.3	248.3	180.9	990.4	1,631.4	4,775.8
1996	235.2	335.7	1,470.7	810.1	552.5	264.4	188.1	1,021.6	1,722.4	5,072.8
1997	253.7	347.8	1,593.3	896.5	573.1	289.8	197.4	1,056.8	1,820.8	5,426.8
1998	273.7	381.6	1,684.6	976.2	601.5	306.0	211.1	1,094.5	1,895.4	5,757.1
1999	287.4	439.3	1,798.4	1,064.5	634.5	327.8	217.8	1,141.2	1,958.9	6,168.3
2000	301.6	458.3	1,931.0	1,140.8	678.4	350.1	229.1	1,202.7	2,081.5	6,532.8
2001	296.9	476.9	2,059.2	1,165.9	739.3	361.5	241.5	1,258.3	2,027.5	6,842.2
2002	304.6	483.0	2,141.9	1,189.0	799.6	381.5	252.5	1,338.4	2,036.9	7,094.3
2003	321.6	491.8	2,260.4	1,235.9	850.6	398.8	264.3	1,414.5	2,126.7	7,430.0
2004	332.9	538.7	2,412.9	1,351.9	909.0	424.3	227.7	1,483.3	2,283.1	7,967.9
			Industry value added as a percentage of GDP (percent)								
1974	3.9	3.4	14.9	5.6	4.3	2.7	2.4	14.8	31.4	53.7
1975	3.6	3.4	15.1	5.7	4.5	2.8	2.3	15.1	30.3	54.6
1976	3.8	3.5	14.9	5.8	4.6	2.8	2.3	14.7	30.7	54.6
1977	3.8	3.5	15.0	6.0	4.6	2.9	2.3	14.4	30.9	54.7
1978	3.8	3.5	15.1	6.2	4.6	3.0	2.3	13.8	31.0	55.2
1979	3.8	3.5	15.2	6.4	4.7	3.0	2.3	13.5	31.2	55.3
1980	3.7	3.5	15.9	6.7	5.0	3.0	2.2	13.8	30.1	56.1
1981	3.5	3.6	15.9	6.8	5.1	3.0	2.2	13.6	30.3	56.1
1982	3.3	3.8	16.6	7.1	5.5	3.1	2.2	14.2	28.4	57.4
1983	3.3	4.0	17.1	7.4	5.6	3.2	2.2	13.9	26.9	59.1
1984	3.3	3.7	17.0	7.7	5.4	3.1	2.3	13.7	27.3	59.0
1985	3.2	3.9	17.3	8.1	5.5	3.2	2.3	13.8	26.2	59.9
1986	3.3	3.9	17.8	8.5	5.6	3.2	2.4	13.9	25.0	61.1
1987	3.2	3.9	17.7	8.7	6.0	3.2	2.4	13.9	24.9	61.2
1988	3.2	3.8	17.8	9.1	6.1	3.3	2.4	13.8	24.7	61.5
1989	3.0	3.8	17.8	9.4	6.3	3.3	2.4	13.7	24.5	61.8
1990	2.9	3.9	18.0	9.8	6.7	3.4	2.5	13.9	23.7	62.4
1991	3.0	3.9	18.4	9.7	7.1	3.4	2.4	14.3	22.6	63.1
1992	2.9	4.0	18.6	9.9	7.3	3.4	2.4	14.2	22.1	63.8
1993	3.0	4.1	18.6	9.9	7.3	3.4	2.5	13.9	21.8	64.2
1994	3.1	4.2	18.4	9.9	7.2	3.3	2.4	13.6	22.2	64.2
1995	3.1	4.2	18.7	10.0	7.2	3.4	2.4	13.4	22.1	64.6
1996	3.0	4.3	18.8	10.4	7.1	3.4	2.4	13.1	22.0	64.9
1997	3.1	4.2	19.2	10.8	6.9	3.5	2.4	12.7	21.9	65.3
1998	3.1	4.4	19.3	11.2	6.9	3.5	2.4	12.5	21.7	65.8
1999	3.1	4.7	19.4	11.5	6.8	3.5	2.3	12.3	21.1	66.6
2000	3.1	4.7	19.7	11.6	6.9	3.6	2.3	12.3	21.2	66.5
2001	2.9	4.7	20.3	11.5	7.3	3.6	2.4	12.4	20.0	67.6
2002	2.9	4.6	20.5	11.4	7.6	3.6	2.4	12.8	19.5	67.8
2003	2.9	4.5	20.6	11.3	7.8	3.6	2.4	12.9	19.4	67.7
2004	2.8	4.6	20.6	11.5	7.7	3.6	2.4	12.6	19.5	67.9

Note (cont'd).—Value added industry data shown in Tables B–12 and B–13 are based on the 1997 North American Industry Classification System (NAICS). GDP by industry data based on the Standard Industrial Classification (SIC) are available from the Department of Commerce, Bureau of Economic Analysis.

Historical data for 1947–73 are available from the U.S. Department of Commerce, Bureau of Economic Analysis. See *Survey of Current Business*, December 2005, for details.

Source: Department of Commerce, Bureau of Economic Analysis.

TABLE B–13.—*Real gross domestic product by industry, value added, and percent changes, 1974–2004*

Year	Gross domestic product	Total private industries	Agriculture, forestry, fishing, and hunting	Mining	Construction	Manufacturing			Utilities	Wholesale trade	Retail trade
						Total manufacturing	Durable goods	Nondurable goods			
	Chain-type quantity indexes for value added (2000=100)										
1974	44.001	41.645	39.532	78.981	75.227	42.094	35.093	54.964	57.065	30.154	33.972
1975	43.916	41.482	45.885	80.253	68.132	39.206	31.649	53.697	60.771	30.899	34.244
1976	46.256	43.911	44.589	80.136	73.128	43.369	34.910	59.644	60.220	31.994	36.890
1977	48.391	46.088	46.430	86.262	74.057	46.745	37.736	64.010	59.909	33.611	38.412
1978	51.085	48.802	45.057	88.929	78.442	49.157	40.159	66.062	59.583	37.065	40.654
1979	52.699	50.606	48.573	79.749	81.174	50.843	40.808	70.282	54.661	39.888	40.701
1980	52.579	50.321	47.543	89.978	74.626	48.190	38.476	67.152	51.968	39.782	38.907
1981	53.904	51.720	59.731	90.260	67.939	50.480	39.563	72.303	51.733	42.074	40.035
1982	52.860	50.422	62.961	86.329	59.460	46.795	35.645	69.864	50.698	42.096	39.951
1983	55.249	52.785	43.338	81.175	62.805	50.455	37.953	76.660	52.706	43.770	44.123
1984	59.220	56.789	57.105	88.849	72.200	55.084	44.042	76.466	57.341	47.143	48.265
1985	61.666	59.383	69.555	93.077	79.043	56.582	45.187	78.688	60.940	49.523	51.232
1986	63.804	61.137	68.605	87.529	81.818	56.516	45.550	77.515	64.406	54.486	54.187
1987	65.958	63.367	71.483	91.661	82.448	60.746	48.859	83.572	72.315	53.070	52.138
1988	68.684	66.299	64.678	99.992	85.435	64.212	52.843	85.425	70.613	56.444	56.545
1989	71.116	68.710	71.099	97.072	87.646	65.033	53.696	86.109	79.002	58.603	58.838
1990	72.451	69.905	74.689	96.157	86.543	64.299	52.963	85.419	84.447	57.318	59.794
1991	72.329	69.779	75.398	97.638	79.137	63.412	51.496	85.835	85.285	59.387	59.483
1992	74.734	72.363	83.114	95.694	80.026	65.508	52.742	89.669	85.362	65.037	62.960
1993	76.731	74.291	72.838	97.020	82.010	68.255	55.173	92.943	85.814	67.135	65.351
1994	79.816	77.765	84.616	105.327	86.586	73.496	60.173	98.369	89.518	71.346	69.806
1995	81.814	79.722	73.099	105.681	86.312	76.819	65.218	97.783	93.835	70.800	72.974
1996	84.842	83.179	80.041	98.850	90.694	79.682	69.120	98.443	95.405	77.261	79.407
1997	88.658	87.362	88.315	102.463	93.267	84.518	75.335	100.438	91.161	85.648	86.039
1998	92.359	91.662	86.287	101.682	97.087	90.181	84.355	99.762	90.481	95.431	90.399
1999	96.469	96.183	89.163	104.300	99.411	94.104	89.627	101.298	94.672	100.412	95.686
2000	100.000	100.000	100.000	100.000	100.000	100.000	100.000	100.000	100.000	100.000	100.000
2001	100.751	100.908	93.661	94.715	100.163	94.436	94.031	95.034	95.081	107.003	106.970
2002	102.362	102.354	98.767	88.719	98.201	97.066	95.663	99.056	99.144	108.059	109.294
2003	105.130	105.178	106.268	87.383	96.895	98.894	99.756	97.827	106.881	110.467	113.202
2004	109.562	110.069	108.139	89.352	99.305	103.638	106.071	100.507	108.054	115.559	120.420
	Percent change from year earlier										
1974	-0.5	-0.9	-2.2	-4.2	-3.6	-4.5	-3.4	-6.2	1.8	-1.2	-4.2
1975	-.2	-.4	16.1	1.6	-9.4	-6.9	-9.8	-2.3	6.5	2.5	.8
1976	5.3	5.9	-2.8	-.1	7.3	10.6	10.3	11.1	-.9	3.5	7.7
1977	4.6	5.0	4.1	7.6	1.3	7.8	8.1	7.3	-.5	5.1	4.1
1978	5.6	5.9	-3.0	3.1	5.9	5.2	6.4	3.2	-.5	10.3	5.8
1979	3.2	3.7	7.8	-10.3	3.5	3.4	1.6	6.4	-8.3	7.6	.1
1980	-.2	-.6	-2.1	12.8	-8.1	-5.2	-5.7	-4.5	-4.9	-.3	-4.4
1981	2.5	2.8	25.6	.3	-9.0	4.8	2.8	7.7	-.5	5.8	2.9
1982	-1.9	-2.5	5.4	-4.4	-12.5	-7.3	-9.9	-3.4	-2.0	.1	-.2
1983	4.5	4.7	-31.2	-6.0	5.6	7.8	6.5	9.7	4.0	4.0	10.4
1984	7.2	7.6	31.8	9.5	15.0	9.2	16.0	-.3	8.8	7.7	9.4
1985	4.1	4.6	21.8	4.8	9.5	2.7	2.6	2.9	6.3	5.0	6.1
1986	3.5	3.0	-1.4	-6.0	3.5	-.1	.8	-1.5	5.7	10.0	5.8
1987	3.4	3.6	4.2	4.7	.8	7.5	7.3	7.8	12.3	-2.6	-3.8
1988	4.1	4.6	-9.5	9.1	3.6	5.7	8.2	2.2	-2.4	6.4	8.5
1989	3.5	3.6	9.9	-2.9	2.6	1.3	1.6	.8	11.9	3.8	4.1
1990	1.9	1.7	5.0	-.9	-1.3	-1.1	-1.4	-.8	6.9	-2.2	1.6
1991	-.2	-.2	.9	1.5	-8.6	-1.4	-2.8	.5	1.0	3.6	-.5
1992	3.3	3.7	10.2	-2.0	1.1	3.3	2.4	4.5	.1	9.5	5.8
1993	2.7	2.7	-12.4	1.4	2.5	4.2	4.6	3.7	.5	3.2	3.8
1994	4.0	4.7	16.2	8.6	5.6	7.7	9.1	5.8	4.3	6.3	6.8
1995	2.5	2.5	-13.6	.3	-.3	4.5	8.4	-.6	4.8	-.8	4.5
1996	3.7	4.3	9.5	-6.5	5.1	3.7	6.0	.7	1.7	9.1	8.8
1997	4.5	5.0	10.3	3.7	2.8	6.1	9.0	2.0	-4.4	10.9	8.4
1998	4.2	4.9	-2.3	-.8	4.1	6.7	12.0	-.7	-.7	11.4	5.1
1999	4.5	4.9	3.3	2.6	2.4	4.4	6.2	1.5	4.6	5.2	5.8
2000	3.7	4.0	12.2	-4.1	.6	6.3	11.6	-1.3	5.6	-.4	4.5
2001	.8	.9	-6.3	-5.3	.2	-5.6	-6.0	-5.0	-4.9	7.0	7.0
2002	1.6	1.4	5.5	-6.3	-2.0	2.8	1.7	4.2	4.3	1.0	2.2
2003	2.7	2.8	7.6	-1.5	-1.3	1.9	4.3	-1.2	7.8	2.2	3.6
2004	4.2	4.7	1.8	2.3	2.5	4.8	6.3	2.7	1.1	4.6	6.4

[1] Consists of agriculture, forestry, fishing, and hunting; mining; construction; and manufacturing.
[2] Consists of utilities; wholesale trade; retail trade; transportation and warehousing; information; finance, insurance, real estate, rental, and leasing; professional and business services; educational services, health care, and social assistance; arts, entertainment, recreation, accommodation, and food services; and other services, except government.

See next page for continuation of table.

TABLE B–13.—*Real gross domestic product by industry, value added, and percent changes, 1974–2004*—Continued

Year	Transportation and warehousing	Information	Finance, insurance, real estate, rental, and leasing	Professional and business services	Educational services, health care, and social assistance	Arts, entertainment, recreation, accommodation, and food services	Other services, except government	Government	Private goods-producing industries [1]	Private services-producing industries [2]
					Chain-type quantity indexes for value added (2000=100)					
1974	41.313	24.289	43.359	30.374	48.961	41.950	68.356	72.251	47.628	38.887
1975	38.471	25.176	45.494	29.732	51.971	42.348	68.213	73.147	45.467	39.687
1976	41.733	26.473	46.720	31.391	54.419	45.554	70.997	74.283	49.103	41.544
1977	43.462	28.460	47.363	34.086	57.878	48.641	71.231	74.973	52.269	43.258
1978	45.697	31.532	50.358	36.884	60.672	52.049	75.107	76.694	54.587	46.163
1979	48.252	34.231	52.965	39.387	63.234	53.512	75.703	77.721	56.085	48.120
1980	47.232	36.394	55.414	40.529	66.887	52.407	74.411	79.023	53.880	48.764
1981	46.178	38.257	56.573	41.554	68.455	54.193	72.329	79.328	55.783	49.923
1982	43.855	38.155	56.986	41.345	68.856	55.695	69.103	79.456	52.029	49.794
1983	49.486	41.017	58.734	44.142	71.153	59.784	72.470	80.178	53.361	52.637
1984	52.121	40.717	61.282	48.913	72.366	62.194	77.498	81.038	59.454	55.727
1985	52.715	42.039	62.812	52.748	73.629	66.167	80.936	83.172	62.569	58.104
1986	53.021	42.672	63.965	56.860	75.166	69.642	82.885	85.105	62.534	60.576
1987	55.690	45.764	65.941	60.050	80.273	68.742	84.221	86.753	66.173	62.256
1988	57.990	47.649	68.652	64.420	80.570	71.515	89.044	88.812	69.104	65.186
1989	59.507	51.150	70.359	68.787	84.002	73.872	92.188	90.984	70.366	68.033
1990	62.281	53.420	71.877	72.073	87.047	76.063	94.369	93.215	69.858	69.877
1991	65.060	54.441	73.051	69.786	89.285	74.232	91.258	93.658	68.214	70.319
1992	68.758	57.568	74.863	72.008	91.728	77.250	92.502	94.134	70.330	73.074
1993	71.988	61.445	76.931	73.224	92.199	78.787	95.195	94.055	72.128	75.047
1994	77.827	65.223	78.506	75.430	92.413	80.604	98.624	94.407	77.818	77.745
1995	80.473	67.996	80.732	77.382	93.503	83.542	99.714	94.250	79.572	79.773
1996	84.585	72.714	82.893	82.053	94.144	86.796	99.072	94.768	82.596	83.377
1997	88.373	74.559	86.786	87.432	94.809	90.310	99.291	95.864	87.229	87.407
1998	91.454	82.252	90.201	91.976	95.603	93.446	101.871	96.923	91.878	91.591
1999	95.301	95.467	94.994	96.898	97.304	96.836	100.236	98.009	95.402	96.434
2000	100.000	100.000	100.000	100.000	100.000	100.000	100.000	100.000	100.000	100.000
2001	97.354	104.034	103.858	99.346	103.186	99.292	98.337	100.794	95.654	102.584
2002	99.531	106.263	104.800	99.192	107.527	101.022	98.667	102.467	96.853	104.107
2003	103.164	109.092	108.409	102.393	110.523	103.997	99.780	103.766	98.009	107.452
2004	107.340	123.022	112.539	108.993	114.026	107.168	101.001	104.766	101.811	112.686
					Percent change from year earlier					
1974	1.0	3.2	5.1	0.8	4.1	−2.5	−3.3	2.6	−4.1	1.1
1975	−6.9	3.7	4.9	−2.1	6.1	.9	−.2	1.2	−4.5	2.1
1976	8.5	5.2	2.7	5.6	4.7	7.6	4.1	1.6	8.0	4.7
1977	4.1	7.5	1.4	8.6	6.4	6.8	.3	.9	6.4	4.1
1978	5.1	10.8	6.3	8.2	4.8	7.0	5.4	2.3	4.4	6.7
1979	5.6	8.6	5.2	6.8	4.2	2.8	.8	1.3	2.7	4.2
1980	−2.1	6.3	4.6	2.9	5.8	−2.1	−1.7	1.7	−3.9	1.3
1981	−2.2	5.1	2.1	2.5	2.3	3.4	−2.8	.4	3.5	2.4
1982	−5.0	−.3	.7	−.5	.6	2.8	−4.5	.2	−6.7	−.3
1983	12.8	7.5	3.1	6.8	3.3	7.3	4.9	.9	2.6	5.7
1984	5.3	−.7	4.3	10.8	1.7	4.0	6.9	1.1	11.4	5.9
1985	1.1	3.2	2.5	7.8	1.7	6.4	4.4	2.6	5.2	4.3
1986	.6	1.5	1.8	7.8	2.1	5.3	2.4	2.3	−.1	4.3
1987	5.0	7.2	3.1	5.6	6.8	−1.3	1.6	1.9	5.8	2.8
1988	4.1	4.1	4.1	7.3	.4	4.0	5.7	2.4	4.4	4.7
1989	2.6	7.3	2.5	6.8	4.3	3.3	3.5	2.4	1.8	4.4
1990	4.7	4.4	2.2	4.8	3.6	3.0	2.4	2.5	−.7	2.7
1991	4.5	1.9	1.6	−3.2	2.6	−2.4	−3.3	.5	−2.4	.6
1992	5.7	5.7	2.5	3.2	2.7	4.1	1.4	.5	3.1	3.9
1993	4.7	6.7	2.8	1.7	.5	2.0	2.9	−.1	2.6	2.7
1994	8.1	6.1	2.0	3.0	.2	2.3	3.6	.4	7.9	3.6
1995	3.4	4.3	2.8	2.6	1.2	3.6	1.1	−.2	2.3	2.6
1996	5.1	6.9	2.7	6.0	.7	3.9	−.6	.5	3.8	4.5
1997	4.5	2.5	4.7	6.6	.7	4.0	.2	1.2	5.6	4.8
1998	3.5	10.3	3.9	5.2	.8	3.5	2.6	1.1	5.3	4.8
1999	4.2	16.1	5.3	5.4	1.8	3.6	−1.6	1.1	3.8	5.3
2000	4.9	4.7	5.3	3.2	2.8	3.3	−.2	2.0	4.8	3.7
2001	−2.6	4.0	3.9	−.7	3.2	−.7	−1.7	.8	−4.3	2.6
2002	2.2	2.1	.9	−.2	4.2	1.7	.3	1.7	1.3	1.5
2003	3.7	2.7	3.4	3.2	2.8	2.9	1.1	1.3	1.2	3.2
2004	4.0	12.8	3.8	6.4	3.2	3.0	1.2	1.0	3.9	4.9

Note.—Data are based on the 1997 North American Industry Classification System (NAICS).
Historical data for 1947–73 are available from the U.S. Department of Commerce, Bureau of Economic Analysis. See *Survey of Current Business*, December 2005, for details.
See Note, Table B–12.

Source: Department of Commerce, Bureau of Economic Analysis.

299

TABLE B–14.—*Gross value added of nonfinancial corporate business, 1959–2005*

[Billions of dollars; quarterly data at seasonally adjusted annual rates]

Year or quarter	Gross value added of non-financial corporate business [1]	Consumption of fixed capital	Net value added Total	Compensation of employees	Taxes on production and imports less subsidies	Net operating surplus Total	Net interest and miscellaneous payments	Business current transfer payments	Corporate profits with inventory valuation and capital consumption adjustments Total	Taxes on corporate income	Profits after tax [2]	Profits before tax	Inventory valuation adjustment	Capital consumption adjustment
1959	266.0	21.1	244.9	170.8	24.4	49.7	2.9	1.3	45.5	20.7	24.8	43.4	-0.3	2.3
1960	276.4	22.6	253.8	180.4	26.6	46.8	3.2	1.4	42.2	19.1	23.1	40.1	-.2	2.3
1961	283.7	23.2	260.5	184.5	27.6	48.4	3.7	1.5	43.2	19.4	23.8	39.9	.3	3.0
1962	309.8	23.9	285.9	199.3	29.9	56.8	4.3	1.7	50.8	20.6	30.2	44.6	.0	6.1
1963	329.9	25.2	304.7	210.1	31.7	62.9	4.7	1.7	56.5	22.8	33.8	49.7	.1	6.8
1964	356.1	26.4	329.7	225.7	33.9	70.2	5.2	2.0	63.0	23.9	39.2	55.9	-.5	7.7
1965	391.2	28.4	362.8	245.4	36.0	81.4	5.8	2.2	73.3	27.1	46.2	66.1	-1.2	8.4
1966	429.0	31.5	397.4	272.9	37.0	87.6	7.0	2.7	77.9	29.5	48.4	71.4	-2.1	8.5
1967	451.2	34.3	416.8	291.1	39.3	86.4	8.4	2.8	75.2	27.8	47.3	67.6	-1.6	9.1
1968	497.8	37.6	460.2	321.9	45.5	92.8	9.7	3.1	80.0	33.5	46.5	74.0	-3.7	9.7
1969	540.5	42.4	498.1	357.1	50.2	90.8	12.7	3.2	74.9	33.3	41.6	71.2	-5.9	9.6
1970	558.3	46.8	511.5	376.5	54.2	80.7	16.6	3.3	60.9	27.3	33.6	58.5	-6.6	8.9
1971	603.0	50.7	552.4	399.4	59.5	93.4	17.6	3.7	72.1	30.0	42.1	67.4	-4.6	9.3
1972	669.5	56.4	613.2	443.9	63.7	105.6	18.6	4.0	83.0	33.8	49.2	79.2	-6.6	10.5
1973	750.8	62.7	688.1	502.2	70.1	115.8	21.8	4.7	89.4	40.4	49.0	99.4	-19.6	9.5
1974	809.8	74.1	735.7	552.2	74.4	109.1	27.5	4.1	77.5	42.8	34.7	110.1	-38.2	5.6
1975	876.7	87.9	788.7	575.5	80.2	133.1	28.4	5.0	99.6	41.9	57.7	110.7	-10.5	-.5
1976	989.7	97.0	892.7	651.4	86.7	154.7	26.0	7.0	121.7	53.5	68.2	138.2	-14.1	-2.4
1977	1,119.4	110.5	1,008.8	735.3	94.6	178.9	28.5	9.0	141.4	60.6	80.9	159.4	-15.7	-2.2
1978	1,272.9	127.8	1,145.1	845.3	102.7	197.0	33.4	9.5	154.1	67.6	86.6	183.7	-23.7	-5.9
1979	1,415.9	147.3	1,268.6	959.9	108.8	200.0	41.8	9.5	148.8	70.6	78.1	197.0	-40.1	-8.1
1980	1,537.1	168.2	1,368.9	1,049.8	121.5	197.6	54.2	10.2	133.2	68.2	65.0	184.0	-42.1	-8.7
1981	1,746.0	191.5	1,554.5	1,161.5	146.7	246.4	67.2	11.4	167.7	66.0	101.7	185.0	-24.6	7.4
1982	1,806.2	211.2	1,594.9	1,203.9	152.9	238.1	77.4	8.8	151.9	48.8	103.1	139.9	-7.5	19.5
1983	1,933.0	217.6	1,715.4	1,266.9	168.0	280.5	77.0	10.5	192.9	61.7	131.2	163.3	-7.4	37.1
1984	2,167.5	230.7	1,936.8	1,406.1	185.0	345.7	86.0	11.7	248.0	75.9	172.0	197.6	-4.0	54.3
1985	2,302.0	247.4	2,054.6	1,504.2	196.6	353.8	91.5	16.1	246.3	71.1	175.2	173.4	.0	72.8
1986	2,387.5	255.3	2,132.2	1,583.1	204.6	344.5	95.1	27.3	222.1	76.2	145.9	149.7	7.1	65.3
1987	2,557.1	266.5	2,290.6	1,687.8	216.8	386.0	96.4	29.9	259.7	94.2	165.5	209.8	-16.2	66.2
1988	2,771.6	281.6	2,490.0	1,812.8	233.8	443.4	109.8	27.4	306.2	104.0	202.3	260.4	-22.2	68.0
1989	2,912.3	301.6	2,610.7	1,914.7	248.2	447.9	142.0	23.0	282.9	101.2	181.7	238.7	-16.3	60.6
1990	3,041.5	319.2	2,722.3	2,012.9	263.5	445.8	146.2	25.4	274.3	98.5	175.8	239.0	-12.9	48.2
1991	3,099.7	341.4	2,758.3	2,048.4	285.7	424.2	135.9	26.7	261.5	88.6	172.9	222.4	4.9	34.2
1992	3,236.0	353.6	2,882.3	2,154.1	302.5	425.7	111.3	25.2	289.2	94.4	194.8	258.2	-2.8	33.8
1993	3,397.8	363.4	3,034.4	2,244.8	318.8	470.8	102.0	29.6	339.2	108.0	231.2	303.3	-4.0	39.9
1994	3,669.5	391.5	3,278.0	2,381.5	349.6	546.9	101.0	30.0	415.9	132.9	283.1	380.1	-12.4	48.3
1995	3,879.5	415.0	3,464.5	2,509.8	356.9	597.8	115.2	30.2	452.5	141.0	311.4	419.3	-18.3	51.5
1996	4,109.5	436.5	3,673.0	2,630.8	369.1	673.1	111.9	38.0	523.2	153.1	370.1	458.5	3.1	61.6
1997	4,401.8	467.1	3,934.7	2,812.9	385.5	736.3	124.0	39.0	573.4	161.9	411.5	494.2	14.1	65.0
1998	4,655.0	493.3	4,161.7	3,045.6	398.7	717.4	143.8	35.2	538.3	158.6	379.7	449.4	20.2	68.7
1999	4,950.8	523.8	4,427.0	3,267.7	416.6	742.7	160.2	45.0	537.6	171.2	366.3	457.9	1.0	78.7
2000	5,272.2	567.8	4,704.3	3,544.4	443.4	716.5	191.7	48.4	476.4	170.2	306.2	423.9	-14.1	66.6
2001	5,293.5	646.8	4,646.7	3,595.9	439.1	611.8	204.0	50.6	357.2	111.7	245.5	310.6	11.3	35.2
2002	5,371.7	643.6	4,728.2	3,611.9	465.5	650.8	167.4	54.0	429.4	97.0	332.3	336.3	-2.2	95.3
2003	5,595.7	652.6	4,943.1	3,703.2	486.5	753.4	166.2	62.4	524.9	126.5	398.3	448.1	-13.3	90.0
2004 *p*	5,995.4	690.3	5,305.1	3,906.8	519.1	879.2	164.9	60.4	653.9	165.9	487.9	573.9	-39.6	119.7
2005 *p*	....	729.2	....	4,173.9	549.8	....	....	43.0	....	....	....	....	....	-55.7
2002: I	5,284.6	643.3	4,641.3	3,576.7	454.3	610.2	186.1	53.6	370.6	78.2	292.3	260.9	13.3	96.4
II	5,358.3	643.4	4,715.0	3,616.8	462.8	635.3	168.5	53.2	413.5	91.9	321.6	317.2	-1.6	97.9
III	5,395.6	643.4	4,752.1	3,626.4	470.2	655.5	160.1	53.8	441.5	102.0	339.5	357.2	-11.8	96.1
IV	5,448.4	644.2	4,804.2	3,627.4	474.8	702.0	155.0	55.2	491.8	116.0	375.8	409.8	-8.8	90.9
2003: I	5,456.5	646.1	4,810.4	3,636.8	478.3	695.2	161.3	59.1	474.8	119.3	355.4	423.7	-25.0	76.0
II	5,541.8	649.6	4,892.2	3,682.2	474.9	735.2	166.1	61.6	507.5	116.7	390.7	414.3	-2.1	95.3
III	5,650.0	654.3	4,995.7	3,726.1	493.1	776.5	168.4	63.7	544.4	128.1	416.3	454.0	-5.1	95.6
IV	5,734.4	660.2	5,074.2	3,767.8	499.8	806.6	168.9	65.0	572.8	141.9	430.9	500.5	-20.8	93.1
2004: I	5,822.0	667.4	5,154.7	3,806.3	509.8	838.5	169.1	66.7	602.7	145.9	456.8	507.9	-28.9	123.8
II	5,922.8	675.7	5,247.1	3,850.5	516.2	880.4	166.2	67.6	646.6	165.2	481.4	571.9	-48.3	123.0
III	6,038.0	722.0	5,316.1	3,928.5	520.6	866.9	162.1	37.9	666.9	171.8	495.1	589.5	-36.9	114.2
IV	6,198.9	696.2	5,502.8	4,042.0	529.9	930.9	162.1	69.5	699.3	180.8	518.5	626.1	-44.4	117.6
2005: I	6,282.8	697.5	5,585.3	4,105.4	537.7	942.2	167.0	58.0	717.1	231.9	485.2	807.6	-39.1	-51.3
II	6,414.0	700.4	5,713.6	4,140.5	547.9	1,025.2	167.3	58.4	799.6	248.6	550.9	865.5	-18.9	-47.0
III	6,512.1	792.8	5,719.3	4,198.8	553.7	966.8	172.8	2.9	791.1	258.0	533.1	890.8	-27.5	-72.2
IV *p*	....	726.0	....	4,251.1	559.9	....	....	52.7	....	....	....	....	....	-52.0

[1] Estimates for nonfinancial corporate business for 2000 and earlier periods are based on the Standard Industrial Classification (SIC); later estimates are based on the North American Industry Classification System (NAICS).
[2] With inventory valuation and capital consumption adjustments.

Source: Department of Commerce, Bureau of Economic Analysis.

[Quarterly data at seasonally adjusted annual rates]

Year or quarter	Gross value added of nonfinancial corporate business (billions of dollars)[1]		Price per unit of real gross value added of nonfinancial corporate business (dollars)[1][2]			Unit nonlabor cost				Corporate profits with inventory valuation and capital consumption adjustments[4]		
	Current dollars	Chained (2000) dollars	Total[2]	Compensation of employees (unit labor cost)	Total	Consumption of fixed capital	Taxes on production and imports[3]	Net interest and miscellaneous payments	Total	Taxes on corporate income	Profits after tax[5]
1959	266.0	980.4	0.271	0.174	0.051	0.022	0.026	0.003	0.046	0.021	0.025
1960	276.4	1,012.0	.273	.178	.053	.022	.028	.003	.042	.019	.023
1961	283.7	1,033.6	.274	.179	.054	.022	.028	.004	.042	.019	.023
1962	309.8	1,120.7	.276	.178	.053	.021	.028	.004	.045	.018	.027
1963	329.9	1,186.7	.278	.177	.053	.021	.028	.004	.048	.019	.028
1964	356.1	1,270.3	.280	.178	.053	.021	.028	.004	.050	.019	.031
1965	391.2	1,375.1	.284	.178	.053	.021	.028	.004	.053	.020	.034
1966	429.0	1,472.6	.291	.185	.053	.021	.027	.005	.053	.020	.033
1967	451.2	1,508.9	.299	.193	.057	.023	.028	.006	.050	.018	.031
1968	497.8	1,604.8	.310	.201	.059	.023	.030	.006	.050	.021	.029
1969	540.5	1,667.6	.324	.214	.065	.025	.032	.008	.045	.020	.025
1970	558.3	1,649.9	.338	.228	.073	.028	.035	.010	.037	.017	.020
1971	603.0	1,716.6	.351	.233	.077	.030	.037	.010	.042	.017	.025
1972	669.5	1,846.4	.363	.240	.078	.031	.037	.010	.045	.018	.027
1973	750.8	1,957.7	.384	.257	.081	.032	.038	.011	.046	.021	.025
1974	809.8	1,925.4	.421	.287	.093	.038	.041	.014	.040	.022	.018
1975	876.7	1,898.8	.462	.303	.106	.046	.045	.015	.052	.022	.030
1976	989.7	2,050.0	.483	.318	.106	.047	.046	.013	.059	.026	.033
1977	1,119.4	2,200.0	.509	.334	.110	.050	.047	.013	.064	.028	.037
1978	1,272.9	2,344.1	.543	.361	.117	.055	.048	.014	.066	.029	.037
1979	1,415.9	2,418.7	.585	.397	.127	.061	.049	.017	.062	.029	.032
1980	1,537.1	2,394.6	.642	.438	.148	.070	.055	.023	.056	.028	.027
1981	1,746.0	2,491.5	.701	.466	.167	.077	.063	.027	.067	.026	.041
1982	1,806.2	2,430.6	.743	.495	.186	.087	.067	.032	.062	.020	.042
1983	1,933.0	2,545.1	.759	.498	.185	.085	.070	.030	.076	.024	.052
1984	2,167.5	2,772.8	.782	.507	.185	.083	.071	.031	.089	.027	.062
1985	2,302.0	2,896.3	.795	.519	.190	.085	.073	.032	.085	.025	.060
1986	2,387.5	2,963.3	.806	.534	.196	.086	.078	.032	.075	.026	.049
1987	2,557.1	3,119.6	.820	.541	.195	.085	.079	.031	.083	.030	.053
1988	2,771.6	3,300.7	.840	.549	.197	.085	.079	.033	.093	.031	.061
1989	2,912.3	3,361.8	.866	.570	.213	.090	.081	.042	.084	.030	.054
1990	3,041.5	3,404.0	.894	.591	.222	.094	.085	.043	.081	.029	.052
1991	3,099.7	3,376.2	.918	.607	.234	.101	.093	.040	.077	.026	.051
1992	3,236.0	3,479.5	.930	.619	.228	.102	.094	.032	.083	.027	.056
1993	3,397.8	3,575.5	.950	.628	.228	.102	.097	.029	.095	.030	.065
1994	3,669.5	3,797.9	.966	.627	.230	.103	.100	.027	.110	.035	.075
1995	3,879.5	3,977.4	.975	.631	.230	.104	.097	.029	.114	.035	.078
1996	4,109.5	4,196.4	.979	.627	.228	.104	.097	.027	.125	.036	.088
1997	4,401.8	4,469.3	.985	.629	.228	.105	.095	.028	.128	.036	.092
1998	4,655.0	4,725.4	.985	.645	.226	.104	.092	.030	.114	.034	.080
1999	4,950.8	5,011.0	.988	.652	.229	.105	.092	.032	.107	.034	.073
2000	5,272.2	5,272.2	1.000	.672	.237	.108	.093	.036	.090	.032	.058
2001	5,293.5	5,224.5	1.013	.688	.257	.124	.094	.039	.068	.021	.047
2002	5,371.7	5,269.7	1.019	.685	.253	.122	.099	.032	.081	.018	.063
2003	5,595.7	5,418.2	1.033	.683	.252	.120	.101	.031	.097	.023	.074
2004	5,995.4	5,714.1	1.049	.684	.251	.121	.101	.029	.114	.029	.085
2002: I	5,284.6	5,194.6	1.017	.689	.258	.124	.098	.036	.071	.015	.056
II	5,358.3	5,265.4	1.018	.687	.252	.122	.098	.032	.079	.017	.061
III	5,395.6	5,296.0	1.019	.685	.250	.121	.099	.030	.083	.019	.064
IV	5,448.4	5,322.8	1.024	.681	.250	.121	.100	.029	.092	.022	.071
2003: I	5,456.5	5,301.9	1.029	.686	.253	.122	.101	.030	.090	.023	.067
II	5,541.8	5,374.5	1.031	.685	.252	.121	.100	.031	.094	.022	.073
III	5,650.0	5,466.9	1.033	.682	.253	.120	.102	.031	.100	.023	.076
IV	5,734.4	5,529.7	1.037	.681	.252	.119	.102	.031	.104	.026	.078
2004: I	5,822.0	5,578.3	1.044	.682	.253	.120	.103	.030	.108	.026	.082
II	5,922.8	5,625.9	1.053	.684	.254	.120	.104	.030	.115	.029	.086
III	6,038.0	5,756.2	1.049	.682	.250	.125	.097	.028	.116	.030	.086
IV	6,198.9	5,895.9	1.051	.686	.247	.118	.102	.027	.119	.031	.088
2005: I	6,282.8	5,943.3	1.057	.691	.245	.117	.100	.028	.121	.039	.082
II	6,414.0	6,046.0	1.061	.685	.244	.116	.100	.028	.132	.041	.091
III	6,512.1	6,107.0	1.066	.688	.249	.130	.091	.028	.130	.042	.087

[1] Estimates for nonfinancial corporate business for 2000 and earlier periods are based on the Standard Industrial Classification (SIC); later estimates are based on the North American Industry Classification System (NAICS).
[2] The implicit price deflator for gross value added of nonfinancial corporate business divided by 100.
[3] Less subsidies plus business current transfer payments.
[4] Unit profits from current production.
[5] With inventory valuation and capital consumption adjustments.

Source: Department of Commerce, Bureau of Economic Analysis.

TABLE B–16.—*Personal consumption expenditures, 1959–2005*

[Billions of dollars; quarterly data at seasonally adjusted annual rates]

Year or quarter	Personal consumption expenditures	Durable goods Total¹	Motor vehicles and parts	Furniture and household equipment	Nondurable goods Total¹	Food	Clothing and shoes	Gasoline and oil	Fuel oil and coal	Services Total¹	Housing²	Household operation Total¹	Electricity and gas	Transportation	Medical care
1959	317.6	42.7	18.9	18.1	148.5	80.6	26.4	11.3	4.0	126.5	45.0	18.7	7.6	10.6	16.4
1960	331.7	43.3	19.7	18.0	152.8	82.3	27.0	12.0	3.8	135.6	48.2	20.3	8.3	11.2	17.7
1961	342.1	41.8	17.8	18.3	156.6	84.0	27.6	12.0	3.8	143.8	51.2	21.2	8.8	11.6	19.0
1962	363.3	46.9	21.5	19.3	162.8	86.1	29.0	12.6	3.8	153.6	54.7	22.4	9.4	12.3	21.2
1963	382.7	51.6	24.4	20.7	168.2	88.2	29.8	13.0	4.0	162.9	58.0	23.6	9.9	12.9	23.0
1964	411.4	56.7	26.0	23.2	178.6	93.5	32.4	13.6	4.1	176.1	61.4	25.0	10.4	13.8	26.4
1965	443.8	63.3	29.9	25.1	191.5	100.7	34.1	14.8	4.4	189.0	65.4	26.5	10.9	14.7	28.6
1966	480.9	68.3	30.3	28.2	208.7	109.3	37.4	16.0	4.7	203.8	69.5	28.1	11.5	15.9	31.5
1967	507.8	70.4	30.0	30.0	217.1	112.4	39.2	17.1	4.8	220.3	74.1	30.0	12.2	17.4	34.7
1968	558.0	80.8	36.1	32.9	235.7	122.2	43.2	18.6	4.7	241.6	79.8	32.3	13.0	19.3	40.1
1969	605.2	85.9	38.4	34.7	253.1	131.5	46.5	20.5	4.6	266.1	86.9	35.0	14.1	21.6	45.8
1970	648.5	85.0	35.5	35.7	272.0	143.8	47.8	21.9	4.4	291.5	94.1	37.8	15.3	24.0	51.7
1971	701.9	96.9	44.5	37.8	285.5	149.7	51.7	23.2	4.6	319.5	102.8	41.1	16.9	26.8	58.4
1972	770.6	110.4	51.1	42.4	308.0	161.4	56.4	24.4	5.1	352.2	112.6	45.4	18.8	29.6	65.6
1973	852.4	123.5	56.1	47.9	343.1	179.6	62.5	28.1	6.3	385.8	123.3	49.9	20.4	31.6	73.3
1974	933.4	122.3	49.5	51.5	384.5	201.8	66.0	36.1	7.8	426.6	134.8	55.8	24.0	34.1	82.3
1975	1,034.4	133.5	54.8	54.5	420.7	223.2	70.8	39.7	8.4	480.2	147.7	64.0	29.2	37.9	95.6
1976	1,151.9	158.9	71.3	60.2	458.3	242.5	76.6	43.0	10.1	534.7	162.2	72.5	33.2	42.5	109.1
1977	1,278.6	181.2	83.5	67.2	497.1	262.6	84.1	46.9	11.1	600.2	180.2	81.8	38.5	48.7	125.3
1978	1,428.5	201.7	93.1	74.3	550.2	289.6	94.3	50.1	11.5	676.6	202.4	91.2	43.0	53.4	143.1
1979	1,592.2	214.4	93.5	82.7	624.5	324.7	101.2	66.2	14.4	753.3	227.3	100.3	47.8	59.9	161.0
1980	1,757.1	214.2	87.0	86.7	696.1	356.0	107.3	86.7	15.4	846.9	256.2	113.7	57.5	65.2	184.4
1981	1,941.1	231.3	95.8	92.1	758.9	383.5	117.2	97.9	15.8	950.8	289.7	126.8	64.8	70.3	216.7
1982	2,077.3	240.2	102.9	93.4	787.6	403.4	120.5	94.1	14.5	1,049.4	315.2	142.5	74.2	72.9	243.3
1983	2,290.6	280.8	126.5	106.6	831.2	423.8	130.9	93.1	13.6	1,178.6	341.0	157.0	82.4	81.1	274.3
1984	2,503.3	326.5	152.1	119.0	884.6	447.4	142.5	94.6	13.9	1,292.2	374.5	169.4	86.5	93.2	303.2
1985	2,720.3	363.5	175.9	128.5	928.7	467.6	152.1	97.2	13.6	1,428.1	412.7	181.8	90.8	104.5	331.5
1986	2,899.7	403.0	194.1	143.0	958.4	492.0	163.1	80.1	11.3	1,538.3	448.4	187.7	89.2	111.1	357.5
1987	3,100.2	421.7	195.0	153.4	1,015.3	515.2	174.4	85.4	11.2	1,663.3	483.7	195.4	90.9	120.9	392.2
1988	3,353.6	453.6	209.4	163.7	1,083.5	553.5	185.5	88.3	11.7	1,816.5	521.5	207.3	96.3	133.4	442.8
1989	3,598.5	471.8	215.3	171.6	1,166.7	591.6	198.9	98.6	11.9	1,960.0	557.4	221.1	101.0	142.0	492.5
1990	3,839.9	474.2	212.8	171.6	1,249.6	636.8	204.1	111.2	12.9	2,115.9	597.9	227.3	101.0	147.7	556.0
1991	3,986.1	453.9	193.5	171.7	1,284.8	657.5	208.7	108.5	12.4	2,247.4	631.1	238.6	107.4	145.3	608.9
1992	4,235.3	483.6	213.0	178.7	1,330.5	669.3	221.9	112.4	12.2	2,421.2	658.5	250.7	108.9	157.7	672.2
1993	4,477.9	526.7	234.0	193.4	1,379.4	691.9	229.9	114.1	12.4	2,571.8	683.9	269.9	118.2	172.7	715.1
1994	4,743.3	582.2	260.5	213.4	1,437.2	720.6	238.1	116.2	12.8	2,723.9	726.1	286.2	120.7	190.6	752.9
1995	4,975.8	611.6	266.7	228.6	1,485.1	740.9	241.7	120.2	13.1	2,879.1	764.4	298.7	122.2	207.7	797.9
1996	5,256.8	652.6	284.9	242.9	1,555.5	768.7	250.2	130.4	14.3	3,048.7	800.1	318.5	129.4	226.5	833.5
1997	5,547.4	692.7	305.1	256.2	1,619.0	796.2	258.1	134.4	13.3	3,235.8	842.6	337.0	131.3	245.7	873.0
1998	5,879.5	750.2	336.1	273.1	1,683.6	829.8	270.9	122.4	11.5	3,445.7	894.6	350.5	128.9	259.5	921.4
1999	6,282.5	817.6	370.8	293.9	1,804.8	873.1	286.3	137.9	11.9	3,660.0	948.4	364.8	130.6	276.4	961.1
2000	6,739.4	863.3	386.5	312.9	1,947.2	925.2	297.7	175.7	15.8	3,928.8	1,006.5	390.1	143.3	291.3	1,026.8
2001	7,055.0	883.7	407.9	312.1	2,017.1	967.9	297.7	171.6	15.4	4,154.3	1,073.7	409.0	156.7	292.8	1,113.8
2002	7,350.7	923.9	429.3	323.1	2,079.6	1,001.9	303.5	164.5	14.2	4,347.2	1,123.1	407.7	152.5	288.4	1,206.2
2003	7,709.9	950.1	439.1	330.3	2,189.0	1,048.5	310.8	192.6	17.0	4,570.8	1,158.0	428.8	166.6	296.8	1,299.4
2004	8,214.3	987.8	441.8	354.1	2,368.3	1,134.7	329.0	230.4	19.5	4,858.2	1,221.1	446.2	175.9	306.9	1,401.1
2005ᵖ	8,745.9	1,025.7	445.8	373.3	2,564.3	1,218.8	345.5	287.2	23.4	5,155.9	1,281.6	482.4	201.6	321.1	1,509.8
2002: I	7,230.3	915.2	422.8	322.0	2,044.9	993.3	303.6	146.7	12.7	4,270.2	1,112.9	400.0	146.5	287.7	1,169.4
II	7,323.0	918.9	422.4	324.9	2,078.9	1,000.3	303.8	167.2	14.1	4,325.2	1,121.1	406.9	153.0	289.0	1,193.4
III	7,396.6	940.1	446.6	322.2	2,085.1	1,002.4	300.2	170.1	14.4	4,371.4	1,126.2	407.9	151.3	287.7	1,218.0
IV	7,453.1	921.5	425.2	323.3	2,109.7	1,011.6	306.5	174.1	15.6	4,421.8	1,132.2	415.9	159.1	289.4	1,244.0
2003: I	7,555.2	919.7	427.2	319.5	2,156.0	1,026.6	302.8	199.9	18.1	4,479.5	1,141.8	424.7	164.2	293.0	1,265.2
II	7,635.3	942.2	438.1	325.9	2,153.1	1,033.7	307.0	185.2	16.1	4,540.0	1,149.5	428.2	167.1	294.9	1,288.6
III	7,782.4	974.7	454.6	335.3	2,213.5	1,058.9	316.1	194.9	16.7	4,594.2	1,162.4	427.9	165.1	298.4	1,308.1
IV	7,866.6	963.6	436.4	340.6	2,233.6	1,074.9	317.3	190.6	17.3	4,669.5	1,178.4	434.3	169.8	300.8	1,335.9
2004: I	8,032.3	974.2	437.0	347.2	2,302.7	1,106.5	326.7	211.3	18.0	4,755.4	1,195.8	440.0	172.9	304.8	1,360.1
II	8,145.6	974.6	432.4	351.7	2,355.2	1,124.8	325.7	234.9	18.2	4,815.9	1,213.9	440.7	171.8	305.6	1,387.1
III	8,263.2	993.8	444.9	356.9	2,378.4	1,141.0	328.3	229.0	20.3	4,891.0	1,230.0	445.9	173.2	308.0	1,415.4
IV	8,416.1	1,008.6	452.8	360.6	2,437.1	1,166.4	335.2	246.5	21.4	4,970.4	1,244.7	457.9	185.9	309.2	1,441.6
2005: I	8,535.8	1,017.3	449.6	366.9	2,476.6	1,184.2	340.5	253.1	22.0	5,041.8	1,260.6	465.3	189.5	312.3	1,470.5
II	8,677.0	1,035.5	458.5	370.0	2,533.7	1,207.1	344.9	273.9	22.5	5,107.8	1,275.3	471.4	192.4	318.5	1,492.6
III	8,844.0	1,050.9	468.7	374.9	2,604.9	1,229.9	343.9	313.9	24.4	5,188.3	1,288.2	484.4	202.1	324.1	1,522.0
IVᵖ	8,926.9	999.0	406.4	381.6	2,642.0	1,254.2	352.6	307.9	24.4	5,285.9	1,302.3	508.4	222.4	329.6	1,554.0

¹ Includes other items not shown separately.
² Includes imputed rental value of owner-occupied housing.

Source: Department of Commerce, Bureau of Economic Analysis.

TABLE B–17.—*Real personal consumption expenditures, 1990–2005*

[Billions of chained (2000) dollars; quarterly data at seasonally adjusted annual rates]

Year or quarter	Personal consumption expenditures	Durable goods			Nondurable goods					Services					
	Total¹	Total¹	Motor vehicles and parts	Furniture and household equipment	Total¹	Food	Clothing and shoes	Gasoline and oil	Fuel oil and coal	Total¹	Housing²	Household operation		Transportation	Medical care
												Total¹	Electricity and gas		
1990	4,770.3	453.5	256.1	119.9	1,484.0	784.4	188.2	141.8	16.7	2,851.7	802.2	266.4	117.4	195.7	797.6
1991	4,778.4	427.9	226.6	121.1	1,480.5	783.3	188.8	140.3	16.6	2,900.0	820.1	269.9	121.1	186.3	824.5
1992	4,934.8	453.0	244.9	127.8	1,510.1	787.9	199.2	146.0	17.0	3,000.8	832.7	277.4	120.4	194.2	863.6
1993	5,099.8	488.4	259.2	141.1	1,550.4	802.2	207.4	149.7	17.4	3,085.7	841.8	291.1	126.8	202.5	877.2
1994	5,290.7	529.4	276.2	156.8	1,603.9	821.8	218.5	151.7	18.2	3,176.6	869.3	303.3	128.8	218.4	887.1
1995	5,433.5	552.6	272.3	173.3	1,638.6	827.1	227.4	154.5	18.7	3,259.9	887.5	312.9	130.2	231.8	906.4
1996	5,619.4	595.9	285.4	193.4	1,680.4	834.7	238.7	157.9	18.4	3,356.0	901.1	327.3	134.7	247.5	922.5
1997	5,831.8	646.9	304.7	216.3	1,725.3	845.2	246.0	162.8	16.9	3,468.0	922.5	340.4	133.7	263.2	942.8
1998	6,125.8	720.3	339.0	244.7	1,794.4	865.6	263.1	170.3	16.0	3,615.0	948.8	357.1	136.7	272.0	970.7
1999	6,438.6	804.6	372.4	280.7	1,876.6	893.6	282.7	176.3	16.4	3,758.0	978.6	371.9	138.1	283.4	989.0
2000	6,739.4	863.3	386.5	312.9	1,947.2	925.2	297.7	175.7	15.8	3,928.8	1,006.5	390.1	143.3	291.3	1,026.8
2001	6,910.4	900.7	405.8	331.8	1,986.7	940.2	303.7	178.3	15.2	4,023.2	1,033.7	391.0	140.9	288.0	1,075.2
2002	7,099.3	964.8	429.0	364.3	2,037.1	954.6	318.3	181.9	15.5	4,100.4	1,042.1	393.2	144.9	280.1	1,136.6
2003	7,306.6	1,028.5	449.7	396.3	2,101.8	980.1	334.1	183.2	15.5	4,183.9	1,048.4	398.2	146.8	280.1	1,184.9
2004	7,588.6	1,089.9	457.0	442.9	2,200.4	1,029.1	355.0	185.9	15.5	4,310.9	1,078.4	405.6	149.2	283.4	1,233.5
2005ᴾ	7,858.1	1,137.7	451.7	485.2	2,298.0	1,081.2	376.6	190.6	14.6	4,438.0	1,103.8	416.8	154.9	287.2	1,291.8
2002: I	7,042.2	948.4	422.1	356.9	2,026.8	950.2	315.9	181.3	14.7	4,069.4	1,044.4	388.0	139.8	281.9	1,113.5
II	7,083.5	956.9	422.5	363.5	2,033.4	954.5	317.0	182.0	15.6	4,095.7	1,043.7	395.1	145.8	281.0	1,129.9
III	7,123.2	983.4	445.6	365.2	2,035.0	954.4	315.7	183.2	15.5	4,109.0	1,041.0	392.4	144.1	279.1	1,144.4
IV	7,148.2	970.4	425.9	371.6	2,053.1	959.5	324.4	181.2	16.3	4,127.4	1,039.3	397.3	149.8	279.0	1,158.8
2003: I	7,192.2	979.1	431.6	372.5	2,069.5	969.2	323.4	181.7	15.7	4,146.5	1,041.3	397.9	148.6	280.6	1,169.8
II	7,256.8	1,014.0	445.9	387.4	2,079.1	970.5	331.1	181.7	14.7	4,169.7	1,044.5	396.4	145.5	279.4	1,180.1
III	7,360.7	1,061.0	466.8	407.5	2,121.2	987.7	340.4	184.0	15.6	4,190.2	1,050.1	395.9	143.8	280.0	1,187.6
IV	7,416.4	1,060.0	454.4	417.7	2,137.3	992.8	341.5	185.3	16.1	4,229.4	1,057.7	402.4	149.2	280.4	1,202.2
2004: I	7,501.4	1,071.6	453.9	428.4	2,171.9	1,015.5	352.6	184.7	15.6	4,269.0	1,067.6	404.2	147.8	283.8	1,211.4
II	7,536.6	1,072.5	448.1	437.1	2,186.1	1,022.5	349.7	185.5	15.4	4,288.6	1,074.6	402.3	146.9	283.5	1,225.5
III	7,617.5	1,100.4	461.4	449.2	2,206.9	1,030.9	354.9	185.4	16.0	4,324.0	1,081.9	403.5	145.6	283.4	1,241.6
IV	7,698.8	1,115.1	464.6	456.8	2,236.5	1,047.4	363.0	188.1	15.0	4,362.1	1,089.5	412.4	154.7	283.0	1,255.4
2005: I	7,764.9	1,122.3	455.0	469.2	2,265.6	1,060.9	367.9	192.1	15.6	4,392.0	1,095.6	414.3	155.2	284.6	1,269.1
II	7,829.5	1,143.9	463.3	475.9	2,285.9	1,072.2	374.4	190.5	14.8	4,417.6	1,101.4	413.8	153.2	286.3	1,282.3
III	7,907.9	1,169.7	477.3	490.5	2,305.8	1,088.7	377.2	188.7	14.4	4,453.5	1,106.6	418.5	155.5	287.6	1,299.6
IVᴾ	7,930.2	1,114.7	411.3	505.2	2,334.7	1,103.0	387.0	190.9	13.6	4,489.1	1,111.5	420.5	155.9	290.5	1,316.1

¹ Includes other items not shown separately.
² Includes imputed rental value of owner-occupied housing.
Note.—See Table B-2 for data for total personal consumption expenditures for 1959-89.
Source: Department of Commerce, Bureau of Economic Analysis.

TABLE B–18.—*Private fixed investment by type, 1959–2005*

[Billions of dollars; quarterly data at seasonally adjusted annual rates]

Year or quarter	Private fixed investment	Nonresidential											Residential		
		Total nonresidential	Structures	Equipment and software									Total residential	Structures	
				Total	Information processing equipment and software				Industrial equipment	Transportation equipment	Other equipment			Total [1]	Single family
					Total	Computers and peripheral equipment	Software	Other							
1959	74.6	46.5	18.1	28.4	4.0	0.0	0.0	4.0	8.5	8.3	7.6		28.1	27.5	16.7
1960	75.7	49.4	19.6	29.8	4.9	.2	.1	4.6	9.4	8.5	7.1		26.3	25.8	14.9
1961	75.2	48.8	19.7	29.1	5.3	.3	.2	4.8	8.8	8.0	7.0		26.4	25.9	14.1
1962	82.0	53.1	20.8	32.3	5.7	.3	.2	5.1	9.3	9.8	7.5		29.0	28.4	15.1
1963	88.1	56.0	21.2	34.8	6.5	.7	.4	5.4	10.0	9.4	8.8		32.1	31.5	16.0
1964	97.2	63.0	23.7	39.2	7.4	.9	.5	5.9	11.4	10.6	9.9		34.3	33.6	17.6
1965	109.0	74.8	28.3	46.5	8.5	1.2	.7	6.7	13.7	13.2	11.0		34.2	33.5	17.8
1966	117.7	85.4	31.3	54.0	10.7	1.7	1.0	8.0	16.2	14.5	12.7		32.3	31.6	16.6
1967	118.7	86.4	31.5	54.9	11.3	1.9	1.2	8.2	16.9	14.3	12.4		32.4	31.6	16.8
1968	132.1	93.4	33.6	59.9	11.9	1.9	1.3	8.7	17.3	17.6	13.0		38.7	37.9	19.5
1969	147.3	104.7	37.7	67.0	14.6	2.4	1.8	10.4	19.1	18.9	14.4		42.6	41.6	19.7
1970	150.4	109.0	40.3	68.7	16.6	2.7	2.3	11.6	20.3	16.2	15.6		41.4	40.2	17.5
1971	169.9	114.1	42.7	71.5	17.3	2.8	2.4	12.2	19.5	18.4	16.3		55.8	54.5	25.8
1972	198.5	128.8	47.2	81.7	19.5	3.5	2.8	13.2	21.4	21.8	19.0		69.7	68.1	32.8
1973	228.6	153.3	55.0	98.3	23.1	3.5	3.2	16.3	26.0	26.6	22.6		75.3	73.6	35.2
1974	235.4	169.5	61.2	108.2	27.0	3.9	3.9	19.2	30.7	26.3	24.3		66.0	64.1	29.7
1975	236.5	173.7	61.4	112.4	28.5	3.6	4.8	20.2	31.3	25.2	27.4		62.7	60.8	29.6
1976	274.8	192.4	65.9	126.4	32.7	4.4	5.2	23.1	34.1	30.0	29.6		82.5	80.4	43.9
1977	339.0	228.7	74.6	154.1	39.2	5.7	5.5	28.0	39.4	39.3	36.3		110.3	107.9	62.2
1978	412.2	280.6	93.6	187.0	48.7	7.6	6.3	34.8	47.7	47.3	43.2		131.6	128.9	72.8
1979	474.9	333.9	117.7	216.2	58.5	10.2	8.1	40.2	56.2	53.6	47.9		141.0	137.8	72.3
1980	485.6	362.4	136.2	226.2	68.8	12.5	9.8	46.4	60.7	48.4	48.3		123.2	119.8	52.9
1981	542.6	420.0	167.3	252.7	81.5	17.1	11.8	52.5	65.5	50.6	55.2		122.6	118.9	52.0
1982	532.1	426.5	177.6	248.9	88.3	18.9	14.0	55.3	62.7	46.8	51.2		105.7	102.0	41.5
1983	570.1	417.2	154.3	262.9	100.1	23.9	16.4	59.8	58.9	53.5	50.4		152.9	148.6	72.5
1984	670.2	489.6	177.4	312.2	121.5	31.6	20.4	69.6	68.1	64.4	58.1		180.6	175.9	86.4
1985	714.4	526.2	194.5	331.7	130.3	33.7	23.8	72.9	72.5	69.0	59.9		188.2	183.1	87.4
1986	739.9	519.8	176.5	343.3	136.8	33.4	25.6	77.7	75.4	70.5	60.7		220.1	214.6	104.1
1987	757.8	524.1	174.2	349.9	141.2	35.8	29.0	76.4	76.7	68.1	63.9		233.7	227.9	117.2
1988	803.1	563.8	182.8	381.0	154.9	38.0	34.2	82.8	84.2	72.9	69.0		239.3	233.2	120.1
1989	847.3	607.7	193.7	414.0	172.6	43.1	41.9	87.6	93.3	67.9	80.2		239.5	233.4	120.9
1990	846.4	622.4	202.9	419.5	177.2	38.6	47.6	90.9	92.1	70.0	80.2		224.0	218.0	112.9
1991	803.3	598.2	183.6	414.6	182.9	37.7	53.7	91.5	89.3	71.5	70.8		205.1	199.4	99.4
1992	848.5	612.1	172.6	439.6	199.9	44.0	57.9	98.1	93.0	74.7	72.0		236.3	230.4	122.0
1993	932.5	666.6	177.2	489.4	217.6	47.9	64.3	105.4	102.2	89.4	80.2		266.0	259.9	140.1
1994	1,033.3	731.4	186.8	544.6	235.2	52.4	68.3	114.6	113.6	107.7	88.1		301.9	295.6	162.3
1995	1,112.9	810.0	207.3	602.8	263.0	66.1	74.6	122.3	129.0	116.1	94.7		302.8	296.5	153.5
1996	1,209.5	875.4	224.6	650.8	290.1	72.8	85.5	131.9	136.5	123.2	101.0		334.1	327.8	170.8
1997	1,317.8	968.7	250.3	718.3	330.3	81.4	107.5	141.4	140.4	135.5	112.1		349.1	342.8	175.2
1998	1,438.4	1,052.6	275.2	777.3	363.4	87.2	124.0	152.2	146.4	144.0	123.5		385.8	379.3	199.4
1999	1,558.8	1,133.9	282.2	851.7	411.0	96.0	152.6	162.4	147.0	167.6	126.0		424.9	417.8	223.8
2000	1,679.0	1,232.1	313.2	918.9	467.6	101.4	176.2	190.0	159.2	160.8	131.2		446.9	439.5	236.8
2001	1,646.1	1,176.8	322.6	854.2	437.0	85.4	174.7	177.0	146.7	141.7	128.8		469.3	461.9	249.1
2002	1,570.2	1,066.3	279.2	787.1	399.4	77.2	167.6	154.5	135.7	126.3	125.7		503.9	496.3	265.9
2003	1,654.9	1,082.4	276.9	805.6	405.7	77.6	170.0	158.2	137.1	127.9	134.8		572.5	564.7	310.6
2004	1,872.6	1,198.8	298.4	900.4	447.0	91.6	178.5	176.9	145.3	151.9	156.2		673.8	665.4	377.6
2005 P	2,084.3	1,328.3	334.5	993.8	489.2	105.6	198.1	185.5	161.0	170.9	172.7		756.0	747.1	420.7
2002: I	1,572.4	1,085.2	292.2	793.0	402.9	79.7	165.9	157.3	136.7	130.6	122.8		487.2	479.6	254.3
II	1,568.8	1,067.8	280.9	787.0	400.3	76.4	167.7	156.2	133.6	126.9	126.1		501.0	493.3	264.0
III	1,566.8	1,061.4	272.1	789.3	403.7	78.1	171.0	154.7	136.0	123.1	126.5		505.4	497.8	267.9
IV	1,572.8	1,050.7	271.7	779.0	390.6	74.8	166.0	149.9	136.4	124.7	127.3		522.1	514.5	277.4
2003: I	1,588.2	1,048.2	268.4	779.8	392.0	73.9	165.6	152.5	140.7	119.0	128.1		540.0	532.4	291.4
II	1,619.7	1,066.8	277.1	789.7	395.3	75.0	166.7	153.6	137.6	127.2	129.5		552.9	545.2	296.2
III	1,683.7	1,098.8	279.0	819.8	412.9	79.1	173.0	160.8	136.9	131.6	138.4		584.9	576.9	313.8
IV	1,728.2	1,116.0	283.0	833.0	422.8	82.3	174.6	165.9	133.3	133.7	143.3		612.2	604.1	341.0
2004: I	1,772.7	1,140.7	285.3	855.3	436.5	86.6	176.1	173.9	139.9	133.3	145.6		632.0	623.8	354.5
II	1,856.6	1,182.7	296.3	886.5	444.3	90.0	176.9	177.4	139.5	150.3	152.4		673.9	665.5	376.7
III	1,908.7	1,219.0	302.1	916.9	450.9	92.3	179.9	178.6	149.3	155.6	161.0		689.7	681.3	388.1
IV	1,952.6	1,252.9	309.8	943.1	456.3	97.5	181.1	177.8	152.6	168.4	165.8		699.7	691.1	390.9
2005: I	1,998.7	1,280.1	315.9	964.3	474.6	102.7	188.3	183.6	161.3	163.8	164.6		718.5	709.7	401.6
II	2,058.5	1,313.5	325.6	987.9	486.6	105.6	197.3	183.6	154.9	172.8	173.7		745.0	736.1	410.3
III	2,119.2	1,348.9	340.2	1,008.7	494.5	105.0	201.3	188.2	161.3	177.9	175.0		770.3	761.3	426.6
IV P	2,160.9	1,370.6	356.3	1,014.3	501.3	109.3	205.5	186.6	166.4	169.0	177.6		790.3	781.1	444.2

[1] Includes other items, not shown separately.

Source: Department of Commerce, Bureau of Economic Analysis.

TABLE B–19.—*Real private fixed investment by type, 1990–2005*

[Billions of chained (2000) dollars; quarterly data at seasonally adjusted annual rates]

Year or quarter	Private fixed investment	Nonresidential										Residential		
		Total nonresidential	Structures	Equipment and software								Structures		
				Total	Information processing equipment and software				Industrial equipment	Transportation equipment	Other equipment	Total residential[2]	Total[2]	Single family
					Total	Computers and peripheral equipment[1]	Software	Other						
1990	886.6	595.1	275.2	355.0	100.7	....	39.9	80.1	109.2	81.0	96.0	298.9	292.6	154.2
1991	829.1	563.2	244.6	345.9	105.9	....	45.1	79.6	102.2	78.8	82.0	270.2	264.0	135.1
1992	878.3	581.3	229.9	371.1	122.2	....	53.0	84.4	104.0	80.2	81.6	307.6	301.4	164.1
1993	953.5	631.9	228.3	417.4	138.2	....	59.3	90.9	112.9	95.1	89.3	332.7	326.4	179.7
1994	1,042.3	689.9	232.3	467.2	155.7	....	65.1	99.4	122.9	111.4	96.5	364.8	358.6	198.9
1995	1,109.6	762.5	247.1	523.1	182.7	....	71.6	107.0	134.9	120.6	101.7	353.1	346.8	180.6
1996	1,209.2	833.6	261.1	578.7	218.9	....	84.1	117.2	139.9	125.4	105.6	381.3	375.1	197.3
1997	1,320.6	934.2	280.1	658.3	269.9	....	108.8	127.3	143.0	135.9	115.8	388.6	382.4	196.6
1998	1,455.0	1,037.8	294.5	745.6	328.9	....	129.4	143.2	148.1	145.4	125.7	418.3	411.9	218.1
1999	1,576.3	1,133.3	293.2	840.2	398.5	....	157.2	158.0	147.9	167.7	126.7	443.6	436.6	234.2
2000	1,679.0	1,232.1	313.2	918.9	467.6	....	176.2	190.0	159.2	160.8	131.2	446.9	439.5	236.8
2001	1,629.4	1,180.5	306.1	874.2	459.0	....	173.8	181.7	145.7	142.8	126.9	448.5	441.1	237.1
2002	1,544.6	1,071.5	253.8	820.2	437.4	....	169.7	161.1	134.5	126.0	122.9	469.9	462.2	246.3
2003	1,600.0	1,085.0	243.1	846.8	459.7	....	175.7	166.2	134.9	123.1	130.7	509.4	501.3	272.6
2004	1,755.1	1,186.7	248.4	947.6	522.4	....	188.8	188.9	139.4	138.7	150.0	561.8	552.9	307.5
2005 ᵖ	1,896.1	1,287.6	253.1	1,049.8	590.8	....	210.2	198.8	148.9	156.5	159.7	602.1	592.7	327.5
2002: I	1,551.5	1,090.3	270.3	820.9	435.0	....	166.3	162.9	135.8	130.4	120.3	459.0	451.4	238.0
II	1,545.9	1,073.3	256.4	819.0	437.1	....	170.2	162.6	132.7	126.1	123.8	469.5	461.8	245.9
III	1,543.2	1,068.0	245.8	825.7	444.2	....	173.4	161.7	134.7	124.1	123.6	471.8	464.2	248.9
IV	1,537.8	1,054.5	242.5	815.4	433.3	....	168.7	157.1	134.9	123.5	124.1	479.3	471.6	252.4
2003: I	1,540.9	1,051.6	237.3	818.7	439.4	....	169.8	159.7	138.8	116.7	124.5	484.8	477.1	257.8
II	1,573.7	1,072.9	244.8	832.0	445.3	....	171.0	161.1	135.6	126.3	125.5	496.0	488.0	262.4
III	1,629.0	1,101.8	244.7	862.4	469.0	....	178.9	169.1	134.5	126.6	134.0	521.2	512.9	276.4
IV	1,656.3	1,113.7	245.5	874.0	485.3	....	183.2	174.9	130.7	122.6	138.8	535.7	527.1	293.8
2004: I	1,684.4	1,135.1	243.4	899.1	504.8	....	185.5	184.7	135.9	121.9	141.3	542.4	533.7	298.0
II	1,744.5	1,171.6	248.5	931.4	517.4	....	186.9	189.5	134.4	136.7	146.4	565.1	556.2	308.2
III	1,780.2	1,204.8	249.4	965.6	527.9	....	190.0	191.1	142.8	142.8	154.3	568.8	559.7	312.0
IV	1,811.3	1,235.1	252.3	994.2	539.7	....	192.8	190.3	144.5	153.3	158.0	571.0	561.8	312.0
2005: I	1,842.2	1,252.2	251.0	1,014.2	565.1	....	199.8	196.3	150.9	148.8	153.9	584.1	574.8	320.5
II	1,884.7	1,279.0	252.7	1,040.9	584.6	....	209.1	196.5	143.2	158.1	160.6	599.3	590.0	323.3
III	1,921.5	1,305.2	254.1	1,067.5	600.2	....	213.7	202.1	148.8	163.3	161.1	610.0	600.6	329.0
IV ᵖ	1,935.9	1,314.2	254.5	1,076.8	613.4	....	218.2	200.5	152.6	155.6	163.1	615.2	605.6	337.4

[1] For details on this component see *Survey of Current Business*, Table 5.3.6, Table 5.3.1 for growth rates, Table 5.3.2 for contributions, and Table 5.3.3 for quantity indexes.

[2] Includes other items, not shown separately.

Source: Department of Commerce, Bureau of Economic Analysis.

TABLE B–20.—*Government consumption expenditures and gross investment by type, 1959–2005*

[Billions of dollars; quarterly data at seasonally adjusted annual rates]

Year or quarter	Total	Federal									State and local			
		Total	National defense				Nondefense				Total	Consumption expenditures	Gross investment	
			Total	Consumption expenditures	Gross investment		Total	Consumption expenditures	Gross investment				Structures	Equipment and software
					Structures	Equipment and software			Structures	Equipment and software				
1959	110.0	65.4	53.8	40.1	2.5	11.2	11.5	9.8	1.5	0.2	44.7	30.7	12.8	1.1
1960	111.6	64.1	53.4	41.0	2.2	10.1	10.7	8.7	1.7	.3	47.5	33.5	12.7	1.2
1961	119.5	67.9	56.5	42.7	2.4	11.5	11.4	9.0	1.9	.6	51.6	36.6	13.8	1.3
1962	130.1	75.3	61.1	46.6	2.0	12.5	14.2	11.3	2.1	.8	54.9	39.0	14.5	1.3
1963	136.4	76.9	61.0	48.3	1.6	11.0	15.9	12.4	2.3	1.2	59.5	41.9	16.0	1.5
1964	143.2	78.5	60.3	48.8	1.3	10.2	18.2	14.0	2.5	1.6	64.8	45.8	17.2	1.8
1965	151.5	80.4	60.6	50.6	1.1	8.9	19.8	15.1	2.8	1.9	71.0	50.2	19.0	1.9
1966	171.8	92.5	71.7	60.0	1.3	10.5	20.8	15.9	2.8	2.1	79.2	56.1	21.0	2.1
1967	192.7	104.8	83.5	70.0	1.2	12.3	21.3	17.1	2.2	1.9	87.9	62.6	23.0	2.3
1968	209.4	111.4	89.3	77.2	1.2	10.9	22.1	18.3	2.1	1.7	98.0	70.4	25.2	2.4
1969	221.5	113.4	89.5	78.2	1.5	9.8	23.8	20.2	1.9	1.7	108.2	79.9	25.6	2.7
1970	233.8	113.5	87.6	76.6	1.3	9.8	25.8	22.1	2.1	1.7	120.3	91.5	25.8	3.0
1971	246.5	113.7	84.6	77.1	1.8	5.7	29.1	24.9	2.5	1.7	132.8	102.7	27.0	3.1
1972	263.5	119.7	87.0	79.5	1.8	5.7	32.7	28.2	2.7	1.8	143.8	113.2	27.1	3.5
1973	281.7	122.5	88.2	79.4	2.1	6.6	34.3	29.4	3.1	1.8	159.2	126.0	29.1	4.1
1974	317.9	134.6	95.6	84.5	2.2	8.9	39.0	33.4	3.4	2.2	183.4	143.7	34.7	4.9
1975	357.7	149.1	103.9	90.9	2.3	10.7	45.1	38.7	4.1	2.4	208.7	165.1	38.1	5.5
1976	383.0	159.7	111.1	95.8	2.1	13.2	48.6	41.4	4.6	2.7	223.3	179.5	38.1	5.7
1977	414.1	175.4	120.9	104.2	2.4	14.4	54.5	46.5	5.0	3.0	238.7	195.9	36.9	5.9
1978	453.6	190.9	130.5	112.7	2.5	15.3	60.4	50.6	6.1	3.7	262.6	213.2	42.8	6.6
1979	500.8	210.6	145.2	123.8	2.5	18.9	65.4	55.1	6.3	4.0	290.2	233.3	49.0	7.8
1980	566.2	243.8	168.0	143.7	3.2	21.1	75.8	63.8	7.1	4.9	322.4	258.4	55.1	8.9
1981	627.5	280.2	196.3	167.3	3.2	25.7	84.0	71.0	7.7	5.3	347.3	282.3	55.4	9.5
1982	680.5	310.8	225.9	191.2	4.0	30.8	84.9	72.1	6.8	6.0	369.7	304.9	54.2	10.6
1983	733.5	342.9	250.7	208.8	4.8	37.1	92.3	77.7	6.7	7.8	390.5	324.1	54.2	12.2
1984	797.0	374.4	281.6	232.9	4.9	43.8	92.8	77.1	7.0	8.7	422.6	347.7	60.5	14.4
1985	879.0	412.8	311.2	253.7	6.2	51.3	101.6	84.7	7.3	9.6	466.2	381.8	67.6	16.8
1986	949.3	438.6	330.9	268.0	6.8	56.1	107.8	90.3	8.0	9.5	510.7	417.9	74.2	18.6
1987	999.5	460.1	350.0	283.6	7.7	58.8	110.0	90.6	9.0	10.4	539.4	440.9	78.8	19.6
1988	1,039.0	462.3	354.9	293.6	7.4	53.9	107.4	88.9	6.8	11.7	576.7	470.4	84.8	21.5
1989	1,099.1	482.2	362.2	299.5	6.4	56.3	120.0	99.7	6.9	13.4	616.9	502.1	88.7	26.0
1990	1,180.2	508.3	374.0	308.1	6.1	59.8	134.3	111.7	8.0	14.6	671.9	544.6	98.5	28.7
1991	1,234.4	527.7	383.2	319.8	4.6	58.8	144.5	119.7	9.2	15.7	706.7	574.6	103.2	28.9
1992	1,271.0	533.9	376.9	315.3	5.2	56.3	157.0	129.8	10.3	16.9	737.0	602.7	104.2	30.1
1993	1,291.2	525.2	362.9	307.6	5.1	50.1	162.4	134.2	11.2	16.9	766.0	630.3	104.5	31.2
1994	1,325.5	519.1	353.7	300.7	5.7	47.2	165.5	140.1	10.5	14.9	806.3	663.3	108.7	34.3
1995	1,369.2	519.2	348.7	297.3	6.3	45.1	170.5	143.2	10.8	16.5	850.0	696.1	117.3	36.7
1996	1,416.0	527.4	354.6	302.5	6.7	45.4	172.8	143.8	11.2	17.9	888.6	724.8	126.8	36.9
1997	1,468.7	530.9	349.6	304.7	5.7	39.2	181.3	153.0	9.8	18.5	937.8	758.9	139.5	39.4
1998	1,518.3	530.4	345.7	300.7	5.1	39.9	184.7	153.9	10.6	20.2	987.9	801.4	143.6	43.0
1999	1,620.8	555.8	360.6	312.9	5.0	42.8	195.2	162.2	10.6	22.4	1,065.0	858.9	159.7	46.4
2000	1,721.6	578.8	370.3	321.5	5.0	43.8	208.5	177.8	8.3	22.3	1,142.8	917.8	176.0	49.0
2001	1,825.6	612.9	392.6	342.4	4.6	45.6	220.3	189.5	8.3	22.5	1,212.8	969.8	192.4	50.6
2002	1,961.1	679.7	437.1	381.7	4.4	51.0	242.5	209.9	9.9	22.8	1,281.5	1,025.3	205.9	50.2
2003	2,091.9	754.8	496.7	436.6	5.1	55.0	258.2	225.3	10.3	22.6	1,337.1	1,074.8	211.6	50.8
2004	2,215.9	827.6	552.7	484.2	5.1	63.4	274.9	241.4	9.4	24.0	1,388.3	1,117.7	217.6	53.0
2005 p	2,359.7	874.8	585.3	514.4	5.2	65.6	289.5	252.8	10.2	26.5	1,484.9	1,192.6	235.8	56.5
2002:I	1,912.0	654.9	418.2	366.8	4.2	47.3	236.6	204.5	9.7	22.5	1,257.2	1,001.8	204.8	50.6
II	1,948.3	675.2	431.1	375.4	4.4	51.3	244.1	209.6	9.7	24.8	1,273.1	1,019.4	203.5	50.2
III	1,971.8	682.0	438.0	379.8	4.5	53.7	243.9	211.6	9.8	22.5	1,289.8	1,033.6	206.0	50.2
IV	2,012.5	706.6	461.1	404.8	4.6	51.7	245.5	213.7	10.3	21.5	1,305.9	1,046.7	209.5	49.8
2003:I	2,054.4	724.0	467.2	409.9	4.7	52.6	256.8	224.9	10.2	21.8	1,330.4	1,070.8	209.6	50.1
II	2,090.5	763.4	507.2	447.0	5.0	55.2	256.3	220.6	10.9	24.7	1,327.1	1,067.8	209.0	50.2
III	2,106.2	761.8	500.3	439.4	5.5	55.5	261.5	229.0	10.6	21.9	1,344.4	1,077.7	215.6	51.1
IV	2,116.5	770.0	512.0	450.0	5.3	56.6	258.0	226.8	9.3	21.9	1,346.5	1,082.9	212.0	51.7
2004:I	2,166.2	808.3	538.7	472.5	5.1	61.1	269.6	238.1	9.1	22.4	1,357.9	1,095.1	210.7	52.1
II	2,205.0	824.6	547.2	479.6	4.7	62.9	277.4	241.5	9.6	26.4	1,380.4	1,108.9	218.7	52.7
III	2,232.5	836.5	562.9	494.6	5.2	63.1	273.6	241.1	9.5	23.0	1,395.9	1,123.9	218.8	53.3
IV	2,260.0	840.8	562.0	490.1	5.2	66.7	278.8	245.1	9.6	24.2	1,419.1	1,143.1	222.0	54.0
2005:I	2,302.0	860.2	575.3	508.9	5.1	61.3	285.0	250.7	9.2	25.0	1,441.7	1,159.0	227.5	55.2
II	2,337.6	869.8	582.5	512.3	5.1	65.1	287.3	250.5	8.7	28.2	1,467.7	1,175.7	235.7	56.3
III	2,392.7	892.2	601.7	528.6	5.1	68.0	290.5	254.3	9.8	26.4	1,500.4	1,205.7	237.7	57.1
IV p	2,406.8	876.9	581.6	507.8	5.5	68.2	295.3	255.7	13.1	26.5	1,529.9	1,230.1	242.2	57.6

Source: Department of Commerce, Bureau of Economic Analysis.

306

TABLE B–21.—*Real government consumption expenditures and gross investment by type, 1990–2005*

[Billions of chained (2000) dollars; quarterly data at seasonally adjusted annual rates]

Year or quarter	Total	Government consumption expenditures and gross investment											
		Federal								State and local			
		National defense				Nondefense							
		Total	Con-sumption expend-itures	Gross investment		Total	Con-sumption expend-itures	Gross investment		Total	Con-sumption expend-itures	Gross investment	
				Struc-tures	Equip-ment and soft-ware			Struc-tures	Equip-ment and soft-ware			Struc-tures	Equip-ment and soft-ware
1990	1,530.0	659.1	479.4	404.9	8.6	64.2	178.6	156.5	10.6	12.9	868.4	714.2	132.1	25.0
1991	1,547.2	658.0	474.2	404.4	6.4	61.8	182.8	158.4	11.8	13.7	886.8	729.0	136.5	24.8
1992	1,555.3	646.6	450.7	383.5	7.0	58.7	195.4	168.2	13.2	15.0	906.5	746.5	137.0	25.9
1993	1,541.1	619.6	425.3	367.2	6.4	51.1	194.1	166.0	14.1	15.0	919.5	761.4	133.9	26.8
1994	1,541.3	596.4	404.6	350.6	7.1	46.8	191.7	167.3	12.7	13.3	943.3	780.6	134.9	29.5
1995	1,549.7	580.3	389.2	338.1	7.4	43.7	191.0	164.7	12.6	14.7	968.3	798.4	139.5	31.7
1996	1,564.9	573.5	383.8	332.2	7.7	43.8	189.6	161.1	12.7	16.4	990.5	812.8	146.3	32.7
1997	1,594.0	567.6	373.0	328.1	6.4	38.9	194.5	166.6	10.9	17.5	1,025.9	834.9	155.8	36.1
1998	1,624.4	561.2	365.3	319.8	5.5	40.1	195.9	164.8	11.5	19.8	1,063.0	866.4	155.6	41.2
1999	1,686.9	573.7	372.2	324.6	5.2	42.5	201.5	168.1	11.1	22.3	1,113.2	900.3	167.0	45.9
2000	1,721.6	578.8	370.3	321.5	5.0	43.8	208.5	177.8	8.3	22.3	1,142.8	917.8	176.0	49.0
2001	1,780.3	601.4	384.9	334.1	4.4	46.4	216.5	185.8	8.0	22.7	1,179.0	941.2	186.0	51.7
2002	1,858.8	643.4	413.2	356.7	4.2	52.6	230.2	197.3	9.3	23.5	1,215.4	969.4	193.5	52.5
2003	1,911.1	687.8	449.7	388.5	4.7	56.7	238.0	204.8	9.4	23.6	1,223.3	975.2	194.3	53.9
2004	1,952.3	723.7	481.3	413.3	4.4	64.4	242.2	208.6	8.3	25.3	1,228.4	979.5	192.8	56.6
2005 P	1,985.1	738.4	492.2	423.0	4.3	65.6	246.0	210.0	8.4	28.0	1,246.5	991.1	196.0	60.5
2002: I	1,832.0	623.2	399.2	346.5	3.9	48.8	224.0	191.8	9.2	22.9	1,208.9	961.9	194.4	52.5
II	1,853.4	641.7	410.2	353.5	4.2	52.9	231.5	196.9	9.2	25.6	1,211.8	967.8	191.6	52.4
III	1,863.9	646.5	414.4	355.2	4.3	55.4	232.2	199.5	9.3	23.3	1,217.5	972.0	192.8	52.7
IV	1,885.8	662.3	428.9	371.5	4.3	53.2	233.4	201.2	9.6	22.3	1,223.6	975.7	195.4	52.3
2003: I	1,884.4	662.8	425.0	366.7	4.3	54.2	237.9	205.5	9.4	22.7	1,221.6	975.3	193.4	52.8
II	1,917.5	696.8	460.1	398.7	4.5	57.0	236.4	200.7	10.1	25.8	1,220.7	975.1	192.3	53.3
III	1,920.1	693.2	452.5	390.5	5.0	57.3	240.6	207.7	9.7	22.9	1,226.8	974.8	197.8	54.4
IV	1,922.6	698.5	461.2	398.2	4.8	58.4	237.0	205.2	8.5	23.1	1,224.1	975.4	193.8	55.1
2004: I	1,938.4	716.5	476.4	409.7	4.5	62.7	239.9	207.9	8.2	23.6	1,221.8	975.3	191.2	55.6
II	1,949.5	722.2	477.4	410.1	4.1	63.9	244.6	208.8	8.5	27.7	1,227.1	977.2	194.2	56.2
III	1,958.4	728.6	487.7	419.8	4.5	63.9	240.6	207.9	8.3	24.3	1,229.6	980.7	192.6	56.9
IV	1,962.8	727.6	483.7	413.4	4.4	66.9	243.6	209.9	8.2	25.5	1,235.0	984.8	193.2	57.6
2005: I	1,971.9	731.8	487.3	421.9	4.3	61.2	244.3	210.4	7.8	26.3	1,239.8	986.8	195.0	58.8
II	1,984.1	736.1	491.7	422.9	4.3	65.2	244.2	208.2	7.2	29.7	1,247.8	988.8	199.9	60.1
III	1,998.1	749.5	503.6	432.2	4.2	68.1	245.6	210.1	8.0	28.0	1,248.5	993.3	195.5	61.0
IV P	1,986.2	736.1	486.2	415.0	4.4	68.0	249.7	211.4	10.6	28.1	1,249.8	995.6	193.7	62.0

Note.—See Table B-2 for data for total government consumption expenditures and gross investment for 1959-89.

Source: Department of Commerce, Bureau of Economic Analysis.

[Billions of dollars, except as noted; seasonally adjusted]

| Quarter | Private inventories[1] | | | | | | | | Final sales of domestic business[3] | Ratio of private inventories to final sales of domestic business | |
	Total[2]	Farm	Mining, utilities, and construc- tion[2]	Manu- fac- turing	Whole- sale trade	Retail trade	Other indus- tries[2]	Non- farm[2]		Total	Nonfarm
Fourth quarter:											
1959	132.9	42.1	....	47.7	16.5	20.5	6.1	90.8	31.6	4.20	2.87
1960	136.2	42.7	....	48.7	16.9	21.9	6.1	93.5	32.7	4.17	2.86
1961	139.6	44.3	....	50.1	17.3	21.3	6.6	95.2	34.3	4.07	2.78
1962	147.2	46.7	....	53.2	18.0	22.7	6.6	100.5	36.0	4.09	2.79
1963	149.7	44.2	....	55.1	19.5	23.9	7.1	105.5	38.3	3.91	2.75
1964	154.3	42.1	....	58.6	20.8	25.2	7.7	112.2	41.2	3.75	2.73
1965	169.3	47.1	....	63.4	22.5	28.0	8.3	122.2	45.3	3.73	2.70
1966	185.7	47.4	....	73.0	25.8	30.6	8.9	138.3	47.8	3.88	2.89
1967	194.9	45.8	....	79.9	28.1	30.9	10.1	149.1	50.3	3.87	2.96
1968	208.2	48.9	....	85.1	29.3	34.2	10.6	159.3	55.4	3.76	2.87
1969	227.7	53.1	....	92.6	32.5	37.5	12.0	174.6	59.1	3.85	2.95
1970	236.0	52.7	....	95.5	36.4	38.5	12.9	183.3	62.4	3.78	2.94
1971	253.9	59.5	....	96.6	39.4	44.7	13.7	194.4	68.0	3.73	2.86
1972	283.9	74.0	....	102.1	43.1	49.8	14.8	209.9	76.3	3.72	2.75
1973	352.2	102.8	....	121.5	51.7	58.4	17.7	249.4	84.3	4.18	2.96
1974	406.3	88.2	....	162.6	66.9	63.9	24.7	318.1	90.4	4.49	3.52
1975	409.3	90.3	....	162.2	66.5	64.4	25.9	319.0	101.7	4.02	3.14
1976	440.1	85.8	....	178.7	74.1	73.0	28.5	354.2	111.9	3.93	3.17
1977	482.4	91.0	....	193.2	84.0	80.9	33.3	391.4	124.8	3.86	3.14
1978	571.4	119.7	....	219.8	99.0	94.1	38.8	451.7	144.7	3.95	3.12
1979	668.2	135.6	....	261.8	119.5	104.7	46.6	532.6	160.1	4.17	3.33
1980	739.8	141.1	....	293.4	139.4	111.7	54.1	598.7	175.0	4.23	3.42
1981	779.2	127.5	....	313.1	148.8	123.2	66.6	651.7	187.7	4.15	3.47
1982	774.1	131.5	....	304.6	147.9	123.2	66.8	642.6	195.8	3.95	3.28
1983	797.6	132.5	....	308.9	153.4	137.6	65.2	665.1	216.8	3.68	3.07
1984	869.3	131.8	....	344.5	169.1	157.0	66.9	737.6	234.8	3.70	3.14
1985	876.1	125.9	....	333.3	175.9	171.4	69.5	750.2	250.7	3.49	2.99
1986	858.0	112.9	....	320.6	182.0	176.2	66.3	745.1	265.7	3.23	2.80
1987	924.2	119.8	....	339.6	195.8	199.1	69.9	804.4	279.3	3.31	2.88
1988	999.2	130.2	....	372.4	213.9	213.2	69.5	869.1	305.6	3.27	2.84
1989	1,044.4	129.6	....	390.5	222.8	231.4	70.1	914.7	324.4	3.22	2.82
1990	1,082.3	133.4	....	404.5	236.8	236.6	71.0	948.9	337.6	3.21	2.81
1991	1,057.2	123.2	....	384.1	239.2	240.2	70.5	934.0	347.6	3.04	2.69
1992	1,082.4	132.9	....	377.6	248.3	249.4	74.3	949.5	372.7	2.90	2.55
1993	1,115.8	132.1	....	380.1	258.6	268.6	76.5	983.7	393.6	2.83	2.50
1994	1,194.3	134.3	....	404.3	281.5	293.6	80.6	1,060.0	416.8	2.87	2.54
1995	1,257.0	130.9	....	424.5	303.7	312.2	85.6	1,126.1	439.2	2.86	2.56
NAICS:											
1996	1,284.4	136.3	31.1	421.0	285.1	328.7	82.1	1,148.1	469.1	2.74	2.45
1997	1,329.5	136.7	33.7	431.7	303.1	337.5	86.9	1,192.9	495.6	2.68	2.41
1998	1,346.8	120.3	37.3	431.5	313.3	353.6	90.9	1,226.5	526.8	2.56	2.33
1999	1,442.2	124.2	39.6	457.7	337.4	383.8	99.5	1,318.0	556.7	2.59	2.37
2000	1,535.9	132.1	44.5	477.0	359.0	409.0	114.4	1,403.8	583.6	2.63	2.41
2001	1,458.3	126.1	47.5	437.9	338.6	395.6	112.6	1,332.2	598.7	2.44	2.23
2002: I	1,460.8	128.3	47.8	437.1	336.0	400.4	111.0	1,332.4	596.0	2.45	2.24
II	1,468.2	125.1	49.1	436.8	338.0	407.5	111.7	1,343.0	598.2	2.45	2.25
III	1,487.6	128.1	48.0	441.0	346.1	412.7	111.5	1,359.4	600.6	2.48	2.26
IV	1,507.8	135.8	49.4	443.6	348.0	419.3	111.7	1,372.0	601.0	2.51	2.28
2003: I	1,536.2	136.5	55.5	450.9	352.3	428.7	112.4	1,399.7	606.6	2.53	2.31
II	1,529.6	136.9	55.6	446.5	348.4	429.5	112.6	1,392.7	614.8	2.49	2.27
III	1,547.5	149.2	56.4	443.9	351.5	434.0	112.6	1,398.3	631.5	2.45	2.21
IV	1,569.3	151.0	58.4	449.7	360.3	437.3	112.6	1,418.3	639.1	2.46	2.22
2004: I	1,606.5	154.2	60.7	460.7	370.9	446.6	113.4	1,452.3	650.6	2.47	2.23
II	1,650.9	160.0	63.3	474.7	380.4	457.5	114.9	1,490.9	661.2	2.50	2.25
III	1,679.7	152.9	66.3	491.7	393.6	458.4	116.9	1,526.8	670.4	2.51	2.28
IV	1,711.7	152.5	70.4	499.6	404.2	465.9	119.1	1,559.3	681.0	2.51	2.29
2005: I	1,761.5	170.1	71.8	512.8	414.9	470.8	121.1	1,591.4	691.3	2.55	2.30
II	1,763.0	165.4	75.9	510.7	419.5	468.8	122.7	1,597.6	707.8	2.49	2.26
III	1,792.3	164.3	80.5	522.9	430.4	469.2	124.9	1,628.0	721.3	2.48	2.26
IV *p*	1,829.0	166.2	90.7	531.5	438.0	476.0	126.5	1,662.8	725.9	2.52	2.29

[1] Inventories at end of quarter. Quarter-to-quarter change calculated from this table is not the current-dollar change in private inventories component of GDP. The former is the difference between two inventory stocks, each valued at its respective end-of-quarter prices. The latter is the change in the physical volume of inventories valued at average prices of the quarter. In addition, changes calculated from this table are at quarterly rates, whereas change in private inventories is stated at annual rates.

[2] Inventories of construction, mining, and utilities establishments are included in other industries through 1995.

[3] Quarterly totals at monthly rates. Final sales of domestic business equals final sales of domestic product less gross output of general government, gross value added of nonprofit institutions, compensation paid to domestic workers, and space rent for owner-occupied housing. Includes a small amount of final sales by farm and by government enterprises.

Note.—The industry classification of inventories is on an establishment basis. Estimates through 1995 are based on the Standard Industrial Classification (SIC). Beginning with 1996, estimates are based on the North American Industry Classification System (NAICS).

Source: Department of Commerce, Bureau of Economic Analysis.

TABLE B–23.—*Real private inventories and domestic final sales by industry, 1959–2005*

[Billions of chained (2000) dollars, except as noted; seasonally adjusted]

Quarter	Private inventories [1] Total [2]	Farm	Mining, utilities, and construction [2]	Manufacturing	Wholesale trade	Retail trade	Other industries [2]	Nonfarm [2]	Final sales of domestic business [3]	Ratio of private inventories to final sales of domestic business Total	Nonfarm
Fourth quarter:											
1959	428.1	106.9	....	143.5	57.6	63.9	29.8	298.7	131.3	3.26	2.27
1960	438.5	108.3	....	145.4	59.1	68.2	30.8	307.5	134.3	3.27	2.29
1961	448.0	110.4	....	149.8	60.7	66.9	33.9	314.4	140.1	3.20	2.24
1962	467.4	111.8	....	159.8	63.4	71.5	33.8	332.7	145.4	3.21	2.29
1963	485.4	112.9	....	165.9	68.4	75.3	36.2	349.7	153.9	3.15	2.27
1964	500.8	109.8	....	175.1	72.5	79.3	38.4	369.4	163.2	3.07	2.26
1965	530.1	111.8	....	187.4	77.4	87.1	40.1	396.8	177.2	2.99	2.24
1966	572.2	110.7	....	212.5	87.7	94.1	41.1	442.0	180.9	3.16	2.44
1967	602.5	112.8	....	229.3	94.7	94.1	46.0	470.4	185.3	3.25	2.54
1968	629.9	116.1	....	239.8	98.0	101.9	47.3	494.1	195.1	3.23	2.53
1969	656.9	116.1	....	250.9	105.1	108.9	49.7	521.9	198.9	3.30	2.62
1970	661.9	114.2	....	250.9	113.0	109.0	50.3	529.7	201.3	3.29	2.63
1971	684.2	117.5	....	247.9	119.1	123.6	52.1	548.3	211.5	3.24	2.59
1972	707.3	117.9	....	254.6	124.6	133.1	54.7	572.5	228.8	3.09	2.50
1973	742.2	119.3	....	273.5	128.1	143.7	57.5	609.1	236.9	3.13	2.57
1974	768.1	115.7	....	294.1	139.7	141.6	61.3	644.2	228.2	3.37	2.82
1975	756.8	120.4	....	286.7	133.7	134.6	62.9	625.0	238.7	3.17	2.62
1976	787.5	119.1	....	300.4	142.7	144.9	63.6	659.0	250.5	3.14	2.63
1977	826.0	125.0	....	308.8	154.1	153.2	68.4	691.1	263.6	3.13	2.62
1978	867.1	126.7	....	322.9	166.9	163.3	72.5	732.0	283.2	3.06	2.58
1979	892.2	130.2	....	335.3	175.0	163.3	72.4	753.5	289.8	3.08	2.60
1980	884.3	124.3	....	335.7	180.0	158.7	71.2	753.5	289.6	3.05	2.60
1981	919.2	132.5	....	340.2	185.1	167.5	79.2	779.0	287.2	3.20	2.71
1982	901.7	138.6	....	325.0	183.0	163.7	76.8	754.4	286.1	3.15	2.64
1983	895.3	124.4	....	324.5	182.7	177.0	75.9	764.6	307.6	2.91	2.49
1984	966.6	129.6	....	352.8	198.5	198.6	77.0	831.2	324.6	2.98	2.56
1985	990.3	135.3	....	346.6	204.9	214.0	81.4	848.7	339.4	2.92	2.50
1986	998.5	133.5	....	342.9	213.2	217.4	84.4	858.8	352.2	2.84	2.44
1987	1,028.8	126.1	....	351.1	220.6	238.5	86.6	896.5	362.6	2.84	2.47
1988	1,049.1	115.4	....	367.6	229.7	246.1	85.2	929.2	381.6	2.75	2.43
1989	1,077.4	115.4	....	381.4	233.6	260.5	81.4	958.0	392.5	2.75	2.44
1990	1,092.8	120.9	....	390.0	242.0	258.9	78.3	971.2	394.0	2.77	2.46
1991	1,092.3	119.4	....	383.5	246.4	259.5	81.4	972.2	394.6	2.77	2.46
1992	1,108.7	125.1	....	378.9	254.8	264.1	83.9	982.5	415.7	2.67	2.36
1993	1,129.4	119.1	....	382.4	261.0	279.4	86.9	1,010.2	429.8	2.63	2.35
1994	1,193.0	130.3	....	394.1	276.7	299.9	91.1	1,062.2	447.2	2.67	2.38
1995	1,222.8	119.6	....	407.8	289.9	312.0	93.3	1,103.5	464.2	2.63	2.38
NAICS:											
1996	1,251.6	126.4	33.6	409.9	273.3	325.9	82.7	1,125.2	488.3	2.56	2.30
1997	1,322.7	129.3	36.1	430.7	298.3	340.6	88.1	1,193.7	509.2	2.60	2.34
1998	1,395.3	130.7	43.3	449.3	320.9	357.9	94.0	1,264.9	538.0	2.59	2.35
1999	1,464.2	127.8	42.7	466.3	340.6	385.5	101.3	1,336.4	563.4	2.60	2.37
2000	1,520.7	126.4	41.1	474.2	358.2	407.1	113.7	1,394.3	581.0	2.62	2.40
2001	1,488.9	126.5	51.7	452.8	347.5	396.3	113.9	1,362.4	583.6	2.55	2.33
2002: I	1,486.4	126.7	51.8	449.1	343.6	401.6	113.1	1,359.6	581.1	2.56	2.34
II	1,487.0	124.4	50.1	446.3	343.6	408.7	113.5	1,362.7	582.6	2.55	2.34
III	1,494.0	124.1	49.2	447.1	346.7	413.4	113.1	1,370.1	584.1	2.56	2.35
IV	1,501.4	124.0	48.1	447.0	348.8	420.6	112.5	1,377.6	582.5	2.58	2.37
2003: I	1,507.4	125.1	48.6	445.8	348.4	427.2	111.9	1,382.5	586.2	2.57	2.36
II	1,507.3	124.7	49.5	444.0	346.9	429.2	112.6	1,382.7	592.8	2.54	2.33
III	1,509.6	124.9	50.9	440.7	347.5	434.0	112.4	1,386.0	606.8	2.49	2.28
IV	1,516.9	124.2	53.2	439.4	350.0	437.3	112.3	1,393.0	611.4	2.48	2.28
2004: I	1,527.4	123.4	52.3	441.7	353.2	443.9	113.1	1,404.7	617.2	2.47	2.28
II	1,543.8	125.0	52.7	443.5	358.3	451.0	113.7	1,419.3	621.7	2.48	2.28
III	1,556.4	126.6	54.1	445.2	366.9	448.5	114.8	1,430.3	629.5	2.47	2.27
IV	1,568.9	126.6	55.0	445.6	373.3	452.7	115.8	1,443.0	636.2	2.47	2.27
2005: I	1,583.4	126.0	55.5	451.8	379.1	454.5	116.6	1,458.4	642.0	2.47	2.27
II	1,583.0	124.9	56.7	449.7	383.2	451.1	117.4	1,459.3	653.7	2.42	2.23
III	1,579.7	123.8	55.8	449.1	385.9	447.7	117.7	1,457.2	661.9	2.39	2.20
IV ᴾ	1,586.1	122.9	55.3	447.4	389.2	453.9	118.7	1,464.9	661.7	2.40	2.21

[1] Inventories at end of quarter. Quarter-to-quarter changes calculated from this table are at quarterly rates, whereas the change in private inventories component of GDP is stated at annual rates.

[2] Inventories of construction, mining, and utilities establishments are included in other industries through 1995.

[3] Quarterly totals at monthly rates. Final sales of domestic business equals final sales of domestic product less gross output of general government, gross value added of nonprofit institutions, compensation paid to domestic workers, and space rent for owner-occupied housing. Includes a small amount of final sales by farm and by government enterprises.

Note.—The industry classification of inventories is on an establishment basis. Estimates through 1995 are based on the Standard Industrial Classification (SIC). Beginning with 1996, estimates are based on the North American Industry Classification System (NAICS).

See *Survey of Current Business*, Tables 5.7.6A and 5.7.6B, for detailed information on calculation of the chained (2000) dollar inventory series.

Source: Department of Commerce, Bureau of Economic Analysis.

[Billions of dollars; quarterly data at seasonally adjusted annual rates]

Year or quarter	Current receipts from rest of the world					Current payments to rest of the world									Balance on current account, NIPA
	Total	Exports of goods and services			Income receipts	Total	Imports of goods and services			Income payments	Current taxes and transfer payments to rest of the world (net)				
		Total	Goods [1]	Services [1]			Total	Goods [1]	Services [1]		Total	From persons (net)	From government (net)	From business (net)	
1959	27.0	22.7	16.5	6.3	4.3	28.2	22.3	15.3	7.0	1.5	4.3	0.5	3.8	0.1	−1.2
1960	31.9	27.0	20.5	6.6	4.9	28.7	22.8	15.2	7.6	1.8	4.1	.5	3.5	.1	3.2
1961	32.9	27.6	20.9	6.7	5.3	28.6	22.7	15.1	7.6	1.8	4.2	.5	3.6	.1	4.3
1962	35.0	29.1	21.7	7.4	5.9	31.1	25.0	16.9	8.1	1.8	4.3	.5	3.6	.1	3.9
1963	37.6	31.1	23.3	7.7	6.5	32.6	26.1	17.7	8.4	2.1	4.4	.7	3.6	.1	5.0
1964	42.3	35.0	26.7	8.3	7.2	34.7	28.1	19.4	8.7	2.3	4.3	.7	3.4	.2	7.5
1965	45.0	37.1	27.8	9.4	7.9	38.8	31.5	22.2	9.3	2.6	4.7	.8	3.7	.2	6.2
1966	49.0	40.9	30.7	10.2	8.1	45.1	37.1	26.3	10.7	3.0	5.0	.8	4.0	.2	3.9
1967	52.1	43.5	32.2	11.3	8.7	48.6	39.9	27.8	12.2	3.3	5.4	1.0	4.1	.2	3.6
1968	58.0	47.9	35.3	12.6	10.1	56.3	46.6	33.9	12.6	4.0	5.7	1.0	4.4	.3	1.7
1969	63.7	51.9	38.3	13.7	11.8	61.9	50.5	36.8	13.7	5.7	5.8	1.1	4.4	.3	1.8
1970	72.5	59.7	44.5	15.2	12.8	68.5	55.8	40.9	14.9	6.4	6.3	1.3	4.7	.4	4.0
1971	77.0	63.0	45.6	17.4	14.0	76.4	62.3	46.6	15.8	6.4	7.6	1.3	5.9	.4	.6
1972	87.1	70.8	51.8	19.0	16.3	90.7	74.2	56.9	17.3	7.7	8.8	1.4	7.0	.5	−3.6
1973	118.8	95.3	73.9	21.3	23.5	109.5	91.2	71.8	19.3	10.9	7.4	1.5	5.2	.7	9.3
1974	156.5	126.7	101.0	25.7	29.8	149.8	127.5	104.5	22.9	14.3	8.1	1.3	5.8	1.0	6.6
1975	166.7	138.7	109.6	29.1	28.0	145.4	122.7	99.0	23.7	15.0	7.6	1.3	5.6	.7	21.4
1976	181.9	149.5	117.8	31.7	32.4	173.0	151.1	124.6	26.5	15.5	6.3	1.3	3.9	1.1	8.9
1977	196.6	159.4	123.7	35.7	37.2	205.6	182.4	152.6	29.8	16.9	6.2	1.3	3.5	1.4	−9.0
1978	233.1	186.9	145.4	41.5	46.3	243.6	212.3	177.4	34.8	24.7	6.7	1.5	3.8	1.4	−10.4
1979	298.5	230.1	184.0	46.1	68.3	297.0	252.7	212.8	39.9	36.4	8.0	1.6	4.3	2.0	1.4
1980	359.9	280.8	225.8	55.0	79.1	348.5	293.8	248.6	45.3	44.9	9.8	1.8	5.5	2.4	11.4
1981	397.3	305.2	239.1	66.1	92.0	390.9	317.8	267.8	49.9	59.1	14.1	5.5	5.4	3.2	6.3
1982	384.2	283.2	215.0	68.2	101.0	384.4	303.2	250.5	52.6	64.5	16.7	6.6	6.7	3.4	−.2
1983	378.9	277.0	207.3	69.7	101.9	410.9	328.6	272.7	56.0	64.8	17.5	6.9	7.2	3.4	−32.1
1984	424.2	302.4	225.6	76.7	121.9	511.2	405.1	336.3	68.8	85.6	20.5	7.8	9.2	3.5	−86.9
1985	414.5	302.0	222.2	79.8	112.4	525.3	417.2	343.3	73.9	85.9	22.2	8.2	11.1	2.9	−110.8
1986	431.9	320.5	226.0	94.5	111.4	571.2	453.3	370.0	83.3	93.6	24.3	9.0	12.2	3.2	−139.2
1987	487.1	363.9	257.5	106.4	123.2	637.9	509.1	414.8	94.3	105.3	23.5	9.9	10.3	3.4	−150.8
1988	596.2	444.1	325.8	118.3	152.1	708.4	554.5	452.1	102.4	128.5	25.5	10.6	10.4	4.5	−112.2
1989	681.0	503.3	369.4	134.0	177.7	769.3	591.5	484.8	106.7	151.5	26.4	11.4	10.4	4.6	−88.3
1990	741.5	552.4	396.6	155.7	189.1	811.5	630.3	508.1	122.3	154.3	26.9	12.0	10.0	4.8	−70.1
1991	765.7	596.8	423.5	173.3	168.9	752.3	624.3	500.7	123.6	138.5	−10.6	13.0	−28.6	5.0	13.5
1992	788.0	635.3	448.0	187.4	152.7	824.9	668.6	544.9	123.6	123.0	33.4	12.3	17.1	3.9	−36.9
1993	812.1	655.8	459.9	195.9	156.2	882.5	720.9	592.8	128.1	124.3	37.3	14.2	17.8	5.4	−70.4
1994	907.3	720.9	510.1	210.8	186.4	1,012.5	814.5	676.8	137.7	160.2	37.8	15.4	15.8	6.6	−105.2
1995	1,046.1	812.2	583.3	228.9	233.9	1,137.1	903.6	757.4	146.1	198.1	35.4	16.2	10.1	9.1	−91.0
1996	1,117.3	868.6	618.3	250.2	248.7	1,217.6	964.8	807.4	157.4	213.7	39.1	18.0	14.1	7.1	−100.3
1997	1,242.0	955.3	687.7	267.6	286.7	1,352.2	1,056.9	885.3	171.5	253.7	41.6	21.0	10.9	9.7	−110.2
1998	1,243.1	955.9	680.9	275.1	287.1	1,430.5	1,115.9	929.0	186.9	265.8	48.8	24.6	11.2	12.9	−187.4
1999	1,312.1	991.2	697.2	294.0	320.8	1,585.9	1,251.7	1,045.5	206.3	287.0	47.2	28.3	11.6	7.3	−273.9
2000	1,478.9	1,096.3	784.3	311.9	382.7	1,875.6	1,475.8	1,243.5	232.3	343.7	56.1	31.5	13.5	11.2	−396.6
2001	1,355.2	1,032.8	731.2	301.6	322.4	1,725.6	1,399.8	1,167.9	231.9	278.8	47.0	33.0	9.5	4.5	−370.4
2002	1,311.6	1,005.9	697.6	308.4	305.7	1,769.9	1,430.3	1,189.3	241.0	275.0	64.5	40.0	14.3	10.3	−458.3
2003	1,389.3	1,045.6	724.3	321.3	343.7	1,893.8	1,546.5	1,283.9	262.6	275.6	71.7	41.2	18.0	12.4	−504.5
2004	1,589.2	1,173.8	818.1	355.7	415.4	2,240.9	1,797.8	1,495.9	301.9	361.7	81.5	42.9	19.7	18.9	−651.7
2005 *P*	....	1,299.2	903.2	396.0	....	2,024.9	1,697.8	327.1		....	89.3	45.8	24.9	18.5	
2002: I	1,270.8	976.4	676.7	299.6	294.5	1,691.9	1,349.5	1,115.4	234.1	268.3	74.1	39.5	23.0	11.6	−421.0
II	1,315.3	1,008.2	703.4	304.8	307.1	1,774.7	1,424.3	1,187.8	236.5	290.5	60.0	39.0	10.4	10.6	−459.4
III	1,340.6	1,022.9	713.0	309.9	317.7	1,804.1	1,456.7	1,214.5	242.2	288.1	59.4	40.2	9.6	9.6	−463.4
IV	1,319.6	1,016.2	697.1	319.1	303.3	1,808.7	1,490.8	1,239.7	251.1	253.3	64.6	41.1	14.1	9.4	−489.1
2003: I	1,335.2	1,018.8	705.8	313.0	316.5	1,864.4	1,521.4	1,266.8	254.6	271.5	71.5	40.8	20.9	9.8	−529.1
II	1,345.1	1,016.1	708.6	307.5	329.1	1,848.4	1,516.6	1,264.3	252.3	262.2	69.5	40.7	18.2	10.6	−503.3
III	1,390.9	1,046.6	723.1	323.5	344.3	1,889.9	1,541.9	1,275.0	266.9	277.0	71.0	39.3	18.7	13.1	−499.0
IV	1,486.0	1,101.1	759.8	341.3	384.9	1,972.5	1,606.1	1,329.5	276.6	291.7	74.7	44.2	14.2	16.3	−486.5
2004: I	1,510.7	1,130.8	786.1	344.7	380.0	2,076.9	1,690.3	1,401.9	288.5	297.0	89.6	43.0	27.3	19.2	−566.2
II	1,564.5	1,163.3	811.5	351.8	401.2	2,213.4	1,776.4	1,478.3	298.1	354.5	82.6	43.5	16.8	22.3	−648.9
III	1,601.9	1,183.8	829.7	354.1	418.1	2,255.1	1,821.8	1,515.0	306.8	369.6	63.6	43.4	17.3	3.0	−653.2
IV	1,679.5	1,217.1	845.0	372.1	462.4	2,418.1	1,902.5	1,588.4	314.1	425.6	90.0	41.7	17.3	31.0	−738.6
2005: I	1,715.4	1,253.2	865.4	387.7	462.3	2,482.4	1,950.6	1,627.6	323.0	422.9	108.8	48.3	31.8	28.7	−767.0
II	1,786.6	1,297.1	904.7	392.5	489.4	2,533.4	1,988.1	1,661.8	326.3	453.9	91.3	44.9	18.2	28.2	−746.8
III	1,835.5	1,314.6	914.8	399.9	520.8	2,576.6	2,045.1	1,718.6	326.4	476.6	54.9	44.4	19.2	−8.7	−741.1
IV *P*	....	1,331.8	928.0	403.8	....	....	2,115.8	1,783.3	332.5	....	102.0	45.7	30.4	25.9	....

[1] Certain goods, primarily military equipment purchased and sold by the Federal Government, are included in services. Beginning with 1986, repairs and alterations of equipment were reclassified from goods to services.

Source: Department of Commerce, Bureau of Economic Analysis.

TABLE B–25.—*Real exports and imports of goods and services, 1990–2005*

[Billions of chained (2000) dollars; quarterly data at seasonally adjusted annual rates]

Year or quarter	Exports of goods and services					Imports of goods and services				
	Total	Goods [1]			Serv-ices [1]	Total	Goods [1]			Serv-ices [1]
		Total	Dura-ble goods	Non-dura-ble goods			Total	Dura-ble goods	Non-dura-ble goods	
1990	552.5	367.2	226.3	145.1	188.7	607.1	469.7	264.7	218.4	142.7
1991	589.1	392.5	243.1	153.7	199.9	603.7	469.3	266.1	215.9	139.0
1992	629.7	421.9	262.5	163.6	210.8	645.6	513.1	294.0	231.9	135.5
1993	650.0	435.6	276.1	162.4	217.5	702.1	564.8	328.8	248.0	139.4
1994	706.5	478.0	309.6	170.1	231.1	785.9	640.0	383.1	266.0	147.3
1995	778.2	533.9	353.6	181.1	245.8	849.1	697.6	427.1	277.0	152.1
1996	843.4	581.1	394.9	186.7	263.5	923.0	762.7	472.8	295.2	160.5
1997	943.7	664.5	466.2	198.7	279.2	1,048.3	872.6	550.3	326.4	175.6
1998	966.5	679.4	481.2	198.5	287.2	1,170.3	974.4	621.8	355.7	195.6
1999	1,008.2	705.2	503.6	201.7	303.2	1,304.4	1,095.2	711.7	384.3	209.1
2000	1,096.3	784.3	569.2	215.1	311.9	1,475.8	1,243.5	820.7	422.8	232.3
2001	1,036.7	736.3	522.2	214.2	300.4	1,435.8	1,204.1	769.4	435.1	231.6
2002	1,013.3	707.0	491.2	216.1	306.0	1,484.6	1,248.2	801.0	447.4	236.5
2003	1,031.2	719.7	499.8	220.2	311.2	1,552.6	1,309.2	835.3	474.2	243.7
2004	1,117.9	783.6	555.7	229.0	334.1	1,719.2	1,452.7	949.7	505.4	267.1
2005 *p*	1,193.3	839.0	606.1	235.6	354.3	1,825.2	1,549.9	1,028.7	526.3	276.6
2002: I	992.8	691.8	478.2	214.1	300.7	1,434.0	1,198.2	769.2	429.4	235.4
II	1,018.0	715.2	497.4	218.1	302.7	1,476.9	1,243.4	802.3	441.4	233.6
III	1,025.2	719.0	502.2	217.1	306.1	1,497.4	1,263.1	814.3	449.2	234.6
IV	1,017.2	702.1	487.2	215.1	314.7	1,530.2	1,287.9	818.4	469.8	242.4
2003: I	1,009.7	704.7	483.7	221.0	304.8	1,520.4	1,279.4	811.9	467.6	241.1
II	1,004.5	704.7	488.4	216.5	299.6	1,532.9	1,299.1	825.6	473.6	234.7
III	1,032.2	720.3	498.6	221.8	311.7	1,548.4	1,302.1	827.1	475.0	246.3
IV	1,078.4	749.3	528.4	221.7	328.8	1,608.6	1,356.3	876.6	480.5	252.7
2004: I	1,091.8	763.1	538.6	225.3	328.5	1,654.8	1,396.6	898.9	498.4	258.8
II	1,110.2	777.7	551.8	227.0	332.3	1,711.9	1,445.2	946.2	501.5	267.2
III	1,125.0	793.1	564.7	229.8	331.8	1,731.5	1,461.9	963.6	501.6	270.2
IV	1,144.5	800.3	567.7	233.8	344.0	1,778.6	1,507.3	990.1	520.2	272.3
2005: I	1,165.5	810.7	576.4	235.6	354.3	1,810.7	1,537.3	1,007.8	532.1	274.8
II	1,195.4	841.3	599.3	243.6	353.9	1,809.6	1,532.9	1,019.2	519.0	277.7
III	1,202.7	847.9	614.2	236.7	354.8	1,820.2	1,546.1	1,037.0	516.6	275.5
IV *p*	1,209.8	855.9	634.7	226.5	354.0	1,860.1	1,583.3	1,050.6	537.3	278.4

[1] Certain goods, primarily military equipment purchased and sold by the Federal Government, are included in services. Beginning with 1986, repairs and alterations of equipment were reclassified from goods to services.

Note.—See Table B-2 for data for total exports of goods and services and total imports of goods and services for 1959-89.

Source: Department of Commerce, Bureau of Economic Analysis.

311

TABLE B–26.—*Relation of gross domestic product, gross national product, net national product, and national income, 1959–2005*

[Billions of dollars; quarterly data at seasonally adjusted annual rates]

Year or quarter	Gross domestic product	Plus: Income receipts from rest of the world	Less: Income payments to rest of the world	Equals: Gross national product	Less: Consumption of fixed capital			Equals: Net national product	Less: Statistical discrepancy	Equals: National income
					Total	Private	Government			
1959	506.6	4.3	1.5	509.3	53.0	38.6	14.5	456.3	0.5	455.8
1960	526.4	4.9	1.8	529.5	55.6	40.5	15.0	473.9	−.9	474.9
1961	544.7	5.3	1.8	548.2	57.2	41.6	15.6	491.0	−.6	491.6
1962	585.6	5.9	1.8	589.7	59.3	42.8	16.5	530.5	.4	530.1
1963	617.7	6.5	2.1	622.2	62.4	44.9	17.5	559.8	−.8	560.6
1964	663.6	7.2	2.3	668.5	65.0	46.9	18.1	603.5	.8	602.7
1965	719.1	7.9	2.6	724.4	69.4	50.5	18.9	655.0	1.6	653.4
1966	787.8	8.1	3.0	792.9	75.6	55.5	20.1	717.3	6.3	711.0
1967	832.6	8.7	3.3	838.0	81.5	59.9	21.6	756.5	4.6	751.9
1968	910.0	10.1	4.0	916.1	88.4	65.2	23.1	827.7	4.6	823.2
1969	984.6	11.8	5.7	990.7	97.9	73.1	24.8	892.8	3.2	889.7
1970	1,038.5	12.8	6.4	1,044.9	106.7	80.0	26.7	938.2	7.3	930.9
1971	1,127.1	14.0	6.4	1,134.7	115.0	86.7	28.3	1,019.7	11.6	1,008.1
1972	1,238.3	16.3	7.7	1,246.8	126.5	97.1	29.5	1,120.3	9.1	1,111.2
1973	1,382.7	23.5	10.9	1,395.3	139.3	107.9	31.4	1,256.0	8.6	1,247.4
1974	1,500.0	29.8	14.3	1,515.5	162.5	126.6	35.9	1,353.0	10.9	1,342.1
1975	1,638.3	28.0	15.0	1,651.3	187.7	147.8	40.0	1,463.6	17.7	1,445.9
1976	1,825.3	32.4	15.5	1,842.1	205.2	162.5	42.6	1,637.0	25.1	1,611.8
1977	2,030.9	37.2	16.9	2,051.2	230.0	184.3	45.7	1,821.2	22.3	1,798.9
1978	2,294.7	46.3	24.7	2,316.3	262.3	212.8	49.5	2,054.0	26.6	2,027.4
1979	2,563.3	68.3	36.4	2,595.3	300.1	245.7	54.5	2,295.1	46.0	2,249.1
1980	2,789.5	79.1	44.9	2,823.7	343.0	281.1	61.8	2,480.7	41.4	2,439.3
1981	3,128.4	92.0	59.1	3,161.4	388.1	317.9	70.1	2,773.3	30.9	2,742.4
1982	3,255.0	101.0	64.5	3,291.5	426.9	349.8	77.1	2,864.6	.3	2,864.3
1983	3,536.7	101.9	64.8	3,573.8	443.8	362.1	81.7	3,130.0	45.7	3,084.2
1984	3,933.2	121.9	85.6	3,969.5	472.6	385.6	87.0	3,496.9	14.6	3,482.3
1985	4,220.3	112.4	85.9	4,246.8	506.7	414.0	92.7	3,740.1	16.7	3,723.4
1986	4,462.8	111.4	93.6	4,480.6	531.3	431.8	99.5	3,949.3	47.0	3,902.3
1987	4,739.5	123.2	105.3	4,757.4	561.9	455.3	106.7	4,195.4	21.7	4,173.7
1988	5,103.8	152.1	128.5	5,127.4	597.6	483.5	114.1	4,529.8	−19.5	4,549.4
1989	5,484.4	177.7	151.5	5,510.6	644.3	522.1	122.2	4,866.3	39.7	4,826.6
1990	5,803.1	189.1	154.3	5,837.9	682.5	551.6	130.9	5,155.4	66.2	5,089.1
1991	5,995.9	168.9	138.5	6,026.3	725.9	586.9	139.1	5,300.4	72.5	5,227.9
1992	6,337.7	152.7	123.0	6,367.4	751.9	607.3	144.6	5,615.5	102.7	5,512.8
1993	6,657.4	156.2	124.3	6,689.3	776.4	624.7	151.8	5,912.9	139.5	5,773.4
1994	7,072.2	184.4	160.2	7,098.4	833.7	675.1	158.6	6,264.7	142.5	6,122.3
1995	7,397.7	233.9	198.1	7,433.4	878.4	713.4	165.0	6,555.1	101.2	6,453.9
1996	7,816.9	248.7	213.7	7,851.9	918.1	748.8	169.3	6,933.8	93.7	6,840.1
1997	8,304.3	286.7	253.7	8,337.3	974.4	800.3	174.1	7,362.8	70.7	7,292.2
1998	8,747.0	287.1	265.8	8,768.3	1,030.2	851.2	179.0	7,738.2	−14.6	7,752.8
1999	9,268.4	320.8	287.0	9,302.2	1,101.3	914.3	187.0	8,200.9	−35.7	8,236.7
2000	9,817.0	382.7	343.7	9,855.9	1,187.8	990.8	197.0	8,668.1	−127.2	8,795.2
2001	10,128.0	322.4	278.8	10,171.6	1,281.5	1,075.5	206.0	8,890.2	−89.6	8,979.8
2002	10,469.6	305.7	275.0	10,500.2	1,292.0	1,080.3	211.6	9,208.3	−21.0	9,229.3
2003	10,971.2	343.7	275.6	11,039.3	1,331.3	1,112.8	218.5	9,708.0	47.1	9,660.9
2004	11,734.3	415.4	361.7	11,788.0	1,435.3	1,206.2	229.1	10,352.8	76.8	10,275.9
2005 ᵖ	12,479.4	....	....	....	1,574.1	1,327.2	246.9	....	....	....
2002: I	10,333.3	294.5	268.3	10,359.5	1,282.0	1,073.1	208.9	9,077.5	−53.6	9,131.1
II	10,426.6	307.1	290.5	10,443.3	1,288.2	1,077.5	210.8	9,155.0	−56.7	9,211.7
III	10,527.4	317.7	288.1	10,557.0	1,294.9	1,082.4	212.5	9,262.1	14.6	9,247.5
IV	10,591.1	303.3	253.3	10,641.1	1,302.7	1,088.4	214.3	9,338.4	11.7	9,326.7
2003: I	10,717.0	316.5	271.5	10,761.9	1,311.8	1,095.7	216.1	9,450.1	16.6	9,433.6
II	10,844.6	329.1	262.2	10,911.4	1,323.8	1,105.8	218.1	9,587.6	14.4	9,573.2
III	11,087.4	344.3	277.0	11,154.8	1,337.2	1,117.8	219.3	9,817.6	85.3	9,732.3
IV	11,236.0	384.9	291.7	11,329.2	1,352.5	1,131.8	220.6	9,976.8	72.0	9,904.8
2004: I	11,457.1	380.0	297.0	11,540.1	1,371.1	1,147.8	223.3	10,169.0	77.8	10,091.2
II	11,666.1	401.2	354.5	11,712.8	1,393.8	1,165.8	228.1	10,319.0	108.1	10,210.9
III	11,818.8	418.1	369.6	11,867.3	1,534.1	1,303.5	230.6	10,333.2	90.8	10,242.4
IV	11,995.2	462.4	425.6	12,032.0	1,442.0	1,207.6	234.5	10,589.9	30.6	10,559.3
2005: I	12,198.8	462.3	422.9	12,238.2	1,448.4	1,210.9	237.5	10,789.8	39.4	10,750.4
II	12,378.0	489.4	453.9	12,413.5	1,457.2	1,216.9	240.4	10,956.3	78.3	10,878.0
III	12,605.7	520.8	476.6	12,650.0	1,863.8	1,603.6	260.2	10,786.2	66.5	10,719.6
IV ᵖ	12,735.3	....	....	....	1,526.9	1,277.3	249.6	....	....	....

Source: Department of Commerce, Bureau of Economic Analysis.

TABLE B–27.—*Relation of national income and personal income, 1959–2005*

[Billions of dollars; quarterly data at seasonally adjusted annual rates]

Year or quarter	National income	Corporate profits with inventory valuation and capital consumption adjustments	Taxes on production and imports less subsidies	Contributions for government social insurance	Net interest and miscellaneous payments on assets	Business current transfer payments (net)	Current surplus of government enterprises	Wage accruals less disbursements	Personal income receipts on assets	Personal current transfer receipts	Personal income
					Less:				Plus:		Equals:
1959	455.8	55.7	40.0	13.8	9.6	1.8	1.0	0.0	34.6	24.2	392.8
1960	474.9	53.8	43.4	16.4	10.6	1.9	.9	.0	37.9	25.7	411.5
1961	491.6	54.9	45.0	17.0	12.5	2.0	.8	.0	40.1	29.5	429.0
1962	530.1	63.3	48.2	19.1	14.2	2.2	.9	.0	44.1	30.4	456.7
1963	560.6	69.0	51.2	21.7	15.2	2.7	1.4	.0	47.9	32.2	479.6
1964	602.7	76.5	54.6	22.4	17.4	3.1	1.3	.0	53.8	33.5	514.6
1965	653.4	87.5	57.8	23.4	19.6	3.6	1.3	.0	59.4	36.2	555.7
1966	711.0	93.2	59.3	31.3	22.4	3.5	1.0	.0	64.1	39.6	603.9
1967	751.9	91.3	64.2	34.9	25.5	3.8	.9	.0	69.0	48.0	648.3
1968	823.2	98.8	72.3	38.7	27.1	4.3	1.2	.0	75.2	56.1	712.0
1969	889.7	95.4	79.4	44.1	32.7	4.9	1.0	.0	84.1	62.3	778.5
1970	930.9	83.6	86.7	46.4	39.1	4.5	.0	.0	93.5	74.7	838.8
1971	1,008.1	98.0	95.9	51.2	43.9	4.3	-.2	.6	101.0	88.1	903.5
1972	1,111.2	112.1	101.4	59.2	47.9	4.9	.5	.0	109.6	97.9	992.7
1973	1,247.4	125.5	112.1	75.5	55.2	6.0	-.4	-.1	124.7	112.6	1,110.7
1974	1,342.1	115.8	121.7	85.2	70.8	7.1	-.9	-.5	146.4	133.3	1,222.6
1975	1,445.9	134.8	131.0	89.3	81.6	9.4	-3.2	.1	162.2	170.0	1,335.0
1976	1,611.8	163.3	141.5	101.3	85.5	9.5	-1.8	.1	178.4	184.0	1,474.8
1977	1,798.9	192.4	152.8	113.1	101.1	8.4	-2.6	.1	205.3	194.2	1,633.2
1978	2,027.4	216.6	162.2	131.3	115.0	10.6	-1.9	.3	234.8	209.6	1,837.7
1979	2,249.1	223.2	171.9	152.7	138.9	13.0	-2.6	-.2	274.7	235.3	2,062.2
1980	2,439.3	201.1	190.9	166.2	181.8	14.4	-4.8	.0	338.7	279.5	2,307.9
1981	2,742.4	226.1	224.5	195.7	232.3	17.6	-4.9	.1	421.9	318.4	2,591.3
1982	2,864.3	209.7	226.4	208.9	271.1	20.1	-4.0	.0	488.4	354.8	2,775.3
1983	3,084.2	264.2	242.5	226.0	285.3	22.5	-3.1	-.4	529.6	383.7	2,960.7
1984	3,482.3	318.6	269.3	257.5	327.1	30.1	-1.9	.2	607.9	400.1	3,289.5
1985	3,723.4	330.3	287.3	281.4	341.3	34.8	.8	-.2	654.0	424.9	3,526.7
1986	3,902.3	319.5	298.9	303.4	366.8	36.6	1.3	.0	695.5	451.0	3,722.4
1987	4,173.7	368.8	317.7	323.1	366.4	33.8	1.2	.0	717.0	467.6	3,947.4
1988	4,549.4	432.6	345.5	361.5	385.3	34.0	2.5	.0	769.3	496.6	4,253.7
1989	4,826.6	426.6	372.1	385.2	432.1	39.2	4.9	.0	878.0	543.4	4,587.8
1990	5,089.1	437.8	398.7	410.1	442.2	39.4	1.6	.1	924.0	595.2	4,878.6
1991	5,227.9	451.2	430.2	430.2	418.2	39.9	5.7	-.1	932.0	666.4	5,051.0
1992	5,512.8	479.3	453.9	455.0	388.5	42.4	7.6	-15.8	910.9	749.4	5,362.0
1993	5,773.4	541.9	467.0	477.7	365.7	40.7	7.2	6.4	901.8	790.1	5,558.5
1994	6,122.3	600.3	513.5	508.2	366.4	43.3	8.6	17.6	950.8	827.3	5,842.5
1995	6,453.9	696.7	524.2	532.8	367.1	46.9	11.4	16.4	1,016.4	877.4	6,152.3
1996	6,840.1	786.2	546.8	555.2	376.2	53.1	12.7	3.6	1,089.2	925.0	6,520.6
1997	7,292.2	868.5	579.1	587.2	415.6	49.9	12.6	-2.9	1,181.7	951.2	6,915.1
1998	7,752.8	801.6	604.4	624.2	487.1	64.7	10.3	-.7	1,283.2	978.6	7,423.0
1999	8,236.7	851.3	629.8	661.4	495.4	67.4	10.1	5.2	1,264.2	1,022.1	7,802.4
2000	8,795.2	817.9	664.6	702.7	559.0	87.1	5.3	.0	1,387.0	1,084.0	8,429.7
2001	8,979.8	767.3	673.3	731.1	566.3	92.8	-1.4	.0	1,380.0	1,193.9	8,724.1
2002	9,229.3	886.3	724.4	750.0	520.9	84.3	.9	.0	1,333.2	1,286.2	8,881.9
2003	9,660.9	1,031.8	754.8	776.6	528.5	81.6	1.3	.0	1,338.7	1,344.0	9,169.1
2004	10,275.9	1,161.5	809.4	822.2	505.5	91.1	-3.0	.0	1,396.5	1,427.5	9,713.3
2005 *P*			847.1	869.4	497.1	79.4	-11.2	.0	1,456.7	1,525.5	10,238.2
2002: I	9,131.1	829.4	706.1	747.1	545.8	91.1	-1.6	.0	1,340.6	1,260.9	8,814.7
II	9,211.7	864.3	720.8	751.1	519.3	85.8	-1.2	.0	1,336.5	1,284.0	8,892.0
III	9,247.5	895.4	733.3	751.1	507.0	81.4	4.0	.0	1,327.4	1,292.7	8,895.4
IV	9,326.7	956.1	737.2	750.9	511.5	78.8	2.3	.0	1,328.5	1,307.1	8,925.5
2003: I	9,433.6	951.5	741.6	765.8	530.9	79.0	4.1	1.4	1,334.6	1,319.8	9,013.7
II	9,573.2	1,005.0	740.1	773.6	532.4	80.5	1.8	-1.4	1,340.5	1,336.9	9,118.6
III	9,732.3	1,057.5	762.1	780.7	528.1	82.5	.4	.0	1,337.6	1,356.8	9,215.4
IV	9,904.8	1,113.1	775.2	786.3	522.7	84.3	-1.1	.0	1,342.1	1,362.3	9,328.7
2004: I	10,091.2	1,147.3	794.8	806.3	519.9	88.2	-1.6	1.5	1,350.4	1,399.6	9,484.8
II	10,210.9	1,162.0	806.0	813.0	512.2	90.7	-2.2	-1.5	1,363.9	1,419.8	9,614.3
III	10,242.4	1,117.2	812.3	825.9	497.5	83.0	-3.0	.0	1,378.2	1,441.5	9,729.2
IV	10,559.3	1,219.5	824.4	843.5	492.7	102.6	-5.2	.0	1,493.6	1,449.2	10,024.8
2005: I	10,750.4	1,288.2	833.2	861.0	498.3	99.0	-6.1	.0	1,407.9	1,488.8	10,073.4
II	10,878.0	1,347.5	848.0	864.9	488.7	99.6	-7.0	.0	1,439.8	1,509.6	10,185.7
III	10,719.6	1,293.1	853.4	872.6	497.6	21.8	-22.8	.0	1,468.9	1,558.1	10,231.0
IV *P*			853.8	879.2	503.8	97.2	-8.8	.0	1,510.3	1,545.5	10,462.6

Source: Department of Commerce, Bureau of Economic Analysis.

[Billions of dollars; quarterly data at seasonally adjusted annual rates]

Year or quarter	National income	Compensation of employees							Proprietors' income with inventory valuation and capital consumption adjustments			Rental income of persons with capital consumption adjustment
		Total	Wage and salary accruals			Supplements to wages and salaries			Total	Farm	Non-farm	
			Total	Government	Other	Total	Employer contributions for employee pension and insurance funds	Employer contributions for government social insurance				
1959	455.8	281.0	259.8	46.1	213.8	21.1	13.3	7.9	50.7	10.0	40.6	16.2
1960	474.9	296.4	272.9	49.2	223.7	23.6	14.3	9.3	50.8	10.5	40.3	17.1
1961	491.6	305.3	280.5	52.5	228.0	24.8	15.2	9.6	53.2	11.0	42.2	17.9
1962	530.1	327.1	299.4	56.3	243.0	27.8	16.6	11.2	55.4	11.0	44.4	18.8
1963	560.6	345.2	314.9	60.0	254.8	30.4	18.0	12.4	56.5	10.8	45.7	19.5
1964	602.7	370.7	337.8	64.9	272.9	32.9	20.3	12.6	59.4	9.6	49.8	19.6
1965	653.4	399.5	363.8	69.9	293.8	35.7	22.7	13.1	63.9	11.8	52.1	20.2
1966	711.0	442.7	400.3	78.4	321.9	42.3	25.5	16.8	68.2	12.8	55.4	20.8
1967	751.9	475.1	429.0	86.5	342.5	46.1	28.1	18.0	69.8	11.5	58.4	21.2
1968	823.2	524.3	472.0	96.7	375.3	52.3	32.4	20.0	74.3	11.5	62.8	20.9
1969	889.7	577.6	518.3	105.6	412.7	59.3	36.5	22.8	77.4	12.6	64.7	21.2
1970	930.9	617.2	551.6	117.2	434.3	65.7	41.8	23.8	78.4	12.7	65.7	21.4
1971	1,008.1	658.9	584.5	126.8	457.8	74.4	47.9	26.4	84.8	13.2	71.6	22.4
1972	1,111.2	725.1	638.8	137.9	500.9	86.4	55.2	31.2	95.9	16.8	79.1	23.4
1973	1,247.4	811.2	708.8	148.8	560.0	102.5	62.7	39.8	113.5	28.9	84.6	24.3
1974	1,342.1	890.2	772.3	160.5	611.8	118.0	73.3	44.7	113.1	23.2	89.9	24.3
1975	1,445.9	949.1	814.8	176.2	638.6	134.3	87.6	46.7	119.5	21.7	97.8	23.7
1976	1,611.8	1,059.3	899.7	188.9	710.8	159.6	105.2	54.4	132.2	17.0	115.2	22.3
1977	1,798.9	1,180.5	994.2	202.6	791.6	186.4	125.3	61.1	145.7	15.7	130.0	20.7
1978	2,027.4	1,336.1	1,121.2	220.0	901.2	214.9	143.4	71.5	166.6	19.6	147.1	22.1
1979	2,249.1	1,500.8	1,255.8	237.1	1,018.7	245.0	162.4	82.6	180.1	21.8	158.3	23.8
1980	2,439.3	1,651.8	1,377.6	261.5	1,116.2	274.2	185.2	88.9	174.1	11.3	162.8	30.0
1981	2,742.4	1,825.8	1,517.5	285.8	1,231.7	308.3	204.7	103.6	183.0	18.7	164.3	38.0
1982	2,864.3	1,925.8	1,593.7	307.5	1,286.2	332.1	222.4	109.8	176.3	13.1	163.3	38.8
1983	3,084.2	2,042.6	1,684.6	324.8	1,359.8	358.0	238.1	119.9	192.5	6.0	186.5	37.8
1984	3,482.3	2,255.6	1,855.1	348.1	1,507.0	400.5	261.5	139.0	243.3	20.6	222.7	40.2
1985	3,723.4	2,424.7	1,995.5	373.9	1,621.6	429.2	281.5	147.7	262.3	20.8	241.5	41.9
1986	3,902.3	2,570.1	2,114.8	397.0	1,717.9	455.3	297.5	157.9	275.7	22.6	253.1	33.5
1987	4,173.7	2,750.2	2,270.7	422.6	1,848.1	479.5	313.2	166.3	302.2	28.7	273.5	33.5
1988	4,549.4	2,967.2	2,452.9	451.3	2,001.6	514.2	329.6	184.6	341.6	26.8	314.7	40.6
1989	4,826.6	3,145.2	2,596.3	480.2	2,116.2	548.9	355.2	193.7	363.3	33.0	330.3	43.1
1990	5,089.1	3,338.2	2,754.0	517.7	2,236.3	584.2	377.8	206.5	380.6	31.9	348.7	50.7
1991	5,227.9	3,445.2	2,823.0	546.8	2,276.2	622.3	407.1	215.1	377.1	26.7	350.4	60.3
1992	5,512.8	3,635.4	2,964.5	569.2	2,395.3	670.9	442.5	228.4	427.6	34.5	393.0	78.0
1993	5,773.4	3,801.4	3,089.2	586.8	2,502.4	712.2	472.4	239.8	453.8	31.2	422.6	95.6
1994	6,122.3	3,997.2	3,249.8	606.2	2,643.5	747.5	493.3	254.1	473.3	33.9	439.4	119.7
1995	6,453.9	4,193.3	3,435.7	625.5	2,810.2	757.7	493.6	264.0	492.1	22.7	469.5	122.1
1996	6,840.1	4,390.5	3,623.2	644.4	2,978.8	767.3	492.5	274.9	543.2	37.3	505.9	131.5
1997	7,292.2	4,661.7	3,874.7	668.1	3,206.6	787.0	497.5	289.5	576.0	34.2	541.8	128.8
1998	7,752.8	5,019.4	4,182.7	697.3	3,485.5	836.7	529.7	307.0	627.8	29.4	598.4	137.5
1999	8,236.7	5,357.1	4,471.4	729.3	3,742.1	885.7	562.4	323.3	678.3	28.6	649.7	147.3
2000	8,795.2	5,782.7	4,829.2	774.7	4,054.5	953.4	609.9	343.5	728.4	22.7	705.7	150.3
2001	8,979.8	5,942.1	4,942.8	815.9	4,126.9	999.3	642.7	356.6	771.9	19.7	752.2	167.4
2002	9,229.3	6,091.2	4,980.9	865.9	4,115.0	1,110.3	745.1	365.2	768.4	10.6	757.8	152.9
2003	9,660.9	6,321.1	5,111.1	903.3	4,207.8	1,210.0	830.0	380.0	810.2	27.7	782.4	131.7
2004	10,275.9	6,687.6	5,389.4	939.5	4,450.0	1,298.1	895.5	402.7	889.6	35.8	853.8	134.2
2005 ᴾ	....	7,113.6	5,711.9	971.4	4,740.4	1,401.8	976.2	425.6	937.8	20.1	917.7	73.9
2002: I	9,131.1	6,025.3	4,961.2	855.4	4,105.7	1,064.2	700.7	363.4	763.0	8.9	754.1	172.1
II	9,211.7	6,091.5	4,989.4	863.7	4,125.7	1,102.1	736.2	365.8	763.5	4.0	759.4	167.7
III ..	9,247.5	6,114.5	4,988.5	869.3	4,119.2	1,126.0	760.1	365.9	769.1	11.0	758.1	142.9
IV ..	9,326.7	6,133.4	4,984.5	875.4	4,109.1	1,148.9	783.2	365.8	778.1	18.4	759.7	129.2
2003: I	9,433.6	6,210.4	5,031.1	895.1	4,135.9	1,179.4	804.8	374.6	778.3	20.5	757.8	137.7
II	9,573.2	6,286.6	5,086.4	902.3	4,184.1	1,200.2	821.6	378.6	801.4	27.2	774.1	125.4
III ..	9,732.3	6,360.1	5,139.8	906.1	4,233.8	1,220.2	838.1	382.1	821.1	28.2	793.0	120.4
IV ..	9,904.8	6,427.4	5,187.3	909.9	4,277.4	1,240.1	855.4	384.7	840.0	35.1	804.8	143.2
2004: I	10,091.2	6,528.2	5,256.3	928.8	4,327.5	1,271.9	877.0	394.9	870.2	44.8	825.4	144.2
II	10,210.9	6,602.1	5,316.6	936.3	4,380.3	1,285.5	887.5	398.0	898.4	44.1	854.2	141.8
III ..	10,242.4	6,724.2	5,422.0	942.8	4,479.2	1,302.3	897.9	404.4	889.1	29.7	859.4	122.1
IV ..	10,559.3	6,895.8	5,562.9	950.0	4,612.9	1,332.9	919.6	413.4	900.9	24.6	876.3	128.7
2005: I	10,750.4	7,001.7	5,629.9	961.8	4,668.1	1,371.8	950.0	421.9	917.9	24.7	893.2	118.0
II	10,878.0	7,060.2	5,672.3	967.3	4,705.0	1,387.9	964.4	423.5	936.6	19.6	917.1	104.4
III ..	10,719.6	7,155.4	5,741.6	975.0	4,766.6	1,413.8	986.8	427.0	932.4	18.0	914.3	−11.1
IV ᴾ	....	7,237.3	5,803.6	981.6	4,822.0	1,433.7	1,003.7	430.0	964.2	17.9	946.3	84.5

See next page for continuation of table.

TABLE B–28.—*National income by type of income, 1959–2005*—Continued

[Billions of dollars; quarterly data at seasonally adjusted annual rates]

Year or quarter	Corporate profits with inventory valuation and capital consumption adjustments									Net interest and miscellaneous payments	Taxes on production and imports	Less: Subsidies	Business current transfer payments (net)	Current surplus of government enterprises
	Profits with inventory valuation adjustment and without capital consumption adjustment								Capital consumption adjustment					
	Total	Profits						Inventory valuation adjustment						
		Total	Profits before tax	Taxes on corporate income	Profits after tax									
					Total	Net dividends	Undistributed profits							
1959	55.7	53.5	53.8	23.7	30.0	12.6	17.5	-0.3	2.2	9.6	41.1	1.1	1.8	1.0
1960	53.8	51.5	51.6	22.8	28.8	13.4	15.5	-.2	2.3	10.6	44.6	1.1	1.9	.9
1961	54.9	51.8	51.6	22.9	28.7	13.9	14.8	.3	3.0	12.5	47.0	2.0	2.0	.8
1962	63.3	57.0	57.0	24.1	32.9	15.0	17.9	.0	6.2	14.2	50.4	2.3	2.2	.9
1963	69.0	62.1	62.1	26.4	35.7	16.2	19.5	.1	6.8	15.2	53.4	2.2	2.7	1.4
1964	76.5	68.6	69.1	28.2	40.9	18.2	22.7	-.5	7.9	17.4	57.3	2.7	3.1	1.3
1965	87.5	78.9	80.2	31.1	49.1	20.2	28.9	-1.2	8.6	19.6	60.8	3.0	3.6	1.3
1966	93.2	84.6	86.7	33.9	52.8	20.7	32.1	-2.1	8.6	22.4	63.3	3.9	3.5	1.0
1967	91.3	82.0	83.5	32.9	50.6	21.5	29.1	-1.6	9.3	25.5	68.0	3.8	3.8	.9
1968	98.8	88.8	92.4	39.6	52.8	23.5	29.3	-3.7	10.0	27.1	76.5	4.2	4.3	1.2
1969	95.4	85.5	91.4	40.0	51.4	24.2	27.2	-5.9	9.9	32.7	84.0	4.5	4.9	1.0
1970	83.6	74.4	81.0	34.8	46.2	24.3	21.9	-6.6	9.2	39.1	91.5	4.8	4.5	.0
1971	98.0	88.3	92.9	38.2	54.7	25.0	29.7	-4.6	9.7	43.9	100.6	4.7	4.3	-.2
1972	112.1	101.2	107.8	42.3	65.5	26.8	38.6	-6.6	10.9	47.9	108.1	6.6	4.9	.5
1973	125.5	115.3	134.8	50.0	84.9	29.9	55.0	-19.6	10.2	55.2	117.3	5.2	6.0	-.4
1974	115.8	109.5	147.8	52.8	95.0	33.2	61.8	-38.2	6.2	70.8	125.0	3.3	7.1	-.9
1975	134.8	135.0	145.5	51.6	93.9	33.0	60.9	-10.5	-.2	81.6	135.5	4.5	9.4	-3.2
1976	163.3	165.6	179.7	65.3	114.4	39.0	75.4	-14.1	-2.3	85.5	146.6	5.1	9.5	-1.8
1977	192.4	194.7	210.4	74.4	136.0	44.8	91.2	-15.7	-2.3	101.1	159.9	7.1	8.4	-2.6
1978	216.6	222.4	246.1	84.9	161.3	50.8	110.5	-23.7	-5.8	115.0	171.2	8.9	10.6	-1.9
1979	223.2	231.8	271.9	90.0	181.9	57.5	124.4	-40.1	-8.5	138.9	180.4	8.5	13.0	-2.6
1980	201.1	211.4	253.5	87.2	166.3	64.1	102.2	-42.1	-10.2	181.8	200.7	9.8	14.4	-4.8
1981	226.1	219.1	243.7	84.3	159.4	73.8	85.6	-24.6	7.0	232.3	236.0	11.5	17.6	-4.9
1982	209.7	191.0	198.5	66.5	132.0	77.7	54.3	-7.5	18.6	271.1	241.3	15.0	20.1	-4.0
1983	264.2	226.5	233.9	80.6	153.3	83.5	69.8	-7.4	37.8	285.3	263.7	21.2	22.5	-3.1
1984	318.6	264.6	268.6	97.5	171.1	90.8	80.3	-4.0	54.0	327.1	290.2	21.0	30.1	-1.9
1985	330.3	257.5	257.4	99.4	158.0	97.6	60.5	.0	72.9	341.3	308.5	21.3	34.8	.8
1986	319.5	253.0	246.0	109.7	136.3	106.2	30.1	7.1	66.5	366.8	323.7	24.8	36.6	1.3
1987	368.8	301.4	317.6	130.4	187.2	112.3	74.9	-16.2	67.5	366.4	347.9	30.2	33.8	1.2
1988	432.6	363.9	386.1	141.6	244.4	129.9	114.5	-22.2	68.7	385.3	374.9	29.4	34.0	2.5
1989	426.6	367.4	383.7	146.1	237.7	158.0	79.7	-16.3	59.2	432.1	399.3	27.2	39.2	4.9
1990	437.8	396.6	409.5	145.4	264.1	169.1	95.0	-12.9	41.2	442.2	425.5	26.8	39.4	1.6
1991	451.2	427.9	423.0	138.6	284.4	180.7	103.7	4.9	23.3	418.2	457.5	27.3	39.9	5.7
1992	479.3	458.3	461.1	148.7	312.4	187.9	124.5	-2.8	21.1	388.5	483.8	29.9	42.4	7.6
1993	541.9	513.1	517.1	171.0	346.1	202.8	143.3	-4.0	28.8	365.7	503.4	36.4	40.7	7.2
1994	600.3	564.6	577.1	193.7	383.3	234.7	148.6	-12.4	35.7	366.4	545.6	32.2	43.3	8.6
1995	696.7	656.0	674.3	218.7	455.6	254.2	201.4	-18.3	40.7	367.1	558.2	34.0	46.9	11.4
1996	786.2	736.1	733.0	231.7	501.4	297.6	203.8	3.1	50.1	376.2	581.1	34.3	53.1	12.7
1997	868.5	812.3	798.2	246.1	552.1	334.5	217.6	14.1	56.2	415.6	612.0	32.9	49.9	12.6
1998	801.6	738.5	718.3	248.3	470.0	351.6	118.3	20.2	63.1	487.1	639.8	35.4	64.7	10.3
1999	851.3	776.8	775.9	258.6	517.2	337.4	179.9	1.0	74.5	495.4	674.0	44.2	67.4	10.1
2000	817.9	759.3	773.4	265.2	508.2	377.9	130.3	-14.1	58.6	559.0	708.9	44.3	87.1	5.3
2001	767.3	719.2	707.9	204.1	503.8	370.9	132.9	11.3	48.1	566.3	728.6	55.3	92.8	-1.4
2002	886.3	766.2	768.4	192.6	575.8	399.2	176.6	-2.2	120.1	520.9	762.8	38.4	84.3	.9
2003	1,031.8	923.9	937.2	232.1	705.1	423.2	281.9	-13.3	107.9	528.5	801.4	46.7	81.6	1.3
2004	1,161.5	1,019.7	1,059.3	271.1	788.2	493.0	295.2	-39.6	141.8	505.5	852.8	43.5	91.1	-3.0
2005ᵖ					514.2				-55.0	497.1	903.2	56.1	79.4	-11.2
2002: I	829.4	707.0	693.8	174.9	518.9	382.5	136.4	13.3	122.4	545.8	746.0	39.9	91.1	-1.6
II	864.3	740.5	742.1	188.5	553.6	396.1	157.5	-1.6	123.8	519.3	757.9	37.0	85.8	-1.2
III	895.4	774.5	786.4	196.9	589.5	406.1	183.4	-11.8	120.8	507.0	771.6	38.3	81.4	4.0
IV	956.1	842.7	851.5	210.2	641.3	412.0	229.3	-8.8	113.4	511.5	775.5	38.3	78.8	2.3
2003: I	951.5	858.0	883.0	223.9	659.1	416.3	242.8	-25.0	93.4	530.9	783.8	42.1	79.0	4.1
II	1,005.0	891.0	893.1	221.7	671.4	419.9	251.5	-2.1	114.0	532.4	794.7	54.6	80.5	1.8
III	1,057.5	944.0	949.0	235.3	713.8	424.6	289.2	-5.1	113.5	528.1	806.6	44.5	82.5	.4
IV	1,113.1	1,002.6	1,023.4	247.5	775.9	432.0	343.9	-20.8	110.5	522.7	820.6	45.4	84.3	-1.1
2004: I	1,147.3	1,001.2	1,030.2	257.9	772.3	445.9	326.4	-28.9	146.1	519.9	837.1	42.3	88.2	-1.6
II	1,162.0	1,016.5	1,064.9	274.7	790.2	460.9	329.2	-48.3	145.4	512.2	847.8	41.8	90.7	-2.2
III	1,117.2	981.3	1,018.2	259.0	759.2	475.9	283.4	-36.9	135.8	497.5	855.5	43.2	83.0	-3.0
IV	1,219.5	1,079.7	1,124.1	293.0	831.1	589.3	241.8	-44.4	139.8	492.7	870.9	46.5	102.6	-5.2
2005: I	1,288.2	1,339.2	1,378.3	362.6	1,015.7	494.9	520.8	-39.1	-51.0	498.3	883.8	50.6	99.0	-6.1
II	1,347.5	1,393.3	1,412.2	372.5	1,039.7	506.3	533.4	-18.9	-45.8	488.7	900.1	52.1	99.6	-7.0
III	1,293.1	1,365.1	1,392.6	360.3	1,032.3	520.1	512.2	-27.5	-72.1	497.6	909.5	56.1	21.8	-22.8
IVᵖ					535.4				-51.1	503.8	919.3	65.6	97.2	-8.8

Source: Department of Commerce, Bureau of Economic Analysis.

[Billions of dollars; quarterly data at seasonally adjusted annual rates]

Year or quarter	Personal income	Total	Compensation of employees, received						Proprietors' income with inventory valuation and capital consumption adjustments			Rental income of persons with capital consumption adjustment
			Wage and salary disbursements			Supplements to wages and salaries						
			Total	Private industries	Government	Total	Employer contributions for employee pension and insurance funds	Employer contributions for government social insurance	Total	Farm	Nonfarm	
1959	392.8	281.0	259.8	213.8	46.1	21.1	13.3	7.9	50.7	10.0	40.6	16.2
1960	411.5	296.4	272.9	223.7	49.2	23.6	14.3	9.3	50.8	10.5	40.3	17.1
1961	429.0	305.3	280.5	228.0	52.5	24.8	15.2	9.6	53.2	11.0	42.2	17.9
1962	456.7	327.1	299.4	243.0	56.3	27.8	16.6	11.2	55.4	11.0	44.4	18.8
1963	479.6	345.2	314.9	254.8	60.0	30.4	18.0	12.4	56.5	10.8	45.7	19.5
1964	514.6	370.7	337.8	272.9	64.9	32.9	20.3	12.6	59.4	9.6	49.8	19.6
1965	555.7	399.5	363.8	293.8	69.9	35.7	22.7	13.1	63.9	11.8	52.1	20.2
1966	603.9	442.7	400.3	321.9	78.4	42.3	25.5	16.8	68.2	12.8	55.4	20.8
1967	648.3	475.1	429.0	342.5	86.5	46.1	28.1	18.0	69.8	11.5	58.4	21.2
1968	712.0	524.3	472.0	375.3	96.7	52.3	32.4	20.0	74.3	11.5	62.8	20.9
1969	778.5	577.6	518.3	412.7	105.6	59.3	36.5	22.8	77.4	12.6	64.7	21.2
1970	838.8	617.2	551.6	434.3	117.2	65.7	41.8	23.8	78.4	12.7	65.7	21.4
1971	903.5	658.3	584.0	457.4	126.6	74.4	47.9	26.4	84.8	13.2	71.6	22.4
1972	992.7	725.1	638.8	501.2	137.6	86.4	55.2	31.2	95.9	16.8	79.1	23.4
1973	1,110.7	811.3	708.8	560.0	148.8	102.5	62.7	39.8	113.5	28.9	84.6	24.3
1974	1,222.6	890.7	772.8	611.8	161.0	118.0	73.3	44.7	113.1	23.2	89.9	24.3
1975	1,335.0	949.0	814.7	638.6	176.1	134.3	87.6	46.7	119.5	21.7	97.8	23.7
1976	1,474.8	1,059.2	899.6	710.8	188.8	159.6	105.2	54.4	132.2	17.0	115.2	22.3
1977	1,633.2	1,180.4	994.1	791.6	202.5	186.4	125.3	61.1	145.7	15.7	130.0	20.7
1978	1,837.7	1,335.8	1,120.9	901.2	219.7	214.9	143.4	71.5	166.6	19.6	147.1	22.1
1979	2,062.2	1,501.0	1,256.0	1,018.7	237.3	245.0	162.4	82.6	180.1	21.8	158.3	23.8
1980	2,307.9	1,651.8	1,377.7	1,116.2	261.5	274.2	185.2	88.9	174.1	11.3	162.8	30.0
1981	2,591.3	1,825.7	1,517.5	1,231.7	285.8	308.3	204.7	103.6	183.0	18.7	164.3	38.0
1982	2,775.3	1,925.9	1,593.7	1,286.2	307.5	332.1	222.4	109.8	176.3	13.1	163.3	38.8
1983	2,960.7	2,043.0	1,685.0	1,359.8	325.2	358.0	238.1	119.9	192.5	6.0	186.5	37.8
1984	3,289.5	2,255.4	1,854.9	1,507.0	347.9	400.5	261.5	139.0	243.3	20.6	222.7	40.2
1985	3,526.7	2,424.9	1,995.7	1,621.6	374.1	429.2	281.5	147.7	262.3	20.8	241.5	41.9
1986	3,722.4	2,570.1	2,114.8	1,717.9	397.0	455.3	297.5	157.9	275.7	22.6	253.1	33.5
1987	3,947.4	2,750.2	2,270.7	1,848.1	422.6	479.5	313.2	166.3	302.2	28.7	273.5	33.5
1988	4,253.7	2,967.2	2,452.9	2,001.6	451.3	514.2	329.6	184.6	341.6	26.8	314.7	40.6
1989	4,587.8	3,145.2	2,596.3	2,116.2	480.2	548.9	355.2	193.7	363.3	33.0	330.3	43.1
1990	4,878.6	3,338.2	2,754.0	2,236.3	517.7	584.2	377.8	206.5	380.6	31.9	348.7	50.7
1991	5,051.0	3,445.3	2,823.0	2,276.2	546.8	622.3	407.1	215.1	377.1	26.7	350.4	60.3
1992	5,362.0	3,651.2	2,980.3	2,411.1	569.2	670.9	442.5	228.4	427.6	34.5	393.0	78.0
1993	5,558.5	3,794.9	3,082.7	2,496.0	586.8	712.2	472.4	239.8	453.8	31.2	422.6	95.6
1994	5,842.5	3,979.6	3,232.1	2,625.9	606.2	747.5	493.3	254.1	473.3	33.9	439.4	119.7
1995	6,152.3	4,177.0	3,419.3	2,793.8	625.5	757.7	493.6	264.0	492.1	22.7	469.5	122.1
1996	6,520.6	4,386.9	3,619.6	2,975.2	644.4	767.3	492.5	274.9	543.2	37.3	505.9	131.5
1997	6,915.1	4,664.6	3,877.6	3,209.5	668.1	787.0	497.5	289.5	576.0	34.2	541.8	128.8
1998	7,423.0	5,020.1	4,183.4	3,486.2	697.3	836.7	529.7	307.0	627.8	29.4	598.4	137.5
1999	7,802.4	5,352.0	4,466.3	3,736.9	729.3	885.7	562.4	323.3	678.3	28.6	649.7	147.3
2000	8,429.7	5,782.7	4,829.2	4,054.5	774.7	953.4	609.9	343.5	728.4	22.7	705.7	150.3
2001	8,724.1	5,942.1	4,942.8	4,126.9	815.9	999.3	642.7	356.6	771.9	19.7	752.2	167.4
2002	8,881.9	6,091.2	4,980.9	4,115.0	865.9	1,110.3	745.1	365.2	768.4	10.6	757.8	152.9
2003	9,169.1	6,321.1	5,111.1	4,207.8	903.3	1,210.0	830.0	380.0	810.2	27.7	782.4	131.7
2004	9,713.3	6,687.6	5,389.4	4,450.0	939.5	1,298.1	895.5	402.7	889.6	35.8	853.8	134.2
2005 ᵖ	10,238.2	7,113.6	5,711.9	4,740.4	971.5	1,401.8	976.2	425.6	937.8	20.1	917.7	73.9
2002: I	8,814.7	6,025.3	4,961.2	4,105.7	855.4	1,064.2	700.7	363.4	763.0	8.9	754.1	172.1
II	8,892.0	6,091.5	4,989.4	4,125.7	863.7	1,102.1	736.2	365.8	763.5	4.0	759.4	167.7
III	8,895.4	6,114.5	4,988.5	4,119.2	869.3	1,126.0	760.1	365.9	769.1	11.0	758.1	142.9
IV	8,925.5	6,133.4	4,984.5	4,109.1	875.4	1,148.9	783.2	365.8	778.1	18.4	759.7	129.2
2003: I	9,013.7	6,209.0	5,029.7	4,135.9	893.7	1,179.4	804.8	374.6	778.3	20.5	757.8	137.7
II	9,118.6	6,288.0	5,087.8	4,184.1	903.7	1,200.2	821.6	378.6	801.4	27.2	774.1	125.4
III	9,215.4	6,360.1	5,139.8	4,233.8	906.1	1,220.2	838.1	382.1	821.1	28.2	793.0	120.4
IV	9,328.7	6,427.4	5,187.3	4,277.4	909.9	1,240.1	855.4	384.7	840.0	35.1	804.8	143.2
2004: I	9,484.8	6,526.7	5,254.8	4,327.5	927.3	1,271.9	877.0	394.9	870.2	44.8	825.4	144.2
II	9,614.3	6,603.6	5,318.1	4,380.3	937.7	1,285.5	887.5	398.0	898.4	44.1	854.2	141.8
III	9,729.2	6,724.2	5,422.0	4,479.2	942.8	1,302.3	897.9	404.4	889.1	29.7	859.4	122.1
IV	10,024.8	6,895.8	5,562.9	4,612.9	950.0	1,332.9	919.6	413.4	900.9	24.6	876.3	128.7
2005: I	10,073.4	7,001.7	5,629.9	4,668.1	961.8	1,371.8	950.0	421.9	917.9	24.7	893.2	118.0
II	10,185.7	7,060.2	5,672.3	4,705.0	967.3	1,387.9	964.4	423.5	936.6	19.6	917.1	104.4
III	10,231.0	7,155.4	5,741.6	4,766.6	975.0	1,413.8	986.8	427.0	932.4	18.0	914.3	−11.1
IV ᵖ	10,462.6	7,237.3	5,803.6	4,822.0	981.6	1,433.7	1,003.7	430.0	964.2	17.9	946.3	84.5

¹ Consists of aid to families with dependent children and, beginning with 1996, assistance programs operating under the Personal Responsibility and Work Opportunity Reconciliation Act of 1996.

See next page for continuation of table.

TABLE B–29.—*Sources of personal income, 1959–2005*—Continued

[Billions of dollars; quarterly data at seasonally adjusted annual rates]

Year or quarter	Personal income receipts on assets			Personal current transfer receipts							Less: Contributions for government social insurance
					Government social benefits to persons						
	Total	Personal interest income	Personal dividend income	Total	Total	Old-age, survivors, disability, and health insurance benefits	Government unemployment insurance benefits	Veterans benefits	Family assistance [1]	Other	Other current transfer receipts, from business (net)	
1959	34.6	22.0	12.6	24.2	22.9	10.2	2.8	4.6	0.9	4.5	1.3	13.8
1960	37.9	24.5	13.4	25.7	24.4	11.1	3.0	4.6	1.0	4.7	1.3	16.4
1961	40.1	26.2	13.9	29.5	28.1	12.6	4.3	5.0	1.1	5.1	1.4	17.0
1962	44.1	29.1	15.0	30.4	28.8	14.3	3.1	4.7	1.3	5.5	1.5	19.1
1963	47.9	31.7	16.2	32.2	30.3	15.2	3.0	4.8	1.4	5.9	1.9	21.7
1964	53.8	35.6	18.2	33.5	31.3	16.0	2.7	4.7	1.5	6.4	2.2	22.4
1965	59.4	39.2	20.2	36.2	33.9	18.1	2.3	4.9	1.7	7.0	2.3	23.4
1966	64.1	43.4	20.7	39.6	37.5	20.8	1.9	4.9	1.9	8.1	2.1	31.3
1967	69.0	47.5	21.5	48.0	45.8	25.8	2.2	5.6	2.3	9.9	2.3	34.9
1968	75.2	51.6	23.5	56.1	53.3	30.5	2.1	5.9	2.8	11.9	2.8	38.7
1969	84.1	59.9	24.2	62.3	59.0	33.1	2.2	6.7	3.5	13.4	3.3	44.1
1970	93.5	69.2	24.3	74.7	71.7	38.6	4.0	7.7	4.8	16.6	2.9	46.4
1971	101.0	75.9	25.0	88.1	85.4	44.7	5.8	8.8	6.2	20.0	2.7	51.2
1972	109.6	82.8	26.8	97.9	94.8	49.8	5.7	9.7	6.9	22.7	3.1	59.2
1973	124.7	94.8	29.9	112.6	108.6	60.9	4.4	10.4	7.2	25.7	3.9	75.5
1974	146.4	113.2	33.2	133.3	128.6	70.3	6.8	11.8	8.0	31.7	4.7	85.2
1975	162.2	129.3	32.9	170.0	163.1	81.5	17.6	14.5	9.3	40.2	6.8	89.3
1976	178.4	139.5	39.0	184.0	177.3	93.3	15.8	14.4	10.1	43.7	6.7	101.3
1977	205.3	160.6	44.7	194.2	189.1	105.3	12.7	13.8	10.6	46.7	5.1	113.1
1978	234.8	184.0	50.7	209.6	203.2	116.9	9.1	13.9	10.8	52.5	6.5	131.3
1979	274.7	217.3	57.4	235.3	227.1	132.5	9.4	14.4	11.1	59.6	8.2	152.7
1980	338.7	274.7	64.0	279.5	270.8	154.8	15.7	15.0	12.5	72.8	8.6	166.2
1981	421.9	348.3	73.6	318.4	307.2	182.1	15.6	16.1	13.1	80.2	11.2	195.7
1982	488.4	410.8	77.6	354.8	342.4	204.6	25.1	16.4	12.9	83.4	12.4	208.9
1983	529.6	446.3	83.3	383.7	369.9	222.2	26.2	16.6	13.8	91.0	13.8	226.0
1984	607.9	517.2	90.6	400.1	380.4	237.8	15.9	16.4	14.5	95.9	19.7	257.5
1985	654.0	556.6	97.4	424.9	402.6	253.0	15.7	16.7	15.2	102.0	22.3	281.4
1986	695.5	589.5	106.0	451.0	428.0	268.9	16.3	16.7	16.1	109.9	22.9	303.4
1987	717.0	604.9	112.2	467.6	447.4	282.6	14.5	16.6	16.4	117.3	20.2	323.1
1988	769.3	639.5	129.7	496.6	476.0	300.2	13.2	16.9	16.9	128.8	20.6	361.5
1989	878.0	720.2	157.8	543.4	519.9	325.6	14.3	17.3	17.5	145.3	23.5	385.2
1990	924.0	755.2	168.8	595.2	573.1	351.8	18.0	17.8	19.2	166.2	22.2	410.1
1991	932.0	751.7	180.3	666.4	648.5	381.7	26.6	18.3	21.1	200.8	17.9	430.2
1992	910.9	723.4	187.4	749.4	729.8	414.4	38.9	19.3	22.2	234.9	19.6	455.0
1993	901.8	699.6	202.2	790.1	775.7	443.4	34.1	20.1	22.8	255.3	14.4	477.7
1994	950.8	716.8	234.0	827.3	812.2	475.4	23.5	20.1	23.2	270.0	15.1	508.2
1995	1,016.4	763.2	253.2	877.4	858.4	506.8	21.4	20.9	22.6	286.7	19.0	532.8
1996	1,089.2	793.0	296.2	925.0	902.1	537.7	22.0	21.7	20.3	300.4	22.9	555.2
1997	1,181.7	848.7	333.0	951.2	931.8	563.2	19.9	22.5	17.9	308.3	19.4	587.2
1998	1,283.2	933.2	349.9	978.6	952.6	575.1	19.5	23.4	17.4	317.3	26.0	624.2
1999	1,264.2	928.6	335.6	1,022.1	988.0	588.9	20.3	24.3	17.9	336.7	34.1	661.4
2000	1,387.0	1,011.0	376.1	1,084.0	1,041.6	620.8	20.3	25.1	18.4	357.0	42.4	702.7
2001	1,380.0	1,011.0	369.0	1,193.9	1,143.9	668.5	31.7	26.7	18.1	398.9	50.0	731.1
2002	1,333.2	936.1	397.2	1,286.2	1,248.9	707.5	53.2	29.6	17.7	440.9	37.3	750.0
2003	1,338.7	917.6	421.1	1,344.0	1,313.5	739.3	52.8	32.0	18.4	471.1	30.5	776.6
2004	1,396.5	905.9	490.6	1,427.5	1,394.5	789.3	36.0	34.2	18.5	516.5	33.0	822.2
2005 *p*	1,456.7	945.0	511.7	1,525.5	1,483.9	845.1	28.9	36.4	18.8	554.7	41.6	869.4
2002: I	1,340.6	960.1	380.5	1,260.9	1,218.6	698.4	42.8	28.8	17.7	430.9	42.3	747.1
II	1,336.5	942.4	394.1	1,284.0	1,245.4	704.5	60.1	29.4	17.6	433.8	38.6	751.1
III	1,327.4	923.3	404.1	1,292.7	1,257.3	710.3	56.8	29.9	17.6	442.7	35.4	751.1
IV	1,328.5	918.4	410.0	1,307.1	1,274.2	716.7	53.1	30.4	17.8	456.2	32.9	750.9
2003: I	1,334.6	920.6	414.0	1,319.8	1,288.2	726.6	51.1	31.5	18.1	460.8	31.6	765.8
II	1,340.5	922.6	417.9	1,336.9	1,306.1	736.0	54.5	31.9	18.3	465.4	30.8	773.6
III	1,337.6	915.1	422.4	1,356.8	1,326.7	742.6	54.4	32.2	18.5	479.1	30.1	780.7
IV	1,342.1	912.2	429.9	1,362.3	1,333.0	751.9	51.3	32.3	18.5	478.9	29.3	786.3
2004: I	1,350.4	906.6	443.9	1,399.6	1,370.6	772.9	43.1	33.8	18.4	502.4	29.0	806.3
II	1,363.9	905.1	458.8	1,419.8	1,390.8	784.9	35.3	34.0	18.5	518.3	28.9	813.0
III	1,378.2	904.7	473.5	1,441.5	1,397.1	793.7	33.3	34.4	18.5	517.1	44.4	825.9
IV	1,493.6	907.4	586.2	1,449.2	1,419.5	805.5	32.4	34.8	18.6	528.2	29.8	843.5
2005: I	1,407.9	915.4	492.5	1,488.8	1,459.7	828.0	29.4	36.2	18.7	547.3	29.1	861.0
II	1,439.8	936.0	503.8	1,509.6	1,480.4	842.2	28.0	36.4	18.7	555.1	29.2	864.9
III	1,468.9	951.2	517.6	1,558.1	1,483.2	850.1	28.5	36.4	18.8	549.3	74.8	872.6
IV *p*	1,510.3	977.5	532.9	1,545.5	1,512.4	860.2	29.7	36.7	18.9	566.9	33.1	879.2

Source: Department of Commerce, Bureau of Economic Analysis.

[Billions of dollars, except as noted; quarterly data at seasonally adjusted annual rates]

Year or quarter	Personal income	Less: Personal current taxes	Equals: Disposable personal income	Less: Personal outlays				Equals: Personal saving	Percent of disposable personal income [2]		
				Total	Personal consumption expenditures	Personal interest payments [1]	Personal current transfer payments		Personal outlays		Personal saving
									Total	Personal consumption expenditures	
1959	392.8	42.3	350.5	323.9	317.6	5.5	0.8	26.7	92.4	90.6	7.6
1960	411.5	46.1	365.4	338.8	331.7	6.2	.8	26.7	92.7	90.8	7.3
1961	429.0	47.3	381.8	349.6	342.1	6.5	1.0	32.2	91.6	89.6	8.4
1962	456.7	51.6	405.1	371.3	363.3	7.0	1.1	33.8	91.7	89.7	8.3
1963	479.6	54.6	425.1	391.8	382.7	7.9	1.2	33.3	92.2	90.0	7.8
1964	514.6	52.1	462.5	421.7	411.4	8.9	1.3	40.8	91.2	89.0	8.8
1965	555.7	57.7	498.1	455.1	443.8	9.9	1.4	43.0	91.4	89.1	8.6
1966	603.9	66.4	537.5	493.1	480.9	10.7	1.6	44.4	91.7	89.5	8.3
1967	648.3	73.0	575.3	520.9	507.8	11.1	2.0	54.4	90.5	88.3	9.5
1968	712.0	87.0	625.0	572.2	558.0	12.2	2.0	52.8	91.6	89.3	8.4
1969	778.5	104.5	674.0	621.4	605.2	14.0	2.2	52.5	92.2	89.8	7.8
1970	838.8	103.1	735.7	666.2	648.5	15.2	2.6	69.5	90.6	88.1	9.4
1971	903.5	101.7	801.8	721.2	701.9	16.6	2.8	80.6	89.9	87.5	10.1
1972	992.7	123.6	869.1	791.9	770.6	18.1	3.1	77.2	91.1	88.7	8.9
1973	1,110.7	132.4	978.3	875.6	852.4	19.8	3.4	102.7	89.5	87.1	10.5
1974	1,222.6	151.0	1,071.6	958.0	933.4	21.2	3.4	113.6	89.4	87.1	10.6
1975	1,335.0	147.6	1,187.4	1,061.9	1,034.4	23.7	3.8	125.6	89.4	87.1	10.6
1976	1,474.8	172.3	1,302.5	1,180.2	1,151.9	23.9	4.4	122.3	90.6	88.4	9.4
1977	1,633.2	197.5	1,435.7	1,310.4	1,278.6	27.0	4.8	125.3	91.3	89.1	8.7
1978	1,837.7	229.4	1,608.3	1,465.8	1,428.5	31.9	5.4	142.5	91.1	88.8	8.9
1979	2,062.2	268.7	1,793.5	1,634.4	1,592.2	36.2	5.9	159.1	91.1	88.8	8.9
1980	2,307.9	298.9	2,009.0	1,807.5	1,757.1	43.6	6.8	201.4	90.0	87.5	10.0
1981	2,591.3	345.2	2,246.1	2,001.8	1,941.1	49.3	11.4	244.3	89.1	86.4	10.9
1982	2,775.3	354.1	2,421.2	2,150.4	2,077.3	59.5	13.6	270.8	88.8	85.8	11.2
1983	2,960.7	352.3	2,608.4	2,374.8	2,290.6	69.2	15.0	233.6	91.0	87.8	9.0
1984	3,289.5	377.4	2,912.0	2,597.3	2,503.3	77.0	16.9	314.8	89.2	86.0	10.8
1985	3,526.7	417.4	3,109.3	2,829.3	2,720.3	90.4	18.6	280.0	91.0	87.5	9.0
1986	3,722.4	437.3	3,285.1	3,016.7	2,899.7	96.1	20.9	268.4	91.8	88.3	8.2
1987	3,947.4	489.1	3,458.3	3,216.9	3,100.2	93.6	23.1	241.4	93.0	89.6	7.0
1988	4,253.7	505.0	3,748.7	3,475.8	3,353.6	96.8	25.4	272.9	92.7	89.5	7.3
1989	4,587.8	566.1	4,021.7	3,734.5	3,598.5	108.2	27.8	287.1	92.9	89.5	7.1
1990	4,878.6	592.8	4,285.8	3,986.4	3,839.9	116.1	30.4	299.4	93.0	89.6	7.0
1991	5,051.0	586.7	4,464.3	4,140.1	3,986.1	118.5	35.6	324.2	92.7	89.3	7.3
1992	5,362.0	610.6	4,751.4	4,385.4	4,235.3	111.8	38.3	366.0	92.3	89.1	7.7
1993	5,558.5	646.6	4,911.9	4,627.9	4,477.9	107.3	42.7	284.0	94.2	91.2	5.8
1994	5,842.5	690.7	5,151.8	4,902.4	4,743.3	112.8	46.3	249.5	95.2	92.1	4.8
1995	6,152.3	744.1	5,408.2	5,157.3	4,975.8	132.7	48.9	250.9	95.4	92.0	4.6
1996	6,520.6	832.1	5,688.5	5,460.0	5,256.8	150.3	52.9	228.4	96.0	92.4	4.0
1997	6,915.1	926.3	5,988.8	5,770.5	5,547.4	163.9	59.2	218.3	96.4	92.6	3.6
1998	7,423.0	1,027.0	6,395.9	6,119.1	5,879.5	174.5	65.2	276.8	95.7	91.9	4.3
1999	7,802.4	1,107.5	6,695.0	6,536.4	6,282.5	181.0	73.0	158.6	97.6	93.8	2.4
2000	8,429.7	1,235.7	7,194.0	7,025.6	6,739.4	204.7	81.5	168.5	97.7	93.7	2.3
2001	8,724.1	1,237.3	7,486.8	7,354.5	7,055.0	212.2	87.2	132.3	98.2	94.2	1.8
2002	8,881.9	1,051.8	7,830.1	7,645.3	7,350.7	196.4	98.2	184.7	97.6	93.9	2.4
2003	9,169.1	999.9	8,169.2	7,996.3	7,709.9	183.2	103.3	172.8	97.9	94.4	2.1
2004	9,713.3	1,049.1	8,664.2	8,512.5	8,214.3	186.7	111.5	151.8	98.2	94.8	1.8
2005 *p*	10,238.2	1,206.9	9,031.3	9,072.8	8,745.9	206.4	120.5	–41.6	100.5	96.8	–.5
2002: I	8,814.7	1,063.2	7,751.5	7,526.1	7,230.3	199.2	96.6	225.4	97.1	93.3	2.9
II	8,892.0	1,050.3	7,841.7	7,620.5	7,323.0	200.6	96.8	221.2	97.2	93.4	2.8
III	8,895.4	1,050.0	7,845.4	7,692.4	7,396.6	197.0	98.9	153.0	98.0	94.3	2.0
IV	8,925.5	1,043.8	7,881.7	7,742.4	7,453.1	188.8	100.5	139.3	98.2	94.6	1.8
2003: I	9,013.7	1,024.3	7,989.4	7,835.4	7,555.2	179.3	101.0	154.0	98.1	94.6	1.9
II	9,118.6	1,026.9	8,091.7	7,922.1	7,635.3	184.8	102.0	169.6	97.9	94.4	2.1
III	9,215.4	940.8	8,274.6	8,069.5	7,782.4	185.2	101.9	205.1	97.5	94.1	2.5
IV	9,328.7	1,007.6	8,321.0	8,158.4	7,866.6	183.4	108.4	162.6	98.0	94.5	2.0
2004: I	9,484.8	1,009.6	8,475.3	8,319.4	8,032.3	178.0	109.2	155.8	98.2	94.8	1.8
II	9,614.3	1,034.0	8,580.3	8,439.1	8,145.6	182.2	111.3	141.2	98.4	94.9	1.6
III	9,729.2	1,058.4	8,670.9	8,566.3	8,263.2	190.3	112.8	104.6	98.8	95.3	1.2
IV	10,024.8	1,094.3	8,930.4	8,725.0	8,416.1	196.2	112.7	205.4	97.7	94.2	2.3
2005: I	10,073.4	1,171.4	8,902.0	8,854.6	8,535.8	198.1	120.8	47.4	99.5	95.9	.5
II	10,185.7	1,206.0	8,979.7	9,001.2	8,677.0	205.3	118.8	–21.5	100.2	96.6	–.2
III	10,231.0	1,215.9	9,015.1	9,173.9	8,844.0	210.0	119.9	–158.9	101.8	98.1	–1.8
IV *p*	10,462.6	1,234.3	9,228.3	9,261.6	8,926.9	212.1	122.7	–33.3	100.4	96.7	–.4

[1] Consists of nonmortgage interest paid by households.
[2] Percents based on data in millions of dollars.

Source: Department of Commerce, Bureau of Economic Analysis.

TABLE B–31.—*Total and per capita disposable personal income and personal consumption expenditures, and per capita gross domestic product, in current and real dollars, 1959–2005*

[Quarterly data at seasonally adjusted annual rates, except as noted]

Year or quarter	Disposable personal income				Personal consumption expenditures				Gross domestic product per capita (dollars)		Popula-tion (thou-sands)[1]
	Total (billions of dollars)		Per capita (dollars)		Total (billions of dollars)		Per capita (dollars)				
	Current dollars	Chained (2000) dollars	Current dollars	Chained (2000) dollars	Current dollars	Chained (2000) dollars	Current dollars	Chained (2000) dollars	Current dollars	Chained (2000) dollars	
1959	350.5	1,715.5	1,979	9,685	317.6	1,554.6	1,793	8,776	2,860	13,782	177,130
1960	365.4	1,759.7	2,022	9,735	331.7	1,597.4	1,835	8,837	2,912	13,840	180,760
1961	381.8	1,819.2	2,078	9,901	342.1	1,630.3	1,862	8,873	2,965	13,932	183,742
1962	405.1	1,908.2	2,171	10,227	363.3	1,711.1	1,947	9,170	3,139	14,552	186,590
1963	425.1	1,979.1	2,246	10,455	382.7	1,781.6	2,022	9,412	3,263	14,971	189,300
1964	462.5	2,122.8	2,410	11,061	411.4	1,888.4	2,144	9,839	3,458	15,624	191,927
1965	498.1	2,253.3	2,563	11,594	443.8	2,007.7	2,283	10,331	3,700	16,420	194,347
1966	537.5	2,371.9	2,734	12,065	480.9	2,121.8	2,446	10,793	4,007	17,290	196,599
1967	575.3	2,475.9	2,895	12,457	507.8	2,185.0	2,555	10,994	4,189	17,533	198,752
1968	625.0	2,588.0	3,114	12,892	558.0	2,310.5	2,780	11,510	4,533	18,196	200,745
1969	674.0	2,668.7	3,324	13,163	605.2	2,396.4	2,985	11,820	4,857	18,573	202,736
1970	735.7	2,781.7	3,587	13,563	648.5	2,451.9	3,162	11,955	5,064	18,391	205,089
1971	801.8	2,907.9	3,860	14,001	701.9	2,545.5	3,379	12,256	5,427	18,771	207,692
1972	869.1	3,046.5	4,140	14,512	770.6	2,701.3	3,671	12,868	5,899	19,555	209,924
1973	978.3	3,252.3	4,616	15,345	852.4	2,833.8	4,022	13,371	6,524	20,484	211,939
1974	1,071.6	3,228.5	5,010	15,094	933.4	2,812.3	4,364	13,148	7,013	20,195	213,898
1975	1,187.4	3,302.6	5,498	15,291	1,034.4	2,876.9	4,789	13,320	7,586	19,961	215,981
1976	1,302.5	3,432.2	5,972	15,738	1,151.9	3,035.5	5,282	13,919	8,369	20,822	218,086
1977	1,435.7	3,552.9	6,517	16,128	1,278.6	3,164.1	5,804	14,364	9,219	21,565	220,289
1978	1,608.3	3,718.8	7,224	16,704	1,428.5	3,303.1	6,417	14,837	10,307	22,526	222,629
1979	1,793.5	3,811.2	7,967	16,931	1,592.2	3,383.4	7,073	15,030	11,387	22,982	225,106
1980	2,009.0	3,857.7	8,822	16,940	1,757.1	3,374.1	7,716	14,816	12,249	22,666	227,726
1981	2,246.1	3,960.0	9,765	17,217	1,941.1	3,422.2	8,439	14,879	13,601	23,007	230,008
1982	2,421.2	4,044.9	10,426	17,418	2,077.3	3,470.3	8,945	14,944	14,017	22,346	232,218
1983	2,608.4	4,177.7	11,131	17,828	2,290.6	3,668.6	9,775	15,656	15,092	23,146	234,333
1984	2,912.0	4,494.1	12,319	19,011	2,503.3	3,863.3	10,589	16,343	16,638	24,593	236,394
1985	3,109.3	4,645.2	13,037	19,476	2,720.3	4,064.0	11,406	17,040	17,695	25,382	238,506
1986	3,285.1	4,791.0	13,649	19,906	2,899.7	4,228.9	12,048	17,570	18,542	26,024	240,683
1987	3,458.3	4,874.5	14,241	20,072	3,100.2	4,369.8	12,766	17,994	19,517	26,664	242,843
1988	3,748.7	5,082.6	15,297	20,740	3,353.6	4,546.9	13,685	18,554	20,827	27,514	245,061
1989	4,021.7	5,224.8	16,257	21,120	3,598.5	4,675.0	14,546	18,898	22,169	28,221	247,387
1990	4,285.8	5,324.2	17,131	21,281	3,839.9	4,770.3	15,349	19,067	23,195	28,429	250,181
1991	4,464.3	5,351.7	17,609	21,109	3,986.1	4,778.4	15,722	18,848	23,650	28,007	253,530
1992	4,751.4	5,536.3	18,494	21,548	4,235.3	4,934.8	16,485	19,208	24,668	28,556	256,922
1993	4,911.9	5,594.2	18,872	21,493	4,477.9	5,099.8	17,204	19,593	25,578	28,940	260,282
1994	5,151.8	5,746.4	19,555	21,812	4,743.3	5,290.7	18,004	20,082	26,844	29,741	263,455
1995	5,408.2	5,905.7	20,287	22,153	4,975.8	5,433.5	18,665	20,382	27,749	30,128	266,588
1996	5,688.5	6,080.9	21,091	22,546	5,256.8	5,619.4	19,490	20,835	28,982	30,881	269,714
1997	5,988.8	6,295.8	21,940	23,065	5,547.4	5,831.8	20,323	21,365	30,424	31,886	272,958
1998	6,395.9	6,663.9	23,161	24,131	5,879.5	6,125.8	21,291	22,183	31,674	32,833	276,154
1999	6,695.0	6,861.3	23,968	24,564	6,282.5	6,438.6	22,491	23,050	33,181	33,904	279,328
2000	7,194.0	7,194.0	25,472	25,472	6,739.4	6,739.4	23,862	23,862	34,759	34,759	282,429
2001	7,486.8	7,333.3	26,236	25,698	7,055.0	6,910.4	24,723	24,216	35,491	34,660	285,366
2002	7,830.1	7,562.2	27,165	26,236	7,350.7	7,099.3	25,502	24,630	36,323	34,863	288,240
2003	8,169.2	7,741.8	28,065	26,596	7,709.9	7,306.6	26,487	25,101	37,691	35,456	291,085
2004	8,664.2	8,004.3	29,475	27,230	8,214.3	7,588.6	27,944	25,816	39,919	36,590	293,951
2005 *P*	9,031.3	8,114.5	30,429	27,340	8,745.9	7,858.1	29,468	26,476	42,047	37,504	296,798
2002: I	7,751.5	7,549.9	26,994	26,292	7,230.3	7,042.2	25,179	24,524	35,985	34,745	287,154
II ...	7,841.7	7,585.2	27,246	26,355	7,323.0	7,083.5	25,444	24,612	36,227	34,855	287,812
III ..	7,845.4	7,555.5	27,187	26,182	7,396.6	7,123.2	25,631	24,684	36,481	34,967	288,575
IV ..	7,881.7	7,559.3	27,241	26,127	7,453.1	7,148.2	25,760	24,706	36,606	34,894	289,328
2003: I	7,989.4	7,605.5	27,552	26,228	7,555.2	7,192.2	26,054	24,803	36,958	34,963	289,977
II ...	8,091.7	7,690.5	27,839	26,459	7,635.3	7,256.8	26,269	24,967	37,311	35,197	290,656
III ..	8,274.6	7,826.2	28,392	26,853	7,782.4	7,360.7	26,703	25,256	38,043	35,722	291,442
IV ..	8,321.0	7,844.8	28,475	26,846	7,866.6	7,416.4	26,921	25,380	38,451	35,941	292,217
2004: I	8,475.3	7,915.1	28,939	27,026	8,032.3	7,501.4	27,426	25,613	39,120	36,236	292,872
II ...	8,580.3	7,938.8	29,231	27,045	8,145.6	7,536.6	27,750	25,675	39,743	36,466	293,540
III ..	8,670.9	7,993.3	29,461	27,159	8,263.2	7,617.5	28,076	25,882	40,157	36,726	294,315
IV ..	8,930.4	8,169.2	30,265	27,685	8,416.1	7,698.8	28,522	26,091	40,651	36,930	295,077
2005: I	8,902.0	8,098.1	30,103	27,384	8,535.8	7,764.9	28,864	26,258	41,251	37,195	295,720
II ...	8,979.7	8,102.6	30,298	27,338	8,677.0	7,829.5	29,276	26,417	41,763	37,415	296,383
III ..	9,015.1	8,060.8	30,338	27,127	8,844.0	7,907.9	29,762	26,612	42,421	37,699	297,155
IV *P*	9,228.3	8,198.0	30,975	27,516	8,926.9	7,930.2	29,963	26,617	42,745	37,705	297,933

[1] Population of the United States including Armed Forces overseas; includes Alaska and Hawaii beginning 1960. Annual data are averages of quarterly data. Quarterly data are averages for the period.

Source: Department of Commerce (Bureau of Economic Analysis and Bureau of the Census).

319

TABLE B–32.—Gross saving and investment, 1959–2005

[Billions of dollars, except as noted; quarterly data at seasonally adjusted annual rates]

Year or quarter	Total gross saving	Total net saving	Net private saving Total	Personal saving	Undistributed corporate profits[1]	Wage accruals less disbursements	Net government saving Total	Federal	State and local	Consumption of fixed capital Total	Private	Government
1959	106.2	53.2	46.0	26.7	19.4	0.0	7.1	3.3	3.8	53.0	38.6	14.5
1960	111.3	55.8	44.3	26.7	17.6	.0	11.5	7.2	4.3	55.6	40.5	15.0
1961	114.3	57.1	50.2	32.2	18.1	.0	6.9	2.6	4.3	57.2	41.6	15.6
1962	124.9	65.7	57.9	33.8	24.1	.0	7.8	2.5	5.2	59.3	42.8	16.5
1963	133.2	70.8	59.7	33.3	26.4	.0	11.1	5.4	5.7	62.4	44.9	17.5
1964	143.4	78.4	71.0	40.8	30.1	.0	7.4	1.0	6.4	65.0	46.9	18.1
1965	158.5	89.1	79.2	43.0	36.2	.0	9.9	3.3	6.5	69.4	50.5	18.9
1966	168.7	93.1	83.1	44.4	38.7	.0	10.0	2.3	7.8	75.6	55.5	20.1
1967	170.5	89.0	91.4	54.4	36.9	.0	−2.4	−9.4	7.0	81.5	59.9	21.6
1968	182.0	93.6	88.4	52.8	35.6	.0	5.2	−2.3	7.5	88.4	65.2	23.1
1969	198.3	100.4	83.7	52.5	31.2	.0	16.7	8.7	8.0	97.9	73.1	24.8
1970	192.7	86.0	94.0	69.5	24.6	.0	−8.1	−15.2	7.1	106.7	80.0	26.7
1971	208.9	93.9	115.8	80.6	34.8	.4	−21.9	−28.4	6.5	115.0	86.7	28.3
1972	237.5	111.0	119.8	77.2	42.9	−.3	−8.8	−24.4	15.6	126.5	97.1	29.5
1973	292.0	152.7	148.3	102.7	45.6	.0	4.4	−11.3	15.7	139.3	107.9	31.4
1974	301.5	139.0	143.4	113.6	29.8	.0	−4.4	−13.8	9.3	162.5	126.6	35.9
1975	297.0	109.2	175.8	125.6	50.2	.0	−66.6	−69.0	2.5	187.7	147.8	40.0
1976	342.1	137.0	181.3	122.3	59.0	.0	−44.4	−51.7	7.4	205.2	162.5	42.6
1977	397.5	167.5	198.5	125.3	73.2	.0	−31.0	−44.1	13.1	230.0	184.3	45.7
1978	478.0	215.7	223.5	142.5	81.0	.0	−7.8	−26.5	18.7	262.3	212.8	49.5
1979	536.7	236.6	234.9	159.1	75.7	.0	1.7	−11.3	13.0	300.1	245.7	54.5
1980	549.4	206.5	251.3	201.4	49.9	.0	−44.8	−53.6	8.8	343.0	281.1	61.8
1981	654.7	266.6	312.3	244.3	68.0	.0	−45.7	−53.3	7.6	388.1	317.9	70.1
1982	629.1	202.2	336.2	270.8	65.4	.0	−134.1	−131.9	−2.2	426.9	349.8	77.1
1983	609.4	165.6	333.7	233.6	100.1	.0	−168.1	−173.0	4.9	443.8	362.1	81.7
1984	773.4	300.9	445.0	314.8	130.3	.0	−144.1	−168.1	23.9	472.6	385.6	87.0
1985	767.5	260.7	413.4	280.0	133.4	.0	−152.6	−175.0	22.3	506.7	414.0	92.7
1986	733.5	202.2	372.0	268.4	103.7	.0	−169.9	−190.8	21.0	531.3	431.8	99.5
1987	796.8	234.9	367.4	241.4	126.1	.0	−132.6	−145.0	12.4	561.9	455.3	106.7
1988	915.0	317.4	434.0	272.9	161.1	.0	−116.6	−134.5	17.9	597.6	483.5	114.1
1989	944.7	300.4	409.7	287.1	122.6	.0	−109.3	−130.1	20.8	644.3	522.1	122.2
1990	940.4	258.0	422.7	299.4	123.3	.0	−164.8	−172.0	7.2	682.5	551.6	130.9
1991	964.1	238.2	456.1	324.2	131.9	.0	−217.9	−213.7	−4.2	725.9	586.9	139.1
1992	948.2	196.3	493.0	366.0	142.7	−15.8	−296.7	−297.4	.7	751.9	607.3	144.6
1993	962.4	186.0	458.6	284.0	168.1	6.4	−272.6	−273.5	.9	776.4	624.7	151.8
1994	1,070.7	237.1	438.9	249.5	171.8	17.6	−201.9	−212.3	10.5	833.7	675.1	158.6
1995	1,184.5	306.2	491.1	250.9	223.8	16.4	−184.9	−197.0	12.0	878.4	713.4	165.0
1996	1,291.1	373.0	489.0	228.4	256.9	3.6	−116.0	−141.8	25.8	918.1	748.8	169.3
1997	1,461.1	486.6	503.3	218.3	287.9	−2.9	−16.7	−55.8	39.1	974.4	800.3	174.1
1998	1,598.7	568.6	477.8	276.8	201.7	−.7	90.8	38.8	52.0	1,030.2	851.2	179.0
1999	1,674.3	573.0	419.0	158.6	255.3	5.2	154.0	103.6	50.4	1,101.3	914.3	187.0
2000	1,770.5	582.7	343.3	168.5	174.8	.0	239.4	189.5	50.0	1,187.8	990.8	197.0
2001	1,657.6	376.1	324.6	132.3	192.3	.0	51.5	46.7	4.8	1,281.5	1,075.5	206.0
2002	1,489.1	197.1	479.2	184.7	294.5	.0	−282.1	−247.9	−34.2	1,292.0	1,080.3	211.6
2003	1,474.1	142.7	549.3	172.8	376.5	.0	−406.5	−382.7	−23.8	1,331.3	1,112.8	218.5
2004	1,572.0	136.8	549.1	151.8	397.3	.0	−412.3	−406.5	−5.9	1,435.3	1,206.2	229.1
2005 ᵖ	....	....	....	−41.6	....	.0	....	....	....	1,574.1	1,327.2	246.9
2002: I	1,535.7	253.7	497.4	225.4	272.0	.0	−243.8	−208.5	−35.3	1,282.0	1,073.1	208.9
II	1,512.6	224.4	500.9	221.2	279.7	.0	−276.5	−241.4	−35.1	1,288.2	1,077.5	210.8
III	1,461.5	166.7	445.4	153.0	292.4	.0	−278.7	−247.3	−31.4	1,294.9	1,082.4	212.5
IV	1,446.6	143.8	473.3	139.3	334.0	.0	−329.5	−294.6	−34.9	1,302.7	1,088.4	214.3
2003: I	1,413.3	101.4	465.2	154.0	311.3	.0	−363.8	−296.0	−67.8	1,311.8	1,095.7	216.1
II	1,456.8	133.0	532.9	169.6	363.4	.0	−399.9	−373.8	−26.1	1,323.8	1,105.8	218.1
III	1,470.0	132.8	602.8	205.1	397.7	.0	−469.9	−456.2	−13.8	1,337.2	1,117.8	219.3
IV	1,556.2	203.7	596.2	162.6	433.6	.0	−392.5	−405.0	12.5	1,352.5	1,131.8	220.6
2004: I	1,534.7	163.6	599.4	155.8	443.5	.0	−435.8	−429.3	−6.5	1,371.1	1,147.8	223.3
II	1,546.4	152.6	567.6	141.2	426.4	.0	−415.0	−413.4	−1.6	1,393.8	1,165.8	228.1
III	1,590.1	56.0	486.9	104.6	382.3	.0	−430.9	−411.6	−19.3	1,534.1	1,303.5	230.6
IV	1,617.0	174.9	542.6	205.4	337.2	.0	−367.7	−371.6	4.0	1,442.0	1,207.6	234.5
2005: I	1,635.5	187.1	478.1	47.4	430.7	.0	−290.9	−298.3	7.4	1,448.4	1,210.9	237.5
II	1,628.4	171.2	447.2	−21.5	468.7	.0	−276.1	−297.3	21.3	1,457.2	1,216.9	240.4
III	1,696.0	−167.8	253.8	−158.9	412.6	.0	−421.6	−415.2	−6.4	1,863.8	1,603.6	260.2
IV ᵖ	....	....	....	−33.3	....	.0	....	....	....	1,526.9	1,277.3	249.6

[1] With inventory valuation and capital consumption adjustments.

See next page for continuation of table.

TABLE B–32.—*Gross saving and investment, 1959–2005*—Continued

[Billions of dollars, except as noted; quarterly data at seasonally adjusted annual rates]

Year or quarter	Gross domestic investment, capital account transactions, and net lending, NIPA							Addenda:						
	Gross domestic investment				Capital account transactions (net)[3]	Net lending or net borrowing (–), NIPA[4]	Statistical discrepancy	Gross private saving	Gross government saving			Net domestic investment	Gross saving as a percent of gross national income	Net saving as a percent of gross national income
	Total	Total	Gross private domestic investment	Gross government investment[2]					Total	Federal	State and local			
1959	106.7	107.8	78.5	29.3	....	–1.2	0.5	84.6	21.6	13.6	8.0	54.8	20.9	10.4
1960	110.4	107.2	78.9	28.3	....	3.2	–.9	84.8	26.5	17.8	8.7	51.6	21.0	10.5
1961	113.8	109.5	78.2	31.3	....	4.3	–.6	91.8	22.5	13.5	9.0	52.3	20.8	10.4
1962	125.3	121.4	88.1	33.3	....	3.9	.4	100.7	24.3	14.0	10.3	62.2	21.2	11.1
1963	132.4	127.4	93.8	33.6	....	5.0	–.8	104.6	28.6	17.5	11.1	65.0	21.4	11.4
1964	144.2	136.7	102.1	34.6	....	7.5	.8	117.9	25.5	13.4	12.1	71.7	21.5	11.7
1965	160.0	153.8	118.2	35.6	....	6.2	1.6	129.7	28.8	16.0	12.8	84.4	21.9	12.3
1966	175.0	171.1	131.3	39.8	....	3.9	6.3	138.6	30.1	15.5	14.6	95.5	21.4	11.8
1967	175.1	171.6	128.6	43.0	....	3.6	4.6	151.3	19.2	4.7	14.5	90.1	20.5	10.7
1968	186.6	184.8	141.2	43.6	....	1.7	4.6	153.7	28.3	12.5	15.8	96.5	20.0	10.3
1969	201.5	199.7	156.4	43.3	....	1.8	3.2	156.8	41.5	24.2	17.3	101.8	20.1	10.2
1970	200.0	196.0	152.4	43.6	....	4.0	7.3	174.1	18.6	.9	17.7	89.3	18.6	8.3
1971	220.5	219.9	178.2	41.8	....	.6	11.6	202.5	6.4	–11.9	18.3	104.9	18.6	8.4
1972	246.6	250.2	207.6	42.6	....	–3.6	9.1	216.8	20.7	–7.7	28.5	123.7	19.2	9.0
1973	300.7	291.3	244.5	46.8	....	9.3	8.6	256.3	35.8	5.8	30.0	152.1	21.1	11.0
1974	312.3	305.7	249.4	56.3	....	6.6	10.9	270.0	31.5	4.5	27.0	143.2	20.0	9.2
1975	314.7	293.3	230.2	63.1	....	21.4	17.7	323.6	–26.6	–49.3	22.7	105.6	18.2	6.7
1976	367.2	358.4	292.0	66.4	....	8.9	25.1	343.8	–1.7	–30.3	28.6	153.2	18.8	7.5
1977	419.8	428.8	361.3	67.5	....	–9.0	22.3	382.8	14.7	–21.0	35.7	198.8	19.6	8.3
1978	504.6	515.0	438.0	77.1	....	–10.4	26.6	436.3	41.7	–1.5	43.2	252.7	20.9	9.4
1979	582.8	581.4	492.9	88.5	....	1.4	46.0	480.5	56.2	15.7	40.5	281.2	21.1	9.3
1980	590.9	579.5	479.3	100.3	....	11.4	41.4	532.4	17.0	–23.6	40.6	236.6	19.7	7.4
1981	685.6	679.3	572.4	106.9	....	6.3	30.9	630.3	24.4	–19.4	43.9	291.2	20.9	8.5
1982	629.4	629.5	517.2	112.3	–0.2	.0	.3	686.0	–56.9	–94.2	37.3	202.6	19.1	6.1
1983	655.1	687.2	564.3	122.9	–.2	–31.8	45.7	695.8	–86.5	–132.3	45.8	243.4	17.3	4.7
1984	788.0	875.0	735.6	139.4	–.2	–86.7	14.6	830.6	–57.2	–123.5	66.3	402.4	19.6	7.6
1985	784.1	895.0	736.2	158.8	–.3	–110.5	16.7	827.3	–59.9	–126.9	67.0	388.3	18.1	6.2
1986	780.5	919.7	746.5	173.2	–.3	–138.9	47.0	803.9	–70.4	–139.2	68.8	388.4	16.5	4.6
1987	818.5	969.2	785.0	184.3	–.4	–150.4	21.7	822.7	–25.9	–89.8	63.9	407.3	16.8	5.0
1988	895.5	1,007.7	821.6	186.1	–.5	–111.7	–19.5	917.5	–2.5	–75.2	72.7	410.1	17.8	6.2
1989	984.3	1,072.6	874.9	197.7	–.3	–88.0	39.7	931.8	12.9	–66.7	79.6	428.4	17.3	5.5
1990	1,006.7	1,076.7	861.0	215.7	6.6	–76.6	66.2	974.3	–33.8	–104.1	70.3	394.2	16.3	4.5
1991	1,036.6	1,023.2	802.9	220.3	4.5	9.0	72.5	1,042.9	–78.8	–141.5	62.7	297.3	16.2	4.0
1992	1,051.0	1,087.9	864.8	223.1	.6	–37.5	102.7	1,100.4	–152.1	–222.7	70.6	336.0	15.1	3.1
1993	1,102.0	1,172.4	953.4	219.0	1.3	–71.7	139.5	1,083.3	–120.8	–195.5	74.7	395.9	14.7	2.8
1994	1,213.2	1,318.4	1,097.1	221.4	1.7	–106.9	142.5	1,114.0	–43.2	–132.2	88.9	484.7	15.4	3.4
1995	1,285.7	1,376.7	1,144.0	232.7	.9	–91.9	101.2	1,204.5	–19.9	–115.1	95.2	498.4	16.2	4.2
1996	1,384.8	1,465.2	1,240.3	244.9	.7	–101.0	93.7	1,237.8	53.3	–59.7	113.0	567.1	16.6	4.8
1997	1,531.7	1,641.9	1,389.8	252.2	1.0	–113.3	70.7	1,303.6	157.5	26.7	130.7	667.5	17.7	5.9
1998	1,584.1	1,771.5	1,509.1	262.4	.7	–188.1	–14.6	1,328.9	269.8	121.6	148.2	741.3	18.2	6.5
1999	1,638.5	1,912.4	1,625.7	286.8	4.8	–278.7	–35.7	1,333.3	341.0	188.5	152.5	811.2	17.9	6.1
2000	1,643.3	2,040.0	1,735.5	304.5	.8	–397.4	–127.2	1,334.1	436.4	276.6	159.8	852.1	17.7	5.8
2001	1,567.9	1,938.3	1,614.3	324.0	1.1	–371.5	–89.6	1,400.1	257.5	134.9	122.6	656.9	16.2	3.7
2002	1,468.1	1,926.4	1,582.1	344.3	1.4	–459.7	–21.0	1,559.6	–70.5	–159.1	88.6	634.4	14.2	1.9
2003	1,521.1	2,025.6	1,670.4	355.3	3.2	–507.7	47.1	1,662.1	–188.0	–292.5	104.5	694.3	13.4	1.3
2004	1,648.9	2,300.6	1,928.1	372.5	1.6	–653.4	76.8	1,755.3	–183.2	–312.7	129.4	865.3	13.4	1.2
2005 P	....	2,499.4	2,099.5	399.9	....							925.4		
2002: I	1,482.1	1,903.1	1,564.1	339.0	1.2	–422.2	–53.6	1,570.5	–34.9	–119.9	85.0	621.1	14.7	2.4
II	1,455.9	1,915.4	1,571.4	343.9	1.2	–460.7	–56.7	1,578.3	–65.7	–152.8	87.0	627.2	14.4	2.1
III	1,476.1	1,939.7	1,592.9	346.8	1.5	–465.1	14.6	1,527.7	–66.2	–158.4	92.2	644.8	13.9	1.6
IV	1,458.3	1,947.4	1,600.1	347.4	1.6	–490.7	11.7	1,561.7	–115.2	–205.1	90.0	644.7	13.6	1.4
2003: I	1,429.8	1,958.9	1,610.0	349.0	1.7	–530.8	16.6	1,560.9	–147.7	–206.4	58.7	647.1	13.2	.9
II	1,471.2	1,974.5	1,619.3	355.2	6.4	–509.6	14.4	1,638.7	–181.9	–283.4	101.6	650.6	13.4	1.2
III	1,555.3	2,054.4	1,694.2	360.1	3.3	–502.4	85.3	1,720.6	–250.6	–365.7	115.1	717.2	13.3	1.2
IV	1,628.2	2,114.7	1,757.9	356.8	1.4	–487.9	72.0	1,728.1	–171.9	–314.3	142.5	762.2	13.8	1.8
2004: I	1,612.5	2,178.7	1,818.2	360.4	1.7	–567.9	77.8	1,747.2	–212.5	–337.6	125.1	807.5	13.4	1.4
II	1,654.5	2,303.4	1,928.5	375.0	1.5	–650.4	108.1	1,733.4	–187.0	–320.0	133.0	909.6	13.3	1.3
III	1,680.9	2,334.0	1,961.2	372.9	1.6	–654.7	90.8	1,790.4	–200.3	–317.3	117.1	799.9	13.5	.5
IV	1,647.6	2,386.2	2,004.5	381.7	1.8	–740.4	30.6	1,750.2	–133.2	–275.7	142.5	944.2	13.5	1.5
2005: I	1,675.0	2,441.9	2,058.5	383.4	17.3	–784.3	39.4	1,688.9	–53.4	–201.4	148.0	993.5	13.4	1.5
II	1,706.6	2,453.5	2,054.4	399.1	.5	–747.3	78.3	1,664.1	–35.7	–199.6	163.9	996.3	13.2	1.4
III	1,762.5	2,503.6	2,099.5	404.1	.5	–741.6	66.5	1,857.4	–161.5	–316.0	154.6	639.8	13.5	–1.3
IV P	....	2,598.8	2,185.7	413.1	....							1,071.9		

[2] For details on government investment, see Table B–20.
[3] Consists of capital transfers and the acquisition and disposal of nonproduced nonfinancial assets.
[4] Prior to 1982, equals the balance on current account, NIPA (see Table B–24).

Source: Department of Commerce, Bureau of Economic Analysis.

TABLE B–33.—*Median money income (in 2004 dollars) and poverty status of families and persons, by race, selected years, 1991–2004*

Year	Families[1]		Below poverty level				Persons below poverty level		Median money income (in 2004 dollars) of persons 15 years old and over with income[2]			
	Number (millions)	Median money income (in 2004 dollars)[2]	Total		Female householder				Males		Females	
			Number (millions)	Percent	Number (millions)	Percent	Number (millions)	Percent	All persons	Year-round full-time workers	All persons	Year-round full-time workers
ALL RACES												
1991	67.2	$48,608	7.7	11.5	4.2	35.6	35.7	14.2	$27,684	$41,023	$14,169	$28,734
1992[3]	68.2	48,255	8.1	11.9	4.3	35.4	38.0	14.8	26,989	40,680	14,136	29,150
1993	68.5	47,578	8.4	12.3	4.4	35.6	39.3	15.1	27,165	40,006	14,220	28,925
1994	69.3	48,895	8.1	11.6	4.2	34.6	38.1	14.5	27,384	39,855	14,456	29,332
1995	69.6	49,987	7.5	10.8	4.1	32.4	36.4	13.8	27,771	39,633	14,930	29,266
1996	70.2	50,705	7.7	11.0	4.2	32.6	36.5	13.7	28,570	40,202	15,361	29,889
1997	70.9	52,307	7.3	10.3	4.0	31.6	35.6	13.3	29,590	41,368	16,082	30,549
1998	71.6	54,091	7.2	10.0	3.8	29.9	34.5	12.7	30,660	41,956	16,700	31,080
1999[4]	73.2	55,350	6.8	9.3	3.6	27.8	32.8	11.9	30,937	42,450	17,347	31,019
2000[5]	73.8	55,647	6.4	8.7	3.3	25.4	31.6	11.3	31,089	42,659	17,619	31,945
2001	74.3	54,857	6.8	9.2	3.5	26.4	32.9	11.7	31,054	42,829	17,729	32,461
2002	75.6	54,285	7.2	9.6	3.6	26.5	34.6	12.1	30,712	42,549	17,659	32,531
2003	76.2	54,096	7.6	10.0	3.9	28.0	35.9	12.5	30,735	42,618	17,723	32,504
2004	77.0	54,061	7.9	10.2	4.0	28.4	37.0	12.7	30,513	41,667	17,629	32,101
WHITE												
1991	57.2	51,102	5.0	8.8	2.2	28.4	23.7	11.3	28,937	41,864	14,500	29,153
1992[3]	57.7	51,022	5.3	9.1	2.2	28.5	25.3	11.9	28,244	41,648	14,465	29,488
1993	57.9	50,592	5.5	9.4	2.4	29.2	26.2	12.2	28,297	40,978	14,503	29,581
1994	58.4	51,545	5.3	9.1	2.3	29.0	25.4	11.7	28,580	40,899	14,663	30,125
1995	58.9	52,492	5.0	8.5	2.2	26.6	24.4	11.2	29,412	41,253	15,159	29,866
1996	58.9	53,649	5.1	8.6	2.3	27.3	24.7	11.2	29,906	41,644	15,536	30,396
1997	59.5	54,872	5.0	8.4	2.3	27.7	24.4	11.0	30,649	42,389	16,187	31,066
1998	60.1	56,736	4.8	8.0	2.1	24.9	23.5	10.5	31,996	43,048	16,917	31,600
1999[4]	61.1	57,898	4.4	7.3	1.9	22.5	22.2	9.8	32,491	44,447	17,401	31,738
2000[5]	61.3	58,167	4.3	7.1	1.8	21.2	21.6	9.5	32,684	44,153	17,637	32,853
2001	61.6	57,695	4.6	7.4	1.9	22.4	22.7	9.9	32,269	43,527	17,769	32,919
Alone[6]												
2002	62.3	57,387	4.9	7.8	2.0	22.6	23.5	10.2	31,914	43,460	17,687	32,983
2003	62.6	57,267	5.1	8.1	2.2	24.0	24.3	10.5	31,558	43,275	17,890	33,057
2004	63.2	56,700	5.3	8.4	2.3	24.8	25.3	10.8	31,335	42,601	17,648	32,683
Alone or in combination[6]												
2002	63.0	57,193	5.0	7.9	2.1	22.6	24.1	10.3	31,844	43,398	17,652	32,970
2003	63.5	57,098	5.2	8.1	2.2	24.2	25.0	10.6	31,482	43,210	17,858	33,045
2004	64.1	56,568	5.4	8.5	2.3	24.9	26.0	10.9	31,269	42,490	17,618	32,649
BLACK												
1991	7.7	29,144	2.3	30.4	1.8	51.2	10.2	32.7	17,531	30,605	11,924	25,879
1992[3]	8.0	27,844	2.5	31.1	1.9	50.2	10.8	33.4	17,237	30,335	11,726	26,729
1993	8.0	27,731	2.5	31.3	1.9	49.9	10.9	33.1	18,801	30,337	12,240	26,152
1994	8.1	31,138	2.2	27.3	1.7	46.2	10.2	30.6	18,889	30,769	13,294	26,007
1995	8.1	31,966	2.1	26.4	1.7	45.1	9.9	29.3	19,701	30,523	13,492	25,946
1996	8.5	31,792	2.2	26.1	1.7	43.7	9.7	28.4	19,768	32,528	14,111	26,359
1997	8.4	33,568	2.0	23.6	1.6	39.8	9.1	26.5	21,238	31,567	15,314	26,717
1998	8.5	34,030	2.0	23.4	1.6	40.8	9.1	26.1	22,361	31,794	15,204	27,619
1999[4]	8.7	36,102	1.9	21.8	1.5	39.2	8.4	23.6	23,170	34,180	16,749	28,497
2000[5]	8.7	36,939	1.7	19.3	1.3	34.3	8.0	22.5	23,411	33,443	17,420	28,245
2001	8.8	35,853	1.8	20.7	1.4	35.2	8.1	22.7	22,907	34,063	17,375	29,129
Alone[6]												
2002	8.9	35,215	1.9	21.5	1.4	35.8	8.6	24.1	22,648	33,541	17,572	29,017
2003	8.9	35,293	2.0	22.3	1.5	36.9	8.8	24.4	22,577	34,327	17,027	28,364
2004	8.9	35,158	2.0	22.8	1.5	37.6	9.0	24.7	22,714	31,732	17,383	29,145
Alone or in combination[6]												
2002	9.1	35,329	2.0	21.4	1.5	35.7	8.9	23.9	22,593	33,577	17,511	29,099
2003	9.1	35,537	2.0	22.1	1.5	36.8	9.1	24.3	22,525	34,363	16,985	28,419
2004	9.1	35,328	2.1	22.8	1.5	37.6	9.4	24.7	22,740	31,724	17,369	29,191

[1] The term "family" refers to a group of two or more persons related by birth, marriage, or adoption and residing together. Every family must include a reference person.

[2] Current dollar median money income adjusted by CPI–U–RS.

[3] Based on 1990 census adjusted population controls; comparable with succeeding years.

[4] Reflects implementation of Census 2000-based population controls comparable with succeeding years.

[5] Reflects household sample expansion.

[6] Data are for white alone; for white alone or in combination; for black alone; and, for black alone or in combination. (Black is also Black or African American.) Beginning with data for 2002 the Current Population Survey allowed respondents to choose more than one race; for earlier years respondents could report only one race group.

Note.—Poverty rates (percent of persons below poverty level) for all races for years not shown above are: 1959, 22.4; 1960, 22.2; 1961, 21.9; 1962, 21.0; 1963, 19.5; 1964, 19.0; 1965, 17.3; 1966, 14.7; 1967, 14.2; 1968, 12.8; 1969, 12.1; 1970, 12.6; 1971, 12.5; 1972, 11.9; 1973, 11.1; 1974, 11.2; 1975, 12.3; 1976, 11.8; 1977, 11.6; 1978, 11.4; 1979, 11.7; 1980, 13.0; 1981, 14.0; 1982, 15.0; 1983, 15.2; 1984, 14.4; 1985, 14.0; 1986, 13.6; 1987, 13.4; 1988, 13.0; 1989, 12.8; and 1990, 13.5.

Poverty thresholds are updated each year to reflect changes in the consumer price index (CPI–U).

For details see "Current Population Reports," Series P–60.

Source: Department of Commerce, Bureau of the Census.

POPULATION, EMPLOYMENT, WAGES, AND PRODUCTIVITY

TABLE B–34.—*Population by age group, 1929–2005*

[Thousands of persons]

July 1	Total	Age (years)						
		Under 5	5-15	16-19	20-24	25-44	45-64	65 and over
1929	121,767	11,734	26,800	9,127	10,694	35,862	21,076	6,474
1933	125,579	10,612	26,897	9,302	11,152	37,319	22,933	7,363
1939	130,880	10,418	25,179	9,822	11,519	39,354	25,823	8,764
1940	132,122	10,579	24,811	9,895	11,690	39,868	26,249	9,031
1941	133,402	10,850	24,516	9,840	11,807	40,383	26,718	9,288
1942	134,860	11,301	24,231	9,730	11,955	40,861	27,196	9,584
1943	136,739	12,016	24,093	9,607	12,064	41,420	27,671	9,867
1944	138,397	12,524	23,949	9,561	12,062	42,016	28,138	10,147
1945	139,928	12,979	23,907	9,361	12,036	42,521	28,630	10,494
1946	141,389	13,244	24,103	9,119	12,004	43,027	29,064	10,828
1947	144,126	14,406	24,468	9,097	11,814	43,657	29,498	11,185
1948	146,631	14,919	25,209	8,952	11,794	44,288	29,931	11,538
1949	149,188	15,607	25,852	8,788	11,700	44,916	30,405	11,921
1950	152,271	16,410	26,721	8,542	11,680	45,672	30,849	12,397
1951	154,878	17,333	27,279	8,446	11,552	46,103	31,362	12,803
1952	157,553	17,312	28,894	8,414	11,350	46,495	31,884	13,203
1953	160,184	17,638	30,227	8,460	11,062	46,786	32,394	13,617
1954	163,026	18,057	31,480	8,637	10,832	47,001	32,942	14,076
1955	165,931	18,566	32,682	8,744	10,714	47,194	33,506	14,525
1956	168,903	19,003	33,994	8,916	10,616	47,379	34,057	14,938
1957	171,984	19,494	35,272	9,195	10,603	47,440	34,591	15,388
1958	174,882	19,887	36,445	9,543	10,756	47,337	35,109	15,806
1959	177,830	20,175	37,368	10,215	10,969	47,192	35,663	16,248
1960	180,671	20,341	38,494	10,683	11,134	47,140	36,203	16,675
1961	183,691	20,522	39,765	11,025	11,483	47,084	36,722	17,089
1962	186,538	20,469	41,205	11,180	11,959	47,013	37,255	17,457
1963	189,242	20,342	41,626	12,007	12,714	46,994	37,782	17,778
1964	191,889	20,165	42,297	12,736	13,269	46,958	38,338	18,127
1965	194,303	19,824	42,938	13,516	13,746	46,912	38,916	18,451
1966	196,560	19,208	43,702	14,311	14,050	47,001	39,534	18,755
1967	198,712	18,563	44,244	14,200	15,248	47,194	40,193	19,071
1968	200,706	17,913	44,622	14,452	15,786	47,721	40,846	19,365
1969	202,677	17,376	44,840	14,800	16,480	48,064	41,437	19,680
1970	205,052	17,166	44,816	15,289	17,202	48,473	41,999	20,107
1971	207,661	17,244	44,591	15,688	18,159	48,936	42,482	20,561
1972	209,896	17,101	44,203	16,039	18,153	50,482	42,898	21,020
1973	211,909	16,851	43,582	16,446	18,521	51,749	43,235	21,525
1974	213,854	16,487	42,989	16,769	18,975	53,051	43,522	22,061
1975	215,973	16,121	42,508	17,017	19,527	54,302	43,801	22,696
1976	218,035	15,617	42,099	17,194	19,986	55,852	44,008	23,278
1977	220,239	15,564	41,298	17,276	20,499	57,561	44,150	23,892
1978	222,585	15,735	40,428	17,288	20,946	59,400	44,286	24,502
1979	225,055	16,063	39,552	17,242	21,297	61,379	44,390	25,134
1980	227,726	16,451	38,838	17,167	21,590	63,470	44,504	25,707
1981	229,966	16,893	38,144	16,812	21,869	65,528	44,500	26,221
1982	232,188	17,228	37,784	16,332	21,902	67,692	44,462	26,787
1983	234,307	17,547	37,526	15,823	21,844	69,733	44,474	27,361
1984	236,348	17,695	37,461	15,295	21,737	71,735	44,547	27,878
1985	238,466	17,842	37,450	15,005	21,478	73,673	44,602	28,416
1986	240,651	17,963	37,404	15,024	20,942	75,651	44,660	29,008
1987	242,804	18,052	37,333	15,215	20,385	77,338	44,854	29,626
1988	245,021	18,195	37,593	15,198	19,846	78,595	45,471	30,124
1989	247,342	18,508	37,972	14,913	19,442	79,943	45,882	30,682
1990	250,132	18,856	38,632	14,466	19,323	81,291	46,316	31,247
1991	253,493	19,208	39,349	13,992	19,414	82,844	46,874	31,812
1992	256,894	19,528	40,161	13,781	19,314	83,201	48,553	32,356
1993	260,255	19,729	40,904	13,953	19,101	83,766	49,899	32,902
1994	263,436	19,777	41,689	14,228	18,758	84,334	51,318	33,331
1995	266,557	19,627	42,510	14,522	18,391	84,933	52,806	33,769
1996	269,667	19,408	43,172	15,057	17,965	85,527	54,396	34,143
1997	272,912	19,233	43,833	15,433	17,992	85,737	56,283	34,402
1998	276,115	19,145	44,332	15,856	18,250	85,663	58,249	34,619
1999	279,295	19,136	44,755	16,164	18,672	85,408	60,362	34,798
2000 [1]	282,402	19,187	45,166	16,205	19,189	85,159	62,419	35,077
2001 [1]	285,329	19,361	45,186	16,248	19,875	84,918	64,414	35,328
2002 [1]	288,173	19,548	45,141	16,302	20,408	84,632	66,557	35,585
2003 [1]	291,028	19,791	45,081	16,359	20,840	84,372	68,642	35,943
2004 [1]	293,907	20,071	44,962	16,534	21,064	84,276	70,705	36,294
2005	296,639	....	....	....	....	....	....	....

[1] Revised total population data are available as follows: 2000, 282,403; 2001, 285,335; 2002, 288,216; 2003, 291,089; and 2004, 293,908.
Note.—Includes Armed Forces overseas beginning 1940. Includes Alaska and Hawaii beginning 1950.
All estimates are consistent with decennial census enumerations.
Source: Department of Commerce, Bureau of the Census.

Year or month	Civilian noninstitutional population[1]	Civilian labor force					Not in labor force	Civilian labor force participation rate[2]	Civilian employment/ population ratio[3]	Unemployment rate, civilian workers[4]
		Total	Employment			Unemployment				
			Total	Agricultural	Nonagricultural					
		Thousands of persons 14 years of age and over							Percent	
1929	....	49,180	47,630	10,450	37,180	1,550	....	....	....	3.2
1933	....	51,590	38,760	10,090	28,670	12,830	....	....	....	24.9
1939	....	55,230	45,750	9,610	36,140	9,480	....	....	....	17.2
1940	99,840	55,640	47,520	9,540	37,980	8,120	44,200	55.7	47.6	14.6
1941	99,900	55,910	50,350	9,100	41,250	5,560	43,990	56.0	50.4	9.9
1942	98,640	56,410	53,750	9,250	44,500	2,660	42,230	57.2	54.5	4.7
1943	94,640	55,540	54,470	9,080	45,390	1,070	39,100	58.7	57.6	1.9
1944	93,220	54,630	53,960	8,950	45,010	670	38,590	58.6	57.9	1.2
1945	94,090	53,860	52,820	8,580	44,240	1,040	40,230	57.2	56.1	1.9
1946	103,070	57,520	55,250	8,320	46,930	2,270	45,550	55.8	53.6	3.9
1947	106,018	60,168	57,812	8,256	49,557	2,356	45,850	56.8	54.5	3.9
		Thousands of persons 16 years of age and over								
1947	101,827	59,350	57,038	7,890	49,148	2,311	42,477	58.3	56.0	3.9
1948	103,068	60,621	58,343	7,629	50,714	2,276	42,447	58.8	56.6	3.8
1949	103,994	61,286	57,651	7,658	49,993	3,637	42,708	58.9	55.4	5.9
1950	104,995	62,208	58,918	7,160	51,758	3,288	42,787	59.2	56.1	5.3
1951	104,621	62,017	59,961	6,726	53,235	2,055	42,604	59.2	57.3	3.3
1952	105,231	62,138	60,250	6,500	53,749	1,883	43,093	59.0	57.3	3.0
1953[5]	107,056	63,015	61,179	6,260	54,919	1,834	44,041	58.9	57.1	2.9
1954	108,321	63,643	60,109	6,205	53,904	3,532	44,678	58.8	55.5	5.5
1955	109,683	65,023	62,170	6,450	55,722	2,852	44,660	59.3	56.7	4.4
1956	110,954	66,552	63,799	6,283	57,514	2,750	44,402	60.0	57.5	4.1
1957	112,265	66,929	64,071	5,947	58,123	2,859	45,336	59.6	57.1	4.3
1958	113,727	67,639	63,036	5,586	57,450	4,602	46,088	59.5	55.4	6.8
1959	115,329	68,369	64,630	5,565	59,065	3,740	46,960	59.3	56.0	5.5
1960[5]	117,245	69,628	65,778	5,458	60,318	3,852	47,617	59.4	56.1	5.5
1961	118,771	70,459	65,746	5,200	60,546	4,714	48,312	59.3	55.4	6.7
1962[5]	120,153	70,614	66,702	4,944	61,759	3,911	49,539	58.8	55.5	5.5
1963	122,416	71,833	67,762	4,687	63,076	4,070	50,583	58.7	55.4	5.7
1964	124,485	73,091	69,305	4,523	64,782	3,786	51,394	58.7	55.7	5.2
1965	126,513	74,455	71,088	4,361	66,726	3,366	52,058	58.9	56.2	4.5
1966	128,058	75,770	72,895	3,979	68,915	2,875	52,288	59.2	56.9	3.8
1967	129,874	77,347	74,372	3,844	70,527	2,975	52,527	59.6	57.3	3.8
1968	132,028	78,737	75,920	3,817	72,103	2,817	53,291	59.6	57.5	3.6
1969	134,335	80,734	77,902	3,606	74,296	2,832	53,602	60.1	58.0	3.5
1970	137,085	82,771	78,678	3,463	75,215	4,093	54,315	60.4	57.4	4.9
1971	140,216	84,382	79,367	3,394	75,972	5,016	55,834	60.2	56.6	5.9
1972[5]	144,126	87,034	82,153	3,484	78,669	4,882	57,091	60.4	57.0	5.6
1973[5]	147,096	89,429	85,064	3,470	81,594	4,365	57,667	60.8	57.8	4.9
1974	150,120	91,949	86,794	3,515	83,279	5,156	58,171	61.3	57.8	5.6
1975	153,153	93,775	85,846	3,408	82,438	7,929	59,377	61.2	56.1	8.5
1976	156,150	96,158	88,752	3,331	85,421	7,406	59,991	61.6	56.8	7.7
1977	159,033	99,009	92,017	3,283	88,734	6,991	60,025	62.3	57.9	7.1
1978[5]	161,910	102,251	96,048	3,387	92,661	6,202	59,659	63.2	59.3	6.1
1979	164,863	104,962	98,824	3,347	95,477	6,137	59,900	63.7	59.9	5.8
1980	167,745	106,940	99,303	3,364	95,938	7,637	60,806	63.8	59.2	7.1
1981	170,130	108,670	100,397	3,368	97,030	8,273	61,460	63.9	59.0	7.6
1982	172,271	110,204	99,526	3,401	96,125	10,678	62,067	64.0	57.8	9.7
1983	174,215	111,550	100,834	3,383	97,450	10,717	62,665	64.0	57.9	9.6
1984	176,383	113,544	105,005	3,321	101,685	8,539	62,839	64.4	59.5	7.5
1985	178,206	115,461	107,150	3,179	103,971	8,312	62,744	64.8	60.1	7.2
1986[5]	180,587	117,834	109,597	3,163	106,434	8,237	62,752	65.3	60.7	7.0
1987	182,753	119,865	112,440	3,208	109,232	7,425	62,888	65.6	61.5	6.2
1988	184,613	121,669	114,968	3,169	111,800	6,701	62,944	65.9	62.3	5.5
1989	186,393	123,869	117,342	3,199	114,142	6,528	62,523	66.5	63.0	5.3
1990[5]	189,164	125,840	118,793	3,223	115,570	7,047	63,324	66.5	62.8	5.6
1991	190,925	126,346	117,718	3,269	114,449	8,628	64,578	66.2	61.7	6.8
1992	192,805	128,105	118,492	3,247	115,245	9,613	64,700	66.4	61.5	7.5
1993	194,838	129,200	120,259	3,115	117,144	8,940	65,638	66.3	61.7	6.9
1994[5]	196,814	131,056	123,060	3,409	119,651	7,996	65,758	66.6	62.5	6.1
1995	198,584	132,304	124,900	3,440	121,460	7,404	66,280	66.6	62.9	5.6
1996	200,591	133,943	126,708	3,443	123,264	7,236	66,647	66.8	63.2	5.4
1997[5]	203,133	136,297	129,558	3,399	126,159	6,739	66,837	67.1	63.8	4.9
1998[5]	205,220	137,673	131,463	3,378	128,085	6,210	67,547	67.1	64.1	4.5
1999[5]	207,753	139,368	133,488	3,281	130,207	5,880	68,385	67.1	64.3	4.2

[1] Not seasonally adjusted.
[2] Civilian labor force as percent of civilian noninstitutional population.
[3] Civilian employment as percent of civilian noninstitutional population.
[4] Unemployed as percent of civilian labor force.

See next page for continuation of table.

TABLE B–35.—*Civilian population and labor force, 1929–2005*—Continued

[Monthly data seasonally adjusted, except as noted]

Year or month	Civilian noninsti- tutional popula- tion [1]	Civilian labor force Total	Employment Total	Agri- cul- tural	Non- agri- cultural	Un- employ- ment	Not in labor force	Civil- ian labor force par- tici- pation rate [2]	Civil- ian em- ploy- ment/ pop- ula- tion ratio [3]	Unem- ploy- ment rate, civil- ian work- ers [4]
			Thousands of persons 16 years of age and over					Percent		
2000 [5][6]	212,577	142,583	136,891	2,464	134,427	5,692	69,994	67.1	64.4	4.0
2001	215,092	143,734	136,933	2,299	134,635	6,801	71,359	66.8	63.7	4.7
2002	217,570	144,863	136,485	2,311	134,174	8,378	72,707	66.6	62.7	5.8
2003 [5]	221,168	146,510	137,736	2,275	135,461	8,774	74,658	66.2	62.3	6.0
2004 [5]	223,357	147,401	139,252	2,232	137,020	8,149	75,956	66.0	62.3	5.5
2005 [5]	226,082	149,320	141,730	2,197	139,532	7,591	76,762	66.0	62.7	5.1
2002: Jan	216,506	143,883	135,698	2,385	133,230	8,184	72,623	66.5	62.7	5.7
Feb	216,663	144,663	136,442	2,397	134,126	8,221	72,000	66.8	63.0	5.7
Mar	216,823	144,485	136,195	2,369	133,816	8,290	72,338	66.6	62.8	5.7
Apr	217,006	144,718	136,136	2,373	133,833	8,582	72,287	66.7	62.7	5.9
May	217,198	144,933	136,546	2,263	134,277	8,387	72,265	66.7	62.9	5.8
June	217,407	144,803	136,415	2,170	134,153	8,388	72,605	66.6	62.7	5.8
July	217,630	144,803	136,410	2,336	134,082	8,392	72,827	66.5	62.7	5.8
Aug	217,866	145,007	136,695	2,132	134,584	8,311	72,859	66.6	62.7	5.7
Sept	218,107	145,562	137,305	2,284	135,108	8,257	72,545	66.7	63.0	5.7
Oct	218,340	145,313	137,001	2,440	134,587	8,312	73,027	66.6	62.7	5.7
Nov	218,548	145,050	136,517	2,255	134,183	8,533	73,499	66.4	62.5	5.9
Dec	218,741	145,065	136,400	2,349	134,073	8,665	73,676	66.3	62.4	6.0
2003: Jan [5]	219,897	145,937	137,424	2,343	135,032	8,513	73,961	66.4	62.5	5.8
Feb [5]	220,114	146,104	137,472	2,240	135,288	8,632	74,011	66.4	62.5	5.9
Mar	220,317	146,004	137,461	2,267	135,223	8,543	74,314	66.3	62.4	5.9
Apr	220,540	146,452	137,637	2,157	135,538	8,816	74,088	66.4	62.4	6.0
May	220,768	146,480	137,547	2,183	135,356	8,933	74,288	66.4	62.3	6.1
June	221,014	147,031	137,784	2,197	135,454	9,246	73,984	66.5	62.3	6.3
July	221,252	146,505	137,478	2,205	135,211	9,027	74,748	66.2	62.1	6.2
Aug	221,507	146,427	137,525	2,304	135,193	8,902	75,080	66.1	62.1	6.1
Sept	221,779	146,546	137,601	2,336	135,373	8,945	75,232	66.1	62.0	6.1
Oct	222,039	146,716	137,986	2,435	135,603	8,730	75,323	66.1	62.1	6.0
Nov	222,279	147,063	138,453	2,364	136,052	8,610	75,216	66.2	62.3	5.9
Dec	222,509	146,773	138,400	2,247	136,153	8,373	75,736	66.0	62.2	5.7
2004: Jan [5]	222,161	146,817	138,472	2,211	136,205	8,345	75,344	66.1	62.3	5.7
Feb	222,357	146,681	138,495	2,227	136,294	8,186	75,675	66.0	62.3	5.6
Mar	222,550	146,849	138,452	2,189	136,291	8,397	75,701	66.0	62.2	5.7
Apr	222,757	146,800	138,659	2,250	136,420	8,140	75,957	65.9	62.2	5.5
May	222,967	147,021	138,843	2,296	136,524	8,178	75,946	65.9	62.3	5.6
June	223,196	147,427	139,181	2,251	136,816	8,247	75,768	66.1	62.4	5.6
July	223,422	147,773	139,591	2,242	137,329	8,182	75,649	66.1	62.5	5.5
Aug	223,677	147,558	139,558	2,317	137,227	8,000	76,119	66.0	62.4	5.4
Sept	223,941	147,476	139,495	2,223	137,391	7,981	76,465	65.9	62.3	5.4
Oct	224,192	147,808	139,768	2,163	137,675	8,040	76,384	65.9	62.3	5.4
Nov	224,422	148,250	140,276	2,192	138,045	7,974	76,172	66.1	62.5	5.4
Dec	224,640	148,173	140,133	2,190	137,944	8,040	76,467	66.0	62.4	5.4
2005: Jan [5]	224,837	147,956	140,234	2,138	138,076	7,723	76,881	65.8	62.4	5.2
Feb	225,041	148,271	140,285	2,161	138,111	7,986	76,770	65.9	62.3	5.4
Mar	225,236	148,217	140,601	2,199	138,416	7,616	77,019	65.8	62.4	5.1
Apr	225,441	148,839	141,196	2,253	138,926	7,644	76,601	66.0	62.6	5.1
May	225,670	149,201	141,571	2,216	139,322	7,629	76,469	66.1	62.7	5.1
June	225,911	149,243	141,750	2,321	139,333	7,493	76,668	66.1	62.7	5.0
July	226,153	149,605	142,111	2,332	139,772	7,494	76,548	66.2	62.8	5.0
Aug	226,421	149,792	142,425	2,157	140,294	7,367	76,629	66.2	62.9	4.9
Sept	226,693	150,083	142,435	2,140	140,287	7,648	76,610	66.2	62.8	5.1
Oct	226,959	150,043	142,625	2,126	140,577	7,418	76,916	66.1	62.8	4.9
Nov	227,204	150,183	142,611	2,154	140,427	7,572	77,021	66.1	62.8	5.0
Dec	227,425	150,153	142,779	2,130	140,638	7,375	77,271	66.0	62.8	4.9

[5] Not strictly comparable with earlier data due to population adjustments or other changes. See *Employment and Earnings* for details on breaks in series.

[6] Beginning in 2000, data for agricultural employment are for agricultural and related industries; data for this series and for non-agricultural employment are not strictly comparable with data for earlier years. Because of independent seasonal adjustment for these two series, monthly data will not add to total civilian employment.

Note.—Labor force data in Tables B–35 through B–44 are based on household interviews and relate to the calendar week including the 12th of the month. For definitions of terms, area samples used, historical comparability of the data, comparability with other series, etc., see *Employment and Earnings*.

Source: Department of Labor, Bureau of Labor Statistics.

TABLE B–36.—*Civilian employment and unemployment by sex and age, 1959–2005*

[Thousands of persons 16 years of age and over; monthly data seasonally adjusted]

Year or month	Civilian employment							Unemployment						
	Total	Males			Females			Total	Males			Females		
		Total	16-19 years	20 years and over	Total	16-19 years	20 years and over		Total	16-19 years	20 years and over	Total	16-19 years	20 years and over
1959	64,630	43,466	2,198	41,267	21,164	1,640	19,524	3,740	2,420	398	2,022	1,320	256	1,063
1960	65,778	43,904	2,361	41,543	21,874	1,768	20,105	3,852	2,486	426	2,060	1,366	286	1,080
1961	65,746	43,656	2,315	41,342	22,090	1,793	20,296	4,714	2,997	479	2,518	1,717	349	1,368
1962	66,702	44,177	2,362	41,815	22,525	1,833	20,693	3,911	2,423	408	2,016	1,488	313	1,175
1963	67,762	44,657	2,406	42,251	23,105	1,849	21,257	4,070	2,472	501	1,971	1,598	383	1,216
1964	69,305	45,474	2,587	42,886	23,831	1,929	21,903	3,786	2,205	487	1,718	1,581	385	1,195
1965	71,088	46,340	2,918	43,422	24,748	2,118	22,630	3,366	1,914	479	1,435	1,452	395	1,056
1966	72,895	46,919	3,253	43,668	25,976	2,468	23,510	2,875	1,551	432	1,120	1,324	405	921
1967	74,372	47,479	3,186	44,294	26,893	2,496	24,397	2,975	1,508	448	1,060	1,468	391	1,078
1968	75,920	48,114	3,255	44,859	27,807	2,526	25,281	2,817	1,419	426	993	1,397	412	985
1969	77,902	48,818	3,430	45,388	29,084	2,687	26,397	2,832	1,403	440	963	1,429	413	1,015
1970	78,678	48,990	3,409	45,581	29,688	2,735	26,952	4,093	2,238	599	1,638	1,855	506	1,349
1971	79,367	49,390	3,478	45,912	29,976	2,730	27,246	5,016	2,789	693	2,097	2,227	568	1,658
1972	82,153	50,896	3,765	47,130	31,257	2,980	28,276	4,882	2,659	711	1,948	2,222	598	1,625
1973	85,064	52,349	4,039	48,310	32,715	3,231	29,484	4,365	2,275	653	1,624	2,089	583	1,507
1974	86,794	53,024	4,103	48,922	33,769	3,345	30,424	5,156	2,714	757	1,957	2,441	665	1,777
1975	85,846	51,857	3,839	48,018	33,989	3,263	30,726	7,929	4,442	966	3,476	3,486	802	2,684
1976	88,752	53,138	3,947	49,190	35,615	3,389	32,226	7,406	4,036	939	3,098	3,369	780	2,588
1977	92,017	54,728	4,174	50,555	37,289	3,514	33,775	6,991	3,667	874	2,794	3,324	789	2,535
1978	96,048	56,479	4,336	52,143	39,569	3,734	35,836	6,202	3,142	813	2,328	3,061	769	2,292
1979	98,824	57,607	4,300	53,308	41,217	3,783	37,434	6,137	3,120	811	2,308	3,018	743	2,276
1980	99,303	57,186	4,085	53,101	42,117	3,625	38,492	7,637	4,267	913	3,353	3,370	755	2,615
1981	100,397	57,397	3,815	53,582	43,000	3,411	39,590	8,273	4,577	962	3,615	3,696	800	2,895
1982	99,526	56,271	3,379	52,891	43,256	3,170	40,086	10,678	6,179	1,090	5,089	4,499	886	3,613
1983	100,834	56,787	3,300	53,487	44,047	3,043	41,004	10,717	6,260	1,003	5,257	4,457	825	3,632
1984	105,005	59,091	3,322	55,769	45,915	3,122	42,793	8,539	4,744	812	3,932	3,794	687	3,107
1985	107,150	59,891	3,328	56,562	47,259	3,105	44,154	8,312	4,521	806	3,715	3,791	661	3,129
1986	109,597	60,892	3,323	57,569	48,706	3,149	45,556	8,237	4,530	779	3,751	3,707	675	3,032
1987	112,440	62,107	3,381	58,726	50,334	3,260	47,074	7,425	4,101	732	3,369	3,324	616	2,709
1988	114,968	63,273	3,492	59,781	51,696	3,313	48,383	6,701	3,655	667	2,987	3,046	558	2,487
1989	117,342	64,315	3,477	60,837	53,027	3,282	49,745	6,528	3,525	658	2,867	3,003	536	2,467
1990	118,793	65,104	3,427	61,678	53,689	3,154	50,535	7,047	3,906	667	3,239	3,140	544	2,596
1991	117,718	64,223	3,044	61,178	53,496	2,862	50,634	8,628	4,946	751	4,195	3,683	608	3,074
1992	118,492	64,440	2,944	61,496	54,052	2,724	51,328	9,613	5,523	806	4,717	4,090	621	3,469
1993	120,259	65,349	2,994	62,355	54,910	2,811	52,099	8,940	5,055	768	4,287	3,885	597	3,288
1994	123,060	66,450	3,156	63,294	56,610	3,005	53,606	7,996	4,367	740	3,627	3,629	580	3,049
1995	124,900	67,377	3,292	64,085	57,523	3,127	54,396	7,404	3,983	744	3,239	3,421	602	2,819
1996	126,708	68,207	3,310	64,897	58,501	3,190	55,311	7,236	3,880	733	3,146	3,356	573	2,783
1997	129,558	69,685	3,401	66,284	59,873	3,260	56,613	6,739	3,577	694	2,882	3,162	577	2,585
1998	131,463	70,693	3,558	67,135	60,771	3,493	57,278	6,210	3,266	686	2,580	2,944	519	2,424
1999	133,488	71,446	3,685	67,761	62,042	3,487	58,555	5,880	3,066	633	2,433	2,814	529	2,285
2000	136,891	73,305	3,671	69,634	63,586	3,519	60,067	5,692	2,975	599	2,376	2,717	483	2,235
2001	136,933	73,196	3,420	69,776	63,737	3,320	60,417	6,801	3,690	650	3,040	3,111	512	2,599
2002	136,485	72,903	3,169	69,734	63,582	3,162	60,420	8,378	4,597	700	3,896	3,781	553	3,228
2003	137,736	73,332	2,917	70,415	64,404	3,002	61,402	8,774	4,906	697	4,209	3,868	554	3,314
2004	139,252	74,524	2,952	71,572	64,728	2,955	61,773	8,149	4,456	664	3,791	3,694	543	3,150
2005	141,730	75,973	2,923	73,050	65,757	3,055	62,702	7,591	4,059	667	3,392	3,531	519	3,013
2004: Jan	138,472	74,344	3,004	71,340	64,128	2,960	61,168	8,345	4,506	640	3,866	3,839	580	3,259
Feb	138,495	74,047	2,941	71,105	64,449	2,954	61,495	8,186	4,449	607	3,841	3,737	562	3,175
Mar	138,452	74,043	2,851	71,192	64,409	2,922	61,487	8,397	4,527	643	3,883	3,870	516	3,354
Apr	138,659	74,081	2,947	71,134	64,578	2,964	61,614	8,140	4,459	672	3,787	3,681	498	3,183
May	138,843	74,082	2,909	71,173	64,761	3,017	61,745	8,178	4,552	667	3,885	3,626	544	3,082
June	139,181	74,462	2,921	71,541	64,719	2,917	61,802	8,247	4,441	642	3,799	3,806	549	3,257
July	139,591	74,769	2,987	71,782	64,822	2,913	61,909	8,182	4,398	647	3,751	3,784	628	3,156
Aug	139,558	74,756	2,977	71,780	64,801	2,937	61,864	8,000	4,417	660	3,757	3,583	545	3,038
Sept	139,495	74,667	2,933	71,733	64,828	2,945	61,883	7,981	4,411	664	3,747	3,570	523	3,048
Oct	139,768	74,850	2,980	71,870	64,918	2,948	61,970	8,040	4,434	713	3,721	3,606	513	3,093
Nov	140,276	75,192	3,051	72,140	65,084	2,971	62,113	7,974	4,398	686	3,712	3,576	500	3,076
Dec	140,133	74,937	2,900	72,037	65,196	3,027	62,169	8,040	4,457	767	3,689	3,583	525	3,058
2005: Jan	140,234	74,980	2,888	72,092	65,254	3,018	62,236	7,723	4,197	639	3,558	3,525	501	3,024
Feb	140,285	75,075	2,829	72,246	65,209	2,989	62,220	7,986	4,415	732	3,683	3,572	508	3,064
Mar	140,601	75,436	2,924	72,513	65,165	3,036	62,129	7,616	4,181	729	3,453	3,434	483	2,952
Apr	141,196	75,773	2,918	72,855	65,423	2,997	62,426	7,644	4,085	738	3,347	3,559	523	3,036
May	141,571	75,998	2,890	73,108	65,573	3,058	62,515	7,629	4,047	711	3,337	3,582	569	3,013
June	141,750	76,099	2,921	73,178	65,652	3,099	62,552	7,493	3,966	673	3,294	3,526	496	3,030
July	142,111	76,258	2,913	73,345	65,853	3,110	62,744	7,494	3,928	654	3,274	3,566	497	3,070
Aug	142,425	76,404	2,924	73,479	66,022	3,121	62,901	7,367	3,951	644	3,307	3,416	539	2,877
Sept	142,435	76,257	2,926	73,331	66,178	3,104	63,074	7,648	4,076	615	3,461	3,572	518	3,055
Oct	142,625	76,396	2,896	73,500	66,229	3,068	63,162	7,418	3,853	573	3,281	3,565	552	3,013
Nov	142,611	76,410	2,970	73,441	66,200	3,031	63,170	7,572	3,984	702	3,282	3,588	535	3,053
Dec	142,779	76,529	3,061	73,468	66,250	3,000	63,249	7,375	3,902	584	3,318	3,473	507	2,966

Note.—See footnote 5 and Note, Table B–35.

Source: Department of Labor, Bureau of Labor Statistics.

—*Civilian employment by demographic characteristic, 1959–2005*

[Thousands of persons 16 years of age and over; monthly data seasonally adjusted]

Year or month	All civilian workers	White[1] Total	Males	Fe-males	Both sexes 16-19	Black and other[1] Total	Males	Fe-males	Both sexes 16-19	Black or African American[1] Total	Males	Fe-males	Both sexes 16-19
1959	64,630	58,006	39,494	18,512	3,475	6,623	3,971	2,652	362				
1960	65,778	58,850	39,755	19,095	3,700	6,928	4,149	2,779	430				
1961	65,746	58,913	39,588	19,325	3,693	6,833	4,068	2,765	414				
1962	66,702	59,698	40,016	19,682	3,774	7,003	4,160	2,843	420				
1963	67,762	60,622	40,428	20,194	3,851	7,140	4,229	2,911	404				
1964	69,305	61,922	41,115	20,807	4,076	7,383	4,359	3,024	440				
1965	71,088	63,446	41,844	21,602	4,562	7,643	4,496	3,147	474				
1966	72,895	65,021	42,331	22,690	5,176	7,877	4,588	3,289	545				
1967	74,372	66,361	42,833	23,528	5,114	8,011	4,646	3,365	568				
1968	75,920	67,750	43,411	24,339	5,195	8,169	4,702	3,467	584				
1969	77,902	69,518	44,048	25,470	5,508	8,384	4,770	3,614	609				
1970	78,678	70,217	44,178	26,039	5,571	8,464	4,813	3,650	574				
1971	79,367	70,878	44,595	26,283	5,670	8,488	4,796	3,692	538				
1972	82,153	73,370	45,944	27,426	6,173	8,783	4,952	3,832	573	7,802	4,368	3,433	509
1973	85,064	75,708	47,085	28,623	6,623	9,356	5,265	4,092	647	8,128	4,527	3,601	570
1974	86,794	77,184	47,674	29,511	6,796	9,610	5,352	4,258	652	8,203	4,527	3,677	554
1975	85,846	76,411	46,697	29,714	6,487	9,435	5,161	4,275	615	7,894	4,275	3,618	507
1976	88,752	78,853	47,775	31,078	6,724	9,899	5,363	4,536	611	8,227	4,404	3,823	508
1977	92,017	81,700	49,150	32,550	7,068	10,317	5,579	4,739	619	8,540	4,565	3,975	508
1978	96,048	84,936	50,544	34,392	7,367	11,112	5,936	5,177	703	9,102	4,796	4,307	571
1979	98,824	87,259	51,452	35,807	7,356	11,565	6,156	5,409	727	9,359	4,923	4,436	579
1980	99,303	87,715	51,127	36,587	7,021	11,588	6,059	5,529	689	9,313	4,798	4,515	547
1981	100,397	88,709	51,315	37,394	6,588	11,688	6,083	5,606	637	9,355	4,794	4,561	505
1982	99,526	87,903	50,287	37,615	5,984	11,624	5,983	5,641	565	9,189	4,637	4,552	428
1983	100,834	88,893	50,621	38,272	5,799	11,941	6,166	5,775	543	9,375	4,753	4,622	416
1984	105,005	92,120	52,462	39,659	5,836	12,885	6,629	6,256	607	10,119	5,124	4,995	474
1985	107,150	93,736	53,046	40,690	5,768	13,414	6,845	6,569	666	10,501	5,270	5,231	532
1986	109,597	95,660	53,785	41,876	5,792	13,937	7,107	6,830	681	10,814	5,428	5,386	536
1987	112,440	97,789	54,647	43,142	5,898	14,652	7,459	7,192	742	11,309	5,661	5,648	587
1988	114,968	99,812	55,550	44,262	6,030	15,156	7,722	7,434	774	11,658	5,824	5,834	601
1989	117,342	101,584	56,352	45,232	5,946	15,757	7,963	7,795	813	11,953	5,928	6,025	625
1990	118,793	102,261	56,703	45,558	5,779	16,533	8,401	8,131	801	12,175	5,995	6,180	598
1991	117,718	101,182	55,797	45,385	5,216	16,536	8,426	8,110	690	12,074	5,961	6,113	494
1992	118,492	101,669	55,959	45,710	4,985	16,823	8,482	8,342	684	12,151	5,930	6,221	492
1993	120,259	103,045	56,656	46,390	5,113	17,214	8,693	8,521	691	12,382	6,047	6,334	494
1994	123,060	105,190	57,452	47,738	5,398	17,870	8,998	8,872	763	12,835	6,241	6,595	552
1995	124,900	106,490	58,146	48,344	5,593	18,409	9,231	9,179	826	13,279	6,422	6,857	586
1996	126,708	107,808	58,888	48,920	5,667	18,900	9,319	9,580	832	13,542	6,456	7,086	613
1997	129,558	109,856	59,998	49,859	5,807	19,701	9,687	10,014	853	13,969	6,607	7,362	631
1998	131,463	110,931	60,604	50,327	6,089	20,532	10,089	10,443	962	14,556	6,871	7,685	736
1999	133,488	112,235	61,139	51,096	6,204	21,253	10,307	10,945	968	14,707	7,027	8,029	691
2000	136,891	114,424	62,289	52,136	6,160					15,156	7,082	8,073	711
2001	136,933	114,430	62,212	52,218	5,817					15,006	6,938	8,068	637
2002	136,485	114,013	61,849	52,164	5,441					14,872	6,959	7,914	611
2003	137,736	114,235	61,866	52,369	5,064					14,739	6,820	7,919	516
2004	139,252	115,239	62,712	52,527	5,039					14,909	6,912	7,997	520
2005	141,730	116,949	63,763	53,186	5,105					15,313	7,155	8,158	536
2004: Jan	138,472	114,648	62,581	52,068	5,119					14,892	6,959	7,933	507
Feb	138,495	114,696	62,382	52,313	5,053					14,887	6,892	7,995	514
Mar	138,452	114,525	62,248	52,276	4,945					14,944	6,931	8,013	507
Apr	138,659	114,783	62,401	52,382	5,061					14,893	6,844	8,049	492
May	138,843	114,974	62,310	52,663	5,079					14,808	6,883	7,925	504
June	139,181	115,204	62,618	52,585	4,985					14,803	6,914	7,889	499
July	139,591	115,608	63,050	52,558	5,066					14,907	6,835	8,072	500
Aug	139,558	115,480	62,915	52,565	5,013					14,939	6,888	8,050	569
Sept	139,495	115,362	62,748	52,614	5,017					14,952	6,930	8,022	533
Oct	139,768	115,653	62,996	52,656	5,036					14,999	6,962	8,037	546
Nov	140,276	115,962	63,191	52,770	5,091					14,938	6,960	7,978	552
Dec	140,133	115,908	63,069	52,840	5,009					14,936	6,927	8,010	515
2005: Jan	140,234	116,072	63,196	52,875	5,058					14,965	6,909	8,056	546
Feb	140,285	116,081	63,248	52,833	5,014					14,941	6,929	8,012	510
Mar	140,601	116,187	63,492	52,694	5,073					15,069	7,026	8,043	558
Apr	141,196	116,624	63,659	52,965	5,042					15,206	7,141	8,064	536
May	141,571	116,845	63,802	53,043	5,080					15,347	7,202	8,145	542
June	141,750	116,811	63,873	52,939	5,131					15,392	7,230	8,163	550
July	142,111	117,168	63,853	53,316	5,126					15,581	7,355	8,225	549
Aug	142,425	117,446	64,004	53,441	5,175					15,476	7,297	8,179	512
Sept	142,435	117,354	63,812	53,542	5,222					15,455	7,241	8,215	490
Oct	142,625	117,396	63,954	53,441	5,074					15,591	7,231	8,360	517
Nov	142,611	117,598	64,054	53,544	5,123					15,299	7,090	8,209	523
Dec	142,792	117,729	64,166	53,564	5,110					15,397	7,193	8,203	598

[1] Beginning in 2003, persons who selected this race group only. Prior to 2003, persons who selected more than one race were included in the group they identified as the main race. Data for black or African American were for black prior to 2003. Data discontinued for black and other series. See *Employment and Earnings*, for details.

Note.—Beginning with data for 2000, since data for all race groups are not shown here, detail will not sum to total. See footnote 5 and Note, Table B–35.

Source: Department of Labor, Bureau of Labor Statistics.

[Thousands of persons 16 years of age and over; monthly data seasonally adjusted]

Year or month	All civilian workers	White[1]				Black and other[1]				Black or African American[1]			
		Total	Males	Fe-males	Both sexes 16-19	Total	Males	Fe-males	Both sexes 16-19	Total	Males	Fe-males	Both sexes 16-19
1959	3,740	2,946	1,903	1,043	525	793	517	276	128	....	....	....	....
1960	3,852	3,065	1,988	1,077	575	788	498	290	138	....	....	....	....
1961	4,714	3,743	2,398	1,345	669	971	599	372	159	....	....	....	....
1962	3,911	3,052	1,915	1,137	580	861	509	352	142	....	....	....	....
1963	4,070	3,208	1,976	1,232	708	863	496	367	176	....	....	....	....
1964	3,786	2,999	1,779	1,220	708	787	426	361	165	....	....	....	....
1965	3,366	2,691	1,556	1,135	705	678	360	318	171	....	....	....	....
1966	2,875	2,255	1,241	1,014	651	622	310	312	186	....	....	....	....
1967	2,975	2,338	1,208	1,130	635	638	300	338	203	....	....	....	....
1968	2,817	2,226	1,142	1,084	644	590	277	313	194	....	....	....	....
1969	2,832	2,260	1,137	1,123	660	571	267	304	193	....	....	....	....
1970	4,093	3,339	1,857	1,482	871	754	380	374	235	....	....	....	....
1971	5,016	4,085	2,309	1,777	1,011	930	481	450	249	....	....	....	....
1972	4,882	3,906	2,173	1,733	1,021	977	486	491	288	906	448	458	279
1973	4,365	3,442	1,836	1,606	955	924	440	484	280	846	395	451	262
1974	5,156	4,097	2,169	1,927	1,104	1,058	544	514	318	965	494	470	297
1975	7,929	6,421	3,627	2,794	1,413	1,507	815	692	355	1,369	741	629	330
1976	7,406	5,914	3,258	2,656	1,364	1,492	779	713	355	1,334	698	637	330
1977	6,991	5,441	2,883	2,558	1,284	1,550	784	766	379	1,393	698	695	354
1978	6,202	4,698	2,411	2,287	1,189	1,505	731	774	394	1,330	641	690	360
1979	6,137	4,664	2,405	2,260	1,193	1,473	714	759	362	1,319	636	683	333
1980	7,637	5,884	3,345	2,540	1,291	1,752	922	830	377	1,553	815	738	343
1981	8,273	6,343	3,580	2,762	1,374	1,930	997	933	388	1,731	891	840	357
1982	10,678	8,241	4,846	3,395	1,534	2,437	1,334	1,104	443	2,142	1,167	975	396
1983	10,717	8,128	4,859	3,270	1,387	2,588	1,401	1,187	441	2,272	1,213	1,059	392
1984	8,539	6,372	3,600	2,772	1,116	2,167	1,144	1,022	384	1,914	1,003	911	353
1985	8,312	6,191	3,426	2,765	1,074	2,121	1,095	1,026	394	1,864	951	913	357
1986	8,237	6,140	3,433	2,708	1,070	2,097	1,097	999	383	1,840	946	894	347
1987	7,425	5,501	3,132	2,369	995	1,924	969	955	353	1,684	826	858	312
1988	6,701	4,944	2,766	2,177	910	1,757	888	869	316	1,547	771	776	288
1989	6,528	4,770	2,636	2,135	863	1,757	889	868	331	1,544	773	772	300
1990	7,047	5,186	2,935	2,251	903	1,860	971	889	308	1,565	806	758	268
1991	8,628	6,560	3,859	2,701	1,029	2,068	1,087	981	330	1,723	890	833	280
1992	9,613	7,169	4,209	2,959	1,037	2,444	1,314	1,130	390	2,011	1,067	944	324
1993	8,940	6,655	3,828	2,827	992	2,285	1,227	1,058	373	1,844	971	872	313
1994	7,996	5,892	3,275	2,617	960	2,104	1,092	1,011	360	1,666	848	818	300
1995	7,404	5,459	2,999	2,460	952	1,945	984	961	394	1,538	762	777	325
1996	7,236	5,300	2,896	2,404	939	1,936	984	952	367	1,592	808	784	310
1997	6,739	4,836	2,641	2,195	912	1,903	935	967	359	1,560	747	813	302
1998	6,210	4,484	2,431	2,053	876	1,726	835	891	329	1,426	671	756	281
1999	5,880	4,273	2,274	1,999	844	1,606	792	814	318	1,309	626	684	268
2000	5,692	4,121	2,177	1,944	795	....	....	....	....	1,241	620	621	230
2001	6,801	4,969	2,754	2,215	845	....	....	....	....	1,416	709	706	260
2002	8,378	6,137	3,459	2,678	925	....	....	....	....	1,693	835	858	260
2003	8,774	6,311	3,643	2,668	909	....	....	....	....	1,787	891	895	255
2004	8,149	5,847	3,282	2,565	890	....	....	....	....	1,729	860	868	241
2005	7,591	5,350	2,931	2,419	845	....	....	....	....	1,700	844	856	267
2004: Jan	8,345	6,047	3,315	2,732	880	....	....	....	....	1,719	853	866	260
Feb	8,186	5,949	3,317	2,632	896	....	....	....	....	1,586	758	828	178
Mar	8,397	6,116	3,400	2,716	862	....	....	....	....	1,701	821	880	217
Apr	8,140	5,952	3,396	2,556	922	....	....	....	....	1,612	782	830	188
May	8,178	5,958	3,482	2,477	921	....	....	....	....	1,645	791	855	230
June	8,247	6,050	3,344	2,707	868	....	....	....	....	1,684	818	866	246
July	8,182	5,776	3,174	2,602	900	....	....	....	....	1,864	920	944	295
Aug	8,000	5,732	3,228	2,504	901	....	....	....	....	1,750	908	843	230
Sept	7,981	5,660	3,184	2,476	873	....	....	....	....	1,732	893	840	214
Oct	8,040	5,618	3,209	2,409	891	....	....	....	....	1,814	919	894	289
Nov	7,974	5,614	3,112	2,502	854	....	....	....	....	1,796	928	868	263
Dec	8,040	5,599	3,163	2,436	936	....	....	....	....	1,808	943	864	249
2005: Jan	7,723	5,419	3,039	2,380	834	....	....	....	....	1,758	875	883	242
Feb	7,986	5,588	3,136	2,452	917	....	....	....	....	1,807	931	876	242
Mar	7,616	5,306	3,037	2,269	850	....	....	....	....	1,733	849	884	275
Apr	7,644	5,383	2,923	2,460	902	....	....	....	....	1,746	872	875	300
May	7,629	5,368	2,933	2,434	907	....	....	....	....	1,713	852	861	304
June	7,493	5,224	2,804	2,420	839	....	....	....	....	1,766	902	863	262
July	7,494	5,263	2,832	2,431	804	....	....	....	....	1,619	793	826	268
Aug	7,367	5,193	2,847	2,345	829	....	....	....	....	1,654	814	840	287
Sept	7,648	5,489	3,024	2,465	801	....	....	....	....	1,613	785	828	242
Oct	7,418	5,415	2,877	2,537	838	....	....	....	....	1,559	774	785	248
Nov	7,572	5,215	2,782	2,433	826	....	....	....	....	1,819	903	916	326
Dec	7,375	5,264	2,855	2,409	789	....	....	....	....	1,582	741	841	194

[1] See footnote 1 and Note, Table B–37.

Note.—See footnote 5 and Note, Table B–35.

Source: Department of Labor, Bureau of Labor Statistics.

TABLE B–39.—*Civilian labor force participation rate and employment/population ratio, 1959–2005*

[Percent;[1] monthly data seasonally adjusted]

Year or month	Labor force participation rate							Employment/population ratio						
	All civilian workers	Males	Females	Both sexes 16–19 years	White[2]	Black and other[2]	Black or African American[2]	All civilian workers	Males	Females	Both sexes 16–19 years	White[2]	Black and other[2]	Black or African American[2]
1959	59.3	83.7	37.1	46.7	58.7	64.3		56.0	79.3	35.0	39.9	55.9	57.5	
1960	59.4	83.3	37.7	47.5	58.8	64.5		56.1	78.9	35.5	40.5	55.9	57.9	
1961	59.3	82.9	38.1	46.9	58.8	64.1		55.4	77.6	35.4	39.1	55.3	56.2	
1962	58.8	82.0	37.9	46.1	58.3	63.2		55.5	77.7	35.6	39.4	55.4	56.3	
1963	58.7	81.4	38.3	45.2	58.2	63.0		55.4	77.1	35.8	37.4	55.3	56.2	
1964	58.7	81.0	38.7	44.5	58.2	63.1		55.7	77.3	36.3	37.3	55.5	57.0	
1965	58.9	80.7	39.3	45.7	58.4	62.9		56.2	77.5	37.1	38.9	56.0	57.8	
1966	59.2	80.4	40.3	48.2	58.7	63.0		56.9	77.9	38.3	42.1	56.8	58.4	
1967	59.6	80.4	41.1	48.4	59.2	62.8		57.3	78.0	39.0	42.2	57.2	58.2	
1968	59.6	80.1	41.6	48.3	59.3	62.2		57.5	77.8	39.6	42.2	57.4	58.0	
1969	60.1	79.8	42.7	49.4	59.9	62.1		58.0	77.6	40.7	43.4	58.0	58.1	
1970	60.4	79.7	43.3	49.9	60.2	61.8		57.4	76.2	40.8	42.3	57.5	56.8	
1971	60.2	79.1	43.4	49.7	60.1	60.9		56.6	74.9	40.4	41.3	56.8	54.9	
1972	60.4	78.9	43.9	51.9	60.4	60.2	59.9	57.0	75.0	41.0	43.5	57.4	54.1	53.7
1973	60.8	78.8	44.7	53.7	60.8	60.5	60.2	57.8	75.5	42.0	45.9	58.2	55.0	54.5
1974	61.3	78.7	45.7	54.8	61.4	60.3	59.8	57.8	74.9	42.6	46.0	58.3	54.3	53.5
1975	61.2	77.9	46.3	54.0	61.5	59.6	58.8	56.1	71.7	42.0	43.3	56.7	51.4	50.1
1976	61.6	77.5	47.3	54.5	61.8	59.8	59.0	56.8	72.0	43.2	44.2	57.5	52.0	50.8
1977	62.3	77.7	48.4	56.0	62.5	60.4	59.8	57.9	72.8	44.5	46.1	58.6	52.5	51.4
1978	63.2	77.9	50.0	57.8	63.3	62.2	61.5	59.3	73.8	46.4	48.3	60.0	54.7	53.6
1979	63.7	77.8	50.9	57.9	63.9	62.2	61.4	59.9	73.8	47.5	48.5	60.6	55.2	53.8
1980	63.8	77.4	51.5	56.7	64.1	61.7	61.0	59.2	72.0	47.7	46.6	60.0	53.6	52.3
1981	63.9	77.0	52.1	55.4	64.3	61.3	60.8	59.0	71.3	48.0	44.6	60.0	52.6	51.3
1982	64.0	76.6	52.6	54.1	64.3	61.6	61.0	57.8	69.0	47.7	41.5	58.8	50.9	49.4
1983	64.0	76.4	52.9	53.5	64.3	62.1	61.5	57.9	68.8	48.0	41.5	58.9	51.0	49.5
1984	64.4	76.4	53.6	53.9	64.6	62.6	62.2	59.5	70.7	49.5	43.7	60.5	53.6	52.3
1985	64.8	76.3	54.5	54.5	65.0	63.3	62.9	60.1	70.9	50.4	44.4	61.0	54.7	53.4
1986	65.3	76.3	55.3	54.7	65.5	63.7	63.3	60.7	71.0	51.4	44.6	61.5	55.4	54.1
1987	65.6	76.2	56.0	54.7	65.8	64.3	63.8	61.5	71.5	52.5	45.5	62.3	56.8	55.6
1988	65.9	76.2	56.6	55.3	66.2	64.0	63.8	62.3	72.0	53.4	46.8	63.1	57.4	56.3
1989	66.5	76.4	57.4	55.9	66.7	64.7	64.2	63.0	72.5	54.3	47.5	63.8	58.2	56.9
1990	66.5	76.4	57.5	53.7	66.9	64.4	64.0	62.8	72.0	54.3	45.3	63.7	57.9	56.7
1991	66.2	75.8	57.4	51.6	66.6	63.8	63.3	61.7	70.4	53.7	42.0	62.6	56.7	55.4
1992	66.4	75.8	57.8	51.3	66.8	64.6	63.9	61.5	69.8	53.8	41.0	62.4	56.4	54.9
1993	66.3	75.4	57.9	51.5	66.8	63.8	63.2	61.7	70.0	54.1	41.7	62.7	56.3	55.0
1994	66.6	75.1	58.8	52.7	67.1	63.9	63.4	62.5	70.4	55.3	43.4	63.5	57.2	56.1
1995	66.6	75.0	58.9	53.5	67.1	64.3	63.7	62.9	70.8	55.6	44.2	63.8	58.1	57.1
1996	66.8	74.9	59.3	52.3	67.2	64.6	64.1	63.2	70.9	56.0	43.5	64.1	58.6	57.4
1997	67.1	75.0	59.8	51.6	67.5	65.2	64.7	63.8	71.3	56.8	43.4	64.6	59.4	58.2
1998	67.1	74.9	59.8	52.8	67.3	66.0	65.6	64.1	71.6	57.1	45.1	64.7	60.9	59.7
1999	67.1	74.7	60.0	52.0	67.3	65.9	65.8	64.3	71.6	57.4	44.7	64.8	61.3	60.6
2000	67.1	74.8	59.9	52.0	67.3		65.8	64.4	71.9	57.5	45.2	64.9		60.9
2001	66.8	74.4	59.8	49.6	67.0		65.3	63.7	70.9	57.0	42.3	64.2		59.7
2002	66.6	74.1	59.6	47.4	66.8		64.8	62.7	69.7	56.3	39.6	63.4		58.1
2003	66.2	73.5	59.5	44.5	66.5		64.3	62.3	68.9	56.1	36.8	63.0		57.4
2004	66.0	73.3	59.2	43.9	66.3		63.8	62.3	69.2	56.0	36.4	63.1		57.2
2005	66.0	73.3	59.3	43.7	66.3		64.2	62.7	69.6	56.2	36.5	63.4		57.7
2004: Jan	66.1	73.6	59.1	44.4	66.4		64.2	62.3	69.4	55.7	36.9	63.0		57.6
Feb	66.0	73.2	59.2	43.7	66.3		63.6	62.3	69.1	56.0	36.4	63.0		57.5
Mar	66.0	73.2	59.2	42.8	66.2		64.2	62.2	69.0	55.9	35.7	62.9		57.6
Apr	65.9	73.1	59.2	43.7	66.2		63.6	62.2	69.0	56.0	36.5	63.0		57.4
May	65.9	73.1	59.2	44.0	66.3		63.3	62.3	68.9	56.1	36.6	63.0		56.9
June	66.1	73.3	59.3	43.3	66.4		63.3	62.4	69.2	56.0	36.0	63.1		56.8
July	66.1	73.5	59.3	44.2	66.4		64.3	62.5	69.4	56.0	36.4	63.3		57.2
Aug	66.0	73.4	59.1	43.9	66.3		63.9	62.4	69.3	56.0	36.4	63.2		57.2
Sept	65.9	73.2	59.0	43.5	66.1		63.8	62.3	69.1	55.9	36.2	63.0		57.1
Oct	65.9	73.3	59.1	44.0	66.2		64.2	62.3	69.2	55.9	36.5	63.1		57.2
Nov	66.1	73.5	59.1	44.3	66.3		63.8	62.5	69.4	56.0	37.0	63.2		56.9
Dec	66.0	73.2	59.2	44.3	66.2		63.7	62.4	69.1	56.1	36.4	63.2		56.9
2005: Jan	65.8	73.0	59.1	43.2	66.2		63.6	62.4	69.1	56.1	36.2	63.2		56.9
Feb	65.9	73.2	59.1	43.3	66.2		63.6	62.3	69.1	56.0	35.7	63.2		56.7
Mar	65.8	73.2	58.9	43.9	66.1		63.7	62.4	69.4	55.9	36.5	63.2		57.1
Apr	66.0	73.4	59.1	43.9	66.3		64.2	62.6	69.6	56.1	36.2	63.4		57.6
May	66.1	73.5	59.2	44.2	66.4		64.5	62.7	69.8	56.2	36.8	63.4		58.0
June	66.1	73.4	59.2	43.9	66.2		64.8	62.7	69.8	56.2	36.8	63.4		58.1
July	66.2	73.4	59.4	43.7	66.4		64.8	62.8	69.8	56.3	36.7	63.5		58.7
Aug	66.2	73.5	59.3	44.0	66.4		64.5	62.9	69.9	56.3	36.8	63.6		58.2
Sept	66.2	73.4	59.5	43.6	66.5		64.1	62.8	69.7	56.5	36.7	63.5		58.1
Oct	66.1	73.2	59.5	43.0	66.4		64.3	62.8	69.7	56.4	36.2	63.4		58.5
Nov	66.3	73.3	59.4	43.9	66.3		64.1	62.8	69.6	56.4	36.4	63.5		57.3
Dec	66.0	73.2	59.3	43.3	66.4		63.5	62.8	69.7	56.4	36.7	63.5		57.6

[1] Civilian labor force or civilian employment as percent of civilian noninstitutional population in group specified.
[2] See footnote 1, Table B–37.

Note.—Data relate to persons 16 years of age and over.
See footnote 5 and Note, Table B–35.

Source: Department of Labor, Bureau of Labor Statistics.

TABLE B–40.—*Civilian labor force participation rate by demographic characteristic, 1965–2005*

[Percent;[1] monthly data seasonally adjusted]

Year or month	All civilian workers	White[2] Total	White Males Total	White Males 16-19 years	White Males 20 years and over	White Females Total	White Females 16-19 years	White Females 20 years and over	Black and other Total	Black and other Males Total	Black and other Males 16-19 years	Black and other Males 20 years and over	Black and other Females Total	Black and other Females 16-19 years	Black and other Females 20 years and over
											Black and other				
1965	58.9	58.4	80.8	54.1	83.9	38.1	39.2	38.0	62.9	79.6	51.3	83.7	48.6	29.5	51.1
1966	59.2	58.7	80.6	55.9	83.6	39.2	42.6	38.8	63.0	79.0	51.4	83.3	49.4	33.5	51.6
1967	59.6	59.2	80.6	56.3	83.5	40.1	42.5	39.8	62.8	78.5	51.1	82.9	49.5	35.2	51.6
1968	59.6	59.3	80.4	55.9	83.2	40.7	43.0	40.4	62.2	77.7	49.7	82.2	49.3	34.8	51.4
1969	60.1	59.9	80.2	56.8	83.0	41.8	44.6	41.5	62.1	76.9	49.6	81.4	49.8	34.6	52.0
1970	60.4	60.2	80.0	57.5	82.8	42.6	45.6	42.2	61.8	76.5	47.4	81.4	49.5	34.1	51.8
1971	60.2	60.1	79.6	57.9	82.3	42.6	45.4	42.3	60.9	74.9	44.7	80.0	49.2	31.2	51.8
1972	60.4	60.4	79.6	60.1	82.0	43.2	48.1	42.7	60.2	73.9	46.0	78.6	48.8	32.3	51.2
											Black or African American[2]				
1972	60.4	60.4	79.6	60.1	82.0	43.2	48.1	42.7	59.9	73.6	46.3	78.5	48.7	32.2	51.2
1973	60.8	60.8	79.4	62.0	81.6	44.1	50.1	43.5	60.2	73.4	45.7	78.4	49.3	34.2	51.6
1974	61.3	61.4	79.4	62.9	81.4	45.2	51.7	44.4	59.8	72.9	46.7	77.6	49.0	33.4	51.4
1975	61.2	61.5	78.7	61.9	80.7	45.9	51.5	45.3	58.8	70.9	42.6	76.0	48.8	34.2	51.1
1976	61.6	61.8	78.4	62.3	80.3	46.9	52.8	46.2	59.0	70.0	41.3	75.4	49.8	32.9	52.5
1977	62.3	62.5	78.5	64.0	80.2	48.0	54.5	47.3	59.8	70.6	43.2	75.6	50.8	32.9	53.6
1978	63.2	63.3	78.6	65.0	80.1	49.4	56.7	48.7	61.5	71.5	44.9	76.2	53.1	37.3	55.5
1979	63.7	63.9	78.6	64.8	80.1	50.5	57.4	49.8	61.4	71.3	43.6	76.3	53.1	36.8	55.4
1980	63.8	64.1	78.2	63.7	79.8	51.2	56.2	50.6	61.0	70.3	43.2	75.1	53.1	34.9	55.6
1981	63.9	64.3	77.9	62.4	79.5	51.9	55.4	51.5	60.8	70.0	41.6	74.5	53.5	34.0	56.0
1982	64.0	64.3	77.4	60.0	79.2	52.4	55.0	52.2	61.0	70.1	39.8	74.7	53.7	33.5	56.2
1983	64.0	64.3	77.1	59.4	78.9	52.7	54.5	52.5	61.5	70.6	39.9	75.2	54.2	33.0	56.8
1984	64.4	64.6	77.1	59.0	78.7	53.3	55.4	53.1	62.2	70.8	41.7	74.8	55.2	35.0	57.6
1985	64.8	65.0	77.0	59.7	78.5	54.1	55.2	54.0	62.9	70.8	44.6	74.4	56.5	37.9	58.6
1986	65.3	65.5	76.9	59.3	78.5	55.0	56.3	54.9	63.3	71.2	43.7	74.8	56.9	39.1	58.9
1987	65.6	65.8	76.8	59.0	78.4	55.7	56.5	55.6	63.8	71.1	43.6	74.7	58.0	39.6	60.0
1988	65.9	66.2	76.9	60.0	78.3	56.4	57.2	56.3	63.8	71.0	43.8	74.6	58.0	37.9	60.1
1989	66.5	66.7	77.1	61.0	78.5	57.2	57.1	57.2	64.2	71.0	44.6	74.4	58.7	40.4	60.6
1990	66.5	66.9	77.1	59.6	78.5	57.4	55.3	57.6	64.0	71.0	40.7	75.0	58.3	36.8	60.6
1991	66.2	66.6	76.5	57.3	78.0	57.4	54.1	57.6	63.3	70.4	37.3	74.6	57.5	33.5	60.0
1992	66.4	66.8	76.5	56.9	78.0	57.7	52.5	58.1	63.9	70.7	40.6	74.3	58.5	35.2	60.8
1993	66.3	66.8	76.2	56.6	77.7	58.0	53.5	58.3	63.2	69.6	39.5	73.2	57.9	34.6	60.2
1994	66.6	67.1	75.9	57.7	77.3	58.9	55.1	59.2	63.4	69.1	40.8	72.5	58.7	36.3	60.9
1995	66.6	67.1	75.7	58.5	77.1	59.0	55.5	59.2	63.7	69.0	40.1	72.5	59.5	39.8	61.4
1996	66.8	67.2	75.8	57.1	77.3	59.1	54.7	59.4	64.1	68.7	39.5	72.3	60.4	38.9	62.6
1997	67.1	67.5	75.9	56.1	77.5	59.5	54.1	59.9	64.7	68.3	37.4	72.2	61.7	39.9	64.0
1998	67.1	67.3	75.6	56.6	77.2	59.4	55.4	59.7	65.6	69.0	40.7	72.5	62.8	42.5	64.8
1999	67.1	67.3	75.6	56.4	77.2	59.6	54.5	59.9	65.8	68.7	38.6	72.4	63.5	38.8	66.1
2000	67.1	67.3	75.5	56.5	77.1	59.5	54.5	59.9	65.8	69.2	39.2	72.8	63.1	39.6	65.4
2001	66.8	67.0	75.1	53.7	76.9	59.4	52.4	59.9	65.3	68.4	37.9	72.1	62.8	37.3	65.2
2002	66.6	66.8	74.8	50.3	76.7	59.3	50.8	60.0	64.8	68.4	37.3	72.1	61.8	34.7	64.4
2003	66.2	66.5	74.2	47.5	76.3	59.2	47.9	59.9	64.3	67.3	31.1	71.5	61.9	33.7	64.6
2004	66.0	66.3	74.1	47.4	76.2	58.9	46.7	59.7	63.8	66.7	30.0	70.9	61.5	32.8	64.2
2005	66.0	66.3	74.1	46.2	76.2	58.9	47.6	59.7	64.2	67.3	32.6	71.3	61.6	32.2	64.4
2004: Jan	66.1	66.4	74.4	48.4	76.4	58.8	47.0	59.6	64.2	67.6	28.5	72.1	61.5	35.3	63.9
Feb	66.0	66.3	74.1	47.6	76.1	58.9	46.9	59.7	63.6	66.1	24.6	70.9	61.6	32.9	64.3
Mar	66.0	66.2	74.0	46.1	76.1	58.9	46.2	59.8	64.2	66.9	29.2	71.2	62.0	30.9	64.9
Apr	65.9	66.2	74.1	48.4	76.1	58.8	46.6	59.7	63.6	65.7	25.4	70.3	61.8	30.9	64.7
May	65.9	66.3	74.0	47.7	76.1	59.0	47.6	59.8	63.3	66.0	26.7	70.5	61.1	34.1	63.6
June	66.1	66.4	74.1	46.6	76.3	59.1	46.3	60.0	63.3	66.4	29.3	70.6	60.8	32.2	63.5
July	66.1	66.4	74.4	47.6	76.4	58.9	47.1	59.8	64.3	66.5	30.6	70.6	62.5	35.0	65.1
Aug	66.0	66.3	74.2	47.3	76.3	58.8	46.5	59.6	63.9	66.7	32.5	70.6	61.6	33.3	64.2
Sept	65.9	66.1	73.9	46.7	76.0	58.7	46.8	59.6	63.8	66.8	31.7	70.8	61.3	29.8	64.2
Oct	65.9	66.2	74.1	48.3	76.1	58.7	45.6	59.6	64.2	67.2	34.2	71.0	61.7	34.3	64.2
Nov	66.1	66.3	74.1	47.8	76.2	58.9	46.3	59.7	63.8	67.2	34.8	70.9	61.0	32.0	63.7
Dec	66.0	66.2	74.0	46.9	76.1	58.8	47.2	59.6	63.7	66.9	31.5	71.0	61.1	30.9	64.0
2005: Jan	65.8	66.2	73.9	46.1	76.1	58.7	47.2	59.6	63.6	66.1	31.6	70.0	61.5	32.7	64.2
Feb	65.9	66.2	74.0	47.7	76.2	58.7	47.7	59.5	63.6	66.6	32.7	70.5	61.1	28.6	64.1
Mar	65.8	66.1	74.2	47.0	76.3	58.4	46.6	59.2	63.7	66.7	35.5	70.2	61.3	32.3	64.0
Apr	66.0	66.3	74.2	46.7	76.3	58.8	47.2	59.6	64.2	67.7	36.9	71.3	61.3	31.1	64.1
May	66.1	66.4	74.3	46.4	76.4	58.8	48.1	59.4	64.5	68.0	35.3	71.7	61.7	33.2	64.4
June	66.1	66.2	74.1	46.2	76.3	58.7	48.0	59.4	64.8	68.5	33.8	72.5	61.7	31.9	64.5
July	66.2	66.4	74.1	45.8	76.2	59.0	47.7	59.8	64.8	68.5	31.4	72.8	61.8	34.5	64.4
Aug	66.2	66.4	74.2	45.9	76.3	59.0	48.7	59.8	64.5	68.1	31.3	72.3	61.5	32.9	64.2
Sept	66.2	66.5	74.1	46.1	76.2	59.2	48.7	59.9	64.1	67.3	28.7	71.7	61.6	30.0	64.6
Oct	66.1	66.4	74.0	45.2	76.2	59.1	47.8	59.9	64.3	67.0	28.1	71.4	62.2	33.0	64.9
Nov	66.1	66.3	73.9	46.3	76.0	59.1	47.1	59.9	64.1	66.7	35.3	70.4	62.0	32.3	64.8
Dec	66.0	66.4	74.0	46.0	76.2	59.0	46.5	59.9	63.5	66.1	30.7	70.2	61.3	32.3	64.1

[1] Civilian labor force as percent of civilian noninstitutional population in group specified.
[2] See footnote 1, Table B–37.
Note.—Data relate to persons 16 years of age and over.
See footnote 5 and Note, Table B–35.

Source: Department of Labor, Bureau of Labor Statistics.

330

TABLE B–41.—*Civilian employment/population ratio by demographic characteristic, 1965–2005*

[Percent;[1] monthly data seasonally adjusted]

Year or month	All civil-ian work-ers	White[2] Total	White Males Total	White Males 16-19 years	White Males 20 years and over	White Females Total	White Females 16-19 years	White Females 20 years and over	Black and other or black or African American[2] Total	Black Males Total	Black Males 16-19 years	Black Males 20 years and over	Black Females Total	Black Females 16-19 years	Black Females 20 years and over
									Black and other						
1965	56.2	56.0	77.9	47.1	81.5	36.2	33.7	36.5	57.8	73.7	39.4	78.7	44.1	20.2	47.3
1966	56.9	56.8	78.3	50.1	81.7	37.5	37.5	37.5	58.4	74.0	40.5	79.2	45.1	23.1	48.2
1967	57.3	57.2	78.4	50.2	81.7	38.3	37.7	38.3	58.2	73.8	38.8	79.4	45.0	24.8	47.9
1968	57.5	57.4	78.3	50.3	81.6	38.9	37.8	39.1	58.0	73.3	38.7	78.9	45.2	24.7	48.2
1969	58.0	58.0	78.2	51.1	81.4	40.1	39.5	40.1	58.1	72.8	39.0	78.4	45.9	25.1	48.9
1970	57.4	57.5	76.8	49.6	80.1	40.3	39.5	40.4	56.8	70.9	35.5	76.8	44.9	22.4	48.2
1971	56.6	56.8	75.7	49.2	79.0	39.9	38.6	40.1	54.9	68.1	31.8	74.2	43.9	20.2	47.3
1972	57.0	57.4	76.0	51.5	79.0	40.7	41.3	40.6	54.1	67.3	32.4	73.2	43.3	19.9	46.7
									Black or African American[2]						
1972	57.0	57.4	76.0	51.5	79.0	40.7	41.3	40.6	53.7	66.8	31.6	73.0	43.0	19.2	46.5
1973	57.8	58.2	76.5	54.3	79.2	41.8	43.6	41.6	54.5	67.5	32.8	73.7	43.8	22.0	47.2
1974	57.8	58.3	75.9	54.4	78.6	42.4	44.3	42.2	53.5	65.8	31.4	71.9	43.5	20.9	46.9
1975	56.1	56.7	73.0	50.6	75.7	42.0	42.5	41.9	50.1	60.6	26.3	66.5	41.6	20.2	44.9
1976	56.8	57.5	73.4	51.5	76.0	43.2	44.2	43.1	50.8	60.6	25.8	66.8	42.8	19.2	46.4
1977	57.9	58.6	74.1	54.4	76.5	44.5	45.9	44.4	51.4	61.4	26.4	67.5	43.3	18.5	47.0
1978	59.3	60.0	75.0	56.3	77.2	46.3	48.5	46.1	53.6	63.3	28.5	69.1	45.8	22.1	49.3
1979	59.9	60.6	75.1	55.7	77.3	47.5	49.4	47.3	53.8	63.4	28.7	69.1	46.0	22.4	49.3
1980	59.2	60.0	73.4	53.4	75.6	47.8	47.9	47.8	52.3	60.4	27.0	65.8	45.7	21.0	49.1
1981	59.0	60.0	72.8	51.3	75.1	48.3	46.2	48.5	51.3	59.1	24.6	64.5	45.1	19.7	48.5
1982	57.8	58.8	70.6	47.0	73.0	48.1	44.6	48.4	49.4	56.0	20.3	61.4	44.2	17.7	47.5
1983	57.9	58.9	70.4	47.4	72.6	48.5	44.5	48.9	49.5	56.3	20.4	61.6	44.1	17.0	47.4
1984	59.5	60.5	72.1	49.1	74.3	49.8	47.0	50.0	52.3	59.2	23.9	64.1	46.7	20.1	49.8
1985	60.1	61.0	72.3	49.9	74.3	50.7	47.1	51.0	53.4	60.0	26.3	64.6	48.1	23.1	50.9
1986	60.7	61.5	72.3	49.6	74.3	51.7	47.9	52.0	54.1	60.6	26.5	65.1	48.8	23.8	51.6
1987	61.5	62.3	72.7	49.9	74.7	52.8	49.0	53.1	55.6	62.0	28.5	66.4	50.3	25.8	53.0
1988	62.3	63.1	73.2	51.7	75.1	53.8	50.2	54.0	56.3	62.7	29.4	67.1	51.2	25.8	53.9
1989	63.0	63.8	73.7	52.6	75.4	54.6	50.5	54.9	56.9	62.8	30.4	67.0	52.0	27.1	54.6
1990	62.8	63.7	73.3	51.0	75.1	54.7	48.3	55.2	56.7	62.6	27.7	67.1	51.9	25.8	54.7
1991	61.7	62.6	71.6	47.2	73.5	54.2	45.9	54.8	55.4	61.3	23.8	65.9	50.6	21.5	53.6
1992	61.5	62.4	71.1	46.4	73.1	54.2	44.2	54.9	54.9	59.9	23.6	64.3	50.8	22.1	53.6
1993	61.7	62.7	71.4	46.6	73.3	54.6	45.7	55.2	55.0	60.0	23.6	64.3	50.9	21.6	53.8
1994	62.5	63.5	71.8	48.3	73.6	55.8	47.5	56.4	56.1	60.8	25.4	65.0	52.3	24.5	55.0
1995	62.9	63.8	72.0	49.4	73.8	56.1	48.1	56.7	57.1	61.7	25.2	66.1	53.4	26.1	56.1
1996	63.2	64.1	72.3	48.2	74.2	56.3	47.6	57.0	57.4	61.1	24.9	65.5	54.4	27.1	57.1
1997	63.8	64.6	72.7	48.1	74.7	57.0	47.2	57.8	58.2	61.4	23.7	66.1	55.6	28.5	58.4
1998	64.1	64.7	72.7	48.6	74.7	57.1	49.3	57.7	59.7	62.9	28.4	67.1	57.2	31.8	59.7
1999	64.3	64.8	72.8	49.3	74.8	57.3	48.3	58.0	60.6	63.1	26.7	67.5	58.6	29.0	61.5
2000	64.4	64.9	73.0	49.5	74.9	57.4	48.8	58.0	60.9	63.6	28.9	67.7	58.6	30.6	61.3
2001	63.7	64.2	72.0	46.2	74.0	57.0	46.5	57.7	59.7	62.1	26.4	66.3	57.8	27.0	60.7
2002	62.7	63.4	70.8	42.3	73.1	56.4	44.1	57.3	58.1	61.1	25.6	65.2	55.8	24.9	58.7
2003	62.3	63.0	70.1	39.4	72.5	56.3	41.5	57.3	57.4	59.5	19.9	64.1	55.6	23.4	58.6
2004	62.3	63.1	70.4	39.7	72.8	56.1	40.3	57.2	57.2	59.3	19.3	63.9	55.5	23.6	58.5
2005	62.7	63.4	70.8	38.8	73.3	56.3	41.8	57.4	57.7	60.2	20.8	64.7	55.7	22.4	58.9
2004: Jan	62.3	63.0	70.6	41.5	72.9	55.8	39.9	57.0	57.6	60.2	16.0	65.3	55.4	26.1	58.2
Feb	62.3	63.0	70.3	40.4	72.7	56.1	40.0	57.2	57.5	59.6	17.2	64.4	55.8	25.5	58.6
Mar	62.2	62.9	70.1	38.6	72.6	56.0	40.0	57.1	57.6	59.8	18.5	64.5	55.9	23.5	58.9
Apr	62.2	63.0	70.2	39.9	72.6	56.1	40.5	57.2	57.4	59.0	17.7	63.7	56.1	23.0	59.1
May	62.3	63.0	70.1	39.1	72.5	56.3	41.7	57.4	56.9	59.2	18.5	63.9	55.1	23.2	58.1
June	62.4	63.1	70.4	39.0	72.8	56.2	40.1	57.3	56.8	59.4	19.4	64.0	54.8	21.9	57.9
July	62.5	63.3	70.8	40.2	73.2	56.1	40.3	57.3	57.2	58.6	19.3	63.1	56.0	21.9	59.2
Aug	62.4	63.2	70.6	39.8	73.0	56.1	39.8	57.3	57.2	59.0	21.5	63.2	55.8	25.4	58.6
Sept	62.3	63.0	70.3	39.3	72.7	56.1	40.3	57.2	57.1	59.2	20.2	63.7	55.5	23.6	58.5
Oct	62.3	63.1	70.5	39.9	72.9	56.1	40.0	57.2	57.4	59.4	21.5	63.7	55.5	23.3	58.5
Nov	62.5	63.2	70.7	40.4	73.0	56.2	40.2	57.3	56.9	59.3	21.8	63.5	55.0	23.4	58.0
Dec	62.4	63.2	70.5	38.4	73.0	56.2	41.0	57.3	56.9	59.7	19.1	63.4	55.2	23.0	58.2
2005: Jan	62.4	63.2	70.5	38.5	73.0	56.2	41.6	57.2	56.9	58.7	22.2	62.8	55.4	22.4	58.5
Feb	62.3	63.2	70.5	37.8	73.1	56.1	41.5	57.2	56.7	58.7	21.2	63.0	55.1	20.3	58.3
Mar	62.4	63.2	70.8	38.7	73.3	56.0	41.6	57.0	57.1	59.5	22.7	63.7	55.2	22.7	58.3
Apr	62.6	63.4	70.9	38.6	73.4	56.2	41.1	57.3	57.6	60.4	22.7	64.7	55.3	20.9	58.5
May	62.7	63.4	71.0	38.3	73.5	56.3	41.9	57.3	58.0	60.8	22.3	65.2	55.8	21.6	59.0
June	62.7	63.4	71.0	38.9	73.5	56.1	42.1	57.1	58.1	60.9	21.1	65.5	55.8	23.3	58.9
July	62.8	63.5	70.9	38.7	73.4	56.5	42.2	57.5	58.7	61.9	19.2	66.8	56.2	25.0	59.1
Aug	62.9	63.6	71.0	38.9	73.5	56.5	42.7	57.5	58.2	61.3	18.9	66.1	55.8	22.2	58.9
Sept	62.8	63.5	71.0	39.0	73.2	56.6	43.2	57.5	58.1	60.7	19.1	65.5	55.9	20.2	59.3
Oct	62.8	63.4	70.8	38.4	73.3	56.4	41.4	57.5	58.5	60.5	18.3	65.3	56.8	23.0	60.0
Nov	62.8	63.4	70.8	39.3	73.3	56.5	41.1	57.6	57.6	60.1	19.5	63.8	55.7	22.1	58.9
Dec	62.8	63.5	70.9	39.7	73.3	56.5	40.5	57.6	57.6	60.0	23.4	64.2	55.6	24.1	58.6

[1] Civilian employment as percent of civilian noninstitutional population in group specified.
[2] See footnote 1, Table B–37.

Note.—Data relate to persons 16 years of age and over.
See footnote 5 and Note, Table B–35.

Source: Department of Labor, Bureau of Labor Statistics.

TABLE B–42.—*Civilian unemployment rate, 1959–2005*

[Percent;[1] monthly data seasonally adjusted, except as noted by NSA]

Year or month	All civilian workers	Males Total	Males 16–19 years	Males 20 years and over	Females Total	Females 16–19 years	Females 20 years and over	Both sexes 16–19 years	White[2]	Black and other[2]	Black or African American[2]	Asian (NSA)[2]	Hispanic or Latino ethnicity[3]	Married men, spouse present	Women who maintain families (NSA)
1959	5.5	5.2	15.3	4.7	5.9	13.5	5.2	14.6	4.8	10.7	....	....	....	3.6	....
1960	5.5	5.4	15.3	4.7	5.9	13.9	5.1	14.7	5.0	10.2	....	....	....	3.7	....
1961	6.7	6.4	17.1	5.7	7.2	16.3	6.3	16.8	6.0	12.4	....	....	....	4.6	....
1962	5.5	5.2	14.7	4.6	6.2	14.6	5.4	14.7	4.9	10.9	....	....	....	3.6	....
1963	5.7	5.2	17.2	4.5	6.5	17.2	5.4	17.2	5.0	10.8	....	....	....	3.4	....
1964	5.2	4.6	15.8	3.9	6.2	16.6	5.2	16.2	4.6	9.6	....	....	....	2.8	....
1965	4.5	4.0	14.1	3.2	5.5	15.7	4.5	14.8	4.1	8.1	....	....	....	2.4	....
1966	3.8	3.2	11.7	2.5	4.8	14.1	3.8	12.8	3.4	7.3	....	....	....	1.9	....
1967	3.8	3.1	12.3	2.3	5.2	13.5	4.2	12.9	3.4	7.4	....	....	....	1.8	4.9
1968	3.6	2.9	11.6	2.2	4.8	14.0	3.8	12.7	3.2	6.7	....	....	....	1.6	4.4
1969	3.5	2.8	11.4	2.1	4.7	13.3	3.7	12.2	3.1	6.4	....	....	....	1.5	4.4
1970	4.9	4.4	15.0	3.5	5.9	15.6	4.8	15.3	4.5	8.2	....	....	....	2.6	5.4
1971	5.9	5.3	16.6	4.4	6.9	17.2	5.7	16.9	5.4	9.9	....	....	....	3.2	7.3
1972	5.6	5.0	15.9	4.0	6.6	16.7	5.4	16.2	5.1	10.0	10.4	....	....	2.8	7.2
1973	4.9	4.2	13.9	3.3	6.0	15.3	4.9	14.5	4.3	9.0	9.4	....	7.5	2.3	7.1
1974	5.6	4.9	15.6	3.8	6.7	16.6	5.5	16.0	5.0	9.9	10.5	....	8.1	2.7	7.0
1975	8.5	7.9	20.1	6.8	9.3	19.7	8.0	19.9	7.8	13.8	14.8	....	12.2	5.1	10.0
1976	7.7	7.1	19.2	5.9	8.6	18.7	7.4	19.0	7.0	13.1	14.0	....	11.5	4.2	10.1
1977	7.1	6.3	17.3	5.2	8.2	18.3	7.0	17.8	6.2	13.1	14.0	....	10.1	3.6	9.4
1978	6.1	5.3	15.8	4.3	7.2	17.1	6.0	16.4	5.2	11.9	12.8	....	9.1	2.8	8.5
1979	5.8	5.1	15.9	4.2	6.8	16.4	5.7	16.1	5.1	11.3	12.3	....	8.3	2.8	8.3
1980	7.1	6.9	18.3	5.9	7.4	17.2	6.4	17.8	6.3	13.1	14.3	....	10.1	4.2	9.2
1981	7.6	7.4	20.1	6.3	7.9	19.0	6.8	19.6	6.7	14.2	15.6	....	10.4	4.3	10.4
1982	9.7	9.9	24.4	8.8	9.4	21.9	8.3	23.2	8.6	17.3	18.9	....	13.8	6.5	11.7
1983	9.6	9.9	23.3	8.9	9.2	21.3	8.1	22.4	8.4	17.8	19.5	....	13.7	6.5	12.2
1984	7.5	7.4	19.6	6.6	7.6	18.0	6.8	18.9	6.5	14.4	15.9	....	10.7	4.6	10.3
1985	7.2	7.0	19.5	6.2	7.4	17.6	6.6	18.6	6.2	13.7	15.1	....	10.5	4.3	10.4
1986	7.0	6.9	19.0	6.1	7.1	17.6	6.2	18.3	6.0	13.1	14.5	....	10.6	4.4	9.8
1987	6.2	6.2	17.8	5.4	6.2	15.9	5.4	16.9	5.3	11.6	13.0	....	8.8	3.9	9.2
1988	5.5	5.5	16.0	4.8	5.6	14.4	4.9	15.3	4.7	10.4	11.7	....	8.2	3.3	8.1
1989	5.3	5.2	15.9	4.5	5.4	14.0	4.7	15.0	4.5	10.0	11.4	....	8.0	3.0	8.1
1990	5.6	5.7	16.3	5.0	5.5	14.7	4.9	15.5	4.8	10.1	11.4	....	8.2	3.4	8.3
1991	6.8	7.2	19.8	6.4	6.4	17.5	5.7	18.7	6.1	11.1	12.5	....	10.0	4.4	9.3
1992	7.5	7.9	21.5	7.1	7.0	18.6	6.3	20.1	6.6	12.7	14.2	....	11.6	5.1	10.0
1993	6.9	7.2	20.4	6.4	6.6	17.5	5.9	19.0	6.1	11.7	13.0	....	10.8	4.4	9.7
1994	6.1	6.2	19.0	5.4	6.0	16.2	5.4	17.6	5.3	10.5	11.5	....	9.9	3.7	8.9
1995	5.6	5.6	18.4	4.8	5.6	16.1	4.9	17.3	4.9	9.6	10.4	....	9.3	3.3	8.0
1996	5.4	5.4	18.1	4.6	5.4	15.2	4.8	16.7	4.7	9.3	10.5	....	8.9	3.0	8.2
1997	4.9	4.9	16.9	4.2	5.0	15.0	4.4	16.0	4.2	8.8	10.0	....	7.7	2.7	8.1
1998	4.5	4.4	16.2	3.7	4.6	12.9	4.1	14.6	3.9	7.8	8.9	....	7.2	2.4	7.2
1999	4.2	4.1	14.7	3.5	4.3	13.2	3.8	13.9	3.7	7.0	8.0	....	6.4	2.2	6.4
2000	4.0	3.9	14.0	3.3	4.1	12.1	3.6	13.1	3.5	....	7.6	3.6	5.7	2.0	5.9
2001	4.7	4.8	16.0	4.2	4.7	13.4	4.1	14.7	4.2	....	8.6	4.5	6.6	2.7	6.6
2002	5.8	5.9	18.1	5.3	5.6	14.9	5.1	16.5	5.1	....	10.2	5.9	7.5	3.6	8.0
2003	6.0	6.3	19.3	5.6	5.7	15.6	5.1	17.5	5.2	....	10.8	6.0	7.7	3.8	8.5
2004	5.5	5.6	18.4	5.0	5.4	15.5	4.9	17.0	4.8	....	10.4	4.4	7.0	3.1	8.0
2005	5.1	5.1	18.6	4.4	5.1	14.5	4.6	16.6	4.4	....	10.0	4.0	6.0	2.8	7.8
2004: Jan	5.7	5.7	17.6	5.1	5.6	16.4	5.1	17.0	5.0	....	10.3	5.2	7.3	3.3	8.3
Feb	5.6	5.7	17.1	5.1	5.5	16.0	4.9	16.6	4.9	....	9.6	4.7	7.4	3.3	8.1
Mar	5.7	5.8	18.4	5.2	5.7	15.0	5.2	16.7	5.1	....	10.2	4.2	7.4	3.2	8.4
Apr	5.5	5.7	18.6	5.1	5.4	14.4	4.9	16.5	4.9	....	9.8	4.4	7.1	3.2	7.5
May	5.6	5.8	18.6	5.2	5.3	15.3	4.8	17.0	4.9	....	10.0	4.2	7.0	3.2	7.4
June	5.6	5.6	18.0	5.0	5.6	15.8	5.0	16.9	5.0	....	10.2	5.0	6.7	3.2	8.2
July	5.5	5.6	17.8	5.0	5.5	17.7	4.8	17.8	4.8	....	11.1	4.3	6.9	3.3	9.0
Aug	5.4	5.6	18.2	5.0	5.2	15.7	4.7	16.9	4.7	....	10.5	3.6	6.9	3.1	8.3
Sept	5.4	5.6	18.5	5.0	5.2	15.1	4.7	16.8	4.7	....	10.4	4.3	7.0	3.0	8.2
Oct	5.4	5.6	19.3	4.9	5.3	14.8	4.8	17.1	4.6	....	10.8	4.8	6.7	3.0	7.8
Nov	5.4	5.5	18.3	4.9	5.2	14.4	4.7	16.5	4.6	....	10.7	4.2	6.6	3.0	7.7
Dec	5.4	5.6	20.9	4.9	5.2	14.8	4.7	17.9	4.6	....	10.8	4.1	6.5	3.0	7.1
2005: Jan	5.2	5.3	18.1	4.7	5.1	14.2	4.6	16.2	4.5	....	10.5	4.2	6.2	3.0	8.2
Feb	5.4	5.6	20.6	4.9	5.2	14.5	4.7	17.6	4.6	....	10.8	4.5	6.3	2.9	8.0
Mar	5.1	5.3	20.0	4.5	5.0	13.7	4.5	16.9	4.4	....	10.3	3.9	5.7	2.9	8.0
Apr	5.1	5.1	20.2	4.4	5.2	14.9	4.6	17.6	4.4	....	10.3	3.9	6.4	2.6	7.7
May	5.1	5.1	19.7	4.4	5.2	15.7	4.6	17.7	4.4	....	10.0	3.9	5.9	2.7	7.9
June	5.0	5.0	18.7	4.3	5.1	13.8	4.6	16.3	4.3	....	10.3	4.0	5.8	2.6	8.2
July	5.0	4.9	18.3	4.3	5.1	13.8	4.7	16.0	4.3	....	9.4	5.2	5.5	2.7	8.8
Aug	4.9	4.9	18.0	4.3	4.9	14.7	4.4	16.4	4.2	....	9.7	3.6	5.8	2.9	7.2
Sept	5.1	5.1	17.4	4.5	5.1	14.3	4.6	15.8	4.5	....	9.5	4.1	6.5	2.7	7.6
Oct	4.9	4.8	16.5	4.3	5.1	15.2	4.6	15.9	4.4	....	9.1	3.1	5.9	2.6	7.3
Nov	5.0	5.0	19.1	4.3	5.1	15.0	4.6	17.1	4.2	....	10.6	3.6	6.1	2.6	7.2
Dec	4.9	4.9	16.0	4.3	5.0	14.4	4.5	15.2	4.3	....	9.3	3.8	6.0	2.6	6.9

[1] Unemployed as percent of civilian labor force in group specified.
[2] See footnote 1, Table B–37.
[3] Persons whose ethnicity is identified as Hispanic or Latino may be of any race.

Note.—Data relate to persons 16 years of age and over.
See footnote 5 and Note, Table B–35.
NSA indicates data are not seasonally adjusted.

Source: Department of Labor, Bureau of Labor Statistics.

TABLE B–43.—*Civilian unemployment rate by demographic characteristic, 1965–2005*

[Percent;[1] monthly data seasonally adjusted]

Year or month	All civilian workers	White[2] Total	White Males Total	White Males 16-19 years	White Males 20 years and over	White Females Total	White Females 16-19 years	White Females 20 years and over	Black Total	Black Males Total	Black Males 16-19 years	Black Males 20 years and over	Black Females Total	Black Females 16-19 years	Black Females 20 years and over
									Black and other						
1965	4.5	4.1	3.6	12.9	2.9	5.0	14.0	4.0	8.1	7.4	23.3	6.0	9.2	31.7	7.5
1966	3.8	3.4	2.8	10.5	2.2	4.3	12.1	3.3	7.3	6.3	21.3	4.9	8.7	31.3	6.6
1967	3.8	3.4	2.7	10.7	2.1	4.6	11.5	3.8	7.4	6.0	23.9	4.3	9.1	29.6	7.1
1968	3.6	3.2	2.6	10.1	2.0	4.3	12.1	3.4	6.7	5.6	22.1	3.9	8.3	28.7	6.3
1969	3.5	3.1	2.5	10.0	1.9	4.2	11.5	3.4	6.4	5.3	21.4	3.7	7.8	27.6	5.8
1970	4.9	4.5	4.0	13.7	3.2	5.4	13.4	4.4	8.2	7.3	25.0	5.6	9.3	34.5	6.9
1971	5.9	5.4	4.9	15.1	4.0	6.3	15.1	5.3	9.9	9.1	28.8	7.3	10.9	35.4	8.7
1972	5.6	5.1	4.5	14.2	3.6	5.9	14.2	4.9	10.0	8.9	29.7	6.9	11.4	38.4	8.8
									Black or African American[2]						
1972	5.6	5.1	4.5	14.2	3.6	5.9	14.2	4.9	10.4	9.3	31.7	7.0	11.8	40.5	9.0
1973	4.9	4.3	3.8	12.3	3.0	5.3	13.0	4.3	9.4	8.0	27.8	6.0	11.1	36.1	8.6
1974	5.6	5.0	4.4	13.5	3.5	6.1	14.5	5.1	10.5	9.8	33.1	7.4	11.3	37.4	8.8
1975	8.5	7.8	7.2	18.3	6.2	8.6	17.4	7.5	14.8	14.8	38.1	12.5	14.8	41.0	12.2
1976	7.7	7.0	6.4	17.3	5.4	7.9	16.4	6.8	14.0	13.7	37.5	11.4	14.3	41.6	11.7
1977	7.1	6.2	5.5	15.0	4.7	7.3	15.9	6.2	14.0	13.3	39.2	10.7	14.9	43.4	12.3
1978	6.1	5.2	4.6	13.5	3.7	6.2	14.4	5.2	12.8	11.8	36.7	9.3	13.8	40.8	11.2
1979	5.8	5.1	4.5	13.9	3.6	5.9	14.0	5.0	12.3	11.4	34.2	9.3	13.3	39.1	10.9
1980	7.1	6.3	6.1	16.2	5.3	6.5	14.8	5.6	14.3	14.5	37.5	12.4	14.0	39.8	11.9
1981	7.6	6.7	6.5	17.9	5.6	6.9	16.6	5.9	15.6	15.7	40.7	13.5	15.6	42.2	13.4
1982	9.7	8.6	8.8	21.7	7.8	8.3	19.0	7.3	18.9	20.1	48.9	17.8	17.6	47.1	15.4
1983	9.6	8.4	8.8	20.2	7.9	7.9	18.3	6.9	19.5	20.3	48.8	18.1	18.6	48.2	16.5
1984	7.5	6.5	6.4	16.8	5.7	6.5	15.2	5.8	15.9	16.4	42.7	14.3	15.4	42.6	13.5
1985	7.2	6.2	6.1	16.5	5.4	6.4	14.8	5.7	15.1	15.3	41.0	13.2	14.9	39.2	13.1
1986	7.0	6.0	6.0	16.3	5.3	6.1	14.9	5.4	14.5	14.8	39.3	12.9	14.2	39.2	12.4
1987	6.2	5.3	5.4	15.5	4.8	5.2	13.4	4.6	13.0	12.7	34.4	11.1	13.2	34.9	11.6
1988	5.5	4.7	4.7	13.9	4.1	4.7	12.3	4.1	11.7	11.7	32.7	10.1	11.7	32.0	10.4
1989	5.3	4.5	4.5	13.7	3.9	4.5	11.5	4.0	11.4	11.5	31.9	10.0	11.4	33.0	9.8
1990	5.6	4.8	4.9	14.3	4.3	4.7	12.6	4.1	11.4	11.9	31.9	10.4	10.9	29.9	9.7
1991	6.8	6.1	6.5	17.6	5.8	5.6	15.2	5.0	12.5	13.0	36.3	11.5	12.0	36.0	10.6
1992	7.5	6.6	7.0	18.5	6.4	6.1	15.8	5.5	14.2	15.2	42.0	13.5	13.2	37.2	11.8
1993	6.9	6.1	6.3	17.7	5.7	5.7	14.7	5.2	13.0	13.8	40.1	12.1	12.1	37.4	10.7
1994	6.1	5.3	5.4	16.3	4.8	5.2	13.8	4.6	11.5	12.0	37.6	10.3	11.0	32.6	9.8
1995	5.6	4.9	4.9	15.6	4.3	4.8	13.4	4.3	10.4	10.6	37.1	8.8	10.2	34.3	8.6
1996	5.4	4.7	4.7	15.5	4.1	4.7	12.9	4.1	10.5	11.1	36.9	9.4	10.0	30.3	8.7
1997	4.9	4.2	4.2	14.3	3.6	4.2	12.8	3.7	10.0	10.2	36.5	8.5	9.9	28.7	8.8
1998	4.5	3.9	3.9	14.1	3.2	3.9	10.9	3.4	8.9	8.9	30.1	7.4	9.0	25.3	7.9
1999	4.2	3.7	3.6	12.6	3.0	3.8	11.3	3.3	8.0	8.2	30.9	6.7	7.8	25.1	6.8
2000	4.0	3.5	3.4	12.3	2.8	3.6	10.4	3.1	7.6	8.0	26.2	6.9	7.1	22.8	6.2
2001	4.7	4.2	4.2	13.9	3.7	4.1	11.4	3.6	8.6	9.3	30.4	8.0	8.1	27.5	7.0
2002	5.8	5.1	5.3	15.9	4.7	4.9	13.1	4.4	10.2	10.7	31.3	9.5	9.8	28.3	8.8
2003	6.0	5.2	5.6	17.1	5.0	4.8	13.3	4.4	10.8	11.6	36.0	10.3	10.2	30.3	9.2
2004	5.5	4.8	5.0	16.3	4.4	4.7	13.6	4.2	10.4	11.1	35.6	9.9	9.8	28.2	8.9
2005	5.1	4.4	4.4	16.1	3.8	4.4	12.3	3.9	10.0	10.5	36.3	9.2	9.5	30.3	8.5
2004: Jan	5.7	5.0	5.0	14.4	4.6	5.0	15.0	4.4	10.3	10.9	43.7	9.4	9.8	26.2	9.0
Feb	5.6	4.9	5.0	15.2	4.6	4.8	14.9	4.2	9.6	9.9	30.0	9.1	9.4	22.5	8.8
Mar	5.7	5.1	5.2	16.2	4.7	4.9	13.4	4.5	10.2	10.6	36.7	9.4	9.9	23.8	9.3
Apr	5.5	4.9	5.2	17.5	4.6	4.7	13.2	4.2	9.8	10.2	30.3	9.4	9.3	25.5	8.6
May	5.6	4.9	5.3	18.1	4.7	4.5	12.5	4.0	10.0	10.3	30.6	9.4	9.7	31.9	8.6
June	5.6	5.0	5.1	16.3	4.5	4.9	13.3	4.4	10.2	10.6	34.0	9.5	9.9	32.1	8.8
July	5.5	4.8	4.8	15.7	4.3	4.7	14.5	4.2	11.1	11.9	36.9	10.6	10.5	37.2	9.1
Aug	5.4	4.7	4.9	16.0	4.3	4.5	14.5	4.0	10.5	11.6	34.0	10.5	9.5	23.8	8.8
Sept	5.4	4.7	4.8	15.9	4.3	4.5	13.7	4.0	10.4	11.4	36.3	10.1	9.5	20.8	9.0
Oct	5.4	4.6	4.8	17.5	4.2	4.4	12.3	3.9	10.8	11.7	37.2	10.3	10.0	32.1	8.9
Nov	5.4	4.6	4.7	15.4	4.2	4.5	13.2	4.1	10.7	11.8	37.3	10.3	9.8	26.8	9.0
Dec	5.4	4.6	4.8	18.2	4.1	4.4	13.2	3.9	10.8	12.0	39.4	10.6	9.7	25.8	9.0
2005: Jan	5.2	4.5	4.6	16.4	4.0	4.3	11.9	3.9	10.5	11.2	29.8	10.3	9.9	31.5	8.8
Feb	5.4	4.6	4.7	18.1	4.1	4.4	12.8	4.0	10.8	11.8	35.0	10.6	9.9	28.9	9.1
Mar	5.1	4.4	4.6	17.7	3.9	4.1	10.9	3.8	10.3	10.8	36.1	9.3	9.9	29.7	9.0
Apr	5.1	4.4	4.4	17.5	3.8	4.4	12.8	4.0	10.3	10.9	38.5	9.2	9.8	32.9	8.7
May	5.1	4.4	4.4	17.4	3.8	4.4	12.9	3.9	10.0	10.6	36.8	9.1	9.6	35.0	8.3
June	5.0	4.3	4.2	15.8	3.7	4.4	12.3	3.9	10.3	11.1	37.5	9.7	9.6	26.9	8.8
July	5.0	4.3	4.2	15.5	3.7	4.4	11.7	4.0	9.4	9.7	38.9	8.3	9.1	27.4	8.2
Aug	4.9	4.2	4.3	15.3	3.7	4.2	12.4	3.7	9.7	10.0	39.5	8.6	9.3	32.6	8.2
Sept	5.1	4.5	4.5	15.3	4.0	4.4	11.4	4.0	9.5	9.8	33.7	8.7	9.2	32.5	8.1
Oct	4.9	4.4	4.3	15.1	3.8	4.5	13.3	4.0	9.1	9.7	35.0	8.5	8.6	30.3	7.5
Nov	5.0	4.2	4.2	15.1	3.8	4.3	12.6	3.9	10.6	11.3	44.9	9.4	10.0	31.5	9.0
Dec	4.9	4.3	4.3	13.8	3.8	4.3	12.9	3.8	9.3	9.3	23.6	8.6	9.3	25.2	8.5

[1] Unemployed as percent of civilian labor force in group specified.
[2] See footnote 1, Table B–37.

Note.—Data relate to persons 16 years of age and over.
See footnote 5 and Note, Table B–35.

Source: Department of Labor, Bureau of Labor Statistics.

TABLE B–44.—*Unemployment by duration and reason, 1959–2005*

[Thousands of persons, except as noted; monthly data seasonally adjusted[1]]

Year or month	Unemployment	Duration of unemployment						Reason for unemployment					
		Less than 5 weeks	5-14 weeks	15-26 weeks	27 weeks and over	Average (mean) duration (weeks)	Median duration (weeks)	Job losers[3]			Job leavers	Reentrants	New entrants
								Total	On layoff	Other			
1959	3,740	1,585	1,114	469	571	14.4	....	....	....	....	....	....	....
1960	3,852	1,719	1,176	503	454	12.8	....	....	....	....	....	....	....
1961	4,714	1,806	1,376	728	804	15.6	....	....	....	....	....	....	....
1962	3,911	1,663	1,134	534	585	14.7	....	....	....	....	....	....	....
1963	4,070	1,751	1,231	535	553	14.0	....	....	....	....	....	....	....
1964	3,786	1,697	1,117	491	482	13.3	....	....	....	....	....	....	....
1965	3,366	1,628	983	404	351	11.8	....	....	....	....	....	....	....
1966	2,875	1,573	779	287	239	10.4	....	....	....	....	....	....	....
1967[2]	2,975	1,634	893	271	177	8.7	2.3	1,229	394	836	438	945	396
1968	2,817	1,594	810	256	156	8.4	4.5	1,070	334	736	431	909	407
1969	2,832	1,629	827	242	133	7.8	4.4	1,017	339	678	436	965	413
1970	4,093	2,139	1,290	428	235	8.6	4.9	1,811	675	1,137	550	1,228	504
1971	5,016	2,245	1,585	668	519	11.3	6.3	2,323	735	1,588	590	1,472	630
1972	4,882	2,242	1,472	601	566	12.0	6.2	2,108	582	1,526	641	1,456	677
1973	4,365	2,224	1,314	483	343	10.0	5.2	1,694	472	1,221	683	1,340	649
1974	5,156	2,604	1,597	574	381	9.8	5.2	2,242	746	1,495	768	1,463	681
1975	7,929	2,940	2,484	1,303	1,203	14.2	8.4	4,386	1,671	2,714	827	1,892	823
1976	7,406	2,844	2,196	1,018	1,348	15.8	8.2	3,679	1,050	2,628	903	1,928	895
1977	6,991	2,919	2,132	913	1,028	14.3	7.0	3,166	865	2,300	909	1,963	953
1978	6,202	2,865	1,923	766	648	11.9	5.9	2,585	712	1,873	874	1,857	885
1979	6,137	2,950	1,946	706	535	10.8	5.4	2,635	851	1,784	880	1,806	817
1980	7,637	3,295	2,470	1,052	820	11.9	6.5	3,947	1,488	2,459	891	1,927	872
1981	8,273	3,449	2,539	1,122	1,162	13.7	6.9	4,267	1,430	2,837	923	2,102	981
1982	10,678	3,883	3,311	1,708	1,776	15.6	8.7	6,268	2,127	4,141	840	2,384	1,185
1983	10,717	3,570	2,937	1,652	2,559	20.0	10.1	6,258	1,780	4,478	830	2,412	1,216
1984	8,539	3,350	2,451	1,104	1,634	18.2	7.9	4,421	1,171	3,250	823	2,184	1,110
1985	8,312	3,498	2,509	1,025	1,280	15.6	6.8	4,139	1,157	2,982	877	2,256	1,039
1986	8,237	3,448	2,557	1,045	1,187	15.0	6.9	4,033	1,090	2,943	1,015	2,160	1,029
1987	7,425	3,246	2,196	943	1,040	14.5	6.5	3,566	943	2,623	965	1,974	920
1988	6,701	3,084	2,007	801	809	13.5	5.9	3,092	851	2,241	983	1,809	816
1989	6,528	3,174	1,978	730	646	11.9	4.8	2,983	850	2,133	1,024	1,843	677
1990	7,047	3,265	2,257	822	703	12.0	5.3	3,387	1,028	2,359	1,041	1,930	688
1991	8,628	3,480	2,791	1,246	1,111	13.7	6.8	4,694	1,292	3,402	1,004	2,139	792
1992	9,613	3,376	2,830	1,453	1,954	17.7	8.7	5,389	1,260	4,129	1,002	2,285	937
1993	8,940	3,262	2,584	1,297	1,798	18.0	8.3	4,848	1,115	3,733	976	2,198	919
1994	7,996	2,728	2,408	1,237	1,623	18.8	9.2	3,815	977	2,838	791	2,786	604
1995	7,404	2,700	2,342	1,085	1,278	16.6	8.3	3,476	1,030	2,446	824	2,525	579
1996	7,236	2,633	2,287	1,053	1,262	16.7	8.3	3,370	1,021	2,349	774	2,512	580
1997	6,739	2,538	2,138	995	1,067	15.8	8.0	3,037	931	2,106	795	2,338	569
1998	6,210	2,622	1,950	763	875	14.5	6.7	2,822	866	1,957	734	2,132	520
1999	5,880	2,568	1,832	755	725	13.4	6.4	2,622	848	1,774	783	2,005	469
2000	5,692	2,558	1,815	669	649	12.6	5.9	2,517	852	1,664	780	1,961	434
2001	6,801	2,853	2,196	951	801	13.1	6.8	3,476	1,067	2,409	835	2,031	459
2002	8,378	2,893	2,580	1,369	1,535	16.6	9.1	4,607	1,124	3,483	866	2,368	536
2003	8,774	2,785	2,612	1,442	1,936	19.2	10.1	4,838	1,121	3,717	818	2,477	641
2004	8,149	2,696	2,382	1,293	1,779	19.6	9.8	4,197	998	3,199	858	2,408	686
2005	7,591	2,667	2,304	1,130	1,490	18.4	8.9	3,667	933	2,734	872	2,386	666
2004: Jan	8,345	2,657	2,397	1,446	1,903	19.8	10.6	4,350	1,027	3,323	815	2,559	677
Feb	8,186	2,419	2,422	1,367	1,865	20.2	10.2	4,258	1,053	3,205	821	2,411	660
Mar	8,397	2,638	2,421	1,333	1,982	19.8	10.2	4,548	1,029	3,519	847	2,429	628
Apr	8,140	2,768	2,387	1,190	1,787	19.6	9.4	4,362	1,005	3,357	825	2,306	638
May	8,178	2,683	2,390	1,274	1,794	19.8	9.9	4,225	963	3,262	851	2,446	705
June	8,247	2,684	2,371	1,325	1,774	19.9	10.8	4,125	1,004	3,121	904	2,443	651
July	8,182	2,868	2,438	1,227	1,709	18.8	8.9	4,243	1,056	3,187	905	2,297	701
Aug	8,000	2,638	2,536	1,247	1,671	19.2	9.4	4,001	977	3,023	890	2,419	711
Sept	7,981	2,760	2,226	1,220	1,718	19.6	9.6	4,007	893	3,114	825	2,414	708
Oct	8,040	2,735	2,297	1,267	1,752	19.6	9.5	4,054	945	3,108	824	2,411	744
Nov	7,974	2,610	2,360	1,258	1,712	19.8	9.7	4,040	955	3,085	865	2,373	704
Dec	8,040	2,887	2,285	1,276	1,650	19.4	9.4	4,029	962	3,067	938	2,367	711
2005: Jan	7,723	2,597	2,348	1,191	1,630	19.2	9.3	3,982	962	3,020	815	2,336	621
Feb	7,986	2,743	2,320	1,236	1,626	19.1	9.2	3,886	960	2,927	950	2,406	741
Mar	7,616	2,498	2,318	1,157	1,636	19.3	9.2	3,759	955	2,804	855	2,368	706
Apr	7,644	2,670	2,271	1,091	1,597	19.6	8.9	3,677	841	2,836	894	2,348	735
May	7,629	2,694	2,270	1,122	1,528	18.6	9.1	3,664	898	2,766	952	2,365	699
June	7,493	2,661	2,339	1,053	1,335	17.2	9.1	3,666	974	2,692	838	2,240	654
July	7,494	2,616	2,452	1,069	1,414	17.7	8.9	3,626	954	2,673	825	2,411	627
Aug	7,367	2,544	2,268	1,229	1,444	18.9	9.4	3,474	874	2,600	839	2,455	633
Sept	7,648	2,751	2,253	1,120	1,464	18.2	8.5	3,697	970	2,726	874	2,423	626
Oct	7,418	2,708	2,263	1,045	1,432	18.0	8.6	3,508	944	2,564	889	2,349	654
Nov	7,572	2,779	2,268	1,108	1,383	17.6	8.5	3,455	899	2,556	900	2,538	679
Dec	7,375	2,764	2,240	1,068	1,350	17.3	8.5	3,486	935	2,552	841	2,430	644

[1] Because of independent seasonal adjustment of the various series, detail will not add to totals.
[2] Data for 1967 by reason for unemployment are not equal to total unemployment.
[3] Beginning January 1994, job losers and persons who completed temporary jobs.

Note.—Data relate to persons 16 years of age and over.
See footnote 5 and Note, Table B-35.

Source: Department of Labor, Bureau of Labor Statistics.

TABLE B–45.—*Unemployment insurance programs, selected data, 1978–2005*

Year or month	All programs			State programs					
	Covered employment [1]	Insured unemployment (weekly average) [2][3]	Total benefits paid (millions of dollars) [2][4]	Insured unemployment [3]	Initial claims	Exhaustions [5]	Insured unemployment as percent of covered employment	Benefits paid	
								Total (millions of dollars) [4]	Average weekly check (dollars) [6]
	Thousands			Weekly average; thousands					
1978	88,804	2,645	9,007	2,359	346	39	3.3	7,717	83.67
1979	92,062	2,592	9,401	2,434	388	39	2.9	8,613	89.67
1980	92,659	3,837	16,175	3,350	488	59	3.9	13,761	98.95
1981	93,300	3,410	15,287	3,047	460	57	3.5	13,262	106.70
1982	91,628	4,592	24,491	4,059	583	80	4.6	20,649	119.34
1983	91,898	3,774	20,968	3,395	438	80	3.9	18,549	123.59
1984	96,474	2,560	13,739	2,475	377	50	2.8	13,237	123.47
1985	99,186	2,699	15,217	2,617	397	49	2.9	14,707	128.11
1986	101,099	2,739	16,563	2,643	378	52	2.8	15,950	135.65
1987	103,936	2,369	14,684	2,300	328	46	2.4	14,211	140.39
1988	107,156	2,135	13,481	2,081	310	38	2.0	13,086	144.74
1989	109,929	2,205	14,569	2,158	330	37	2.1	14,205	151.43
1990	111,500	2,575	18,387	2,522	388	45	2.4	17,932	161.20
1991	109,606	3,406	26,327	3,342	447	67	3.2	25,479	169.56
1992	110,167	3,348	[7] 26,035	3,245	408	74	3.1	25,056	173.38
1993	112,146	2,845	[7] 22,629	2,751	341	62	2.6	21,661	179.41
1994	115,255	2,746	22,508	2,670	340	57	2.4	21,537	181.91
1995	118,068	2,639	21,991	2,572	357	51	2.3	21,226	187.04
1996	120,567	2,656	22,495	2,595	356	53	2.2	21,820	189.27
1997	121,044	2,370	20,324	2,323	323	48	1.9	19,735	192.84
1998	124,184	2,260	19,941	2,222	321	44	1.8	19,431	200.58
1999	127,042	2,223	21,024	2,188	298	44	1.7	20,563	212.10
2000	129,877	2,146	20,983	2,110	301	41	1.6	20,507	221.01
2001	129,636	3,012	32,228	2,974	404	54	2.3	31,680	238.07
2002	128,234	3,624	[8] 42,980	3,585	407	85	2.8	42,132	256.79
2003	127,796	3,573	[8] 42,413	3,531	404	85	2.8	41,358	261.67
2004	129,278	2,999	[8] 35,297	2,950	345	68	2.3	34,432	262.50
2005 p	....	2,710	....	2,663	328	55	....	....	....
2004: Jan	....	3,709	3,696.7	3,160	355	82	2.5	3,608.3	264.44
Feb	....	3,982	3,630.8	3,131	356	79	2.5	3,561.5	266.02
Mar	....	3,576	3,880.9	3,036	344	77	2.4	3,811.8	266.00
Apr	....	2,974	3,007.0	2,982	345	73	2.4	2,943.0	263.99
May	....	2,846	2,650.9	2,938	344	70	2.3	2,592.5	263.05
June	....	2,871	2,856.8	2,924	343	68	2.3	2,794.0	260.10
July	....	2,726	2,630.9	2,888	340	65	2.3	2,572.7	258.05
Aug	....	2,917	2,773.7	2,875	339	66	2.3	2,706.0	255.63
Sept	....	2,403	2,391.1	2,846	343	56	2.3	2,329.4	261.80
Oct	....	2,429	2,224.2	2,797	339	57	2.2	2,161.9	262.19
Nov	....	2,624	2,543.6	2,756	336	59	2.2	2,473.4	261.36
Dec	....	2,696	2,826.5	2,738	332	55	2.2	2,753.4	264.25
2005: Jan	....	3,659	3,378.7	2,723	329	66	2.2	3,303.4	268.39
Feb	....	3,262	3,085.7	2,674	309	58	2.1	3,019.4	271.74
Mar	....	2,958	3,336.7	2,652	337	57	2.1	3,250.9	272.14
Apr	....	2,662	2,614.4	2,593	323	60	2.0	2,553.8	270.13
May	....	2,589	2,544.6	2,590	334	59	2.0	2,480.7	268.95
June	....	2,411	2,466.4	2,600	323	53	2.0	2,404.9	266.53
July	....	2,619	2,400.7	2,582	317	57	2.0	2,338.3	263.30
Aug	....	2,494	2,619.7	2,581	318	54	2.0	2,544.4	262.78
Sept	....	2,228	2,196.1	2,774	398	46	2.2	2,132.8	263.75
Oct	....	2,634	2,383.8	2,825	350	53	2.2	2,317.1	259.01
Nov	....	2,475	2,453.7	2,703	323	49	2.1	2,384.0	261.12
Dec p	....	2,617	2,651.4	2,672	318	49	2.1	2,578.6	267.20

** Monthly data are seasonally adjusted.

[1] Through 1996 includes persons under the State, UCFE (Federal employee, effective January 1955), RRB (Railroad Retirement Board) programs, and UCX (unemployment compensation for ex-servicemembers, effective October 1958) programs. Beginning 1997, covered employment data are State and UCFE programs only. Workers covered by State programs account for about 97 percent of wage and salary earners. Covered employment data beginning 2001 are based on the North American Industry Classification System (NAICS). Prior data are based on the Standard Industrial Classification (SIC).

[2] Includes State, UCFE, RR, and UCX. Also includes Federal and State extended benefit programs. Does not include FSB (Federal supplemental benefits), SUA (special unemployment assistance), Federal Supplemental Compensation, Emergency Unemployment Compensation, and TEUC (Temporary Extended Unemployment Compensation) programs.

[3] Covered workers who have completed at least 1 week of unemployment.

[4] Annual data are net amounts and monthly data are gross amounts.

[5] Individuals receiving final payments in benefit year.

[6] For total unemployment only.

[7] Including Emergency Unemployment Compensation, total benefits paid for 1992 and 1993 would be approximately (in millions of dollars): for 1992, 39,990 and for 1993, 34,876.

[8] Including Temporary Extended Unemployment Compensation, total benefits paid (not including RRB program) would be approximately (in millions of dollars): for 2002, 52,709; 2003, 63,097; and 2004, 37,932.

Note.—Insured unemployment and initial claims programs include Puerto Rican sugar cane workers.

Source: Department of Labor, Employment and Training Administration.

[Thousands of persons; monthly data seasonally adjusted]

Year or month	Total	Goods-producing industries						Service-providing industries		
		Total	Natural re-sources and mining	Con-struc-tion	Manufacturing			Total	Trade, transpor-tation, and utilities [1]	
					Total	Dura ble goods	Non-dura ble goods		Total	Retail trade
1959	53,374	19,163	789	3,050	15,325	8,988	6,337	34,211	10,960	5,453
1960	54,296	19,182	771	2,973	15,438	9,071	6,367	35,114	11,147	5,589
1961	54,105	18,647	728	2,908	15,011	8,711	6,300	35,458	11,040	5,560
1962	55,659	19,203	709	2,997	15,498	9,099	6,399	36,455	11,215	5,672
1963	56,764	19,385	694	3,060	15,631	9,226	6,405	37,379	11,367	5,781
1964	58,391	19,733	697	3,148	15,888	9,414	6,474	38,658	11,677	5,977
1965	60,874	20,595	694	3,284	16,617	9,973	6,644	40,279	12,139	6,262
1966	64,020	21,740	690	3,371	17,680	10,803	6,878	42,280	12,611	6,530
1967	65,931	21,882	679	3,305	17,897	10,952	6,945	44,049	12,950	6,711
1968	68,023	22,292	671	3,410	18,211	11,137	7,074	45,731	13,334	6,977
1969	70,512	22,893	683	3,637	18,573	11,396	7,177	47,619	13,853	7,295
1970	71,006	22,179	677	3,654	17,848	10,762	7,086	48,827	14,144	7,463
1971	71,335	21,602	658	3,770	17,174	10,229	6,944	49,734	14,318	7,657
1972	73,798	22,299	672	3,957	17,669	10,630	7,039	51,499	14,788	8,038
1973	76,912	23,450	693	4,167	18,589	11,414	7,176	53,462	15,349	8,371
1974	78,389	23,364	755	4,095	18,514	11,432	7,082	55,025	15,693	8,536
1975	77,069	21,318	802	3,608	16,909	10,266	6,643	55,751	15,606	8,600
1976	79,502	22,025	832	3,662	17,531	10,640	6,891	57,477	16,128	8,966
1977	82,593	22,972	865	3,940	18,167	11,132	7,035	59,620	16,765	9,359
1978	86,826	24,156	902	4,322	18,932	11,770	7,162	62,670	17,658	9,879
1979	89,932	24,997	1,008	4,562	19,426	12,220	7,206	64,935	18,303	10,180
1980	90,528	24,263	1,077	4,454	18,733	11,679	7,054	66,265	18,413	10,244
1981	91,289	24,118	1,180	4,304	18,634	11,611	7,023	67,172	18,604	10,364
1982	89,677	22,550	1,163	4,024	17,363	10,610	6,753	67,127	18,457	10,372
1983	90,280	22,110	997	4,065	17,048	10,326	6,722	68,171	18,668	10,635
1984	94,530	23,435	1,014	4,501	17,920	11,050	6,870	71,095	19,653	11,223
1985	97,511	23,585	974	4,793	17,819	11,034	6,784	73,926	20,379	11,733
1986	99,474	23,318	829	4,937	17,552	10,795	6,757	76,156	20,795	12,078
1987	102,088	23,470	771	5,090	17,609	10,767	6,842	78,618	21,302	12,419
1988	105,345	23,909	770	5,233	17,906	10,969	6,938	81,436	21,974	12,808
1989	108,014	24,045	750	5,309	17,985	11,004	6,981	83,969	22,510	13,108
1990	109,487	23,723	765	5,263	17,695	10,736	6,959	85,764	22,666	13,182
1991	108,374	22,588	739	4,780	17,068	10,219	6,849	85,787	22,281	12,896
1992	108,726	22,095	689	4,608	16,799	9,945	6,854	86,631	22,125	12,828
1993	110,844	22,219	666	4,779	16,774	9,900	6,873	88,625	22,378	13,021
1994	114,291	22,774	659	5,095	17,021	10,131	6,890	91,517	23,128	13,491
1995	117,298	23,156	641	5,274	17,241	10,372	6,869	94,142	23,834	13,897
1996	119,708	23,410	637	5,536	17,237	10,485	6,752	96,299	24,239	14,143
1997	122,776	23,886	654	5,813	17,419	10,704	6,716	98,890	24,700	14,389
1998	125,930	24,354	645	6,149	17,560	10,910	6,650	101,576	25,186	14,609
1999	128,993	24,465	598	6,545	17,322	10,830	6,492	104,528	25,771	14,970
2000	131,785	24,649	599	6,787	17,263	10,876	6,388	107,136	26,225	15,280
2001	131,826	23,873	606	6,826	16,441	10,335	6,107	107,952	25,983	15,239
2002	130,341	22,557	583	6,716	15,259	9,483	5,775	107,784	25,497	15,025
2003	129,999	21,816	572	6,735	14,510	8,963	5,547	108,182	25,287	14,917
2004	131,480	21,884	591	6,964	14,329	8,923	5,406	109,596	25,510	15,035
2005 ^P	133,631	22,141	629	7,233	14,279	8,950	5,329	111,490	25,833	15,174
2004: Jan	130,372	21,703	575	6,845	14,283	8,855	5,428	108,669	25,348	14,962
Feb	130,466	21,699	577	6,841	14,281	8,864	5,417	108,767	25,367	14,977
Mar	130,786	21,773	585	6,897	14,291	8,873	5,418	109,013	25,441	15,021
Apr	131,123	21,825	589	6,913	14,323	8,902	5,421	109,298	25,481	15,038
May	131,373	21,888	592	6,949	14,347	8,925	5,422	109,485	25,511	15,052
June	131,479	21,890	591	6,955	14,344	8,931	5,413	109,589	25,536	15,061
July	131,562	21,902	596	6,965	14,341	8,926	5,415	109,660	25,536	15,048
Aug	131,750	21,946	595	6,985	14,366	8,965	5,401	109,804	25,537	15,043
Sept	131,880	21,947	597	6,998	14,352	8,957	5,395	109,933	25,555	15,038
Oct	132,162	21,982	595	7,043	14,344	8,960	5,384	110,180	25,581	15,057
Nov	132,294	21,996	599	7,060	14,337	8,954	5,383	110,298	25,621	15,081
Dec	132,449	22,022	602	7,086	14,334	8,957	5,377	110,427	25,620	15,077
2005: Jan	132,573	22,004	607	7,090	14,307	8,942	5,365	110,569	25,652	15,081
Feb	132,873	22,066	612	7,133	14,321	8,962	5,359	110,807	25,714	15,125
Mar	132,995	22,093	619	7,159	14,315	8,957	5,358	110,902	25,743	15,129
Apr	133,287	22,130	623	7,207	14,300	8,954	5,346	111,157	25,797	15,158
May	133,413	22,138	624	7,213	14,301	8,961	5,340	111,275	25,842	15,186
June	133,588	22,134	628	7,230	14,276	8,947	5,329	111,454	25,854	15,197
July	133,865	22,134	629	7,235	14,270	8,940	5,330	111,731	25,922	15,249
Aug	134,013	22,159	632	7,267	14,260	8,945	5,315	111,854	25,910	15,231
Sept	134,030	22,164	636	7,284	14,244	8,934	5,310	111,866	25,870	15,183
Oct	134,055	22,197	641	7,299	14,257	8,954	5,303	111,858	25,870	15,178
Nov ^P	134,360	22,250	644	7,341	14,265	8,958	5,307	112,110	25,905	15,190
Dec ^P	134,468	22,262	647	7,332	14,283	8,973	5,310	112,206	25,880	15,175

[1] Includes wholesale trade, transportation and warehousing, and utilities, not shown separately.

Note.—Data in Tables B–46 and B–47 are based on reports from employing establishments and relate to full- and part-time wage and salary workers in nonagricultural establishments who received pay for any part of the pay period that includes the 12th of the month. Not comparable with labor force data (Tables B–35 through B–44), which include proprietors, self-employed persons, unpaid family workers, and private household workers; which count persons as employed when they are not at work because of industrial disputes, bad

See next page for continuation of table.

TABLE B–46.—*Employees on nonagricultural payrolls, by major industry, 1959–2005*—Continued

[Thousands of persons; monthly data seasonally adjusted]

Year or month	Infor-ma-tion	Finan-cial activi-ties	Profes-sional and busi-ness services	Educa-tion and health services	Leisure and hos-pitality	Other services	Government Total	Government Federal	Government State	Government Local
1959	1,718	2,454	3,591	2,822	3,365	1,107	8,192	2,342	1,484	4,366
1960	1,728	2,532	3,694	2,937	3,460	1,152	8,464	2,381	1,536	4,547
1961	1,693	2,590	3,744	3,030	3,468	1,188	8,706	2,391	1,607	4,708
1962	1,723	2,656	3,885	3,172	3,557	1,243	9,004	2,455	1,669	4,881
1963	1,735	2,731	3,990	3,288	3,639	1,288	9,341	2,473	1,747	5,121
1964	1,766	2,811	4,137	3,438	3,772	1,346	9,711	2,463	1,856	5,392
1965	1,824	2,878	4,306	3,587	3,951	1,404	10,191	2,495	1,996	5,700
1966	1,908	2,961	4,517	3,770	4,127	1,475	10,910	2,690	2,141	6,080
1967	1,955	3,087	4,720	3,986	4,269	1,558	11,525	2,852	2,302	6,371
1968	1,991	3,234	4,918	4,191	4,453	1,638	11,972	2,871	2,442	6,660
1969	2,048	3,404	5,156	4,428	4,670	1,731	12,330	2,893	2,533	6,904
1970	2,041	3,532	5,267	4,577	4,789	1,789	12,687	2,865	2,664	7,158
1971	2,009	3,651	5,328	4,675	4,914	1,827	13,012	2,828	2,747	7,437
1972	2,056	3,784	5,523	4,863	5,121	1,900	13,465	2,815	2,859	7,790
1973	2,135	3,920	5,774	5,092	5,341	1,990	13,862	2,794	2,923	8,146
1974	2,160	4,023	5,974	5,322	5,471	2,078	14,303	2,858	3,039	8,407
1975	2,061	4,047	6,034	5,497	5,544	2,144	14,820	2,882	3,179	8,758
1976	2,111	4,155	6,287	5,756	5,794	2,244	15,001	2,863	3,273	8,865
1977	2,185	4,348	6,587	6,052	6,065	2,359	15,258	2,859	3,377	9,023
1978	2,287	4,599	6,972	6,427	6,411	2,505	15,812	2,893	3,474	9,446
1979	2,375	4,843	7,312	6,767	6,631	2,637	16,068	2,894	3,541	9,633
1980	2,361	5,025	7,544	7,072	6,721	2,755	16,375	3,000	3,610	9,765
1981	2,382	5,163	7,782	7,357	6,840	2,865	16,180	2,922	3,640	9,619
1982	2,317	5,209	7,848	7,515	6,874	2,924	15,982	2,884	3,640	9,458
1983	2,253	5,334	8,039	7,766	7,078	3,021	16,011	2,915	3,662	9,434
1984	2,398	5,553	8,464	8,193	7,489	3,186	16,159	2,943	3,734	9,482
1985	2,437	5,815	8,871	8,657	7,869	3,366	16,533	3,014	3,832	9,687
1986	2,445	6,128	9,211	9,061	8,156	3,523	16,838	3,044	3,893	9,901
1987	2,507	6,385	9,608	9,515	8,446	3,699	17,156	3,089	3,967	10,100
1988	2,585	6,500	10,090	10,063	8,778	3,907	17,540	3,124	4,076	10,339
1989	2,622	6,562	10,555	10,616	9,062	4,116	17,927	3,136	4,182	10,609
1990	2,688	6,614	10,848	10,984	9,288	4,261	18,415	3,196	4,305	10,914
1991	2,677	6,558	10,714	11,506	9,256	4,249	18,545	3,110	4,355	11,081
1992	2,641	6,540	10,970	11,891	9,437	4,240	18,787	3,111	4,408	11,267
1993	2,668	6,709	11,495	12,303	9,732	4,350	18,989	3,063	4,488	11,438
1994	2,738	6,867	12,174	12,807	10,100	4,428	19,275	3,018	4,576	11,682
1995	2,843	6,827	12,844	13,289	10,501	4,572	19,432	2,949	4,635	11,849
1996	2,940	6,969	13,462	13,683	10,777	4,690	19,539	2,877	4,606	12,056
1997	3,084	7,178	14,335	14,087	11,018	4,825	19,664	2,806	4,582	12,276
1998	3,218	7,462	15,147	14,446	11,232	4,976	19,909	2,772	4,612	12,525
1999	3,419	7,648	15,957	14,798	11,543	5,087	20,307	2,769	4,709	12,829
2000	3,631	7,687	16,666	15,109	11,862	5,168	20,790	2,865	4,786	13,139
2001	3,629	7,807	16,476	15,645	12,036	5,258	21,118	2,764	4,905	13,449
2002	3,395	7,847	15,976	16,199	11,986	5,372	21,513	2,766	5,029	13,718
2003	3,188	7,977	15,987	16,588	12,173	5,401	21,583	2,761	5,002	13,820
2004	3,138	8,052	16,414	16,954	12,479	5,431	21,618	2,728	4,985	13,905
2005 ᵖ	3,142	8,227	16,935	17,344	12,748	5,467	21,795	2,719	5,030	14,046
2004: Jan	3,139	7,989	16,138	16,766	12,351	5,405	21,533	2,729	4,961	13,843
Feb	3,143	7,997	16,153	16,787	12,367	5,402	21,551	2,731	4,971	13,849
Mar	3,136	8,005	16,184	16,833	12,412	5,420	21,582	2,730	4,974	13,878
Apr	3,142	8,021	16,305	16,871	12,443	5,428	21,607	2,745	4,975	13,887
May	3,146	8,037	16,384	16,913	12,474	5,434	21,586	2,729	4,967	13,890
June	3,151	8,051	16,415	16,936	12,486	5,443	21,571	2,731	4,963	13,887
July	3,144	8,043	16,453	16,963	12,497	5,438	21,586	2,726	4,976	13,884
Aug	3,135	8,058	16,470	17,010	12,508	5,441	21,645	2,730	4,987	13,928
Sept	3,127	8,083	16,514	17,019	12,522	5,436	21,677	2,730	5,000	13,947
Oct	3,131	8,093	16,614	17,081	12,546	5,434	21,700	2,723	5,007	13,970
Nov	3,133	8,107	16,611	17,108	12,571	5,441	21,706	2,728	5,015	13,963
Dec	3,127	8,128	16,674	17,142	12,589	5,447	21,700	2,706	5,020	13,974
2005: Jan	3,123	8,150	16,694	17,178	12,611	5,451	21,710	2,717	5,025	13,968
Feb	3,127	8,165	16,775	17,186	12,650	5,457	21,733	2,720	5,027	13,986
Mar	3,134	8,167	16,796	17,210	12,662	5,459	21,731	2,724	5,024	13,983
Apr	3,152	8,182	16,843	17,243	12,723	5,472	21,745	2,718	5,026	14,001
May	3,146	8,189	16,851	17,289	12,736	5,468	21,754	2,722	5,023	14,009
June	3,146	8,208	16,906	17,336	12,765	5,479	21,760	2,719	5,026	14,015
July	3,146	8,227	16,964	17,377	12,801	5,477	21,817	2,719	5,034	14,064
Aug	3,147	8,248	16,983	17,418	12,830	5,469	21,849	2,718	5,033	14,098
Sept	3,153	8,265	17,037	17,455	12,762	5,468	21,856	2,718	5,039	14,099
Oct	3,142	8,289	17,051	17,443	12,755	5,458	21,850	2,716	5,037	14,097
Nov ᵖ	3,146	8,304	17,127	17,480	12,808	5,466	21,874	2,718	5,045	14,111
Dec ᵖ	3,149	8,316	17,160	17,505	12,831	5,477	21,888	2,712	5,057	14,119

Note (cont'd).—weather, etc., even if they are not paid for the time off; which are based on a sample of the working-age population; and which count persons only once—as employed, unemployed, or not in the labor force. In the data shown here, persons who work at more than one job are counted each time they appear on a payroll.

Establishment data for employment, hours, and earnings are classified based on the 2002 North American Industry Classification System (NAICS).

For further description and details see *Employment and Earnings*.

Source: Department of Labor, Bureau of Labor Statistics.

TABLE B–47.—*Hours and earnings in private nonagricultural industries, 1959–2005* [1]

[Monthly data seasonally adjusted]

Year or month	Average weekly hours			Average hourly earnings			Average weekly earnings, total private			
	Total private	Manufacturing		Total private		Manu-facturing (current dollars)	Level		Percent change from year earlier	
		Total	Over-time	Current dollars	1982 dollars [2]		Current dollars	1982 dollars [2]	Current dollars	1982 dollars [2]
1959	....	40.3	2.7	....	....	$2.08	....	....	....	....
1960	....	39.8	2.5	....	....	2.15	....	....	....	....
1961	....	39.9	2.4	....	....	2.20	....	....	....	....
1962	....	40.5	2.8	....	....	2.27	....	....	....	....
1963	....	40.6	2.8	....	....	2.34	....	....	....	....
1964	38.5	40.8	3.1	$2.53	$7.86	2.41	$97.41	$302.52	....	....
1965	38.6	41.2	3.6	2.63	8.04	2.49	101.52	310.46	4.2	2.6
1966	38.5	41.4	3.9	2.73	8.13	2.60	105.11	312.83	3.5	.8
1967	37.9	40.6	3.3	2.85	8.21	2.71	108.02	311.30	2.8	−.5
1968	37.7	40.7	3.5	3.02	8.37	2.89	113.85	315.37	5.4	1.3
1969	37.5	40.6	3.6	3.22	8.45	3.07	120.75	316.93	6.1	.5
1970	37.0	39.8	2.9	3.40	8.46	3.23	125.80	312.94	4.2	−1.3
1971	36.8	39.9	2.9	3.63	8.64	3.45	133.58	318.05	6.2	1.6
1972	36.9	40.6	3.4	3.90	8.99	3.70	143.91	331.59	7.7	4.3
1973	36.9	40.7	3.8	4.14	8.98	3.97	152.77	331.39	6.2	−.1
1974	36.4	40.0	3.2	4.43	8.65	4.31	161.25	314.94	5.6	−5.0
1975	36.0	39.5	2.6	4.73	8.48	4.71	170.28	305.16	5.6	−3.1
1976	36.1	40.1	3.1	5.06	8.58	5.09	182.67	309.61	7.3	1.5
1977	35.9	40.3	3.4	5.44	8.66	5.55	195.30	310.99	6.9	.4
1978	35.8	40.4	3.6	5.87	8.67	6.05	210.15	310.41	7.6	−.2
1979	35.6	40.2	3.3	6.33	8.40	6.57	225.35	298.87	7.2	−3.7
1980	35.2	39.7	2.8	6.84	7.99	7.15	240.77	281.27	6.8	−5.9
1981	35.2	39.8	2.8	7.43	7.88	7.86	261.54	277.35	8.6	−1.4
1982	34.7	38.9	2.3	7.86	7.86	8.36	272.74	272.74	4.3	−1.7
1983	34.9	40.1	2.9	8.19	7.95	8.70	285.83	277.50	4.8	1.7
1984	35.1	40.7	3.4	8.48	7.95	9.05	297.65	279.22	4.1	.6
1985	34.9	40.5	3.3	8.73	7.91	9.40	304.68	276.23	2.4	−1.1
1986	34.7	40.7	3.4	8.92	7.96	9.59	309.52	276.11	1.6	−.0
1987	34.7	40.9	3.7	9.13	7.86	9.77	316.81	272.88	2.4	−1.2
1988	34.6	41.0	3.8	9.43	7.81	10.05	326.28	270.32	3.0	−.9
1989	34.5	40.9	3.8	9.80	7.75	10.35	338.10	267.27	3.6	−1.1
1990	34.3	40.5	3.8	10.19	7.66	10.78	349.29	262.43	3.3	−1.8
1991	34.1	40.4	3.8	10.50	7.58	11.13	358.06	258.34	2.5	−1.6
1992	34.2	40.7	4.0	10.76	7.55	11.40	367.83	257.95	2.7	−.2
1993	34.3	41.1	4.4	11.03	7.52	11.70	378.40	258.12	2.9	.1
1994	34.5	41.7	5.0	11.32	7.53	12.04	390.73	259.97	3.3	.7
1995	34.3	41.3	4.7	11.64	7.53	12.34	399.53	258.43	2.3	−.6
1996	34.3	41.3	4.8	12.03	7.57	12.75	412.74	259.58	3.3	.4
1997	34.5	41.7	5.1	12.49	7.68	13.14	431.25	265.22	4.5	2.2
1998	34.5	41.4	4.8	13.00	7.89	13.45	448.04	271.87	3.9	2.5
1999	34.3	41.4	4.8	13.47	8.00	13.85	462.49	274.64	3.2	1.0
2000	34.3	41.3	4.7	14.00	8.03	14.32	480.41	275.62	3.9	.4
2001	34.0	40.3	4.0	14.53	8.11	14.76	493.20	275.38	2.7	−.1
2002	33.9	40.5	4.2	14.95	8.24	15.29	506.07	278.83	2.6	1.3
2003	33.7	40.4	4.2	15.35	8.27	15.74	517.30	278.72	2.2	−.0
2004	33.7	40.8	4.6	15.67	8.23	16.14	528.56	277.61	2.2	−.4
2005 ᵖ	33.8	40.7	4.5	16.11	8.17	16.56	543.86	275.93	2.9	−.6
2004:Jan	33.8	41.0	4.5	15.48	8.27	15.94	523.22	279.50	1.9	.1
Feb	33.8	41.0	4.5	15.51	8.25	15.98	524.24	279.00	1.9	.4
Mar	33.7	40.9	4.6	15.54	8.23	16.01	523.70	277.38	1.5	.0
Apr	33.7	40.8	4.5	15.58	8.24	16.07	525.05	277.66	2.5	.4
May	33.8	41.0	4.6	15.62	8.21	16.08	527.96	277.44	2.6	−.3
June	33.6	40.7	4.5	15.64	8.20	16.12	525.50	275.42	2.0	−1.1
July	33.7	40.8	4.6	15.70	8.23	16.16	529.09	277.45	2.3	−.6
Aug	33.7	40.9	4.6	15.74	8.25	16.22	530.44	278.01	2.5	−.0
Sept	33.8	40.8	4.6	15.77	8.25	16.29	533.03	278.93	3.0	.6
Oct	33.8	40.7	4.5	15.81	8.22	16.27	534.38	277.89	2.9	−.3
Nov	33.7	40.5	4.5	15.82	8.21	16.29	533.13	276.52	2.1	−1.6
Dec	33.7	40.5	4.5	15.85	8.23	16.34	534.15	277.19	2.9	−.5
2005:Jan	33.7	40.7	4.5	15.90	8.24	16.37	535.83	277.78	2.4	−.6
Feb	33.7	40.6	4.6	15.91	8.22	16.42	536.17	276.95	2.3	−.7
Mar	33.7	40.4	4.5	15.95	8.19	16.43	537.52	276.08	2.6	−.5
Apr	33.8	40.5	4.4	16.00	8.16	16.47	540.80	275.92	3.0	−.6
May	33.7	40.4	4.4	16.03	8.19	16.53	540.21	275.90	2.3	−.6
June	33.7	40.4	4.4	16.07	8.21	16.55	541.56	276.59	3.1	.4
July	33.7	40.5	4.5	16.14	8.20	16.55	543.92	276.24	2.8	−.4
Aug	33.7	40.5	4.5	16.17	8.16	16.65	544.93	275.08	2.7	−1.1
Sept	33.8	40.7	4.5	16.19	8.06	16.59	547.22	272.38	2.7	−2.3
Oct	33.8	41.0	4.6	16.28	8.10	16.70	550.26	273.63	3.0	−1.5
Nov ᵖ	33.8	40.8	4.5	16.29	8.16	16.70	550.60	275.85	3.3	−.2
Dec ᵖ	33.7	40.7	4.5	16.34	8.19	16.71	550.66	276.16	3.1	−.4

[1] For production or nonsupervisory workers; total includes private industry groups shown in Table B-46.
[2] Current dollars divided by the consumer price index for urban wage earners and clerical workers on a 1982=100 base.

Note.—See Note, Table B-46.

Source: Department of Labor, Bureau of Labor Statistics.

TABLE B-48.—*Employment cost index, private industry, 1984–2005*

Year and month	Total private Total compensation	Wages and salaries	Benefits[1]	Goods-producing Total compensation	Wages and salaries	Benefits[1]	Service-producing Total compensation	Wages and salaries	Benefits[1]	Manufacturing Total compensation	Wages and salaries	Benefits[1]	Nonmanufacturing Total compensation	Wages and salaries	Benefits[1]
					Index, June 1989=100; not seasonally adjusted										
December:															
1984	84.0	84.8	81.7	85.4	86.4	83.2	82.9	83.7	80.4	85.0	86.1	82.7	83.4	84.2	81.1
1985	87.3	88.3	84.6	88.2	89.4	85.7	86.6	87.7	83.6	87.8	89.2	85.0	87.0	88.0	84.4
1986	90.1	91.1	87.5	91.0	92.3	88.3	89.3	90.3	86.8	90.7	92.1	87.5	89.7	90.6	87.5
1987	93.1	94.1	90.5	93.8	95.2	90.9	92.6	93.4	90.2	93.4	95.2	89.8	92.9	93.7	91.0
1988	97.6	98.0	96.7	97.9	98.2	97.3	97.3	97.8	96.1	97.6	98.1	96.6	97.5	97.8	96.8
1989	102.3	102.0	102.6	102.1	102.0	102.6	102.3	102.2	102.6	102.0	101.9	102.3	102.3	102.2	102.8
1990	107.0	106.1	109.4	107.0	105.8	109.9	107.0	106.3	109.0	107.2	106.2	109.5	106.9	106.1	109.3
1991	111.7	110.0	116.2	111.9	109.7	116.7	111.6	110.2	115.7	112.2	110.3	116.1	111.5	109.8	116.2
1992	115.6	112.9	122.2	116.1	112.8	123.4	115.2	113.0	121.2	116.5	113.7	122.6	115.1	112.6	122.0
1993	119.8	116.4	128.3	120.6	116.1	130.3	119.3	116.6	126.7	121.3	117.3	130.0	119.0	116.0	127.4
1994	123.5	119.7	133.0	124.3	119.6	134.8	122.8	119.7	131.5	125.1	120.8	134.3	122.6	119.1	132.3
1995	126.7	123.1	135.9	127.3	122.9	137.1	126.2	123.2	134.7	128.3	124.3	136.7	125.9	122.5	135.3
1996	130.6	127.3	138.6	130.9	126.8	139.7	130.2	127.5	137.4	132.1	128.4	139.8	129.8	126.8	137.9
1997	135.1	132.3	141.8	134.1	130.6	141.5	135.3	133.1	141.4	135.3	132.2	141.7	134.7	132.1	141.5
1998	139.8	137.4	145.2	137.8	135.2	143.2	140.5	138.4	145.7	138.9	136.8	142.7	139.7	137.4	145.8
1999	144.6	142.2	150.2	142.5	139.7	148.2	145.3	143.3	150.7	143.6	141.5	147.8	144.5	142.1	150.7
2000	150.9	147.7	158.6	148.8	145.2	156.2	151.7	148.9	159.4	149.3	146.5	154.8	151.1	147.9	159.7
2001	157.2	153.3	166.7	154.4	150.5	162.6	158.2	154.5	168.4	154.6	151.7	160.4	157.6	153.5	168.8
2002	162.3	157.5	174.6	160.1	155.0	171.0	163.1	158.6	175.9	160.5	156.5	168.9	162.5	157.5	176.3
2003	168.8	162.3	185.8	166.5	158.7	183.8	169.7	163.9	186.2	167.1	160.1	182.3	169.0	162.6	186.7
2004	175.2	166.2	198.7	174.3	162.4	201.2	175.3	167.9	196.5	175.4	164.0	200.4	174.7	166.6	197.6
2005: Mar	177.2	167.4	203.3	176.9	163.6	207.0	177.1	169.0	200.5	178.2	165.3	206.7	176.5	167.7	201.6
June	178.5	168.4	204.9	178.5	164.8	209.4	178.1	170.0	201.6	179.6	166.4	208.8	177.6	168.7	203.0
Sept	179.6	169.5	206.4	179.7	166.0	210.9	179.3	171.1	203.1	180.7	167.4	210.1	178.9	169.8	204.6
					Index, June 1989=100; seasonally adjusted										
2004: Mar	171.5	163.5	190.9	170.7	159.9	192.1	171.9	165.1	190.2	170.9	161.3	192.2	170.8	163.8	190.5
June	173.1	164.5	194.1	172.4	160.9	195.0	173.5	166.0	193.5	172.7	162.4	195.6	172.3	164.7	193.7
Sept	174.8	165.7	196.7	174.6	162.3	198.9	174.9	167.2	195.3	174.8	163.8	199.8	173.7	165.9	195.7
Dec	176.2	166.4	199.9	176.3	162.4	203.5	176.2	168.2	197.7	176.6	164.0	203.5	175.1	166.9	198.7
2005: Mar	177.3	167.4	202.0	177.1	163.6	205.3	177.3	169.1	200.1	177.3	165.3	204.4	176.4	167.8	201.1
June	178.4	168.4	203.6	178.9	164.8	208.2	178.2	169.9	200.9	179.1	166.4	207.4	177.4	168.6	202.3
Sept	179.8	169.4	206.2	180.9	166.0	211.7	179.4	170.8	202.9	180.6	167.4	210.8	178.7	169.5	204.6
					Percent change from 12 months earlier, not seasonally adjusted										
December:															
1984	4.9	4.2	6.5	4.7	3.8	6.3	5.1	4.4	6.9	5.2	4.4	6.7	4.8	4.0	6.4
1985	3.9	4.1	3.5	3.3	3.5	3.0	4.5	4.8	4.0	3.3	3.6	2.8	4.3	4.5	4.1
1986	3.2	3.2	3.4	3.2	3.2	3.0	3.1	3.0	3.8	3.3	3.3	2.9	3.1	3.0	3.7
1987	3.3	3.3	3.4	3.1	3.1	2.9	3.7	3.4	3.9	3.0	3.4	2.6	3.6	3.4	4.0
1988	4.8	4.1	6.9	4.4	3.2	7.0	5.1	4.7	6.5	4.5	3.0	7.6	5.0	4.4	6.4
1989	4.8	4.1	6.1	4.3	3.9	5.4	5.1	4.5	6.8	4.5	3.9	5.9	4.9	4.5	6.2
1990	4.6	4.0	6.6	4.8	3.7	7.1	4.6	4.0	6.2	5.1	4.2	7.0	4.5	3.8	6.3
1991	4.4	3.7	6.2	4.6	3.7	6.2	4.3	3.7	6.1	4.7	3.9	6.0	4.3	3.5	6.3
1992	3.5	2.6	5.2	3.8	2.8	5.7	3.2	2.5	4.8	3.8	3.1	5.6	3.2	2.6	5.0
1993	3.6	3.1	5.0	3.9	2.9	5.6	3.6	3.2	4.5	4.1	3.2	6.0	3.4	3.0	4.4
1994	3.1	2.8	3.7	3.1	3.0	3.5	2.9	2.7	3.8	3.1	3.0	3.3	3.0	2.7	3.8
1995	2.6	2.8	2.2	2.4	2.8	1.7	2.8	2.9	2.4	2.6	2.9	1.8	2.7	2.9	2.3
1996	3.1	3.4	2.0	2.8	3.2	1.9	3.2	3.5	2.0	3.0	3.3	2.3	3.1	3.5	1.9
1997	3.4	3.9	2.3	2.4	3.0	1.3	3.9	4.4	2.9	2.4	3.0	1.4	3.8	4.2	2.6
1998	3.5	3.9	2.4	2.8	3.5	1.2	3.8	4.0	3.0	2.7	3.5	.7	3.7	4.0	3.0
1999	3.4	3.5	3.4	3.4	3.3	3.4	3.4	3.5	3.4	3.4	3.4	3.4	3.4	3.4	3.4
2000	4.4	3.9	5.6	4.4	3.9	5.4	4.4	3.9	5.8	4.0	3.5	4.7	4.6	4.1	6.0
2001	4.2	3.8	5.1	3.8	3.7	4.1	4.3	3.8	5.6	3.5	3.5	3.6	4.3	3.8	5.7
2002	3.2	2.7	4.7	3.7	3.0	5.2	3.1	2.7	4.5	3.8	3.2	5.3	3.1	2.6	4.4
2003	4.0	3.0	6.4	4.0	2.4	7.5	4.0	3.3	5.9	4.1	2.3	7.9	4.0	3.2	5.9
2004	3.8	2.4	6.9	4.7	2.3	9.5	3.3	2.4	5.5	5.0	2.4	9.9	3.4	2.5	5.8
2005: Mar	3.4	2.4	5.8	3.9	2.3	6.9	3.2	2.4	5.2	3.8	2.5	6.3	3.3	2.4	5.6
June	3.2	2.4	4.9	3.9	2.4	6.7	2.8	2.3	3.9	3.7	2.5	6.0	3.0	2.4	4.5
Sept	3.0	2.2	4.8	3.7	2.3	6.5	2.6	2.1	3.9	3.3	2.2	5.5	2.9	2.2	4.5
					Percent change from 3 months earlier, seasonally adjusted										
2004: Mar	1.1	0.6	2.2	1.7	0.8	3.4	0.8	0.5	1.5	1.6	0.7	3.9	0.8	0.6	1.5
June	.9	.6	1.7	1.0	.6	1.5	.9	.5	1.7	1.1	.7	1.8	.9	.5	1.7
Sept	1.0	.7	1.3	1.3	.9	2.0	.8	.7	.9	1.2	.9	2.1	.8	.7	1.0
Dec	.8	.4	1.6	1.0	.1	2.3	.7	.6	1.2	1.0	.1	1.9	.8	.6	1.5
2005: Mar	.6	.6	1.1	.5	.7	.9	.6	.5	1.2	.4	.8	.4	.7	.5	1.2
June	.6	.6	.8	1.0	.7	1.4	.5	.5	.4	1.0	.7	1.5	.6	.5	.6
Sept	.8	.6	1.3	1.1	.7	1.7	.7	.7	1.0	.8	.6	1.6	.7	.5	1.1

[1] Employer costs for employee benefits.

Note.—The employment cost index is a measure of the change in the cost of labor, free from the influence of employment shifts among occupations and industries.

Data exclude farm and household workers.

Source: Department of Labor, Bureau of Labor Statistics.

TABLE B–49.—*Productivity and related data, business sector, 1959–2005*

[Index numbers, 1992=100; quarterly data seasonally adjusted]

Year or quarter	Output per hour of all persons		Output[1]		Hours of all persons[2]		Compensation per hour[3]		Real compensation per hour[4]		Unit labor costs		Implicit price deflator[5]	
	Business sector	Nonfarm business sector	Business sector	Nonfarm business sector	Business sector	Nonfarm business sector	Business sector	Nonfarm business sector	Business sector	Nonfarm business sector	Business sector	Nonfarm business sector	Business sector	Nonfarm business sector
1959	48.0	51.3	31.4	31.2	65.5	60.9	13.3	13.9	59.4	61.8	27.8	27.1	26.8	26.3
1960	48.9	51.9	32.0	31.8	65.6	61.2	13.9	14.5	60.8	63.3	28.4	27.9	27.1	26.6
1961	50.6	53.5	32.7	32.4	64.6	60.6	14.4	15.0	62.5	64.8	28.5	28.0	27.3	26.8
1962	52.9	55.9	34.8	34.6	65.8	61.9	15.1	15.6	64.6	66.7	28.5	27.8	27.6	27.1
1963	54.9	57.8	36.4	36.2	66.2	62.6	15.6	16.1	66.1	68.1	28.4	27.8	27.7	27.3
1964	56.8	59.6	38.7	38.7	68.1	64.9	16.2	16.6	67.7	69.3	28.5	27.9	28.1	27.6
1965	58.8	61.4	41.4	41.4	70.5	67.4	16.8	17.1	69.1	70.5	28.6	27.9	28.5	28.0
1966	61.2	63.6	44.2	44.4	72.3	69.8	17.9	18.2	71.7	72.6	29.3	28.6	29.2	28.6
1967	62.5	64.7	45.1	45.1	72.1	69.8	19.0	19.2	73.5	74.5	30.3	29.7	30.0	29.5
1968	64.7	66.9	47.3	47.5	73.2	71.0	20.5	20.7	76.2	77.1	31.7	31.0	31.2	30.7
1969	65.0	67.0	48.8	48.9	75.0	73.0	21.9	22.1	77.3	78.1	33.7	33.0	32.6	32.1
1970	66.3	68.0	48.7	48.9	73.5	71.9	23.6	23.7	78.8	79.2	35.6	34.9	34.1	33.5
1971	69.0	70.7	50.6	50.7	73.3	71.7	25.1	25.2	80.2	80.7	36.3	35.7	35.5	35.0
1972	71.2	73.1	53.9	54.1	75.6	74.0	26.7	26.9	82.6	83.2	37.4	36.8	36.8	36.1
1973	73.4	75.3	57.6	58.0	78.5	77.1	28.9	29.1	84.3	84.8	39.4	38.6	38.7	37.4
1974	72.2	74.2	56.8	57.3	78.7	77.2	31.7	31.9	83.3	83.8	43.9	43.0	42.4	41.2
1975	74.8	76.2	56.3	56.3	75.3	73.9	34.9	35.1	84.1	84.5	46.7	46.1	46.6	45.6
1976	77.1	78.7	60.0	60.2	77.8	76.5	38.0	38.1	86.4	86.6	49.2	48.4	49.0	48.1
1977	78.4	80.0	63.3	63.6	80.8	79.5	41.0	41.2	87.6	88.0	52.2	51.5	52.0	51.2
1978	79.3	81.0	67.3	67.8	84.9	83.7	44.5	44.8	89.1	89.6	56.2	55.3	55.6	54.6
1979	79.3	80.7	69.6	70.0	87.8	86.6	48.9	49.1	89.3	89.7	61.7	60.8	60.4	59.2
1980	79.1	80.6	68.8	69.2	87.0	85.9	54.1	54.4	89.1	89.5	68.4	67.5	65.8	64.9
1981	80.8	81.7	70.7	70.7	87.6	86.6	59.3	59.7	89.3	89.8	73.5	73.1	71.8	71.1
1982	80.1	80.8	68.6	68.4	85.6	84.7	63.6	64.0	90.4	90.8	79.4	79.1	75.9	75.5
1983	83.0	84.5	72.3	72.9	87.1	86.3	66.3	66.6	90.3	90.9	79.8	78.9	78.5	77.9
1984	85.2	86.1	78.6	78.9	92.2	91.6	69.1	69.5	90.7	91.1	81.2	80.7	80.8	80.1
1985	87.1	87.4	82.2	82.2	94.3	94.0	72.5	72.6	92.0	92.2	83.2	83.1	82.7	82.5
1986	89.8	90.1	85.3	85.4	95.0	94.7	76.2	76.4	95.0	95.2	84.9	84.8	84.1	83.9
1987	90.3	90.6	88.3	88.4	97.7	97.6	79.1	79.2	95.3	95.4	87.6	87.4	85.9	85.7
1988	91.7	92.1	92.1	92.4	100.4	100.4	83.1	83.1	96.6	96.6	90.6	90.3	88.6	88.3
1989	92.6	92.7	95.4	95.7	103.1	103.2	85.3	85.2	95.1	95.0	92.1	91.9	91.9	91.5
1990	94.5	94.5	96.9	97.1	102.6	102.7	90.6	90.4	96.3	96.0	96.0	95.7	95.1	94.9
1991	95.9	96.1	96.1	96.3	100.2	100.2	95.1	95.0	97.4	97.4	99.1	98.9	98.2	98.1
1992	100.0	100.0	100.0	100.0	100.0	100.0	100.0	100.0	100.0	100.0	100.0	100.0	100.0	100.0
1993	100.4	100.4	103.1	103.4	102.7	102.9	102.2	102.0	99.7	99.5	101.8	101.6	102.1	102.1
1994	101.5	101.6	108.2	108.3	106.7	106.5	103.7	103.7	99.1	99.1	102.2	102.1	103.9	104.0
1995	101.6	102.1	111.4	111.8	109.6	109.4	105.9	106.0	98.8	98.9	104.2	103.7	105.7	105.8
1996	104.7	104.9	116.5	116.8	111.3	111.4	109.6	109.5	99.6	99.5	104.7	104.5	107.4	107.3
1997	106.7	106.6	122.7	122.8	115.0	115.3	113.1	112.9	100.6	100.4	106.1	105.9	109.0	109.1
1998	109.7	109.5	128.6	128.9	117.3	117.7	120.0	119.7	105.3	105.0	109.4	109.3	109.7	109.9
1999	112.9	112.6	135.2	135.6	119.7	120.4	125.8	125.2	108.1	107.5	111.4	111.2	110.7	111.1
2000	116.1	115.6	140.5	140.8	121.0	121.8	134.5	134.0	111.9	111.4	115.9	115.9	112.7	113.3
2001	119.0	118.5	141.0	141.3	118.4	119.3	140.2	139.3	113.4	112.6	117.8	117.5	114.9	115.4
2002	123.8	123.3	143.1	143.4	115.6	116.3	145.0	144.2	115.4	114.8	117.1	117.0	116.1	116.7
2003	128.6	128.0	147.9	148.2	115.0	115.8	150.7	149.9	117.3	116.7	117.2	117.1	117.7	118.2
2004	133.0	132.3	154.9	155.3	116.5	117.4	157.7	156.7	119.5	118.7	118.6	118.4	120.6	120.7
2001: I	117.2	116.6	141.1	141.4	120.4	121.3	138.8	138.0	113.0	112.4	118.5	118.4	114.1	114.6
II	118.8	118.2	141.4	141.9	119.1	120.0	139.9	138.9	113.0	112.2	117.8	117.5	114.9	115.4
III	119.2	118.7	140.3	140.8	117.7	118.7	140.5	139.5	113.3	112.5	117.9	117.6	115.2	115.6
IV	121.1	120.5	141.0	141.2	116.4	117.2	141.5	140.6	114.2	113.5	116.9	116.7	115.6	116.0
2002: I	122.7	122.5	141.9	142.5	115.7	116.3	143.5	142.7	115.4	114.8	116.9	116.5	115.6	116.0
II	123.2	122.7	142.6	143.0	115.7	116.5	145.0	144.2	115.7	115.0	117.7	117.5	115.9	116.6
III	124.6	123.9	143.8	144.1	115.4	116.3	145.7	144.8	115.7	114.9	116.9	116.9	116.2	116.9
IV	124.7	124.0	144.0	144.1	115.5	116.2	145.8	145.0	115.1	114.5	116.9	116.9	116.7	117.3
2003: I	125.6	124.9	144.6	144.8	115.2	115.9	147.8	147.0	115.5	114.9	117.7	117.7	117.2	117.9
II	127.9	126.9	146.4	146.5	114.5	115.4	150.3	149.3	117.3	116.5	117.5	117.6	117.4	118.0
III	130.5	129.9	149.8	150.2	114.8	115.6	152.0	151.2	118.0	117.4	116.4	116.4	117.9	118.3
IV	130.6	130.1	150.8	151.2	115.5	116.2	152.8	152.2	118.4	117.9	117.0	116.9	118.3	118.6
2004: I	131.7	130.8	152.6	152.8	115.9	116.8	154.4	153.5	118.5	117.8	117.3	117.3	119.4	119.6
II	132.8	132.2	154.1	154.5	116.1	116.8	155.7	154.9	118.2	117.6	117.2	117.1	120.5	120.6
III	133.3	132.7	155.8	156.3	116.9	117.8	158.2	157.2	119.6	118.8	118.7	118.5	120.7	121.0
IV	134.3	133.5	157.2	157.7	117.1	118.2	162.5	161.0	121.8	120.7	121.0	120.7	121.5	121.8
2005: I	135.3	134.5	158.9	159.4	117.5	118.5	164.4	163.2	122.5	121.6	121.5	121.3	122.3	122.7
II	135.5	135.3	160.4	161.2	118.4	119.2	164.3	163.6	121.2	120.6	121.2	120.9	123.1	123.5
III	137.3	136.8	162.4	163.1	118.3	119.2	166.0	165.0	121.0	120.2	120.9	120.6	123.9	124.4

[1] Output refers to real gross domestic product in the sector.
[2] Hours at work of all persons engaged in the sector, including hours of proprietors and unpaid family workers. Estimates based primarily on establishment data.
[3] Wages and salaries of employees plus employers' contributions for social insurance and private benefit plans. Also includes an estimate of wages, salaries, and supplemental payments for the self-employed.
[4] Hourly compensation divided by the consumer price index for all urban consumers for recent quarters. The trend from 1978–2004 is based on the consumer price index research series (CPI–U–RS).
[5] Current dollar output divided by the output index.

Source: Department of Labor, Bureau of Labor Statistics.

TABLE B–50.—*Changes in productivity and related data, business sector, 1959–2005*

[Percent change from preceding period; quarterly data at seasonally adjusted annual rates]

Year or quarter	Output per hour of all persons		Output[1]		Hours of all persons[2]		Compensation per hour[3]		Real compensation per hour[4]		Unit labor costs		Implicit price deflator[5]	
	Business sector	Nonfarm business sector	Business sector	Nonfarm business sector	Business sector	Nonfarm business sector	Business sector	Nonfarm business sector	Business sector	Nonfarm business sector	Business sector	Nonfarm business sector	Business sector	Nonfarm business sector
1959	3.8	3.8	8.1	8.6	4.2	4.6	4.1	3.9	3.4	3.2	0.3	0.1	0.8	1.3
1960	1.7	1.2	1.9	1.7	.2	.6	4.2	4.3	2.4	2.5	2.4	3.1	1.1	1.2
1961	3.5	3.1	1.9	2.0	-1.5	-1.1	3.9	3.3	2.8	2.3	.4	.2	.8	.8
1962	4.6	4.5	6.4	6.8	1.8	2.2	4.4	4.0	3.4	3.0	-.1	-.5	1.0	1.0
1963	3.9	3.5	4.6	4.7	.7	1.1	3.6	3.4	2.2	2.1	-.3	-.1	.6	.7
1964	3.4	3.0	6.4	6.7	2.9	3.7	3.8	3.1	2.4	1.8	.4	.2	1.1	1.3
1965	3.5	3.1	7.0	7.1	3.4	3.9	3.7	3.3	2.1	1.7	.2	.2	1.6	1.3
1966	4.1	3.6	6.8	7.1	2.6	3.5	6.7	5.9	3.8	3.0	2.6	2.3	2.5	2.3
1967	2.2	1.7	1.9	1.7	-.3	-.0	5.7	5.8	2.5	2.7	3.4	4.0	2.7	3.2
1968	3.4	3.4	5.0	5.2	1.5	1.8	8.1	7.8	3.7	3.5	4.5	4.3	4.0	4.0
1969	.5	.1	3.0	3.0	2.5	2.9	7.0	6.8	1.4	1.3	6.5	6.6	4.6	4.5
1970	2.0	1.5	-.0	-.1	-2.0	-1.6	7.7	7.2	1.9	1.4	5.6	5.6	4.4	4.5
1971	4.1	4.0	3.8	3.8	-.3	-.2	6.3	6.4	1.8	1.9	2.1	2.3	4.2	4.3
1972	3.2	3.3	6.5	6.7	3.1	3.2	6.3	6.5	3.0	3.2	3.0	3.1	3.6	3.2
1973	3.0	3.1	7.0	7.3	3.8	4.1	8.4	8.1	2.1	1.8	5.2	4.9	5.2	3.6
1974	-1.6	-1.5	-1.4	-1.4	.2	.1	9.6	9.8	-1.3	-1.2	11.4	11.4	9.6	10.2
1975	3.5	2.7	-1.0	-1.7	-4.3	-4.3	10.2	10.1	1.0	.9	6.5	7.1	9.8	10.8
1976	3.1	3.3	6.6	7.0	3.3	3.6	8.6	8.4	2.7	2.5	5.3	5.0	5.3	5.6
1977	1.7	1.6	5.6	5.6	3.8	3.9	8.0	8.1	1.4	1.5	6.2	6.4	6.0	6.3
1978	1.1	1.3	6.3	6.6	5.1	5.2	8.7	8.9	1.7	1.8	7.5	7.5	7.1	6.7
1979	-.0	-.3	3.4	3.2	3.4	3.6	9.7	9.6	.3	.2	9.8	10.0	8.5	8.4
1980	-.2	-.2	-1.1	-1.0	-.9	-.8	10.8	10.8	-.2	-.2	11.0	11.0	8.9	9.6
1981	2.1	1.4	2.8	2.1	.7	.7	9.6	9.8	.2	.4	7.4	8.3	9.2	9.6
1982	-.8	-1.0	-3.0	-3.2	-2.3	-2.2	7.2	7.1	1.2	1.1	8.0	8.2	5.7	6.2
1983	3.6	4.5	5.4	6.5	1.8	1.9	4.1	4.2	-.0	.0	.6	-.3	3.4	3.1
1984	2.7	2.0	8.7	8.2	5.8	6.1	4.4	4.2	.4	.2	1.7	2.2	2.9	2.9
1985	2.3	1.5	4.6	4.2	2.3	2.6	4.8	4.6	1.4	1.2	2.5	3.0	2.4	3.0
1986	3.0	3.1	3.7	3.9	.7	.8	5.2	5.2	3.3	3.3	2.1	2.0	1.6	1.7
1987	.6	.5	3.5	3.6	2.9	3.0	3.7	3.7	.3	.3	3.1	3.2	2.2	2.2
1988	1.5	1.7	4.3	4.6	2.7	2.9	5.1	4.9	1.4	1.2	3.5	3.2	3.1	3.0
1989	1.0	.7	3.7	3.5	2.7	2.7	2.7	2.6	-1.6	-1.6	1.7	1.8	3.7	3.6
1990	2.0	1.9	1.5	1.5	-.5	-.4	6.3	6.1	1.2	1.1	4.1	4.1	3.6	3.7
1991	1.5	1.7	-.8	-.8	-2.3	-2.4	4.9	5.1	1.2	1.4	3.3	3.4	3.2	3.4
1992	4.3	4.1	4.0	3.9	-.2	-.2	5.2	5.2	2.6	2.7	.9	1.1	1.8	1.9
1993	.4	.4	3.1	3.3	2.7	2.9	2.2	2.0	-.3	-.5	1.8	1.6	2.1	2.1
1994	1.0	1.2	5.0	4.8	3.9	3.5	1.5	1.7	-.6	-.4	.4	.5	1.8	1.9
1995	.2	.5	2.9	3.2	2.7	2.7	2.1	2.1	-.3	-.3	1.9	1.6	1.8	1.7
1996	3.0	2.7	4.6	4.5	1.6	1.8	3.5	3.4	.8	.7	.5	.7	1.6	1.4
1997	1.9	1.6	5.3	5.2	3.3	3.5	3.2	3.1	1.1	.9	1.3	1.4	1.5	1.7
1998	2.8	2.8	4.8	5.0	2.0	2.1	6.1	6.0	4.6	4.5	3.2	3.1	.6	.7
1999	3.0	2.8	5.1	5.2	2.1	2.3	4.8	4.6	2.7	2.5	1.8	1.8	.9	1.1
2000	2.8	2.7	3.9	3.8	1.1	1.1	7.0	7.0	3.5	3.6	4.0	4.2	1.8	1.9
2001	2.5	2.5	.3	.4	-2.2	-2.0	4.2	4.0	1.4	1.1	1.6	1.4	2.0	1.9
2002	4.0	4.0	1.5	1.5	-2.4	-2.5	3.4	3.5	1.8	1.9	-.5	-.5	1.0	1.1
2003	3.9	3.8	3.4	3.3	-.5	-.5	3.9	4.0	1.6	1.6	.0	.2	1.4	1.3
2004	3.4	3.4	4.8	4.8	1.3	1.4	4.6	4.5	1.9	1.8	1.2	1.1	2.4	2.1
2001: I	-.5	-.4	-1.1	-1.1	-.6	-.7	6.9	6.8	3.0	2.8	7.4	7.2	2.7	2.5
II	5.5	5.6	.8	1.2	-4.4	-4.2	3.0	2.5	-.2	-.6	-2.4	-3.0	3.0	2.7
III	1.4	1.5	-3.1	-2.9	-4.4	-4.3	2.0	1.8	1.1	1.0	.6	.4	1.0	.7
IV	6.6	6.5	1.8	1.2	-4.5	-5.0	2.8	3.2	3.4	3.8	-3.6	-3.1	1.3	1.5
2002: I	5.3	6.5	2.6	3.5	-2.5	-2.8	5.6	5.6	4.1	4.5	.3	-.4	.2	-.0
II	1.8	.8	2.1	1.4	.3	.6	4.4	4.2	1.1	.9	2.6	3.4	1.0	2.0
III	4.8	4.1	3.6	3.1	-1.1	-.9	2.0	1.8	-.1	-.3	-2.6	-2.2	1.0	.9
IV	.1	.2	.5	.1	.3	-.0	.1	.4	-1.9	-1.6	.0	.2	1.7	1.6
2003: I	2.8	3.1	1.7	2.0	-1.1	-1.1	5.5	5.8	1.3	1.5	2.6	2.6	1.8	1.9
II	7.6	6.6	4.9	4.7	-2.6	-1.8	7.0	6.2	6.5	5.8	-.6	-.3	.6	.4
III	8.4	9.6	9.9	10.4	1.3	.8	4.5	5.1	2.3	2.9	-3.6	-4.1	1.6	1.0
IV	.3	.8	2.6	2.8	2.3	2.0	2.3	2.7	1.4	1.8	2.1	2.0	1.6	.8
2004: I	3.4	2.1	4.9	4.2	1.5	2.0	4.2	3.5	.3	-.5	.8	1.3	3.7	3.6
II	3.4	4.5	4.0	4.6	.6	.1	3.3	3.7	-1.0	-.7	-.1	-.8	3.8	3.2
III	1.4	1.3	4.4	4.6	3.0	3.3	6.5	6.1	4.8	4.4	5.0	4.8	.7	1.5
IV	3.1	2.5	3.6	3.9	.5	1.4	11.3	10.2	7.5	6.4	7.9	7.6	2.4	2.6
2005: I	2.9	3.2	4.4	4.3	1.4	1.1	4.7	5.5	2.3	3.1	1.7	2.2	2.7	3.0
II	.8	2.1	4.0	4.4	3.1	2.2	-.1	.9	-4.0	-3.1	-.9	-1.2	2.6	2.7
III	5.4	4.7	5.0	4.8	-.4	.1	4.2	3.7	-.8	-1.4	-1.1	-1.0	2.8	3.1

[1] Output refers to real gross domestic product in the sector.
[2] Hours at work of all persons engaged in the sector. See footnote 2, Table B–49.
[3] Wages and salaries of employees plus employers' contributions for social insurance and private benefit plans. Also includes an estimate of wages, salaries, and supplemental payments for the self-employed.
[4] Hourly compensation divided by a consumer price index. See footnote 4, Table B–49.
[5] Current dollar output divided by the output index.

Note.—Percent changes are based on original data and may differ slightly from percent changes based on indexes in Table B–49.

Source: Department of Labor, Bureau of Labor Statistics.

TABLE B–51.—*Industrial production indexes, major industry divisions, 1959–2005*

[2002=100; monthly data seasonally adjusted]

Year or month	Total industrial production [1]	Manufacturing				Mining	Utilities
		Total [1]	Durable	Nondurable	Other (non-NAICS) [1]		
1959	25.5	23.2					
1960	26.0	23.7					
1961	26.2	23.8					
1962	28.4	25.9					
1963	30.1	27.4					
1964	32.1	29.3					
1965	35.3	32.5					
1966	38.4	35.4					
1967	39.2	36.1					
1968	41.4	38.1					
1969	43.3	39.8					
1970	41.9	38.0					
1971	42.5	38.6					
1972	46.6	42.7	31.6	61.0	65.6	106.8	50.3
1973	50.4	46.5	35.5	63.8	67.6	107.4	53.2
1974	50.2	46.4	35.3	64.1	68.0	105.8	53.0
1975	45.7	41.5	30.6	59.5	64.8	103.3	54.0
1976	49.3	45.2	33.4	64.9	66.8	104.0	56.4
1977	53.1	49.1	36.7	69.4	73.2	106.4	58.7
1978	56.0	52.1	39.6	71.8	75.7	109.8	60.2
1979	57.7	53.7	41.6	72.2	77.3	113.1	61.6
1980	56.2	51.7	39.7	70.0	79.9	115.1	62.0
1981	56.9	52.3	40.2	70.6	81.8	118.1	62.9
1982	54.0	49.5	36.7	69.6	82.8	112.3	60.9
1983	55.4	51.7	38.5	72.8	85.0	106.4	61.4
1984	60.4	56.9	44.0	76.2	88.9	113.3	65.0
1985	61.2	57.9	45.0	76.6	92.4	111.1	66.4
1986	61.8	59.1	45.8	78.9	94.2	103.0	67.0
1987	64.9	62.4	48.4	83.1	99.7	103.9	70.1
1988	68.2	65.6	51.8	85.9	99.3	106.5	74.1
1989	68.8	66.1	52.4	86.4	97.8	105.3	76.4
1990	69.4	66.6	52.5	87.8	96.7	106.9	77.9
1991	68.3	65.3	50.9	87.4	92.8	104.5	79.8
1992	70.3	67.7	53.5	89.7	91.0	102.2	79.7
1993	72.6	70.1	56.5	91.0	91.8	102.2	82.6
1994	76.5	74.3	61.5	94.1	90.9	104.6	84.2
1995	80.2	78.3	66.8	95.8	90.9	104.4	87.2
1996	83.6	81.8	72.4	96.1	90.2	106.2	89.7
1997	89.7	88.8	81.2	99.6	97.7	108.0	89.7
1998	94.9	94.7	89.8	101.1	104.1	106.4	92.0
1999	99.3	99.7	97.6	101.8	107.4	101.2	94.7
2000	103.5	104.3	105.3	102.4	109.5	103.5	97.4
2001	99.9	99.9	100.2	99.0	103.1	104.5	97.0
2002	100.0	100.0	100.0	100.0	100.0	100.0	100.0
2003	100.6	100.5	102.3	98.9	97.0	99.8	102.0
2004	104.7	105.4	109.8	101.0	98.8	99.5	103.1
2005 ᴾ	108.1	109.5	116.9	101.8	101.6	97.2	105.6
2004: Jan	102.7	102.6	106.2	99.3	95.5	101.0	104.2
Feb	103.5	103.6	107.4	99.8	97.6	99.8	105.4
Mar	103.2	103.7	107.6	99.9	97.5	100.0	101.0
Apr	104.0	104.6	108.4	100.8	98.6	99.7	102.0
May	105.0	105.5	109.2	101.8	99.2	99.8	104.4
June	104.4	104.9	109.0	100.8	98.2	99.4	103.9
July	105.0	105.7	110.2	101.3	99.0	100.3	102.2
Aug	105.3	106.4	111.0	101.6	101.1	99.3	100.5
Sept	105.1	106.0	110.9	101.1	99.3	97.2	103.1
Oct	105.8	106.9	112.1	101.8	99.0	97.9	102.8
Nov	106.0	106.9	112.1	101.8	99.1	99.9	103.0
Dec	106.7	107.5	112.9	101.9	101.1	100.4	105.2
2005: Jan	106.9	108.1	113.7	102.1	102.5	99.9	102.9
Feb	107.4	108.6	114.8	102.2	101.5	100.9	101.7
Mar	107.3	108.2	114.2	101.9	102.4	100.4	104.8
Apr	107.2	108.3	114.3	101.9	102.5	100.5	103.1
May	107.4	108.7	115.0	101.9	103.2	99.8	102.9
June	108.3	109.0	115.5	102.1	102.0	100.8	108.3
July	108.3	109.1	115.9	102.1	101.0	99.8	108.1
Aug	108.6	109.5	117.3	101.5	100.9	99.2	108.4
Sept	107.2	108.9	117.5	100.1	100.4	90.3	108.1
Oct ᴾ	108.2	110.9	120.8	100.7	101.5	88.3	104.9
Nov ᴾ	109.1	111.4	120.7	102.0	100.2	92.5	105.3
Dec ᴾ	109.8	111.6	120.6	102.6	100.0	94.8	108.2

[1] Total industry and total manufacturing series include manufacturing as defined in the North American Industry Classification System (NAICS) plus those industries—logging, and newspaper, periodical, book and directory-publishing—that have traditionally been considered to be manufacturing and included in the industrial sector.

Note.—Data based on the North American Industry Classification System; see footnote 1.

Source: Board of Governors of the Federal Reserve System.

TABLE B–52.—*Industrial production indexes, market groupings, 1959–2005*

[2002=100; monthly data seasonally adjusted]

Year or month	Total indus- trial pro- duc- tion	Final products								Nonindustrial supplies			Materials		
		Total	Consumer goods				Equipment			Total	Con- struc- tion	Busi- ness	Total	Non- en- ergy	Ener- gy
			Total	Auto- motive prod- ucts	Other dura- ble goods	Non- durable goods	Total[1]	Busi- ness	De- fense and space						
1959	25.5	25.0	30.7	19.0	19.2	37.0	17.9	13.0	49.1	26.2	38.1	21.2	25.0		51.1
1960	26.0	25.9	31.8	21.7	19.4	38.2	18.4	13.4	50.5	26.4	37.2	22.0	25.4		51.8
1961	26.2	26.1	32.5	19.8	20.0	39.4	18.1	13.0	51.3	26.9	37.5	22.6	25.4		52.2
1962	28.4	28.3	34.7	24.0	21.7	41.3	20.2	14.1	59.4	28.5	39.8	24.0	27.7		54.0
1963	30.1	29.9	36.6	26.3	23.4	43.2	21.4	14.8	64.1	30.1	41.7	25.6	29.5		57.2
1964	32.1	31.6	38.7	27.6	25.6	45.3	22.6	16.6	62.0	32.1	44.2	27.4	31.8		59.5
1965	35.3	34.7	41.7	33.9	29.0	47.2	25.6	19.0	68.6	34.1	46.9	29.2	35.5		62.2
1966	38.4	38.0	43.8	33.8	31.9	49.5	29.8	22.0	80.7	36.2	48.9	31.5	38.7		66.1
1967	39.2	39.5	44.9	29.7	32.3	52.0	31.7	22.4	92.0	37.7	50.2	33.1	38.3	31.5	68.4
1968	41.4	41.4	47.6	35.4	34.6	54.1	32.6	23.4	92.2	39.9	52.8	35.2	40.8	33.8	71.6
1969	43.3	42.7	49.4	35.6	36.9	55.9	33.4	24.9	87.8	42.1	55.1	37.4	43.2	35.9	75.2
1970	41.9	41.2	48.8	29.9	35.8	56.9	31.1	24.0	74.3	41.4	53.1	37.5	41.7	33.8	78.9
1971	42.5	41.6	51.6	38.1	37.9	58.5	29.1	22.9	66.8	42.7	54.8	38.7	42.4	34.4	79.6
1972	46.6	45.1	55.8	41.1	43.4	62.2	31.8	26.0	65.0	47.7	62.2	42.6	46.6	38.5	82.6
1973	50.4	48.6	58.3	44.7	46.3	64.2	36.2	30.0	71.5	51.0	67.5	45.2	50.8	42.7	84.7
1974	50.2	48.5	56.6	38.6	43.6	64.2	38.0	31.7	73.9	50.5	65.9	45.1	50.7	42.6	84.3
1975	45.7	45.6	54.4	37.1	38.1	63.1	34.4	28.0	74.9	45.3	55.8	41.6	45.2	36.6	83.5
1976	49.3	48.8	58.8	42.3	42.8	67.0	36.1	29.7	72.8	48.4	60.2	44.2	49.2	40.8	85.4
1977	53.1	52.7	62.5	47.9	47.9	69.5	40.3	34.3	65.1	52.5	65.6	47.9	52.6	44.2	88.1
1978	56.0	55.9	64.5	47.6	50.1	71.9	44.8	38.8	65.6	55.4	69.3	50.5	55.2	47.1	89.1
1979	57.7	57.8	63.5	42.9	50.3	71.5	50.1	43.8	70.3	57.2	71.0	52.3	56.8	48.4	91.6
1980	56.2	57.5	61.1	33.0	46.7	71.6	52.3	44.5	83.9	54.8	65.7	51.0	54.6	45.5	92.3
1981	56.9	58.9	61.5	34.1	47.0	71.9	54.7	45.8	91.2	55.4	64.5	52.3	54.9	45.7	93.2
1982	54.0	57.6	61.3	33.1	43.6	73.1	52.1	41.9	109.1	53.4	58.6	51.7	50.7	41.2	89.2
1983	55.4	58.5	63.6	38.4	47.1	74.0	51.4	41.8	109.7	56.3	62.6	54.1	52.1	44.0	86.4
1984	60.4	63.4	66.5	43.0	52.7	75.5	58.9	48.2	124.6	61.2	68.2	58.8	57.0	49.1	91.8
1985	61.2	65.1	67.1	43.0	52.7	76.4	61.9	50.2	139.6	62.8	69.9	60.4	57.0	49.1	91.3
1986	61.8	66.1	69.5	46.2	55.8	78.2	61.0	49.3	148.2	64.9	72.3	62.4	57.0	50.1	87.7
1987	64.9	69.0	72.3	49.2	58.7	81.0	63.9	52.4	151.1	68.8	76.7	66.1	60.0	53.4	89.8
1988	68.2	72.5	75.1	51.9	61.7	83.7	68.6	57.2	152.0	71.1	78.4	68.6	63.3	56.8	92.9
1989	68.8	73.2	75.4	53.9	62.4	83.4	70.0	59.0	152.0	71.8	78.0	69.6	63.8	57.2	93.8
1990	69.4	73.9	75.8	50.5	62.3	84.8	71.2	61.0	145.8	72.9	77.3	71.3	64.2	57.3	95.7
1991	68.3	72.9	75.7	47.2	60.5	86.0	68.8	59.8	135.2	71.1	73.0	70.4	63.3	56.1	95.8
1992	70.3	74.6	77.9	55.2	63.2	86.7	69.5	62.1	125.5	73.2	76.0	72.1	65.4	58.9	94.9
1993	72.6	77.0	80.6	61.0	68.8	87.9	71.3	64.5	118.6	75.7	79.4	74.4	67.6	61.6	95.1
1994	76.5	80.3	84.4	68.3	75.4	90.1	74.0	68.2	111.5	79.4	85.2	77.3	72.1	66.7	96.7
1995	80.2	83.6	86.9	70.4	79.7	92.2	78.6	73.8	108.2	82.4	87.0	80.7	76.3	71.4	98.1
1996	83.6	86.7	88.7	72.6	83.6	93.4	84.1	80.5	104.5	85.6	90.9	83.6	80.0	75.6	99.6
1997	89.7	92.2	91.9	78.0	88.8	95.6	94.3	92.3	102.2	91.2	95.3	89.7	86.7	83.9	99.5
1998	94.9	97.4	95.1	83.2	94.8	97.7	103.7	102.8	105.9	96.4	100.2	95.0	92.0	90.3	99.9
1999	99.3	100.1	97.1	91.2	100.1	97.7	107.8	108.6	103.1	100.2	102.7	99.3	98.0	97.8	99.7
2000	103.5	103.1	99.0	93.4	103.5	99.2	113.3	116.6	92.2	104.3	105.0	104.0	103.7	104.5	101.1
2001	99.9	100.7	97.8	90.5	97.9	99.3	107.9	108.4	100.1	99.9	100.2	99.8	99.0	98.6	100.0
2002	100.0	100.0	100.0	100.0	100.0	100.0	100.0	100.0	100.0	100.0	100.0	100.0	100.0	100.0	100.0
2003	100.6	101.0	101.0	107.1	100.5	99.8	100.9	100.0	105.0	100.3	99.1	100.7	100.4	100.6	99.6
2004	104.7	105.1	103.1	109.3	104.4	101.6	110.0	109.4	113.1	104.1	104.6	103.9	104.6	106.5	99.6
2005 ᵖ	108.1	109.6	105.4	112.4	105.7	103.8	120.6	119.4	125.6	107.8	108.5	107.5	106.6	110.2	97.8
2004: Jan	102.7	103.1	102.7	111.6	104.3	100.5	104.2	103.7	106.4	101.9	102.4	101.7	102.5	103.2	100.6
Feb	103.5	104.1	103.4	111.2	104.3	101.5	105.9	105.3	108.6	102.7	102.3	102.8	103.2	104.3	100.2
Mar	103.2	103.6	102.5	110.4	103.7	100.6	106.4	105.7	109.5	102.3	102.7	102.2	103.1	104.6	99.3
Apr	104.0	104.5	103.2	110.7	104.7	101.3	107.9	107.2	110.9	103.3	103.5	103.2	103.8	105.2	99.8
May	105.0	105.3	103.8	108.8	105.2	102.5	108.9	108.3	112.1	104.4	104.9	104.1	104.9	106.3	101.0
June	104.4	104.3	102.4	105.8	104.4	101.3	109.4	108.8	112.0	104.1	104.6	103.8	104.5	106.3	99.8
July	105.0	105.0	102.3	105.7	104.4	101.2	111.8	111.3	114.2	104.7	105.7	104.3	105.1	107.2	99.7
Aug	105.3	105.6	103.2	109.5	104.6	101.7	111.5	110.9	114.6	104.9	105.7	104.5	105.2	107.8	98.4
Sept	105.1	105.2	102.6	107.0	103.8	101.4	112.1	111.3	116.1	104.4	104.2	104.5	105.1	107.7	98.2
Oct	105.8	106.3	103.6	110.7	104.5	101.9	113.4	112.6	116.7	105.1	106.1	104.7	105.6	108.3	98.5
Nov	106.0	106.5	103.7	109.9	104.4	102.2	113.8	112.9	117.6	105.2	105.7	105.0	105.9	108.3	99.3
Dec	106.7	107.2	104.1	110.1	104.1	102.9	115.0	114.1	119.0	106.2	106.1	106.2	106.5	108.8	100.4
2005: Jan	106.9	107.3	103.9	108.2	104.3	102.9	116.1	115.2	119.4	106.5	106.0	106.7	106.7	109.6	99.4
Feb	107.4	108.2	104.7	113.9	105.0	102.8	117.0	115.9	121.6	106.2	106.4	106.1	107.0	109.7	99.7
Mar	107.3	108.2	104.6	110.3	104.7	103.4	117.4	116.3	122.5	106.4	106.2	106.5	106.8	109.4	99.8
Apr	107.2	108.0	104.1	107.8	103.9	103.3	118.1	116.8	124.5	106.9	107.5	106.7	106.5	109.2	99.2
May	107.4	108.5	104.6	109.3	104.6	103.5	118.8	117.9	124.1	106.9	107.5	106.7	106.5	109.3	99.2
June	108.3	109.6	105.8	111.7	104.9	104.7	119.5	118.4	124.9	107.4	106.9	107.6	107.3	109.5	101.3
July	108.3	109.7	105.2	109.5	104.4	104.4	121.2	120.0	126.8	107.4	107.5	107.4	107.2	109.8	100.3
Aug	108.6	110.0	105.4	114.4	105.2	103.9	121.4	120.1	127.4	108.0	108.2	107.9	107.4	110.2	100.0
Sept	107.2	109.4	106.4	117.8	107.0	103.9	117.0	115.1	124.6	108.4	109.8	107.8	104.5	109.4	92.8
Oct ᵖ	108.2	111.3	106.0	117.3	108.5	103.3	124.9	123.5	128.1	109.1	111.7	108.1	104.8	110.8	90.8
Nov ᵖ	109.1	111.1	105.3	111.1	108.2	103.6	126.3	125.1	128.4	109.9	112.7	108.8	106.7	112.0	94.1
Dec ᵖ	109.8	111.4	105.5	108.0	107.8	104.5	126.8	125.7	130.6	110.0	111.6	109.3	108.0	112.7	96.6

[1] Includes other items, not shown separately.

Note.—See footnote 1 and Note, Table B–51.

Source: Board of Governors of the Federal Reserve System.

TABLE B–53.—*Industrial production indexes, selected manufacturing industries, 1967–2005*

[2002=100; monthly data seasonally adjusted]

Year or month	Durable manufacturing								Nondurable manufacturing					
	Primary metal		Fabricated metal products	Machinery	Computer and electronic products		Transportation equipment		Apparel	Paper	Printing and support	Chemical	Plastics and rubber products	Food
	Total	Iron and steel products			Total	Selected high-technology[1]	Total	Motor vehicles and parts						
1967	....	....	....	....	....	0.3	....	....	....	....	....	....	....	....
1968	....	....	....	....	....	.3	....	....	....	....	....	....	....	....
1969	....	....	....	....	....	.3	....	....	....	....	....	....	....	....
1970	....	....	....	....	....	.3	....	....	....	....	....	....	....	....
1971	....	....	....	....	....	.3	....	....	....	....	....	....	....	....
1972	120.9	128.7	69.3	68.4	1.5	.4	53.2	44.2	159.5	66.1	51.5	48.3	35.2	58.5
1973	140.6	154.3	76.6	79.0	1.7	.4	60.8	50.6	164.4	71.4	54.1	52.9	39.6	58.7
1974	144.2	165.0	75.4	82.9	1.9	.5	56.0	43.4	153.0	74.5	52.5	55.0	38.6	59.3
1975	111.8	122.4	65.1	72.3	1.7	.5	50.8	37.8	149.7	64.6	49.0	48.3	33.0	58.1
1976	118.7	127.0	69.8	75.5	2.0	.6	56.8	48.3	158.1	71.1	52.6	54.1	36.5	62.8
1977	119.8	124.0	75.7	82.4	2.5	.8	61.7	55.0	168.1	74.2	57.0	58.8	42.9	64.0
1978	127.4	133.2	79.4	88.8	3.1	1.0	65.7	57.3	173.0	77.6	60.3	61.7	44.4	65.0
1979	130.4	137.9	82.9	93.8	3.8	1.3	66.5	52.5	163.9	78.7	62.1	63.1	43.8	65.3
1980	114.4	116.9	78.2	89.3	4.6	1.5	59.0	38.6	166.4	78.6	62.6	59.6	39.0	66.5
1981	114.6	121.2	77.7	88.4	5.3	1.8	56.9	37.6	165.4	79.6	64.2	60.5	41.3	67.4
1982	80.9	74.5	69.6	74.0	6.0	2.1	52.2	33.9	167.6	78.4	69.0	56.7	40.5	70.0
1983	82.8	75.1	70.2	66.9	6.9	2.5	57.6	43.3	172.5	83.4	74.2	60.6	44.1	70.8
1984	90.8	82.7	76.4	77.9	8.6	3.3	65.2	52.0	175.0	87.6	80.8	64.1	50.9	72.1
1985	83.9	76.8	77.5	78.1	9.2	3.5	68.7	54.0	168.2	85.9	84.0	63.6	52.9	74.8
1986	81.9	75.0	77.0	76.9	9.6	3.6	70.3	53.9	170.1	89.4	88.2	66.5	55.1	75.9
1987	88.2	85.3	78.4	78.3	10.8	4.3	72.8	55.9	171.2	92.4	94.8	71.8	61.0	77.5
1988	98.8	99.3	82.4	86.2	11.9	5.0	77.3	59.7	168.1	96.1	97.8	75.8	63.7	79.5
1989	96.6	95.8	81.7	89.3	12.2	5.3	78.8	59.1	159.9	97.1	98.2	77.3	65.9	79.7
1990	95.4	94.7	80.7	87.1	13.2	6.0	76.4	55.5	156.6	97.0	101.9	79.1	67.7	82.1
1991	89.5	86.5	77.0	81.8	13.7	6.4	73.3	53.1	157.5	97.3	98.7	78.8	67.0	83.6
1992	91.7	90.6	79.4	81.6	15.5	7.7	76.0	60.4	160.6	99.6	104.1	80.0	72.1	85.2
1993	96.1	96.0	82.4	87.6	17.1	9.1	78.2	66.8	164.5	100.8	104.4	81.0	77.2	87.5
1994	103.5	103.6	89.6	96.0	20.3	11.8	81.8	76.7	167.8	105.1	105.5	83.0	83.6	88.0
1995	104.5	105.2	95.1	102.7	26.4	16.6	81.9	79.0	168.0	106.7	107.1	84.4	85.7	90.2
1996	107.0	107.7	98.6	106.2	33.6	23.3	83.4	79.6	163.4	103.3	107.9	86.1	88.6	88.4
1997	111.6	111.0	103.0	112.2	45.2	34.6	91.0	85.8	161.3	105.5	110.0	91.2	94.0	90.8
1998	113.5	110.8	106.3	115.0	58.3	48.4	99.0	90.2	152.6	106.4	111.2	92.7	97.4	94.8
1999	113.2	111.6	107.1	112.7	77.2	70.5	104.4	100.1	146.2	107.2	112.3	94.6	102.5	95.8
2000	109.5	110.5	111.3	118.4	102.5	100.7	99.5	99.5	139.1	105.0	113.0	96.0	103.6	97.5
2001	99.1	99.9	103.2	104.8	103.6	102.6	95.7	90.6	119.1	99.0	106.0	94.3	97.6	97.5
2002	100.0	100.0	100.0	100.0	100.0	100.0	100.0	100.0	100.0	100.0	100.0	100.0	100.0	100.0
2003	97.6	99.0	98.6	99.0	112.6	117.6	101.8	104.0	91.7	95.9	95.8	99.7	99.4	99.6
2004	103.4	108.4	103.2	110.7	130.7	141.2	105.6	108.0	87.6	98.0	96.0	102.8	102.5	100.8
2005ᴾ	100.5	101.8	106.8	115.6	156.6	171.5	111.2	111.9	84.4	97.8	97.7	102.6	104.8	103.3
2004:Jan	98.5	102.6	100.7	104.1	121.3	130.5	105.3	109.0	88.7	95.5	95.2	100.5	100.1	99.4
Feb	101.2	105.4	101.2	107.4	123.6	133.5	106.0	109.3	89.1	95.9	95.4	100.8	100.9	99.9
Mar	101.6	106.2	100.9	108.0	125.0	135.0	105.4	108.6	89.7	95.7	94.9	101.5	101.0	99.9
Apr	101.6	104.0	102.3	109.3	125.3	135.5	105.8	108.9	90.1	97.5	95.3	102.5	102.3	100.7
May	103.2	106.5	103.4	110.6	128.2	138.3	104.8	107.2	89.3	98.4	95.9	102.9	103.6	101.7
June	103.4	106.2	103.5	111.0	129.8	140.4	103.2	104.9	88.3	98.5	96.2	102.3	103.5	100.4
July	106.4	112.2	104.0	113.5	131.9	142.4	103.5	104.5	85.8	99.5	96.7	103.1	103.5	101.3
Aug	104.7	110.3	104.3	111.8	134.4	145.7	106.0	108.4	84.9	98.6	96.6	103.8	103.0	101.5
Sept	105.2	112.0	103.8	112.8	136.1	147.6	104.7	106.5	86.3	98.7	95.6	103.4	102.3	101.6
Oct	105.3	112.4	104.8	113.3	136.4	147.0	107.3	109.8	85.9	99.2	96.2	104.4	103.6	101.2
Nov	105.8	112.9	104.6	113.1	136.9	147.8	107.4	109.2	86.8	99.1	96.8	104.1	102.8	101.2
Dec	104.4	110.2	104.6	113.1	139.7	151.0	108.1	110.0	86.2	99.0	97.2	104.5	103.3	101.2
2005:Jan	103.8	108.1	105.4	114.1	144.3	157.8	107.2	108.6	85.3	99.9	97.9	103.8	104.0	102.3
Feb	101.9	105.5	105.3	114.0	146.8	160.4	111.1	113.4	85.1	99.6	97.0	104.6	103.7	102.7
Mar	102.3	104.5	105.0	114.3	147.4	160.4	109.1	109.8	84.3	99.8	96.4	103.8	103.5	102.5
Apr	99.5	99.3	105.5	114.3	149.5	163.1	108.6	107.9	84.6	98.2	96.5	104.1	103.8	102.5
May	98.9	96.4	105.7	114.5	152.2	166.2	109.4	108.8	82.3	96.8	97.0	103.9	103.1	103.2
June	95.5	92.4	105.6	115.0	153.6	167.9	111.0	111.4	81.9	97.8	96.5	103.9	102.9	103.0
July	95.3	90.5	106.1	116.3	156.5	171.6	109.8	109.2	83.7	96.6	97.9	103.7	103.2	104.2
Aug	98.2	98.9	106.6	114.1	160.1	176.7	112.7	113.1	84.0	96.2	97.2	102.7	104.1	102.7
Sept	101.8	103.7	106.8	116.1	162.1	179.6	108.8	116.3	84.5	96.5	97.9	97.5	106.5	103.5
Octᴾ	102.1	104.4	109.1	119.2	165.1	181.3	115.3	116.1	83.8	98.8	98.3	99.1	106.2	103.5
Novᴾ	102.7	108.1	109.7	119.6	169.4	185.4	112.2	110.5	85.2	97.6	98.8	101.1	107.8	104.7
Decᴾ	103.8	110.2	109.3	120.2	173.4	190.4	110.6	107.4	87.0	96.3	98.2	102.2	108.2	106.2

[1] Computers and office equipment, communications equipment, and semiconductors and related electronic components.

Note.—See footnote 1 and Note, Table B–51.

Source: Board of Governors of the Federal Reserve System.

TABLE B–54.—*Capacity utilization rates, 1959–2005*

[Percent [1]; monthly data seasonally adjusted]

Year or month	Total industry [2]	Manufacturing				Mining	Utilities	Stage-of-process		
		Total [2]	Durable goods	Non-durable goods	Other (non-NAICS) [2]			Crude	Primary and semi-finished	Finished
1959		81.6							83.0	81.1
1960		80.1							79.8	80.5
1961		77.3							77.9	77.2
1962		81.4							81.5	81.6
1963		83.5							83.8	83.4
1964		85.6							87.8	84.6
1965		89.5							91.0	88.8
1966		91.1							91.4	91.1
1967	87.0	87.2	87.5	86.3		81.2	94.5	81.1	85.0	88.2
1968	87.3	87.1	87.3	86.5		83.6	95.1	83.4	86.8	87.0
1969	87.4	86.6	86.9	86.2		86.8	96.8	85.7	88.1	85.4
1970	81.2	79.4	77.5	82.2		89.3	96.3	85.2	81.5	77.9
1971	79.6	77.9	75.1	81.9		88.0	94.7	84.4	81.6	75.3
1972	84.6	83.3	81.8	85.3	85.7	90.9	95.2	88.6	88.1	79.4
1973	88.4	87.6	88.5	86.6	84.7	92.0	94.3	90.6	92.2	83.0
1974	85.2	84.4	84.7	84.2	82.7	91.1	87.4	91.3	87.4	80.2
1975	75.6	73.5	71.6	76.0	77.2	89.2	84.5	83.9	75.1	73.5
1976	79.6	78.1	76.2	80.9	77.4	89.7	85.2	87.1	80.0	76.4
1977	83.1	82.2	80.9	84.1	83.4	89.7	85.3	89.0	84.3	79.5
1978	84.8	84.3	83.9	84.9	85.1	89.8	84.2	88.3	85.9	82.1
1979	85.0	84.2	84.5	83.6	85.3	91.1	85.5	89.3	85.8	82.0
1980	80.7	78.7	77.6	79.4	87.3	91.5	85.1	89.1	78.6	79.6
1980	79.7	77.1	75.3	78.8	87.7	91.4	84.3	89.5	77.1	78.0
1982	73.7	71.0	66.6	76.7	86.8	83.7	80.4	82.0	70.4	73.6
1983	74.7	73.4	68.4	79.8	87.4	78.5	79.7	78.7	74.2	73.4
1984	80.4	79.4	76.7	82.4	89.6	84.7	82.9	84.9	81.1	77.6
1985	79.4	78.3	75.8	80.8	90.5	83.3	83.1	83.1	79.9	77.1
1986	78.6	78.3	75.3	81.8	88.8	76.5	82.3	78.4	79.9	77.1
1987	81.2	81.0	77.6	84.8	90.7	79.6	83.9	82.7	83.0	78.5
1988	84.2	84.0	82.0	86.3	88.5	83.6	86.1	86.5	86.0	81.3
1989	83.6	83.1	81.4	85.2	85.4	84.9	86.6	87.2	84.9	81.0
1990	82.4	81.6	79.1	84.4	83.9	86.9	86.0	88.2	82.6	80.3
1991	79.6	78.3	75.0	82.3	81.6	84.9	86.8	85.3	79.7	77.9
1992	80.4	79.6	77.1	82.5	80.8	84.4	85.2	85.2	81.3	78.1
1993	81.4	80.4	78.8	82.2	82.5	85.8	87.7	85.3	83.6	78.0
1994	83.6	82.8	82.1	83.8	82.2	87.6	88.8	87.4	86.7	79.1
1995	83.9	83.0	82.4	83.9	82.1	87.9	89.9	88.5	86.7	79.4
1996	83.0	81.8	81.4	82.4	80.9	90.3	90.4	88.2	85.6	78.7
1997	83.9	83.0	82.5	83.3	85.1	91.3	89.1	89.7	85.8	80.2
1998	82.7	81.7	80.9	82.1	86.8	89.1	91.1	87.0	83.9	80.4
1999	81.9	80.8	80.5	80.5	86.9	86.3	92.4	86.6	84.1	78.5
2000	81.8	80.3	80.3	79.4	87.5	90.9	92.2	88.4	84.4	77.3
2001	76.3	74.1	71.7	76.2	82.7	90.9	88.7	85.6	77.5	72.8
2002	75.1	73.3	70.0	76.9	81.9	86.7	87.5	84.0	77.1	71.2
2003	75.7	73.7	70.7	76.7	82.1	88.0	86.2	84.9	77.4	71.7
2004	78.6	77.1	75.0	79.1	84.4	88.1	84.7	86.8	80.6	74.3
2005 *p*	80.0	78.8	77.4	79.9	86.1	86.8	85.9	85.5	81.7	76.9
2004: Jan	77.2	75.3	73.0	77.5	81.7	89.2	86.7	85.9	79.3	72.9
Feb	77.8	76.0	73.8	78.0	83.6	88.2	87.4	85.6	80.0	73.5
Mar	77.6	76.1	73.9	78.1	83.5	88.3	83.6	86.1	79.5	73.4
Apr	78.1	76.7	74.4	78.8	84.4	88.1	84.1	86.5	80.0	74.1
May	78.8	77.3	74.9	79.7	84.9	88.2	85.9	86.9	81.0	74.5
June	78.4	76.9	74.7	78.9	84.0	87.9	85.3	86.9	80.8	73.6
July	78.8	77.4	75.4	79.4	84.6	88.8	83.7	87.7	80.9	74.2
Aug	79.0	77.9	75.9	79.6	86.3	88.0	82.1	87.1	81.0	74.7
Sept	78.7	77.5	75.6	79.2	84.7	86.2	84.2	86.0	81.0	74.3
Oct	79.2	78.1	76.3	79.8	84.3	86.9	83.8	86.6	81.2	75.2
Nov	79.3	78.0	76.1	79.8	84.4	88.7	83.9	88.2	81.0	75.2
Dec	79.7	78.3	76.4	80.0	86.0	89.3	85.6	88.5	81.7	75.5
2005: Jan	79.8	78.6	76.8	80.2	87.2	88.9	83.7	88.2	81.7	75.6
Feb	80.0	78.9	77.3	80.2	86.2	89.9	82.7	88.8	81.4	76.4
Mar	79.9	78.5	76.7	80.0	87.0	89.5	85.2	88.5	81.4	76.1
Apr	79.7	78.4	76.5	80.0	87.0	89.7	83.8	88.2	81.2	76.0
May	79.8	78.6	76.7	80.0	87.6	89.1	83.7	87.6	81.0	76.5
June	80.3	78.7	76.8	80.2	86.6	90.0	88.0	88.4	81.7	76.8
July	80.2	78.6	76.8	80.2	85.7	89.1	88.0	87.5	81.6	76.8
Aug	80.3	78.8	77.4	79.7	85.6	88.6	88.2	86.8	81.8	77.1
Sept	79.1	78.2	77.2	78.7	85.1	80.7	88.0	78.2	81.9	76.6
Oct *p*	79.8	79.5	79.1	79.2	86.1	78.9	85.4	78.0	82.0	78.2
Nov *p*	80.3	79.6	78.8	80.2	84.9	82.6	85.8	81.9	82.3	78.0
Dec *p*	80.7	79.6	78.4	80.6	84.7	84.7	88.1	84.1	82.4	78.1

[1] Output as percent of capacity.
[2] See footnote 1 and Note, Table B–51.

Source: Board of Governors of the Federal Reserve System.

[Value put in place, billions of dollars; monthly data at seasonally adjusted annual rates]

Year or month	Total new construc-tion	Private construction										Public construction		
		Total	Residential buildings[1]		Nonresidential buildings and other construction							Total	Federal	State and local
			Total[2]	New housing units[3]	Total	Lodg-ing	Office	Com-mer-cial[4]	Manu-fac-turing	Other[5]			
1964	75.1	54.9	30.5	24.1	24.4	....	....	....	....	....	20.2	3.7	16.5
1965	81.9	60.0	30.2	23.8	29.7	....	....	....	....	....	21.9	3.9	18.0
1966	85.8	61.9	28.6	21.8	33.3	....	....	....	....	....	23.8	3.8	20.0
1967	87.2	61.8	28.7	21.5	33.1	....	....	....	....	....	25.4	3.3	22.1
1968	96.8	69.4	34.2	26.7	35.2	....	....	....	....	....	27.4	3.2	24.2
1969	104.9	77.2	37.2	29.2	39.9	....	....	....	....	....	27.8	3.2	24.6
1970	105.9	78.0	35.9	27.1	42.1	....	....	....	....	....	27.9	3.1	24.8
1971	122.4	92.7	48.5	38.7	44.2	....	....	....	....	....	29.7	3.8	25.9
1972	139.1	109.1	60.7	50.1	48.4	....	....	....	....	....	30.0	4.2	25.8
1973	153.8	121.4	65.1	54.6	56.3	....	....	....	....	....	32.3	4.7	27.6
1974	155.2	117.0	56.0	43.4	61.1	....	....	....	....	....	38.1	5.1	33.0
1975	152.6	109.3	51.6	36.3	57.8	....	....	....	....	....	43.3	6.1	37.2
1976	172.1	128.2	68.3	50.8	59.9	....	....	....	....	....	44.0	6.8	37.2
1977	200.5	157.4	92.0	72.2	65.4	....	....	....	....	....	43.1	7.1	36.0
1978	239.9	189.7	109.8	85.6	79.9	....	....	....	....	....	50.1	8.1	42.0
1979	272.9	216.2	116.4	89.3	99.8	....	....	....	....	....	56.6	8.6	48.1
1980	273.9	210.3	100.4	69.6	109.9	....	....	....	....	....	63.6	9.6	54.0
1981	289.1	224.4	99.2	69.4	125.1	....	....	....	....	....	64.7	10.4	54.3
1982	279.3	216.3	84.7	57.0	131.6	....	....	....	....	....	63.1	10.0	53.1
1983	311.9	248.4	125.8	95.0	122.6	....	....	....	....	....	63.5	10.6	52.9
1984	370.2	300.0	155.0	114.6	144.9	....	....	....	....	....	70.2	11.2	59.0
1985	403.4	325.6	160.5	115.9	165.1	....	....	....	....	....	77.8	12.0	65.8
1986	433.5	348.9	190.7	135.2	158.2	....	....	....	....	....	84.6	12.4	72.2
1987	446.6	356.0	199.7	142.7	156.3	....	....	....	....	....	90.6	14.1	76.6
1988	462.0	367.3	204.5	142.4	162.8	....	....	....	....	....	94.7	12.3	82.5
1989	477.5	379.3	204.3	143.2	175.1	....	....	....	....	....	98.2	12.2	86.0
1990	476.8	369.3	191.1	132.1	178.2	....	....	....	....	....	107.5	12.1	95.4
1991	432.6	322.5	166.3	114.6	156.2	....	....	....	....	....	110.1	12.8	97.3
1992	463.7	347.8	199.4	135.1	148.4	....	....	....	....	....	115.8	14.4	101.5
1993	491.0	375.1	225.1	150.9	150.0	4.6	20.0	34.4	23.4	67.7	116.0	14.4	101.5
1994	539.2	419.0	258.6	176.4	160.4	4.7	20.4	39.6	28.8	66.9	120.2	14.4	105.8
1995	557.8	427.9	247.4	171.4	180.5	7.1	23.0	44.1	35.4	70.9	129.9	15.8	114.2
1996	615.9	476.6	281.1	191.1	195.5	10.9	26.5	49.4	38.1	70.6	139.3	15.3	123.9
1997	653.4	502.7	289.0	198.1	213.7	12.9	32.8	53.1	37.6	77.3	150.7	14.1	136.6
1998	706.3	552.0	314.6	224.0	237.4	14.8	40.4	55.7	40.5	86.0	154.3	14.3	140.0
1999	769.5	599.7	350.6	251.3	249.2	16.0	45.1	59.4	35.1	93.7	169.7	14.0	155.7
2000	835.3	649.8	374.5	265.0	275.3	16.3	52.4	64.1	37.6	104.9	185.5	14.2	171.4
2001	868.3	662.2	388.3	279.4	273.9	14.5	49.7	63.6	37.8	108.2	206.1	15.1	191.0
2002	876.8	659.7	421.9	298.8	237.7	10.5	35.3	59.0	22.7	110.2	217.2	16.6	200.6
2003	925.1	701.6	475.9	345.7	225.7	9.9	30.6	57.2	21.4	106.5	223.5	17.9	205.6
2004	1,027.7	798.5	563.4	416.1	235.1	11.5	33.1	61.6	23.5	105.4	229.3	18.0	211.3
2004: Jan	966.2	747.1	524.8	386.1	222.4	8.6	31.2	56.7	21.7	104.2	219.0	17.3	201.7
Feb	965.9	749.6	522.0	385.4	227.6	9.9	32.5	56.9	22.7	105.6	216.3	16.1	200.1
Mar	998.8	769.3	535.9	396.1	233.4	10.9	33.1	57.4	22.0	110.1	229.5	18.0	211.5
Apr	1,010.9	779.6	546.4	405.3	233.2	11.2	33.8	58.9	22.0	107.3	231.3	18.9	212.4
May	1,019.1	788.7	558.3	416.1	230.4	11.3	33.7	61.3	22.5	101.7	230.4	19.0	211.4
June	1,022.9	790.4	561.8	417.2	228.5	11.7	33.4	62.2	20.9	100.4	232.5	17.6	214.9
July	1,037.5	803.5	567.7	419.5	235.7	12.0	34.3	64.1	22.5	102.9	234.0	18.2	215.8
Aug	1,044.4	815.3	580.2	429.8	235.1	12.5	32.7	63.0	22.8	104.1	229.1	18.3	210.7
Sept	1,048.7	820.7	576.8	429.1	243.8	12.8	32.5	64.1	23.3	111.2	228.0	18.3	209.7
Oct	1,048.5	821.1	581.7	430.0	239.4	12.9	33.0	64.1	25.5	103.9	227.4	15.5	211.9
Nov	1,063.4	827.8	585.1	429.4	242.7	12.6	32.8	63.9	27.2	106.3	235.5	18.8	216.7
Dec	1,073.5	839.8	597.8	432.3	242.0	12.2	32.8	64.1	28.2	104.7	233.7	18.3	215.4
2005: Jan	1,083.7	853.3	610.0	440.7	243.3	11.6	33.6	64.2	27.3	106.6	230.4	17.4	212.9
Feb	1,103.6	863.5	621.4	446.6	242.1	11.6	34.1	63.0	27.4	106.1	240.1	17.5	222.6
Mar	1,106.4	864.1	619.7	448.0	244.3	12.0	34.7	64.5	29.0	104.1	242.3	17.5	224.9
Apr	1,102.1	859.4	613.3	449.3	246.1	12.8	35.0	66.7	28.4	103.2	242.7	16.3	226.4
May	1,106.4	859.7	615.8	455.6	243.9	11.7	34.8	66.8	28.0	102.6	246.7	16.1	230.6
June	1,101.4	854.1	613.3	462.4	240.7	10.9	34.9	64.7	27.9	102.4	247.3	17.4	229.8
July	1,107.7	860.3	617.3	468.0	242.9	11.3	35.0	66.3	26.7	103.7	247.5	17.7	229.7
Aug	1,121.5	871.3	622.4	472.8	248.9	11.5	34.6	68.1	29.2	105.4	250.3	19.3	231.0
Sept	1,135.6	886.7	636.2	483.1	250.5	11.9	36.1	67.9	29.0	105.7	248.9	17.1	231.8
Oct[p]	1,144.2	891.0	642.1	488.9	249.0	11.7	34.4	68.4	29.8	104.7	253.2	18.7	234.5
Nov[p]	1,146.4	892.4	641.9	495.1	250.5	11.8	35.2	70.3	29.0	104.3	253.9	17.7	236.2

[1] Includes farm residential buildings.
[2] Includes residential improvements, not shown separately.
[3] New single- and multi-family units.
[4] Including farm.
[5] Health care, educational, religious, public safety, amusement and recreation, transportation, communication, power, highway and street, sewage and waste disposal, water supply, and conservation and development.

Note.—Data beginning 1993 reflect reclassification.

Source: Department of Commerce, Bureau of the Census.

TABLE B–56.—*New private housing units started, authorized, completed and houses sold, 1959–2005*

[Thousands; monthly data at seasonally adjusted annual rates]

Year or month	New housing units started				New housing units authorized [1]				New housing units completed	New houses sold
	Type of structure				Type of structure					
	Total	1 unit	2 to 4 units [2]	5 units or more	Total	1 unit	2 to 4 units	5 units or more		
1959	1,517.0	1,234.0	283.0		1,208.3	938.3	77.1	192.9		
1960	1,252.2	994.7	257.5		998.0	746.1	64.6	187.4		
1961	1,313.0	974.3	338.7		1,064.2	722.8	67.6	273.8		
1962	1,462.9	991.4	471.5		1,186.6	716.2	87.1	383.3		
1963	1,603.2	1,012.4	590.8		1,334.7	750.2	118.9	465.6		560
1964	1,528.8	970.5	108.3	450.0	1,285.8	720.1	100.8	464.9		565
1965	1,472.8	963.7	86.7	422.5	1,240.6	709.9	84.8	445.9		575
1966	1,164.9	778.6	61.2	325.1	971.9	563.2	61.0	347.7		461
1967	1,291.6	843.9	71.7	376.1	1,141.0	650.6	73.0	417.5		487
1968	1,507.6	899.4	80.7	527.3	1,353.4	694.7	84.3	574.4	1,319.8	490
1969	1,466.8	810.6	85.1	571.2	1,322.3	624.8	85.2	612.4	1,399.0	448
1970	1,433.6	812.9	84.9	535.9	1,351.5	646.8	88.1	616.7	1,418.4	485
1971	2,052.2	1,151.0	120.5	780.9	1,924.6	906.1	132.9	885.7	1,706.1	656
1972	2,356.6	1,309.2	141.2	906.2	2,218.9	1,033.1	148.6	1,037.2	2,003.9	718
1973	2,045.3	1,132.0	118.2	795.0	1,819.5	882.1	117.0	820.5	2,100.5	634
1974	1,337.7	888.1	68.0	381.6	1,074.4	643.8	64.3	366.2	1,728.5	519
1975	1,160.4	892.2	64.0	204.3	939.2	675.5	63.9	199.8	1,317.2	549
1976	1,537.5	1,162.4	85.8	289.2	1,296.2	893.6	93.1	309.5	1,377.2	646
1977	1,987.1	1,450.9	121.7	414.4	1,690.0	1,126.1	121.3	442.7	1,657.1	819
1978	2,020.3	1,433.3	125.1	462.0	1,800.5	1,182.6	130.6	487.3	1,867.5	817
1979	1,745.1	1,194.1	122.0	429.0	1,551.8	981.5	125.4	444.8	1,870.8	709
1980	1,292.2	852.2	109.5	330.5	1,190.6	710.4	114.5	365.7	1,501.6	545
1981	1,084.2	705.4	91.2	287.7	985.5	564.3	101.8	319.4	1,265.7	436
1982	1,062.2	662.6	80.1	319.6	1,000.5	546.4	88.3	365.8	1,005.5	412
1983	1,703.0	1,067.6	113.5	522.0	1,605.2	901.5	133.6	570.1	1,390.3	623
1984	1,749.5	1,084.2	121.4	543.9	1,681.8	922.4	142.6	616.8	1,652.2	639
1985	1,741.8	1,072.4	93.5	576.0	1,733.3	956.6	120.1	656.6	1,703.3	688
1986	1,805.4	1,179.4	84.0	542.0	1,769.4	1,077.6	108.4	583.5	1,756.4	750
1987	1,620.5	1,146.4	65.1	408.7	1,534.8	1,024.4	89.3	421.1	1,668.8	671
1988	1,488.1	1,081.3	58.7	348.0	1,455.6	993.8	75.7	386.1	1,529.8	676
1989	1,376.1	1,003.3	55.3	317.6	1,338.4	931.7	67.0	339.8	1,422.8	650
1990	1,192.7	894.8	37.6	260.4	1,110.8	793.9	54.3	262.6	1,308.0	534
1991	1,013.9	840.4	35.6	137.9	948.8	753.5	43.1	152.1	1,090.8	509
1992	1,199.7	1,029.9	30.9	139.0	1,094.9	910.7	45.8	138.4	1,157.5	610
1993	1,287.6	1,125.7	29.4	132.6	1,199.1	986.5	52.3	160.2	1,192.7	666
1994	1,457.0	1,198.4	35.2	223.5	1,371.6	1,068.5	62.2	241.0	1,346.9	670
1995	1,354.1	1,076.2	33.8	244.1	1,332.5	997.3	63.7	271.5	1,312.6	667
1996	1,476.8	1,160.9	45.3	270.8	1,425.6	1,069.5	65.8	290.3	1,412.9	757
1997	1,474.0	1,133.7	44.5	295.8	1,441.1	1,062.4	68.5	310.3	1,400.5	804
1998	1,616.9	1,271.4	42.6	302.9	1,612.3	1,187.6	69.2	355.5	1,474.2	886
1999	1,640.9	1,302.4	31.9	306.6	1,663.5	1,246.7	65.8	351.1	1,604.9	880
2000	1,568.7	1,230.9	38.7	299.1	1,592.3	1,198.1	64.9	329.3	1,573.7	877
2001	1,602.7	1,273.3	36.6	292.8	1,636.7	1,235.6	66.0	335.2	1,570.8	908
2002	1,704.9	1,358.6	38.5	307.9	1,747.7	1,332.6	73.7	341.4	1,648.4	973
2003	1,847.7	1,499.0	33.5	315.2	1,889.2	1,460.9	82.5	345.8	1,678.7	1,086
2004	1,955.8	1,610.5	42.3	303.0	2,070.1	1,613.4	90.4	366.2	1,841.9	1,203
2005 ᵖ	2,064.7	1,714.3	40.9	309.5	2,147.6	1,681.2	84.0	382.5	1,930.3	1,282
2004: Jan	1,927	1,562	30	335	1,963	1,546	94	323	1,734	1,155
Feb	1,852	1,485	29	338	1,984	1,574	90	320	1,716	1,158
Mar	2,007	1,638	32	337	2,064	1,633	101	330	1,793	1,253
Apr	1,968	1,624	36	308	2,069	1,610	92	367	1,956	1,162
May	1,974	1,649	56	269	2,129	1,660	88	381	1,909	1,243
June	1,827	1,526	26	275	2,014	1,606	83	325	1,857	1,205
July	1,986	1,661	64	261	2,114	1,625	105	384	1,888	1,104
Aug	2,025	1,689	68	268	2,058	1,606	85	367	1,909	1,165
Sept	1,912	1,555	31	326	2,039	1,593	78	368	1,784	1,223
Oct	2,062	1,666	41	355	2,093	1,603	87	403	1,841	1,306
Nov	1,807	1,484	39	284	2,093	1,588	90	415	1,725	1,175
Dec	2,050	1,713	48	289	2,081	1,620	90	371	1,911	1,247
2005: Jan	2,188	1,769	48	371	2,136	1,635	84	417	1,883	1,194
Feb	2,228	1,808	52	368	2,093	1,624	83	386	1,922	1,247
Mar	1,833	1,550	34	249	2,021	1,552	85	384	1,797	1,307
Apr	2,027	1,640	47	340	2,148	1,640	78	430	1,944	1,269
May	2,041	1,724	37	280	2,062	1,628	85	349	2,097	1,293
June	2,065	1,716	37	312	2,132	1,653	87	392	1,963	1,298
July	2,062	1,732	36	294	2,171	1,690	99	382	1,889	1,371
Aug	2,081	1,719	43	319	2,138	1,676	86	376	1,933	1,274
Sept	2,160	1,791	59	310	2,219	1,767	88	364	1,953	1,249
Oct	2,051	1,732	33	286	2,103	1,707	82	314	1,948	1,358
Nov ᵖ	2,121	1,798	33	290	2,163	1,724	81	358	1,882	1,233
Dec ᵖ	1,933	1,577	34	322	2,075	1,645	81	349	1,953	1,269

[1] Authorized by issuance of local building permits in permit-issuing places: beginning 2004, 20,000 places; 19,000 for 1994–2003; 17,000 for 1984–93; 16,000 for 1978–83; 14,000 for 1972–77; 13,000 for 1967–71; 12,000 for 1963–66; and 10,000 prior to 1963.

[2] Monthly data derived.

Note.—Data beginning 1999 for new housing units started and completed and for new houses sold are based on new estimation methods and are not directly comparable with earlier data.

Source: Department of Commerce, Bureau of the Census.

[Amounts in millions of dollars; monthly data seasonally adjusted]

Year or month	Total manufacturing and trade			Manufacturing			Merchant wholesalers			Retail trade			Retail and food services sales
	Sales[1]	Inventories[2]	Ratio[3]	Sales[1]	Inventories[2]	Ratio[3]	Sales[1]	Inventories[2]	Ratio[3]	Sales[1,4]	Inventories[2]	Ratio[3]	
SIC:[5]													
1965	80,283	120,929	1.51	40,995	68,207	1.66	15,611	18,317	1.17	23,677	34,405	1.45	....
1966	87,187	136,824	1.57	44,870	77,986	1.74	16,987	20,765	1.22	25,330	38,073	1.50	....
1967	90,820	145,681	1.60	46,486	84,646	1.82	19,576	25,786	1.32	24,757	35,249	1.42	....
1968	98,685	156,611	1.59	50,229	90,560	1.80	21,012	27,166	1.29	27,445	38,885	1.42	....
1969	105,690	170,400	1.61	53,501	98,145	1.83	22,818	29,800	1.31	29,371	42,455	1.45	....
1970	108,221	178,594	1.65	52,805	101,599	1.92	24,167	33,354	1.38	31,249	43,641	1.40	....
1971	116,895	188,991	1.62	55,906	102,567	1.83	26,492	36,568	1.38	34,497	49,856	1.45	....
1972	131,081	203,227	1.55	63,027	108,121	1.72	29,866	40,297	1.35	38,189	54,809	1.44	....
1973	153,677	234,406	1.53	72,931	124,499	1.71	38,115	46,918	1.23	42,631	62,989	1.48	....
1974	177,912	287,144	1.61	84,790	157,625	1.86	47,982	58,667	1.22	45,141	70,852	1.57	....
1975	182,198	288,992	1.59	86,589	159,708	1.84	46,634	57,774	1.24	48,975	71,510	1.46	....
1976	204,150	318,345	1.56	98,797	174,636	1.77	50,698	64,622	1.27	54,655	79,087	1.45	....
1977	229,513	350,706	1.53	113,201	188,378	1.66	56,136	73,179	1.30	60,176	89,149	1.48	....
1978	260,320	400,931	1.54	126,905	211,691	1.67	66,413	86,934	1.31	67,002	102,306	1.53	....
1979	297,701	452,640	1.52	143,936	242,157	1.68	79,051	99,679	1.26	74,713	110,804	1.48	....
1980	327,233	508,924	1.56	154,391	265,215	1.72	93,099	122,631	1.32	79,743	121,078	1.52	....
1981	355,822	545,786	1.53	168,129	283,413	1.69	101,180	129,654	1.28	86,514	132,719	1.53	....
1982	347,625	573,908	1.67	163,351	311,852	1.95	95,211	127,428	1.36	89,062	134,628	1.49	....
1983	369,286	590,287	1.56	172,547	312,379	1.78	99,225	130,075	1.28	97,514	147,833	1.44	....
1984	410,124	649,780	1.53	190,682	339,516	1.73	112,199	142,452	1.23	107,243	167,812	1.49	....
1985	422,583	664,039	1.56	194,538	334,749	1.73	113,459	147,409	1.28	114,586	181,881	1.52	....
1986	430,419	662,738	1.55	194,657	322,654	1.68	114,960	153,574	1.32	120,803	186,510	1.56	....
1987	457,735	709,848	1.50	206,326	338,109	1.59	122,968	163,903	1.29	128,442	207,836	1.55	....
1988	497,157	767,222	1.49	224,619	369,374	1.57	134,521	178,801	1.30	138,017	219,047	1.54	....
1989	527,039	815,455	1.52	236,698	391,212	1.63	143,760	187,009	1.28	146,581	237,234	1.58	....
1990	545,909	840,594	1.52	242,686	405,073	1.65	149,506	195,833	1.29	153,718	239,688	1.56	....
1991	542,815	834,609	1.53	239,847	390,950	1.65	148,306	200,448	1.33	154,661	243,211	1.54	....
1992	567,176	842,809	1.48	250,394	382,510	1.54	154,150	208,302	1.32	162,632	251,997	1.52	....
NAICS:[5]													
1992	541,017	836,555	1.52	242,002	378,732	1.57	148,639	198,884	1.31	150,376	258,939	1.67	167,327
1993	567,951	863,467	1.50	251,708	379,650	1.50	155,405	206,774	1.30	160,838	277,043	1.67	178,842
1994	610,510	926,578	1.46	269,843	399,926	1.44	165,981	223,958	1.29	174,686	302,694	1.66	193,489
1995	655,297	985,395	1.48	289,973	424,896	1.44	181,369	240,473	1.30	183,955	320,026	1.71	203,423
1996	687,557	1,004,682	1.46	299,766	430,593	1.43	191,936	243,194	1.27	195,855	330,895	1.66	216,097
1997	724,012	1,045,825	1.42	319,558	443,723	1.37	199,788	260,713	1.26	204,666	341,389	1.64	226,170
1998	742,386	1,078,402	1.43	324,984	449,182	1.38	203,495	273,910	1.32	214,356	355,310	1.62	237,043
1999	786,597	1,138,602	1.40	335,991	463,709	1.35	217,449	291,290	1.30	233,157	383,603	1.59	256,914
2000	834,353	1,197,793	1.41	350,715	481,651	1.36	235,053	309,820	1.29	248,584	406,322	1.59	274,061
2001	822,999	1,140,044	1.43	335,242	447,583	1.40	231,939	297,182	1.32	255,819	395,279	1.58	282,330
2002	823,870	1,142,517	1.37	326,713	423,265	1.31	235,368	300,671	1.26	261,789	418,581	1.55	289,472
2003	850,144	1,160,136	1.35	331,654	418,536	1.27	245,539	306,556	1.23	272,951	435,044	1.54	302,066
2004	936,136	1,249,976	1.30	364,465	450,637	1.20	278,196	339,639	1.17	293,476	459,700	1.54	325,145
2004: Jan	882,057	1,160,617	1.32	342,696	418,985	1.22	258,049	306,364	1.19	281,312	435,268	1.55	311,973
Feb	888,982	1,169,540	1.32	342,327	421,149	1.23	263,485	310,581	1.18	283,170	437,810	1.55	313,973
Mar	919,851	1,178,635	1.28	358,320	423,155	1.18	271,880	312,803	1.15	289,651	442,677	1.53	320,815
Apr	917,654	1,186,243	1.29	357,831	425,094	1.19	273,761	312,981	1.14	286,062	448,168	1.57	317,103
May	928,045	1,194,376	1.29	359,378	429,200	1.19	275,440	317,009	1.15	293,227	448,167	1.53	324,439
June	927,942	1,206,898	1.30	363,501	433,106	1.19	275,861	320,389	1.16	288,580	453,403	1.57	319,926
July	935,235	1,219,242	1.30	365,217	437,473	1.20	277,722	325,410	1.17	292,296	456,359	1.56	323,929
Aug	945,827	1,230,178	1.30	371,976	440,509	1.18	281,122	329,038	1.17	292,729	460,631	1.57	324,257
Sept	947,748	1,229,158	1.30	368,539	441,152	1.20	281,412	330,201	1.17	297,797	457,805	1.54	329,876
Oct	958,291	1,234,960	1.29	373,313	445,357	1.19	284,409	334,739	1.18	300,569	454,864	1.51	332,904
Nov	964,138	1,247,803	1.29	375,710	450,148	1.20	287,839	338,711	1.18	300,589	458,944	1.53	332,874
Dec	975,644	1,249,976	1.28	380,511	450,637	1.18	291,456	339,639	1.17	303,677	459,700	1.51	336,432
2005: Jan	978,620	1,260,850	1.29	382,257	456,853	1.20	292,430	343,126	1.17	303,933	460,871	1.52	336,785
Feb	975,100	1,267,111	1.30	378,367	459,282	1.21	290,976	345,294	1.19	305,757	462,535	1.51	338,991
Mar	983,324	1,272,133	1.29	384,622	461,291	1.20	291,624	347,275	1.19	307,078	463,567	1.51	340,075
Apr	991,433	1,275,463	1.29	383,583	461,687	1.20	295,487	349,626	1.18	312,363	464,150	1.49	346,081
May	993,287	1,277,275	1.29	386,344	461,219	1.19	295,647	350,764	1.19	311,296	465,292	1.49	344,933
June	1,001,155	1,276,804	1.28	386,436	461,511	1.19	297,096	352,337	1.19	317,623	462,956	1.46	351,320
July	1,008,882	1,271,304	1.26	386,858	464,221	1.20	298,514	352,670	1.18	323,510	454,413	1.40	357,285
Aug	1,015,597	1,276,131	1.26	395,009	463,115	1.17	303,781	354,386	1.17	316,807	458,630	1.45	350,742
Sept	1,022,252	1,282,217	1.25	393,566	463,591	1.18	311,199	356,354	1.15	317,487	462,272	1.46	351,802
Oct	1,028,132	1,287,238	1.25	396,181	466,414	1.18	314,028	357,212	1.14	317,923	463,612	1.46	352,541
Nov *ᵖ*	1,029,174	1,293,509	1.26	397,047	467,144	1.18	311,714	358,647	1.15	320,413	467,718	1.46	355,387

[1] Annual data are averages of monthly not seasonally adjusted figures.

[2] Seasonally adjusted, end of period. Inventories beginning January 1982 for manufacturing and December 1980 for wholesale and retail trade are not comparable with earlier periods.

[3] Inventory/sales ratio. Annual data are: beginning 1982, averages of monthly ratios; for 1965–81, ratio of December inventories to monthly average sales for the year; and for earlier years, weighted averages. Monthly ratios are inventories at end of month to sales for month.

[4] Food services included on SIC basis and excluded on NAICS basis. See last column for retail and food services sales.

[5] Effective in 2001, data classified based on North American Industry Classification System (NAICS). Data on NAICS basis available beginning 1992. Earlier data based on Standard Industrial Classification (SIC). Data include semiconductors.

Note.—Earlier data are not strictly comparable with data beginning 1967 for wholesale and retail trade.

Source: Department of Commerce, Bureau of the Census.

TABLE B–58.—*Manufacturers' shipments and inventories, 1965–2005*

[Millions of dollars; monthly data seasonally adjusted]

Year or month	Shipments [1]			Inventories [2]								
					Durable goods industries				Nondurable goods industries			
	Total	Durable goods industries	Nondurable goods industries	Total	Total	Materials and supplies	Work in process	Finished goods	Total	Materials and supplies	Work in process	Finished goods
SIC:[3]												
1965	40,995	22,193	18,802	68,207	42,189	13,298	18,055	10,836	26,018	10,487	3,825	11,706
1966	44,870	24,617	20,253	77,986	49,852	15,464	21,908	12,480	28,134	11,197	4,226	12,711
1967	46,486	25,233	21,253	84,646	54,896	16,423	24,933	13,540	29,750	11,760	4,431	13,559
1968	50,229	27,624	22,605	90,560	58,732	17,344	27,213	14,175	31,828	12,328	4,852	14,648
1969	53,501	29,403	24,098	98,145	64,598	18,636	30,282	15,680	33,547	12,753	5,120	15,674
1970	52,805	28,156	24,649	101,599	66,651	19,149	29,745	17,757	34,948	13,168	5,271	16,509
1971	55,906	29,924	25,982	102,567	66,136	19,679	28,550	17,907	36,431	13,686	5,678	17,067
1972	63,027	33,987	29,040	108,121	70,067	20,807	30,713	18,547	38,054	14,677	5,998	17,379
1973	72,931	39,635	33,296	124,499	81,192	25,944	35,490	19,758	43,307	18,147	6,729	18,431
1974	84,790	44,173	40,617	157,625	101,493	35,070	42,530	23,893	56,132	23,744	8,189	24,199
1975	86,589	43,598	42,991	159,708	102,590	33,903	43,227	25,460	57,118	23,565	8,834	24,719
1976	98,797	50,623	48,174	174,636	111,988	37,457	46,074	28,457	62,648	25,847	9,929	26,872
1977	113,201	59,168	54,033	188,378	120,877	40,186	50,226	30,465	67,501	27,387	10,961	29,153
1978	126,905	67,731	59,174	211,691	138,181	45,198	58,848	34,135	73,510	29,619	12,085	31,806
1979	143,936	75,927	68,009	242,157	160,734	52,670	69,325	38,739	81,423	32,814	13,910	34,699
1980	154,391	77,419	76,972	265,215	174,788	55,173	76,945	42,670	90,427	36,606	15,884	37,937
1981	168,129	83,727	84,402	283,413	186,443	57,998	80,998	47,447	96,970	38,165	16,194	42,611
1982	163,351	79,212	84,139	311,852	200,444	59,136	86,707	54,601	111,408	44,039	18,612	48,757
1983	172,547	85,481	87,066	312,379	199,854	60,325	86,899	52,630	112,525	44,816	18,691	49,018
1984	190,682	97,940	92,742	339,516	221,330	66,031	98,251	57,048	118,186	45,692	19,328	53,166
1985	194,538	101,279	93,259	334,749	218,193	63,904	98,162	56,127	116,556	44,106	19,442	53,008
1986	194,657	103,238	91,419	322,654	211,997	61,331	97,000	53,666	110,657	42,335	18,124	50,198
1987	206,326	108,128	98,198	338,109	220,799	63,562	102,393	54,844	117,310	45,319	19,270	52,721
1988	224,619	118,458	106,161	369,374	242,468	69,611	112,958	59,899	126,906	49,396	20,559	56,951
1989	236,698	123,158	113,540	391,212	257,513	72,435	122,251	62,827	133,699	50,674	21,653	61,372
1990	242,686	123,776	118,910	405,073	263,209	73,559	124,130	65,520	141,864	52,645	22,817	66,402
1991	239,847	121,000	118,847	390,950	250,019	70,834	114,960	64,225	140,931	53,011	22,815	65,105
1992	250,394	128,489	121,905	382,510	238,105	69,459	104,424	64,222	144,405	54,007	23,532	66,866
NAICS:[3]												
1992	242,002	126,572	115,430	378,732	238,008	69,764	104,001	64,243	140,724	53,239	23,338	64,147
1993	251,708	133,712	117,996	379,650	238,627	72,681	101,779	64,167	141,023	54,342	23,341	63,340
1994	269,843	147,005	122,838	399,926	253,054	78,593	106,347	68,114	146,872	57,230	24,417	65,225
1995	289,973	158,568	131,405	424,896	267,375	85,512	106,511	75,352	157,521	60,802	25,783	70,936
1996	299,766	164,883	134,883	430,593	272,533	86,259	110,448	75,826	158,060	59,173	26,461	72,426
1997	319,558	178,949	140,610	443,723	281,119	92,300	109,873	78,946	162,604	60,220	28,514	73,870
1998	324,984	185,966	139,019	449,182	290,735	93,587	115,195	81,953	158,447	58,259	27,085	73,103
1999	335,991	193,895	142,096	463,709	296,591	97,886	114,095	84,610	167,118	61,103	28,808	77,207
2000	350,715	197,807	152,908	481,651	306,743	106,107	111,194	89,442	174,908	61,503	30,107	83,298
2001	335,242	183,592	151,650	447,583	279,602	94,157	103,330	82,115	167,981	58,230	27,617	82,134
2002	326,713	177,341	149,372	423,265	260,427	87,323	92,867	79,822	162,838	56,572	28,207	78,059
2003	331,654	178,164	153,490	418,536	253,559	83,897	91,862	77,800	164,977	57,557	28,517	78,903
2004	364,465	196,508	167,957	450,637	274,800	94,073	96,704	84,023	175,837	59,830	29,009	86,998
2004: Jan	342,696	184,413	158,283	418,985	253,486	84,038	92,063	77,385	165,499	57,812	28,695	78,992
Feb	342,327	186,455	155,872	421,149	254,184	84,591	92,152	77,441	166,965	58,524	29,013	79,428
Mar	358,320	195,675	162,645	423,155	255,537	85,791	92,099	77,647	167,618	58,379	29,340	79,899
Apr	357,831	193,562	164,269	425,094	257,157	87,176	92,670	77,311	167,937	58,484	29,560	79,893
May	359,378	192,750	166,628	429,200	259,110	87,419	93,049	78,642	170,090	58,390	28,891	82,809
June	363,501	195,759	167,742	433,106	262,103	88,649	93,941	79,513	171,003	58,494	29,224	83,285
July	365,217	195,468	169,749	437,473	264,967	89,969	95,079	79,919	172,506	59,324	28,712	84,470
Aug	371,976	199,813	172,163	440,509	267,232	90,483	95,123	81,626	173,277	59,334	28,663	85,280
Sept	368,539	199,408	169,131	441,152	268,297	91,076	94,323	82,898	172,855	59,211	28,105	85,539
Oct	373,313	198,980	174,333	445,357	270,894	92,560	95,398	82,936	174,463	59,772	28,406	86,285
Nov	375,710	199,412	176,298	450,148	274,026	93,809	96,868	83,349	176,122	59,905	28,731	87,486
Dec	380,511	207,145	173,366	450,637	274,800	94,073	96,704	84,023	175,837	59,830	29,009	86,998
2005: Jan	382,257	206,217	176,040	456,853	278,433	95,534	97,708	85,191	178,420	60,525	28,109	89,786
Feb	378,367	203,141	175,226	459,282	280,129	95,484	98,776	85,869	179,153	60,586	28,740	89,827
Mar	384,622	204,445	180,177	461,291	281,005	95,717	98,528	86,760	180,286	61,134	29,102	90,050
Apr	383,583	204,389	179,194	461,687	281,087	96,020	98,164	86,903	180,600	61,099	28,401	91,100
May	386,344	205,944	180,400	461,219	281,584	96,028	98,321	87,235	179,635	61,211	27,946	90,478
June	386,436	206,451	179,985	461,511	280,518	95,896	97,938	86,684	180,993	61,480	28,073	91,440
July	386,858	205,013	181,845	464,221	282,815	95,506	99,581	87,728	181,406	61,489	27,815	92,102
Aug	395,009	209,844	185,165	463,115	282,007	95,405	98,740	87,862	181,108	61,914	27,844	91,350
Sept	393,566	209,831	183,735	463,591	282,301	95,566	99,316	87,419	181,290	61,931	27,938	91,421
Oct	396,181	212,334	183,847	466,414	283,704	95,729	100,326	87,649	182,710	62,316	28,708	91,686
Nov[P]	397,047	212,409	184,638	467,144	285,228	96,154	101,083	87,991	181,916	61,810	28,905	91,201

[1] Annual data are averages of monthly not seasonally adjusted figures.
[2] Seasonally adjusted, end of period. Data beginning 1982 are not comparable with earlier data.
[3] Effective in 2001, data classified based on North American Industry Classification System (NAICS). Data on NAICS basis available beginning 1992. Earlier data based on Standard Industrial Classification (SIC).
Data include semiconductors.

Source: Department of Commerce, Bureau of the Census.

[Amounts in millions of dollars; monthly data seasonally adjusted]

Year or month	New orders[1]				Unfilled orders[2]			Unfilled orders—shipments ratio[2]		
	Total	Durable goods industries		Non-durable goods industries	Total	Durable goods industries	Non-durable goods industries	Total	Durable goods industries	Non-durable goods industries
		Total	Capital goods, non-defense							
SIC:[3]										
1965	42,137	23,286	....	18,851	78,249	74,459	3,790	3.25	3.86	0.79
1966	46,420	26,163	....	20,258	96,846	93,002	3,844	3.74	4.48	.75
1967	47,067	25,803	....	21,265	103,711	99,735	3,976	3.66	4.37	.73
1968	50,657	28,051	6,314	22,606	108,377	104,393	3,984	3.79	4.58	.69
1969	53,990	29,876	7,046	24,114	114,341	110,161	4,180	3.71	4.45	.69
1970	52,022	27,340	6,072	24,682	105,008	100,412	4,596	3.61	4.36	.76
1971	55,921	29,905	6,682	26,016	105,247	100,225	5,022	3.32	4.00	.76
1972	64,182	35,038	7,745	29,144	119,349	113,034	6,315	3.26	3.85	.86
1973	76,003	42,627	9,926	33,376	156,561	149,204	7,357	3.80	4.51	.91
1974	87,327	46,862	11,594	40,465	187,043	181,519	5,524	4.09	4.93	.62
1975	85,139	41,957	9,886	43,181	169,546	161,664	7,882	3.69	4.45	.82
1976	99,513	51,307	11,490	48,206	178,128	169,857	8,271	3.24	3.88	.74
1977	115,109	61,035	13,681	54,073	202,024	193,323	8,701	3.24	3.85	.71
1978	131,629	72,278	17,588	59,351	259,169	248,281	10,888	3.57	4.20	.81
1979	147,604	79,483	21,154	68,121	303,593	291,321	12,272	3.89	4.62	.82
1980	156,359	79,392	21,135	76,967	327,416	315,202	12,214	3.85	4.58	.75
1981	168,025	83,654	21,806	84,371	326,547	314,707	11,840	3.87	4.68	.69
1982	162,140	78,064	19,213	84,077	311,887	300,798	11,089	3.84	4.74	.62
1983	175,451	88,140	19,624	87,311	347,273	333,114	14,159	3.53	4.29	.69
1984	192,879	100,164	23,669	92,715	373,529	359,651	13,878	3.60	4.37	.64
1985	195,706	102,356	24,545	93,351	387,196	372,097	15,099	3.67	4.47	.68
1986	195,204	103,647	23,982	91,557	393,515	376,699	16,816	3.59	4.41	.70
1987	209,389	110,809	26,094	98,579	430,426	408,688	21,738	3.63	4.43	.83
1988	228,270	122,076	31,108	106,194	474,154	452,150	22,004	3.64	4.46	.76
1989	239,572	126,055	32,988	113,516	508,849	487,098	21,751	3.96	4.85	.77
1990	244,507	125,583	33,331	118,924	531,131	509,124	22,007	4.15	5.15	.76
1991	238,805	119,849	30,471	118,957	519,199	495,802	23,397	4.08	5.07	.79
1992	248,212	126,308	31,524	121,905	492,893	469,381	23,512	3.51	4.30	.75
NAICS:[3]										
1992	....	128,672	40,681	....	....	450,975	....	....	4.85	....
1993	246,668	128,672	40,681	....	....	425,833	....	....	4.35	....
1994	266,641	143,803	45,175	....	....	434,941	....	....	4.01	....
1995	285,542	154,137	51,011	....	....	447,487	....	....	3.86	....
1996	297,282	162,399	54,066	....	....	488,915	....	....	4.15	....
1997	314,986	174,377	60,697	....	....	513,202	....	....	4.04	....
1998	317,345	178,327	62,133	....	....	496,385	....	....	3.78	....
1999	329,770	187,674	64,392	....	....	505,750	....	....	3.74	....
2000	346,789	193,881	69,278	....	....	549,646	....	....	4.03	....
2001	326,435	174,786	58,232	....	....	511,596	....	....	4.21	....
2002	318,008	168,636	52,442	....	....	468,123	....	....	4.05	....
2003	329,219	175,729	54,847	....	....	505,626	....	....	4.06	....
2004	361,177	193,220	61,073	....	....	547,944	....	....	3.94	....
2004: Jan	336,711	178,428	53,765	....	....	505,686	....	....	4.10	....
Feb	337,355	181,483	53,813	....	....	506,979	....	....	4.09	....
Mar	361,145	198,500	62,962	....	....	516,232	....	....	3.99	....
Apr	354,388	190,119	58,295	....	....	519,325	....	....	4.03	....
May	356,415	189,787	59,396	....	....	523,228	....	....	4.05	....
June	359,932	192,190	59,679	....	....	526,286	....	....	4.00	....
July	364,652	194,903	66,582	....	....	532,903	....	....	4.00	....
Aug	367,598	195,435	61,282	....	....	535,674	....	....	3.99	....
Sept	364,352	195,221	62,490	....	....	538,394	....	....	4.01	....
Oct	366,812	192,479	60,162	....	....	538,987	....	....	4.01	....
Nov	375,215	198,917	65,347	....	....	545,701	....	....	4.07	....
Dec	375,820	202,454	66,430	....	....	547,944	....	....	3.94	....
2005: Jan	372,642	196,602	64,908	....	....	545,812	....	....	3.90	....
Feb	374,908	199,682	66,527	....	....	549,247	....	....	3.98	....
Mar	376,107	195,930	63,297	....	....	547,243	....	....	3.92	....
Apr	376,033	196,839	66,012	....	....	546,771	....	....	3.93	....
May	391,656	211,256	78,376	....	....	559,106	....	....	3.99	....
June	395,324	215,339	76,688	....	....	574,800	....	....	4.09	....
July	385,553	203,708	70,886	....	....	580,753	....	....	4.18	....
Aug	396,767	211,602	73,722	....	....	589,978	....	....	4.12	....
Sept	391,151	207,416	67,293	....	....	594,816	....	....	4.19	....
Oct	397,614	213,767	71,771	....	....	603,370	....	....	4.16	....
Nov *p*	407,711	223,073	85,809	....	....	621,432	....	....	4.27	....

[1] Annual data are averages of monthly not seasonally adjusted figures.
[2] Unfilled orders are seasonally adjusted, end of period. Ratios are unfilled orders at end of period to shipments for period (excludes industries with no unfilled orders). Annual ratios relate to seasonally adjusted data for December.
[3] Effective in 2001, data classified based on North American Industry Classification System (NAICS). Data on NAICS basis available beginning 1992. Earlier data based on the Standard Industrial Classification (SIC).
Data on SIC basis include semiconductors. Data on NAICS basis do not include semiconductors.

Note.—For data beginning 1992 on NAICS basis, since there are no unfilled orders for manufacturers' nondurable goods, manufacturers' nondurable new orders and nondurable shipments are the same (see Table B–58).

Source: Department of Commerce, Bureau of the Census.

PRICES

TABLE B–60.—*Consumer price indexes for major expenditure classes, 1959–2005*

[For all urban consumers; 1982-84=100, except as noted]

Year or month	All items (CPI-U)	Food and beverages Total[1]	Food	Apparel	Housing	Transportation	Medical care	Entertainment	Recreation[2]	Education and communication[2]	Other goods and services	Energy[3]
1959	29.1		29.7	45.0		29.8	21.5					21.9
1960	29.6		30.0	45.7		29.8	22.3					22.4
1961	29.9		30.4	46.1		30.1	22.9					22.5
1962	30.2		30.6	46.3		30.8	23.5					22.6
1963	30.6		31.1	46.9		30.9	24.1					22.6
1964	31.0		31.5	47.3		31.4	24.6					22.5
1965	31.5		32.2	47.8		31.9	25.2					22.9
1966	32.4		33.8	49.0		32.3	26.3					23.3
1967	33.4	35.0	34.1	51.0	30.8	33.3	28.2	40.7			35.1	23.8
1968	34.8	36.2	35.3	53.7	32.0	34.3	29.9	43.0			36.9	24.2
1969	36.7	38.1	37.1	56.8	34.0	35.7	31.9	45.2			38.7	24.8
1970	38.8	40.1	39.2	59.2	36.4	37.5	34.0	47.5			40.9	25.5
1971	40.5	41.4	40.4	61.1	38.0	39.5	36.1	50.0			42.9	26.5
1972	41.8	43.1	42.1	63.2	39.4	39.9	37.3	51.5			44.7	27.2
1973	44.4	48.8	48.2	64.6	41.2	41.2	38.8	52.9			46.4	29.4
1974	49.3	55.5	55.1	69.4	45.8	45.8	42.4	56.9			49.8	38.1
1975	53.8	60.2	59.8	72.5	50.7	50.1	47.5	62.0			53.9	42.1
1976	56.9	62.1	61.6	75.2	53.8	55.1	52.0	65.1			57.0	45.1
1977	60.6	65.8	65.5	78.6	57.4	59.0	57.0	68.3			60.4	49.4
1978	65.2	72.2	72.0	81.4	62.4	61.7	61.8	71.9			64.3	52.5
1979	72.6	79.9	79.9	84.9	70.1	70.5	67.5	76.7			68.9	65.7
1980	82.4	86.7	86.8	90.9	81.1	83.1	74.9	83.6			75.2	86.0
1981	90.9	93.5	93.6	95.3	90.4	93.2	82.9	90.1			82.6	97.7
1982	96.5	97.3	97.4	97.8	96.9	97.0	92.5	96.0			91.1	99.2
1983	99.6	99.5	99.4	100.2	99.5	99.3	100.6	100.1			101.1	99.9
1984	103.9	103.2	103.2	102.1	103.6	103.7	106.8	103.8			107.9	100.9
1985	107.6	105.6	105.6	105.0	107.7	106.4	113.5	107.9			114.5	101.6
1986	109.6	109.1	109.0	105.9	110.9	102.3	122.0	111.6			121.4	88.2
1987	113.6	113.5	113.5	110.6	114.2	105.4	130.1	115.3			128.5	88.6
1988	118.3	118.2	118.2	115.4	118.5	108.7	138.6	120.3			137.0	89.3
1989	124.0	124.9	125.1	118.6	123.0	114.1	149.3	126.5			147.7	94.3
1990	130.7	132.1	132.4	124.1	128.5	120.5	162.8	132.4			159.0	102.1
1991	136.2	136.8	136.3	128.7	133.6	123.8	177.0	138.4			171.6	102.5
1992	140.3	138.7	137.9	131.9	137.5	126.5	190.1	142.3			183.3	103.0
1993	144.5	141.6	140.9	133.7	141.2	130.4	201.4	145.8	90.7	85.5	192.9	104.2
1994	148.2	144.9	144.3	133.4	144.8	134.3	211.0	150.1	92.7	88.8	198.5	104.6
1995	152.4	148.9	148.4	132.0	148.5	139.1	220.5	153.9	94.5	92.2	206.9	105.2
1996	156.9	153.7	153.3	131.7	152.8	143.0	228.2	159.1	97.4	95.3	215.4	110.1
1997	160.5	157.7	157.3	132.9	156.8	144.3	234.6	162.5	99.6	98.4	224.8	111.5
1998	163.0	161.1	160.7	133.0	160.4	141.6	242.1		101.1	100.3	237.7	102.9
1999	166.6	164.6	164.1	131.3	163.9	144.4	250.6		102.0	101.2	258.3	106.6
2000	172.2	168.4	167.8	129.6	169.6	153.3	260.8		103.3	102.5	271.1	124.6
2001	177.1	173.6	173.1	127.3	176.4	154.3	272.8		104.9	105.2	282.6	129.3
2002	179.9	176.8	176.2	124.0	180.3	152.9	285.6		106.2	107.9	293.2	121.7
2003	184.0	180.5	180.0	120.9	184.8	157.6	297.1		107.5	109.8	298.7	136.5
2004	188.9	186.6	186.2	120.4	189.5	163.1	310.1		108.6	111.6	304.7	151.4
2005	195.3	191.2	190.7	119.5	195.7	173.9	323.2		109.4	113.7	313.4	177.1
2004: Jan	185.2	184.3	183.8	115.8	186.3	157.0	303.6		107.9	111.1	301.4	137.4
Feb	186.2	184.5	184.1	118.6	187.0	158.8	306.0		108.4	111.2	302.3	140.6
Mar	187.4	184.9	184.4	123.5	187.9	160.5	307.5		108.8	111.1	303.1	143.1
Apr	188.0	185.0	184.5	124.3	188.4	161.8	308.3		109.0	110.9	303.6	145.9
May	189.1	186.5	186.1	123.4	188.9	165.2	309.0		108.8	110.6	303.8	154.1
June	189.7	186.8	186.3	120.1	190.3	165.7	310.0		108.9	110.8	304.1	159.7
July	189.4	187.2	186.8	115.9	190.9	164.0	311.0		108.7	110.9	305.1	156.3
Aug	189.5	187.3	186.8	116.5	191.2	162.9	311.6		108.5	111.7	305.5	155.3
Sept	189.9	187.2	186.7	121.2	191.0	162.9	312.3		108.6	112.9	306.3	154.3
Oct	190.9	188.4	187.9	124.1	191.0	166.4	313.3		108.7	112.5	306.8	157.7
Nov	191.0	188.6	188.2	123.0	190.8	167.2	314.1		108.7	112.7	307.0	158.6
Dec	190.3	188.9	188.5	118.8	190.7	164.8	314.9		108.5	112.6	307.8	153.7
2005: Jan	190.7	189.5	189.1	116.1	191.8	164.0	316.8		108.9	112.7	309.3	151.9
Feb	191.8	189.3	188.8	118.7	192.7	166.1	319.3		109.0	112.8	310.8	155.2
Mar	193.3	189.6	189.1	123.5	194.1	168.8	320.7		109.0	112.7	311.2	160.8
Apr	194.6	190.7	190.2	123.7	194.4	173.2	321.5		109.2	112.9	311.6	170.9
May	194.4	191.1	190.6	122.4	194.5	172.1	322.2		109.5	112.7	312.5	169.4
June	194.5	190.9	190.4	118.3	195.5	171.8	322.9		109.1	112.8	312.5	171.4
July	195.4	191.3	190.8	113.8	196.6	174.4	324.1		109.1	112.9	314.1	178.5
Aug	196.4	191.3	190.9	115.8	196.9	177.7	323.9		109.3	113.7	314.4	186.6
Sept	198.8	191.8	191.4	120.5	197.0	186.5	324.6		109.7	115.3	315.0	208.0
Oct	199.2	192.5	192.1	127.0	198.4	184.0	326.2		109.9	115.1	315.3	204.3
Nov	197.6	192.8	192.4	121.5	198.5	175.6	328.1		109.8	115.3	316.2	187.6
Dec	196.8	193.2	192.9	117.5	198.3	172.7	328.4		109.7	115.3	317.3	180.0

[1] Includes alcoholic beverages, not shown separately.
[2] December 1997=100.
[3] Household fuels—gas (piped), electricity, fuel oil, etc.—and motor fuel. Motor oil, coolant, etc. also included through 1982.

Note.—Data beginning 1983 incorporate a rental equivalence measure for homeowners' costs.
Series reflect changes in composition and renaming beginning in 1998, and formula and methodology changes beginning in 1999.

Source: Department of Labor, Bureau of Labor Statistics.

TABLE B-61.—*Consumer price indexes for selected expenditure classes, 1959–2005*

[For all urban consumers; 1982-84=100, except as noted]

Year or month	Food and beverages Total[1]	Food			Housing Total	Shelter			Fuels and utilities				Furnishings and operations
		Total	At home	Away from home		Total[2]	Rent of primary residence	Owners' equivalent rent of primary residence[3]	Total[2]	Fuels			
										Total	Fuel oil and other fuels	Gas (piped) and electricity	
1959	....	29.7	31.2	24.8	....	24.7	38.2	....	25.4	....		13.9	22.4	....
1960	....	30.0	31.5	25.4	....	25.2	38.7	....	26.0	....	13.8	23.3	....
1961	....	30.4	31.8	26.0	....	25.4	39.2	....	26.3	....	14.1	23.5	....
1962	....	30.6	32.0	26.7	....	25.8	39.7	....	26.3	....	14.2	23.5	....
1963	....	31.1	32.4	27.3	....	26.1	40.1	....	26.6	....	14.4	23.5	....
1964	....	31.5	32.7	27.8	....	26.5	40.5	....	26.6	....	14.4	23.5	....
1965	....	32.2	33.5	28.4	....	27.0	40.9	....	26.6	....	14.6	23.5	....
1966	....	33.8	35.2	29.7	....	27.8	41.5	....	26.7	....	15.0	23.6	....
1967	35.0	34.1	35.1	31.3	30.8	28.8	42.2	....	27.1	21.4	15.5	23.7	42.0
1968	36.2	35.3	36.3	32.9	32.0	30.1	43.3	....	27.4	21.7	16.0	23.9	43.6
1969	38.1	37.1	38.0	34.9	34.0	32.6	44.7	....	28.0	22.1	16.3	24.3	45.2
1970	40.1	39.2	39.9	37.5	36.4	35.5	46.5	....	29.1	23.1	17.0	25.4	46.8
1971	41.4	40.4	40.9	39.4	38.0	37.0	48.7	....	31.1	24.7	18.2	27.1	48.6
1972	43.1	42.1	42.7	41.0	39.4	38.7	50.4	....	32.5	25.7	18.3	28.5	49.7
1973	48.8	48.2	49.7	44.2	41.2	40.5	52.5	....	34.3	27.5	21.1	29.9	51.1
1974	55.5	55.1	57.1	49.8	45.8	44.4	55.2	....	40.7	34.4	33.2	34.5	56.8
1975	60.2	59.8	61.8	54.5	50.7	48.8	58.0	....	45.4	39.4	36.4	40.1	63.4
1976	62.1	61.6	63.1	58.2	53.8	51.5	61.1	....	49.4	43.3	38.8	44.7	67.3
1977	65.8	65.5	66.8	62.6	57.4	54.9	64.8	....	54.7	49.0	43.9	50.5	70.4
1978	72.2	72.0	73.8	68.3	62.4	60.5	69.3	....	58.5	53.0	46.2	55.0	74.7
1979	79.9	79.9	81.8	75.9	70.1	68.9	74.3	....	64.8	61.3	62.4	61.0	79.9
1980	86.7	86.8	88.4	83.4	81.1	81.0	80.9	....	75.4	74.8	86.1	71.4	86.3
1981	93.5	93.6	94.8	90.9	90.4	90.5	87.9	....	86.4	87.2	104.6	81.9	93.0
1982	97.3	97.4	98.1	95.8	96.9	96.9	94.6	....	94.9	95.6	103.4	93.2	98.0
1983	99.5	99.4	99.1	100.0	99.5	99.1	100.1	102.5	100.2	100.5	97.2	101.5	100.2
1984	103.2	103.2	102.8	104.2	103.6	104.0	105.3	107.3	104.8	104.0	99.4	105.4	101.9
1985	105.6	105.6	104.3	108.3	107.7	109.8	111.8	113.2	106.5	104.5	95.9	107.1	103.8
1986	109.1	109.0	107.3	112.5	110.9	115.8	118.3	119.4	104.1	99.2	77.6	105.7	105.2
1987	113.5	113.5	111.9	117.0	114.2	121.3	123.1	124.8	103.0	97.3	77.9	103.8	107.1
1988	118.2	118.2	116.6	121.8	118.5	127.1	127.8	131.1	104.4	98.0	78.1	104.6	109.4
1989	124.9	125.1	124.2	127.4	123.0	132.8	132.8	137.4	107.8	100.9	81.7	107.5	111.2
1990	132.1	132.4	132.3	133.4	128.5	140.0	138.4	144.8	111.6	104.5	99.3	109.3	113.3
1991	136.8	136.3	135.8	137.9	133.6	146.3	143.3	150.4	115.3	106.7	94.6	112.6	116.0
1992	138.7	137.9	136.8	140.7	137.5	151.2	146.9	155.5	117.8	108.1	90.7	114.8	118.0
1993	141.6	140.9	140.1	143.2	141.2	155.7	150.3	160.5	121.3	111.2	90.3	118.5	119.3
1994	144.9	144.3	144.1	145.7	144.8	160.5	154.0	165.8	122.8	111.7	88.8	119.2	121.0
1995	148.9	148.4	148.8	149.0	148.5	165.7	157.8	171.3	123.7	111.5	88.1	119.2	123.0
1996	153.7	153.3	154.3	152.7	152.8	171.0	162.0	176.8	127.5	115.2	99.2	122.1	124.7
1997	157.7	157.3	158.1	157.0	156.8	176.3	166.7	181.9	130.8	117.9	99.8	125.1	125.4
1998	161.1	160.7	161.1	161.1	160.4	182.1	172.1	187.8	128.5	113.7	90.0	121.2	126.6
1999	164.6	164.1	164.2	165.1	163.9	187.3	177.5	192.9	128.8	113.5	91.4	120.9	126.7
2000	168.4	167.8	167.9	169.0	169.6	193.4	183.9	198.7	137.9	122.8	129.7	128.0	128.2
2001	173.6	173.1	173.4	173.9	176.4	200.6	192.1	206.3	150.2	135.4	129.3	142.4	129.1
2002	176.8	176.2	175.6	178.3	180.3	208.1	199.7	214.7	143.6	127.2	115.5	134.4	128.3
2003	180.5	180.0	179.4	182.1	184.8	213.1	205.5	219.9	154.5	138.2	139.5	145.0	126.1
2004	186.6	186.2	186.2	187.5	189.5	218.8	211.0	224.9	161.9	144.4	160.5	150.6	125.5
2005	191.2	190.7	189.8	193.4	195.7	224.4	217.3	230.2	179.0	161.6	208.6	166.5	126.1
2004: Jan	184.3	183.8	184.0	184.9	186.3	215.2	208.3	222.6	156.3	139.2	149.9	145.5	125.3
Feb	184.5	184.1	184.0	185.5	187.0	216.0	208.8	222.9	156.9	139.5	155.1	145.5	125.7
Mar	184.9	184.4	184.3	185.8	187.9	217.8	209.2	223.3	155.2	137.6	152.5	143.5	125.7
Apr	185.0	184.5	184.1	186.2	188.4	218.4	209.7	223.9	155.6	138.0	149.6	144.2	125.6
May	186.5	186.1	186.6	186.7	188.9	218.7	210.2	224.3	158.1	140.4	150.4	146.8	125.4
June	186.8	186.3	186.8	187.0	190.3	219.2	210.7	224.7	165.5	148.5	150.7	155.8	125.6
July	187.2	186.8	187.1	187.8	190.9	220.0	211.2	225.1	166.6	149.5	151.1	156.9	125.2
Aug	187.3	186.8	186.7	188.4	191.2	220.3	211.9	225.7	167.7	150.5	157.4	157.6	124.8
Sept	187.2	186.7	186.1	188.9	191.0	220.2	212.4	226.1	166.7	149.3	161.6	156.0	125.0
Oct	188.4	187.9	187.9	189.4	191.0	220.6	212.8	226.5	162.8	144.9	177.3	150.0	126.1
Nov	188.6	188.2	188.1	189.6	190.8	219.9	213.2	226.8	165.6	147.8	186.6	152.7	125.8
Dec	188.9	188.5	188.5	189.9	190.7	219.8	213.9	227.2	165.7	148.0	183.7	153.0	125.5
2005: Jan	189.5	189.1	188.9	190.8	191.8	221.0	214.5	227.8	166.9	149.0	181.2	154.3	126.1
Feb	189.3	188.8	188.0	191.4	192.7	222.5	215.0	228.4	166.4	148.1	188.5	152.9	126.1
Mar	189.6	189.1	188.1	191.7	194.1	224.4	215.5	228.7	166.7	148.4	195.5	152.7	126.1
Apr	190.7	190.2	189.8	192.1	194.4	224.4	216.0	229.0	169.6	151.5	199.5	155.9	126.3
May	191.1	190.6	190.3	192.6	194.5	224.0	216.4	229.4	171.7	153.7	193.9	158.7	126.7
June	190.9	190.4	189.4	193.2	195.5	224.5	216.8	229.7	177.4	159.9	195.0	165.6	126.0
July	191.3	190.8	189.8	193.6	196.6	225.6	217.5	230.2	180.1	162.6	202.9	168.1	125.9
Aug	191.3	190.9	189.5	194.2	196.9	225.6	218.0	230.7	181.8	164.4	209.8	169.5	125.8
Sept	191.8	191.4	190.0	194.6	197.0	224.4	218.6	231.2	188.9	172.1	235.9	176.4	125.7
Oct	192.5	192.1	190.8	195.2	198.4	225.7	219.3	231.7	192.8	176.2	241.1	180.7	125.9
Nov	192.8	192.4	191.0	195.6	198.5	225.4	220.0	232.2	194.6	178.0	231.5	183.4	126.1
Dec	193.2	192.9	191.7	196.0	198.3	225.6	220.5	232.8	191.6	174.7	227.8	180.0	126.4

[1] Includes alcoholic beverages, not shown separately.
[2] Includes other items, not shown separately.
[3] December 1982=100.

See next page for continuation of table.

352

TABLE B–61.—*Consumer price indexes for selected expenditure classes, 1959–2005*—Continued

[For all urban consumers; 1982-84=100, except as noted]

Year or month	Transportation								Medical care		
	Total	Private transportation						Public transportation	Total	Medical care commodities	Medical care services
		Total²	New vehicles		Used cars and trucks	Motor fuel	Motor vehicle maintenance and repair				
			Total²	New cars							
1959	29.8	30.8	52.3	52.2	26.8	23.7	26.0	21.5	21.5	46.8	18.7
1960	29.8	30.6	51.6	51.5	25.0	24.4	26.5	22.2	22.3	46.9	19.5
1961	30.1	30.8	51.6	51.5	26.0	24.1	27.1	23.2	22.9	46.3	20.2
1962	30.8	31.4	51.4	51.3	28.4	24.3	27.5	24.0	23.5	45.6	20.9
1963	30.9	31.6	51.1	51.0	28.7	24.2	27.8	24.3	24.1	45.2	21.5
1964	31.4	32.0	50.9	50.9	30.0	24.1	28.2	24.7	24.6	45.1	22.0
1965	31.9	32.5	49.8	49.7	29.8	25.1	28.7	25.2	25.2	45.0	22.7
1966	32.3	32.9	48.9	48.8	29.0	25.6	29.2	26.1	26.3	45.1	23.9
1967	33.3	33.8	49.3	49.3	29.9	26.4	30.4	27.4	28.2	44.9	26.0
1968	34.3	34.8	50.7	50.7	....	26.8	32.1	28.7	29.9	45.0	27.9
1969	35.7	36.0	51.5	51.5	30.9	27.6	34.1	30.9	31.9	45.4	30.2
1970	37.5	37.5	53.1	53.0	31.2	27.9	36.6	35.2	34.0	46.5	32.3
1971	39.5	39.4	55.3	55.2	33.0	28.1	39.3	37.8	36.1	47.3	34.7
1972	39.9	39.7	54.8	54.7	33.1	28.4	41.1	39.3	37.3	47.4	35.9
1973	41.2	41.0	54.8	54.8	35.2	31.2	43.2	39.7	38.8	47.5	37.5
1974	45.8	46.2	58.0	57.9	36.7	42.2	47.6	40.6	42.4	49.2	41.4
1975	50.1	50.6	63.0	62.9	43.8	45.1	53.7	43.5	47.5	53.3	46.6
1976	55.1	55.6	67.0	66.9	50.3	47.0	57.6	47.8	52.0	56.5	51.3
1977	59.0	59.7	70.5	70.4	54.7	49.7	61.9	50.0	57.0	60.2	56.4
1978	61.7	62.5	75.9	75.8	55.8	51.8	67.0	51.5	61.8	64.4	61.2
1979	70.5	71.7	81.9	81.8	60.2	70.1	73.7	54.9	67.5	69.0	67.2
1980	83.1	84.2	88.5	88.4	62.3	97.4	81.5	69.0	74.9	75.4	74.8
1981	93.2	93.8	93.9	93.7	76.9	108.5	89.2	85.6	82.9	83.7	82.8
1982	97.0	97.1	97.5	97.4	88.8	102.8	96.0	94.9	92.5	92.3	92.6
1983	99.3	99.3	99.9	99.9	98.7	99.4	100.3	99.5	100.6	100.2	100.7
1984	103.7	103.6	102.6	102.8	112.5	97.9	103.8	105.7	106.8	107.5	106.7
1985	106.4	106.2	106.1	106.1	113.7	98.7	106.8	110.5	113.5	115.2	113.2
1986	102.3	101.2	110.6	110.6	108.8	77.1	110.3	117.0	122.0	122.8	121.9
1987	105.4	104.2	114.4	114.6	113.1	80.2	114.8	121.1	130.1	131.0	130.0
1988	108.7	107.6	116.5	116.9	118.0	80.9	119.7	123.3	138.6	139.9	138.3
1989	114.1	112.9	119.2	119.2	120.4	88.5	124.9	129.5	149.3	150.8	148.9
1990	120.5	118.8	121.4	121.0	117.6	101.2	130.1	142.6	162.8	163.4	162.7
1991	123.8	121.9	126.0	125.3	118.1	99.4	136.0	148.9	177.0	176.8	177.1
1992	126.5	124.6	129.2	128.4	123.2	99.0	141.3	151.4	190.1	188.1	190.5
1993	130.4	127.5	132.7	131.5	133.9	98.0	145.9	167.0	201.4	195.0	202.9
1994	134.3	131.4	137.6	136.0	141.7	98.5	150.2	172.0	211.0	200.7	213.4
1995	139.1	136.3	141.0	139.0	156.5	100.0	154.0	175.9	220.5	204.5	224.2
1996	143.0	140.0	143.7	141.4	157.0	106.3	158.4	181.9	228.2	210.4	232.4
1997	144.3	141.0	144.3	141.7	151.1	106.2	162.7	186.7	234.6	215.3	239.1
1998	141.6	137.9	143.4	140.7	150.6	92.2	167.1	190.3	242.1	221.8	246.8
1999	144.4	140.5	142.9	139.6	152.0	100.7	171.9	197.7	250.6	230.7	255.1
2000	153.3	149.1	142.8	139.6	155.8	129.3	177.3	209.6	260.8	238.1	266.0
2001	154.3	150.0	142.1	138.9	158.7	124.7	183.5	210.6	272.8	247.6	278.8
2002	152.9	148.8	140.0	137.3	152.0	116.6	190.2	207.4	285.6	256.4	292.9
2003	157.6	153.6	137.9	134.7	142.9	135.8	195.6	209.3	297.1	262.8	306.0
2004	163.1	159.4	137.1	133.9	133.3	160.4	200.2	209.1	310.1	269.3	321.3
2005	173.9	170.2	137.9	135.2	139.4	195.7	206.9	217.3	323.2	276.0	336.7
2004: Jan	157.0	153.2	138.0	134.7	130.8	136.7	198.2	206.3	303.6	265.5	313.8
Feb	158.8	154.9	138.3	134.8	131.0	143.1	198.2	208.1	306.0	266.7	316.6
Mar	160.5	156.6	137.9	134.6	131.2	150.5	198.5	209.9	307.5	267.3	318.4
Apr	161.8	157.9	137.6	134.3	131.3	155.9	198.6	211.5	308.3	268.5	319.2
May	165.2	161.5	137.4	134.4	131.8	170.5	199.0	210.7	309.0	269.1	319.8
June	165.7	161.9	137.2	134.2	130.6	173.3	199.7	212.3	310.0	269.6	321.0
July	164.0	160.0	135.9	133.0	132.1	165.2	200.3	214.4	311.0	269.9	322.3
Aug	162.9	159.1	134.9	132.0	133.8	162.0	200.8	209.7	311.6	270.0	323.1
Sept	162.9	159.4	134.9	131.9	136.5	161.2	200.7	205.3	312.3	270.3	323.7
Oct	166.4	162.9	135.9	133.0	136.8	173.1	201.7	206.5	313.3	271.7	324.8
Nov	167.2	163.6	137.9	134.9	136.7	171.9	202.9	208.6	314.1	271.2	326.0
Dec	164.8	161.3	138.8	135.5	137.3	161.2	203.3	205.4	314.9	270.8	327.3
2005: Jan	164.0	160.5	139.8	136.4	137.5	156.4	204.0	204.4	316.8	271.6	329.5
Feb	166.1	162.6	139.9	136.4	137.6	164.3	203.9	205.9	319.3	272.8	332.5
Mar	168.8	165.2	139.1	135.7	137.7	175.9	204.7	210.1	320.7	273.2	334.3
Apr	173.2	169.6	138.8	135.6	138.1	193.9	205.0	215.0	321.5	273.5	335.2
May	172.1	168.3	138.7	135.5	138.8	188.2	205.6	218.0	322.2	274.6	335.9
June	171.8	167.7	138.1	135.1	139.9	185.5	206.1	222.4	322.9	275.6	336.3
July	174.4	170.3	136.3	133.9	141.0	197.5	206.7	226.1	324.1	276.3	337.8
Aug	177.7	173.8	135.0	132.7	142.0	212.7	207.3	223.3	323.9	276.8	337.3
Sept	186.5	183.1	135.8	133.6	141.5	249.5	208.7	220.7	324.6	277.7	337.9
Oct	184.0	180.5	137.1	135.1	140.6	237.1	209.8	222.7	326.2	278.9	339.7
Nov	175.6	171.8	138.0	136.1	139.4	199.7	210.5	220.8	328.1	280.3	341.7
Dec	172.7	168.9	138.3	136.6	139.2	187.3	210.7	217.6	328.4	280.8	342.0

Source: Department of Labor, Bureau of Labor Statistics.

TABLE B–62.—*Consumer price indexes for commodities, services, and special groups, 1960–2005*

[For all urban consumers; 1982-84=100, except as noted]

Year or month	All items (CPI-U)	Commodities		Services		Special indexes				All items		
		All commodities	Commodities less food	All services	Services less medical care services	All items less food	All items less energy	All items less food and energy	All items less medical care	CPI-U-X1 (Dec. 1982= 97.6)[1]	CPI-U-RS (Dec. 1977= 100)[2]	C-CPI-U (Dec. 1999= 100)[3]
1960	29.6	33.6	36.0	24.1	25.0	29.7	30.4	30.6	30.2	32.2	....	....
1961	29.9	33.8	36.1	24.5	25.4	30.0	30.7	31.0	30.5	32.5	....	....
1962	30.2	34.1	36.3	25.0	25.9	30.3	31.1	31.4	30.8	32.8	....	....
1963	30.6	34.4	36.6	25.5	26.3	30.7	31.5	31.8	31.1	33.3	....	....
1964	31.0	34.8	36.9	26.0	26.8	31.1	32.0	32.3	31.5	33.7	....	....
1965	31.5	35.2	37.2	26.6	27.4	31.6	32.5	32.7	32.0	34.2	....	....
1966	32.4	36.1	37.7	27.6	28.3	32.3	33.5	33.5	33.0	35.2	....	....
1967	33.4	36.8	38.6	28.8	29.3	33.4	34.4	34.7	33.7	36.3	....	....
1968	34.8	38.1	40.0	30.3	30.8	34.9	35.9	36.3	35.1	37.7	....	....
1969	36.7	39.9	41.7	32.4	32.9	36.8	38.0	38.4	37.0	39.4	....	....
1970	38.8	41.7	43.4	35.0	35.6	39.0	40.3	40.8	39.2	41.3	....	....
1971	40.5	43.2	45.1	37.0	37.5	40.8	42.0	42.7	40.8	43.1	....	....
1972	41.8	44.5	46.1	38.4	38.9	42.0	43.4	44.0	42.1	44.4	....	....
1973	44.4	47.8	47.7	40.1	40.6	43.7	46.1	45.6	44.8	47.2	....	....
1974	49.3	53.5	52.8	43.8	44.3	48.0	50.6	49.4	49.8	51.9	....	....
1975	53.8	58.2	57.6	48.0	48.3	52.5	55.1	53.9	54.3	56.2	....	....
1976	56.9	60.7	60.5	52.0	52.2	56.0	58.2	57.4	57.2	59.4	....	....
1977	60.6	64.2	63.8	56.0	55.9	59.6	61.9	61.0	60.8	63.2	....	....
1978	65.2	68.8	67.5	60.8	60.7	63.9	66.7	65.5	65.4	67.5	104.3	....
1979	72.6	76.6	75.3	67.5	67.5	71.2	73.4	71.9	72.9	74.0	114.1	....
1980	82.4	86.0	85.7	77.9	78.2	81.5	81.9	80.8	82.8	82.3	126.7	....
1981	90.9	93.2	93.1	88.1	88.7	90.4	90.1	89.2	91.4	90.1	138.6	....
1982	96.5	97.0	96.9	96.0	96.4	96.3	96.1	95.8	96.8	95.6	146.8	....
1983	99.6	99.8	100.0	99.4	99.2	99.7	99.6	99.6	99.6	99.6	152.9	....
1984	103.9	103.2	103.1	104.6	104.4	104.0	104.3	104.6	103.7	103.9	159.0	....
1985	107.6	105.4	105.2	109.9	109.6	108.0	108.4	109.1	107.2	107.6	164.3	....
1986	109.6	104.4	101.7	115.4	114.6	109.8	112.6	113.5	108.8	109.6	167.3	....
1987	113.6	107.7	104.3	120.2	119.1	113.6	117.2	118.2	112.6	113.6	173.0	....
1988	118.3	111.5	107.7	125.7	124.3	118.3	122.3	123.4	117.0	118.3	179.3	....
1989	124.0	116.7	112.0	131.9	130.1	123.7	128.1	129.0	122.4	124.0	187.0	....
1990	130.7	122.8	117.4	139.2	136.8	130.3	134.7	135.5	128.8	130.7	196.3	....
1991	136.2	126.6	121.3	146.3	143.3	136.1	140.9	142.1	133.8	136.2	203.4	....
1992	140.3	129.1	124.2	152.0	148.4	140.8	145.4	147.3	137.5	140.3	208.5	....
1993	144.5	131.5	126.3	157.9	153.6	145.1	150.0	152.2	141.2	144.5	213.7	....
1994	148.2	133.8	127.9	163.1	158.4	149.0	154.1	156.5	144.7	148.2	218.2	....
1995	152.4	136.4	129.8	168.7	163.5	153.1	158.7	161.2	148.6	152.4	223.5	....
1996	156.9	139.9	132.6	174.1	168.7	157.5	163.1	165.6	152.8	156.9	229.5	....
1997	160.5	141.8	133.4	179.4	173.9	161.1	167.1	169.5	156.3	160.5	234.4	....
1998	163.0	141.9	132.0	184.2	178.4	163.4	170.9	173.4	158.6	163.0	237.7	....
1999	166.6	144.4	134.0	188.8	182.7	167.0	174.4	177.0	162.0	166.6	242.7	....
2000	172.2	149.2	139.2	195.3	188.9	173.0	178.6	181.3	167.3	172.2	250.8	102.0
2001	177.1	150.7	138.9	203.4	196.6	177.8	183.5	186.1	171.9	177.1	257.8	104.3
2002	179.9	149.7	136.0	209.8	202.5	180.5	187.7	190.5	174.3	179.9	261.9	105.6
2003	184.0	151.2	136.5	216.5	208.7	184.7	190.6	193.2	178.1	184.0	267.9	107.8
2004	188.9	154.7	138.8	222.8	214.5	189.4	194.4	196.6	182.7	188.9	275.1	110.2
2005	195.3	160.2	144.5	230.1	221.2	196.0	198.7	200.9	188.7	195.3	284.4	113.3
2004: Jan	185.2	151.1	134.7	219.1	211.0	185.5	191.9	194.0	179.1	185.2	269.7	108.3
Feb	186.2	152.3	136.3	219.9	211.7	186.6	192.7	194.9	180.1	186.2	271.2	108.9
Mar	187.4	153.7	138.0	221.0	212.7	188.0	193.7	196.1	181.3	187.4	272.9	109.6
Apr	188.0	154.3	138.9	221.5	213.2	188.6	194.1	196.5	181.8	188.0	273.8	109.9
May	189.1	156.0	140.6	221.9	213.6	189.6	194.3	196.5	182.9	189.1	275.3	110.3
June	189.7	155.8	140.3	223.3	215.0	190.3	194.4	196.6	183.5	189.7	276.2	110.6
July	189.4	154.5	138.2	224.1	215.8	189.9	194.5	196.6	183.2	189.4	275.9	110.5
Aug	189.5	154.2	137.7	224.5	216.2	189.9	194.7	196.8	183.2	189.5	275.9	110.5
Sept	189.9	154.9	138.8	224.5	216.1	190.4	195.2	197.4	183.6	189.9	276.5	110.8
Oct	190.9	157.1	141.4	224.5	216.0	191.4	196.0	198.2	184.6	190.9	278.0	111.3
Nov	191.0	157.2	141.4	224.6	216.1	191.5	196.0	198.1	184.7	191.0	278.2	111.3
Dec	190.3	155.8	139.3	224.6	216.0	190.6	195.8	197.8	183.9	190.3	277.1	110.9
2005: Jan	190.7	155.4	138.6	225.6	217.0	190.9	196.4	198.4	184.2	190.7	277.7	111.1
Feb	191.8	156.5	140.2	226.8	218.0	192.3	197.3	199.5	185.3	191.8	279.3	111.7
Mar	193.3	158.2	142.5	228.0	219.2	194.0	198.3	200.7	186.8	193.3	281.5	112.5
Apr	194.6	160.3	144.9	228.6	219.7	195.3	198.6	200.9	188.1	194.6	283.4	113.1
May	194.4	159.8	144.0	228.8	219.9	195.1	198.6	200.8	187.9	194.4	283.1	113.1
June	194.5	158.9	142.8	229.8	220.9	195.2	198.5	200.6	187.9	194.5	283.2	113.0
July	195.4	159.5	143.5	230.9	222.0	196.1	198.7	200.8	188.8	195.4	284.5	113.4
Aug	196.4	161.1	145.7	231.3	222.5	197.3	198.9	201.0	189.8	196.4	286.0	113.8
Sept	198.8	165.6	151.8	231.7	222.8	200.0	199.2	201.3	192.3	198.8	289.5	114.7
Oct	199.2	165.1	150.8	233.0	224.1	200.4	200.1	202.3	192.6	199.2	290.1	115.0
Nov	197.6	161.5	145.6	233.5	224.4	198.5	200.2	202.3	190.9	197.6	287.7	114.4
Dec	196.8	160.0	143.3	233.2	224.2	197.4	200.1	202.1	190.0	196.8	286.6	114.0

[1] CPI-U-X1 is a rental equivalence approach to homeowners' costs for the CPI-U for years prior to 1983, the first year for which the official index incorporates such a measure. CPI-U-X1 is rebased to the December 1982 value of the CPI-U (1982-84=100) and is identical with CPI-U data from December 1982 forward. Data prior to 1967 estimated by moving the series at the same rate as the CPI-U for each year.

[2] CPI research series using current methods (CPI-U-RS) introduced in June 1999. Data for 2005 are preliminary. All data are subject to revision annually.

[3] Chained consumer price index introduced in August 2002. Data for 2004 and 2005 are subject to revision.

Source: Department of Labor, Bureau of Labor Statistics.

TABLE B–63.—*Changes in special consumer price indexes, 1960–2005*

[For all urban consumers; percent change]

Year or month	All items (CPI-U)		All items less food		All items less energy		All items less food and energy		All items less medical care	
	Dec. to Dec.¹	Year to year	Dec. to Dec.¹	Year to year	Dec. to Dec.¹	Year to year	Dec. to Dec.¹	Year to year	Dec. to Dec.¹	Year to year
1960	1.4	1.7	1.0	1.7	1.3	1.7	1.0	1.3	1.3	1.3
1961	.7	1.0	1.3	1.0	.7	1.0	1.3	1.3	.3	1.0
1962	1.3	1.0	1.0	1.0	1.3	1.3	1.3	1.3	1.3	1.0
1963	1.6	1.3	1.6	1.3	1.9	1.3	1.6	1.3	1.6	1.0
1964	1.0	1.3	1.0	1.3	1.3	1.6	1.2	1.6	1.0	1.3
1965	1.9	1.6	1.6	1.6	1.9	1.6	1.5	1.2	1.9	1.6
1966	3.5	2.9	3.5	2.2	3.4	3.1	3.3	2.4	3.4	3.1
1967	3.0	3.1	3.3	3.4	3.2	2.7	3.8	3.6	2.7	2.1
1968	4.7	4.2	5.0	4.5	4.9	4.4	5.1	4.6	4.7	4.2
1969	6.2	5.5	5.6	5.4	6.5	5.8	6.2	5.8	6.1	5.4
1970	5.6	5.7	6.6	6.0	5.4	6.1	6.6	6.3	5.2	5.9
1971	3.3	4.4	3.0	4.6	3.4	4.2	3.1	4.7	3.2	4.1
1972	3.4	3.2	2.9	2.9	3.5	3.3	3.0	3.0	3.4	3.2
1973	8.7	6.2	5.6	4.0	8.2	6.2	4.7	3.6	9.1	6.4
1974	12.3	11.0	12.2	9.8	11.7	9.8	11.1	8.3	12.2	11.2
1975	6.9	9.1	7.3	9.4	6.6	8.9	6.7	9.1	6.7	9.0
1976	4.9	5.8	6.1	6.7	4.8	5.6	6.1	6.5	4.5	5.3
1977	6.7	6.5	6.4	6.4	6.7	6.4	6.5	6.3	6.7	6.3
1978	9.0	7.6	8.3	7.2	9.1	7.8	8.5	7.4	9.1	7.6
1979	13.3	11.3	14.0	11.4	11.1	10.0	11.3	9.8	13.4	11.5
1980	12.5	13.5	13.0	14.5	11.7	11.6	12.2	12.4	12.5	13.6
1981	8.9	10.3	9.8	10.9	8.5	10.0	9.5	10.4	8.8	10.4
1982	3.8	6.2	4.1	6.5	4.2	6.7	4.5	7.4	3.6	5.9
1983	3.8	3.2	4.1	3.5	4.5	3.6	4.8	4.0	3.6	2.9
1984	3.9	4.3	3.9	4.3	4.4	4.7	4.7	5.0	3.9	4.1
1985	3.8	3.6	4.1	3.8	4.0	3.9	4.3	4.3	3.5	3.4
1986	1.1	1.9	.5	1.7	3.8	3.9	3.8	4.0	.7	1.5
1987	4.4	3.6	4.6	3.5	4.1	4.1	4.2	4.1	4.3	3.5
1988	4.4	4.1	4.2	4.1	4.7	4.4	4.7	4.4	4.2	3.9
1989	4.6	4.8	4.5	4.6	4.6	4.7	4.4	4.5	4.5	4.6
1990	6.1	5.4	6.3	5.3	5.2	5.2	5.2	5.0	5.9	5.2
1991	3.1	4.2	3.3	4.5	3.9	4.6	4.4	4.9	2.7	3.9
1992	2.9	3.0	3.2	3.5	3.0	3.2	3.3	3.7	2.7	2.8
1993	2.7	3.0	2.7	3.1	3.1	3.2	3.2	3.3	2.6	2.7
1994	2.7	2.6	2.6	2.7	2.6	2.7	2.6	2.8	2.5	2.5
1995	2.5	2.8	2.7	2.8	2.9	3.0	3.0	3.0	2.5	2.7
1996	3.3	3.0	3.1	2.9	2.9	2.8	2.6	2.7	3.3	2.8
1997	1.7	2.3	1.8	2.3	2.1	2.5	2.2	2.4	1.6	2.3
1998	1.6	1.6	1.5	1.4	2.4	2.3	2.4	2.3	1.5	1.5
1999	2.7	2.2	2.8	2.2	2.0	2.0	1.9	2.1	2.6	2.1
2000	3.4	3.4	3.5	3.6	2.6	2.4	2.6	2.4	3.3	3.3
2001	1.6	2.8	1.3	2.8	2.8	2.7	2.7	2.6	1.4	2.7
2002	2.4	1.6	2.6	1.5	1.8	2.3	1.9	2.4	2.2	1.4
2003	1.9	2.3	1.5	2.3	1.5	1.5	1.1	1.4	1.8	2.2
2004	3.3	2.7	3.4	2.5	2.2	2.0	2.2	1.8	3.2	2.6
2005	3.4	3.4	3.6	3.5	2.2	2.2	2.2	2.2	3.3	3.3
Percent change from preceding month										
	Unadjusted	Seasonally adjusted	Unadjusted	Seasonally adjusted	Unadjusted	Seasonally adjusted	Unadjusted	Seasonally adjusted	Unadjusted	Seasonally adjusted
2004: Jan	0.5	0.5	0.6	0.5	0.2	0.2	0.2	0.2	0.5	0.4
Feb	.5	.3	.6	.3	.4	.2	.5	.2	.6	.3
Mar	.6	.4	.8	.5	.5	.3	.6	.3	.7	.5
Apr	.3	.2	.3	.3	.2	.2	.2	.2	.3	.2
May	.6	.6	.5	.5	.1	.3	0	.2	.6	.6
June	.3	.3	.4	.3	.1	.2	.1	.1	.3	.3
July	-.2	-.1	-.2	-.1	.1	.1	0	.1	-.2	-.1
Aug	.1	.1	0	.1	.1	.1	.1	.1	0	0
Sept	.2	.2	.3	.2	.3	.3	.3	.3	.2	.2
Oct	.5	.6	.5	.6	.4	.3	.4	.2	.5	.6
Nov	.1	.3	.1	.3	0	.2	-.1	.2	.1	.2
Dec	-.4	0	-.5	-.1	-.1	.1	-.2	.2	-.4	0
2005: Jan	.2	.1	.2	.1	.3	.2	.3	.2	.2	.1
Feb	.6	.4	.7	.4	.5	.2	.6	.3	.6	.3
Mar	.8	.6	.9	.7	.5	.4	.6	.4	.8	.6
Apr	.7	.5	.7	.5	.2	.2	.1	.0	.7	.5
May	-.1	-.1	-.1	-.1	0	.2	-.0	.2	-.1	-.1
June	.1	0	.1	0	-.1	.1	-.1	.1	0	0
July	.5	.5	.5	.6	.1	.2	.1	.1	.5	.5
Aug	.5	.5	.6	.6	.1	.1	.1	.1	.5	.6
Sept	1.2	1.2	1.4	1.4	.2	.2	.1	.1	1.3	1.3
Oct	.2	.2	.2	.2	.5	.3	.5	.2	.2	.2
Nov	-.8	-.6	-.9	-.7	.0	.3	0	.2	-.9	-.7
Dec	-.4	-.1	-.6	-.1	-.0	.2	-.1	.1	-.5	-.1

¹ Changes from December to December are based on unadjusted indexes.

Source: Department of Labor, Bureau of Labor Statistics.

TABLE B–64.—*Changes in consumer price indexes for commodities and services, 1929–2005*

[For all urban consumers; percent change]

Year	All items (CPI-U)		Commodities				Services				Medical care[2]		Energy[3]	
			Total		Food		Total		Medical care					
	Dec. to Dec.[1]	Year to year	Dec. to Dec.[1]	Year to year	Dec. to Dec.[1]	Year to year	Dec. to Dec.[1]	Year to year	Dec. to Dec.[1]	Year to year	Dec. to Dec.[1]	Year to year	Dec. to Dec.[1]	Year to year
1929	0.6	0	....	....	2.5	1.2	....	....	....	....	....	....	....	....
1933	.8	−5.1	....	....	6.9	−2.8	....	....	....	....	....	....	....	....
1939	0	−1.4	−0.7	−2.0	−2.5	−2.5	0	0	1.2	1.2	1.0	0	....	....
1940	.7	.7	1.4	.7	2.5	1.7	.8	.8	0	0	0	1.0	....	....
1941	9.9	5.0	13.3	6.7	15.7	9.2	2.4	.8	1.2	0	1.0	0	....	....
1942	9.0	10.9	12.9	14.5	17.9	17.6	2.3	3.1	3.5	3.5	3.8	2.9	....	....
1943	3.0	6.1	4.2	9.3	3.0	11.0	2.3	2.3	5.6	4.5	4.6	4.7	....	....
1944	2.3	1.7	2.0	1.0	0	−1.2	2.2	2.2	3.2	4.3	2.6	3.6	....	....
1945	2.2	2.3	2.9	3.0	3.5	2.4	.7	1.5	3.1	3.1	2.6	2.6	....	....
1946	18.1	8.3	24.8	10.6	31.3	14.5	3.6	1.4	9.0	5.1	8.3	5.0	....	....
1947	8.8	14.4	10.3	20.5	11.3	21.7	5.6	4.3	6.4	8.7	6.9	8.0	....	....
1948	3.0	8.1	1.7	7.2	−.8	8.3	5.9	6.1	6.9	7.1	5.8	6.7	....	....
1949	−2.1	−1.2	−4.1	−2.7	−3.9	−4.2	3.7	5.1	1.6	3.3	1.4	2.8	....	....
1950	5.9	1.3	7.8	.7	9.8	1.6	3.6	3.0	4.0	2.4	3.4	2.0	....	....
1951	6.0	7.9	5.9	9.0	7.1	11.0	5.2	5.3	5.3	4.7	5.8	5.3	....	....
1952	.8	1.9	−.9	1.3	−1.0	1.8	4.4	4.5	5.8	6.7	4.3	5.0	....	....
1953	.7	.8	−.3	−.3	−1.1	−1.4	4.2	4.3	3.4	3.5	3.5	3.6	....	....
1954	−.7	.7	−1.6	−.9	−1.8	−.4	2.0	3.1	2.6	3.4	2.3	2.9	....	....
1955	.4	−.4	−.3	−.9	−.7	−1.4	2.0	2.0	3.2	2.6	3.3	2.2	....	....
1956	3.0	1.5	2.6	1.0	2.9	.7	3.4	2.5	3.8	3.8	3.2	3.8	....	....
1957	2.9	3.3	2.8	3.2	2.8	3.2	4.2	4.3	4.8	4.3	4.7	4.2	....	....
1958	1.8	2.8	1.2	2.1	2.4	4.5	2.7	3.7	4.6	5.3	4.5	4.6	−0.9	0
1959	1.7	.7	.6	0	−1.0	−1.7	3.9	3.1	4.9	4.5	3.8	4.4	4.7	1.9
1960	1.4	1.7	1.2	.9	3.1	1.0	2.5	3.4	3.7	4.3	3.2	3.7	1.3	2.3
1961	.7	1.0	0	.6	−.7	1.3	2.1	1.7	3.5	3.6	3.1	2.7	−1.3	.4
1962	1.3	1.0	.9	.9	1.3	.7	1.6	2.0	2.9	3.5	2.2	2.6	2.2	.4
1963	1.6	1.3	1.5	.9	2.0	1.6	2.4	2.0	2.8	2.9	2.5	2.6	−.9	0
1964	1.0	1.3	.9	1.2	1.3	1.3	1.6	2.0	2.3	2.3	2.1	2.1	0	−.4
1965	1.9	1.6	1.4	1.1	3.5	2.2	2.7	2.3	3.6	3.2	2.8	2.4	1.8	1.8
1966	3.5	2.9	2.5	2.6	4.0	5.0	4.8	3.8	8.3	5.3	6.7	4.4	1.7	1.7
1967	3.0	3.1	2.5	1.9	1.2	.9	4.3	4.3	8.0	8.8	6.3	7.2	1.7	2.1
1968	4.7	4.2	4.0	3.5	4.4	3.5	5.8	5.2	7.1	7.3	6.2	6.0	1.7	1.7
1969	6.2	5.5	5.4	4.7	7.0	5.1	7.7	6.9	7.3	8.2	6.2	6.7	2.9	2.5
1970	5.6	5.7	3.9	4.5	2.3	5.7	8.1	8.0	8.1	7.0	7.4	6.6	4.8	2.8
1971	3.3	4.4	2.8	3.6	4.3	3.1	4.1	5.7	5.4	7.4	4.6	6.2	3.1	3.9
1972	3.4	3.2	3.4	3.0	4.6	4.2	3.4	3.8	3.7	3.5	3.3	3.3	2.6	2.6
1973	8.7	6.2	10.4	7.4	20.3	14.5	6.2	4.4	6.0	4.5	5.3	4.0	17.0	8.1
1974	12.3	11.0	12.8	11.9	12.0	14.3	11.4	9.2	13.2	10.4	12.6	9.3	21.6	29.6
1975	6.9	9.1	6.2	8.8	6.6	8.5	8.2	9.6	10.3	12.6	9.8	12.0	11.4	10.5
1976	4.9	5.8	3.3	4.3	.5	3.0	7.2	8.3	10.8	10.1	10.0	9.5	7.1	7.1
1977	6.7	6.5	6.1	5.8	8.1	6.3	8.0	7.7	9.0	9.9	8.9	9.6	7.2	9.5
1978	9.0	7.6	8.8	7.2	11.8	9.9	9.3	8.6	9.3	8.5	8.8	8.4	7.9	6.3
1979	13.3	11.3	13.0	11.3	10.2	11.0	13.6	11.0	10.5	9.8	10.1	9.2	37.5	25.1
1980	12.5	13.5	11.0	12.3	10.2	8.6	14.2	15.4	10.1	11.3	9.9	11.0	18.0	30.9
1981	8.9	10.3	6.0	8.4	4.3	7.8	13.0	13.1	12.6	10.7	12.5	10.7	11.9	13.6
1982	3.8	6.2	3.6	4.1	3.1	4.1	4.3	9.0	11.2	11.8	11.0	11.6	1.3	1.5
1983	3.8	3.2	2.9	2.9	2.7	2.1	4.8	3.5	6.2	8.7	6.4	8.8	−.5	.7
1984	3.9	4.3	2.7	3.4	3.8	3.8	5.4	5.2	5.8	6.0	6.1	6.2	.2	1.0
1985	3.8	3.6	2.5	2.1	2.6	2.3	5.1	5.1	6.8	6.1	6.8	6.3	1.8	.7
1986	1.1	1.9	−2.0	−.9	3.8	3.2	4.5	5.0	7.9	7.7	7.7	7.5	−19.7	−13.2
1987	4.4	3.6	4.6	3.2	3.5	4.1	4.3	4.2	5.6	6.6	5.8	6.6	8.2	.5
1988	4.4	4.1	3.8	3.5	5.2	4.1	4.8	4.6	6.9	6.4	6.9	6.5	.5	.8
1989	4.6	4.8	4.1	4.7	5.6	5.8	5.1	4.9	8.6	7.7	8.5	7.7	5.1	5.6
1990	6.1	5.4	6.6	5.2	5.3	5.8	5.7	5.5	9.9	9.3	9.6	9.0	18.1	8.3
1991	3.1	4.2	1.2	3.1	1.9	2.9	4.6	5.1	8.0	8.9	7.9	8.7	−7.4	.4
1992	2.9	3.0	2.0	2.0	1.5	1.2	3.6	3.9	7.0	7.6	6.6	7.4	2.0	.5
1993	2.7	3.0	1.5	1.9	2.9	2.2	3.8	3.9	5.9	6.5	5.4	5.9	−1.4	1.2
1994	2.7	2.6	2.3	1.7	2.9	2.4	2.9	3.3	5.4	5.2	4.9	4.8	2.2	.4
1995	2.5	2.8	1.4	1.9	2.1	2.8	3.5	3.4	4.4	5.1	3.9	4.5	−1.3	.6
1996	3.3	3.0	3.2	2.6	4.3	3.3	3.3	3.2	3.2	3.7	3.0	3.5	8.6	4.7
1997	1.7	2.3	.2	1.4	1.5	2.6	2.8	3.0	2.9	2.9	2.8	2.8	−3.4	1.3
1998	1.6	1.6	.4	.1	2.3	2.2	2.6	2.7	3.2	3.2	3.4	3.2	−8.8	−7.7
1999	2.7	2.2	2.7	1.8	1.9	2.1	2.6	2.5	3.6	3.4	3.7	3.5	13.4	3.6
2000	3.4	3.4	2.7	3.3	2.8	2.3	3.9	3.4	4.6	4.3	4.2	4.1	14.2	16.9
2001	1.6	2.8	−1.4	1.0	2.8	3.2	3.7	4.1	4.8	4.8	4.7	4.6	−13.0	3.8
2002	2.4	1.6	1.2	−.7	1.5	1.8	3.2	3.1	5.6	5.1	5.0	4.7	10.7	−5.9
2003	1.9	2.3	.5	1.0	3.6	2.2	2.8	3.2	4.2	4.5	3.7	4.0	6.9	12.2
2004	3.3	2.7	3.6	2.3	2.7	3.4	3.1	2.9	4.9	5.0	4.2	4.4	16.6	10.9
2005	3.4	3.4	2.7	3.6	2.3	2.4	3.8	3.3	4.5	4.8	4.3	4.2	17.1	17.0

[1] Changes from December to December are based on unadjusted indexes.
[2] Commodities and services.
[3] Household fuels—gas (piped), electricity, fuel oil, etc.,—and motor fuel. Motor oil, coolant, etc., also included through 1982.

Source: Department of Labor, Bureau of Labor Statistics.

TABLE B-65.—*Producer price indexes by stage of processing, 1959–2005*

[1982=100]

Year or month	Total finished goods	Finished goods								Total finished consumer goods
		Consumer foods			Finished goods excluding consumer foods					
		Total	Crude	Processed	Total	Consumer goods			Capital equipment	
						Total	Durable	Non-durable		
1959	33.1	34.8	37.3	34.7	....	33.3	43.9	28.2	32.7	33.3
1960	33.4	35.5	39.8	35.2	....	33.5	43.8	28.4	32.8	33.6
1961	33.4	35.4	38.0	35.3	....	33.4	43.6	28.4	32.9	33.6
1962	33.5	35.7	38.4	35.6	....	33.4	43.4	28.4	33.0	33.7
1963	33.4	35.3	37.8	35.2	....	33.4	43.1	28.5	33.1	33.5
1964	33.5	35.4	38.9	35.2	....	33.3	43.3	28.4	33.4	33.6
1965	34.1	36.8	39.0	36.8	....	33.6	43.2	28.8	33.8	34.2
1966	35.2	39.2	41.5	39.2	....	34.1	43.4	29.3	34.6	35.4
1967	35.6	38.5	39.6	38.8	35.0	34.7	44.1	30.0	35.8	35.6
1968	36.6	40.0	42.5	40.0	35.9	35.5	45.1	30.6	37.0	36.5
1969	38.0	42.4	45.9	42.3	36.9	36.3	45.9	31.5	38.3	37.9
1970	39.3	43.8	46.0	43.9	38.2	37.4	47.2	32.5	40.1	39.1
1971	40.5	44.5	45.8	44.7	39.6	38.7	48.9	33.5	41.7	40.2
1972	41.8	46.9	48.0	47.2	40.4	39.4	50.0	34.1	42.8	41.5
1973	45.6	56.5	63.6	55.8	42.0	41.2	50.9	36.1	44.2	46.0
1974	52.6	64.4	71.6	63.9	44.8	48.2	55.5	44.0	50.5	53.1
1975	58.2	69.8	71.7	70.3	54.7	53.2	61.0	48.9	58.2	58.2
1976	60.8	69.6	76.7	69.0	58.1	56.5	63.7	52.4	62.1	60.4
1977	64.7	73.3	79.5	72.7	62.2	60.6	67.4	56.8	66.1	64.3
1978	69.8	79.9	85.8	79.4	66.7	64.9	73.6	60.0	71.3	69.4
1979	77.6	87.3	92.3	86.8	74.6	73.5	80.8	69.3	77.5	77.5
1980	88.0	92.4	93.9	92.3	86.7	87.1	91.0	85.1	85.8	88.6
1981	96.1	97.8	104.4	97.2	95.6	96.1	96.4	95.8	94.6	96.6
1982	100.0	100.0	100.0	100.0	100.0	100.0	100.0	100.0	100.0	100.0
1983	101.6	101.0	102.4	100.9	101.8	101.2	102.8	100.5	102.8	101.3
1984	103.7	105.4	111.4	104.9	103.2	102.2	104.5	101.1	105.2	103.3
1985	104.7	104.6	102.9	104.8	104.6	103.3	106.5	101.7	107.5	103.8
1986	103.2	107.3	105.6	107.4	101.9	98.5	108.9	93.3	109.7	101.4
1987	105.4	109.5	107.1	109.6	104.0	100.7	111.5	94.9	111.7	103.6
1988	108.0	112.6	109.8	112.7	106.5	103.1	113.8	97.3	114.3	106.2
1989	113.6	118.7	119.6	118.6	111.8	108.9	117.6	103.8	118.8	112.1
1990	119.2	124.4	123.0	124.4	117.4	115.3	120.4	111.5	122.9	118.2
1991	121.7	124.1	119.3	124.4	120.9	118.7	123.9	115.0	126.7	120.5
1992	123.2	123.3	107.6	124.4	123.1	120.8	125.7	117.3	129.1	121.7
1993	124.7	125.7	114.4	126.5	124.4	121.7	128.0	117.6	131.4	123.0
1994	125.5	126.8	111.3	127.9	125.1	121.6	130.9	116.2	134.1	123.3
1995	127.9	129.0	118.8	129.8	127.5	124.0	132.7	118.8	136.7	125.6
1996	131.3	133.6	129.2	133.8	130.5	127.6	134.2	123.3	138.3	129.5
1997	131.8	134.5	126.6	135.1	130.9	128.2	133.7	124.3	138.2	130.2
1998	130.7	134.3	127.2	134.8	129.5	126.4	132.9	122.2	137.6	128.9
1999	133.0	135.1	125.5	135.9	132.3	130.5	133.0	127.9	137.6	132.0
2000	138.0	137.2	123.5	138.3	138.1	138.4	133.9	138.7	138.8	138.2
2001	140.7	141.3	127.7	142.4	140.4	141.4	134.0	142.8	139.7	141.5
2002	138.9	140.1	128.5	141.0	138.3	138.8	133.0	139.8	139.1	139.4
2003	143.3	145.9	130.0	147.2	142.4	144.7	133.1	148.4	139.5	145.3
2004	148.5	152.7	138.2	153.9	147.2	150.9	135.0	156.6	141.4	151.7
2005	155.7	155.6	139.4	156.9	155.5	162.0	136.7	172.1	144.7	160.5
2004: Jan	145.4	148.1	141.5	148.6	144.5	147.4	134.3	151.7	140.5	147.8
Feb	145.3	148.4	134.8	149.5	144.3	147.3	134.2	151.6	140.2	147.8
Mar	146.3	150.7	145.8	151.0	144.9	148.0	134.7	152.4	140.5	149.0
Apr	147.3	152.7	130.8	154.5	145.7	149.1	134.4	154.3	140.6	150.4
May	148.9	155.5	132.6	157.4	147.0	150.9	134.8	156.7	140.8	152.5
June	148.7	155.0	120.0	158.0	146.8	150.5	134.9	156.0	141.1	152.0
July	148.5	152.3	117.5	155.2	147.2	151.4	133.6	158.0	140.7	151.9
Aug	148.5	152.2	127.3	154.3	147.3	151.3	133.6	157.9	141.2	151.8
Sept	148.7	152.7	140.2	153.7	147.5	151.5	133.5	158.2	141.2	152.1
Oct	152.0	155.1	162.9	154.3	150.9	155.6	137.8	162.1	143.4	155.7
Nov	151.7	154.7	159.0	154.2	150.7	155.3	137.4	161.8	143.4	155.4
Dec	150.6	154.9	146.4	155.5	149.2	153.0	137.2	158.5	143.6	153.8
2005: Jan	151.4	154.2	131.4	156.1	150.5	154.6	137.8	160.7	144.1	154.8
Feb	152.1	155.4	142.3	156.4	151.0	155.5	137.0	162.4	143.9	155.7
Mar	153.6	156.3	145.5	157.2	152.6	157.8	137.0	165.7	144.2	157.6
Apr	154.4	156.3	144.6	157.2	153.6	159.2	136.9	167.9	144.5	158.7
May	154.3	156.7	140.3	158.0	153.5	158.8	136.8	167.4	144.7	158.5
June	154.2	155.5	137.0	157.1	153.6	159.3	135.6	168.7	144.2	158.6
July	155.5	154.4	128.0	156.6	155.5	162.1	135.8	172.6	144.4	160.2
Aug [1]	156.3	154.0	126.3	156.3	155.6	163.8	135.4	175.4	144.4	161.4
Sept	158.9	155.9	141.0	157.1	159.4	168.0	135.5	181.4	144.5	164.9
Oct	161.0	155.6	135.7	157.2	162.1	171.3	138.0	185.1	145.9	167.2
Nov	158.4	155.9	142.9	156.9	158.8	166.5	137.1	178.5	145.5	163.8
Dec	158.8	157.1	157.9	157.0	158.9	166.7	137.0	178.9	145.5	164.3

[1] Data have been revised through August 2005; data are subject to revision 4 months after date of original publication.

See next page for continuation of table.

TABLE B–65.—*Producer price indexes by stage of processing, 1959–2005*—Continued

[1982=100]

| Year or month | Intermediate materials, supplies, and components | | | | | | | | Crude materials for further processing | | | | |
| | Total | Foods and feeds[2] | Other | Materials and components | | Processed fuels and lubricants | Containers | Supplies | Total | Foodstuffs and feedstuffs | Other | | |
				For manufacturing	For construction						Total	Fuel	Other
1959	30.8	.....	30.5	33.3	32.9	16.2	33.0	33.5	31.1	38.8	.....	10.4	28.1
1960	30.8	.....	30.7	33.3	32.7	16.6	33.4	33.3	30.4	38.4	.....	10.5	26.9
1961	30.6	.....	30.3	32.9	32.2	16.8	33.2	33.7	30.2	37.9	.....	10.5	27.2
1962	30.6	.....	30.2	32.7	32.1	16.7	33.6	34.5	30.5	38.6	.....	10.4	27.1
1963	30.7	.....	30.1	32.7	32.2	16.6	33.2	35.0	29.9	37.5	.....	10.5	26.7
1964	30.8	.....	30.3	33.1	32.5	16.2	32.9	34.7	29.6	36.6	.....	10.5	27.2
1965	31.2	.....	30.7	33.6	32.8	16.5	33.5	35.0	31.1	39.2	.....	10.6	27.7
1966	32.0	.....	31.3	34.3	33.6	16.8	34.5	36.5	33.1	42.7	.....	10.9	28.3
1967	32.2	41.8	31.7	34.5	34.0	16.9	35.0	36.8	31.3	40.3	21.1	11.3	26.5
1968	33.0	41.5	32.5	35.3	35.7	16.5	35.9	37.1	31.8	40.9	21.6	11.5	27.1
1969	34.1	42.9	33.6	36.5	37.7	16.6	37.2	37.8	33.9	44.1	22.5	12.0	28.4
1970	35.4	45.6	34.8	38.0	38.3	17.7	39.0	39.7	35.2	45.2	23.8	13.8	29.1
1971	36.8	46.7	36.2	38.9	40.8	19.5	40.8	40.8	36.0	46.1	24.7	15.7	29.4
1972	38.2	49.5	37.7	40.4	43.0	20.1	42.7	42.5	39.9	51.5	27.0	16.8	32.3
1973	42.4	70.3	40.6	44.1	46.5	22.2	45.2	51.7	54.5	72.6	34.3	18.6	42.9
1974	52.5	83.6	50.5	56.0	55.0	33.6	53.3	56.8	61.4	76.4	44.1	24.8	54.5
1975	58.0	81.6	56.6	61.7	60.1	39.4	60.0	61.8	61.6	77.4	43.7	30.6	50.0
1976	60.9	77.4	60.0	64.0	64.1	42.3	63.1	65.8	63.4	76.8	48.2	34.5	54.9
1977	64.9	79.6	64.1	67.4	69.3	47.7	65.9	69.3	65.5	77.5	51.7	42.0	56.3
1978	69.5	84.8	68.6	72.0	76.5	49.9	71.0	72.9	73.4	87.3	57.5	48.2	61.9
1979	78.4	94.5	77.4	80.9	84.2	61.6	79.4	80.2	85.9	100.0	69.6	57.3	75.5
1980	90.3	105.5	89.4	91.7	91.3	85.0	89.1	89.9	95.3	104.6	84.6	69.4	91.8
1981	98.6	104.6	98.2	98.7	97.9	100.6	96.7	96.9	103.0	103.9	101.8	84.8	109.8
1982	100.0	100.0	100.0	100.0	100.0	100.0	100.0	100.0	100.0	100.0	100.0	100.0	100.0
1983	100.6	103.6	100.5	101.2	102.8	95.4	100.4	101.8	101.3	101.8	100.7	105.1	98.8
1984	103.1	105.7	103.0	104.1	105.6	95.7	105.9	104.1	103.5	104.7	102.2	105.1	101.0
1985	102.7	97.3	103.0	103.3	107.3	92.8	109.0	104.4	95.8	94.8	96.9	102.7	94.3
1986	99.1	96.2	99.3	102.2	108.1	72.7	110.3	105.6	87.7	93.2	81.6	92.2	76.0
1987	101.5	99.2	101.7	105.3	109.8	73.3	114.5	107.7	93.7	96.2	87.9	84.1	88.5
1988	107.1	109.5	106.9	113.2	116.1	71.2	120.1	113.7	96.0	106.1	85.5	82.1	85.9
1989	112.0	113.8	111.9	118.1	121.3	76.4	125.4	118.1	103.1	111.2	93.4	85.3	95.8
1990	114.5	113.3	114.5	118.7	122.9	85.9	127.7	119.4	108.9	113.1	101.5	84.8	107.3
1991	114.4	111.1	114.6	118.1	124.5	85.3	128.1	121.4	101.2	105.5	94.6	82.9	97.5
1992	114.7	110.7	114.9	117.9	126.5	84.5	127.7	122.7	100.4	105.1	93.5	84.0	94.2
1993	116.2	112.7	116.4	118.9	132.0	84.7	126.4	125.0	102.4	108.4	94.7	87.1	94.1
1994	118.5	114.8	118.7	122.1	136.6	83.1	129.7	127.0	101.8	106.5	94.8	82.4	97.0
1995	124.9	114.8	125.5	130.4	142.1	84.2	148.8	132.1	102.7	105.8	96.8	72.1	105.8
1996	125.7	128.1	125.6	128.6	143.6	90.0	141.1	135.9	113.8	121.5	104.5	92.6	105.7
1997	125.6	125.4	125.7	128.3	146.5	89.3	136.0	135.9	111.1	112.2	106.4	101.3	103.5
1998	123.0	116.2	123.4	126.1	146.8	81.1	140.8	134.8	96.8	103.9	88.4	86.7	84.5
1999	123.2	111.1	123.9	124.6	148.9	84.6	142.5	134.2	98.2	98.7	94.3	91.2	91.1
2000	129.2	111.7	130.1	128.1	150.7	102.0	151.6	136.9	120.6	100.2	130.4	136.9	118.0
2001	129.7	115.9	130.5	127.4	150.6	104.5	153.1	138.7	121.0	106.1	126.8	154.4	110.5
2002	127.8	115.5	128.5	126.1	151.3	96.3	152.1	138.9	108.1	99.5	114.4	117.3	101.0
2003	133.7	125.9	134.2	129.7	153.6	112.6	153.7	141.5	135.3	113.5	148.2	185.7	116.9
2004	142.6	137.1	143.0	137.9	166.4	124.3	159.3	146.7	159.0	127.0	179.2	211.4	149.2
2005	153.9	133.8	155.0	145.8	176.6	149.8	167.0	151.9	182.1	122.6	223.2	279.1	176.8
2004:Jan	136.2	132.2	136.5	131.9	156.2	116.8	153.9	143.2	147.8	117.1	167.3	207.9	133.3
Feb	137.3	133.7	137.6	133.2	159.0	116.8	153.7	143.8	150.1	122.2	167.3	200.2	137.7
Mar	138.3	137.0	138.4	134.3	161.9	116.5	154.1	144.8	152.9	131.7	164.8	182.9	143.8
Apr	140.2	143.2	140.2	136.2	164.7	118.4	154.9	146.4	155.7	135.4	166.6	191.8	141.4
May	142.0	147.7	141.9	137.4	166.9	122.3	156.7	147.2	161.8	141.1	172.9	208.4	141.5
June	142.8	144.9	142.8	137.7	166.9	124.9	158.9	147.3	163.0	137.4	178.0	229.8	136.8
July	143.5	142.3	143.7	138.1	167.5	126.4	159.7	148.0	162.5	130.9	182.2	219.9	148.9
Aug	144.8	136.3	145.3	139.4	169.8	128.5	162.0	147.6	162.2	124.8	186.6	214.0	158.9
Sept	145.3	134.4	145.9	140.6	170.9	126.9	163.5	147.9	154.4	122.0	174.9	186.9	156.8
Oct	146.5	131.9	147.3	141.5	170.8	130.8	164.6	147.9	160.5	120.1	187.3	194.1	171.4
Nov	147.4	130.7	148.3	142.0	170.7	134.0	164.9	148.1	171.5	119.5	207.1	256.8	165.2
Dec	146.9	131.0	147.8	142.8	171.3	128.9	165.2	148.5	165.7	121.5	195.3	243.8	155.0
2005:Jan	148.0	132.0	148.9	143.9	173.1	129.5	165.5	149.6	163.0	123.8	188.7	217.0	160.3
Feb	148.8	131.7	149.7	144.4	174.7	130.9	166.1	150.0	162.5	121.5	189.7	217.8	161.4
Mar	150.4	133.3	151.3	145.2	175.1	136.0	166.9	150.7	170.4	127.7	198.7	221.7	172.8
Apr	151.5	133.6	152.5	144.9	175.4	141.5	167.5	151.1	175.0	124.9	208.9	252.4	170.6
May	151.0	135.0	151.9	144.7	175.0	139.5	167.3	151.4	170.6	126.2	200.2	237.1	166.1
June	151.7	134.8	152.6	144.3	175.5	142.9	167.4	151.7	167.0	122.0	197.1	223.5	169.3
July	153.2	134.9	154.1	144.6	175.7	149.3	166.8	152.0	175.4	120.9	212.8	250.1	177.7
Aug[1]	153.9	134.4	154.9	144.4	175.4	153.4	166.8	152.2	181.8	119.6	225.1	265.0	187.8
Sept	157.5	133.6	158.7	146.5	177.0	165.2	165.7	152.3	198.4	120.6	253.5	332.8	191.8
Oct	161.9	134.4	163.3	148.6	179.3	179.7	166.2	153.4	211.1	120.6	275.9	394.1	190.3
Nov	159.8	133.8	161.1	148.8	180.9	167.1	168.4	153.8	207.6	120.7	269.7	389.3	183.8
Dec	159.3	133.8	160.6	149.2	181.8	163.0	169.6	154.0	202.4	123.2	258.4	348.3	190.3

[2] Intermediate materials for food manufacturing and feeds.

Source: Department of Labor, Bureau of Labor Statistics.

TABLE B–66.—*Producer price indexes by stage of processing, special groups, 1974–2005*

[1982=100]

Year or month	Finished goods						Intermediate materials, supplies, and components				Crude materials for further processing			
				Excluding foods and energy										
	Total	Foods	Energy	Total	Capital equip-ment	Con-sumer goods exclud-ing foods and energy	Total	Foods and feeds[1]	Energy	Other	Total	Food-stuffs and feed-stuffs	Energy	Other
1974	52.6	64.4	26.2	53.6	50.5	55.5	52.5	83.6	33.1	54.0	61.4	76.4	27.8	83.3
1975	58.2	69.8	30.7	59.7	58.2	60.6	58.0	81.6	38.7	60.2	61.6	77.4	33.3	69.3
1976	60.8	69.6	34.3	63.1	62.1	63.7	60.9	77.4	41.5	63.8	63.4	76.8	35.3	80.2
1977	64.7	73.3	39.7	66.9	66.1	67.3	64.9	79.6	46.8	67.6	65.5	77.5	40.4	79.8
1978	69.8	79.9	42.3	71.9	71.3	72.2	69.5	84.8	49.1	72.5	73.4	87.3	45.2	87.8
1979	77.6	87.3	57.1	78.3	77.5	78.8	78.4	94.5	61.1	80.7	85.9	100.0	54.9	106.2
1980	88.0	92.4	85.2	87.1	85.8	87.8	90.3	105.5	84.9	90.3	95.3	104.6	73.1	113.1
1981	96.1	97.8	101.5	94.6	94.6	94.6	98.6	104.6	100.5	97.7	103.0	103.9	97.7	111.7
1982	100.0	100.0	100.0	100.0	100.0	100.0	100.0	100.0	100.0	100.0	100.0	100.0	100.0	100.0
1983	101.6	101.0	95.2	103.0	102.8	103.1	100.6	103.6	95.3	101.6	101.3	101.8	98.7	105.3
1984	103.7	105.4	91.2	105.5	105.2	105.7	103.1	105.7	95.5	104.7	103.5	104.7	98.0	111.7
1985	104.7	104.6	87.6	108.1	107.5	108.4	102.7	97.3	92.6	105.2	95.8	94.8	93.3	104.9
1986	103.2	107.3	63.0	110.6	109.7	111.1	99.1	96.2	72.6	104.9	87.7	93.2	71.8	103.1
1987	105.4	109.5	61.8	113.3	111.7	114.2	101.5	99.2	73.0	107.8	93.7	96.2	75.0	115.7
1988	108.0	112.6	59.8	117.0	114.3	118.5	107.1	109.5	70.9	115.2	96.0	106.1	67.7	133.0
1989	113.6	118.7	65.7	122.1	118.8	124.0	112.0	113.8	76.1	120.2	103.1	111.2	75.9	137.9
1990	119.2	124.4	75.0	126.6	122.9	128.8	114.5	113.3	85.5	120.9	108.9	113.1	85.9	136.3
1991	121.7	124.1	78.1	131.1	126.7	133.7	114.4	111.1	85.1	121.4	101.2	105.5	80.4	128.2
1992	123.2	123.3	77.8	134.2	129.1	137.3	114.7	110.7	84.3	122.0	100.4	105.1	78.8	128.4
1993	124.7	125.7	78.0	135.8	131.4	138.5	116.2	112.7	84.6	123.8	102.4	108.4	76.7	140.2
1994	125.5	126.8	77.0	137.1	134.1	139.0	118.5	114.8	83.0	127.1	101.8	106.5	72.1	156.2
1995	127.9	129.0	78.1	140.0	136.7	141.9	124.9	114.8	84.1	135.2	102.7	105.8	69.4	173.6
1996	131.3	133.6	83.2	142.0	138.3	144.3	125.7	128.1	89.8	134.0	113.8	121.5	85.0	155.8
1997	131.8	134.5	83.4	142.4	138.2	145.1	125.6	125.4	89.0	134.2	111.1	112.2	87.3	156.5
1998	130.7	134.3	75.1	143.7	137.6	147.7	123.0	116.2	80.8	133.5	96.8	103.9	68.6	142.1
1999	133.0	135.1	78.8	146.1	137.6	151.7	123.2	111.1	84.3	133.1	98.2	98.7	78.5	135.2
2000	138.0	137.2	94.1	148.0	138.8	154.0	129.2	111.7	101.7	136.6	120.6	100.2	122.1	145.2
2001	140.7	141.3	96.7	150.0	139.7	156.9	129.7	115.9	104.1	136.4	121.0	106.1	122.3	130.7
2002	138.9	140.1	88.8	150.2	139.1	157.6	127.8	115.5	95.9	135.8	108.1	99.5	102.0	135.7
2003	143.3	145.9	102.0	150.5	139.5	157.9	133.7	125.9	111.9	138.5	135.3	113.5	147.2	152.5
2004	148.5	152.7	113.0	152.7	141.4	160.3	142.6	137.1	123.2	146.5	159.0	127.0	174.4	193.0
2005	155.7	155.6	132.7	156.4	144.7	164.4	153.9	133.8	149.1	154.5	182.1	122.6	233.8	202.4
2004: Jan	145.4	148.1	106.0	151.8	140.5	159.4	136.2	132.2	115.8	140.4	147.8	117.1	163.5	179.3
Feb	145.3	148.4	105.7	151.7	140.2	159.4	137.3	133.7	115.8	141.7	150.1	122.2	158.9	189.9
Mar	146.3	150.7	107.0	152.0	140.5	159.7	138.3	137.0	115.6	142.9	152.9	131.7	153.0	195.2
Apr	147.3	152.7	109.5	152.1	140.6	159.8	140.2	143.2	117.3	144.6	155.7	135.4	158.8	187.6
May	148.9	155.5	113.6	152.2	140.8	159.9	142.0	147.7	121.1	145.7	161.8	141.1	172.1	177.9
June	148.7	155.0	112.5	152.3	141.1	160.0	142.8	144.9	123.7	146.2	163.0	137.4	180.0	176.3
July	148.5	152.3	115.4	151.9	140.7	159.4	143.5	142.3	125.1	146.8	162.5	130.9	177.9	195.4
Aug	148.5	152.2	115.0	152.2	141.2	159.6	144.8	136.3	127.1	148.3	162.2	124.8	181.9	200.8
Sept	148.7	152.7	115.1	152.3	141.2	159.7	145.3	134.4	125.8	149.5	154.4	122.0	166.6	197.4
Oct	152.0	155.1	121.1	154.7	143.4	162.2	146.5	131.9	129.9	150.1	160.5	120.1	181.8	203.5
Nov	151.7	154.7	120.1	154.7	143.4	162.3	147.4	130.7	132.7	150.6	171.5	119.5	208.3	207.9
Dec	150.6	154.9	114.5	154.9	143.6	162.5	146.9	131.0	128.4	151.1	165.7	121.5	192.7	204.9
2005: Jan	151.4	154.2	116.4	155.8	144.1	163.8	148.0	132.0	129.0	152.3	163.0	123.8	183.9	203.3
Feb	152.1	155.4	118.6	155.7	143.9	163.7	148.8	131.7	130.0	153.1	162.5	121.5	186.6	200.2
Mar	153.6	156.3	123.8	155.9	144.2	163.7	150.4	133.3	134.9	153.8	170.4	127.7	199.7	199.9
Apr	154.4	156.3	126.9	156.1	144.5	164.0	151.5	133.6	139.8	153.9	175.0	124.9	212.6	204.0
May	154.3	156.7	125.5	156.4	144.7	164.3	151.0	135.0	138.5	153.5	170.6	126.2	203.1	196.9
June	154.2	155.5	127.4	155.9	144.2	163.8	151.7	134.8	142.3	153.3	167.0	122.0	202.1	188.9
July	155.5	154.4	133.2	156.2	144.4	164.2	153.2	134.9	148.7	153.5	175.4	120.9	224.0	190.2
Aug[2]	156.3	154.0	137.3	156.1	144.4	164.1	153.9	134.4	153.0	153.3	181.8	119.6	237.5	200.1
Sept	158.9	155.9	147.1	156.2	144.5	164.0	157.5	133.6	164.9	154.8	198.4	120.6	273.9	210.3
Oct	161.0	155.6	152.7	157.6	145.9	165.5	161.9	134.4	179.3	156.6	211.1	120.6	307.9	205.7
Nov	158.4	155.9	141.5	157.4	145.5	165.5	159.8	133.8	166.4	157.4	207.6	120.7	295.0	215.1
Dec	158.8	157.1	141.9	157.5	145.5	165.6	159.3	133.8	162.4	157.9	202.4	123.2	279.0	214.8

[1] Intermediate materials for food manufacturing and feeds.
[2] Data have been revised through August 2005; data are subject to revision 4 months after date of original publication.

Source: Department of Labor, Bureau of Labor Statistics.

TABLE B–67.—*Producer price indexes for major commodity groups, 1959–2005*

[1982=100]

Year or month	Farm products and processed foods and feeds			Industrial commodities				
	Total	Farm products	Processed foods and feeds	Total	Textile products and apparel	Hides, skins, leather, and related products	Fuels and related products and power	Chemicals and allied products[1]
1959	37.6	40.2	35.6	30.5	48.1	35.9	13.7	34.8
1960	37.7	40.1	35.6	30.5	48.6	34.6	13.9	34.8
1961	37.7	39.7	36.2	30.4	47.8	34.9	14.0	34.5
1962	38.1	40.4	36.5	30.4	48.2	35.3	14.0	33.9
1963	37.7	39.6	36.8	30.3	48.2	34.3	13.9	33.5
1964	37.5	39.0	36.7	30.5	48.5	34.4	13.5	33.6
1965	39.0	40.7	38.0	30.9	48.8	35.9	13.8	33.9
1966	41.6	43.7	40.2	31.5	48.9	39.4	14.1	34.0
1967	40.2	41.3	39.8	32.0	48.9	38.1	14.4	34.2
1968	41.1	42.3	40.6	32.8	50.7	39.3	14.3	34.1
1969	43.4	45.0	42.7	33.9	51.8	41.5	14.6	34.2
1970	44.9	45.8	44.6	35.2	52.4	42.0	15.3	35.0
1971	45.8	46.6	45.5	36.5	53.3	43.4	16.6	35.6
1972	49.2	51.6	48.0	37.8	55.5	50.0	17.1	35.6
1973	63.9	72.7	58.9	40.3	60.5	54.5	19.4	37.6
1974	71.3	77.4	68.0	49.2	68.0	55.2	30.1	50.2
1975	74.0	77.0	72.6	54.9	67.4	56.5	35.4	62.0
1976	73.6	78.8	70.8	58.4	72.4	63.9	38.3	64.0
1977	75.9	79.4	74.0	62.5	75.3	68.3	43.6	65.9
1978	83.0	87.7	80.6	67.0	78.1	76.1	46.5	68.0
1979	92.3	99.6	88.5	75.7	82.5	96.1	58.9	76.0
1980	98.3	102.9	95.9	88.0	89.7	94.7	82.8	89.0
1981	101.1	105.2	98.9	97.4	97.6	99.3	100.2	98.4
1982	100.0	100.0	100.0	100.0	100.0	100.0	100.0	100.0
1983	102.0	102.4	101.8	101.1	100.3	103.2	95.9	100.3
1984	105.5	105.5	105.4	103.3	102.7	109.0	94.8	102.9
1985	100.7	95.1	103.5	103.7	102.9	108.9	91.4	103.7
1986	101.2	92.9	105.4	100.0	103.2	113.0	69.8	102.6
1987	103.7	95.5	107.9	102.6	105.1	120.4	70.2	106.4
1988	110.0	104.9	112.7	106.3	109.2	131.4	66.7	116.3
1989	115.4	110.9	117.8	111.6	112.3	136.3	72.9	123.0
1990	118.6	112.2	121.9	115.8	115.0	141.7	82.3	123.6
1991	116.4	105.7	121.9	116.5	116.3	138.9	81.2	125.6
1992	115.9	103.6	122.1	117.4	117.8	140.4	80.4	125.9
1993	118.4	107.1	124.0	119.0	118.0	143.7	80.0	128.2
1994	119.1	106.3	125.5	120.7	118.3	148.5	77.8	132.1
1995	120.5	107.4	127.0	125.5	120.8	153.7	78.0	142.5
1996	129.7	122.4	133.3	127.3	122.4	150.5	85.8	142.1
1997	127.0	112.9	134.0	127.7	122.6	154.2	86.1	143.6
1998	122.7	104.6	131.6	124.8	122.9	148.0	75.3	143.9
1999	120.3	98.4	131.1	126.5	121.1	146.0	80.5	144.2
2000	122.0	99.5	133.1	134.8	121.4	151.5	103.5	151.0
2001	126.2	103.8	137.3	135.7	121.3	158.4	105.3	151.8
2002	123.9	99.0	136.2	132.4	119.9	157.6	93.2	151.9
2003	132.8	111.5	143.4	139.1	119.8	162.3	112.9	161.8
2004	142.0	123.3	151.2	147.6	121.0	164.5	126.9	174.4
2005	141.2	118.4	153.1	160.2	122.8	165.3	156.4	191.2
2004: Jan	136.8	117.4	146.4	142.2	120.3	165.4	118.9	166.6
Feb	138.4	120.4	147.3	142.8	120.1	165.1	118.0	167.5
Mar	142.8	129.1	149.4	143.3	120.2	164.8	117.5	168.0
Apr	145.6	129.6	153.3	144.8	120.5	163.1	120.4	170.1
May	149.3	135.1	156.1	146.5	121.0	162.8	126.0	170.9
June	147.2	129.7	155.8	147.3	121.0	163.2	127.8	172.2
July	143.8	124.4	153.3	148.2	121.1	165.0	129.4	173.7
Aug	140.6	119.0	151.4	149.3	121.0	165.0	130.7	176.5
Sept	139.9	118.7	150.4	149.1	121.4	165.0	127.7	179.4
Oct	140.0	119.2	150.3	151.8	121.6	165.0	134.6	181.0
Nov	139.5	118.0	150.1	153.5	121.8	164.9	139.7	183.0
Dec	140.2	118.4	151.1	152.0	121.6	165.1	132.7	183.9
2005: Jan	140.6	118.8	151.8	152.7	122.1	165.3	132.3	185.5
Feb	140.5	117.6	152.3	153.6	122.1	165.5	134.2	186.4
Mar	143.0	123.0	153.4	155.6	122.3	165.6	140.9	188.9
Apr	142.2	120.7	153.3	157.2	122.5	164.8	146.5	189.0
May	143.1	121.5	154.3	156.3	122.6	164.8	143.7	188.4
June	141.3	118.3	153.2	156.6	122.8	165.7	146.0	187.2
July	140.4	116.3	153.0	159.1	122.7	165.8	154.8	189.3
Aug [2]	139.6	114.5	152.7	160.8	122.8	165.6	160.7	189.9
Sept	140.5	116.4	153.1	165.5	123.2	165.2	176.2	193.6
Oct	140.6	115.4	153.8	170.3	123.3	165.1	190.4	198.7
Nov	140.8	117.1	153.1	167.5	123.9	165.5	177.4	198.5
Dec	142.1	120.8	153.3	166.6	123.6	165.0	173.1	199.0

[1] Prices for some items in this grouping are lagged and refer to 1 month earlier than the index month.
[2] Data have been revised through August 2005; data are subject to revision 4 months after date of original publication.

See next page for continuation of table.

TABLE B–67.—*Producer price indexes for major commodity groups, 1959–2005*—Continued

[1982=100]

Year or month	Rubber and plastic products	Lumber and wood products	Pulp, paper, and allied products	Metals and metal products	Machinery and equipment	Furniture and household durables	Non-metallic mineral products	Transportation equipment — Total	Transportation equipment — Motor vehicles and equipment	Miscellaneous products
				Industrial commodities—Continued						
1959	42.6	34.7	33.7	30.6	32.8	48.0	30.3	....	39.9	33.4
1960	42.7	33.5	34.0	30.6	33.0	47.8	30.4	....	39.3	33.6
1961	41.1	32.0	33.0	30.5	33.0	47.5	30.5	....	39.2	33.7
1962	39.9	32.2	33.4	30.2	33.0	47.2	30.5	....	39.2	33.9
1963	40.1	32.8	33.1	30.3	33.1	46.9	30.3	....	38.9	34.2
1964	39.6	33.5	33.0	31.1	33.3	47.1	30.4	....	39.1	34.4
1965	39.7	33.7	33.3	32.0	33.7	46.8	30.4	....	39.2	34.7
1966	40.5	35.2	34.2	32.8	34.7	47.4	30.7	....	39.2	35.3
1967	41.4	35.1	34.6	33.2	35.9	48.3	31.2	....	39.8	36.2
1968	42.8	39.8	35.0	34.0	37.0	49.7	32.4	....	40.9	37.0
1969	43.6	44.0	36.0	36.0	38.2	50.7	33.6	40.4	41.7	38.1
1970	44.9	39.9	37.5	38.7	40.0	51.9	35.3	41.9	43.3	39.8
1971	45.2	44.7	38.1	39.4	41.4	53.1	38.2	44.2	45.7	40.8
1972	45.3	50.7	39.3	40.9	42.3	53.8	39.4	45.5	47.0	41.5
1973	46.6	62.2	42.3	44.0	43.7	55.7	40.7	46.1	47.4	43.3
1974	56.4	64.5	52.5	57.0	50.0	61.8	47.8	50.3	51.4	48.1
1975	62.2	62.1	59.0	61.5	57.9	67.5	54.4	56.7	57.6	53.4
1976	66.0	72.2	62.1	65.0	61.3	70.3	58.2	60.5	61.2	55.6
1977	69.4	83.0	64.6	69.3	65.2	73.2	62.6	64.6	65.2	59.4
1978	72.4	96.9	67.7	75.3	70.3	77.5	69.6	69.5	70.0	66.7
1979	80.5	105.5	75.9	86.0	76.7	82.8	77.6	75.3	75.8	75.5
1980	90.1	101.5	86.3	95.0	86.0	90.7	88.4	82.9	83.1	93.6
1981	96.4	102.8	94.8	99.6	94.4	95.9	96.7	94.3	94.6	96.1
1982	100.0	100.0	100.0	100.0	100.0	100.0	100.0	100.0	100.0	100.0
1983	100.8	107.9	103.3	101.8	102.7	103.4	101.6	102.8	102.2	104.8
1984	102.3	108.0	110.3	104.8	105.1	105.7	105.4	105.2	104.1	107.0
1985	101.9	106.6	113.3	104.4	107.2	107.1	108.6	107.9	106.4	109.4
1986	101.9	107.2	116.1	103.2	108.8	108.2	110.0	110.5	109.1	111.6
1987	103.0	112.8	121.8	107.1	110.4	109.9	110.0	112.5	111.7	114.9
1988	109.3	118.9	130.4	118.7	113.2	113.1	111.2	114.3	113.1	120.2
1989	112.6	126.7	137.8	124.1	117.4	116.9	112.6	117.7	116.2	126.5
1990	113.6	129.7	141.2	122.9	120.7	119.2	114.7	121.5	118.2	134.2
1991	115.1	132.1	142.9	120.2	123.0	121.2	117.2	126.4	122.1	140.8
1992	115.1	146.6	145.2	119.2	123.4	122.2	117.3	130.4	124.9	145.3
1993	116.0	174.0	147.3	119.2	124.0	123.7	120.0	133.7	128.0	145.4
1994	117.6	180.0	152.5	124.8	125.1	126.1	124.2	137.2	131.4	141.9
1995	124.3	178.1	172.2	134.5	126.6	128.2	129.0	139.7	133.0	145.4
1996	123.8	176.1	168.7	131.0	126.5	130.4	131.0	141.7	134.1	147.7
1997	123.2	183.8	167.9	131.8	125.9	130.8	133.2	141.6	132.7	150.9
1998	122.6	179.1	171.7	127.8	124.9	131.3	135.4	141.2	131.4	156.0
1999	122.5	183.6	174.1	124.6	124.3	131.7	138.9	141.8	131.7	156.0
2000	125.5	178.2	183.7	128.1	124.0	132.6	142.5	143.8	132.3	170.8
2001	127.2	174.4	184.8	125.4	123.7	133.2	144.3	145.2	131.5	181.3
2002	126.8	173.3	185.9	125.9	122.9	133.5	146.2	144.6	129.9	182.4
2003	130.1	177.4	190.0	129.2	121.9	133.9	148.2	145.7	129.6	179.6
2004	133.8	195.6	195.7	149.6	122.1	135.1	153.2	148.6	131.0	183.2
2005	143.9	196.4	202.5	160.8	123.7	139.5	163.3	151.0	131.4	195.5
2004: Jan	130.8	183.3	191.2	135.9	121.4	133.6	149.5	147.8	130.9	181.3
Feb	131.4	189.0	192.2	140.2	121.4	133.9	150.5	147.7	130.6	181.4
Mar	131.6	194.1	192.9	143.9	121.6	133.7	150.5	148.0	130.9	181.8
Apr	132.0	197.7	193.9	146.5	122.0	134.0	151.1	147.7	130.3	182.1
May	132.4	201.6	194.7	147.0	122.1	134.5	151.9	148.0	130.8	181.9
June	132.9	198.4	195.4	147.3	122.2	134.9	152.6	148.4	130.9	182.5
July	133.4	196.5	196.2	151.3	122.1	134.9	153.4	147.2	129.1	182.8
Aug	133.9	202.1	197.3	154.0	122.2	135.6	154.4	147.4	128.9	183.4
Sept	135.1	202.5	198.4	154.7	122.3	135.6	155.5	147.3	128.6	184.3
Oct	136.5	196.7	198.3	157.1	122.5	135.9	155.8	151.8	134.4	184.6
Nov	137.3	191.9	198.7	158.6	122.5	137.0	156.3	151.1	133.3	185.4
Dec	138.3	193.0	199.1	159.0	122.6	137.2	156.6	151.3	133.2	186.8
2005: Jan	139.7	194.6	200.8	160.1	123.1	137.5	159.2	151.9	133.6	189.5
Feb	140.6	198.2	201.5	160.5	123.3	138.2	160.3	151.0	132.4	191.5
Mar	141.2	198.6	202.1	160.4	123.5	138.6	160.8	151.0	132.0	192.2
Apr	141.7	198.3	202.1	161.1	123.7	138.7	162.1	151.0	132.0	192.8
May	141.9	195.2	202.2	159.4	123.7	139.2	162.7	151.0	131.7	193.4
June	142.4	197.6	202.6	157.6	123.7	139.3	163.1	149.7	130.0	194.4
July	142.4	196.0	202.6	157.4	123.8	139.8	164.8	150.1	130.3	195.3
Aug[2]	142.4	194.1	202.3	158.4	123.9	139.6	165.4	150.0	129.8	196.1
Sept	143.3	197.4	202.7	161.0	124.0	139.9	166.7	150.1	129.8	198.2
Oct	147.1	198.0	203.2	161.8	124.2	140.1	167.5	152.9	133.2	200.1
Nov	152.3	194.1	203.9	165.2	123.8	141.0	169.4	151.8	131.7	200.7
Dec	152.3	195.3	204.2	166.7	123.7	141.9	169.5	151.3	131.0	202.1

Source: Department of Labor, Bureau of Labor Statistics.

TABLE B–68.—*Changes in producer price indexes for finished goods, 1965–2005*

[Percent change]

Year or month	Total finished goods Dec. to Dec.[1]	Total finished goods Year to year	Finished consumer foods Dec. to Dec.[1]	Finished consumer foods Year to year	Finished goods excluding consumer foods — Total Dec. to Dec.[1]	Total Year to year	Consumer goods Dec. to Dec.[1]	Consumer goods Year to year	Capital equipment Dec. to Dec.[1]	Capital equipment Year to year	Finished energy goods Dec. to Dec.[1]	Finished energy goods Year to year	Finished goods excluding foods and energy Dec. to Dec.[1]	Finished goods excluding foods and energy Year to year
1965	3.3	1.8	9.1	4.0			0.9	0.9	1.5	1.2				
1966	2.0	3.2	1.3	6.5			1.8	1.5	3.8	2.4				
1967	1.7	1.1	-.3	-1.8			2.0	1.8	3.1	3.5				
1968	3.1	2.8	4.6	3.9	2.5	2.6	2.0	2.3	3.0	3.4				
1969	4.9	3.8	8.1	6.0	3.3	2.8	2.8	2.3	4.8	3.5				
1970	2.1	3.4	-2.3	3.3	4.3	3.5	3.8	3.0	4.8	4.7				
1971	3.3	3.1	5.8	1.6	2.0	3.7	2.1	3.5	2.4	4.0				
1972	3.9	3.2	7.9	5.4	2.3	2.0	2.1	1.8	2.1	2.6				
1973	11.7	9.1	22.7	20.5	6.6	4.0	7.5	4.6	5.1	3.3				
1974	18.3	15.4	12.8	14.0	21.1	16.2	20.3	17.0	22.7	14.3			17.7	11.4
1975	6.6	10.6	5.6	8.4	7.2	12.1	6.8	10.4	8.1	15.2	16.3	17.2	6.0	11.4
1976	3.8	4.5	-2.5	-.3	6.2	6.2	6.0	6.2	6.5	6.7	11.6	11.7	5.7	5.7
1977	6.7	6.4	6.9	5.3	6.8	7.1	6.7	7.3	7.2	6.4	12.0	15.7	6.2	6.0
1978	9.3	7.9	11.7	9.0	8.3	7.2	8.5	7.1	8.0	7.9	8.5	6.5	8.4	7.5
1979	12.8	11.2	7.4	9.3	14.8	11.8	17.6	13.3	8.8	8.7	58.1	35.0	9.4	8.9
1980	11.8	13.4	7.5	5.8	13.4	16.2	14.1	18.5	11.4	10.7	27.9	49.2	10.8	11.2
1981	7.1	9.2	1.5	5.8	8.7	10.3	8.6	10.3	9.2	10.3	14.1	19.1	7.7	8.6
1982	3.6	4.1	2.0	2.2	4.2	4.6	4.2	4.1	3.9	5.7	-.1	-1.5	4.9	5.7
1983	.6	1.6	2.3	1.0	0	1.8	-.9	1.2	2.0	2.8	-9.2	-4.8	1.9	3.0
1984	1.7	2.1	3.5	4.4	1.1	1.4	.8	1.0	1.8	2.3	-4.2	-4.2	2.0	2.4
1985	1.8	1.0	.6	-.8	2.2	1.4	2.1	1.1	2.7	2.2	-.2	-3.9	2.7	2.5
1986	-2.3	-1.4	2.8	2.6	-4.0	-2.6	-6.6	-4.6	2.1	2.0	-38.1	-28.1	2.7	2.3
1987	2.2	2.1	-.2	2.1	3.2	2.1	4.1	2.2	1.3	1.8	11.2	-1.9	2.1	2.4
1988	4.0	2.5	5.7	2.8	3.2	2.4	3.1	2.4	3.6	2.3	-3.6	-3.2	4.3	3.3
1989	4.9	5.2	5.2	5.4	4.8	5.0	5.3	5.6	3.8	3.9	9.5	9.9	4.2	4.4
1990	5.7	4.9	2.6	4.8	6.9	5.0	8.7	5.9	3.4	3.5	30.7	14.2	3.5	3.7
1991	-.1	2.1	-1.5	-.2	.3	3.0	-.7	2.9	2.5	3.1	-9.6	4.1	3.1	3.6
1992	1.6	1.2	1.6	-.6	1.6	1.8	1.6	1.8	1.7	1.9	-.3	-.4	2.0	2.4
1993	.2	1.2	2.4	1.9	-.4	1.1	-1.4	.7	1.8	1.8	-4.1	.3	.4	1.2
1994	1.7	.6	1.1	.9	1.9	.6	2.0	-.1	2.0	2.1	3.5	-1.3	1.6	1.0
1995	2.3	1.9	1.9	1.7	2.3	1.9	2.3	2.0	2.2	1.9	1.1	1.4	2.6	2.1
1996	2.8	2.7	3.4	3.6	2.6	2.4	3.7	2.9	.4	1.2	11.7	6.5	.6	1.4
1997	-1.2	.4	-.8	.7	-1.2	.3	-1.5	.5	-.6	-.1	-6.4	.2	0	.3
1998	0	-.8	.1	-.1	-.1	-1.1	-.1	-1.4	0	-.4	-11.7	-10.0	2.5	.9
1999	2.9	1.8	.8	.6	3.5	2.2	5.1	3.2	.3	0	18.1	4.9	.9	1.7
2000	3.6	3.8	1.7	1.6	4.1	4.4	5.5	6.1	1.2	.9	16.6	19.4	1.3	1.3
2001	-1.6	2.0	1.8	3.0	-2.6	1.7	-3.9	2.2	0	.6	-17.1	2.8	.9	1.4
2002	1.2	-1.3	-.6	-.8	1.7	-1.5	2.9	-1.8	-.6	-.4	12.3	-8.2	-.5	.1
2003	4.0	3.2	7.7	4.1	3.0	3.0	4.1	4.3	.8	.3	11.4	14.9	1.0	.2
2004	4.2	3.6	3.1	4.7	4.5	3.4	5.5	4.3	2.4	1.4	13.4	10.8	2.3	1.5
2005	5.4	4.8	1.4	1.9	6.5	5.6	9.0	7.4	1.3	2.3	23.9	17.4	1.7	2.4

Percent change from preceding month

	Unadjusted	Seasonally adjusted	Unadjusted	Seasonally adjusted	Unadjusted	Seasonally adjusted	Unadjusted	Seasonally adjusted	Unadjusted	Seasonally adjusted	Unadjusted	Seasonally adjusted	Unadjusted	Seasonally adjusted
2004:Jan	0.6	0.3	-1.5	-1.5	1.2	0.8	1.7	1.0	0.2	0.2	5.0	2.6	0.3	0.3
Feb	-.1	-.1	.2	.1	-.1	-.1	-.1	-.1	-.2	-.2	-.3	-.4	-.1	-.1
Mar	.7	.5	1.5	1.4	.4	.3	.5	.3	.2	.4	1.2	.3	.2	.3
Apr	.7	.7	1.3	1.3	.6	.6	.7	.7	.1	.1	2.3	1.8	.1	.3
May	1.1	.6	1.8	1.4	.9	.3	1.2	.5	.1	.2	3.7	1.4	.1	.1
June	-.1	-.1	-.3	-.4	-.1	.1	-.3	-.1	.2	.4	-1.0	-.8	.1	.3
July	-.1	.1	-1.7	-1.5	.3	.5	.6	.7	-.3	-.1	2.6	2.5	-.3	-.1
Aug	0	.1	-.1	-.2	.1	.1	-.1	.1	.4	.4	-.3	.3	.2	.3
Sept	.1	.3	.3	.5	.1	.1	.1	.1	0	.2	.1	-.2	.1	.3
Oct	2.2	1.5	1.6	1.5	2.3	1.4	2.7	2.0	1.6	.3	5.2	5.7	1.6	.3
Nov	-.2	.7	-.3	.3	-.1	.8	-.2	1.0	0	.2	-.8	2.7	0	.3
Dec	-.7	-.3	.1	.2	-1.0	-.4	-1.5	-.7	.1	.3	-4.7	-2.4	.1	.2
2005:Jan	.5	.1	-.5	-.5	.9	.3	1.0	.3	.3	.4	1.7	-1.0	.6	.7
Feb	.5	.4	.8	.6	.3	.4	.6	.6	-.1	-.1	1.9	1.8	-.1	-.1
Mar	1.0	.8	.6	.6	1.1	.9	1.5	1.2	.2	.3	4.4	3.3	.1	.2
Apr	.5	.5	0	-.2	.7	.7	.9	.8	.2	.3	2.5	1.8	.1	.3
May	-.1	-.5	.3	-.2	-.1	-.6	-.3	-.9	.1	.3	-1.1	-3.3	.2	.3
June	-.1	0	-.8	-.8	.1	.3	.3	.5	-.3	-.3	1.5	1.8	-.3	-.2
July	.8	1.0	-.7	-.5	1.2	1.4	1.8	1.8	.1	.3	4.6	4.6	.2	.4
Aug[2]	.5	.6	-.3	-.3	.7	.8	1.0	1.3	0	0	3.1	3.6	-.1	0
Sept	1.7	1.7	1.2	1.4	1.8	1.8	2.6	2.5	.1	.3	7.1	6.9	.1	.1
Oct	1.3	.7	-.2	-.1	1.7	.9	2.0	1.4	1.0	-.2	3.8	4.1	.9	-.3
Nov	-1.6	-.7	.2	.5	-2.0	-1.0	-2.8	-1.4	-.3	-.1	-7.3	-4.0	-.1	.1
Dec	.3	.9	.8	.9	.1	.9	.1	1.3	0	.1	.3	3.1	.1	.1

[1] Changes from December to December are based on unadjusted indexes.
[2] Data have been revised through August 2005; data are subject to revision 4 months after date of original publication.

Source: Department of Labor, Bureau of Labor Statistics.

TABLE B–69.—*Money stock and debt measures, 1959–2005*
[Averages of daily figures, except debt end-of-period basis; billions of dollars, seasonally adjusted]

Year and month	M1 — Sum of currency, demand deposits, travelers checks, and other checkable deposits (OCDs)	M2 — M1 plus retail MMMF balances, savings deposits (including MMDAs), and small time deposits	M3 — M2 plus large time deposits, RPs, Euro-dollars, and institution-only MMMF balances	Debt[1] — Debt of domestic nonfinancial sectors	Percent change — From year or 6 months earlier[2] M1	M2	M3	From previous period[3] Debt
December:								
1959	140.0	297.8	299.7	689.5	....	....	....	7.8
1960	140.7	312.4	315.2	724.3	0.5	4.9	5.2	5.0
1961	145.2	335.5	340.8	767.8	3.2	7.4	8.1	6.0
1962	147.8	362.7	371.3	820.6	1.8	8.1	8.9	6.9
1963	153.3	393.2	405.9	876.0	3.7	8.4	9.3	6.8
1964	160.3	424.7	442.4	940.0	4.6	8.0	9.0	7.3
1965	167.8	459.2	482.1	1,007.2	4.7	8.1	9.0	7.1
1966	172.0	480.2	505.4	1,074.7	2.5	4.6	4.8	6.7
1967	183.3	524.8	557.9	1,152.7	6.6	9.3	10.4	7.3
1968	197.4	566.8	607.2	1,242.8	7.7	8.0	8.8	7.8
1969	203.9	587.9	615.9	1,330.1	3.3	3.7	1.4	7.0
1970	214.4	626.5	677.1	1,420.2	5.1	6.6	9.9	6.8
1971	228.3	710.3	776.0	1,555.2	6.5	13.4	14.6	9.5
1972	249.2	802.3	885.9	1,711.2	9.2	13.0	14.2	10.0
1973	262.9	855.5	985.0	1,895.5	5.5	6.6	11.2	10.7
1974	274.2	902.1	1,069.9	2,069.9	4.3	5.4	8.6	9.2
1975	287.1	1,016.2	1,170.2	2,261.8	4.7	12.6	9.4	9.3
1976	306.2	1,152.0	1,309.9	2,505.3	6.7	13.4	11.9	10.8
1977	330.9	1,270.3	1,470.4	2,826.6	8.1	10.3	12.3	12.8
1978	357.3	1,366.0	1,644.5	3,211.2	8.0	7.5	11.8	13.8
1979	381.8	1,473.7	1,808.7	3,603.0	6.9	7.9	10.0	12.2
1980	408.5	1,599.8	1,995.5	3,953.5	7.0	8.6	10.3	9.5
1981	436.7	1,755.4	2,254.5	4,361.7	6.9	9.7	13.0	10.4
1982	474.8	1,910.3	2,460.6	4,783.4	8.7	8.8	9.1	10.1
1983	521.4	2,126.5	2,697.4	5,359.2	9.8	11.3	9.6	12.0
1984	551.6	2,310.0	2,990.6	6,146.2	5.8	8.6	10.9	14.8
1985	619.8	2,495.7	3,208.1	7,127.3	12.4	8.0	7.3	15.7
1986	724.7	2,732.3	3,499.1	7,970.6	16.9	9.5	9.1	11.9
1987	750.2	2,831.5	3,686.5	8,673.9	3.5	3.6	5.4	9.0
1988	786.7	2,994.5	3,928.8	9,458.1	4.9	5.8	6.6	9.1
1989	792.9	3,158.5	4,077.1	10,162.1	.8	5.5	3.8	7.3
1990	824.7	3,278.8	4,154.7	10,845.2	4.0	3.8	1.9	6.5
1991	897.1	3,379.7	4,210.3	11,306.2	8.8	3.1	1.3	4.3
1992	1,025.0	3,433.1	4,222.6	11,821.9	14.3	1.6	.3	4.5
1993	1,129.7	3,484.3	4,285.6	12,400.4	10.2	1.5	1.5	4.8
1994	1,150.3	3,497.6	4,369.8	12,975.4	1.8	.4	2.0	4.6
1995	1,126.8	3,640.6	4,636.3	13,656.6	-2.0	4.1	6.1	5.3
1996	1,080.0	3,815.3	4,985.5	14,368.4	-4.2	4.8	7.5	5.2
1997	1,072.2	4,031.7	5,460.9	15,129.1	-.7	5.7	9.5	5.3
1998	1,094.9	4,383.7	6,051.9	16,149.9	2.1	8.7	10.8	6.7
1999	1,123.1	4,648.7	6,551.5	17,215.3	2.6	6.0	8.3	6.4
2000	1,087.6	4,931.3	7,117.6	18,051.6	-3.2	6.1	8.6	4.8
2001	1,182.1	5,450.3	8,035.0	19,146.8	8.7	10.5	12.9	6.1
2002	1,219.2	5,800.3	8,569.2	20,465.9	3.1	6.4	6.6	6.9
2003	1,304.2	6,079.4	8,874.0	22,149.6	7.0	4.8	3.6	8.1
2004	1,372.1	6,422.1	9,435.8	24,090.5	5.2	5.6	6.3	8.7
2005	1,368.9	6,680.5	10,169.3	....	-.2	4.0	7.8	....
2004: Jan	1,306.0	6,088.3	8,931.9	....	2.4	.5	.9	....
Feb	1,319.9	6,132.1	9,002.0	....	3.9	.4	1.8	....
Mar	1,329.6	6,173.0	9,082.4	22,658.2	5.1	2.4	3.9	9.2
Apr	1,339.4	6,216.9	9,151.4	....	6.5	4.3	5.7	....
May	1,336.5	6,280.6	9,245.6	....	6.1	6.6	8.2	....
June	1,341.2	6,288.8	9,277.6	23,083.4	5.7	6.9	9.1	7.5
July	1,343.5	6,295.4	9,284.6	....	5.7	6.8	7.9	....
Aug	1,354.1	6,317.3	9,316.3	....	5.2	6.0	7.0	....
Sept	1,360.5	6,346.9	9,353.8	23,578.9	4.6	5.6	6.0	8.3
Oct	1,360.8	6,369.2	9,361.4	....	3.2	4.9	4.6	....
Nov	1,374.1	6,404.0	9,397.5	....	5.6	3.9	3.3	....
Dec	1,372.1	6,422.1	9,435.8	24,090.5	4.6	4.2	3.4	8.7
2005: Jan	1,367.0	6,436.4	9,492.1	....	3.5	4.5	4.5	....
Feb	1,369.5	6,455.7	9,536.5	....	2.3	4.4	4.7	....
Mar	1,373.0	6,475.8	9,570.2	24,668.4	1.8	4.1	4.6	9.6
Apr	1,365.7	6,482.7	9,625.6	....	.7	3.6	5.6	....
May	1,370.7	6,492.1	9,669.6	....	-.5	2.8	5.8	....
June	1,369.5	6,518.3	9,729.2	25,168.0	-.4	3.0	6.2	8.1
July	1,362.5	6,538.5	9,766.0	....	-.7	3.2	5.8	....
Aug	1,370.4	6,568.9	9,868.8	....	.1	3.5	7.0	....
Sept	1,367.4	6,600.0	9,955.7	25,742.1	-.8	3.8	8.1	9.1
Oct	1,369.2	6,629.6	10,037.7	....	.5	4.5	8.6	....
Nov	1,370.0	6,652.0	10,088.3	....	-.1	4.9	8.7	....
Dec	1,368.9	6,680.5	10,169.3	....	-.1	5.0	9.0	....

[1] Consists of outstanding credit market debt of the U.S. Government, State and local governments, and private nonfinancial sectors.
[2] Annual changes are from December to December; monthly changes are from 6 months earlier at a simple annual rate.
[3] Annual changes are from fourth quarter to fourth quarter. Quarterly changes are from previous quarter at annual rate.
Source: Board of Governors of the Federal Reserve System.

TABLE B–70.—*Components of money stock measures, 1959–2005*

[Averages of daily figures; billions of dollars, seasonally adjusted]

Year and month	Currency	Nonbank travelers checks	Demand deposits	Other checkable deposits (OCDs)	Small denomination time deposits [1]	Savings deposits, including money market deposit accounts (MMDAs) [2]
December:						
1959	28.8	0.3	110.8	0.0	11.4	146.5
1960	28.7	.3	111.6	.0	12.5	159.1
1961	29.3	.4	115.5	.0	14.8	175.5
1962	30.3	.4	117.1	.0	20.1	194.8
1963	32.2	.4	120.6	.1	25.5	214.4
1964	33.9	.5	125.8	.1	29.2	235.2
1965	36.0	.5	131.3	.1	34.5	256.9
1966	38.0	.6	133.4	.1	55.0	253.1
1967	40.0	.6	142.5	.1	77.8	263.7
1968	43.0	.7	153.6	.1	100.5	268.9
1969	45.7	.8	157.3	.2	120.4	263.7
1970	48.6	.9	164.7	.1	151.2	261.0
1971	52.0	1.0	175.1	.2	189.7	292.2
1972	56.2	1.2	191.6	.2	231.6	321.4
1973	60.8	1.4	200.3	.3	265.8	326.8
1974	67.0	1.7	205.1	.4	287.9	338.6
1975	72.8	2.1	211.3	.9	337.9	388.9
1976	79.5	2.6	221.5	2.7	390.7	453.2
1977	87.4	2.9	236.4	4.2	445.5	492.2
1978	96.0	3.3	249.5	8.5	521.0	481.9
1979	104.8	3.5	256.6	16.8	634.3	423.8
1980	115.3	3.9	261.2	28.1	728.5	400.3
1981	122.5	4.1	231.4	78.7	823.1	343.9
1982	132.5	4.1	234.1	104.1	850.9	400.1
1983	146.2	4.7	238.5	132.1	784.1	684.9
1984	156.1	5.0	243.4	147.1	888.8	704.7
1985	167.8	5.6	267.0	179.5	885.7	815.3
1986	180.4	6.1	302.9	235.2	858.4	940.9
1987	196.7	6.6	287.7	259.2	921.0	937.4
1988	212.0	7.0	287.1	280.6	1,037.1	926.4
1989	222.3	6.9	278.6	285.1	1,151.3	893.7
1990	246.5	7.7	276.8	293.7	1,173.4	922.9
1991	267.1	7.7	289.7	332.6	1,065.6	1,044.6
1992	292.2	8.2	340.0	384.6	868.1	1,187.2
1993	321.6	8.0	385.4	414.7	782.0	1,219.4
1994	354.0	8.6	383.6	404.2	816.4	1,150.0
1995	372.2	9.0	389.0	356.6	931.4	1,134.2
1996	394.1	8.8	401.6	275.5	946.9	1,272.9
1997	424.5	8.4	393.8	245.4	968.3	1,399.9
1998	459.8	8.5	377.0	249.6	952.0	1,605.1
1999	517.8	8.6	353.4	243.3	954.5	1,740.3
2000	531.2	8.3	309.9	238.2	1,044.8	1,877.9
2001	581.1	8.0	335.7	257.4	973.7	2,312.8
2002	626.2	7.8	306.1	279.1	892.0	2,778.8
2003	662.3	7.7	324.7	309.5	809.6	3,169.4
2004	697.3	7.6	340.3	327.0	816.8	3,519.9
2005	723.8	7.3	321.0	316.9	973.7	3,620.5
2004: Jan	663.9	7.8	320.5	313.8	807.0	3,193.2
Feb	665.6	7.8	327.9	318.6	804.5	3,234.2
Mar	667.4	7.8	332.4	322.0	801.8	3,277.9
Apr	670.2	7.8	339.7	321.7	798.6	3,323.0
May	673.6	7.7	332.9	322.2	793.8	3,393.1
June	677.8	7.7	330.2	325.6	792.7	3,403.5
July	684.9	7.6	325.0	325.9	793.6	3,417.8
Aug	686.5	7.6	332.7	327.4	797.3	3,430.5
Sept	689.9	7.6	338.3	324.7	801.2	3,456.5
Oct	692.9	7.6	334.1	326.3	806.4	3,482.7
Nov	697.7	7.6	340.0	328.7	811.1	3,504.5
Dec	697.3	7.6	340.3	327.0	816.8	3,519.9
2005: Jan	699.0	7.5	336.4	324.1	829.0	3,528.6
Feb	700.8	7.5	338.6	322.6	841.1	3,538.4
Mar	702.9	7.5	339.3	323.4	854.7	3,543.6
Apr	703.9	7.5	331.0	323.3	869.4	3,541.7
May	705.8	7.5	332.8	324.7	885.9	3,533.9
June	708.4	7.4	334.2	319.6	900.7	3,548.0
July	710.0	7.3	327.4	317.8	914.9	3,560.2
Aug	712.8	7.4	330.0	320.2	929.3	3,569.4
Sept	716.1	7.3	324.2	319.8	942.5	3,585.1
Oct	717.4	7.3	325.9	318.5	952.6	3,597.3
Nov	720.3	7.3	323.4	319.0	963.9	3,603.8
Dec	723.8	7.3	321.0	316.9	973.7	3,620.5

[1] Small denomination deposits are those issued in amounts of less than $100,000.
[2] Data prior to 1982 are savings deposits only; MMDA data begin December 1982.

See next page for continuation of table.

[Averages of daily figures; billions of dollars, seasonally adjusted]

Year and month	Money market mutual fund (MMMF) balances		Large denomination time deposits [3]	Overnight and term repurchase agreements (RPs) (net)	Overnight and term Eurodollars (net)
	Retail	Institution only			
December:					
1959	0.0	0.0	1.2	0.0	0.7
1960	.0	.0	2.0	.0	.8
1961	.0	.0	3.9	.0	1.5
1962	.0	.0	7.0	.0	1.6
1963	.0	.0	10.8	.0	1.9
1964	.0	.0	15.2	.0	2.4
1965	.0	.0	21.2	.0	1.8
1966	.0	.0	23.1	.0	2.2
1967	.0	.0	30.9	.0	2.2
1968	.0	.0	37.4	.0	2.9
1969	.0	.0	20.4	4.9	2.7
1970	.0	.0	45.2	3.0	2.4
1971	.0	.0	57.7	5.2	2.9
1972	.0	.0	73.3	6.6	3.8
1973	.1	.0	110.9	12.8	5.8
1974	1.4	.2	144.7	14.5	8.5
1975	2.4	.5	129.7	13.8	10.0
1976	1.8	.6	118.1	24.0	15.2
1977	1.8	1.0	145.2	32.2	21.7
1978	5.8	3.5	195.6	44.4	35.1
1979	33.9	10.4	223.1	48.8	52.7
1980	62.5	16.0	260.2	58.1	61.4
1981	151.7	38.2	304.3	67.8	88.8
1982	184.5	48.8	325.6	71.8	104.2
1983	136.1	40.9	316.1	97.3	116.6
1984	164.9	62.3	402.2	107.3	108.9
1985	174.9	65.3	421.7	121.2	104.2
1986	208.4	86.2	419.0	145.8	115.7
1987	222.8	93.7	461.9	178.0	121.5
1988	244.3	93.8	512.4	196.5	131.7
1989	320.6	112.0	528.1	169.1	109.4
1990	357.7	139.6	481.7	151.5	103.3
1991	372.4	188.5	418.6	131.1	92.3
1992	352.8	212.8	355.7	141.5	79.5
1993	353.1	216.8	339.2	172.6	72.8
1994	380.9	210.8	378.9	196.3	86.3
1995	448.2	264.4	438.9	198.3	94.0
1996	515.5	324.2	521.1	210.3	114.6
1997	591.4	396.9	631.1	253.9	147.5
1998	731.7	541.2	683.7	293.2	150.2
1999	830.9	638.2	758.9	334.9	170.8
2000	921.1	791.9	836.9	362.3	195.2
2001	981.7	1,196.7	802.9	373.7	211.4
2002	910.2	1,247.7	817.2	473.4	230.7
2003	796.1	1,117.4	887.1	494.8	295.3
2004	713.2	1,068.4	1,073.3	492.6	379.4
2005	717.4	1,136.2	1,359.4	563.0	430.2
2004: Jan	782.2	1,118.8	917.6	504.8	302.4
Feb	773.5	1,116.0	922.9	521.0	310.1
Mar	763.6	1,123.8	943.5	526.1	316.0
Apr	755.9	1,127.6	962.0	520.0	324.9
May	757.2	1,132.1	983.6	522.3	327.0
June	751.4	1,126.4	996.0	536.9	329.5
July	740.5	1,112.2	1,013.5	526.5	337.0
Aug	735.3	1,105.9	1,024.5	524.7	343.8
Sept	728.7	1,094.6	1,031.6	526.7	354.1
Oct	719.4	1,075.7	1,038.6	510.2	367.6
Nov	714.2	1,071.1	1,050.6	501.0	370.8
Dec	713.2	1,068.4	1,073.3	492.6	379.4
2005: Jan	711.8	1,062.5	1,127.4	473.1	392.7
Feb	706.7	1,054.1	1,141.9	489.3	395.5
Mar	704.5	1,049.3	1,153.1	487.8	404.2
Apr	705.9	1,057.5	1,196.7	483.8	405.0
May	701.6	1,057.9	1,208.6	504.7	406.3
June	700.2	1,069.1	1,235.5	504.3	402.1
July	700.9	1,078.6	1,223.0	517.6	408.4
Aug	699.8	1,091.3	1,265.7	525.1	417.7
Sept	705.1	1,107.4	1,292.5	534.2	421.6
Oct	710.6	1,119.3	1,322.9	545.0	421.0
Nov	714.2	1,120.6	1,335.6	554.3	425.9
Dec	717.4	1,136.2	1,359.4	563.0	430.2

[3] Large denomination deposits are those issued in amounts of more than $100,000.

Note.—See also Table B–69.
Source: Board of Governors of the Federal Reserve System.

TABLE B–71.—*Aggregate reserves of depository institutions and the monetary base, 1959–2005*

[Averages of daily figures [1]; millions of dollars; seasonally adjusted, except as noted]

Year and month	Adjusted for changes in reserve requirements [2]					Borrowings of depository institutions from the Federal Reserve (NSA)				
	Reserves of depository institutions				Mone-tary base	Total	Primary	Secondary	Seasonal	Adjust-ment
	Total	Nonbor-rowed	Required	Excess (NSA)						
December:										
1959	11,109	10,168	10,603	506	40,880	941	....	....	....	941
1960	11,247	11,172	10,503	743	40,977	74	....	....	....	74
1961	11,499	11,366	10,915	584	41,853	133	....	....	....	133
1962	11,604	11,344	11,033	572	42,957	260	....	....	....	260
1963	11,730	11,397	11,239	490	45,003	332	....	....	....	332
1964	12,011	11,747	11,605	406	47,161	264	....	....	....	264
1965	12,316	11,872	11,892	423	49,620	444	....	....	....	444
1966	12,223	11,690	11,884	339	51,565	532	....	....	....	532
1967	13,180	12,952	12,805	375	54,579	228	....	....	....	228
1968	13,767	13,021	13,341	426	58,357	746	....	....	....	746
1969	14,168	13,049	13,882	286	61,569	1,119	....	....	....	1,119
1970	14,558	14,225	14,309	249	65,013	332	....	....	....	332
1971	15,230	15,104	15,049	182	69,108	126	....	....	....	126
1972	16,645	15,595	16,361	284	75,167	1,050	....	....	....	1,050
1973	17,021	15,723	16,717	304	81,073	1,298	....	....	41	1,257
1974	17,550	16,823	17,292	258	87,535	727	....	....	32	548
1975	17,822	17,692	17,556	266	93,887	130	....	....	14	104
1976	18,388	18,335	18,115	274	101,515	53	....	....	13	40
1977	18,990	18,420	18,800	190	110,324	569	....	....	55	514
1978	19,753	18,885	19,521	232	120,445	868	....	....	135	734
1979	20,720	19,248	20,279	442	131,143	1,473	....	....	82	1,390
1980	22,015	20,325	21,501	514	142,004	1,690	....	....	116	1,571
1981	22,443	21,807	22,124	319	149,021	636	....	....	54	433
1982	23,600	22,966	23,100	500	160,127	634	....	....	33	415
1983	25,367	24,593	24,806	561	175,467	774	....	....	96	676
1984	26,913	23,727	26,078	835	187,238	3,186	....	....	113	469
1985	31,569	30,250	30,505	1,063	203,562	1,318	....	....	56	763
1986	38,840	38,014	37,667	1,173	223,425	827	....	....	38	486
1987	38,913	38,135	37,893	1,019	239,837	777	....	....	93	201
1988	40,453	38,738	39,392	1,061	256,892	1,716	....	....	130	342
1989	40,486	40,221	39,545	941	267,755	265	....	....	84	162
1990	41,766	41,440	40,101	1,664	293,287	326	....	....	76	227
1991	45,515	45,323	44,526	989	317,557	192	....	....	38	153
1992	54,421	54,297	53,267	1,154	350,919	124	....	....	18	105
1993	60,567	60,485	59,497	1,070	386,594	82	....	....	31	51
1994	59,454	59,245	58,295	1,159	418,325	209	....	....	100	109
1995	56,483	56,226	55,193	1,290	434,585	257	....	....	40	217
1996	50,183	50,028	48,766	1,416	452,081	155	....	....	68	87
1997	46,873	46,549	45,189	1,685	479,946	324	....	....	79	245
1998	45,515	45,398	44,001	1,514	514,077	117	....	....	15	101
1999	42,009	41,778	40,802	1,297	593,635	[3]320	....	....	67	179
2000	38,792	38,582	37,364	1,428	584,831	210	....	....	111	99
2001	41,496	41,429	39,846	1,650	635,401	67	....	....	33	34
2002	40,441	40,361	38,432	2,009	681,386	80	....	....	45	35
2003	42,772	42,726	41,729	1,043	720,101	46	17	0	29	....
2004	46,795	46,733	44,886	1,909	758,973	63	11	0	52	....
2005	44,798	44,630	42,847	1,951	786,383	169	97	0	72	....
2004: Jan	43,004	42,898	42,112	892	721,878	106	93	0	13	....
Feb	42,915	42,873	41,718	1,196	723,993	42	28	0	14	....
Mar	44,662	44,610	42,855	1,807	726,571	51	23	0	28	....
Apr	45,788	45,702	43,980	1,808	730,639	86	29	0	57	....
May	45,643	45,531	43,956	1,686	734,231	112	9	0	103	....
June	46,284	46,104	44,351	1,933	738,990	180	40	0	140	....
July	46,400	46,155	44,681	1,719	746,307	245	42	0	203	....
Aug	45,481	45,229	43,898	1,583	747,704	251	18	0	233	....
Sept	46,488	46,153	44,833	1,655	751,823	335	97	0	238	....
Oct.	46,344	46,164	44,587	1,757	754,730	179	15	0	164	....
Nov	46,368	46,185	44,584	1,784	759,302	183	105	0	78	....
Dec	46,795	46,733	44,886	1,909	758,973	63	11	0	52	....
2005: Jan	47,475	47,413	45,734	1,741	760,531	62	39	0	23	....
Feb	45,969	45,927	44,472	1,497	763,479	42	26	0	16	....
Mar	46,804	46,755	45,021	1,783	765,712	49	13	0	37	....
Apr	46,559	46,428	44,884	1,675	766,942	132	52	0	80	....
May	45,873	45,734	44,336	1,537	768,134	139	6	0	133	....
June	46,670	46,421	44,887	1,782	771,123	249	85	0	164	....
July	46,085	45,660	44,343	1,741	772,865	425	176	12	237	....
Aug	44,540	44,178	42,918	1,622	774,705	362	63	3	297	....
Sept	45,720	45,388	43,673	2,047	777,801	332	12	5	315	....
Oct	44,784	44,500	42,883	1,900	780,069	284	35	29	220	....
Nov	44,705	44,579	42,909	1,797	783,668	126	20	0	106	....
Dec	44,798	44,630	42,847	1,951	786,383	169	97	0	72	....

[1] Data are prorated averages of biweekly (maintenance period) averages of daily figures.
[2] Aggregate reserves incorporate adjustments for discontinuities associated with regulatory changes to reserve requirements. For details on aggregate reserves series see *Federal Reserve Bulletin*.
[3] Total includes borrowing under the terms and conditions established for the Century Date Change Special Liquidity Facility in effect from October 1, 1999 through April 7, 2000.

Note.—NSA indicates data are not seasonally adjusted.

Source: Board of Governors of the Federal Reserve System.

TABLE B–72.—*Bank credit at all commercial banks, 1959–2005*

[Monthly average; billions of dollars, seasonally adjusted [1]]

Year and month	Total bank credit	Securities in bank credit			Loans and leases in bank credit						
		Total securities	U.S. Treasury and agency securities	Other securities	Total loans and leases [2]	Commercial and industrial	Real estate			Consumer	Security	Other
							Total	Revolving home equity	Other			
December:												
1959	189.5	77.4	61.9	15.5	112.1	39.5	28.1	....	....	24.1	5.0	15.4
1960	197.6	79.5	63.9	15.6	118.1	42.4	28.7	....	....	26.3	5.2	15.6
1961	213.1	88.2	70.4	17.9	124.8	44.1	30.2	....	....	27.6	6.1	16.8
1962	231.0	92.2	70.7	21.5	138.8	47.7	34.0	....	....	30.3	6.6	20.2
1963	250.7	92.6	67.4	25.2	158.1	52.5	38.9	....	....	34.2	7.9	24.6
1964	270.4	94.7	66.7	28.1	175.6	58.7	43.5	....	....	39.5	8.3	25.7
1965	297.1	96.1	64.3	31.9	201.0	69.5	48.9	....	....	45.0	8.0	29.7
1966	318.6	97.2	61.0	36.2	221.4	79.3	53.8	....	....	47.7	8.3	32.4
1967	350.5	111.4	70.7	40.6	239.2	86.5	58.2	....	....	51.2	9.6	33.8
1968	390.5	121.9	73.8	48.1	268.6	96.5	64.8	....	....	57.7	10.5	39.2
1969	401.6	112.4	64.2	48.2	289.2	106.9	69.9	....	....	62.6	10.0	39.8
1970	434.4	129.7	73.4	56.3	304.6	111.6	72.9	....	....	65.3	10.4	44.5
1971	485.2	147.5	79.8	67.7	337.6	118.0	81.7	....	....	73.3	10.9	53.9
1972	555.3	160.6	85.4	75.2	394.7	133.6	98.8	....	....	85.4	14.4	62.5
1973	638.6	168.4	89.7	78.7	470.1	162.8	119.4	....	119.4	98.3	11.2	78.4
1974	701.7	173.8	87.9	85.9	527.9	193.0	132.5	....	132.5	102.1	10.6	89.6
1975	732.9	206.7	117.9	88.9	526.2	184.3	137.2	....	137.2	104.6	12.7	87.5
1976	790.7	228.6	137.3	91.3	562.1	186.3	151.3	....	151.3	115.9	17.7	91.0
1977	876.0	236.3	137.4	98.9	639.7	205.8	178.0	....	178.0	138.1	20.7	97.2
1978	989.4	242.2	138.4	103.8	747.2	239.0	213.5	....	213.5	164.6	19.1	110.9
1979	1,111.4	260.7	147.2	113.4	850.7	282.2	245.0	....	245.0	184.5	17.4	121.6
1980	1,207.1	296.8	173.2	123.6	910.3	314.5	265.7	....	265.7	179.2	17.2	133.6
1981	1,302.7	311.1	181.8	129.3	991.6	353.3	287.5	....	287.5	182.7	20.2	148.0
1982	1,412.3	338.6	204.7	133.9	1,073.7	396.4	303.8	....	303.8	188.2	23.6	161.7
1983	1,566.7	403.8	263.4	140.4	1,163.0	419.1	334.8	....	334.8	213.2	26.5	169.4
1984	1,733.4	406.6	262.9	143.7	1,326.9	479.4	380.8	....	380.8	253.6	34.1	179.0
1985	1,922.2	455.9	273.8	182.2	1,466.3	506.5	431.0	....	431.0	294.5	42.9	191.4
1986	2,106.6	510.0	312.8	197.2	1,596.5	544.0	499.9	....	499.9	314.5	38.6	199.5
1987	2,255.3	535.0	338.9	196.1	1,720.2	575.0	595.7	32.2	563.5	327.7	34.8	187.0
1988	2,432.7	561.7	366.0	195.7	1,871.0	611.7	676.4	42.6	633.8	354.8	40.3	187.9
1989	2,602.2	584.7	399.5	185.2	2,017.5	642.7	769.2	53.5	715.6	375.3	40.9	189.3
1990	2,749.7	634.9	456.0	178.9	2,114.9	645.6	856.6	66.4	790.2	380.8	44.4	187.4
1991	2,856.4	747.2	566.9	180.3	2,109.2	623.4	882.8	74.3	808.5	363.9	53.9	185.2
1992	2,954.1	841.8	664.9	176.9	2,112.3	599.4	906.0	78.5	827.5	356.3	63.4	187.2
1993	3,112.4	915.6	730.8	184.8	2,196.7	590.3	947.0	78.1	868.9	387.6	86.4	185.5
1994	3,318.2	939.9	721.6	218.3	2,378.3	650.3	1,010.7	80.5	930.2	448.2	75.8	193.3
1995	3,601.0	984.0	701.1	282.9	2,617.0	723.8	1,089.5	84.5	1,004.9	491.4	83.2	229.1
1996	3,756.9	984.4	702.6	281.8	2,772.5	784.0	1,141.2	90.9	1,050.3	512.4	75.3	259.6
1997	4,099.3	1,098.7	755.6	343.1	3,000.6	853.4	1,243.3	105.0	1,138.3	502.6	94.4	306.9
1998	4,532.8	1,237.0	797.6	439.5	3,295.8	946.7	1,333.6	103.9	1,229.6	496.9	145.3	373.3
1999	4,763.3	1,282.8	815.6	467.2	3,480.5	998.0	1,471.8	101.5	1,370.3	490.6	149.8	370.2
2000	5,216.4	1,348.2	792.4	555.8	3,868.2	1,085.9	1,651.2	130.0	1,521.2	539.3	177.3	414.4
2001	5,417.7	1,487.4	849.0	638.4	3,930.3	1,024.3	1,778.6	155.7	1,623.0	556.0	146.0	425.4
2002	5,884.6	1,721.6	1,029.1	692.5	4,163.0	960.8	2,022.0	213.5	1,808.5	586.2	190.2	403.7
2003	6,251.3	1,850.3	1,104.8	745.5	4,401.0	900.4	2,216.5	280.8	1,935.7	643.4	215.2	425.6
2004	6,793.5	1,937.2	1,150.2	787.0	4,856.3	924.4	2,547.6	399.9	2,147.8	695.2	215.9	473.1
2005	7,483.6	2,045.6	1,132.9	912.7	5,438.0	1,044.6	2,902.6	436.2	2,466.3	704.4	261.5	525.0
2004: Jan ...	6,321.8	1,855.3	1,106.3	749.0	4,466.5	901.8	2,242.3	291.2	1,951.1	651.7	234.1	436.6
Feb ..	6,442.7	1,930.8	1,170.9	760.0	4,511.8	900.1	2,264.3	297.6	1,966.7	653.9	244.7	448.9
Mar ..	6,520.6	1,980.7	1,204.9	775.8	4,539.9	889.4	2,305.1	308.2	1,996.9	658.5	245.5	441.5
Apr ..	6,541.0	1,953.6	1,200.2	753.4	4,587.4	885.1	2,362.5	318.1	2,044.4	658.8	240.7	440.2
May	6,550.0	1,930.8	1,189.3	741.5	4,619.1	884.7	2,397.7	328.1	2,069.6	659.8	235.2	441.7
June	6,589.9	1,934.6	1,189.1	745.5	4,655.3	888.5	2,411.7	338.2	2,073.5	662.7	248.9	443.5
July ..	6,602.3	1,909.6	1,180.9	728.7	4,692.7	894.6	2,421.2	348.1	2,073.1	691.3	238.1	447.6
Aug ..	6,632.7	1,915.2	1,182.6	732.5	4,717.5	902.9	2,439.8	359.2	2,080.6	691.7	232.1	451.1
Sept	6,702.5	1,925.4	1,177.0	748.4	4,777.1	906.2	2,465.5	370.5	2,095.0	693.6	247.5	464.2
Oct ..	6,713.8	1,918.2	1,148.1	770.1	4,795.7	906.8	2,499.4	384.5	2,114.9	689.6	241.6	458.3
Nov ..	6,759.5	1,924.6	1,145.9	778.7	4,834.9	915.2	2,524.6	394.2	2,130.4	685.6	236.8	472.7
Dec ..	6,793.5	1,937.2	1,150.2	787.0	4,856.3	924.4	2,547.6	399.9	2,147.8	695.2	215.9	473.1
2005: Jan ...	6,892.7	1,991.3	1,182.3	809.0	4,901.4	942.9	2,572.3	407.3	2,165.0	702.7	200.5	482.9
Feb ..	6,999.4	2,039.6	1,217.6	821.9	4,959.8	953.0	2,600.7	409.9	2,190.8	700.6	220.5	484.9
Mar ..	7,084.7	2,058.3	1,218.1	840.2	5,026.4	960.7	2,654.9	418.3	2,236.5	708.5	226.2	476.1
Apr ..	7,112.4	2,044.9	1,193.8	851.1	5,067.5	974.3	2,682.3	423.0	2,259.3	711.2	223.9	475.7
May	7,166.6	2,072.4	1,200.0	872.4	5,094.2	985.2	2,691.2	426.9	2,264.3	704.3	237.1	476.4
June	7,221.2	2,055.6	1,172.4	883.2	5,165.6	990.3	2,734.7	431.5	2,303.2	707.1	248.4	485.1
July ..	7,281.2	2,063.3	1,177.5	885.9	5,217.9	1,004.1	2,787.7	437.9	2,349.8	710.5	232.5	483.0
Aug ..	7,360.5	2,066.7	1,174.4	892.4	5,293.8	1,014.0	2,825.1	439.5	2,385.6	717.2	245.3	492.2
Sept	7,409.0	2,078.1	1,166.4	911.6	5,330.9	1,018.1	2,840.9	438.7	2,402.2	719.9	246.7	505.3
Oct ..	7,420.4	2,069.2	1,159.0	910.2	5,351.2	1,025.2	2,864.8	436.8	2,427.9	708.7	241.8	510.8
Nov ..	7,438.4	2,058.3	1,141.6	916.7	5,380.1	1,033.0	2,877.3	436.8	2,440.5	709.2	246.6	514.1
Dec ..	7,483.6	2,045.6	1,132.9	912.7	5,438.0	1,044.6	2,902.6	436.2	2,466.3	704.4	261.5	525.0

[1] Data are prorated averages of Wednesday values for domestically chartered commercial banks, branches and agencies of foreign banks, New York State investment companies (through September 1996), and Edge Act and agreement corporations.
[2] Excludes Federal funds sold to, reverse repurchase agreements (RPs) with, and loans to commercial banks in the United States.
Source: Board of Governors of the Federal Reserve System.

[Percent per annum]

Year and month	U.S. Treasury securities					Corporate bonds (Moody's)		High-grade munici-pal bonds (Stand-ard & Poor's)	New-home mort-gage yields[4]	Prime rate charged by banks[5]	Discount window (Federal Reserve Bank of New York)[5][6]		Federal funds rate[7]
	Bills (new issues)[1]		Constant maturities[2]										
	3-month	6-month	3-year	10-year	30-year	Aaa[3]	Baa				Primary credit	Adjust-ment credit	
1929	....	....	....	....	....	4.73	5.90	4.27	....	5.50-6.00	....	5.16	....
1933	0.515	....	....	....	....	4.49	7.76	4.71	....	1.50-4.00	....	2.56	....
1939	.023	....	....	....	....	3.01	4.96	2.76	....	1.50	....	1.00	....
1940	.014	....	....	....	....	2.84	4.75	2.50	....	1.50	....	1.00	....
1941	.103	....	....	....	....	2.77	4.33	2.10	....	1.50	....	1.00	....
1942	.326	....	....	....	....	2.83	4.28	2.36	....	1.50	....	[8]1.00	....
1943	.373	....	....	....	....	2.73	3.91	2.06	....	1.50	....	[8]1.00	....
1944	.375	....	....	....	....	2.72	3.61	1.86	....	1.50	....	[8]1.00	....
1945	.375	....	....	....	....	2.62	3.29	1.67	....	1.50	....	[8]1.00	....
1946	.375	....	....	....	....	2.53	3.05	1.64	....	1.50	....	[8]1.00	....
1947	.594	....	....	....	....	2.61	3.24	2.01	....	1.50-1.75	....	1.00	....
1948	1.040	....	....	....	....	2.82	3.47	2.40	....	1.75-2.00	....	1.34	....
1949	1.102	....	....	....	....	2.66	3.42	2.21	....	2.00	....	1.50	....
1950	1.218	....	....	....	....	2.62	3.24	1.98	....	2.07	....	1.59	....
1951	1.552	....	....	....	....	2.86	3.41	2.00	....	2.56	....	1.75	....
1952	1.766	....	....	....	....	2.96	3.52	2.19	....	3.00	....	1.75	....
1953	1.931	....	2.47	2.85	....	3.20	3.74	2.72	....	3.17	....	1.99	....
1954	.953	....	1.63	2.40	....	2.90	3.51	2.37	....	3.05	....	1.60	....
1955	1.753	....	2.47	2.82	....	3.06	3.53	2.53	....	3.16	....	1.89	1.78
1956	2.658	....	3.19	3.18	....	3.36	3.88	2.93	....	3.77	....	2.77	2.73
1957	3.267	....	3.98	3.65	....	3.89	4.71	3.60	....	4.20	....	3.12	3.11
1958	1.839	....	2.84	3.32	....	3.79	4.73	3.56	....	3.83	....	2.15	1.57
1959	3.405	3.832	4.46	4.33	....	4.38	5.05	3.95	....	4.48	....	3.36	3.30
1960	2.928	3.247	3.98	4.12	....	4.41	5.19	3.73	....	4.82	....	3.53	3.22
1961	2.378	2.605	3.54	3.88	....	4.35	5.08	3.46	....	4.50	....	3.00	1.96
1962	2.778	2.908	3.47	3.95	....	4.33	5.02	3.18	....	4.50	....	3.00	2.68
1963	3.157	3.253	3.67	4.00	....	4.26	4.86	3.23	5.89	4.50	....	3.23	3.18
1964	3.549	3.686	4.03	4.19	....	4.40	4.83	3.22	5.83	4.50	....	3.55	3.50
1965	3.954	4.055	4.22	4.28	....	4.49	4.87	3.27	5.81	4.54	....	4.04	4.07
1966	4.881	5.082	5.23	4.92	....	5.13	5.67	3.82	6.25	5.63	....	4.50	5.11
1967	4.321	4.630	5.03	5.07	....	5.51	6.23	3.98	6.46	5.61	....	4.19	4.22
1968	5.339	5.470	5.68	5.65	....	6.18	6.94	4.51	6.97	6.30	....	5.16	5.66
1969	6.677	6.853	7.02	6.67	....	7.03	7.81	5.81	7.81	7.96	....	5.87	8.20
1970	6.458	6.562	7.29	7.35	....	8.04	9.11	6.51	8.45	7.91	....	5.95	7.18
1971	4.348	4.511	5.65	6.16	....	7.39	8.56	5.70	7.74	5.72	....	4.88	4.66
1972	4.071	4.466	5.72	6.21	....	7.21	8.16	5.27	7.60	5.25	....	4.50	4.43
1973	7.041	7.178	6.95	6.84	....	7.44	8.24	5.18	7.96	8.03	....	6.44	8.73
1974	7.886	7.926	7.82	7.56	....	8.57	9.50	6.09	8.92	10.81	....	7.83	10.50
1975	5.838	6.122	7.49	7.99	....	8.83	10.61	6.89	9.00	7.86	....	6.25	5.82
1976	4.989	5.266	6.77	7.61	....	8.43	9.75	6.49	9.00	6.84	....	5.50	5.04
1977	5.265	5.510	6.69	7.42	7.75	8.02	8.97	5.56	9.02	6.83	....	5.46	5.54
1978	7.221	7.572	8.29	8.41	8.49	8.73	9.49	5.90	9.56	9.06	....	7.46	7.93
1979	10.041	10.017	9.71	9.44	9.28	9.63	10.69	6.39	10.78	12.67	....	10.28	11.19
1980	11.506	11.374	11.55	11.46	11.27	11.94	13.67	8.51	12.66	15.27	....	11.77	13.36
1981	14.029	13.776	14.44	13.91	13.45	14.17	16.04	11.23	14.70	18.87	....	13.42	16.38
1982	10.686	11.084	12.92	13.00	12.76	13.79	16.11	11.57	15.14	14.86	....	11.02	12.26
1983	8.63	8.75	10.45	11.10	11.18	12.04	13.55	9.47	12.57	10.79	....	8.50	9.09
1984	9.58	9.80	11.89	12.44	12.41	12.71	14.19	10.15	12.38	12.04	....	8.80	10.23
1985	7.48	7.66	9.64	10.62	10.79	11.37	12.72	9.18	11.55	9.93	....	7.69	8.10
1986	5.98	6.03	7.06	7.68	7.78	9.02	10.39	7.38	10.17	8.33	....	6.33	6.81
1987	5.82	6.05	7.68	8.39	8.59	9.38	10.58	7.73	9.31	8.21	....	5.66	6.66
1988	6.69	6.92	8.26	8.85	8.96	9.71	10.83	7.76	9.19	9.32	....	6.20	7.57
1989	8.12	8.04	8.55	8.49	8.45	9.26	10.18	7.24	10.13	10.87	....	6.93	9.21
1990	7.51	7.47	8.26	8.55	8.61	9.32	10.36	7.25	10.05	10.01	....	6.98	8.10
1991	5.42	5.49	6.82	7.86	8.14	8.77	9.80	6.89	9.32	8.46	....	5.45	5.69
1992	3.45	3.57	5.30	7.01	7.67	8.14	8.98	6.41	8.24	6.25	....	3.25	3.52
1993	3.02	3.14	4.44	5.87	6.59	7.22	7.93	5.63	7.20	6.00	....	3.00	3.02
1994	4.29	4.66	6.27	7.09	7.37	7.96	8.62	6.19	7.49	7.15	....	3.60	4.21
1995	5.51	5.59	6.25	6.57	6.88	7.59	8.20	5.95	7.87	8.83	....	5.21	5.83
1996	5.02	5.09	5.99	6.44	6.71	7.37	8.05	5.75	7.80	8.27	....	5.02	5.30
1997	5.07	5.18	6.10	6.35	6.61	7.26	7.86	5.55	7.71	8.44	....	5.00	5.46
1998	4.81	4.85	5.14	5.26	5.58	6.53	7.22	5.12	7.07	8.35	....	4.92	5.35
1999	4.66	4.76	5.49	5.65	5.87	7.04	7.87	5.43	7.04	8.00	....	4.62	4.97
2000	5.85	5.92	6.22	6.03	5.94	7.62	8.36	5.77	7.52	9.23	....	5.73	6.24
2001	3.45	3.39	4.09	5.02	5.49	7.08	7.95	5.19	7.00	6.91	....	3.40	3.88
2002	1.62	1.69	3.10	4.61	....	6.49	7.80	5.05	6.43	4.67	....	1.17	1.67
2003	1.02	1.06	2.10	4.01	....	5.67	6.77	4.73	5.80	4.12	2.12	....	1.13
2004	1.38	1.58	2.78	4.27	....	5.63	6.39	4.63	5.77	4.34	2.34	....	1.35
2005	3.16	3.40	3.93	4.29	....	5.24	6.06	4.29	5.94	6.19	4.19	....	3.22

[1] Rate on new issues within period; bank-discount basis.

[2] Yields on the more actively traded issues adjusted to constant maturities by the Department of the Treasury. In February 2002, the Department of the Treasury discontinued publication of the 30-year series.

[3] Beginning December 7, 2001, data for corporate Aaa series are industrial bonds only.

[4] Effective rate (in the primary market) on conventional mortgages, reflecting fees and charges as well as contract rate and assuming, on the average, repayment at end of 10 years. Rates beginning January 1973 not strictly comparable with prior rates.

See next page for continuation of table.

TABLE B-73.—*Bond yields and interest rates, 1929-2005*—Continued

[Percent per annum]

Year and month	U.S. Treasury securities — Bills (new issues)[1] 3-month	6-month	Constant maturities[2] 3-year	10-year	30-year	Corporate bonds (Moody's) Aaa[3]	Baa	High-grade municipal bonds (Standard & Poor's)	New-home mortgage yields[4]	Prime rate charged by banks[5]	Discount window (Federal Reserve Bank of New York)[5][6] Primary credit High-low	Adjustment credit High-low	Federal funds rate[7]
2001:													
Jan	5.27	5.04	4.77	5.16	5.54	7.15	7.93	5.15	7.20	9.50-9.00		6.00-5.00	5.98
Feb	4.93	4.78	4.71	5.10	5.45	7.10	7.87	5.21	7.10	8.50-8.50		5.00-5.00	5.49
Mar	4.50	4.36	4.43	4.89	5.34	6.98	7.84	5.19	7.04	8.50-8.00		5.00-4.50	5.31
Apr	3.92	3.89	4.42	5.14	5.65	7.20	8.07	5.33	7.07	8.00-7.50		4.50-4.00	4.80
May	3.67	3.66	4.51	5.39	5.78	7.29	8.07	5.35	7.12	7.50-7.00		4.00-3.50	4.21
June	3.48	3.44	4.35	5.28	5.67	7.18	7.97	5.24	7.12	7.00-6.75		3.50-3.25	3.97
July	3.54	3.48	4.31	5.24	5.61	7.13	7.97	5.22	7.11	6.75-6.75		3.25-3.25	3.77
Aug	3.39	3.31	4.04	4.97	5.48	7.02	7.85	5.06	7.15	6.75-6.50		3.25-3.00	3.65
Sept	2.87	2.84	3.45	4.73	5.48	7.17	8.03	5.09	6.89	6.50-6.00		3.00-2.50	3.07
Oct	2.22	2.19	3.14	4.57	5.32	7.03	7.91	5.07	6.73	6.00-5.50		2.50-2.00	2.49
Nov	1.93	1.94	3.22	4.65	5.12	6.97	7.81	5.06	6.63	5.50-5.00		2.00-1.50	2.09
Dec	1.72	1.81	3.62	5.09	5.48	6.76	8.05	5.28	6.79	5.00-4.75		1.50-1.25	1.82
2002:													
Jan	1.66	1.74	3.56	5.04	5.45	6.55	7.87	5.19	6.87	4.75-4.75		1.25-1.25	1.73
Feb	1.73	1.83	3.55	4.91		6.51	7.89	5.14	6.82	4.75-4.75		1.25-1.25	1.74
Mar	1.81	2.02	4.14	5.28		6.81	8.11	5.27	6.76	4.75-4.75		1.25-1.25	1.73
Apr	1.72	1.97	4.01	5.21		6.76	8.03	5.27	6.74	4.75-4.75		1.25-1.25	1.75
May	1.74	1.88	3.80	5.16		6.75	8.09	5.22	6.59	4.75-4.75		1.25-1.25	1.75
June	1.71	1.83	3.49	4.93		6.63	7.95	5.11	6.47	4.75-4.75		1.25-1.25	1.75
July	1.68	1.71	3.01	4.65		6.53	7.90	5.01	6.37	4.75-4.75		1.25-1.25	1.73
Aug	1.63	1.62	2.52	4.26		6.37	7.58	4.92	6.26	4.75-4.75		1.25-1.25	1.74
Sept	1.63	1.61	2.32	3.87		6.15	7.40	4.73	6.17	4.75-4.75		1.25-1.25	1.75
Oct	1.60	1.57	2.25	3.94		6.32	7.73	4.85	6.09	4.75-4.75		1.25-1.25	1.75
Nov	1.26	1.29	2.32	4.05		6.31	7.62	4.98	6.08	4.75-4.25		1.25-0.75	1.34
Dec	1.20	1.26	2.23	4.03		6.21	7.45	4.91	6.04	4.25-4.25		0.75-0.75	1.24
2003:													
Jan	1.17	1.21	2.18	4.05		6.17	7.35	4.88	6.12	4.25-4.25	2.25-2.25	0.75-0.75	1.24
Feb	1.16	1.18	2.05	3.90		5.95	7.06	4.80	5.82	4.25-4.25	2.25-2.25		1.26
Mar	1.13	1.12	1.98	3.81		5.89	6.95	4.72	5.75	4.25-4.25	2.25-2.25		1.25
Apr	1.14	1.15	2.06	3.96		5.74	6.85	4.71	5.92	4.25-4.25	2.25-2.25		1.26
May	1.08	1.09	1.75	3.57		5.22	6.38	4.35	5.75	4.25-4.25	2.25-2.25		1.26
June	0.95	0.94	1.51	3.33		4.97	6.19	4.32	5.51	4.25-4.00	2.25-2.00		1.22
July	0.90	0.95	1.93	3.98		5.49	6.62	4.71	5.53	4.00-4.00	2.00-2.00		1.01
Aug	0.96	1.04	2.44	4.45		5.88	7.01	5.08	5.77	4.00-4.00	2.00-2.00		1.03
Sept	0.95	1.02	2.23	4.27		5.72	6.79	4.91	5.97	4.00-4.00	2.00-2.00		1.01
Oct	0.93	1.01	2.26	4.29		5.70	6.73	4.84	5.92	4.00-4.00	2.00-2.00		1.01
Nov	0.94	1.02	2.45	4.30		5.65	6.66	4.74	5.92	4.00-4.00	2.00-2.00		1.00
Dec	0.90	1.00	2.44	4.27		5.62	6.60	4.65	5.59	4.00-4.00	2.00-2.00		0.98
2004:													
Jan	0.89	0.98	2.27	4.15		5.54	6.44	4.53	5.48	4.00-4.00	2.00-2.00		1.00
Feb	0.92	0.99	2.25	4.08		5.50	6.27	4.48	5.72	4.00-4.00	2.00-2.00		1.01
Mar	0.94	0.99	2.00	3.83		5.33	6.11	4.39	5.42	4.00-4.00	2.00-2.00		1.00
Apr	0.94	1.06	2.57	4.35		5.73	6.46	4.84	5.49	4.00-4.00	2.00-2.00		1.00
May	1.04	1.31	3.10	4.72		6.04	6.75	5.03	5.77	4.00-4.00	2.00-2.00		1.00
June	1.27	1.58	3.26	4.73		6.01	6.78	5.00	5.81	4.25-4.00	2.25-2.00		1.03
July	1.35	1.68	3.05	4.50		5.82	6.62	4.82	5.96	4.25-4.25	2.25-2.25		1.26
Aug	1.48	1.72	2.88	4.28		5.65	6.46	4.65	5.88	4.50-4.25	2.50-2.25		1.43
Sept	1.65	1.86	2.83	4.13		5.46	6.27	4.49	5.72	4.75-4.50	2.75-2.50		1.61
Oct	1.75	2.00	2.85	4.10		5.47	6.21	4.43	5.82	4.75-4.75	2.75-2.75		1.76
Nov	2.06	2.26	3.09	4.19		5.52	6.20	4.48	5.91	5.00-4.75	3.00-2.75		1.93
Dec	2.20	2.45	3.21	4.23		5.47	6.15	4.40	6.02	5.25-5.00	3.25-3.00		2.16
2005:													
Jan	2.32	2.60	3.39	4.22		5.36	6.02	4.28	6.01	5.25-5.25	3.25-3.25		2.28
Feb	2.53	2.76	3.54	4.17		5.20	5.82	4.14	5.75	5.50-5.25	3.50-3.25		2.50
Mar	2.75	3.00	3.91	4.50		5.40	6.06	4.42	5.82	5.75-5.50	3.75-3.50		2.63
Apr	2.79	3.06	3.79	4.34		5.33	6.05	4.31	5.84	5.75-5.75	3.75-3.75		2.79
May	2.86	3.10	3.72	4.14		5.15	6.01	4.16	5.82	6.00-5.75	4.00-3.75		3.00
June	2.99	3.13	3.69	4.00		4.96	5.86	4.08	5.76	6.25-6.00	4.25-4.00		3.04
July	3.22	3.41	3.91	4.18		5.06	5.95	4.15	5.76	6.25-6.25	4.25-4.25		3.26
Aug	3.45	3.67	4.08	4.26		5.09	5.96	4.21	5.83	6.50-6.25	4.50-4.25		3.50
Sept	3.47	3.68	3.96	4.20		5.13	6.03	4.28	5.99	6.75-6.50	4.75-4.50		3.62
Oct	3.70	3.98	4.29	4.46		5.35	6.30	4.49	6.03	6.75-6.75	4.75-4.75		3.78
Nov	3.90	4.16	4.43	4.54		5.42	6.39	4.53	6.20	7.00-7.00	5.00-5.00		4.00
Dec	3.89	4.19	4.39	4.47		5.37	6.32	4.43	6.39	7.25-7.00	5.25-5.00		4.16

[5] For monthly data, high and low for the period. Prime rate for 1929-33 and 1947-48 are ranges of the rate in effect during the period.
[6] Primary credit replaced adjustment credit as the Federal Reserve's principal discount window lending program effective January 9, 2003.
[7] Since July 19, 1975, the daily effective rate is an average of the rates on a given day weighted by the volume of transactions at these rates. Prior to that date, the daily effective rate was the rate considered most representative of the day's transactions, usually the one at which most transactions occurred.
[8] From October 30, 1942, to April 24, 1946, a preferential rate of 0.50 percent was in effect for advances secured by Government securities maturing in 1 year or less.

Sources: Department of the Treasury, Board of Governors of the Federal Reserve System, Federal Housing Finance Board, Moody's Investors Service, and Standard & Poor's.

TABLE B–74.—*Credit market borrowing, 1997–2005*

[Billions of dollars; quarterly data at seasonally adjusted annual rates]

Item	1997	1998	1999	2000	2001	2002	2003	2004
NONFINANCIAL SECTORS								
DOMESTIC	762.2	1,020.8	1,027.3	825.2	1,094.6	1,319.1	1,651.3	1,926.1
FEDERAL GOVERNMENT	23.1	−52.6	−71.2	−295.9	−5.6	257.6	396.0	361.9
Treasury securities	23.2	−54.6	−71.0	−294.9	−5.1	257.1	398.4	362.5
Budget agency securities and mortgages	−.1	2.0	−.2	−1.0	−.5	.5	−2.4	−.6
NONFEDERAL, BY INSTRUMENT	739.1	1,073.4	1,098.6	1,121.1	1,100.2	1,061.6	1,255.2	1,564.2
Commercial paper	13.7	24.4	37.4	48.1	−88.3	−64.2	−40.0	15.8
Municipal securities and loans	56.9	84.2	54.4	23.6	122.9	159.4	135.1	133.1
Corporate bonds	150.5	235.2	221.7	162.6	347.7	132.3	158.3	77.7
Bank loans n.e.c.	106.4	111.4	82.2	98.2	−81.6	−87.0	−80.2	33.6
Other loans and advances	43.1	68.5	26.1	79.6	8.9	20.3	10.0	25.0
Mortgages	299.1	454.0	563.8	540.8	658.3	813.7	983.6	1,188.0
Home	234.9	348.9	418.0	401.0	496.1	672.8	782.0	972.7
Multifamily residential	7.2	26.2	39.2	26.8	40.6	37.2	69.9	47.8
Commercial	53.8	72.2	100.6	106.1	113.9	96.0	123.6	159.4
Farm	3.2	6.7	6.1	6.9	7.7	7.7	8.1	8.1
Consumer credit	69.4	95.8	113.0	168.1	132.3	87.1	88.4	91.0
NONFEDERAL, BY SECTOR	739.1	1,073.4	1,098.6	1,121.1	1,100.2	1,061.6	1,255.2	1,564.2
Household sector	304.9	419.1	487.5	551.1	600.5	736.2	825.2	1,011.7
Nonfinancial business	392.7	586.6	572.6	554.5	393.9	181.5	312.3	434.3
Corporate	291.8	396.5	373.3	346.2	220.7	25.2	148.4	258.2
Nonfarm noncorporate	94.7	179.9	194.3	197.1	162.7	148.5	156.1	164.6
Farm	6.2	10.3	5.0	11.2	10.5	7.9	7.7	11.5
State and local governments	41.5	67.7	38.5	15.5	105.8	143.9	117.8	118.2
FOREIGN BORROWING IN THE UNITED STATES	69.9	37.2	19.0	63.0	−43.8	70.8	54.3	82.2
Commercial paper	3.7	7.8	16.3	31.7	−14.2	36.1	22.3	63.7
Bonds	59.6	28.8	79.9	21.2	−18.5	31.6	41.9	19.2
Bank loans n.e.c.	8.5	6.6	.5	11.4	−7.3	5.3	−7.7	2.5
Other loans and advances	−1.8	−6.0	−5.7	−1.3	−3.8	−2.3	−2.1	−3.1
NONFINANCIAL DOMESTIC AND FOREIGN BORROWING	832.2	1,058.0	1,046.3	888.2	1,050.8	1,389.9	1,705.6	2,008.3
FINANCIAL SECTORS								
BY INSTRUMENT	570.5	1,019.6	1,015.6	778.4	877.5	823.3	1,009.2	799.1
Open market paper	166.7	161.0	176.2	131.7	−45.3	−63.5	−63.8	34.2
GSE issues (government-sponsored enterprises)	99.1	278.9	318.8	235.2	304.1	219.8	243.7	65.0
Agency- and GSE-backed mortgage pool securities	114.6	192.7	274.6	199.7	338.5	326.8	330.5	53.0
Corporate bonds	126.4	243.5	144.8	160.7	239.4	323.7	463.9	534.7
Bank loans n.e.c.	13.3	28.5	−12.8	3.8	13.0	1.5	−4.8	12.4
Other loans and advances	35.6	90.2	107.1	42.5	25.5	6.8	31.2	74.1
Mortgages	14.9	24.8	6.9	4.9	2.2	8.2	8.3	25.6
BY SECTOR	570.5	1,019.6	1,015.6	778.4	877.5	823.3	1,009.2	799.1
Commercial banking	46.1	72.9	67.2	60.0	52.9	49.7	49.2	77.7
U.S.-chartered commercial banks	29.5	52.8	41.8	36.8	30.2	29.9	13.9	18.1
Foreign banking offices in U.S.	−2.4	−4.8	−.4	−.0	−.9	−.4	−.1	.1
Bank holding companies	19.0	24.9	25.8	23.2	23.6	20.3	35.4	59.5
Savings institutions	19.7	52.2	48.0	27.3	−2.0	−23.4	6.1	64.4
Government-sponsored enterprises	99.1	278.9	318.8	235.2	304.1	219.8	243.7	65.0
Agency- and GSE-backed mortgage pools	114.6	192.7	274.6	199.7	338.5	326.8	330.5	53.0
Asset-backed securities issuers	133.7	254.7	146.8	157.2	230.4	181.9	219.5	321.8
Finance companies	33.8	57.1	70.7	81.9	1.3	42.2	118.2	117.9
REITS (real estate investment trusts)	39.6	62.7	12.3	2.6	3.2	24.5	31.9	97.6
Brokers and dealers	8.1	7.2	−17.2	15.6	1.4	−1.7	6.4	15.2
Funding corporations	79.9	40.0	91.6	−.3	−54.6	−.5	−1.4	−18.9
Other [1]	−4.2	1.2	3.0	−.7	2.2	4.0	5.1	5.3
ALL SECTORS								
BY INSTRUMENT	1,402.6	2,077.6	2,061.9	1,666.6	1,928.3	2,213.2	2,714.7	2,807.5
Open market paper	184.1	193.1	229.9	211.6	−147.8	−91.5	−81.6	113.6
Treasury securities	23.2	−54.6	−71.0	−294.9	−5.1	257.1	398.4	362.5
Agency- and GSE-backed securities	213.6	473.6	593.1	433.9	642.1	547.2	571.9	117.5
Municipal securities	56.9	84.2	54.4	23.6	122.9	159.4	135.1	133.1
Corporate and foreign bonds	336.4	507.5	374.5	344.5	568.6	487.6	664.1	631.6
Bank loans n.e.c.	128.2	146.5	69.8	113.3	−75.8	−80.2	−92.6	48.5
Other loans and advances	76.9	152.7	127.5	120.8	30.6	24.7	39.1	96.0
Mortgages	314.0	478.8	570.7	545.6	660.5	821.9	991.9	1,213.6
Consumer credit	69.4	95.8	113.0	168.1	132.3	87.1	88.4	91.0

[1] Credit unions, life insurance companies, and mortgage companies.

See next page for continuation of table.

TABLE B–74.—*Credit market borrowing, 1997–2005*—Continued

[Billions of dollars; quarterly data at seasonally adjusted annual rates]

Item	2004				2005		
	I	II	III	IV	I	II	III
NONFINANCIAL SECTORS							
DOMESTIC	2,034.4	1,701.0	1,922.8	2,046.3	2,311.7	1,998.3	2,296.6
FEDERAL GOVERNMENT	502.9	367.2	266.3	311.2	630.7	5.8	231.9
Treasury securities	501.9	370.8	266.5	310.9	631.5	7.2	232.3
Budget agency securities and mortgages	1.1	−3.6	−.2	.3	−.7	−1.4	−.4
NONFEDERAL, BY INSTRUMENT	1,531.5	1,333.8	1,656.4	1,735.2	1,680.9	1,992.4	2,064.6
Commercial paper	33.8	32.3	22.4	−25.4	53.7	9.2	4.6
Municipal securities and loans	174.0	70.2	157.3	130.9	224.9	127.7	240.5
Corporate bonds	114.2	6.7	51.7	138.3	34.3	30.1	82.7
Bank loans n.e.c.	−38.4	85.3	−31.5	119.1	88.5	210.3	42.1
Other loans and advances	14.3	−15.3	.2	100.7	84.0	70.2	23.4
Mortgages	1,143.8	1,092.9	1,334.6	1,180.6	1,137.8	1,459.7	1,554.3
Home	964.7	889.6	1,097.9	938.6	918.7	1,137.4	1,225.3
Multifamily residential	23.7	67.5	42.3	57.6	30.9	64.2	30.6
Commercial	148.4	125.3	185.2	178.6	183.1	246.7	289.5
Farm	7.1	10.4	9.1	5.9	5.1	11.4	8.8
Consumer credit	89.7	61.8	121.7	90.9	57.7	85.2	117.0
NONFEDERAL, BY SECTOR	1,531.5	1,333.8	1,656.4	1,735.2	1,680.9	1,992.4	2,064.6
Household sector	1,024.4	968.7	1,063.3	990.4	929.4	1,158.4	1,235.9
Nonfinancial business	351.1	314.0	447.9	624.3	549.3	728.3	608.0
Corporate	207.4	131.8	261.5	432.0	351.4	429.8	362.3
Nonfarm noncorporate	137.5	169.0	168.1	183.8	195.0	281.5	220.6
Farm	6.2	13.1	18.3	8.5	2.9	17.0	25.1
State and local governments	156.0	51.1	145.2	120.5	202.2	105.7	220.7
FOREIGN BORROWING IN THE UNITED STATES	84.2	−63.6	97.5	210.7	17.6	87.5	111.7
Commercial paper	99.6	−30.1	24.4	160.7	13.7	33.6	116.7
Bonds	−4.3	−40.1	86.8	34.4	−4.6	60.7	−3.5
Bank loans n.e.c.	−6.7	7.0	−9.0	18.5	12.1	−5.3	5.2
Other loans and advances	−4.3	−.4	−4.8	−2.9	−3.5	−1.6	−6.7
NONFINANCIAL DOMESTIC AND FOREIGN BORROWING	2,118.7	1,637.4	2,020.2	2,257.0	2,329.3	2,085.7	2,408.3
FINANCIAL SECTORS							
BY INSTRUMENT	710.8	926.0	727.4	832.2	598.5	1,302.3	683.8
Open market paper	129.6	−2.5	−31.4	41.1	122.1	473.2	140.2
GSE issues (government-sponsored enterprises)	.6	211.9	93.1	−45.5	−209.6	−84.2	−243.9
Agency- and GSE-backed mortgage pool securities	126.7	88.0	62.1	−64.6	64.7	123.5	178.4
Corporate bonds	331.0	490.3	554.6	762.8	563.3	680.1	538.9
Bank loans n.e.c.	17.5	−25.8	44.2	13.6	5.8	−24.0	39.5
Other loans and advances	79.1	148.1	−15.7	85.1	27.0	114.5	10.8
Mortgages	26.5	15.9	20.6	39.6	25.2	19.3	19.9
BY SECTOR	710.8	926.0	727.4	832.2	598.5	1,302.3	683.8
Commercial banking	182.7	6.8	60.1	61.2	163.0	41.4	82.7
U.S.-chartered commercial banks	80.0	−9.5	−.8	2.6	75.4	19.3	30.8
Foreign banking offices in U.S.	−.1	.2	.5	−.0	−.3	.6	.3
Bank holding companies	102.8	16.1	60.4	58.7	87.9	21.4	51.7
Savings institutions	1.1	166.6	−7.0	96.9	−30.6	82.4	−7.1
Government-sponsored enterprises	.6	211.9	93.1	−45.5	−209.6	−84.2	−243.9
Agency- and GSE-backed mortgage pools	126.7	88.0	62.1	−64.6	64.7	123.5	178.4
Asset-backed securities issuers	147.1	355.1	417.0	367.9	430.3	688.4	620.6
Finance companies	111.2	−8.4	115.5	253.2	75.8	−23.6	12.6
REITS (real estate investment trusts)	67.1	63.9	42.1	217.6	76.2	92.8	65.5
Brokers and dealers	51.9	2.5	33.2	−26.6	11.2	−5.2	18.0
Funding corporations	25.6	32.1	−89.6	−43.6	17.6	381.4	−43.9
Other [1]	−3.0	7.6	1.0	158.8	−.1	5.4	.7
ALL SECTORS							
BY INSTRUMENT	2,829.5	2,563.4	2,747.7	3,089.2	2,927.8	3,388.0	3,092.0
Open market paper	263.0	−.3	15.4	176.4	189.4	516.0	261.5
Treasury securities	501.9	370.8	266.5	310.9	631.5	7.2	232.3
Agency- and GSE-backed securities	128.3	296.3	155.1	−109.8	−145.7	37.9	−65.8
Municipal securities	174.0	70.2	157.3	130.9	224.9	127.7	240.5
Corporate and foreign bonds	440.9	456.8	693.0	935.5	593.1	770.9	618.1
Bank loans n.e.c.	−27.6	66.5	3.7	151.3	106.4	180.9	86.8
Other loans and advances	89.1	132.4	−20.3	182.9	107.5	183.1	27.5
Mortgages	1,170.3	1,108.8	1,355.1	1,220.2	1,163.0	1,478.9	1,574.1
Consumer credit	89.7	61.8	121.7	90.9	57.7	85.2	117.0

Source: Board of Governors of the Federal Reserve System.

[Billions of dollars]

End of year or quarter	All proper-ties	Farm proper-ties	Nonfarm properties				Nonfarm properties by type of mortgage					
							Government underwritten				Conventional[2]	
			Total	1- to 4-family houses	Multi-family proper-ties	Com-mercial proper-ties	Total[1]	1- to 4-family houses			Total	1- to 4-family houses
								Total	FHA insured	VA guar-anteed		
1949	62.3	5.6	56.7	37.3	8.6	10.8	17.1	15.0	6.9	8.1	39.6	22.3
1950	72.7	6.0	66.6	45.1	10.1	11.5	22.1	18.8	8.5	10.3	44.6	26.2
1951	82.1	6.6	75.6	51.6	11.5	12.5	26.6	22.9	9.7	13.2	49.0	28.8
1952	91.4	7.2	84.2	58.6	12.3	13.4	29.3	25.4	10.8	14.6	55.0	33.2
1953	101.2	7.7	93.5	66.1	12.9	14.6	32.1	28.1	12.0	16.1	61.4	38.0
1954	113.7	8.1	105.6	75.8	13.5	16.3	36.2	32.1	12.8	19.3	69.4	43.7
1955	130.1	9.0	121.1	88.4	14.3	18.4	42.9	38.9	14.3	24.6	78.1	49.5
1956	144.7	9.8	134.8	99.2	14.9	20.8	47.8	43.9	15.5	28.4	87.0	55.3
1957	156.7	10.4	146.3	107.8	15.3	23.2	51.6	47.2	16.5	30.7	94.8	60.6
1958	172.0	11.1	160.9	117.9	16.8	26.2	55.2	50.1	19.7	30.4	105.8	67.8
1959	190.9	12.1	178.8	130.9	18.7	29.2	59.3	53.8	23.8	30.0	119.5	77.1
1960	207.5	12.8	194.7	141.9	20.3	32.4	62.3	56.4	26.7	29.7	132.3	85.5
1961	228.1	13.9	214.2	154.7	23.0	36.5	65.6	59.1	29.5	29.6	148.6	95.5
1962	251.6	15.2	236.4	169.4	25.8	41.2	69.4	62.2	32.3	29.9	167.1	107.3
1963	278.7	16.8	261.9	186.6	29.0	46.3	73.4	65.9	35.0	30.9	188.5	120.7
1964	306.2	18.9	287.3	203.6	33.6	50.1	77.2	69.2	38.3	30.9	210.1	134.3
1965	333.7	21.2	312.5	220.8	37.2	54.5	81.2	73.1	42.0	31.1	231.3	147.6
1966	356.9	23.1	333.8	233.3	40.3	60.3	84.1	76.1	44.8	31.3	249.7	157.2
1967	381.6	25.1	356.5	247.7	43.9	64.8	88.2	79.9	47.4	32.5	268.3	167.8
1968	411.5	27.5	383.9	265.2	47.3	71.4	93.4	84.4	50.6	33.8	290.5	180.8
1969	442.3	29.4	412.9	283.6	52.2	77.1	100.2	90.2	54.5	35.7	312.7	193.4
1970	474.4	30.5	443.9	297.8	60.1	86.0	109.2	97.3	59.9	37.3	334.7	200.6
1971	525.1	32.4	492.7	326.2	70.1	96.4	120.7	105.2	65.7	39.5	372.0	221.0
1972	598.1	35.4	562.8	366.7	82.8	113.3	131.1	113.0	68.2	44.7	431.7	253.8
1973	673.4	39.8	633.6	407.9	93.2	132.6	135.0	116.2	66.2	50.0	498.6	291.6
1974	734.0	44.9	689.1	440.7	100.0	148.3	140.2	121.3	65.1	56.2	548.8	319.4
1975	793.5	49.9	743.7	482.0	100.7	161.0	147.0	127.7	66.1	61.6	596.7	354.2
1976	880.3	55.4	824.9	544.8	105.9	174.2	154.0	133.5	66.5	67.0	670.9	411.3
1977	1,012.0	63.8	948.2	640.6	114.3	193.3	161.7	141.6	68.0	73.6	786.4	499.0
1978	1,164.6	72.8	1,091.9	752.2	125.2	214.5	176.4	153.4	71.4	82.0	915.5	598.8
1979	1,330.0	86.8	1,243.3	868.8	135.0	239.4	199.0	172.9	81.0	92.0	1,044.3	695.9
1980	1,464.8	97.5	1,367.3	966.2	141.1	259.9	225.1	195.2	93.6	101.6	1,142.2	771.1
1981	1,590.1	107.2	1,482.9	1,044.1	139.2	299.7	238.9	207.6	101.3	106.2	1,244.0	836.5
1982	1,675.5	111.3	1,564.2	1,089.5	141.1	333.6	248.9	217.9	108.0	109.9	1,315.3	871.6
1983	1,869.1	113.7	1,755.3	1,211.6	154.3	389.4	279.8	248.8	127.4	121.4	1,475.5	962.8
1984	2,113.1	112.4	2,000.7	1,351.4	177.4	471.9	294.8	265.9	136.7	129.1	1,705.8	1,085.5
1985	2,376.8	105.9	2,271.0	1,523.5	205.9	541.6	328.3	288.8	153.0	135.8	1,942.7	1,234.7
1986	2,663.3	95.1	2,568.3	1,726.4	239.3	602.5	370.5	328.6	185.5	143.1	2,197.8	1,397.8
1987	3,001.5	87.7	2,913.7	1,953.6	262.1	698.0	431.4	387.9	235.5	152.4	2,482.3	1,565.7
1988	3,319.6	83.0	3,236.6	2,188.1	279.0	769.6	459.7	414.2	258.8	155.4	2,776.9	1,773.9
1989	3,591.3	80.5	3,510.8	2,421.5	289.9	799.5	486.8	440.1	282.8	157.3	3,024.0	1,981.4
1990	3,807.4	78.9	3,728.5	2,619.5	288.3	820.7	517.9	470.9	310.9	160.0	3,210.5	2,148.6
1991	3,952.9	79.2	3,873.7	2,781.7	284.9	807.1	537.2	493.3	330.6	162.7	3,336.4	2,288.4
1992	4,062.5	79.7	3,982.7	2,947.3	272.0	763.4	533.3	489.8	326.0	163.8	3,449.4	2,457.6
1993	4,195.7	80.7	4,115.0	3,106.0	269.1	739.9	513.4	469.5	303.2	166.2	3,601.6	2,636.6
1994	4,363.4	83.3	4,280.0	3,283.2	269.6	727.2	559.3	514.2	336.8	177.3	3,720.7	2,769.0
1995	4,550.2	85.0	4,465.2	3,451.2	275.5	738.5	584.3	537.1	352.3	184.7	3,881.0	2,914.2
1996	4,819.5	87.6	4,731.9	3,674.7	288.0	769.2	620.3	571.2	379.2	192.0	4,111.6	3,103.5
1997	5,133.1	90.4	5,042.8	3,910.6	301.1	831.7	656.7	605.7	405.7	200.0	4,386.1	3,304.3
1998	5,611.5	96.7	5,514.8	4,258.5	334.5	921.9	674.1	623.8	417.9	205.9	4,840.8	3,634.7
1999	6,215.2	103.9	6,111.3	4,673.9	375.8	1,061.6	731.5	678.8	462.3	216.5	5,379.8	3,995.1
2000	6,760.5	110.2	6,650.3	5,075.2	405.6	1,169.4	773.1	720.0	499.9	220.1	5,877.2	4,355.3
2001	7,421.0	117.8	7,303.1	5,571.3	447.8	1,284.0	772.7	718.5	497.4	221.2	6,530.5	4,852.8
2002	8,243.0	125.5	8,117.5	6,244.1	486.7	1,386.7	759.3	704.0	486.2	217.7	7,358.2	5,540.2
2003	9,235.0	133.6	9,101.5	7,026.1	557.2	1,518.2	709.2	653.3	438.7	214.6	8,392.3	6,372.8
2004	10,463.2	141.7	10,321.5	8,013.7	609.0	1,698.8	661.5	605.4	398.1	207.3	9,660.0	7,408.4
2004: I	9,490.1	135.3	9,354.8	7,235.3	564.8	1,554.7	702.1	646.3	433.2	213.1	8,652.7	6,589.0
II	9,776.7	138.3	9,638.4	7,465.8	582.0	1,590.5	687.6	631.7	422.0	209.7	8,950.8	6,834.2
III	10,142.1	140.5	10,001.6	7,768.3	594.0	1,639.3	676.2	620.3	411.6	208.7	9,325.4	7,148.0
IV	10,463.2	141.7	10,321.5	8,013.7	609.0	1,698.8	661.5	605.4	398.1	207.3	9,660.0	7,408.4
2005: I	10,716.1	143.0	10,573.1	8,210.2	617.6	1,745.3	647.9	591.6	386.1	205.5	9,925.2	7,618.6
II	11,093.9	146.2	10,947.7	8,502.0	632.4	1,813.3	633.4	577.2	372.7	204.4	10,314.3	7,924.8
III *p*	11,499.7	148.3	11,351.4	8,821.5	641.6	1,888.3	619.1	562.5	359.3	203.2	10,732.3	8,259.0

[1] Includes FHA insured multifamily properties, not shown separately.

[2] Derived figures. Total includes multifamily properties, not shown separately, and commercial properties not shown here but are the same as nonfarm properties—commercial properties.

Source: Board of Governors of the Federal Reserve System, based on data from various Government and private organizations.

TABLE B–76.—*Mortgage debt outstanding by holder, 1949–2005*

[Billions of dollars]

End of year or quarter	Total	Major financial institutions				Other holders	
		Total	Savings institu- tions [1]	Commer- cial banks [2]	Life insur- ance com- panies	Federal and related agen- cies [3]	Indi- viduals and others [4]
1949	62.3	42.9	18.3	11.6	12.9	2.0	17.5
1950	72.7	51.7	21.9	13.7	16.1	2.6	18.4
1951	82.1	59.5	25.5	14.7	19.3	3.3	19.3
1952	91.4	67.0	29.8	16.0	21.3	3.9	20.4
1953	101.2	75.1	34.8	17.0	23.3	4.4	21.7
1954	113.7	85.8	41.1	18.7	26.0	4.7	23.2
1955	130.1	99.5	48.9	21.2	29.4	5.3	25.3
1956	144.7	111.4	55.5	22.9	33.0	6.2	27.1
1957	156.7	120.0	61.2	23.6	35.2	7.7	29.1
1958	172.0	131.7	68.9	25.8	37.1	8.0	32.3
1959	190.9	145.6	78.1	28.2	39.2	10.2	35.1
1960	207.5	157.6	86.9	28.9	41.8	11.5	38.4
1961	228.1	172.7	98.0	30.6	44.2	12.2	43.1
1962	251.6	192.6	111.1	34.7	46.9	12.6	46.3
1963	278.7	217.4	127.2	39.6	50.5	11.8	49.5
1964	306.2	241.3	141.9	44.3	55.2	12.2	52.7
1965	333.7	265.0	154.9	50.0	60.0	13.5	55.2
1966	356.9	281.2	161.8	54.8	64.6	17.5	58.2
1967	381.6	299.2	172.3	59.5	67.4	20.9	61.4
1968	411.5	320.3	184.3	66.1	70.0	25.1	66.1
1969	442.3	339.8	196.4	71.4	72.0	31.1	71.4
1970	474.4	356.7	208.3	74.1	74.4	38.3	79.4
1971	525.1	395.2	236.2	83.4	75.5	46.3	83.6
1972	598.1	450.8	273.6	100.2	76.9	54.5	92.8
1973	673.4	506.3	305.0	120.1	81.3	64.7	102.4
1974	734.0	544.1	324.2	133.6	86.2	82.2	107.7
1975	793.5	582.9	355.8	137.9	89.2	101.1	109.6
1976	880.3	649.3	404.6	153.1	91.6	116.7	114.4
1977	1,012.0	747.0	469.4	180.8	96.8	140.5	124.5
1978	1,164.6	849.8	528.0	215.7	106.2	170.6	144.3
1979	1,330.0	939.9	574.6	246.9	118.4	216.0	174.2
1980	1,464.8	998.6	603.1	264.5	131.1	256.8	209.4
1981	1,590.1	1,042.8	618.5	286.5	137.7	289.4	257.9
1982	1,675.5	1,023.4	578.1	303.4	142.0	355.4	296.7
1983	1,869.1	1,109.9	626.6	332.3	151.0	433.3	325.8
1984	2,113.1	1,247.8	709.7	381.4	156.7	490.6	374.7
1985	2,376.8	1,363.5	760.5	431.2	171.8	580.9	432.4
1986	2,663.3	1,476.5	778.0	504.7	193.8	733.7	453.1
1987	3,001.5	1,667.6	860.5	594.8	212.4	857.9	475.9
1988	3,319.6	1,834.3	924.5	676.9	232.9	937.8	547.6
1989	3,591.3	1,935.2	910.3	770.7	254.2	1,067.3	588.8
1990	3,807.4	1,918.8	801.6	849.3	267.9	1,258.9	629.7
1991	3,952.9	1,846.2	705.4	881.3	259.5	1,422.5	684.2
1992	4,062.5	1,770.4	627.9	900.5	242.0	1,558.1	733.9
1993	4,195.7	1,770.1	598.4	947.8	223.9	1,682.8	742.8
1994	4,363.4	1,824.7	596.2	1,012.7	215.8	1,788.0	750.7
1995	4,550.2	1,900.1	596.8	1,090.2	213.1	1,878.7	771.5
1996	4,819.5	1,981.9	628.3	1,145.4	208.2	2,006.1	831.5
1997	5,133.1	2,084.0	631.8	1,245.3	206.8	2,111.4	937.7
1998	5,611.5	2,194.6	644.0	1,337.0	213.6	2,310.9	1,106.1
1999	6,215.2	2,394.3	668.1	1,495.4	230.8	2,613.3	1,207.6
2000	6,760.5	2,619.0	723.0	1,660.1	235.9	2,834.4	1,307.1
2001	7,421.0	2,790.9	758.0	1,789.8	243.0	3,205.0	1,425.1
2002	8,243.0	3,089.4	781.0	2,058.4	250.0	3,592.2	1,561.4
2003	9,235.0	3,387.2	870.2	2,256.0	260.9	4,026.3	1,821.6
2004	10,463.2	3,925.7	1,057.0	2,595.3	273.3	4,096.0	2,441.5
2004: I	9,490.1	3,517.8	926.3	2,329.3	262.2	4,053.3	1,919.0
II	9,776.7	3,665.3	965.3	2,435.9	264.1	4,067.0	2,044.4
III	10,142.1	3,793.2	1,007.9	2,517.4	267.9	4,092.1	2,256.9
IV	10,463.2	3,925.7	1,057.0	2,595.3	273.3	4,096.0	2,441.5
2005: I	10,716.1	4,033.1	1,068.0	2,690.4	274.7	4,101.7	2,581.2
II	11,093.9	4,181.2	1,112.9	2,790.4	277.8	4,121.1	2,791.6
III p	11,499.7	4,317.5	1,140.8	2,896.2	280.5	4,167.3	3,014.9

[1] Includes savings banks and savings and loan associations. Data reported by Federal Savings and Loan Insurance Corporation-insured institutions include loans in process for 1987 and exclude loans in process beginning 1988.

[2] Includes loans held by nondeposit trust companies, but not by bank trust departments.

[3] Includes Ginnie Mae—Government National Mortgage Association (GNMA), Federal Housing Administration, Veterans Administration, Farmers Home Administration (FmHA), Federal Deposit Insurance Corporation, Resolution Trust Corporation (through 1995), and in earlier years Reconstruction Finance Corporation, Homeowners Loan Corporation, Federal Farm Mortgage Corporation, and Public Housing Administration. Also includes U.S.-sponsored agencies such as Fannie Mae—Federal National Mortgage Association (FNMA), Federal Land Banks, Freddie Mac— Federal Home Loan Mortgage Corporation (FHLMC), Federal Agricultural Mortgage Corporation (beginning 1994), Federal Home Loan Banks (beginning 1997), and mortgage pass-through securities issued or guaranteed by GNMA, FHLMC, FNMA or FmHA. Other U.S. agencies (amounts small or current separate data not readily available) included with "individuals and others."

[4] Includes private mortgage pools.

Source: Board of Governors of the Federal Reserve System, based on data from various Government and private organizations.

TABLE B–77.—*Consumer credit outstanding, 1955–2005*

[Amount outstanding (end of month); millions of dollars, seasonally adjusted]

Year and month	Total consumer credit [1]	Revolving	Nonrevolving [2]
December:			
1955	41,869.0	....	41,869.0
1956	45,448.2	....	45,448.2
1957	48,078.3	....	48,078.3
1958	48,394.3	....	48,394.3
1959	56,010.7	....	56,010.7
1960	60,025.3	....	60,025.3
1961	62,248.5	....	62,248.5
1962	68,126.7	....	68,126.7
1963	76,581.4	....	76,581.4
1964	85,959.6	....	85,959.6
1965	95,954.7	....	95,954.7
1966	101,788.2	....	101,788.2
1967	106,842.6	....	106,842.6
1968	117,399.1	2,041.5	115,357.5
1969	127,156.2	3,604.8	123,551.3
1970	131,551.6	4,961.5	126,590.1
1971	146,930.2	8,245.3	138,684.8
1972	166,189.1	9,379.2	156,809.9
1973	190,086.3	11,342.2	178,744.1
1974	198,917.8	13,241.3	185,676.6
1975	204,002.0	14,495.3	189,506.7
1976	225,721.6	16,489.1	209,232.5
1977	260,562.7	37,414.8	223,147.9
1978	306,100.4	45,691.0	260,409.4
1979	348,589.1	53,596.4	294,992.7
1980	351,920.1	54,970.1	296,950.0
1981	371,301.4	60,928.0	310,373.4
1982	389,848.7	66,348.3	323,500.4
1983	437,068.9	79,027.2	358,041.6
1984	517,279.0	100,385.6	416,893.3
1985	599,711.2	124,465.8	475,245.4
1986	654,750.2	141,068.2	513,682.1
1987	686,318.8	160,853.9	525,464.9
1988[3]	731,917.8	184,593.1	547,324.6
1989	794,612.2	211,229.8	583,382.3
1990	808,230.6	238,642.6	569,587.9
1991	798,029.0	263,768.6	534,260.4
1992	806,118.7	278,449.7	527,669.0
1993	865,650.6	309,908.0	555,742.6
1994	997,126.9	365,569.6	631,557.3
1995	1,140,994.5	443,491.8	697,502.7
1996	1,242,862.5	499,624.6	743,238.0
1997	1,320.091.3	536,721.0	783,370.3
1998	1,415,787.3	576,468.3	839,319.0
1999	1,528,029.3	604,468.1	923,561.2
2000	1,704,510.1	675,653.3	1,028,856.8
2001	1,835,563.3	713,328.0	1,122,235.2
2002	1,921,852.1	732,665.2	1,189,186.9
2003	2,009,850.0	752,792.4	1,257,057.6
2004	2,098,996.3	781,056.6	1,317,939.7
2004: Jan	2,019,751.2	755,543.9	1,264,207.3
Feb	2,023,358.1	756,004.8	1,267,353.3
Mar	2,032,067.5	759,615.4	1,272,452.1
Apr	2,029,622.2	750,513.3	1,279,109.0
May	2,034,662.6	751,621.6	1,283,041.0
June	2,046,968.9	759,878.4	1,287,090.5
July	2,055,657.4	766,641.2	1,289,016.2
Aug	2,063.693.1	769,423.1	1,294,270.0
Sept	2,076,716.0	777,305.3	1,299,410.6
Oct	2,094,537.5	786,238.3	1,308,299.2
Nov	2,092,756.0	779,498.5	1,313,257.5
Dec	2,098,996.3	781,056.6	1,317,939.7
2005: Jan	2,104,393.5	786,449.1	1,317,944.4
Feb	2,109,642.4	783,443.8	1,326,198.6
Mar	2,113,397.8	780,426.9	1,332,970.9
Apr	2,124,650.7	785,864.5	1,338,786.3
May	2,125,589.9	784,684.4	1,340,905.5
June	2,136,441.6	789,323.1	1,347,118.5
July	2,148,412.9	790,680.1	1,357,732.8
Aug	2,160,082.4	795,340.6	1,364,741.8
Sept	2,165,048.7	800,665.2	1,364,383.4
Oct	2,156,644.4	798,802.8	1,357,841.6
Nov[p]	2,155,995.6	799,138.0	1,356,857.6

[1] Covers most short- and intermediate-term credit extended to individuals. Credit secured by real estate is excluded.
[2] Includes automobile loans and all other loans not included in revolving credit, such as loans for mobile homes, education, boats, trailers, or vacations. These loans may be secured or unsecured. Beginning 1977 includes student loans extended by the Federal Government and by SLM Holding Corporation.
[3] Data newly available in January 1989 result in breaks in these series between December 1988 and subsequent months.

Source: Board of Governors of the Federal Reserve System.

GOVERNMENT FINANCE

TABLE B–78.—*Federal receipts, outlays, surplus or deficit, and debt, fiscal years, 1940–2007*

[Billions of dollars; fiscal years]

Fiscal year or period	Total			On-budget			Off-budget			Federal debt (end of period)		Addendum: Gross domestic product
	Receipts	Outlays	Surplus or deficit (–)	Receipts	Outlays	Surplus or deficit (–)	Receipts	Outlays	Surplus or deficit (–)	Gross Federal	Held by the public	
1940	6.5	9.5	–2.9	6.0	9.5	–3.5	0.6	–0.0	0.6	50.7	42.8	96.8
1941	8.7	13.7	–4.9	8.0	13.6	–5.6	.7	.0	.7	57.5	48.2	114.1
1942	14.6	35.1	–20.5	13.7	35.1	–21.3	.9	.1	.8	79.2	67.8	144.3
1943	24.0	78.6	–54.6	22.9	78.5	–55.6	1.1	.1	1.0	142.6	127.8	180.3
1944	43.7	91.3	–47.6	42.5	91.2	–48.7	1.3	.1	1.2	204.1	184.8	209.2
1945	45.2	92.7	–47.6	43.8	92.6	–48.7	1.3	.1	1.2	260.1	235.2	221.4
1946	39.3	55.2	–15.9	38.1	55.0	–17.0	1.2	.2	1.0	271.0	241.9	222.7
1947	38.5	34.5	4.0	37.1	34.2	2.9	1.5	.3	1.2	257.1	224.3	233.2
1948	41.6	29.8	11.8	39.9	29.4	10.5	1.6	.4	1.2	252.0	216.3	256.0
1949	39.4	38.8	.6	37.7	38.4	–.7	1.7	.4	1.3	252.6	214.3	271.1
1950	39.4	42.6	–3.1	37.3	42.0	–4.7	2.1	.5	1.6	256.9	219.0	273.0
1951	51.6	45.5	6.1	48.5	44.2	4.3	3.1	1.3	1.8	255.3	214.3	320.6
1952	66.2	67.7	–1.5	62.6	66.0	–3.4	3.6	1.7	1.9	259.1	214.8	348.6
1953	69.6	76.1	–6.5	65.5	73.8	–8.3	4.1	2.3	1.8	266.0	218.4	372.9
1954	69.7	70.9	–1.2	65.1	67.9	–2.8	4.6	2.9	1.7	270.8	224.5	377.3
1955	65.5	68.4	–3.0	60.4	64.5	–4.1	5.1	4.0	1.1	274.4	226.6	394.6
1956	74.6	70.6	3.9	68.2	65.7	2.5	6.4	5.0	1.5	272.7	222.2	427.2
1957	80.0	76.6	3.4	73.2	70.6	2.6	6.8	6.0	.8	272.3	219.3	450.3
1958	79.6	82.4	–2.8	71.6	74.9	–3.3	8.0	7.5	.5	279.7	226.3	460.5
1959	79.2	92.1	–12.8	71.0	83.1	–12.1	8.3	9.0	–.7	287.5	234.7	491.5
1960	92.5	92.2	.3	81.9	81.3	.5	10.6	10.9	–.2	290.5	236.8	517.9
1961	94.4	97.7	–3.3	82.3	86.0	–3.8	12.1	11.7	.4	292.6	238.4	530.8
1962	99.7	106.8	–7.1	87.4	93.3	–5.9	12.3	13.5	–1.3	302.9	248.0	567.6
1963	106.6	111.3	–4.8	92.4	96.4	–4.0	14.2	15.0	–.8	310.3	254.0	598.7
1964	112.6	118.5	–5.9	96.2	102.8	–6.5	16.4	15.7	.6	316.1	256.8	640.4
1965	116.8	118.2	–1.4	100.1	101.7	–1.6	16.7	16.5	.2	322.3	260.8	687.1
1966	130.8	134.5	–3.7	111.7	114.8	–3.1	19.1	19.7	–.6	328.5	263.7	752.9
1967	148.8	157.5	–8.6	124.4	137.0	–12.6	24.4	20.4	4.0	340.4	266.6	811.8
1968	153.0	178.1	–25.2	128.1	155.8	–27.7	24.9	22.3	2.6	368.7	289.5	866.6
1969	186.9	183.6	3.2	157.9	158.4	–.5	29.0	25.2	3.7	365.8	278.1	948.6
1970	192.8	195.6	–2.8	159.3	168.0	–8.7	33.5	27.6	5.9	380.9	283.2	1,012.2
1971	187.1	210.2	–23.0	151.3	177.3	–26.1	35.8	32.8	3.0	408.2	303.0	1,079.9
1972	207.3	230.7	–23.4	167.4	193.5	–26.1	39.9	37.2	2.7	435.9	322.4	1,178.3
1973	230.8	245.7	–14.9	184.7	200.0	–15.2	46.1	45.7	.3	466.3	340.9	1,307.6
1974	263.2	269.4	–6.1	209.3	216.5	–7.2	53.9	52.9	1.1	483.9	343.7	1,439.3
1975	279.1	332.3	–53.2	216.6	270.8	–54.1	62.5	61.6	.9	541.9	394.7	1,560.7
1976	298.1	371.8	–73.7	231.7	301.1	–69.4	66.4	70.7	–4.3	629.0	477.4	1,736.5
Transition quarter ...	81.2	96.0	–14.7	63.2	77.3	–14.1	18.0	18.7	–.7	643.6	495.5	456.7
1977	355.6	409.2	–53.7	278.7	328.7	–49.9	76.8	80.5	–3.7	706.4	549.1	1,974.3
1978	399.6	458.7	–59.2	314.2	369.6	–55.4	85.4	89.2	–3.8	776.6	607.1	2,217.0
1979	463.3	504.0	–40.7	365.3	404.9	–39.6	98.0	99.1	–1.1	829.5	640.3	2,500.7
1980	517.1	590.9	–73.8	403.9	477.0	–73.1	113.2	113.9	–.7	909.0	711.9	2,726.7
1981	599.3	678.2	–79.0	469.1	543.0	–73.9	130.2	135.3	–5.1	994.8	789.4	3,054.7
1982	617.8	745.7	–128.0	474.3	594.9	–120.6	143.5	150.9	–7.4	1,137.3	924.6	3,227.6
1983	600.6	808.4	–207.8	453.2	660.9	–207.7	147.3	147.4	–.1	1,371.7	1,137.3	3,440.7
1984	666.5	851.9	–185.4	500.4	685.7	–185.3	166.1	166.2	–.1	1,564.6	1,307.0	3,840.2
1985	734.1	946.4	–212.3	547.9	769.4	–221.5	186.2	176.9	9.2	1,817.4	1,507.3	4,141.5
1986	769.2	990.4	–221.2	569.0	806.9	–237.9	200.2	183.5	16.7	2,120.5	1,740.6	4,412.4
1987	854.4	1,004.1	–149.7	641.0	809.3	–168.4	213.4	194.8	18.6	2,346.0	1,889.8	4,647.1
1988	909.3	1,064.5	–155.2	667.8	860.1	–192.3	241.5	204.4	37.1	2,601.1	2,051.6	5,008.6
1989	991.2	1,143.8	–152.6	727.5	932.9	–205.4	263.7	210.9	52.8	2,867.8	2,190.7	5,400.5
1990	1,032.1	1,253.1	–221.0	750.4	1,028.1	–277.6	281.7	225.1	56.6	3,206.3	2,411.6	5,735.4
1991	1,055.1	1,324.3	–269.2	761.2	1,082.6	–321.4	293.9	241.7	52.2	3,598.2	2,689.0	5,935.1
1992	1,091.3	1,381.6	–290.3	788.9	1,129.3	–340.4	302.4	252.3	50.1	4,001.8	2,999.7	6,239.9
1993	1,154.5	1,409.5	–255.1	842.5	1,142.9	–300.4	311.9	266.6	45.3	4,351.0	3,248.4	6,575.5
1994	1,258.7	1,461.9	–203.2	923.7	1,182.5	–258.8	335.0	279.4	55.7	4,643.3	3,433.1	6,961.3
1995	1,351.9	1,515.9	–164.0	1,000.9	1,227.2	–226.4	351.1	288.7	62.4	4,920.6	3,604.4	7,325.8
1996	1,453.2	1,560.6	–107.4	1,085.7	1,259.7	–174.0	367.5	300.9	66.6	5,181.5	3,734.1	7,694.1
1997	1,579.4	1,601.3	–21.9	1,187.4	1,290.7	–103.2	392.0	310.6	81.4	5,369.2	3,772.3	8,182.4
1998	1,722.0	1,652.7	69.3	1,306.2	1,336.1	–29.9	415.8	316.6	99.2	5,478.2	3,721.1	8,627.9
1999	1,827.6	1,702.0	125.6	1,383.2	1,381.3	1.9	444.5	320.8	123.7	5,605.5	3,632.4	9,125.3
2000	2,025.5	1,789.2	236.2	1,544.9	1,458.5	86.4	480.6	330.8	149.8	5,628.7	3,409.8	9,709.8
2001	1,991.4	1,863.2	128.2	1,483.9	1,516.4	–32.4	507.5	346.8	160.7	5,769.9	3,319.6	10,057.9
2002	1,853.4	2,011.2	–157.8	1,338.1	1,655.5	–317.4	515.3	355.7	159.7	6,198.4	3,540.4	10,377.4
2003	1,782.5	2,160.1	–377.6	1,258.7	1,797.1	–538.4	523.8	363.0	160.8	6,760.0	3,913.4	10,805.5
2004	1,880.3	2,293.0	–412.7	1,345.5	1,913.5	–568.0	534.7	379.5	155.2	7,354.7	4,295.5	11,546.0
2005	2,153.9	2,472.2	–318.3	1,576.4	2,070.0	–493.6	577.5	402.2	175.3	7,905.3	4,592.2	12,290.4
2006 (estimates)	2,285.5	2,708.7	–423.2	1,675.5	2,277.7	–602.1	610.0	431.0	179.0	8,611.5	5,018.9	13,030.2
2007 (estimates)	2,415.9	2,770.1	–354.2	1,773.5	2,317.0	–543.4	642.3	453.1	189.2	9,295.4	5,391.5	13,760.9

Note.—Through fiscal year 1976, the fiscal year was on a July 1–June 30 basis; beginning October 1976 (fiscal year 1977), the fiscal year is on an October 1–September 30 basis. The transition quarter is the 3-month period from July 1, 1976 through September 30, 1976. See *Budget of the United States Government, Fiscal Year 2007*, for additional information.

Sources: Department of Commerce (Bureau of Economic Analysis), Department of the Treasury, and Office of Management and Budget.

375

TABLE B–79.—*Federal receipts, outlays, surplus or deficit, and debt, as percent of gross domestic product, fiscal years 1934–2007*

[Percent; fiscal years]

Fiscal year or period	Receipts	Outlays		Surplus or deficit (−)	Federal debt (end of period)	
		Total	National defense		Gross Federal	Held by public
1934	4.8	10.7		−5.9		
1935	5.2	9.2		−4.0		
1936	5.0	10.5		−5.5		
1937	6.1	8.6		−2.5		
1938	7.6	7.7		−.1		
1939	7.1	10.3		−3.2	54.2	46.6
1940	6.8	9.8	1.7	−3.0	52.4	44.2
1941	7.6	12.0	5.6	−4.3	50.4	42.3
1942	10.1	24.3	17.8	−14.2	54.9	47.0
1943	13.3	43.6	37.0	−30.3	79.1	70.9
1944	20.9	43.6	37.8	−22.7	97.6	88.3
1945	20.4	41.9	37.5	−21.5	117.5	106.2
1946	17.6	24.8	19.2	−7.2	121.7	108.6
1947	16.5	14.8	5.5	1.7	110.3	96.2
1948	16.2	11.6	3.6	4.6	98.4	84.5
1949	14.5	14.3	4.9	.2	93.2	79.1
1950	14.4	15.6	5.0	−1.1	94.1	80.2
1951	16.1	14.2	7.4	1.9	79.6	66.9
1952	19.0	19.4	13.2	−.4	74.3	61.6
1953	18.7	20.4	14.2	−1.7	71.3	58.6
1954	18.5	18.8	13.1	−.3	71.8	59.5
1955	16.6	17.3	10.8	−.8	69.5	57.4
1956	17.5	16.5	10.0	.9	63.8	52.0
1957	17.8	17.0	10.1	.8	60.5	48.7
1958	17.3	17.9	10.2	−.6	60.7	49.2
1959	16.1	18.7	10.0	−2.6	58.5	47.8
1960	17.9	17.8	9.3	.1	56.1	45.7
1961	17.8	18.4	9.3	−.6	55.1	44.9
1962	17.6	18.8	9.2	−1.3	53.4	43.7
1963	17.8	18.6	8.9	−.8	51.8	42.4
1964	17.6	18.5	8.6	−.9	49.4	40.1
1965	17.0	17.2	7.4	−.2	46.9	38.0
1966	17.4	17.9	7.7	−.5	43.6	35.0
1967	18.3	19.4	8.8	−1.1	41.9	32.8
1968	17.7	20.6	9.5	−2.9	42.5	33.4
1969	19.7	19.4	8.7	.3	38.6	29.3
1970	19.0	19.3	8.1	−.3	37.6	28.0
1971	17.3	19.5	7.3	−2.1	37.8	28.1
1972	17.6	19.6	6.7	−2.0	37.0	27.4
1973	17.7	18.8	5.9	−1.1	35.7	26.1
1974	18.3	18.7	5.5	−.4	33.6	23.9
1975	17.9	21.3	5.5	−3.4	34.7	25.3
1976	17.2	21.4	5.2	−4.2	36.2	27.5
Transition quarter	17.8	21.0	4.9	−3.2	35.2	27.1
1977	18.0	20.7	4.9	−2.7	35.8	27.8
1978	18.0	20.7	4.7	−2.7	35.0	27.4
1979	18.5	20.2	4.7	−1.6	33.2	25.6
1980	19.0	21.7	4.9	−2.7	33.3	26.1
1981	19.6	22.2	5.2	−2.6	32.6	25.8
1982	19.1	23.1	5.7	−4.0	35.2	28.6
1983	17.5	23.5	6.1	−6.0	39.9	33.1
1984	17.4	22.2	5.9	−4.8	40.7	34.0
1985	17.7	22.9	6.1	−5.1	43.9	36.4
1986	17.4	22.4	6.2	−5.0	48.1	39.4
1987	18.4	21.6	6.1	−3.2	50.5	40.7
1988	18.2	21.3	5.8	−3.1	51.9	41.0
1989	18.4	21.2	5.6	−2.8	53.1	40.6
1990	18.0	21.8	5.2	−3.9	55.9	42.0
1991	17.8	22.3	4.6	−4.5	60.6	45.3
1992	17.5	22.1	4.8	−4.7	64.1	48.1
1993	17.6	21.4	4.4	−3.9	66.2	49.4
1994	18.1	21.0	4.0	−2.9	66.7	49.3
1995	18.5	20.7	3.7	−2.2	67.2	49.2
1996	18.9	20.3	3.5	−1.4	67.3	48.5
1997	19.3	19.6	3.3	−.3	65.6	46.1
1998	20.0	19.2	3.1	.8	63.5	43.1
1999	20.0	18.7	3.0	1.4	61.4	39.8
2000	20.9	18.4	3.0	2.4	58.0	35.1
2001	19.8	18.5	3.0	1.3	57.4	33.0
2002	17.9	19.4	3.4	−1.5	59.7	34.1
2003	16.5	20.0	3.7	−3.5	62.6	36.2
2004	16.3	19.9	3.9	−3.6	63.7	37.2
2005	17.5	20.1	4.0	−2.6	64.3	37.4
2006 (estimates)	17.5	20.8	4.1	−3.2	66.1	38.5
2007 (estimates)	17.6	20.1	3.8	−2.6	67.5	39.2

Note.—See Note, Table B–78.

Sources: Department of the Treasury and Office of Management and Budget.

TABLE B–80.—*Federal receipts and outlays, by major category, and surplus or deficit, fiscal years 1940–2007*

[Billions of dollars; fiscal years]

Fiscal year or period	Receipts (on-budget and off-budget)					Outlays (on-budget and off-budget)										Surplus or deficit (−) (on-budget and off-budget)
	Total	Individual income taxes	Corporation income taxes	Social insurance and retirement receipts	Other	Total	National defense		International affairs	Health	Medicare	Income security	Social security	Net interest	Other	
							Total	Department of Defense, military								
1940	6.5	0.9	1.2	1.8	2.7	9.5	1.7		0.1	0.1		1.5	0.0	0.9	5.3	−2.9
1941	8.7	1.3	2.1	1.9	3.3	13.7	6.4		.1	.1		1.9	.1	.9	4.1	−4.9
1942	14.6	3.3	4.7	2.5	4.2	35.1	25.7		1.0	.1		1.8	.1	1.1	5.4	−20.5
1943	24.0	6.5	9.6	3.0	4.9	78.6	66.7		1.3	.1		1.7	.2	1.5	7.0	−54.6
1944	43.7	19.7	14.8	3.5	5.7	91.3	79.1		1.4	.2		1.5	.2	2.2	6.6	−47.6
1945	45.2	18.4	16.0	3.5	7.3	92.7	83.0		1.9	.2		1.1	.3	3.1	3.1	−47.6
1946	39.3	16.1	11.9	3.1	8.2	55.2	42.7		1.9	.2		2.4	.4	4.1	3.6	−15.9
1947	38.5	17.9	8.6	3.4	8.5	34.5	12.8		5.8	.2		2.8	.5	4.2	8.2	4.0
1948	41.6	19.3	9.7	3.8	8.8	29.8	9.1		4.6	.2		2.5	.6	4.3	8.5	11.8
1949	39.4	15.6	11.2	3.8	8.9	38.8	13.2		6.1	.2		3.2	.7	4.5	11.1	.6
1950	39.4	15.8	10.4	4.3	8.9	42.6	13.7		4.7	.3		4.1	.8	4.8	14.2	−3.1
1951	51.6	21.6	14.1	5.7	10.2	45.5	23.6		3.6	.3		3.4	1.6	4.7	8.4	6.1
1952	66.2	27.9	21.2	6.4	10.6	67.7	46.1		2.7	.3		3.7	2.1	4.7	8.1	−1.5
1953	69.6	29.8	21.2	6.8	11.7	76.1	52.8		2.1	.3		3.8	2.7	5.2	9.1	−6.5
1954	69.7	29.5	21.1	7.2	11.9	70.9	49.3		1.6	.3		4.4	3.4	4.8	7.1	−1.2
1955	65.5	28.7	17.9	7.9	11.0	68.4	42.7		2.2	.3		5.1	4.4	4.9	8.9	−3.0
1956	74.6	32.2	20.9	9.3	12.2	70.6	42.5		2.4	.4		4.7	5.5	5.1	10.1	3.9
1957	80.0	35.6	21.2	10.0	13.2	76.6	45.4		3.1	.5		5.4	6.7	5.4	10.1	3.4
1958	79.6	34.7	20.1	11.2	13.6	82.4	46.8		3.4	.5		7.5	8.2	5.6	10.3	−2.8
1959	79.2	36.7	17.3	11.7	13.5	92.1	49.0		3.1	.7		8.2	9.7	5.8	15.5	−12.8
1960	92.5	40.7	21.5	14.7	15.6	92.2	48.1		3.0	.8		7.4	11.6	6.9	14.4	.3
1961	94.4	41.3	21.0	16.4	15.7	97.7	49.6		3.2	.9		9.7	12.5	6.7	15.2	−3.3
1962	99.7	45.6	20.5	17.0	16.5	106.8	52.3	50.1	5.6	1.2		9.2	14.4	6.9	17.2	−7.1
1963	106.6	47.6	21.6	19.8	17.6	111.3	53.4	51.1	5.3	1.5		9.3	15.8	7.7	18.3	−4.8
1964	112.6	48.7	23.5	22.0	18.5	118.5	54.8	52.6	4.9	1.8		9.7	16.6	8.2	22.6	−5.9
1965	116.8	48.8	25.5	22.2	20.3	118.2	50.6	48.8	5.3	1.8		9.5	17.5	8.6	25.0	−1.4
1966	130.8	55.4	30.1	25.5	19.8	134.5	58.1	56.6	5.6	2.5	0.1	9.7	20.7	9.4	28.5	−3.7
1967	148.8	61.5	34.0	32.6	20.7	157.5	71.4	70.1	5.6	3.4	2.7	10.3	21.7	10.3	32.1	−8.6
1968	153.0	68.7	28.7	33.9	21.7	178.1	81.9	80.4	5.3	4.4	4.6	11.8	23.9	11.1	35.1	−25.2
1969	186.9	87.2	36.7	39.0	23.9	183.6	82.5	80.8	4.6	5.2	5.7	13.1	27.3	12.7	32.6	3.2
1970	192.8	90.4	32.8	44.4	25.2	195.6	81.7	80.1	4.3	5.9	6.2	15.7	30.3	14.4	37.2	−2.8
1971	187.1	86.2	26.8	47.3	26.8	210.2	78.9	77.5	4.2	6.8	6.6	22.9	35.9	14.8	40.0	−23.0
1972	207.3	94.7	32.2	52.6	27.8	230.7	79.2	77.6	4.8	8.7	7.5	27.7	40.2	15.5	47.3	−23.4
1973	230.8	103.2	36.2	63.1	28.3	245.7	76.7	75.0	4.1	9.4	8.1	28.3	49.1	17.3	52.8	−14.9
1974	263.2	119.0	38.6	75.1	30.6	269.4	79.3	77.9	5.7	10.7	9.6	33.7	55.9	21.4	52.9	−6.1
1975	279.1	122.4	40.6	84.5	31.5	332.3	86.5	84.9	7.1	12.9	12.9	50.2	64.7	23.2	74.8	−53.2
1976	298.1	131.6	41.4	90.8	34.3	371.8	89.6	87.9	6.4	15.7	15.8	60.8	73.9	26.7	82.7	−73.7
Transition quarter	81.2	38.8	8.5	25.2	8.8	96.0	22.3	21.8	2.5	3.9	4.3	15.0	19.8	6.9	21.4	−14.7
1977	355.6	157.6	54.9	106.5	36.6	409.2	97.2	95.1	6.4	17.3	19.3	61.1	85.1	29.9	93.0	−53.7
1978	399.6	181.0	60.0	121.0	37.7	458.7	104.5	102.3	7.5	18.5	22.8	61.5	93.9	35.5	114.7	−59.2
1979	463.3	217.8	65.7	138.9	40.8	504.0	116.3	113.6	7.5	20.5	26.5	66.4	104.1	42.6	120.2	−40.7
1980	517.1	244.1	64.6	157.8	50.6	590.9	134.0	130.9	12.7	23.2	32.1	86.6	118.5	52.5	131.3	−73.8
1981	599.3	285.9	61.1	182.7	69.5	678.2	157.5	153.9	13.1	26.9	39.1	100.3	139.6	68.8	133.0	−79.0
1982	617.8	297.7	49.2	201.5	69.3	745.7	185.3	180.7	12.3	27.4	46.6	108.2	156.0	85.0	125.0	−128.0
1983	600.6	288.9	37.0	209.0	65.6	808.4	209.9	204.4	11.8	28.6	52.6	123.0	170.7	89.8	121.8	−207.8
1984	666.5	298.4	56.9	239.4	71.8	851.9	227.4	220.9	15.9	30.4	57.5	113.4	178.2	111.1	117.9	−185.4
1985	734.1	334.5	61.3	265.2	73.1	946.4	252.7	245.1	16.2	33.5	65.8	129.0	188.6	129.5	131.0	−212.3
1986	769.2	349.0	63.1	283.9	73.2	990.4	273.4	265.4	14.2	35.9	70.2	120.6	198.8	136.0	141.4	−221.2
1987	854.4	392.6	83.9	303.3	74.6	1,004.1	282.0	273.9	11.6	40.0	75.1	124.1	207.4	138.6	125.3	−149.7
1988	909.3	401.2	94.5	334.3	79.3	1,064.5	290.4	281.9	10.5	44.5	78.9	130.4	219.3	151.8	138.8	−155.2
1989	991.2	445.7	103.3	359.4	82.8	1,143.8	303.6	294.8	9.6	48.4	85.0	137.4	232.5	169.0	158.4	−152.6
1990	1,032.1	466.9	93.5	380.0	91.7	1,253.1	299.3	289.7	13.8	57.7	98.1	148.7	248.6	184.3	202.6	−221.0
1991	1,055.1	467.8	98.1	396.0	93.2	1,324.3	273.3	262.3	15.9	71.2	104.5	172.5	269.0	194.4	223.6	−269.2
1992	1,091.3	476.0	100.3	413.7	101.4	1,381.6	298.4	286.8	16.1	89.5	119.0	199.6	287.6	199.3	172.2	−290.3
1993	1,154.5	509.7	117.5	428.3	99.0	1,409.5	291.1	278.5	17.2	99.4	130.6	210.0	304.6	198.7	158.0	−255.1
1994	1,258.7	543.1	140.4	461.5	113.8	1,461.9	281.6	268.6	17.1	107.1	144.7	217.2	319.6	202.9	171.7	−203.2
1995	1,351.9	590.2	157.0	484.5	120.2	1,515.9	272.1	259.4	16.4	115.4	159.9	223.8	335.8	232.1	160.3	−164.0
1996	1,453.2	656.4	171.8	509.4	115.5	1,560.6	265.8	253.1	13.5	119.4	174.2	229.7	349.7	241.1	167.3	−107.4
1997	1,579.4	737.5	182.3	539.4	120.3	1,601.3	270.5	258.3	15.2	123.8	190.0	235.0	365.3	244.0	157.4	−21.9
1998	1,722.0	828.6	188.7	571.8	132.9	1,652.7	268.5	256.1	13.1	131.4	192.8	237.8	379.2	241.1	188.8	69.3
1999	1,827.6	879.5	184.7	611.8	151.7	1,702.0	274.9	261.3	15.2	141.1	190.4	242.5	390.0	229.8	218.1	125.6
2000	2,025.5	1,004.5	207.3	652.9	160.9	1,789.2	294.5	281.2	17.2	154.5	197.1	253.7	409.4	222.9	239.8	236.2
2001	1,991.4	994.3	151.1	694.0	152.0	1,863.2	304.9	290.3	16.5	172.3	217.4	269.8	433.0	206.2	243.3	128.2
2002	1,853.4	858.3	148.0	700.8	146.2	2,011.2	348.6	332.0	22.4	196.5	230.9	312.7	456.0	170.9	273.2	−157.8
2003	1,782.5	793.7	131.8	713.0	144.1	2,160.1	404.9	387.3	21.2	219.6	249.4	334.6	474.7	153.1	302.6	−377.6
2004	1,880.3	809.0	189.4	733.4	148.5	2,293.0	455.9	436.5	26.9	240.1	269.4	333.1	495.5	160.2	311.9	−412.7
2005	2,153.9	927.2	278.3	794.1	154.2	2,472.2	495.3	474.2	34.6	250.6	298.6	345.8	523.3	184.0	339.9	−318.3
2006 [1]	2,285.5	997.6	277.1	841.1	169.7	2,708.7	535.9	512.1	34.8	268.8	343.0	360.6	554.7	220.1	390.8	−423.2
2007 [1]	2,415.9	1,096.4	260.6	884.1	174.8	2,770.1	527.4	504.9	33.3	280.9	392.0	367.2	585.9	247.3	336.0	−354.2

[1] Estimates.

Note.—See Note, Table B–78.

Sources: Department of the Treasury and Office of Management and Budget.

TABLE B–81.—*Federal receipts, outlays, surplus or deficit, and debt, fiscal years 2002–2007*

[Millions of dollars; fiscal years]

Description	Actual 2002	Actual 2003	Actual 2004	Actual 2005	Estimates 2006	Estimates 2007
RECEIPTS AND OUTLAYS:						
Total receipts	1,853,395	1,782,532	1,880,279	2,153,859	2,285,491	2,415,852
Total outlays	2,011,153	2,160,117	2,293,006	2,472,205	2,708,677	2,770,097
Total surplus or deficit (–)	–157,758	–377,585	–412,727	–318,346	–423,186	–354,245
On-budget receipts	1,338,074	1,258,690	1,345,534	1,576,383	1,675,526	1,773,533
On-budget outlays	1,655,491	1,797,108	1,913,495	2,069,994	2,277,667	2,316,952
On-budget surplus or deficit (–)	–317,417	–538,418	–567,961	–493,611	–602,141	–543,419
Off-budget receipts	515,321	523,842	534,745	577,476	609,965	642,319
Off-budget outlays	355,662	363,009	379,511	402,211	431,010	453,145
Off-budget surplus or deficit (–)	159,659	160,833	155,234	175,265	178,955	189,174
OUTSTANDING DEBT, END OF PERIOD:						
Gross Federal debt	6,198,401	6,760,014	7,354,673	7,905,316	8,611,473	9,295,438
Held by Federal Government accounts	2,657,974	2,846,570	3,059,129	3,313,088	3,592,551	3,903,951
Held by the public	3,540,427	3,913,443	4,295,544	4,592,229	5,018,922	5,391,487
Federal Reserve System	604,191	656,116	700,341	736,360	....	....
Other	2,936,235	3,257,327	3,595,203	3,855,869	....	....
RECEIPTS: ON-BUDGET AND OFF-BUDGET	1,853,395	1,782,532	1,880,279	2,153,859	2,285,491	2,415,852
Individual income taxes	858,345	793,699	808,959	927,222	997,599	1,096,366
Corporation income taxes	148,044	131,778	189,371	278,282	277,122	260,567
Social insurance and retirement receipts	700,760	712,978	733,407	794,125	841,087	884,126
On-budget	185,439	189,136	198,662	216,649	231,122	241,807
Off-budget	515,321	523,842	534,745	577,476	609,965	642,319
Excise taxes	66,989	67,524	69,855	73,094	73,511	74,608
Estate and gift taxes	26,507	21,959	24,831	24,764	27,523	23,700
Customs duties and fees	18,602	19,862	21,083	23,379	25,887	28,069
Miscellaneous receipts	34,148	34,732	32,773	32,993	42,762	48,416
Deposits of earnings by Federal Reserve System	23,683	21,878	19,652	19,297	27,455	32,679
All other	10,465	12,854	13,121	13,696	15,307	15,737
OUTLAYS: ON-BUDGET AND OFF-BUDGET	2,011,153	2,160,117	2,293,006	2,472,205	2,708,677	2,770,097
National defense	348,555	404,920	455,908	495,335	535,943	527,428
International affairs	22,351	21,209	26,891	34,592	34,750	33,274
General science, space and technology	20,767	20,873	23,053	23,674	23,996	25,445
Energy	475	–735	–166	429	2,621	972
Natural resources and environment	29,454	29,703	30,725	28,023	32,731	31,049
Agriculture	21,966	22,497	15,440	26,566	26,846	25,733
Commerce and housing credit	–399	735	5,273	7,574	9,087	11,177
On-budget	252	5,980	9,403	9,365	7,665	7,749
Off-budget	–651	–5,245	–4,130	–1,791	1,422	3,428
Transportation	61,833	67,069	64,627	67,894	71,637	76,294
Community and regional development	12,981	18,850	15,822	26,264	52,025	28,159
Education, training, employment, and social services	70,544	82,568	87,948	97,526	109,651	87,576
Health	196,544	219,576	240,134	250,612	268,789	280,941
Medicare	230,855	249,433	269,360	298,638	342,987	392,000
Income security	312,720	334,632	333,059	345,847	360,632	367,206
Social security	455,980	474,680	495,548	523,305	554,740	585,940
On-budget	13,969	13,279	14,348	16,526	16,032	18,314
Off-budget	442,011	461,401	481,200	506,779	538,708	567,626
Veterans benefits and services	50,984	57,022	59,779	70,151	70,410	73,946
Administration of justice	35,061	35,340	45,576	40,019	41,342	44,344
General government	16,925	23,054	22,321	16,994	19,085	20,170
Net interest	170,949	153,073	160,245	183,986	220,053	247,315
On-budget	247,769	236,618	246,473	275,822	317,496	353,063
Off-budget	–76,820	–83,545	–86,228	–91,836	–97,443	–105,748
Allowances	....	....	....	....	3,726	5,464
Undistributed offsetting receipts	–47,392	–54,382	–58,537	–65,224	–72,374	–94,336
On-budget	–38,514	–44,780	–47,206	–54,283	–60,697	–82,175
Off-budget	–8,878	–9,602	–11,331	–10,941	–11,677	–12,161

Note.—See Note, Table B–78.

Sources: Department of the Treasury and Office of Management and Budget.

TABLE B-82.—*Federal and State and local government current receipts and expenditures, national income and product accounts (NIPA), 1959–2005*

[Billions of dollars; quarterly data at seasonally adjusted annual rates]

Year or quarter	Total government			Federal Government			State and local government			Adden-dum: Grants-in-aid to State and local govern-ments
	Current receipts	Current expendi-tures	Net govern-ment saving (NIPA)	Current receipts	Current expendi-tures	Net Federal Govern-ment saving (NIPA)	Current receipts	Current expendi-tures	Net State and local govern-ment saving (NIPA)	
1959	123.0	115.8	7.1	87.0	83.6	3.3	40.6	36.9	3.8	3.8
1960	134.4	122.9	11.5	93.9	86.7	7.2	44.5	40.2	4.3	4.0
1961	139.0	132.1	6.9	95.5	92.8	2.6	48.1	43.8	4.3	4.5
1962	150.6	142.8	7.8	103.6	101.1	2.5	52.0	46.8	5.2	5.0
1963	162.2	151.1	11.1	111.8	106.4	5.4	56.0	50.3	5.7	5.6
1964	166.6	159.2	7.4	111.8	110.8	1.0	61.3	54.9	6.4	6.5
1965	180.3	170.4	9.9	120.9	117.6	3.3	66.5	60.0	6.5	7.2
1966	202.8	192.8	10.0	137.9	135.7	2.3	74.9	67.2	7.8	10.1
1967	217.6	220.0	-2.4	146.9	156.2	-9.4	82.5	75.5	7.0	11.7
1968	252.0	246.8	5.2	171.2	173.5	-2.3	93.5	86.0	7.5	12.7
1969	283.4	266.7	16.7	192.5	183.8	8.7	105.5	97.5	8.0	14.6
1970	286.7	294.8	-8.1	186.0	201.1	-15.2	120.1	113.0	7.1	19.3
1971	303.4	325.3	-21.9	191.7	220.0	-28.4	134.9	128.5	6.5	23.2
1972	346.8	355.5	-8.8	220.1	244.4	-24.4	158.4	142.8	15.6	31.7
1973	390.0	385.6	4.4	250.4	261.7	-11.3	174.3	158.6	15.7	34.8
1974	431.3	435.8	-4.4	279.5	293.3	-13.8	188.1	178.7	9.3	36.3
1975	441.6	508.2	-66.6	277.2	346.2	-69.0	209.6	207.1	2.5	45.1
1976	505.5	549.9	-44.4	322.5	374.3	-51.7	233.7	226.3	7.4	50.7
1977	566.8	597.7	-31.0	363.4	407.5	-44.1	259.9	246.8	13.1	56.6
1978	645.6	653.4	-7.8	423.5	450.0	-26.5	287.6	268.9	18.7	65.5
1979	728.2	726.5	1.7	486.2	497.5	-11.3	308.4	295.4	13.0	66.3
1980	798.0	842.8	-44.8	532.1	585.7	-53.6	338.2	329.4	8.8	72.3
1981	917.2	962.9	-45.7	619.4	672.7	-53.3	370.2	362.7	7.6	72.5
1982	938.5	1,072.6	-134.1	616.6	748.5	-131.9	391.4	393.6	-2.2	69.5
1983	999.4	1,167.5	-168.1	642.3	815.4	-173.0	428.6	423.7	4.9	71.6
1984	1,112.5	1,256.6	-144.1	709.0	877.1	-168.1	480.2	456.2	23.9	76.7
1985	1,213.5	1,366.1	-152.6	773.3	948.2	-175.0	521.1	498.7	22.3	80.9
1986	1,289.3	1,459.1	-169.9	815.2	1,006.0	-190.8	561.6	540.7	21.0	87.6
1987	1,403.2	1,535.8	-132.6	896.6	1,041.6	-145.0	590.6	578.1	12.4	83.9
1988	1,502.2	1,618.7	-116.6	958.2	1,092.7	-134.5	635.5	617.6	17.9	91.6
1989	1,626.3	1,735.6	-109.3	1,037.4	1,167.5	-130.1	687.3	666.5	20.8	98.3
1990	1,707.8	1,872.6	-164.8	1,081.5	1,253.5	-172.0	737.8	730.5	7.2	111.4
1991	1,758.8	1,976.7	-217.9	1,101.3	1,315.0	-213.7	789.2	793.3	-4.2	131.6
1992	1,843.7	2,140.4	-296.7	1,147.2	1,444.6	-297.4	845.7	845.0	.7	149.1
1993	1,945.8	2,218.4	-272.6	1,222.5	1,496.0	-273.5	886.9	886.0	.9	163.7
1994	2,089.0	2,290.8	-201.9	1,320.8	1,533.1	-212.3	942.9	932.4	10.5	174.7
1995	2,212.6	2,397.6	-184.9	1,406.5	1,603.5	-197.0	990.2	978.2	12.0	184.1
1996	2,376.1	2,492.1	-116.0	1,524.0	1,665.8	-141.8	1,043.3	1,017.5	25.8	191.2
1997	2,551.9	2,568.6	-16.7	1,653.1	1,708.9	-55.8	1,097.4	1,058.3	39.1	198.6
1998	2,724.2	2,633.4	90.8	1,773.8	1,734.9	38.8	1,163.2	1,111.2	52.0	212.8
1999	2,895.0	2,741.0	154.0	1,891.2	1,787.6	103.6	1,236.7	1,186.3	50.4	232.9
2000	3,125.9	2,886.5	239.4	2,053.8	1,864.4	189.5	1,319.5	1,269.5	50.0	247.3
2001	3,113.1	3,061.6	51.5	2,016.2	1,969.5	46.7	1,373.0	1,368.2	4.8	276.1
2002	2,958.7	3,240.8	-282.1	1,853.2	2,101.1	-247.9	1,410.1	1,444.3	-34.2	304.6
2003	3,018.1	3,424.7	-406.5	1,868.6	2,251.4	-382.7	1,488.6	1,512.4	-23.8	339.1
2004	3,208.2	3,620.6	-412.3	1,974.8	2,381.3	-406.5	1,581.7	1,587.5	-5.9	348.3
2005 ᵖ	....	3,875.6	....	....	2,547.5	....	....	1,685.9	....	357.8
2002: I	2,934.2	3,178.0	-243.8	1,845.9	2,054.4	-208.5	1,379.7	1,415.0	-35.3	291.4
II	2,947.4	3,223.9	-276.5	1,854.1	2,095.5	-241.4	1,396.4	1,431.5	-35.1	303.1
III	2,972.3	3,251.0	-278.7	1,856.1	2,103.4	-247.3	1,422.7	1,454.2	-31.4	306.6
IV	2,981.1	3,310.5	-329.5	1,856.6	2,151.1	-294.6	1,441.7	1,476.6	-34.9	317.2
2003: I	3,001.3	3,365.1	-363.8	1,881.4	2,177.4	-296.0	1,433.1	1,500.9	-67.8	313.2
II	3,026.3	3,426.2	-399.9	1,896.3	2,270.1	-373.8	1,474.6	1,500.7	-26.1	344.6
III	2,972.1	3,442.1	-469.9	1,808.9	2,265.1	-456.2	1,507.6	1,521.4	-13.8	344.4
IV	3,072.9	3,465.4	-392.5	1,887.9	2,292.9	-405.0	1,539.0	1,526.5	12.5	354.0
2004: I	3,122.0	3,557.8	-435.8	1,917.8	2,347.2	-429.3	1,546.8	1,553.2	-6.5	342.6
II	3,181.2	3,596.3	-415.0	1,951.4	2,364.9	-413.4	1,579.7	1,581.3	-1.6	349.9
III	3,208.0	3,638.9	-430.9	1,975.4	2,387.0	-411.6	1,574.5	1,593.8	-19.3	341.9
IV	3,321.6	3,689.2	-367.7	2,054.6	2,426.2	-371.6	1,625.7	1,621.7	4.0	358.7
2005: I	3,497.2	3,788.1	-290.9	2,196.6	2,494.9	-298.3	1,656.7	1,649.4	7.4	356.1
II	3,564.3	3,840.3	-276.1	2,227.9	2,525.2	-297.3	1,694.9	1,673.7	21.3	358.6
III	3,478.8	3,900.4	-421.6	2,148.5	2,563.7	-415.2	1,684.3	1,690.8	-6.4	354.1
IV ᵖ	....	3,973.7	....	....	2,606.2	....	....	1,729.9	....	362.4

Note.—Federal grants-in-aid to State and local governments are reflected in Federal current expenditures and State and local current receipts. Total government current receipts and expenditures have been adjusted to eliminate this duplication.

Source: Department of Commerce, Bureau of Economic Analysis.

TABLE B–83.—*Federal and State and local government current receipts and expenditures, national income and product accounts (NIPA), by major type, 1959–2005*

[Billions of dollars; quarterly data at seasonally adjusted annual rates]

Year or quarter	Current receipts									Current expenditures					Net government saving
	Total	Current tax receipts				Contributions for government social insurance	Income receipts on assets	Current transfer receipts	Current surplus of government enterprises	Total [2]	Consumption expenditures	Current transfer payments	Interest payments	Subsidies	
		Total [1]	Personal current taxes	Taxes on production and imports	Taxes on corporate income										
1959	123.0	107.1	42.3	41.1	23.6	13.8	0.3	0.8	1.0	115.8	80.7	26.8	7.3	1.1	7.1
1960	134.4	113.4	46.1	44.6	22.7	16.4	2.7	.9	.9	122.9	83.3	28.0	10.4	1.1	11.5
1961	139.0	117.1	47.3	47.0	22.8	17.0	2.9	1.1	.8	132.1	88.2	31.8	10.2	2.0	6.9
1962	150.6	126.1	51.6	50.4	24.0	19.1	3.2	1.2	.9	142.8	96.8	32.6	11.1	2.3	7.8
1963	162.2	134.4	54.6	53.4	26.2	21.7	3.4	1.3	1.4	151.1	102.7	34.1	12.0	2.2	11.1
1964	166.6	137.6	52.1	57.3	28.0	22.4	3.7	1.6	1.3	159.2	108.6	34.9	12.9	2.7	7.4
1965	180.3	149.5	57.7	60.8	30.9	23.4	4.1	1.9	1.3	170.4	115.9	37.8	13.7	3.0	9.9
1966	202.8	163.5	66.4	63.3	33.7	31.3	4.7	2.2	1.0	192.8	132.0	41.8	15.1	3.9	10.0
1967	217.6	173.9	73.0	68.0	32.7	34.9	5.5	2.5	.9	220.0	149.7	50.1	16.4	3.8	−2.4
1968	252.0	203.2	87.0	76.5	39.4	38.7	6.4	2.6	1.2	246.8	165.8	58.1	18.8	4.2	5.2
1969	283.4	228.5	104.5	84.0	39.7	44.1	7.0	2.7	1.0	266.7	178.2	63.7	20.2	4.5	16.7
1970	286.7	229.3	103.1	91.5	34.4	46.4	8.2	2.9	.0	294.8	190.2	76.8	23.1	4.8	−8.1
1971	303.4	240.4	101.7	100.6	37.7	51.2	9.0	3.1	−.2	325.3	204.7	91.6	24.5	4.7	−21.9
1972	346.8	274.0	123.6	108.1	41.9	59.2	9.5	3.6	.5	355.5	220.8	102.2	26.3	6.6	−8.8
1973	390.0	299.4	132.4	117.3	49.3	75.5	11.6	3.9	−.4	385.6	234.8	114.2	31.3	5.2	4.4
1974	431.3	328.3	151.0	125.0	51.8	85.2	14.4	4.5	−.9	435.8	261.7	134.7	35.6	3.3	−4.4
1975	441.6	334.4	147.6	135.5	50.9	89.3	16.1	5.1	−3.2	508.2	294.6	169.2	40.0	4.5	−66.6
1976	505.5	383.8	172.3	146.6	64.2	101.3	16.3	5.8	−1.8	549.9	316.6	181.9	46.3	5.1	−44.4
1977	566.8	431.2	197.5	159.9	73.0	113.1	18.4	6.8	−2.6	597.7	346.6	193.3	50.8	7.1	−31.0
1978	645.6	485.0	229.4	171.2	83.5	131.3	23.2	8.0	−1.9	653.4	376.5	207.9	60.2	8.9	−7.8
1979	728.2	538.2	268.7	180.4	88.0	152.7	30.8	9.1	−2.6	726.5	412.3	232.6	72.9	8.5	1.7
1980	798.0	586.0	298.9	200.7	84.8	166.2	39.9	10.7	−4.8	842.8	465.9	278.0	89.1	9.8	−44.8
1981	917.2	663.9	345.2	236.0	81.1	195.7	50.2	12.3	−4.9	962.9	520.6	314.2	116.7	11.5	−45.7
1982	938.5	659.9	354.1	241.3	63.1	208.9	58.9	14.8	−4.0	1,072.6	568.2	350.5	138.9	15.0	−134.1
1983	999.4	694.5	352.3	263.7	77.2	226.0	65.3	16.8	−3.1	1,167.5	610.6	378.4	156.9	21.2	−168.1
1984	1,112.5	763.0	377.4	290.2	94.0	257.5	74.3	19.6	−1.9	1,256.6	657.6	390.9	187.3	21.0	−144.1
1985	1,213.5	824.3	417.4	308.5	96.5	281.4	84.0	23.0	.8	1,366.1	720.2	415.7	208.8	21.3	−152.6
1986	1,289.3	869.2	437.3	323.7	106.5	303.4	89.8	25.6	1.3	1,459.1	776.1	441.9	216.3	24.8	−169.9
1987	1,403.2	966.1	489.1	347.9	127.1	323.1	86.1	26.8	1.2	1,535.8	815.2	459.7	230.8	30.2	−132.6
1988	1,502.2	1,019.4	505.0	374.9	137.2	361.5	90.5	28.2	2.5	1,618.7	852.8	488.8	247.7	29.4	−116.6
1989	1,626.3	1,109.7	566.1	399.3	141.5	385.2	94.3	32.2	4.9	1,735.6	901.4	533.1	274.0	27.2	−109.3
1990	1,707.8	1,161.9	592.8	425.5	140.6	410.1	98.7	35.6	1.6	1,872.6	964.4	586.1	295.3	26.8	−164.8
1991	1,758.8	1,180.3	586.7	457.5	133.6	430.2	98.1	44.6	5.7	1,976.7	1,014.1	622.5	312.7	27.3	−217.9
1992	1,843.7	1,240.2	610.6	483.8	143.1	455.0	90.5	50.5	7.6	2,140.4	1,047.8	749.5	313.2	29.9	−296.7
1993	1,945.8	1,318.2	646.6	503.4	165.4	477.7	87.6	55.1	7.2	2,218.4	1,072.2	796.3	313.6	36.4	−272.6
1994	2,089.0	1,426.1	690.7	545.6	186.7	508.2	86.6	59.5	8.6	2,290.8	1,104.1	831.2	323.4	32.2	−201.9
1995	2,212.6	1,517.2	744.1	558.2	211.0	532.8	92.1	59.1	11.4	2,397.6	1,136.5	872.5	354.6	34.0	−184.9
1996	2,376.1	1,642.0	832.1	581.1	223.6	555.2	100.2	66.0	12.7	2,492.1	1,171.1	921.4	365.3	34.3	−116.0
1997	2,551.9	1,780.5	926.3	612.0	237.1	587.2	103.7	67.9	12.6	2,568.6	1,216.6	947.8	371.4	32.9	−16.7
1998	2,724.2	1,911.7	1,027.0	639.8	239.2	624.2	102.4	75.5	10.3	2,633.4	1,256.0	969.6	372.4	35.4	90.8
1999	2,895.0	2,036.2	1,107.5	674.0	248.8	661.4	106.8	80.6	10.1	2,741.0	1,334.0	1,005.5	357.3	44.2	154.0
2000	3,125.9	2,206.8	1,235.7	708.9	255.0	702.7	117.4	93.7	5.3	2,886.5	1,417.1	1,062.4	362.8	44.3	239.4
2001	3,113.1	2,168.0	1,237.3	728.6	194.9	731.1	113.7	101.8	−1.4	3,061.6	1,501.6	1,160.6	344.1	55.3	51.5
2002	2,958.7	2,004.5	1,051.8	762.8	182.6	750.0	98.4	104.9	.9	3,240.8	1,616.9	1,270.4	315.1	38.4	−282.1
2003	3,018.1	2,031.8	999.9	801.4	221.9	776.6	97.6	110.9	1.3	3,424.7	1,736.7	1,340.0	301.4	46.7	−406.5
2004	3,208.2	2,169.9	1,049.1	852.8	258.9	822.2	99.0	120.1	−3.0	3,620.6	1,843.4	1,423.4	310.3	43.5	−412.3
2005 [p]	....	1,206.9	903.2	....	....	869.4	102.2	108.4	−11.2	3,875.6	1,959.8	1,518.5	341.3	56.1	....
2002: I	2,934.2	1,981.6	1,063.2	746.0	165.4	747.1	103.4	103.8	−1.6	3,178.0	1,573.1	1,248.6	316.4	39.9	−243.8
II	2,947.4	1,994.0	1,050.3	757.9	178.6	751.1	99.1	104.3	−1.2	3,223.9	1,604.3	1,263.0	319.5	37.0	−276.5
III	2,972.3	2,015.5	1,050.0	771.6	186.7	751.1	96.4	105.2	4.0	3,251.0	1,624.9	1,274.1	313.6	38.3	−278.7
IV	2,981.1	2,026.9	1,043.8	775.5	199.9	750.9	94.9	106.1	2.3	3,310.5	1,665.2	1,296.0	311.0	38.3	−329.5
2003: I	3,001.3	2,029.1	1,024.3	783.8	214.1	765.8	94.6	107.7	4.1	3,365.1	1,705.5	1,316.1	302.8	42.1	−363.8
II	3,026.3	2,043.7	1,026.9	794.7	212.3	773.6	97.3	109.8	1.8	3,426.2	1,735.4	1,334.2	300.7	54.6	−399.9
III	2,972.1	1,980.3	940.8	806.6	225.2	780.7	98.7	112.1	.4	3,442.1	1,746.1	1,353.1	298.4	44.5	−469.9
IV	3,072.9	2,073.9	1,007.6	820.6	236.3	786.3	99.6	114.2	−1.1	3,465.4	1,759.7	1,356.5	303.7	45.4	−392.5
2004: I	3,122.0	2,102.3	1,009.6	837.1	246.5	806.3	97.6	117.5	−1.6	3,557.8	1,805.8	1,407.1	304.2	42.3	−435.8
II	3,181.2	2,152.3	1,034.0	847.8	262.1	813.0	98.2	119.9	−2.2	3,596.3	1,830.1	1,416.2	306.8	41.8	−415.0
III	3,208.0	2,168.6	1,058.4	855.5	246.9	825.9	99.2	117.2	−3.0	3,638.9	1,859.6	1,422.2	313.8	43.2	−430.9
IV	3,321.6	2,256.5	1,094.3	870.9	280.1	843.5	101.0	125.7	−5.2	3,689.2	1,878.2	1,448.0	316.5	46.5	−367.7
2005: I	3,497.2	2,413.0	1,171.4	883.8	348.1	861.0	101.2	128.2	−6.1	3,788.1	1,918.6	1,501.2	317.8	50.6	−290.9
II	3,564.3	2,473.2	1,206.0	900.1	358.5	864.9	103.1	130.1	−7.0	3,840.3	1,938.5	1,507.1	342.6	52.1	−276.1
III	3,478.8	2,481.6	1,215.9	909.5	346.2	872.6	102.2	45.1	−22.8	3,900.4	1,988.6	1,512.4	343.3	56.1	−421.6
IV [p]	....		1,234.3	919.3	....	879.2	102.3	130.3	−8.8	3,973.7	1,993.7	1,553.1	361.4	65.6	....

[1] Includes taxes from the rest of the world, not shown separately.
[2] Includes an item for the difference between wage accruals and disbursements, not shown separately.

Source: Department of Commerce, Bureau of Economic Analysis.

TABLE B–84.—*Federal Government current receipts and expenditures, national income and product accounts (NIPA), 1959–2005*

[Billions of dollars; quarterly data at seasonally adjusted annual rates]

| | Current receipts | | | | | | | | Current expenditures | | | | | |
| Year or quarter | Total | Current tax receipts | | | | Contributions for government social insurance | Income receipts on assets | Current transfer receipts | Current surplus of government enterprises | Total [2] | Consumption expenditures | Current transfer payments [3] | Interest payments | Subsidies | Net Federal Government saving |
		Total [1]	Personal current taxes	Taxes on production and imports	Taxes on corporate income										
1959	87.0	73.3	38.5	12.2	22.5	13.4	0.0	0.4	−0.1	83.6	50.0	26.2	6.3	1.1	3.3
1960	93.9	76.5	41.8	13.1	21.4	16.0	1.4	.4	−.3	86.7	49.8	27.5	8.4	1.1	7.2
1961	95.5	77.5	42.7	13.2	21.5	16.5	1.5	.5	−.5	92.8	51.6	31.3	7.9	2.0	2.6
1962	103.6	83.3	46.5	14.2	22.5	18.6	1.7	.5	−.5	101.1	57.8	32.3	8.6	2.3	2.5
1963	111.8	88.6	49.1	14.7	24.6	21.0	1.8	.6	−.3	106.4	60.8	34.1	9.3	2.2	5.4
1964	111.8	87.8	46.0	15.5	26.1	21.7	1.8	.7	−.3	110.8	62.8	35.2	10.0	2.7	1.0
1965	120.9	95.7	51.1	15.5	28.9	22.7	1.9	1.1	−.3	117.6	65.7	38.3	10.6	3.0	3.3
1966	137.9	104.8	58.6	14.5	31.4	30.5	2.1	1.2	−.6	135.7	75.9	44.2	11.6	3.9	2.3
1967	146.9	109.9	64.4	15.2	30.0	34.0	2.5	1.1	−.6	156.2	87.1	52.6	12.7	3.8	−9.4
1968	171.2	129.8	76.4	17.0	36.1	37.8	2.9	1.1	−.3	173.5	95.4	59.3	14.6	4.1	−2.3
1969	192.5	146.1	91.7	17.9	36.1	43.1	2.7	1.1	−.5	183.8	98.4	65.1	15.8	4.5	8.7
1970	186.0	138.0	88.9	18.2	30.6	45.3	3.1	1.1	−1.5	201.1	98.6	80.0	17.7	4.8	−15.2
1971	191.7	138.7	85.8	19.1	33.5	50.0	3.5	1.1	−1.6	220.0	102.0	95.5	17.9	4.6	−28.4
1972	220.1	158.4	102.8	18.6	36.6	57.9	3.6	1.3	−1.1	244.4	107.7	111.9	18.8	6.6	−24.4
1973	250.4	173.1	109.6	19.9	43.3	74.0	3.8	1.3	−1.8	261.7	108.9	124.9	22.8	5.1	−11.3
1974	279.5	192.2	126.5	20.2	45.1	83.5	4.2	1.4	−1.8	293.3	118.0	145.7	26.0	3.2	−13.8
1975	277.2	187.0	120.7	22.2	43.6	87.5	4.9	1.5	−3.6	346.2	129.6	183.5	28.9	4.3	−69.0
1976	322.5	218.1	141.2	21.6	54.6	99.1	5.9	1.6	−2.2	374.3	137.2	198.5	33.8	4.9	−51.7
1977	363.4	247.4	162.2	22.9	61.6	110.3	6.7	1.9	−2.9	407.5	150.7	212.9	37.1	6.9	−44.1
1978	423.5	286.9	188.9	25.6	71.4	127.9	8.5	2.4	−2.1	450.0	163.3	232.7	45.3	8.7	−26.5
1979	486.2	326.2	224.6	26.0	74.4	148.9	10.7	2.8	−2.3	497.5	179.0	254.6	55.7	8.2	−11.3
1980	532.1	355.9	250.0	34.0	70.3	162.6	13.7	3.5	−3.6	585.7	207.5	299.1	69.7	9.4	−53.6
1981	619.4	408.1	290.6	50.3	65.7	191.8	18.3	3.8	−2.5	672.7	238.3	329.5	93.9	11.1	−53.3
1982	616.6	386.8	295.0	41.4	49.0	204.9	22.2	5.2	−2.4	748.5	263.3	358.8	111.8	14.5	−131.9
1983	642.3	393.6	286.2	44.8	61.3	221.8	23.8	6.0	−2.9	815.4	286.5	383.0	124.6	20.8	−173.0
1984	709.0	425.7	301.4	47.8	75.2	252.8	26.6	7.3	−3.4	877.1	310.0	396.5	150.3	20.6	−168.1
1985	773.3	460.6	336.0	46.4	76.3	276.5	29.1	9.4	−2.4	948.2	338.4	419.3	169.4	20.9	−175.0
1986	815.2	479.6	350.1	44.0	83.8	297.5	31.4	8.2	−1.5	1,006.0	358.2	445.1	178.2	24.5	−190.8
1987	896.6	544.0	392.5	46.3	103.2	315.9	27.9	10.7	−2.0	1,041.6	374.3	452.9	184.6	29.9	−145.0
1988	958.2	566.7	402.9	50.3	111.1	353.1	30.0	10.8	−2.3	1,092.7	382.5	481.9	199.3	29.0	−134.5
1989	1,037.4	621.7	451.5	50.2	117.2	376.3	28.6	12.4	−1.6	1,167.5	399.2	522.0	219.3	26.8	−130.1
1990	1,081.5	642.8	470.2	51.4	118.1	400.1	30.2	13.5	−5.1	1,253.5	419.8	569.9	237.5	26.4	−172.0
1991	1,101.3	636.1	461.3	62.2	109.9	418.6	30.1	17.9	−1.4	1,315.0	439.5	597.6	250.9	26.9	−213.7
1992	1,147.2	660.4	475.3	63.7	118.8	441.8	25.7	19.4	−.1	1,444.6	445.2	718.7	251.3	29.5	−297.4
1993	1,222.5	713.4	505.5	66.7	138.5	463.6	26.2	21.1	−1.8	1,496.0	441.9	764.7	253.4	36.0	−273.5
1994	1,320.8	781.9	542.7	79.4	156.7	493.7	23.4	22.3	−.4	1,533.1	440.8	799.2	261.3	31.8	−212.3
1995	1,406.5	845.1	586.0	75.9	179.3	519.2	23.7	19.1	−.6	1,603.5	440.5	839.0	290.4	33.7	−197.0
1996	1,524.0	932.4	663.4	73.2	190.6	542.8	26.9	23.1	−1.2	1,665.8	446.3	888.3	297.3	34.0	−141.8
1997	1,653.1	1,030.6	744.3	78.2	203.0	576.4	25.9	19.9	.3	1,708.9	457.7	918.8	300.0	32.4	−55.8
1998	1,773.8	1,116.8	825.8	81.1	204.2	613.8	21.5	21.5	.1	1,734.9	454.6	946.5	298.8	35.0	38.8
1999	1,891.2	1,195.7	893.0	83.9	213.0	651.6	21.5	22.7	−.3	1,787.6	475.1	986.1	282.7	43.8	103.6
2000	2,053.8	1,313.6	999.1	87.8	219.4	691.7	25.2	25.7	−2.3	1,864.4	499.3	1,038.1	283.3	43.8	189.5
2001	2,016.2	1,252.2	994.5	85.8	164.7	717.5	24.9	27.1	−5.5	1,969.5	531.9	1,131.4	258.6	47.6	46.7
2002	1,853.2	1,075.5	830.5	87.3	150.5	734.3	20.2	24.8	−1.6	2,101.1	591.5	1,243.0	229.1	37.5	−247.9
2003	1,868.6	1,059.2	774.3	89.7	186.7	759.1	22.7	25.7	1.9	2,251.4	661.9	1,327.7	215.2	46.5	−382.7
2004	1,974.8	1,122.4	801.8	94.0	217.4	802.5	21.9	28.6	−.5	2,381.3	725.7	1,391.2	221.5	43.0	−406.5
2005 ᵖ			932.2	97.2		849.5	23.1	7.4	−3.7	2,547.5	767.2	1,475.6	249.1	55.6	
2002: I	1,845.9	1,071.3	843.1	84.9	136.3	732.1	21.1	25.7	−4.3	2,054.4	571.3	1,215.1	229.9	38.1	−208.5
II	1,854.1	1,077.5	835.2	87.7	147.4	735.5	20.1	24.9	−3.9	2,095.5	585.0	1,240.7	233.3	36.5	−241.4
III	1,856.1	1,075.4	825.8	88.5	153.9	735.0	19.8	24.5	1.4	2,103.4	591.4	1,247.6	227.7	36.7	−247.3
IV	1,856.6	1,078.0	818.0	88.0	164.2	734.4	19.9	24.0	.3	2,151.1	618.5	1,268.5	225.4	38.7	−294.6
2003: I	1,881.4	1,084.4	806.7	90.1	180.7	749.0	19.5	24.8	3.7	2,177.4	634.7	1,285.0	217.0	42.0	−296.0
II	1,896.3	1,089.6	811.2	89.7	178.8	756.4	22.8	25.5	2.1	2,270.1	667.6	1,332.1	214.9	54.2	−373.8
III	1,808.9	994.5	708.8	88.8	189.1	762.9	24.0	26.2	1.4	2,265.1	668.4	1,339.0	212.2	45.5	−456.2
IV	1,887.9	1,068.2	770.6	90.2	198.1	768.0	24.6	26.5	.6	2,292.9	676.8	1,354.8	216.8	44.4	−405.0
2004: I	1,917.8	1,080.7	771.3	93.4	206.9	787.2	22.0	27.6	.3	2,347.2	710.7	1,379.3	216.9	41.8	−429.3
II	1,951.4	1,108.1	786.3	93.4	219.9	793.5	21.5	28.1	.3	2,364.9	721.1	1,382.8	218.4	41.3	−413.4
III	1,975.4	1,119.4	810.0	94.0	207.5	806.0	21.8	28.7	−.4	2,387.0	735.7	1,384.0	224.5	42.8	−411.6
IV	2,054.6	1,181.3	839.7	95.1	235.3	823.4	22.2	30.0	−2.3	2,426.2	735.1	1,419.0	226.1	46.1	−371.6
2005: I	2,196.6	1,305.1	908.3	95.4	291.7	841.1	23.0	30.4	−2.9	2,494.9	759.6	1,458.7	226.6	50.1	−298.3
II	2,227.9	1,331.8	924.3	98.3	300.8	845.1	24.3	30.2	−3.6	2,525.2	762.8	1,459.9	250.8	51.6	−297.3
III	2,148.5	1,338.7	940.5	97.5	290.7	852.6	22.8	−61.4	−4.3	2,563.7	782.9	1,474.4	250.8	55.6	−415.2
IV ᵖ			955.7	97.5		859.1	22.4	30.6	−3.8	2,606.2	763.6	1,509.2	268.3	65.1	

[1] Includes taxes from the rest of the world, not shown separately.
[2] Includes an item for the difference between wage accruals and disbursements, not shown separately.
[3] Includes Federal grants-in-aid to state and local governments. See Table B–82 for data on Federal grants-in-aid.

Source: Department of Commerce, Bureau of Economic Analysis.

TABLE B–85.—*State and local government current receipts and expenditures, national income and product accounts (NIPA), 1959–2005*

[Billions of dollars; quarterly data at seasonally adjusted annual rates]

Year or quarter	Current receipts									Current expenditures					Net State and local government saving
	Total	Current tax receipts				Contributions for government social insurance	Income receipts on assets	Current transfer receipts [1]	Current surplus of government enterprises	Total [2]	Consumption expenditures	Government social benefit payments to persons	Interest payments	Subsidies	
		Total	Personal current taxes	Taxes on production and imports	Taxes on corporate income										
1959	40.6	33.8	3.8	28.8	1.2	0.4	1.1	4.2	1.1	36.9	30.7	4.3	1.8	0.0	3.8
1960	44.5	37.0	4.2	31.5	1.2	.5	1.3	4.5	1.2	40.2	33.5	4.6	2.1	.0	4.3
1961	48.1	39.7	4.6	33.8	1.3	.5	1.4	5.2	1.3	43.8	36.6	5.0	2.2	.0	4.3
1962	52.0	42.8	5.0	36.3	1.5	.5	1.5	5.8	1.4	46.8	39.0	5.3	2.4	.0	5.2
1963	56.0	45.8	5.4	38.7	1.7	.6	1.6	6.4	1.6	50.3	41.9	5.7	2.7	.0	5.7
1964	61.3	49.8	6.1	41.8	1.8	.7	1.9	7.3	1.6	54.9	45.8	6.2	2.9	.0	6.4
1965	66.5	53.9	6.6	45.3	2.0	.8	2.2	8.0	1.7	60.0	50.2	6.7	3.1	.0	6.5
1966	74.9	58.8	7.8	48.8	2.2	.8	2.6	11.1	1.6	67.2	56.1	7.6	3.4	.0	7.8
1967	82.5	64.0	8.6	52.8	2.6	.9	3.0	13.1	1.5	75.5	62.6	9.2	3.7	.0	7.0
1968	93.5	73.4	10.6	59.5	3.3	.9	3.5	14.2	1.5	86.0	70.4	11.4	4.2	.0	7.5
1969	105.5	82.5	12.8	66.0	3.6	1.0	4.3	16.2	1.5	97.5	79.9	13.2	4.4	.0	8.0
1970	120.1	91.3	14.2	73.3	3.7	1.1	5.2	21.1	1.5	113.0	91.5	16.1	5.3	.0	7.1
1971	134.9	101.7	15.9	81.5	4.3	1.2	5.5	25.2	1.4	128.5	102.7	19.3	6.5	.0	6.5
1972	158.4	115.6	20.9	89.4	5.3	1.3	5.9	34.0	1.6	142.8	113.2	22.0	7.5	.1	15.6
1973	174.3	126.3	22.8	97.4	6.0	1.5	7.8	37.3	1.5	158.6	126.0	24.1	8.5	.1	15.7
1974	188.1	136.0	24.5	104.8	6.7	1.7	10.2	39.3	.9	178.7	143.7	25.3	9.6	.1	9.3
1975	209.6	147.4	26.9	113.2	7.3	1.8	11.2	48.7	.4	207.1	165.1	30.8	11.1	.2	2.5
1976	233.7	165.7	31.1	125.0	9.6	2.2	10.4	55.0	.4	226.3	179.5	34.1	12.5	.2	7.4
1977	259.9	183.7	35.4	136.9	11.4	2.8	11.7	61.4	.3	246.8	195.9	37.0	13.7	.2	13.1
1978	287.6	198.2	40.5	145.6	12.1	3.4	14.7	71.1	.3	268.9	213.2	40.8	14.9	.2	18.7
1979	308.4	212.0	44.0	154.4	13.6	3.9	20.1	72.7	−.3	295.4	233.3	44.3	17.2	.3	13.0
1980	338.2	230.0	48.9	166.7	14.5	3.6	26.3	79.5	−1.2	329.4	258.4	51.2	19.4	.4	8.8
1981	370.2	255.8	54.6	185.7	15.4	3.9	32.0	81.0	−2.4	362.7	282.3	57.1	22.8	.4	7.6
1982	391.4	273.2	59.1	200.0	14.0	4.0	36.7	79.1	−1.6	393.6	304.9	61.2	27.1	.5	−2.2
1983	428.6	300.9	66.1	218.9	15.9	4.1	41.4	82.4	−.2	423.7	324.1	66.9	32.3	.4	4.9
1984	480.2	337.3	76.0	242.5	18.8	4.7	47.7	89.0	1.5	456.2	347.7	71.2	37.0	.4	23.9
1985	521.1	363.7	81.4	262.1	20.2	4.9	54.9	94.5	1.2	498.7	381.8	77.3	39.4	.3	22.3
1986	561.6	389.5	87.2	279.7	22.7	6.0	58.4	105.0	2.8	540.7	417.9	84.3	38.2	.3	21.0
1987	590.6	422.1	96.6	301.6	23.9	7.2	58.1	100.0	3.1	578.1	440.9	90.7	46.2	.3	12.4
1988	635.5	452.8	102.1	324.6	26.0	8.4	60.5	109.0	4.8	617.6	470.4	98.5	48.4	.4	17.9
1989	687.3	488.0	114.6	349.1	24.2	9.0	65.7	118.1	6.5	666.5	502.1	109.3	54.6	.4	20.8
1990	737.8	519.1	122.6	374.1	22.5	10.0	68.4	133.5	6.7	730.5	544.6	127.7	57.9	.4	7.2
1991	789.2	544.3	125.3	395.3	23.6	11.6	68.0	158.2	7.1	793.3	574.6	156.5	61.7	.4	−4.2
1992	845.7	579.8	135.3	420.1	24.4	13.1	64.8	180.3	7.7	845.0	602.7	180.0	61.9	.4	.7
1993	886.9	604.7	141.1	436.8	26.9	14.1	61.4	197.7	9.0	886.0	630.3	195.2	60.2	.4	.9
1994	942.9	644.2	148.0	466.3	30.0	14.5	63.2	211.9	9.0	932.4	663.3	206.7	62.0	.3	10.5
1995	990.2	672.1	158.1	482.4	31.7	13.6	68.4	224.1	12.0	978.2	696.1	217.6	64.2	.3	12.0
1996	1,043.3	709.6	168.7	507.9	33.0	12.5	73.3	234.1	13.9	1,017.5	724.8	224.3	68.1	.3	25.8
1997	1,097.4	749.9	182.0	533.8	34.1	10.8	77.8	246.6	12.3	1,058.3	758.9	227.6	71.4	.4	39.1
1998	1,163.2	794.9	201.2	558.8	34.9	10.4	80.9	266.8	10.2	1,111.2	801.4	235.8	73.6	.4	52.0
1999	1,236.7	840.4	214.5	590.2	35.8	9.8	85.3	290.8	10.4	1,186.3	858.9	252.4	74.6	.4	50.4
2000	1,319.5	893.2	236.6	621.1	35.5	11.0	92.2	315.4	7.7	1,269.5	917.8	271.7	79.5	.5	50.0
2001	1,373.0	915.8	242.7	642.8	30.2	13.6	88.8	350.8	4.0	1,368.2	969.8	305.2	85.5	7.7	4.8
2002	1,410.1	929.0	221.3	675.5	32.2	15.8	78.2	384.7	2.5	1,444.3	1,025.3	332.0	86.0	.9	−34.2
2003	1,488.6	972.6	225.6	711.7	35.3	17.5	74.9	424.3	−.6	1,512.4	1,074.8	351.3	86.2	.1	−23.8
2004	1,581.7	1,047.6	247.2	758.8	41.5	19.7	77.1	439.8	−2.5	1,587.5	1,117.7	380.5	88.9	.5	−5.9
2005[P]	....	....	274.7	806.0	....	19.9	79.1	458.8	−7.5	1,685.9	1,192.6	400.7	92.1	.5	....
2002:I	1,379.7	910.3	220.1	661.1	29.1	15.0	82.3	369.5	2.7	1,415.0	1,001.8	324.9	86.5	1.8	−35.3
II	1,396.4	916.5	215.1	670.2	31.2	15.0	79.0	382.5	2.7	1,431.5	1,019.4	325.4	86.2	.6	−35.1
III	1,422.7	940.1	224.2	683.2	32.8	16.1	76.5	387.4	2.6	1,454.2	1,033.6	333.0	85.9	1.7	−31.4
IV	1,441.7	949.0	225.8	687.5	35.6	16.5	75.0	399.3	2.0	1,476.6	1,046.7	344.7	85.7	−.4	−34.9
2003:I	1,433.1	944.7	217.7	693.7	33.4	16.7	75.1	396.1	.4	1,500.9	1,070.8	344.3	85.8	.1	−67.8
II	1,474.6	954.1	215.8	705.0	33.4	17.2	74.6	428.9	−.3	1,500.7	1,067.8	346.7	85.8	.4	−26.1
III	1,507.6	985.8	231.9	717.8	36.0	17.7	74.7	430.4	−1.0	1,521.4	1,077.7	358.5	86.2	−.9	−13.8
IV	1,539.0	1,005.7	237.0	730.5	38.2	18.3	75.0	441.7	−1.7	1,526.5	1,082.9	355.8	86.9	1.0	12.5
2004:I	1,546.8	1,021.5	238.3	743.7	39.5	19.1	75.6	432.5	−1.9	1,553.2	1,095.1	370.4	87.3	.5	−6.5
II	1,579.7	1,044.2	247.7	754.3	42.2	19.6	76.7	441.8	−2.5	1,581.3	1,108.9	383.5	88.4	.5	−1.6
III	1,574.5	1,049.3	248.4	761.5	39.4	19.9	77.4	430.5	−2.6	1,593.8	1,123.9	380.2	89.3	.5	−19.3
IV	1,625.7	1,075.2	254.6	775.8	44.8	20.1	78.8	454.5	−2.9	1,621.7	1,143.1	387.7	90.4	.5	4.0
2005:I	1,656.7	1,107.9	263.1	788.4	56.4	19.9	78.2	453.9	−3.2	1,649.4	1,159.0	398.6	91.2	.5	7.4
II	1,694.9	1,141.4	281.8	801.8	57.7	19.8	78.8	458.4	−3.5	1,673.7	1,175.7	405.7	91.8	.5	21.3
III	1,684.3	1,142.9	275.4	812.0	55.5	19.9	79.4	460.6	−18.5	1,690.8	1,205.7	392.1	92.4	.5	−6.4
IV[P]	....	....	278.6	821.9	....	20.1	79.9	462.1	−4.9	1,729.9	1,230.1	406.3	93.0	.5	....

[1] Includes Federal grants-in-aid. See Table B–82 for data on Federal grants-in-aid.
[2] Includes an item for the difference between wage accruals and disbursements, not shown separately.

Source: Department of Commerce, Bureau of Economic Analysis.

TABLE B–86.—*State and local government revenues and expenditures, selected fiscal years, 1927–2003*

[Millions of dollars]

Fiscal year [1]	General revenues by source [2]							General expenditures by function [2]				
	Total	Property taxes	Sales and gross receipts taxes	Individual income taxes	Corporation net income taxes	Revenue from Federal Government	All other [3]	Total	Education	Highways	Public welfare	All other [4]
1927	7,271	4,730	470	70	92	116	1,793	7,210	2,235	1,809	151	3,015
1932	7,267	4,487	752	74	79	232	1,643	7,765	2,311	1,741	444	3,269
1934	7,678	4,076	1,008	80	49	1,016	1,449	7,181	1,831	1,509	889	2,952
1936	8,395	4,093	1,484	153	113	948	1,604	7,644	2,177	1,425	827	3,215
1938	9,228	4,440	1,794	218	165	800	1,811	8,757	2,491	1,650	1,069	3,547
1940	9,609	4,430	1,982	224	156	945	1,872	9,229	2,638	1,573	1,156	3,862
1942	10,418	4,537	2,351	276	272	858	2,123	9,190	2,586	1,490	1,225	3,889
1944	10,908	4,604	2,289	342	451	954	2,269	8,863	2,793	1,200	1,133	3,737
1946	12,356	4,986	2,986	422	447	855	2,661	11,028	3,356	1,672	1,409	4,591
1948	17,250	6,126	4,442	543	592	1,861	3,685	17,684	5,379	3,036	2,099	7,170
1950	20,911	7,349	5,154	788	593	2,486	4,541	22,787	7,177	3,803	2,940	8,867
1952	25,181	8,652	6,357	998	846	2,566	5,763	26,098	8,318	4,650	2,788	10,342
1953	27,307	9,375	6,927	1,065	817	2,870	6,252	27,910	9,390	4,987	2,914	10,619
1954	29,012	9,967	7,276	1,127	778	2,966	6,897	30,701	10,557	5,527	3,060	11,557
1955	31,073	10,735	7,643	1,237	744	3,131	7,584	33,724	11,907	6,452	3,168	12,197
1956	34,667	11,749	8,691	1,538	890	3,335	8,465	36,711	13,220	6,953	3,139	13,399
1957	38,164	12,864	9,467	1,754	984	3,843	9,252	40,375	14,134	7,816	3,485	14,940
1958	41,219	14,047	9,829	1,759	1,018	4,865	9,699	44,851	15,919	8,567	3,818	16,547
1959	45,306	14,983	10,437	1,994	1,001	6,377	10,516	48,887	17,283	9,592	4,136	17,876
1960	50,505	16,405	11,849	2,463	1,180	6,974	11,634	51,876	18,719	9,428	4,404	19,325
1961	54,037	18,002	12,463	2,613	1,266	7,131	12,563	56,201	20,574	9,844	4,720	21,063
1962	58,252	19,054	13,494	3,037	1,308	7,871	13,489	60,206	22,216	10,357	5,084	22,549
1963	62,890	20,089	14,456	3,269	1,505	8,722	14,850	64,816	23,776	11,136	5,481	24,423
1962-63	62,269	19,833	14,446	3,267	1,505	8,663	13,977	63,977	23,729	11,150	5,420	23,678
1963-64	68,443	21,241	15,762	3,791	1,695	10,002	15,951	69,302	26,286	11,664	5,766	25,586
1964-65	74,000	22,583	17,118	4,090	1,929	11,029	17,250	74,678	28,563	12,221	6,315	27,579
1965-66	83,036	24,670	19,085	4,760	2,038	13,214	19,269	82,843	33,287	12,770	6,757	30,029
1966-67	91,197	26,047	20,530	5,825	2,227	15,370	21,198	93,350	37,919	13,932	8,218	33,281
1967-68	101,264	27,747	22,911	7,308	2,518	17,181	23,599	102,411	41,158	14,481	9,857	36,915
1968-69	114,550	30,673	26,519	8,908	3,180	19,153	26,117	116,728	47,238	15,417	12,110	41,963
1969-70	130,756	34,054	30,322	10,812	3,738	21,857	29,973	131,332	52,718	16,427	14,679	47,508
1970-71	144,927	37,852	33,233	11,900	3,424	26,146	32,372	150,674	59,413	18,095	18,226	54,940
1971-72	167,535	42,877	37,518	15,227	4,416	31,342	36,156	168,549	65,813	19,021	21,117	62,598
1972-73	190,222	45,283	42,047	17,994	5,425	39,264	40,210	181,357	69,713	18,615	23,582	69,447
1973-74	207,670	47,705	46,098	19,491	6,015	41,820	46,542	198,959	75,833	19,946	25,085	78,095
1974-75	228,171	51,491	49,815	21,454	6,642	47,034	51,735	230,722	87,858	22,528	28,156	92,180
1975-76	256,176	57,001	54,547	24,575	7,273	55,589	57,191	256,731	97,216	23,907	32,604	103,004
1976-77	285,157	62,527	60,641	29,246	9,174	62,444	61,125	274,215	102,780	23,058	35,906	112,472
1977-78	315,960	66,422	67,596	33,176	10,738	69,592	68,435	296,984	110,758	24,609	39,140	122,478
1978-79	343,236	64,944	74,247	36,932	12,128	75,164	79,822	327,517	119,448	28,440	41,898	137,731
1979-80	382,322	68,499	79,927	42,080	13,321	83,029	95,467	369,086	133,211	33,311	47,288	155,276
1980-81	423,404	74,969	85,971	46,426	14,143	90,294	111,599	407,449	145,784	34,603	54,105	172,957
1981-82	457,654	82,067	93,613	50,738	15,028	87,282	128,925	436,733	154,282	34,520	57,996	189,935
1982-83	486,753	89,105	100,247	55,129	14,258	90,007	138,008	466,516	163,876	36,655	60,906	205,080
1983-84	542,730	96,457	114,097	64,529	17,141	96,935	153,571	505,008	176,108	39,419	66,414	223,068
1984-85	598,121	103,757	126,376	70,361	19,152	106,158	172,317	553,899	192,686	44,989	71,479	244,745
1985-86	641,486	111,709	135,005	74,365	19,994	113,099	187,314	605,623	210,819	49,368	75,868	269,568
1986-87	686,860	121,203	144,091	83,935	22,425	114,857	200,350	657,134	226,619	52,355	82,650	295,510
1987-88	726,762	132,212	156,452	88,350	23,663	117,602	208,482	704,921	242,683	55,621	89,090	317,527
1988-89	786,129	142,400	166,336	97,806	25,926	125,824	227,838	762,360	263,898	58,105	97,879	342,479
1989-90	849,502	155,613	177,885	105,640	23,566	136,802	249,996	834,818	288,148	61,057	110,518	375,094
1990-91	902,207	167,999	185,570	109,341	22,242	154,099	262,955	908,108	309,302	64,937	130,402	403,467
1991-92	979,137	180,337	197,731	115,638	23,880	179,174	282,376	981,253	324,652	67,351	158,723	430,526
1992-93	1,041,643	189,744	209,649	123,235	26,417	198,663	293,935	1,030,434	342,287	68,370	170,705	449,072
1993-94	1,100,490	197,141	223,628	128,810	28,320	215,492	307,099	1,077,665	353,287	72,067	183,394	468,916
1994-95	1,169,505	203,451	237,268	137,931	31,406	228,771	330,677	1,149,863	378,273	77,109	196,703	497,779
1995-96	1,222,821	209,440	248,993	146,844	32,009	234,891	350,645	1,193,276	398,859	79,092	197,354	517,971
1996-97	1,289,232	218,877	261,418	159,042	33,820	244,847	371,228	1,249,984	418,416	82,062	203,779	545,727
1997-98	1,365,762	230,150	274,883	175,630	34,412	255,048	395,639	1,318,042	450,365	87,214	208,120	572,343
1998-99	1,434,464	240,107	290,993	189,309	33,922	270,628	409,505	1,402,369	483,259	91,038	218,957	607,134
1999-2000	1,541,322	249,178	309,290	211,661	36,059	291,950	443,186	1,506,797	521,612	101,336	237,336	646,512
2000-01	1,647,161	263,689	320,217	226,334	35,296	324,033	477,592	1,626,066	563,575	107,235	261,622	693,634
2001-02	1,684,879	279,191	324,123	202,832	28,152	360,546	490,035	1,736,866	594,694	115,295	285,464	741,413
2002-03	1,763,212	296,683	337,787	199,407	31,369	389,264	508,702	1,821,917	621,335	117,696	310,783	772,102

[1] Fiscal years not the same for all governments. See Note.
[2] Excludes revenues or expenditures of publicly owned utilities and liquor stores, and of insurance-trust activities. Intergovernmental receipts and payments between State and local governments are also excluded.
[3] Includes other taxes and charges and miscellaneous revenues.
[4] Includes expenditures for libraries, hospitals, health, employment security administration, veterans' services, air transportation, water transport and terminals, parking facilities, transit subsidies, police protection, fire protection, correction, protective inspection and regulation, sewerage, natural resources, parks and recreation, housing and community development, solid waste management, financial administration, judicial and legal, general public buildings, other government administration, interest on general debt, and general expenditures, n.e.c.
Note.—Except for States listed, data for fiscal years listed from 1962-63 to 2002-03 are the aggregation of data for government fiscal years that ended in the 12-month period from July 1 to June 30 of those years (Texas used August and Alabama and Michigan used September). Data for 1963 and earlier years include data for governments fiscal years ending during that particular calendar year.
Data prior to 1952 are not available for intervening years.
Source: Department of Commerce, Bureau of the Census.

End of year or month	Total Treasury securities outstanding [1]	Marketable							Nonmarketable				
		Total [2]	Treasury bills	Treasury notes	Treasury bonds	Treasury inflation-protected securities			Total	U.S. savings securities [3]	Foreign series [4]	Government account series	Other [5]
						Total	Notes	Bonds					
Fiscal year:													
1967	322.3	[6] 210.7	58.5	49.1	97.4				111.6	51.2	1.5	56.2	2.7
1968	344.4	226.6	64.4	71.1	91.1				117.8	51.7	3.7	59.5	2.8
1969	351.7	226.1	68.4	78.9	78.8				125.6	51.7	4.1	66.8	3.1
1970	369.0	232.6	76.2	93.5	63.0				136.4	51.3	4.8	76.3	4.1
1971	396.3	245.5	86.7	104.8	54.0				150.8	53.0	9.3	82.8	5.8
1972	425.4	257.2	94.6	113.4	49.1				168.2	55.9	19.0	89.6	3.7
1973	456.4	263.0	100.1	117.8	45.1				193.4	59.4	28.5	101.7	3.7
1974	473.2	266.6	105.0	128.4	33.1				206.7	61.9	25.0	115.4	4.3
1975	532.1	315.6	128.6	150.3	36.8				216.5	65.5	23.2	124.2	3.6
1976	619.3	392.6	161.2	191.8	39.6				226.7	69.7	21.5	130.6	4.9
1977	697.6	443.5	156.1	241.7	45.7				254.1	75.4	21.8	140.1	16.8
1978	767.0	485.2	160.9	267.9	56.4				281.8	79.8	21.7	153.3	27.1
1979	819.0	506.7	161.4	274.2	71.1				312.3	80.4	28.1	176.4	27.4
1980	906.4	594.5	199.8	310.9	83.8				311.9	72.7	25.2	189.8	24.2
1981	996.5	683.2	223.4	363.6	96.2				313.3	68.0	20.5	201.1	23.7
1982	1,140.9	824.4	277.9	442.9	103.6				316.5	67.3	14.6	210.5	24.1
1983	1,375.8	1,024.0	340.7	557.5	125.7				351.8	70.0	11.5	234.7	35.6
1984	1,559.6	1,176.6	356.8	661.7	158.1				383.0	72.8	8.8	259.5	41.8
1985	1,821.0	1,360.2	384.2	776.4	199.5				460.8	77.0	6.6	313.9	63.3
1986	2,122.7	[2] 1,564.3	410.7	896.9	241.7				558.4	85.6	4.1	365.9	102.8
1987	2,347.8	[2] 1,676.0	378.3	1,005.1	277.6				671.8	97.0	4.4	440.7	129.8
1988	2,599.9	[2] 1,802.9	398.5	1,089.6	299.9				797.0	106.2	6.3	536.5	148.0
1989	2,836.3	[2] 1,892.8	406.6	1,133.2	338.0				943.5	114.0	6.8	663.7	159.0
1990	3,210.9	[2] 2,092.8	482.5	1,218.1	377.2				1,118.2	122.2	36.0	779.4	180.6
1991	3,662.8	[2] 2,390.7	564.6	1,387.7	423.4				1,272.1	133.5	41.6	908.4	188.5
1992	4,061.8	[2] 2,677.5	634.3	1,566.3	461.8				1,384.3	148.3	37.0	1,011.0	188.0
1993	4,408.6	[2] 2,904.9	658.4	1,734.2	497.4				1,503.7	167.0	42.5	1,114.3	179.9
1994	4,689.5	[2] 3,091.6	697.3	1,867.5	511.8				1,597.9	176.4	42.0	1,211.7	167.8
1995	4,950.6	[2] 3,260.4	742.5	1,980.3	522.6				1,690.2	181.2	41.0	1,324.3	143.8
1996	5,220.8	[2] 3,418.4	761.2	2,098.7	543.5				1,802.4	184.1	37.5	1,454.7	126.1
1997	5,407.5	[2] 3,439.6	701.9	2,122.2	576.2	24.4	24.4		1,967.9	182.7	34.9	1,608.5	141.9
1998	5,518.7	[2] 3,331.0	637.6	2,009.1	610.4	58.8	41.9	17.0	2,187.7	180.8	35.1	1,777.3	194.4
1999	5,647.2	[2] 3,233.0	653.2	1,828.8	643.7	92.4	67.6	24.8	2,414.2	180.0	31.0	2,005.2	198.1
2000	5,622.1	[2] 2,992.8	616.2	1,611.3	635.3	115.0	81.6	33.4	2,629.3	177.7	25.4	2,242.9	183.3
2001	5,807.5	[2] 2,930.7	734.9	1,433.0	613.0	134.9	95.1	39.7	2,876.7	186.5	18.3	2,492.1	179.9
2002	6,228.2	[2] 3,136.7	868.3	1,521.6	593.0	138.9	93.7	45.1	3,091.5	193.3	12.5	2,707.3	178.4
2003	6,783.2	3,460.7	918.2	1,799.5	576.9	166.1	120.0	46.1	3,322.5	201.6	11.0	2,912.2	197.7
2004	7,379.1	3,846.1	961.5	2,109.6	552.0	223.0			3,533.0	204.2	5.9	3,130.0	192.9
2005	7,932.7	[2] 4,084.9	914.3	2,328.8	520.7	307.1			3,847.8	203.6	3.1	3,380.6	260.5
2004: Jan	7,009.2	3,581.8	907.9	1,921.8	564.4	187.7	141.5	46.2	3,427.4	204.3	5.9	3,016.8	200.5
Feb	7,091.9	3,662.9	958.2	1,952.7	564.4	187.5	141.3	46.2	3,429.1	204.5	6.7	3,019.7	198.2
Mar	7,131.1	3,721.2	985.0	1,983.5	564.4	188.4	142.0	46.4	3,409.9	204.5	6.7	3,008.6	190.0
Apr	7,133.8	3,697.4	933.4	2,001.1	564.4	198.5	151.8	46.7	3,436.4	204.5	6.7	3,029.0	196.1
May	7,196.4	3,744.6	958.1	2,030.7	556.1	199.7	152.8	47.0	3,451.8	204.7	6.4	3,045.2	195.5
June	7,274.3	3,755.5	946.8	2,052.3	556.1	200.4			3,518.8	204.6	6.4	3,111.7	196.0
July	7,316.6	3,808.5	962.5	2,067.3	556.1	222.6			3,508.1	204.6	6.4	3,105.7	191.4
Aug	7,351.0	3,840.7	976.8	2,088.6	552.1	223.3			3,510.2	204.2	5.9	3,110.6	189.5
Sept	7,379.1	3,846.1	961.5	2,109.6	552.0	223.0			3,533.0	204.2	5.9	3,130.0	192.9
Oct	7,429.7	3,902.7	981.9	2,124.6	552.0	244.2			3,526.9	204.3	5.9	3,121.6	195.2
Nov	7,525.2	[2] 3,963.6	1,030.8	2,134.4	539.6	244.7			3,561.6	204.4	5.9	3,158.9	192.4
Dec	7,596.1	[2] 3,959.8	1,003.2	2,157.1	539.5	245.9			3,636.4	204.5	5.9	3,230.6	195.5
2005: Jan	7,627.7	[2] 3,975.0	986.8	2,167.3	539.5	267.3			3,652.8	204.4	6.2	3,243.6	198.5
Feb	7,713.1	[2] 4,054.3	1,030.9	2,205.9	537.2	266.3			3,658.8	204.5	6.2	3,249.4	198.8
Mar	7,776.9	[2] 4,103.8	1,059.1	2,226.7	537.2	266.8			3,673.1	204.2	6.1	3,248.9	213.9
Apr	7,764.5	[2] 4,070.7	991.3	2,241.7	537.2	286.5			3,693.9	204.2	6.0	3,259.6	224.0
May	7,777.9	[2] 4,050.2	961.3	2,256.1	530.1	288.7			3,727.7	204.3	5.9	3,282.2	235.4
June	7,836.5	[2] 4,031.1	923.4	2,273.1	530.0	290.7			3,805.4	204.2	3.0	3,356.3	241.9
July	7,887.6	[2] 4,077.9	942.2	2,286.1	530.0	305.6			3,809.7	204.1	3.0	3,354.4	248.2
Aug	7,926.9	[2] 4,106.5	953.3	2,312.7	520.7	305.8			3,820.5	203.8	3.0	3,360.9	252.8
Sept	7,932.7	[2] 4,084.9	914.3	2,328.8	520.7	307.1			3,847.8	203.6	3.1	3,380.6	260.5
Oct	8,027.1	[2] 4,131.3	936.6	2,336.0	520.7	324.0			3,895.8	203.9	3.1	3,426.7	262.1
Nov	8,092.3	[2] 4,185.3	986.9	2,339.8	516.6	327.9			3,907.1	204.6	3.0	3,432.8	266.7
Dec	8,170.4	[2] 4,184.0	963.9	2,360.8	516.6	328.7			3,986.5	205.2	3.8	3,506.6	270.9

[1] Data beginning January 2001 are interest-bearing and noninterest-bearing securities; prior data are interest-bearing securities only.

[2] Includes Federal Financing Bank securities, not shown separately.

[3] Through 1996, series is U.S. savings bonds. Beginning 1997, includes U.S. retirement plan bonds, U.S. individual retirement bonds, and U.S. savings notes previously included in "other" nonmarketable securities.

[4] Nonmarketable certificates of indebtedness, notes, bonds, and bills in the Treasury foreign series of dollar-denominated and foreign-currency denominated issues.

[5] Includes depository bonds, retirement plan bonds, Rural Electrification Administration bonds, State and local bonds, special issues held only by U.S. Government agencies and trust funds and the Federal home loan banks and for the period July 2003 through February 2004, depositary compensation securities.

[6] Includes $5,610 million in certificates not shown separately.

Note.—Through fiscal year 1976, the fiscal year was on a July 1-June 30 basis; beginning October 1976 (fiscal year 1977), the fiscal year is on an October 1-September 30 basis.

Source: Department of the Treasury.

TABLE B–88.—*Maturity distribution and average length of marketable interest-bearing public debt securities held by private investors, 1967–2005*

End of year or month	Amount outstanding, privately held	Maturity class					Average length [1]	
		Within 1 year	1 to 5 years	5 to 10 years	10 to 20 years	20 years and over		
		Millions of dollars					Years	Months
Fiscal year:								
1967	150,321	56,561	53,584	21,057	6,153	12,968	5	1
1968	159,671	66,746	52,295	21,850	6,110	12,670	4	5
1969	156,008	69,311	50,182	18,078	6,097	12,337	4	2
1970	157,910	76,443	57,035	8,286	7,876	8,272	3	8
1971	161,863	74,803	58,557	14,503	6,357	7,645	3	6
1972	165,978	79,509	57,157	16,033	6,358	6,922	3	3
1973	167,869	84,041	54,139	16,385	8,741	4,564	3	1
1974	164,862	87,150	50,103	14,197	9,930	3,481	2	11
1975	210,382	115,677	65,852	15,385	8,857	4,611	2	8
1976	279,782	150,296	90,578	24,169	8,087	6,652	2	7
1977	326,674	161,329	113,319	33,067	8,428	10,531	2	11
1978	356,501	163,819	132,993	33,500	11,383	14,805	3	3
1979	380,530	181,883	127,574	32,279	18,489	20,304	3	7
1980	463,717	220,084	156,244	38,809	25,901	22,679	3	9
1981	549,863	256,187	182,237	48,743	32,569	30,127	4	0
1982	682,043	314,436	221,783	75,749	33,017	37,058	3	11
1983	862,631	379,579	294,955	99,174	40,826	48,097	4	1
1984	1,017,488	437,941	332,808	130,417	49,664	66,658	4	6
1985	1,185,675	472,661	402,766	159,383	62,853	88,012	4	11
1986	1,354,275	506,903	467,348	189,995	70,664	119,365	5	3
1987	1,445,366	483,582	526,746	209,160	72,862	153,016	5	9
1988	1,555,208	524,201	552,993	232,453	74,186	171,375	5	9
1989	1,654,660	546,751	578,333	247,428	80,616	201,532	6	0
1990	1,841,903	626,297	630,144	267,573	82,713	235,176	6	1
1991	2,113,799	713,778	761,243	280,574	84,900	273,304	6	0
1992	2,363,802	808,705	866,329	295,921	84,706	308,141	5	11
1993	2,562,336	858,135	978,714	306,663	94,345	324,479	5	10
1994	2,719,861	877,932	1,128,322	289,998	88,208	335,401	5	8
1995	2,870,781	1,002,875	1,157,492	290,111	87,297	333,006	5	4
1996	3,011,185	1,058,558	1,212,258	306,643	111,360	322,366	5	3
1997	2,998,846	1,017,913	1,206,993	321,622	154,205	298,113	5	5
1998	2,856,637	940,572	1,105,175	319,331	157,347	334,212	5	10
1999	2,728,011	915,145	962,644	378,163	149,703	322,356	6	0
2000	2,469,152	858,903	791,540	355,382	167,082	296,246	6	2
2001	2,328,302	900,178	650,522	329,247	174,653	273,702	6	1
2002	2,492,821	939,986	802,032	311,176	203,816	235,811	5	6
2003	2,804,092	1,057,049	955,239	351,552	243,755	196,497	5	1
2004	3,145,244	1,127,850	1,150,979	414,728	243,036	208,652	4	11
2005	3,334,411	1,100,783	1,279,646	499,386	281,229	173,367	4	10
2004: Jan	2,889,890	1,086,110	1,000,107	363,307	243,755	196,611	5	0
Feb	2,967,133	1,149,251	998,984	378,812	243,520	196,566	4	11
Mar	3,046,725	1,178,142	1,038,873	389,481	243,520	196,709	4	10
Apr	3,019,341	1,125,763	1,054,136	389,995	243,520	196,928	4	11
May	3,035,769	1,153,189	1,043,862	398,095	243,436	197,187	4	11
June	3,067,768	1,136,300	1,082,581	408,129	243,436	197,323	4	11
July	3,088,164	1,147,439	1,070,294	418,436	243,436	208,560	4	11
Aug	3,145,333	1,148,585	1,137,991	406,590	243,436	208,731	4	11
Sept	3,145,244	1,127,850	1,150,979	414,728	243,036	208,652	4	11
Oct	3,166,311	1,143,145	1,137,251	434,604	242,636	208,675	4	10
Nov	3,233,704	1,177,963	1,159,725	444,697	250,625	200,694	4	10
Dec	3,225,653	1,149,591	1,170,576	453,993	250,625	200,868	4	10
2005: Jan	3,240,748	1,132,991	1,195,479	452,642	269,863	189,773	4	10
Feb	3,322,699	1,184,006	1,231,825	456,120	269,036	181,712	4	9
Mar	3,372,393	1,211,253	1,244,945	465,335	269,072	181,789	4	8
Apr	3,310,933	1,143,168	1,253,939	462,850	268,951	182,025	4	9
May	3,311,486	1,132,636	1,250,391	477,013	269,100	182,346	4	10
June	3,292,256	1,095,354	1,260,365	485,465	268,443	182,629	4	10
July	3,314,952	1,130,292	1,233,071	494,373	274,618	182,599	4	10
Aug	3,361,958	1,143,059	1,273,564	490,944	281,161	173,230	4	9
Sept	3,334,411	1,100,783	1,279,646	499,386	281,229	173,367	4	10
Oct	3,376,594	1,136,101	1,278,315	508,135	280,839	173,203	4	9
Nov	3,426,982	1,201,621	1,248,485	526,593	276,571	173,712	4	9
Dec	3,399,628	1,176,549	1,237,702	534,929	276,633	173,815	4	9

[1] In 2002, the average length calculation was revised to include Treasury inflation-protected securities.

Note.—Through fiscal year 1976, the fiscal year was on a July 1-June 30 basis; beginning October 1976 (fiscal year 1977), the fiscal year is on an October 1-September 30 basis.

Source: Department of the Treasury.

[Billions of dollars]

End of month	Total public debt [1]	Federal Reserve and Government ac- counts [2]	Held by private investors									
			Total privately held	De- posi- tory insti- tu- tions [3]	U.S. savings bonds [4]	Pension funds		Insur- ance compa- nies	Mutual funds [6]	State and local govern- ments	Foreign and inter- nation- al [7]	Other inves- tors [8]
						Pri- vate [5]	State and local govern- ments					
1994: Mar	4,575.9	1,476.0	3,099.9	397.4	175.0	120.1	224.3	233.4	212.8	443.4	661.1	632.3
June	4,645.8	1,547.5	3,098.3	383.8	177.1	129.4	220.6	238.0	204.6	425.2	659.9	659.7
Sept	4,692.8	1,562.8	3,130.0	364.0	178.6	136.4	217.4	243.7	201.6	398.2	682.0	708.1
Dec	4,800.2	1,622.6	3,177.6	339.6	179.9	140.1	215.6	240.1	209.4	370.0	667.3	815.6
1995: Mar	4,864.1	1,619.3	3,244.8	353.0	181.4	141.8	225.0	244.2	210.6	350.5	707.0	831.4
June	4,951.4	1,690.1	3,261.3	340.0	182.6	142.7	217.2	245.0	202.5	313.7	762.5	855.2
Sept	4,974.0	1,688.0	3,286.0	330.8	183.5	142.1	211.3	245.2	211.6	304.3	820.4	836.8
Dec	4,988.7	1,681.0	3,307.7	315.4	185.0	142.9	208.2	241.5	225.1	289.8	835.2	864.6
1996: Mar	5,117.8	1,731.1	3,386.7	322.1	185.8	144.5	213.5	239.4	240.9	283.6	908.1	848.7
June	5,161.1	1,806.7	3,354.4	318.7	186.5	144.8	221.1	229.5	230.6	283.3	929.7	810.3
Sept	5,224.8	1,831.6	3,393.2	310.9	186.8	141.5	213.4	226.8	226.8	263.7	993.4	829.9
Dec	5,323.2	1,892.0	3,431.2	296.6	187.0	140.2	212.8	214.1	227.4	257.0	1,102.1	794.0
1997: Mar	5,380.9	1,928.7	3,452.2	317.3	186.5	141.7	211.1	181.8	221.9	248.1	1,157.6	786.2
June	5,376.2	1,998.9	3,377.3	300.1	186.3	142.2	214.9	183.1	216.8	243.3	1,182.7	707.8
Sept	5,413.1	2,011.5	3,401.6	292.8	186.2	143.2	223.5	186.8	221.6	235.2	1,230.5	681.7
Dec	5,502.4	2,087.8	3,414.6	300.3	186.5	144.4	219.0	176.6	232.4	239.3	1,241.6	674.5
1998: Mar	5,542.4	2,104.9	3,437.5	308.3	186.2	136.9	212.1	169.4	234.7	238.1	1,250.5	701.2
June	5,547.9	2,198.6	3,349.3	290.9	186.0	129.9	213.2	160.6	230.7	258.5	1,256.0	623.4
Sept	5,526.2	2,213.0	3,313.2	244.4	186.0	121.5	207.8	151.3	231.8	271.8	1,224.2	674.3
Dec	5,614.2	2,280.2	3,334.0	237.4	186.6	113.6	212.6	141.7	253.5	280.8	1,278.7	629.2
1999: Mar	5,651.6	2,324.1	3,327.5	247.4	186.5	110.8	211.5	137.5	254.0	288.6	1,272.3	619.0
June	5,638.8	2,439.6	3,199.2	240.6	186.5	114.1	213.8	133.6	227.9	298.8	1,258.8	525.1
Sept	5,656.3	2,480.9	3,175.4	241.2	186.2	117.2	204.8	128.0	224.4	299.6	1,281.4	492.6
Dec	5,776.1	2,542.2	3,233.9	248.6	186.4	118.9	198.8	123.4	228.7	305.1	1,268.7	555.3
2000: Mar	5,773.4	2,590.6	3,182.8	237.7	185.3	114.7	196.9	120.0	222.2	307.1	1,106.9	691.9
June	5,685.9	2,698.6	2,987.3	222.2	184.6	115.3	194.9	116.5	204.5	310.1	1,082.0	557.2
Sept	5,674.2	2,737.9	2,936.3	220.5	184.3	115.2	185.5	113.7	205.7	308.7	1,057.9	544.8
Dec	5,662.2	2,781.8	2,880.4	201.5	184.8	113.7	179.1	110.2	221.8	310.9	1,034.2	524.3
2001: Mar	5,773.7	2,880.9	2,892.8	188.0	184.8	115.6	177.3	109.1	221.8	317.9	1,029.9	548.4
June	5,726.8	3,004.2	2,722.6	188.1	185.5	116.3	183.1	108.1	218.7	325.7	1,000.5	396.8
Sept	5,807.5	3,027.8	2,779.7	189.1	186.4	119.7	166.8	106.8	232.5	321.9	1,005.5	450.9
Dec	5,943.4	3,123.9	2,819.5	181.5	190.3	121.1	155.1	105.7	259.4	329.3	1,051.2	426.1
2002: Mar	6,006.0	3,156.8	2,849.2	187.6	191.9	123.7	163.3	114.0	266.0	328.7	1,067.1	407.0
June	6,126.5	3,276.7	2,849.8	204.6	192.7	125.6	153.9	122.0	253.8	334.4	1,135.4	327.4
Sept	6,228.2	3,303.5	2,924.8	210.4	193.3	131.2	156.3	130.4	256.6	339.3	1,200.8	306.5
Dec	6,405.7	3,387.2	3,018.5	222.8	194.9	135.0	158.9	139.7	280.9	355.6	1,246.8	283.9
2003: Mar	6,460.8	3,390.8	3,069.9	153.1	196.9	139.0	162.1	139.5	296.5	350.7	1,286.3	345.8
June	6,670.1	3,505.4	3,164.7	145.4	199.1	138.2	161.3	138.7	302.8	348.7	1,382.8	347.6
Sept	6,783.2	3,515.3	3,268.0	146.9	201.5	139.9	162.7	137.4	287.8	357.9	1,454.2	379.6
Dec	6,998.0	3,620.1	3,377.9	154.0	203.8	141.2	162.8	136.5	281.5	363.9	1,533.0	401.1
2004: Mar	7,131.1	3,628.3	3,502.8	165.0	204.5	143.3	164.9	141.0	281.6	373.7	1,677.1	351.6
June	7,274.3	3,742.8	3,531.5	161.6	204.6	146.4	163.3	144.1	259.4	379.7	1,777.5	294.8
Sept	7,379.1	3,772.0	3,607.0	141.0	204.2	150.8	159.0	147.4	255.7	379.4	1,836.6	332.9
Dec	7,596.1	3,929.0	3,667.1	128.1	204.4	151.5	158.7	149.7	254.9	386.1	1,890.7	343.1
2005: Mar	7,776.9	3,921.6	3,855.4	142.9	204.2	153.8	158.6	153.4	262.3	407.1	1,983.5	389.7
June	7,836.5	4,033.5	3,803.0	127.9	204.2	157.6	159.3	154.6	249.1	430.6	2,016.2	303.5
Sept	7,932.7	4,067.8	3,864.9	....	203.6	.....	.....	.....	.....	.....	2,069.0	....

[1] Face value.

[2] Federal Reserve holdings exclude Treasury securities held under repurchase agreements.

[3] Includes commercial banks, savings institutions, and credit unions.

[4] Current accrual value.

[5] Includes Treasury securities held by the Federal Employees Retirement System Thrift Savings Plan "G Fund."

[6] Includes money market mutual funds, mutual funds, and closed-end investment companies.

[7] Includes nonmarketable foreign series Treasury securities and Treasury deposit funds. Excludes Treasury securities held under repurchase agreements in custody accounts at the Federal Reserve Bank of New York.

Estimates reflect benchmarks to this series at differing intervals.

[8] Includes individuals, Government-sponsored enterprises, brokers and dealers, bank personal trusts and estates, corporate and noncorporate businesses, and other investors.

Note.—Data shown in this table are as of December 2005.

Source: Department of the Treasury.

CORPORATE PROFITS AND FINANCE

TABLE B–90.—*Corporate profits with inventory valuation and capital consumption adjustments, 1959–2005*

[Billions of dollars; quarterly data at seasonally adjusted annual rates]

Year or quarter	Corporate profits with inventory valuation and capital consumption adjustments	Taxes on corporate income	Corporate profits after tax with inventory valuation and capital consumption adjustments		
			Total	Net dividends	Undistributed profits with inventory valuation and capital consumption adjustments
1959	55.7	23.7	32.0	12.6	19.4
1960	53.8	22.8	31.0	13.4	17.6
1961	54.9	22.9	32.0	13.9	18.1
1962	63.3	24.1	39.2	15.0	24.1
1963	69.0	26.4	42.6	16.2	26.4
1964	76.5	28.2	48.3	18.2	30.1
1965	87.5	31.1	56.4	20.2	36.2
1966	93.2	33.9	59.3	20.7	38.7
1967	91.3	32.9	58.4	21.5	36.9
1968	98.8	39.6	59.2	23.5	35.6
1969	95.4	40.0	55.4	24.2	31.2
1970	83.6	34.8	48.9	24.3	24.6
1971	98.0	38.2	59.9	25.0	34.8
1972	112.1	42.3	69.7	26.8	42.9
1973	125.5	50.0	75.5	29.9	45.6
1974	115.8	52.8	63.0	33.2	29.8
1975	134.8	51.6	83.2	33.0	50.2
1976	163.3	65.3	98.1	39.0	59.0
1977	192.4	74.4	118.0	44.8	73.2
1978	216.6	84.9	131.8	50.8	81.0
1979	223.2	90.0	133.2	57.5	75.7
1980	201.1	87.2	113.9	64.1	49.9
1981	226.1	84.3	141.8	73.8	68.0
1982	209.7	66.5	143.2	77.7	65.4
1983	264.2	80.6	183.6	83.5	100.1
1984	318.6	97.5	221.1	90.8	130.3
1985	330.3	99.4	230.9	97.6	133.4
1986	319.5	109.7	209.8	106.2	103.7
1987	368.8	130.4	238.4	112.3	126.1
1988	432.6	141.6	291.0	129.9	161.1
1989	426.6	146.1	280.5	158.0	122.6
1990	437.8	145.4	292.4	169.1	123.3
1991	451.2	138.6	312.6	180.7	131.9
1992	479.3	148.7	330.6	187.9	142.7
1993	541.9	171.0	370.9	202.8	168.1
1994	600.3	193.7	406.5	234.7	171.8
1995	696.7	218.7	478.0	254.2	223.8
1996	786.2	231.7	554.5	297.6	256.9
1997	868.5	246.1	622.4	334.5	287.9
1998	801.6	248.3	553.3	351.6	201.7
1999	851.3	258.6	592.6	337.4	255.3
2000	817.9	265.2	552.7	377.9	174.8
2001	767.3	204.1	563.2	370.9	192.3
2002	886.3	192.6	693.7	399.2	294.5
2003	1,031.8	232.1	799.7	423.2	376.5
2004	1,161.5	271.1	890.3	493.0	397.3
2005 ᵖ	....	....	....	514.2	....
2002: I	829.4	174.9	654.5	382.5	272.0
II	864.3	188.5	675.8	396.1	279.7
III	895.4	196.9	698.5	406.1	292.4
IV	956.1	210.2	746.0	412.0	334.0
2003: I	951.5	223.9	727.6	416.3	311.3
II	1,005.0	221.7	783.3	419.9	363.4
III	1,057.5	235.3	822.2	424.6	397.7
IV	1,113.1	247.5	865.6	432.0	433.6
2004: I	1,147.3	257.9	889.4	445.9	443.5
II	1,162.0	274.7	887.3	460.9	426.4
III	1,117.2	259.0	858.2	475.9	382.3
IV	1,219.5	293.0	926.4	589.3	337.2
2005: I	1,288.2	362.6	925.6	494.9	430.7
II	1,347.5	372.5	975.0	506.3	468.7
III	1,293.1	360.3	932.8	520.1	412.6
IV ᵖ	....	....	....	535.4	....

Source: Department of Commerce, Bureau of Economic Analysis.

TABLE B–91.—*Corporate profits by industry, 1959–2005*

[Billions of dollars; quarterly data at seasonally adjusted annual rates]

Year or quarter	Total	Corporate profits with inventory valuation adjustment and without capital consumption adjustment											Rest of the world
		Domestic industries												
		Financial			Nonfinancial									
		Total	Fed-eral Re-serve banks	Other	Total	Manu-fac-tur-ing[1]	Trans-porta-tion[2]	Utili-ties	Whole-sale trade	Retail trade	In-for-ma-tion	Other	
SIC:[3]													
1959	53.5	50.8	7.6	0.7	6.9	43.2	26.5	7.1	....	2.9	3.3	....	3.4	2.7
1960	51.5	48.3	8.4	.9	7.5	39.9	23.8	7.5	....	2.5	2.8	....	3.3	3.1
1961	51.8	48.5	8.3	.8	7.6	40.2	23.4	7.9	....	2.5	3.0	....	3.4	3.3
1962	57.0	53.3	8.6	.9	7.7	44.7	26.3	8.5	....	2.8	3.4	....	3.6	3.8
1963	62.1	58.1	8.3	1.0	7.3	49.8	29.7	9.5	....	2.8	3.6	....	4.1	4.1
1964	68.6	64.1	8.8	1.1	7.6	55.4	32.6	10.2	....	3.4	4.5	....	4.7	4.5
1965	78.9	74.2	9.3	1.3	8.0	64.9	39.8	11.0	....	3.8	4.9	....	5.4	4.7
1966	84.6	80.1	10.7	1.7	9.1	69.3	42.6	12.0	....	4.0	4.9	....	5.9	4.5
1967	82.0	77.2	11.2	2.0	9.2	66.0	39.2	10.9	....	4.1	5.7	....	6.1	4.8
1968	88.8	83.2	12.8	2.5	10.3	70.4	41.9	11.0	....	4.6	6.4	....	6.6	5.6
1969	85.5	78.9	13.6	3.1	10.5	65.3	37.3	10.7	....	4.9	6.4	....	6.1	6.6
1970	74.4	67.3	15.4	3.5	11.9	52.0	27.5	8.3	....	4.4	6.0	....	5.8	7.1
1971	88.3	80.4	17.6	3.3	14.3	62.8	35.1	8.9	....	5.2	7.2	....	6.4	7.9
1972	101.2	91.7	19.1	3.3	15.8	72.6	41.9	9.5	....	6.9	7.4	....	7.0	9.5
1973	115.3	100.4	20.5	4.5	16.0	79.9	47.2	9.1	....	8.2	6.6	....	8.7	14.9
1974	109.5	92.1	20.2	5.7	14.5	71.9	41.4	7.6	....	11.5	2.3	....	9.1	17.5
1975	135.0	120.4	20.2	5.6	14.6	100.2	55.2	11.0	....	13.8	8.2	....	12.0	14.6
1976	165.6	149.0	25.0	5.9	19.1	124.1	71.3	15.3	....	12.9	10.5	....	14.0	16.5
1977	194.7	175.6	31.9	6.1	25.8	143.7	79.3	18.6	....	15.6	12.4	....	17.8	19.1
1978	222.4	199.6	39.5	7.6	31.9	160.0	90.5	21.8	....	15.6	12.3	....	19.8	22.9
1979	231.8	197.2	40.3	9.4	30.9	156.8	89.6	17.0	....	18.8	9.8	....	21.6	34.6
1980	211.4	175.9	34.0	11.8	22.2	141.9	78.3	18.4	....	17.2	6.2	....	21.8	35.5
1981	219.1	189.4	29.1	14.4	14.7	160.3	91.1	20.3	....	22.4	9.9	....	16.7	29.7
1982	191.0	158.5	26.0	15.2	10.8	132.4	67.1	23.1	....	19.6	13.4	....	9.2	32.6
1983	226.5	191.4	35.5	14.6	20.9	155.9	76.2	29.5	....	21.0	18.7	....	10.4	35.1
1984	264.6	228.1	34.4	16.4	18.0	193.7	91.8	40.1	....	29.5	21.1	....	11.1	36.6
1985	257.5	219.4	45.9	16.3	29.5	173.5	84.3	33.8	....	23.9	22.2	....	9.2	38.1
1986	253.0	213.5	56.8	15.5	41.2	156.8	57.9	35.8	....	24.1	23.5	....	15.5	39.5
1987	301.4	253.4	59.8	15.7	44.1	193.5	86.3	41.9	....	18.6	23.4	....	23.4	48.0
1988	363.9	306.9	68.7	17.6	51.1	238.2	121.2	48.4	....	20.1	20.3	....	28.3	57.0
1989	367.4	300.3	77.9	20.2	57.8	222.3	110.9	43.3	....	21.8	20.8	....	25.5	67.1
1990	396.6	320.5	94.4	21.4	73.0	226.1	113.1	44.2	....	19.2	20.7	....	29.0	76.1
1991	427.9	351.4	124.2	20.3	103.9	227.3	98.0	53.3	....	21.7	26.7	....	27.5	76.5
1992	458.3	385.2	129.8	17.8	111.9	255.4	99.5	58.4	....	25.1	32.6	....	39.7	73.1
1993	513.1	436.1	136.8	16.2	120.6	299.3	115.6	69.5	....	26.3	39.1	....	48.9	76.9
1994	564.6	487.6	119.9	18.1	101.8	367.7	147.0	83.2	....	30.9	46.2	....	60.4	77.1
1995	656.0	563.2	162.2	22.5	139.7	401.0	173.7	85.8	....	27.3	43.1	....	71.2	92.8
1996	736.1	634.2	172.6	22.1	150.5	461.6	188.8	91.3	....	39.8	51.9	....	89.7	101.9
1997	812.3	701.4	193.0	23.8	169.2	508.4	209.0	84.2	....	47.6	64.2	....	103.4	110.9
1998	738.5	635.5	195.4	25.2	140.7	469.6	173.5	78.9	....	52.3	73.4	....	91.5	103.0
1999	776.8	655.3	196.4	26.3	170.1	458.9	175.2	56.8	....	52.6	74.6	....	99.7	121.5
2000	759.3	613.6	203.8	30.8	173.0	409.8	166.3	43.8	....	56.9	70.1	....	72.8	145.7
NAICS:[3]														
1998	738.5	635.5	165.4	25.2	140.2	470.1	157.0	21.0	32.7	53.2	66.4	20.1	119.8	103.0
1999	776.8	655.3	194.3	26.3	168.0	461.1	150.6	16.1	33.1	55.5	65.2	10.5	130.1	121.5
2000	759.3	613.6	200.2	30.8	169.4	413.4	144.3	14.9	24.4	59.7	59.6	−17.6	128.2	145.7
2001	719.2	549.5	227.6	28.3	199.3	322.0	52.6	1.3	24.7	52.1	71.0	−25.6	145.9	169.7
2002	766.2	610.4	276.4	23.7	252.7	334.0	48.2	−.9	10.6	49.3	79.4	−8.5	155.8	155.8
2003	923.9	747.9	313.0	20.2	292.8	434.9	80.7	8.1	11.4	56.3	87.7	−1.9	192.4	176.0
2004	1,019.7	834.8	306.0	20.3	280.3	524.2	118.9	8.4	12.1	63.5	90.0	17.0	224.3	184.9
2003:I	858.0	703.5	304.8	22.0	282.8	398.7	70.9	4.6	12.3	48.6	81.4	−7.0	187.9	154.5
II	891.0	721.2	309.0	20.9	288.2	412.2	68.0	9.8	10.4	50.3	90.4	−4.3	187.7	169.8
III	944.0	769.2	320.4	19.5	300.9	448.9	79.2	8.9	10.7	62.1	90.3	4.9	192.6	174.7
IV	1,002.6	797.6	317.9	18.5	299.4	479.7	104.8	9.3	12.3	64.1	88.8	−1.1	201.5	205.0
2004:I	1,001.2	803.0	324.1	19.4	304.7	479.0	97.3	11.0	11.0	56.8	97.5	−6.5	211.8	198.2
II	1,016.5	839.7	316.1	19.3	296.8	523.6	107.3	15.0	11.7	61.3	92.9	20.3	215.1	176.9
III	981.3	795.5	242.8	20.2	222.7	552.7	116.2	6.1	11.4	69.1	81.9	33.0	235.0	185.9
IV	1,079.7	901.1	319.4	22.2	297.1	581.7	154.7	1.7	14.1	66.9	87.7	21.0	235.6	178.6
2005:I	1,339.2	1,145.7	377.2	23.1	354.2	768.5	170.2	22.9	23.7	81.4	104.6	46.7	318.9	193.5
II	1,393.3	1,196.1	349.5	26.2	323.2	846.6	204.7	27.9	26.4	98.1	109.1	53.5	326.9	197.2
III	1,365.1	1,142.0	278.7	27.0	251.7	863.3	218.6	32.9	19.7	95.4	116.9	50.2	329.6	223.1

[1] See Table B–92 for industrial detail.

[2] Data on SIC basis include transportation and utilities. On NAICS basis included transportation and warehousing. Utilities classified separately in NAICS (as shown beginning 1998).

[3] Industry data for SIC are based on the 1987 SIC for data beginning 1987 and on the 1972 SIC for earlier data shown. Data on NAICS basis are based on the 1997 NAICS.

Note.—Industry data on SIC (Standard Industrial Classification) basis and NAICS (North American Industry Classification System) basis are not necessarily the same and are not strictly comparable.

Source: Department of Commerce, Bureau of Economic Analysis.

TABLE B–92.—*Corporate profits of manufacturing industries, 1959–2005*

[Billions of dollars; quarterly data at seasonally adjusted annual rates]

Year or quarter	Total manufacturing	Corporate profits with inventory valuation adjustment and without capital consumption adjustment											
		Durable goods [2]							Nondurable goods [2]				
		Total [1]	Fabricated metal products	Machinery	Computer and electronic products	Electrical equipment, appliances, and components	Motor vehicles, bodies and trailers, and parts	Other	Total	Food and beverage and tobacco products	Chemical products	Petroleum and coal products	Other
SIC:[3]													
1959	26.5	13.7	1.1	2.2	....	1.7	3.0	3.5	12.9	2.5	3.5	2.6	4.3
1960	23.8	11.6	.8	1.8	....	1.3	3.0	2.7	12.2	2.2	3.1	2.6	4.2
1961	23.4	11.3	1.0	1.9	....	1.3	2.5	2.9	12.1	2.4	3.3	2.3	4.2
1962	26.3	14.1	1.2	2.4	....	1.5	4.0	3.4	12.3	2.4	3.2	2.2	4.4
1963	29.7	16.4	1.3	2.6	....	1.6	4.9	4.0	13.3	2.7	3.7	2.2	4.7
1964	32.6	18.1	1.5	3.3	....	1.7	4.6	4.4	14.5	2.7	4.1	2.4	5.3
1965	39.8	23.3	2.1	4.0	....	2.7	6.2	5.2	16.5	2.9	4.6	2.9	6.1
1966	42.6	24.1	2.4	4.6	....	3.0	5.2	5.2	18.6	3.3	4.9	3.4	6.9
1967	39.2	21.3	2.5	4.2	....	3.0	4.0	4.9	18.0	3.3	4.3	4.0	6.4
1968	41.9	22.5	2.3	4.2	....	2.9	5.5	5.6	19.4	3.2	5.3	3.8	7.1
1969	37.3	19.2	2.0	3.8	....	2.3	4.8	4.9	18.1	3.1	4.6	3.4	7.0
1970	27.5	10.5	1.1	3.1	....	1.3	1.3	2.9	17.0	3.2	3.9	3.7	6.1
1971	35.1	16.6	1.5	3.1	....	2.0	5.2	4.1	18.5	3.6	4.5	3.8	6.6
1972	41.9	22.7	2.2	4.5	....	2.9	6.0	5.6	19.2	3.0	5.3	3.3	7.6
1973	47.2	25.1	2.7	4.9	....	3.2	5.9	6.2	22.0	2.5	6.2	5.4	7.9
1974	41.4	15.3	1.8	3.3	....	.6	.7	4.0	26.1	2.6	5.3	10.9	7.3
1975	55.2	20.6	3.3	5.1	....	2.6	2.3	4.7	34.5	8.6	6.4	10.1	9.5
1976	71.3	31.4	3.9	6.9	....	3.8	7.4	7.3	39.9	7.1	8.2	13.5	11.1
1977	79.3	37.9	4.5	8.6	....	5.9	9.4	8.5	41.4	6.9	7.8	13.1	13.6
1978	90.5	45.4	5.0	10.7	....	6.7	9.0	10.5	45.1	6.2	8.3	15.8	14.8
1979	89.6	37.1	5.3	9.5	....	5.6	4.7	8.5	52.5	5.8	7.2	24.8	14.7
1980	78.3	18.9	4.4	8.0	....	5.2	−4.3	2.7	59.5	6.1	5.7	34.7	13.1
1981	91.1	19.5	4.5	9.0	....	5.2	.3	−2.6	71.6	9.2	8.0	40.0	14.5
1982	67.1	5.0	2.7	3.1	....	1.7	.0	2.1	62.1	7.3	5.1	34.7	15.0
1983	76.2	19.5	3.1	4.0	....	3.5	5.3	8.4	56.7	6.3	7.4	23.9	19.1
1984	91.8	39.3	4.7	6.0	....	5.1	9.2	14.6	52.6	6.8	8.2	17.6	20.1
1985	84.3	29.7	4.9	5.7	....	2.6	7.4	10.1	54.6	8.8	6.6	18.7	20.5
1986	57.9	26.3	5.2	.8	....	2.7	4.6	12.1	31.7	7.5	7.5	−4.7	21.3
1987	86.3	40.7	5.5	5.4	....	5.9	3.7	17.6	45.6	11.4	14.4	−1.5	21.3
1988	121.2	54.1	6.5	11.1	....	7.7	6.2	16.5	67.1	12.0	18.6	12.7	23.7
1989	110.9	51.2	6.4	12.2	....	9.3	2.7	14.2	59.7	11.1	18.2	6.5	23.9
1990	113.1	43.8	6.0	11.8	....	8.5	−1.9	15.9	69.2	14.3	16.8	16.4	21.7
1991	98.0	34.4	5.3	5.7	....	10.0	−5.4	17.3	63.6	18.1	16.2	7.3	22.0
1992	99.5	40.6	6.2	7.5	....	10.4	−1.0	17.4	59.0	18.2	16.0	−.9	25.6
1993	115.6	55.8	7.4	7.5	....	15.2	6.0	19.4	59.7	16.4	15.9	2.7	24.7
1994	147.0	74.4	11.1	9.1	....	22.8	7.8	21.3	72.6	19.9	23.2	1.2	28.3
1995	173.7	80.9	11.8	14.8	....	21.5	.0	25.8	92.8	27.1	27.9	7.1	30.6
1996	188.8	90.6	14.5	16.9	....	20.1	4.2	29.2	98.2	22.1	26.4	15.0	34.7
1997	209.0	103.1	17.0	16.7	....	25.3	4.8	33.0	105.9	24.6	32.3	17.3	31.7
1998	173.5	87.3	16.4	19.5	....	8.9	5.9	30.1	86.2	21.9	26.5	6.7	31.1
1999	175.2	78.8	16.2	12.4	....	5.3	7.3	35.3	96.4	28.1	25.2	4.3	38.9
2000	166.3	64.8	15.4	16.3	....	4.7	−1.5	28.8	101.5	25.7	16.0	29.1	30.7
NAICS:[3]													
1998	157.0	83.4	16.7	15.6	3.9	6.1	6.4	34.6	73.6	21.8	25.1	4.9	21.8
1999	150.6	72.3	16.5	12.4	−6.5	6.3	7.3	36.4	78.3	30.7	23.0	1.8	22.7
2000	144.3	60.0	15.5	8.2	4.0	5.6	−1.0	27.7	84.3	25.4	14.2	26.9	17.8
2001	52.6	−25.4	9.9	2.7	−48.5	1.9	−9.2	17.8	78.0	28.0	12.6	29.6	7.8
2002	48.2	−9.9	8.9	1.7	−35.3	−.1	−5.0	20.0	58.1	24.9	18.4	1.6	13.2
2003	80.7	−4.1	8.5	1.4	−16.1	1.9	−11.6	11.9	84.8	23.5	20.8	23.6	16.9
2004	118.9	34.8	10.3	1.0	−3.2	.3	−3.4	29.9	84.0	24.0	13.5	31.0	15.6
2003: I	70.9	−7.3	6.0	−1.1	−20.9	3.3	−2.3	7.6	78.3	20.2	20.3	24.6	13.2
II	68.0	−10.4	9.2	1.2	−18.0	2.6	−14.1	8.7	78.3	21.6	18.8	21.6	16.3
III	79.2	−8.7	8.4	3.0	−16.1	.9	−17.9	12.9	88.0	22.9	23.8	22.1	19.1
IV	104.8	10.1	10.5	2.4	−9.7	.8	−12.4	18.5	94.6	29.3	20.3	25.9	19.1
2004: I	97.3	11.2	9.3	1.8	−8.0	−4.7	−6.6	19.4	86.2	28.1	15.1	27.7	15.2
II	107.3	27.1	9.1	1.4	−5.8	2.0	−7.7	28.1	80.3	23.7	14.4	27.6	14.6
III	116.2	42.2	9.8	3.4	1.3	−3.0	−.7	31.4	73.9	23.4	16.3	19.5	14.7
IV	154.7	58.8	13.1	−2.6	−.2	6.8	1.3	40.5	95.9	20.5	8.4	49.2	17.8
2005: I	170.2	35.5	8.8	.9	.5	−1.3	−20.8	47.3	134.7	39.6	18.8	62.8	13.5
II	204.7	59.9	11.4	2.9	4.2	5.5	−15.7	51.6	144.8	37.7	20.5	66.3	20.3
III	218.6	62.0	15.7	7.6	6.7	8.6	−25.3	48.8	156.6	40.8	22.7	70.8	22.3

[1] For SIC data, includes primary metal industries, not shown separately.
[2] Industry groups shown in column headings reflect NAICS classification for data beginning 1998. For data on SIC basis, the industry groups would be, machinery—industrial machinery and equipment; electrical equipment, appliances, and components—electronic and other electric equipment; motor vehicles, bodies and trailers, and parts—motor vehicles and equipment; food and beverage and tobacco products—food and kindred products; and chemical products—chemicals and allied products.
[3] See footnote 3 and Note, Table B–91.

Source: Department of Commerce, Bureau of Economic Analysis.

TABLE B–93.—*Sales, profits, and stockholders' equity, all manufacturing corporations, 1965–2005*

[Billions of dollars]

Year or quarter	All manufacturing corporations				Durable goods industries				Nondurable goods industries			
	Sales (net)	Profits		Stock-holders' equity[2]	Sales (net)	Profits		Stock-holders' equity[2]	Sales (net)	Profits		Stock-holders' equity[2]
		Before income taxes[1]	After income taxes			Before income taxes[1]	After income taxes			Before income taxes[1]	After income taxes	
1965	492.2	46.5	27.5	211.7	257.0	26.2	14.5	105.4	235.2	20.3	13.0	106.3
1966	554.2	51.8	30.9	230.3	291.7	29.2	16.4	115.2	262.4	22.6	14.6	115.1
1967	575.4	47.8	29.0	247.6	300.6	25.7	14.6	125.0	274.8	22.0	14.4	122.6
1968	631.9	55.4	32.1	265.9	335.5	30.6	16.5	135.6	296.4	24.8	15.5	130.3
1969	694.6	58.1	33.2	289.9	366.5	31.5	16.9	147.6	328.1	26.6	16.4	142.3
1970	708.8	48.1	28.6	306.8	363.1	23.0	12.9	155.1	345.7	25.2	15.7	151.7
1971	751.1	52.9	31.0	320.8	381.8	26.5	14.5	160.4	369.3	26.5	16.5	160.5
1972	849.5	63.2	36.5	343.4	435.8	33.6	18.4	171.4	413.7	29.6	18.0	172.0
1973	1,017.2	81.4	48.1	374.1	527.3	43.6	24.8	188.7	489.9	37.8	23.3	185.4
1973: IV	275.1	21.4	13.0	386.4	140.1	10.8	6.3	194.7	135.0	10.6	6.7	191.7
New series:												
1973: IV	236.6	20.6	13.2	368.0	122.7	10.1	6.2	185.8	113.9	10.5	7.0	182.1
1974	1,060.6	92.1	58.7	395.0	529.0	41.1	24.7	196.0	531.6	51.0	34.1	199.0
1975	1,065.2	79.9	49.1	423.4	521.1	35.3	21.4	208.1	544.1	44.6	27.7	215.3
1976	1,203.2	104.9	64.5	462.7	589.6	50.7	30.8	224.3	613.7	54.3	33.7	238.4
1977	1,328.1	115.1	70.4	496.7	657.3	57.9	34.8	239.9	670.8	57.2	35.5	256.8
1978	1,496.4	132.5	81.1	540.5	760.7	69.6	41.8	262.6	735.7	62.9	39.3	277.9
1979	1,741.8	154.2	98.7	600.5	865.7	72.4	45.2	292.5	876.1	81.8	53.5	308.0
1980	1,912.8	145.8	92.6	668.1	889.1	57.4	35.6	317.7	1,023.7	88.4	56.9	350.4
1981	2,144.7	158.6	101.3	743.4	979.5	67.2	41.6	350.4	1,165.2	91.3	59.6	393.0
1982	2,039.4	108.2	70.9	770.2	913.1	34.7	21.7	355.5	1,126.4	73.6	49.3	414.7
1983	2,114.3	133.1	85.8	812.8	973.5	48.7	30.0	372.4	1,140.8	84.4	55.8	440.4
1984	2,335.0	165.6	107.6	864.2	1,107.6	75.5	48.9	395.6	1,227.5	90.0	58.8	468.5
1985	2,331.4	137.0	87.6	866.2	1,142.6	61.5	38.6	420.9	1,188.8	75.6	49.1	445.3
1986	2,220.9	129.3	83.1	874.7	1,125.5	52.1	32.6	436.3	1,095.4	77.2	50.5	438.4
1987	2,378.2	173.0	115.6	900.9	1,178.0	78.0	53.0	444.3	1,200.3	95.1	62.6	456.6
1988[3]	2,596.2	215.3	153.8	957.6	1,284.7	91.6	66.9	468.7	1,311.5	123.7	86.8	488.9
1989	2,745.1	187.6	135.1	999.0	1,356.6	75.1	55.5	501.3	1,388.5	112.6	79.6	497.7
1990	2,810.7	158.1	110.1	1,043.8	1,357.2	57.3	40.7	515.0	1,453.5	100.8	69.4	528.9
1991	2,761.1	98.7	66.4	1,064.1	1,304.0	13.9	7.2	506.8	1,457.1	84.8	59.3	557.4
1992[4]	2,890.2	31.4	22.1	1,034.7	1,389.8	–33.7	–24.0	473.9	1,500.4	65.1	46.0	560.8
1993	3,015.1	117.9	83.2	1,039.7	1,490.2	38.9	27.4	482.7	1,524.9	79.0	55.7	557.1
1994	3,255.8	243.5	174.9	1,110.1	1,657.6	121.0	87.1	533.3	1,598.2	122.5	87.8	576.8
1995	3,528.3	274.5	198.2	1,240.6	1,807.7	130.6	94.3	613.7	1,720.6	143.9	103.9	627.0
1996	3,757.6	306.6	224.9	1,348.0	1,941.6	146.6	106.1	673.9	1,816.0	160.0	118.8	674.2
1997	3,920.0	331.4	244.5	1,462.7	2,075.8	167.0	121.4	743.4	1,844.2	164.4	123.1	719.3
1998	3,949.4	314.7	234.4	1,482.9	2,168.8	175.1	127.8	779.9	1,780.7	139.6	106.5	703.0
1999	4,148.9	355.3	257.8	1,569.3	2,314.2	198.8	140.3	869.6	1,834.6	156.5	117.5	699.7
2000	4,548.2	381.1	275.3	1,823.1	2,457.4	190.7	131.8	1,054.3	2,090.8	190.5	143.5	768.7
2000: IV	1,163.6	69.2	46.8	1,892.4	620.4	31.2	19.3	1,101.5	543.2	38.0	27.4	790.9
NAICS:[5]												
2000: IV	1,128.8	62.1	41.7	1,833.8	623.0	26.9	15.4	1,100.0	505.8	35.2	26.3	733.8
2001	4,295.0	83.2	36.2	1,843.0	2,321.2	–69.0	–76.1	1,080.5	1,973.8	152.2	112.3	762.5
2002	4,216.4	195.5	134.7	1,804.0	2,260.6	45.9	21.6	1,024.8	1,955.8	149.6	113.1	779.2
2003	4,397.2	305.7	237.0	1,952.2	2,282.7	117.6	88.2	1,040.8	2,114.5	188.1	148.9	911.5
2004	4,935.2	446.5	347.1	2,200.9	2,539.0	199.2	155.8	1,207.3	2,396.3	247.3	191.4	993.6
2003: I	1,072.0	77.2	58.2	1,842.3	548.3	21.8	14.6	991.0	523.7	55.4	43.6	851.3
II	1,096.9	77.1	57.8	1,937.8	572.9	29.9	21.8	1,019.7	524.0	47.2	36.0	918.0
III	1,109.4	70.4	52.6	1,956.1	569.7	29.0	22.0	1,032.5	539.8	41.4	30.6	923.5
IV	1,118.8	81.0	68.4	2,072.8	591.8	36.9	29.7	1,119.8	527.0	44.1	38.7	953.0
2004: I	1,145.9	97.3	75.3	2,113.0	593.6	44.2	34.3	1,157.4	552.3	53.1	41.0	955.6
II	1,248.7	122.3	94.6	2,177.1	644.6	57.7	45.8	1,197.8	604.1	64.6	48.8	979.4
III	1,251.0	117.7	89.8	2,220.9	638.9	49.8	37.2	1,216.9	612.0	67.9	52.6	1,004.1
IV	1,289.7	109.2	87.4	2,292.4	661.8	47.5	38.5	1,257.1	627.9	61.7	49.0	1,035.3
2005: I	1,269.0	116.0	89.8	2,315.3	641.4	44.9	34.1	1,260.7	627.7	71.0	55.7	1,054.6
II	1,376.5	136.6	105.9	2,366.8	690.7	61.9	47.2	1,286.2	685.8	74.6	58.7	1,080.6
III	1,409.4	136.3	103.6	2,411.5	686.1	54.6	41.2	1,303.4	723.3	81.8	62.4	1,108.1

[1] In the old series, "income taxes" refers to Federal income taxes only, as State and local income taxes had already been deducted. In the new series, no income taxes have been deducted.

[2] Annual data are average equity for the year (using four end-of-quarter figures).

[3] Beginning 1988, profits before and after income taxes reflect inclusion of minority stockholders' interest in net income before and after income taxes.

[4] Data for 1992 (most significantly 1992:I) reflect the early adoption of Financial Accounting Standards Board Statement 106 (Employer's Accounting for Post-Retirement Benefits Other Than Pensions) by a large number of companies during the fourth quarter of 1992. Data for 1993 (1993:I) also reflect adoption of Statement 106. Corporations must show the cumulative effect of a change in accounting principle in the first quarter of the year in which the change is adopted.

[5] Data based on the North American Industry Classification System (NAICS). Other data shown are based on the Standard Industrial Classification (SIC).

Note.—Data are not necessarily comparable from one period to another due to changes in accounting principles, industry classifications, sampling procedures, etc. For explanatory notes concerning compilation of the series, see "Quarterly Financial Report for Manufacturing, Mining, and Trade Corporations," Department of Commerce, Bureau of the Census.

Source: Department of Commerce, Bureau of the Census.

TABLE B–94.—*Relation of profits after taxes to stockholders' equity and to sales, all manufacturing corporations, 1955–2005*

Year or quarter	Ratio of profits after income taxes (annual rate) to stockholders' equity—percent [1]			Profits after income taxes per dollar of sales—cents		
	All manufacturing corporations	Durable goods industries	Nondurable goods industries	All manufacturing corporations	Durable goods industries	Nondurable goods industries
1955	12.6	13.8	11.4	5.4	5.7	5.1
1956	12.3	12.8	11.8	5.3	5.2	5.3
1957	10.9	11.3	10.6	4.8	4.8	4.9
1958	8.6	8.0	9.2	4.2	3.9	4.4
1959	10.4	10.4	10.4	4.8	4.8	4.9
1960	9.2	8.5	9.8	4.4	4.0	4.8
1961	8.9	8.1	9.6	4.3	3.9	4.7
1962	9.8	9.6	9.9	4.5	4.4	4.7
1963	10.3	10.1	10.4	4.7	4.5	4.9
1964	11.6	11.7	11.5	5.2	5.1	5.4
1965	13.0	13.8	12.2	5.6	5.7	5.5
1966	13.4	14.2	12.7	5.6	5.6	5.6
1967	11.7	11.7	11.8	5.0	4.8	5.3
1968	12.1	12.2	11.9	5.1	4.9	5.2
1969	11.5	11.4	11.5	4.8	4.6	5.0
1970	9.3	8.3	10.3	4.0	3.5	4.5
1971	9.7	9.0	10.3	4.1	3.8	4.5
1972	10.6	10.8	10.5	4.3	4.2	4.4
1973	12.8	13.1	12.6	4.7	4.7	4.8
1973: IV	13.4	12.9	14.0	4.7	4.5	5.0
New series:						
1973: IV	14.3	13.3	15.3	5.6	5.0	6.1
1974	14.9	12.6	17.1	5.5	4.7	6.4
1975	11.6	10.3	12.9	4.6	4.1	5.1
1976	13.9	13.7	14.2	5.4	5.2	5.5
1977	14.2	14.5	13.8	5.3	5.3	5.3
1978	15.0	16.0	14.2	5.4	5.5	5.3
1979	16.4	15.4	17.4	5.7	5.2	6.1
1980	13.9	11.2	16.3	4.8	4.0	5.6
1981	13.6	11.9	15.2	4.7	4.2	5.1
1982	9.2	6.1	11.9	3.5	2.4	4.4
1983	10.6	8.1	12.7	4.1	3.1	4.9
1984	12.5	12.4	12.5	4.6	4.4	4.8
1985	10.1	9.2	11.0	3.8	3.4	4.1
1986	9.5	7.5	11.5	3.7	2.9	4.6
1987	12.8	11.9	13.7	4.9	4.5	5.2
1988 [2]	16.1	14.3	17.8	5.9	5.2	6.6
1989	13.5	11.1	16.0	4.9	4.1	5.7
1990	10.6	7.9	13.1	3.9	3.0	4.8
1991	6.2	1.4	10.6	2.4	.5	4.1
1992 [3]	2.1	−5.1	8.2	.8	−1.7	3.1
1993	8.0	5.7	10.0	2.8	1.8	3.7
1994	15.8	16.3	15.2	5.4	5.3	5.5
1995	16.0	15.4	16.6	5.6	5.2	6.0
1996	16.7	15.7	17.6	6.0	5.5	6.5
1997	16.7	16.3	17.1	6.2	5.8	6.7
1998	15.8	16.4	15.2	5.9	5.9	6.0
1999	16.4	16.1	16.8	6.2	6.1	6.4
2000	15.1	12.5	18.7	6.1	5.4	6.9
2000: IV	9.9	7.0	13.9	4.0	3.1	5.1
NAICS: [4]						
2000: IV	9.1	5.6	14.3	3.7	2.5	5.2
2001	2.0	−7.0	14.7	.8	−3.3	5.7
2002	7.5	2.1	14.5	3.2	1.0	5.8
2003	12.1	8.5	16.3	5.4	3.9	7.0
2004	15.8	12.9	19.3	7.0	6.1	8.0
2003: I	12.6	5.9	20.5	5.4	2.7	8.3
II	11.9	8.6	15.7	5.3	3.8	6.9
III	10.8	8.5	13.3	4.7	3.9	5.7
IV	13.2	10.6	16.3	6.1	5.0	7.3
2004: I	14.2	11.8	17.2	6.6	5.8	7.4
II	17.4	15.3	19.9	7.6	7.1	8.1
III	16.2	12.2	21.0	7.2	5.8	8.6
IV	15.3	12.2	18.9	6.8	5.8	7.8
2005: I	15.5	10.8	21.1	7.1	5.3	8.9
II	17.9	14.7	21.7	7.7	6.8	8.6
III	17.2	12.6	22.5	7.3	6.0	8.6

[1] Annual ratios based on average equity for the year (using four end-of-quarter figures). Quarterly ratios based on equity at end of quarter.
[2] See footnote 3, Table B–93.
[3] See footnote 4, Table B–93.
[4] See footnote 5, Table B–93.
Note.—Based on data in millions of dollars.
See Note, Table B–93.
Source: Department of Commerce, Bureau of the Census.

TABLE B–95.—*Historical stock prices and yields, 1949–2003*

Year	Common stock prices [1]									Common stock yields (S&P) (percent) [5]	
	New York Stock Exchange indexes [2]						Dow Jones industrial average [2]	Standard & Poor's composite index (1941–43=10) [2]	Nasdaq composite index (Feb. 5, 1971=100) [2]	Dividend-price ratio [6]	Earnings-price ratio [7]
	Composite (Dec. 31, 2002= 5,000) [3]	December 31, 1965=50									
		Composite	Industrial	Transportation	Utility [4]	Finance					
1949	....	9.02	....	....	....	....	179.48	15.23	....	6.59	15.48
1950	....	10.87	....	....	....	....	216.31	18.40	....	6.57	13.99
1951	....	13.08	....	....	....	....	257.64	22.34	....	6.13	11.82
1952	....	13.81	....	....	....	....	270.76	24.50	....	5.80	9.47
1953	....	13.67	....	....	....	....	275.97	24.73	....	5.80	10.26
1954	....	16.19	....	....	....	....	333.94	29.69	....	4.95	8.57
1955	....	21.54	....	....	....	....	442.72	40.49	....	4.08	7.95
1956	....	24.40	....	....	....	....	493.01	46.62	....	4.09	7.55
1957	....	23.67	....	....	....	....	475.71	44.38	....	4.35	7.89
1958	....	24.56	....	....	....	....	491.66	46.24	....	3.97	6.23
1959	....	30.73	....	....	....	....	632.12	57.38	....	3.23	5.78
1960	....	30.01	....	....	....	....	618.04	55.85	....	3.47	5.90
1961	....	35.37	....	....	....	....	691.55	66.27	....	2.98	4.62
1962	....	33.49	....	....	....	....	639.76	62.38	....	3.37	5.82
1963	....	37.51	....	....	....	....	714.81	69.87	....	3.17	5.50
1964	....	43.76	....	....	....	....	834.05	81.37	....	3.01	5.32
1965	....	47.39	....	....	....	....	910.88	88.17	....	3.00	5.59
1966	487.92	46.15	46.18	50.26	90.81	44.45	873.60	85.26	....	3.40	6.63
1967	536.84	50.77	51.97	53.51	90.86	49.82	879.12	91.93	....	3.20	5.73
1968	585.47	55.37	58.00	50.58	88.38	65.85	906.00	98.70	....	3.07	5.67
1969	578.01	54.67	57.44	46.96	85.60	70.49	876.72	97.84	....	3.24	6.08
1970	483.39	45.72	48.03	32.14	74.47	60.00	753.19	83.22	....	3.83	6.45
1971	573.33	54.22	57.92	44.35	79.05	70.38	884.76	98.29	107.44	3.14	5.41
1972	637.52	60.29	65.73	50.17	76.95	78.35	950.71	109.20	128.52	2.84	5.50
1973	607.11	57.42	63.08	37.74	75.38	70.12	923.88	107.43	109.90	3.06	7.12
1974	463.54	43.84	48.08	31.89	59.58	49.67	759.37	82.85	76.29	4.47	11.59
1975	483.55	45.73	50.52	31.10	63.00	47.14	802.49	86.16	77.20	4.31	9.15
1976	575.85	54.46	60.44	39.57	73.94	52.94	974.92	102.01	89.90	3.77	8.90
1977	567.66	53.69	57.86	41.09	81.84	55.25	894.63	98.20	98.71	4.62	10.79
1978	567.81	53.70	58.23	43.50	78.44	56.65	820.23	96.02	117.53	5.28	12.03
1979	616.68	58.32	64.76	47.34	76.41	61.42	844.40	103.01	136.57	5.47	13.46
1980	720.15	68.10	78.70	60.61	74.69	64.25	891.41	118.78	168.61	5.26	12.66
1981	782.62	74.02	85.44	72.61	77.81	73.52	932.92	128.05	203.18	5.20	11.96
1982	728.84	68.93	78.18	60.41	79.49	71.99	884.36	119.71	188.97	5.81	11.60
1983	979.52	92.63	107.45	89.36	93.99	95.34	1,190.34	160.41	285.43	4.40	8.03
1984	977.33	92.46	108.01	85.63	92.89	89.28	1,178.48	160.46	248.88	4.64	10.02
1985	1,142.97	108.09	123.79	104.11	113.49	114.21	1,328.23	186.84	290.19	4.25	8.12
1986	1,438.02	136.00	155.85	119.87	142.72	147.20	1,792.76	236.34	366.96	3.49	6.09
1987	1,709.79	161.70	195.31	140.39	148.59	146.48	2,275.99	286.83	402.57	3.08	5.48
1988	1,585.14	149.91	180.95	134.12	143.53	127.26	2,060.82	265.79	374.43	3.64	8.01
1989	1,903.36	180.02	216.23	175.28	174.87	151.88	2,508.91	322.84	437.81	3.45	7.42
1990	1,939.47	183.46	225.78	158.62	181.20	133.26	2,678.94	334.59	409.17	3.61	6.47
1991	2,181.72	206.33	258.14	173.99	185.32	150.82	2,929.33	376.18	491.69	3.24	4.79
1992	2,421.51	229.01	284.62	201.09	198.91	179.26	3,284.29	415.74	599.26	2.99	4.22
1993	2,638.96	249.58	299.99	242.49	228.90	216.42	3,522.06	451.41	715.16	2.78	4.46
1994	2,687.02	254.12	315.25	247.29	209.06	209.73	3,793.77	460.42	751.65	2.82	5.83
1995	3,078.56	291.15	367.34	269.41	220.30	238.45	4,493.76	541.72	925.19	2.56	6.09
1996	3,787.20	358.17	453.98	327.33	249.77	303.89	5,742.89	670.50	1,164.96	2.19	5.24
1997	4,827.35	456.54	574.52	414.60	283.82	424.48	7,441.15	873.43	1,469.49	1.77	4.57
1998	5,818.26	550.26	681.57	468.69	378.12	516.35	8,625.52	1,085.50	1,794.91	1.49	3.46
1999	6,546.81	619.16	774.78	491.60	473.73	530.86	10,464.88	1,327.33	2,728.15	1.25	3.17
2000	6,805.89	643.66	810.63	413.60	477.65	553.13	10,734.90	1,427.22	3,783.67	1.15	3.63
2001	6,397.85	605.07	748.26	443.59	377.30	595.61	10,189.13	1,194.18	2,035.00	1.32	2.95
2002	5,578.89	527.62	657.37	431.10	260.85	555.27	9,226.43	993.94	1,539.73	1.61	2.92
2003	5,447.46	(3)	633.18	436.51	237.77	565.75	8,993.59	965.23	1,647.17	1.77	3.84

[1] Averages of daily closing prices.

[2] Includes stocks as follows: for NYSE, all stocks listed; for Dow Jones industrial average, 30 stocks; for S&P composite index, 500 stocks; and for Nasdaq composite index, over 5,000.

[3] The NYSE relaunched the composite index on January 9, 2003, incorporating new definitions, methodology, and base value. (The composite index based on December 31, 1965=50 was discontinued.) Subset indexes on financial, energy, and health care were released by the NYSE on January 8, 2004 (see Table B–96). NYSE indexes shown in this table for industrials, utilities, transportation, and finance were discontinued.

[4] Effective April 1993, the NYSE doubled the value of the utility index to facilitate trading of options and futures on the index. Annual indexes prior to 1993 reflect the doubling.

[5] Based on 500 stocks in the S&P composite index.

[6] Aggregate cash dividends (based on latest known annual rate) divided by aggregate market value based on Wednesday closing prices. Monthly data are averages of weekly figures; annual data are averages of monthly figures.

[7] Quarterly data are ratio of earnings (after taxes) for 4 quarters ending with particular quarter to price index for last day of that quarter. Annual data are averages of quarterly ratios.

Sources: New York Stock Exchange (NYSE), Dow Jones & Co., Inc., Standard & Poor's (S&P), and Nasdaq Stock Market.

TABLE B–96.—*Common stock prices and yields, 2000–2005*

Year or month	Common stock prices[1] New York Stock Exchange indexes[2][3] (December 31, 2002=5,000) Composite	Financial	Energy	Health Care	Dow Jones industrial average[2]	Standard & Poor's composite index (1941-43=10)[2]	Nasdaq composite index (Feb. 5, 1971=100)[2]	Common stock yields (S&P) (percent)[4] Dividend-price ratio[5]	Earnings-price ratio[6]
2000	6,805.89				10,734.90	1,427.22	3,783.67	1.15	3.63
2001	6,397.85				10,189.13	1,194.18	2,035.00	1.32	2.95
2002	5,578.89				9,226.43	993.94	1,539.73	1.61	2.92
2003	5,447.46	5,583.00	5,273.90	5,288.67	8,993.59	965.23	1,647.17	1.77	3.84
2004	6,612.62	6,822.18	6,952.36	5,924.80	10,317.39	1,130.65	1,986.53	1.72	4.89
2005	7,349.00	7,383.70	9,377.84	6,283.96	10,547.67	1,207.23	2,099.32	1.83	
2001: Jan	6,878.79				10,682.74	1,335.63	2,656.86	1.16	
Feb	6,852.31				10,774.57	1,305.75	2,449.57	1.22	
Mar	6,380.65				10,081.32	1,185.85	1,986.66	1.33	3.92
Apr	6,418.94				10,234.52	1,189.84	1,933.93	1.32	
May	6,814.16				11,004.96	1,270.37	2,181.13	1.23	
June	6,670.56				10,767.20	1,238.71	2,112.05	1.27	3.00
July	6,485.53				10,444.50	1,204.45	2,033.98	1.30	
Aug	6,391.99				10,314.68	1,178.51	1,929.71	1.34	
Sept	5,756.20				9,042.56	1,044.64	1,573.31	1.48	2.72
Oct	5,879.37				9,220.75	1,076.59	1,656.43	1.45	
Nov	6,083.09				9,721.82	1,129.68	1,870.06	1.38	
Dec	6,162.59				9,979.88	1,144.93	1,977.71	1.36	2.15
2002: Jan	6,151.15				9,923.80	1,140.21	1,976.77	1.38	
Feb	6,022.23				9,891.05	1,100.67	1,799.72	1.43	
Mar	6,352.08				10,500.95	1,153.79	1,863.05	1.37	2.15
Apr	6,212.88				10,165.18	1,112.03	1,758.80	1.42	
May	6,087.85				10,080.48	1,079.27	1,660.31	1.47	
June	5,755.89				9,492.44	1,014.05	1,505.49	1.58	2.70
July	5,139.94				8,616.52	903.59	1,346.09	1.76	
Aug	5,200.62				8,685.48	912.55	1,327.36	1.72	
Sept	4,980.65				8,160.78	867.81	1,251.07	1.80	3.68
Oct	4,862.70				8,048.12	854.63	1,241.91	1.86	
Nov	5,104.89				8,625.72	909.93	1,409.15	1.73	
Dec	5,075.76				8,526.66	899.18	1,387.15	1.77	3.14
2003: Jan	5,055.78	5,092.08	4,900.65	5,043.19	8,474.59	895.84	1,389.56	1.80	
Feb	4,738.56	4,723.86	4,802.42	4,788.19	7,916.18	837.62	1,313.26	1.95	
Mar	4,724.22	4,685.40	4,855.44	4,854.73	7,977.73	846.62	1,348.50	1.93	3.57
Apr	4,977.45	5,357.20	5,036.82	5,078.71	8,332.09	890.03	1,409.83	1.83	
May	5,269.96	5,357.20	5,190.65	5,316.27	8,623.41	935.96	1,524.18	1.75	
June	5,583.42	5,690.39	5,522.45	5,557.87	9,098.07	988.00	1,631.75	1.66	3.55
July	5,567.94	5,790.61	5,276.08	5,457.98	9,154.39	992.54	1,716.85	1.71	
Aug	5,580.87	5,776.36	5,368.25	5,263.19	9,284.78	989.53	1,724.82	1.78	
Sept	5,748.42	5,897.76	5,453.23	5,402.56	9,492.54	1,019.44	1,856.22	1.73	3.87
Oct	5,894.39	6,187.33	5,552.99	5,428.31	9,682.46	1,038.73	1,907.89	1.71	
Nov	5,989.42	6,282.53	5,474.84	5,521.85	9,762.20	1,049.90	1,939.25	1.69	
Dec	6,239.14	6,475.68	5,973.31	5,751.14	10,124.66	1,080.64	1,956.98	1.67	4.38
2004: Jan	6,569.76	6,827.35	6,323.29	6,000.57	10,540.05	1,132.52	2,098.00	1.62	
Feb	6,661.38	6,978.62	6,337.87	6,134.16	10,601.50	1,143.36	2,048.36	1.63	
Mar	6,574.75	6,914.60	6,455.53	5,908.76	10,323.73	1,123.98	1,979.48	1.68	4.62
Apr	6,600.77	6,792.05	6,638.65	6,028.53	10,418.40	1,133.08	2,021.32	1.68	
May	6,371.44	6,495.19	6,572.79	6,022.12	10,083.81	1,102.78	1,930.09	1.74	
June	6,548.06	6,683.10	6,780.86	6,063.65	10,364.90	1,132.76	2,000.98	1.70	4.92
July	6,443.45	6,569.52	6,971.57	5,823.34	10,152.09	1,105.85	1,912.42	1.77	
Aug	6,352.83	6,566.19	6,866.75	5,733.68	10,032.80	1,088.94	1,821.54	1.81	
Sept	6,551.90	6,773.95	7,270.08	5,890.05	10,204.67	1,117.66	1,884.73	1.78	5.18
Oct	6,608.98	6,792.44	7,593.71	5,668.02	10,001.60	1,118.07	1,938.25	1.79	
Nov	6,933.75	7,118.40	7,773.26	5,818.20	10,411.76	1,168.94	2,062.87	1.74	
Dec	7,134.42	7,354.73	7,843.99	6,006.46	10,673.38	1,199.21	2,149.53	1.72	4.83
2005: Jan	7,056.85	7,282.65	7,841.24	5,970.34	10,539.51	1,181.41	2,071.87	1.77	
Feb	7,241.89	7,377.10	8,646.71	6,052.78	10,723.82	1,199.63	2,065.74	1.76	
Mar	7,275.51	7,274.12	9,077.38	6,148.03	10,682.09	1,194.90	2,030.43	1.79	5.11
Apr	7,077.97	7,014.98	8,793.74	6,253.05	10,283.19	1,164.42	1,957.49	1.86	
May	7,094.02	7,092.20	8,513.39	6,432.30	10,377.18	1,178.28	2,005.22	1.86	
June	7,238.96	7,199.86	9,122.87	6,408.88	10,486.66	1,202.26	2,074.02	1.83	5.32
July	7,389.23	7,373.25	9,607.53	6,342.76	10,545.38	1,222.24	2,145.14	1.82	
Aug	7,482.93	7,374.01	10,034.26	6,383.81	10,554.27	1,224.27	2,157.85	1.82	
Sept	7,584.49	7,435.85	10,672.51	6,412.24	10,532.54	1,225.91	2,144.61	1.84	5.42
Oct	7,373.23	7,368.60	9,915.63	6,270.83	10,324.31	1,191.96	2,087.09	1.90	
Nov	7,585.75	7,800.01	9,998.62	6,297.57	10,695.25	1,237.37	2,202.84	1.85	
Dec	7,787.22	8,011.76	10,310.18	6,434.97	10,827.79	1,262.02	2,246.09	1.84	

[1] Averages of daily closing prices.
[2] Includes stocks as follows: for NYSE, all stocks listed (in 2005, about 2,800); for Dow Jones Industrial average, 30 stocks; for S&P composite index, 500 stocks; and for Nasdaq composite index, in 2005, over 3,100.
[3] The NYSE relaunched the composite index on January 9, 2003, incorporating new definitions, methodology, and base value. Subset indexes on financial, energy, and health care were released by the NYSE on January 8, 2004.
[4] Based on 500 stocks in the S&P composite index.
[5] Aggregate cash dividends (based on latest known annual rate) divided by aggregate market value based on Wednesday closing prices. Monthly data are averages of weekly figures, annual data are averages of monthly figures.
[6] Quarterly data are ratio of earnings (after taxes) for 4 quarters ending with particular quarter to price index for last day of that quarter. Annual data are averages of quarterly ratios.

Sources: New York Stock Exchange (NYSE), Dow Jones & Co., Inc., Standard & Poor's (S&P), and Nasdaq Stock Market.

TABLE B–97.—*Farm income, 1945–2005*

[Billions of dollars]

Year	Income of farm operators from farming							
	Gross farm income						Produc-tion expenses	Net farm income
	Total[1]	Cash marketing receipts			Value of inventory changes[3]	Direct Government payments[4]		
		Total	Livestock and products	Crops[2]				
1945	25.4	21.7	12.0	9.7	−0.4	0.7	13.1	12.3
1946	29.6	24.8	13.8	11.0	.0	.8	14.5	15.1
1947	32.4	29.6	16.5	13.1	−1.8	.3	17.0	15.4
1948	36.5	30.2	17.1	13.1	1.7	.3	18.8	17.7
1949	30.8	27.8	15.4	12.4	−.9	.2	18.0	12.8
1950	33.1	28.4	16.1	12.4	.8	.3	19.5	13.6
1951	38.3	32.8	19.6	13.2	1.2	.3	22.3	15.9
1952	37.7	32.5	18.2	14.3	.9	.3	22.8	14.9
1953	34.4	31.0	16.9	14.1	−.6	.2	21.5	13.0
1954	34.2	29.8	16.3	13.6	.5	.3	21.8	12.4
1955	33.4	29.5	16.0	13.5	.2	.2	22.2	11.3
1956	33.9	30.4	16.4	14.0	−.5	.6	22.7	11.2
1957	34.8	29.7	17.4	12.3	.6	1.0	23.7	11.1
1958	39.0	33.5	19.2	14.2	.8	1.1	25.8	13.2
1959	37.9	33.6	18.9	14.7	.0	.7	27.2	10.7
1960	38.6	34.0	19.0	15.0	.4	.7	27.4	11.2
1961	40.5	35.2	19.5	15.7	.3	1.5	28.6	12.0
1962	42.3	36.5	20.2	16.3	.6	1.7	30.3	12.1
1963	43.4	37.5	20.0	17.4	.6	1.7	31.6	11.8
1964	42.3	37.3	19.9	17.4	−.8	2.2	31.8	10.5
1965	46.5	39.4	21.9	17.5	1.0	2.5	33.6	12.9
1966	50.5	43.4	25.0	18.4	−.1	3.3	36.5	14.0
1967	50.5	42.8	24.4	18.4	.7	3.1	38.2	12.3
1968	51.8	44.2	25.5	18.7	.1	3.5	39.5	12.3
1969	56.4	48.2	28.6	19.6	.1	3.8	42.1	14.3
1970	58.8	50.5	29.5	21.0	.0	3.7	44.5	14.4
1971	62.1	52.7	30.5	22.3	1.4	3.1	47.1	15.0
1972	71.1	61.1	35.6	25.5	.9	4.0	51.7	19.5
1973	98.9	86.9	45.8	41.1	3.4	2.6	64.6	34.4
1974	98.2	92.4	41.3	51.1	−1.6	.5	71.0	27.3
1975	100.6	88.9	43.1	45.8	3.4	.8	75.0	25.5
1976	102.9	95.4	46.3	49.0	−1.5	.7	82.7	20.2
1977	108.8	96.2	47.6	48.6	1.1	1.8	88.9	19.9
1978	128.4	112.4	59.2	53.2	1.9	3.0	103.2	25.2
1979	150.7	131.5	69.2	62.3	5.0	1.4	123.3	27.4
1980	149.3	139.7	68.0	71.7	−6.3	1.3	133.1	16.1
1981	166.3	141.6	69.2	72.5	6.5	1.9	139.4	26.9
1982	164.1	142.6	70.3	72.3	−1.4	3.5	140.3	23.8
1983	153.9	136.8	69.6	67.2	−10.9	9.3	139.6	14.3
1984	168.0	142.8	72.9	69.9	6.0	8.4	142.0	26.0
1985	161.1	144.0	70.1	73.9	−2.3	7.7	132.6	28.5
1986	156.1	135.4	71.6	63.8	−2.2	11.8	125.0	31.1
1987	168.4	141.8	76.0	65.8	−2.3	16.7	130.4	38.0
1988	177.9	151.3	79.6	71.6	−4.1	14.5	138.3	39.6
1989	191.6	160.5	83.6	76.9	3.8	10.9	145.1	46.5
1990	197.8	169.3	89.1	80.2	3.3	9.3	151.5	46.3
1991	192.0	168.0	85.8	82.2	−.2	8.2	151.8	40.2
1992	201.1	172.0	85.8	86.3	4.2	9.2	150.4	50.7
1993	205.0	178.3	90.5	87.8	−4.2	13.4	158.3	46.7
1994	216.1	181.4	88.3	93.1	8.3	7.9	163.5	52.6
1995	210.9	188.2	87.2	101.0	−5.0	7.3	171.1	39.8
1996	235.8	199.4	92.9	106.5	7.9	7.3	176.9	59.0
1997	238.0	207.8	96.5	111.3	.6	7.5	186.7	51.3
1998	232.6	196.5	94.2	102.2	−.6	12.4	185.5	47.1
1999	235.0	187.8	95.7	92.1	−.2	21.5	187.2	47.7
2000	242.0	192.1	99.6	92.5	1.6	22.9	193.1	48.9
2001	248.7	200.1	106.7	93.3	1.1	20.7	197.1	51.5
2002	229.9	195.0	94.0	101.0	−3.4	11.2	193.4	36.6
2003	259.8	216.6	105.6	111.0	−2.5	17.2	200.3	59.5
2004	292.3	241.2	123.5	117.8	7.0	13.3	209.8	82.5
2005 *p*	293.4	239.6	123.7	115.9	−1.3	22.7	221.9	71.5

[1] Cash marketing receipts, Government payments, value of changes in inventories, other farm related cash income, and nonmoney income produced by farms including imputed rent of operator residences.
[2] Crop receipts include proceeds received from commodities placed under Commodity Credit Corporation loans.
[3] Physical changes in beginning and ending year inventories of crop and livestock commodities valued at weighted average market prices during the year.
[4] Includes only Government payments made directly to farmers.

Note.—Data for 2005 are forecasts.

Source: Department of Agriculture, Economic Research Service.

[Billions of dollars]

| End of year | Total assets | Physical assets | | | | | Financial assets | | | Claims | | | |
| | | Real estate | Livestock and poultry[1] | Machinery and motor vehicles | Crops[2] | Purchased inputs[3] | Total[4] | Investments in cooperatives | Other[4] | Total claims | Real estate debt[5] | Nonreal estate debt[6] | Proprietors' equity |
			Nonreal estate										
1950	121.6	75.4	17.1	12.3	7.1		9.7	2.7	7.0	121.6	5.2	5.7	110.7
1951	136.0	83.8	19.5	14.3	8.2		10.2	2.9	7.3	136.0	5.7	6.9	123.4
1952	133.1	85.1	14.8	15.0	7.9		10.3	3.2	7.1	133.1	6.2	7.1	119.8
1953	128.7	84.3	11.7	15.6	6.8		10.3	3.3	7.0	128.7	6.6	6.3	115.8
1954	132.6	87.8	11.2	15.7	7.5		10.4	3.5	6.9	132.6	7.1	6.7	118.8
1955	137.0	93.0	10.6	16.3	6.5		10.6	3.7	6.9	137.0	7.8	7.3	121.9
1956	145.7	100.3	11.0	16.9	6.8		10.7	4.0	6.7	145.7	8.5	7.4	129.8
1957	154.5	106.4	13.9	17.0	6.4		10.8	4.2	6.6	154.5	9.0	8.2	137.3
1958	168.7	114.6	17.7	18.1	6.9		11.4	4.5	6.9	168.7	9.7	9.4	149.6
1959	172.9	121.2	15.2	19.3	6.2		11.0	4.8	6.2	172.9	10.6	10.7	151.6
1960	174.4	123.3	15.6	19.1	6.4		10.0	4.2	5.8	174.4	11.3	11.1	151.9
1961	181.6	129.1	16.4	19.3	6.5		10.4	4.5	5.9	181.6	12.3	11.8	157.5
1962	188.9	134.6	17.3	19.9	6.5		10.5	4.6	5.9	188.9	13.5	13.2	162.2
1963	196.7	142.4	15.9	20.4	7.4		10.7	5.0	5.7	196.7	15.0	14.6	167.1
1964	204.2	150.5	14.5	21.2	7.0		11.0	5.2	5.8	204.2	16.9	15.3	172.1
1965	220.8	161.5	17.6	22.4	7.9		11.4	5.4	6.0	220.8	18.9	16.9	185.0
1966	234.0	171.2	19.0	24.1	8.1		11.6	5.7	6.0	234.0	20.7	18.5	194.8
1967	246.1	180.9	18.8	26.3	8.0		12.0	5.8	6.1	246.1	22.6	19.6	203.9
1968	257.2	189.4	20.2	27.7	7.4		12.4	6.1	6.3	257.2	24.7	19.2	213.2
1969	267.8	195.3	22.8	28.6	8.3		12.8	6.4	6.4	267.8	26.4	20.0	221.4
1970	278.8	202.4	23.7	30.4	8.7		13.7	7.2	6.5	278.8	27.2	21.3	230.3
1971	301.8	217.6	27.3	32.4	10.0		14.5	7.9	6.7	301.8	28.8	24.0	248.9
1972	339.9	243.0	33.7	34.6	12.9		15.7	8.7	6.9	339.9	31.4	26.7	281.8
1973	418.5	298.3	42.4	39.7	21.4		16.8	9.7	7.1	418.5	35.2	31.6	351.7
1974[7]	449.2	335.6	24.6	48.5	22.5		18.1	11.2	6.9	449.2	39.6	35.1	374.5
1975	510.8	383.6	29.4	57.4	20.5		19.9	13.0	6.9	510.8	43.8	39.8	427.3
1976	590.7	456.5	29.0	63.3	20.6		21.3	14.3	6.9	590.7	48.5	45.7	496.5
1977	651.5	509.3	31.9	69.3	20.4		20.5	13.5	7.0	651.5	55.8	52.6	543.1
1978	777.7	601.8	50.1	78.8	23.8		23.2	16.1	7.1	777.7	63.4	60.4	653.9
1979	914.7	706.1	61.4	91.9	29.9		25.4	18.1	7.3	914.7	75.8	71.7	767.2
1980	1,000.4	782.8	60.6	97.5	32.8		26.7	19.3	7.4	1,000.4	85.3	77.2	838.0
1981	997.9	785.6	53.5	101.1	29.5		28.2	20.6	7.6	997.9	93.9	83.8	820.2
1982	962.5	750.0	53.0	103.9	25.9		29.7	21.9	7.8	962.5	96.8	87.2	778.5
1983	959.3	753.4	49.5	101.7	23.7		30.9	22.8	8.1	959.3	98.1	88.1	773.1
1984	897.8	661.8	49.5	125.8	26.1	2.0	32.6	24.3	8.3	897.8	101.4	87.4	709.0
1985	775.9	586.2	46.3	86.1	22.9	1.2	33.3	24.3	9.0	775.9	94.1	78.1	603.8
1986	722.0	542.4	47.8	79.0	16.3	2.1	34.4	24.4	10.0	722.0	84.1	67.2	570.7
1987	756.5	563.7	58.0	78.7	17.8	3.2	35.2	25.3	9.9	756.5	75.8	62.7	618.0
1988	788.5	582.3	62.2	81.0	23.7	3.5	35.9	25.6	10.4	788.5	70.8	62.3	655.4
1989	813.7	600.1	66.2	84.1	23.9	2.6	36.7	26.3	10.4	813.7	68.8	62.3	682.7
1990	840.6	619.1	70.9	86.3	23.2	2.8	38.3	27.5	10.9	840.6	67.6	63.5	709.5
1991	844.2	624.8	68.1	85.9	22.2	2.6	40.5	28.7	11.8	844.2	67.4	64.4	712.3
1992	867.8	640.8	71.0	84.8	24.2	3.9	43.0	29.4	13.6	867.8	67.9	63.7	736.2
1993	909.2	677.6	72.8	85.4	23.3	3.8	46.3	31.0	15.3	909.2	68.4	65.9	774.9
1994	934.7	704.1	67.9	86.8	23.3	5.0	47.6	32.1	15.5	934.7	69.9	69.0	795.8
1995	965.7	740.5	57.8	87.6	27.4	3.4	49.1	34.1	15.0	965.7	71.7	71.3	822.8
1996	1,002.9	769.5	60.3	88.0	31.7	4.4	49.0	34.9	14.1	1,002.9	74.4	74.2	854.3
1997	1,051.3	808.2	67.1	88.7	32.7	4.9	49.6	35.7	13.9	1,051.3	78.5	78.4	894.4
1998	1,083.4	840.4	63.4	89.8	29.9	5.0	54.7	40.5	14.2	1,083.4	83.1	81.5	918.7
1999	1,138.8	887.0	73.2	89.8	28.3	4.0	56.5	41.9	14.6	1,138.8	87.2	80.5	971.1
2000	1,203.2	946.4	76.8	90.1	27.9	4.9	57.1	43.0	14.1	1,203.2	91.1	86.5	1,025.6
2001	1,255.9	996.2	78.5	92.8	25.2	4.2	58.9	43.6	15.3	1,255.9	96.0	89.7	1,070.2
2002	1,304.0	1,045.7	75.6	93.6	23.1	5.6	60.4	44.7	15.8	1,304.0	103.4	90.0	1,110.7
2003	1,378.8	1,111.8	78.5	95.9	24.4	5.6	62.4	45.6	16.9	1,378.8	108.0	90.0	1,180.8
2004	1,500.8	1,227.1	79.4	98.7	24.4	5.7	65.5			1,500.8	114.3	92.7	1,293.9

[1] Excludes commercial broilers; excludes horses and mules beginning 1959; excludes turkeys beginning 1986.
[2] Non-Commodity Credit Corporation (CCC) crops held on farms plus value above loan rate for crops held under CCC.
[3] Includes fertilizer, chemicals, fuels, parts, feed, seed, and other supplies.
[4] Beginning in 2004, data available only for total financial assets. Data through 2003 for other financial assets are currency and demand deposits.
[5] Includes CCC storage and drying facilities loans.
[6] Does not include CCC crop loans.
[7] Beginning 1974, data are for farms included in the new farm definition, that is, places with sales of $1,000 or more annually.

Note.—Data exclude operator households.
Beginning 1959, data include Alaska and Hawaii.

Source: Department of Agriculture, Economic Research Service.

TABLE B–99.—*Farm output and productivity indexes, 1948–2004*

[1996=100]

| Year | Farm output | | | | Productivity indicators | |
| | Total | Primary output | | Secondary output | Farm output per unit of total factor input | Farm output per unit of labor input |
		Livestock and products	Crops			
1948	41	44	42	20	42	13
1949	41	47	40	18	40	13
1950	41	49	38	17	40	13
1951	43	52	40	18	41	15
1952	44	53	41	20	42	15
1953	45	54	42	21	43	16
1954	45	56	41	21	44	17
1955	46	58	42	23	44	18
1956	47	59	42	25	45	19
1957	46	58	41	29	45	20
1958	49	59	46	35	47	22
1959	51	62	46	53	48	24
1960	53	62	49	57	50	26
1961	53	65	48	56	51	27
1962	54	65	49	55	51	27
1963	56	67	51	56	52	29
1964	55	69	49	51	53	31
1965	57	67	52	51	54	32
1966	56	68	51	50	53	34
1967	58	70	53	52	56	38
1968	59	70	55	48	56	39
1969	60	70	57	46	56	40
1970	60	73	54	40	56	41
1971	64	74	61	40	60	45
1972	64	75	61	39	60	45
1973	67	76	65	42	62	48
1974	63	75	59	40	58	45
1975	66	70	67	41	64	48
1976	67	74	67	41	63	50
1977	71	75	72	40	67	54
1978	73	75	75	45	65	56
1979	78	77	82	44	67	59
1980	75	80	75	39	64	58
1981	81	82	86	32	72	63
1982	82	81	87	51	74	69
1983	71	83	67	53	65	61
1984	81	82	85	51	77	72
1985	85	84	89	60	82	82
1986	82	84	83	58	80	78
1987	84	86	84	68	83	78
1988	80	88	74	84	80	73
1989	86	88	84	91	87	82
1990	90	89	90	92	91	91
1991	90	92	89	97	90	91
1992	96	94	97	95	98	99
1993	91	95	88	100	92	99
1994	101	99	104	98	98	94
1995	96	101	92	108	92	89
1996	100	100	100	100	100	100
1997	104	101	105	111	101	105
1998	105	104	104	126	101	112
1999	108	107	105	133	102	115
2000	108	108	107	120	107	122
2001	108	107	106	126	107	124
2002	107	110	102	126	107	122
2003	108	110	105	122	111	131
2004	112	110	114	116	117	144

Note.—Farm output includes primary agricultural activities and certain secondary activities that are closely linked to agricultural production for which information on production and input use cannot be separately observed.
See Table B–100 for farm inputs.

Source: Department of Agriculture, Economic Research Service.

TABLE B–100.—*Farm input use, selected inputs, 1948–2005*

Year	Farm employment (thousands)[1]			Crops harvested (millions of acres)[3]	Total farm input	Capital input		Labor input			Materials input				
	Total	Self-employed and unpaid family workers[2]	Hired workers			Total	Durable equipment	Total	Hired labor	Self-employed	Total	Feed and seed	Energy	Agricultural chemicals	Purchased services
1948	9,759	7,433	2,326	356	97	108	66	326	279	349	48	60	77	20	43
1949	9,633	7,392	2,241	360	101	109	78	318	259	347	54	62	86	21	41
1950	9,283	6,965	2,318	345	102	112	90	306	270	324	55	62	88	25	43
1951	8,653	6,464	2,189	344	103	115	100	294	261	311	57	65	88	25	47
1952	8,441	6,301	2,140	349	104	117	109	287	255	304	58	64	93	26	51
1953	7,904	5,817	2,087	348	104	119	114	275	248	289	58	66	94	26	48
1954	7,893	5,782	2,111	346	102	120	120	270	234	288	56	61	97	27	47
1955	7,719	5,675	2,044	340	105	120	122	264	230	281	60	69	101	28	49
1956	7,367	5,451	1,916	324	105	120	124	247	210	267	63	71	101	30	51
1957	6,966	5,046	1,920	324	104	119	122	229	201	244	64	75	99	29	52
1958	6,667	4,705	1,962	324	105	118	121	219	203	227	68	79	105	30	54
1959	6,565	4,621	1,944	324	107	118	121	217	198	227	71	80	106	34	74
1960	6,155	4,260	1,895	324	106	118	123	205	198	208	71	80	109	34	72
1961	5,994	4,135	1,859	302	104	118	121	200	197	201	70	77	112	37	70
1962	5,841	3,997	1,844	295	106	118	119	201	197	202	72	80	113	41	71
1963	5,500	3,700	1,800	298	106	118	119	192	196	190	74	83	116	45	70
1964	5,206	3,585	1,621	298	105	119	121	181	177	182	74	81	123	49	68
1965	4,964	3,465	1,499	298	104	119	123	176	167	181	74	80	121	50	69
1966	4,574	3,224	1,350	294	105	119	126	164	150	170	78	86	120	55	69
1967	4,303	3,036	1,267	306	105	120	131	154	139	161	80	87	119	62	72
1968	4,207	2,974	1,233	300	106	121	137	153	135	162	81	88	123	66	71
1969	4,050	2,843	1,207	290	107	121	139	151	136	158	85	92	126	74	68
1970	3,951	2,727	1,224	293	107	120	140	144	137	147	86	95	126	79	65
1971	3,868	2,665	1,203	305	106	120	142	142	136	145	86	92	122	86	65
1972	3,870	2,664	1,206	294	107	119	142	141	135	144	88	95	118	94	64
1973	3,947	2,702	1,245	321	108	119	145	140	137	141	91	96	111	110	69
1974	3,919	2,588	1,331	328	108	120	153	140	146	136	90	96	97	115	69
1975	3,818	2,481	1,337	336	104	121	159	137	148	131	83	91	102	79	70
1976	3,741	2,369	1,372	337	107	123	164	135	150	128	88	95	111	89	74
1977	3,660	2,347	1,313	345	106	124	170	131	146	124	86	91	112	88	75
1978	3,682	2,410	1,272	338	113	126	175	129	137	125	97	104	119	92	88
1979	3,549	2,320	1,229	348	116	127	182	131	143	126	102	110	107	100	93
1980	3,512	2,302	1,210	352	116	130	189	128	141	121	102	116	98	100	83
1981	3,328	2,241	1,087	366	112	128	190	128	141	121	96	111	91	94	79
1982	3,267	2,142	1,125	362	111	127	187	119	126	114	96	113	88	83	88
1983	3,082	1,991	1,091	306	110	125	178	117	139	106	97	114	88	77	86
1984	2,943	1,930	1,013	348	106	120	170	114	130	105	93	103	92	90	83
1985	2,723	1,753	970	342	103	119	161	103	113	98	92	104	85	83	85
1986	2,686	1,740	946	325	102	115	150	105	109	103	91	104	101	81	78
1987	2,681	1,717	964	302	100	111	139	107	112	105	90	101	96	78	81
1988	2,685	1,725	960	297	100	109	131	109	117	105	91	99	102	78	81
1989	2,627	1,709	918	318	98	107	125	105	108	103	90	95	95	84	87
1990	2,541	1,649	892	322	99	105	121	99	109	93	94	102	92	88	84
1991	2,548	1,682	866	318	100	105	118	100	110	94	96	103	95	93	88
1992	2,506	1,640	866	319	98	103	114	97	103	94	95	102	94	93	85
1993	2,367	1,510	857	308	99	103	110	92	101	88	100	105	97	95	96
1994	2,614	1,774	840	321	103	101	106	107	101	111	102	106	100	94	100
1995	2,598	1,730	868	314	105	101	103	107	103	110	106	111	104	94	104
1996	2,434	1,602	832	326	100	100	100	100	100	100	100	100	100	100	100
1997	2,434	1,557	877	333	103	100	98	99	105	96	106	107	104	103	106
1998	2,285	1,405	880	327	104	99	98	94	106	87	113	116	115	105	112
1999	2,255	1,326	929	327	105	99	98	93	112	84	115	122	104	104	115
2000	2,139	1,249	890	324	102	98	98	89	106	79	110	120	94	103	108
2001	2,084	1,211	873	321	101	98	98	87	104	78	110	116	99	100	111
2002	2,129	1,243	886	316	100	98	99	88	105	79	108	114	106	99	104
2003	2,017	1,181	836	324	97	97	100	83	96	76	105	116	85	93	100
2004	2,013	1,188	825	321	96	97	102	78	85	75	104	117	82	94	101
2005 *p*	....	....	780	321	....	....	....	....	....	....	....	....	....	....	....

[1] Persons involved in farmwork. Total farm employment is the sum of self-employed and unpaid family workers and hired workers shown here.

[2] Data from *Current Population Survey* (CPS), Department of Commerce (Census Bureau), adjusted for multiple jobholders by Department of Labor (Bureau of Labor Statistics).

[3] Acreage harvested plus acreages in fruits, tree nuts, and vegetables and minor crops. Includes double-cropping.

Source: Department of Agriculture, Economic Research Service.

TABLE B–101.—*Agricultural price indexes and farm real estate value, 1975–2005*

[1990-92=100, except as noted]

Year or month	Prices received by farmers			Prices paid by farmers												Addendum: Average farm real estate value per acre (dollars) [3]
				All commodities, services, interest, taxes, and wage rates [1]	Production items											
	All farm products	Crops	Livestock and products		Total [2]	Feed	Livestock and poultry	Fertilizer	Agricultural chemicals	Fuels	Farm machinery	Farm services	Rent	Wage rates	
1975	73	88	62	47	55	83	39	87	72	40	38	48		44	340
1976	75	87	64	50	59	83	47	74	78	43	43	52		48	397
1977	73	83	64	53	61	82	48	72	71	46	47	57		51	474
1978	83	89	78	58	67	80	65	72	66	48	51	60		55	531
1979	94	98	90	66	76	89	88	77	67	61	56	66		60	628
1980	98	107	89	75	85	98	85	96	71	86	63	81		65	737
1981	100	111	89	82	92	110	80	104	77	98	70	89		70	819
1982	94	98	90	86	94	99	78	105	83	97	76	96		74	823
1983	98	108	88	86	92	107	76	100	87	94	81	82		76	788
1984	101	111	91	89	94	112	73	103	90	93	85	86		77	801
1985	91	98	86	86	91	95	74	98	90	93	85	85		78	713
1986	87	87	88	85	86	88	73	90	89	76	83	83		81	640
1987	89	86	91	87	87	83	85	86	87	76	85	84		85	599
1988	99	104	93	91	90	104	91	94	89	77	89	85		87	632
1989	104	109	100	96	95	110	93	99	93	83	94	91		95	668
1990	104	103	105	99	99	103	102	97	95	100	96	96	96	96	683
1991	100	101	99	100	100	98	102	103	101	104	100	98	100	100	703
1992	98	101	97	101	101	99	96	100	103	96	104	103	104	105	713
1993	101	102	100	104	104	102	104	96	109	93	107	110	100	108	736
1994	100	105	95	106	106	106	94	105	112	89	113	110	108	111	798
1995	102	112	92	109	108	103	82	121	116	89	120	115	117	114	844
1996	112	127	99	115	115	129	75	125	119	102	125	116	128	117	887
1997	107	115	98	118	119	125	94	121	121	106	128	116	136	123	926
1998	102	107	97	115	113	111	88	112	122	84	132	115	120	129	974
1999	96	97	95	115	111	100	95	105	121	93	135	116	113	135	1,030
2000	96	96	97	120	116	102	110	110	120	134	139	119	110	140	1,090
2001	102	99	106	123	120	109	111	123	121	119	144	121	117	146	1,150
2002	98	105	90	124	119	112	102	108	119	112	148	120	119	153	1,210
2003	107	111	103	128	124	114	109	124	121	140	151	123	120	157	1,270
2004	119	117	122	134	132	121	128	141	120	163	162	124	120	161	1,360
2005	116	113	120	140	139	116	140	163	120	224	171	128	123	165	1,510
2004: Jan	112	114	110	130	127	117	113	131	121	145	156	123	120	163	1,360
Feb	117	122	112	131	127	121	110	134	121	137	156	123	120	163	....
Mar	122	122	122	132	129	124	115	137	121	142	161	123	120	163	....
Apr	125	124	126	133	131	131	121	137	121	151	161	123	120	159	....
May	129	124	133	135	133	135	126	136	120	159	161	124	120	159	....
June	128	123	133	135	133	130	134	137	120	151	161	125	120	159	....
July	124	120	128	135	133	128	136	138	120	161	161	125	120	162	....
Aug	120	119	122	135	133	119	137	142	120	170	161	125	120	162	....
Sept	116	114	118	135	133	116	138	143	120	175	164	125	120	162	....
Oct	114	111	118	136	134	111	141	148	119	204	165	124	120	161	....
Nov	115	112	119	135	133	109	137	151	119	196	167	124	120	161	....
Dec	111	104	120	134	132	109	133	153	119	167	167	124	120	161	....
2005: Jan	112	103	121	137	134	113	134	156	118	173	167	126	123	169	1,510
Feb	114	107	119	137	134	110	134	156	118	184	169	127	123	169	....
Mar	119	117	121	139	136	114	138	157	117	210	171	127	123	169	....
Apr	122	122	122	139	138	116	141	158	120	210	171	127	123	161	....
May	120	118	122	139	138	117	140	159	120	203	171	127	123	161	....
June	120	122	118	140	139	120	139	159	120	216	171	129	123	161	....
July	118	117	118	141	140	123	136	160	120	224	171	129	123	162	....
Aug	117	116	117	141	140	120	133	159	121	241	172	129	123	162	....
Sept	117	112	122	142	141	116	138	163	121	264	171	129	123	162	....
Oct	111	103	122	144	144	116	148	167	122	302	171	129	123	166	....
Nov	113	105	121	143	142	114	149	176	122	240	172	128	123	166	....
Dec	114	109	119	143	142	115	147	186	123	226	172	128	123	166	....

[1] Includes items used for family living, not shown separately.
[2] Includes other production items not shown separately.
[3] Average for 48 States. Annual data are: March 1 for 1975, February 1 for 1976-81, April 1 for 1982-85, February 1 for 1986-89, and January 1 for 1990-2005.

Note.—Data on a 1990-92 base prior to 1975 have not been calculated by Department of Agriculture.

Source: Department of Agriculture, National Agricultural Statistics Service.

TABLE B–102.—*U.S. exports and imports of agricultural commodities, 1945–2005*

[Billions of dollars]

Year	Exports							Imports					Agricultural trade balance
	Total¹	Feed grains	Food grains²	Oil-seeds and products	Cotton	Tobacco	Animals and products	Total¹	Fruits, nuts, and vegetables³	Animals and products	Coffee	Cocoa beans and products	
1945	2.3	(⁴)	0.4	(⁴)	0.3	0.2	0.9	1.7	0.1	0.4	0.3	(⁴)	0.5
1946	3.1	0.1	.7	(⁴)	.5	.4	.9	2.3	.2	.4	.5	0.1	.8
1947	4.0	.4	1.4	0.1	.4	.3	.7	2.8	.1	.4	.6	.2	1.2
1948	3.5	.1	1.5	.2	.5	.2	.5	3.1	.2	.6	.7	.2	.3
1949	3.6	.3	1.1	.3	.9	.3	.4	2.9	.2	.4	.8	.1	.7
1950	2.9	.2	.6	.2	1.0	.3	.3	4.0	.2	.7	1.1	.2	−1.1
1951	4.0	.3	1.1	.3	1.1	.3	.5	5.2	.2	1.1	1.4	.2	−1.1
1952	3.4	.3	1.1	.2	.9	.2	.3	4.5	.2	.7	1.4	.2	−1.1
1953	2.8	.3	.7	.2	.5	.3	.4	4.2	.2	.6	1.5	.2	−1.3
1954	3.1	.2	.5	.3	.8	.3	.5	4.0	.2	.5	1.5	.3	−.9
1955	3.2	.3	.6	.4	.5	.4	.6	4.0	.2	.5	1.4	.2	−.8
1956	4.2	.4	1.0	.5	.7	.3	.7	4.0	.2	.4	1.4	.2	.2
1957	4.5	.3	1.0	.5	1.0	.4	.7	4.0	.2	.5	1.4	.2	.6
1958	3.9	.5	.8	.4	.7	.4	.5	3.9	.2	.7	1.2	.2	(⁴)
1959	4.0	.6	.9	.6	.4	.3	.6	4.1	.2	.8	1.1	.2	−.1
1960	4.8	.5	1.2	.6	1.0	.4	.6	3.8	.2	.6	1.0	.2	1.0
1961	5.0	.5	1.4	.6	.9	.4	.6	3.7	.2	.7	1.0	.2	1.3
1962	5.0	.8	1.3	.7	.5	.4	.6	3.9	.2	.9	1.0	.2	1.1
1963	5.6	.8	1.5	.8	.6	.4	.7	4.0	.3	.9	1.0	.2	1.6
1964	6.3	.9	1.7	1.0	.7	.4	.8	4.1	.3	.8	1.2	.2	2.3
1965	6.2	1.1	1.4	1.2	.5	.4	.8	4.1	.3	.9	1.1	.1	2.1
1966	6.9	1.3	1.8	1.2	.4	.5	.7	4.5	.4	1.2	1.1	.1	2.4
1967	6.4	1.1	1.5	1.3	.5	.5	.7	4.5	.4	1.1	1.0	.2	1.9
1968	6.3	.9	1.4	1.3	.5	.5	.7	5.0	.5	1.3	1.2	.2	1.3
1969	6.0	.9	1.2	1.3	.3	.6	.8	5.0	.5	1.4	.9	.2	1.1
1970	7.3	1.1	1.4	1.9	.4	.5	.9	5.8	.5	1.6	1.2	.3	1.5
1971	7.7	1.0	1.3	2.2	.6	.5	1.0	5.8	.6	1.5	1.2	.2	1.9
1972	9.4	1.5	1.8	2.4	.5	.7	1.1	6.5	.7	1.8	1.3	.2	2.9
1973	17.7	3.5	4.7	4.3	.9	.7	1.6	8.4	.8	2.6	1.7	.3	9.3
1974	21.9	4.6	5.4	5.7	1.3	.8	1.8	10.2	.8	2.2	1.6	.5	11.7
1975	21.9	5.2	6.2	4.5	1.0	.9	1.7	9.3	.8	1.8	1.7	.5	12.6
1976	23.0	6.0	4.7	5.1	1.0	.9	2.4	11.0	.9	2.3	2.9	.6	12.0
1977	23.6	4.9	3.6	6.6	1.5	1.1	2.7	13.4	1.2	2.3	4.2	1.0	10.2
1978	29.4	5.9	5.5	8.2	1.7	1.4	3.0	14.8	1.5	3.1	4.0	1.4	14.6
1979	34.7	7.7	6.3	8.9	2.2	1.2	3.8	16.7	1.7	3.9	4.2	1.2	18.0
1980	41.2	9.8	7.9	9.4	2.9	1.3	3.8	17.4	1.7	3.8	4.2	.9	23.8
1981	43.3	9.4	9.6	9.6	2.3	1.5	4.2	16.9	2.0	3.5	2.9	.9	26.4
1982	36.6	6.4	7.9	9.1	2.0	1.5	3.9	15.3	2.3	3.7	2.9	.7	21.3
1983	36.1	7.3	7.4	8.7	1.8	1.5	3.8	16.5	2.3	3.8	2.8	.8	19.6
1984	37.8	8.1	7.5	8.4	2.4	1.5	4.2	19.3	3.1	4.1	3.3	1.1	18.5
1985	29.0	6.0	4.5	5.8	1.6	1.5	4.1	20.0	3.5	4.2	3.3	1.4	9.1
1986	26.2	3.1	3.8	6.5	.8	1.2	4.5	21.5	3.6	4.5	4.6	1.1	4.7
1987	28.7	3.8	3.8	6.4	1.6	1.1	5.2	20.4	3.6	4.9	2.9	1.2	8.3
1988	37.1	5.9	5.9	7.7	2.0	1.3	6.4	21.0	3.8	5.2	2.5	1.0	16.1
1989	40.1	7.7	7.1	6.4	2.2	1.3	6.4	21.9	4.4	5.0	2.4	1.0	18.2
1990	39.5	7.0	4.8	5.7	2.8	1.4	6.6	22.9	4.9	5.6	1.9	1.1	16.6
1991	39.3	5.7	4.2	6.4	2.5	1.4	7.1	22.9	5.0	5.5	1.9	1.1	16.5
1992	43.1	5.7	5.4	7.2	2.0	1.7	8.0	24.8	5.2	5.7	1.7	1.1	18.3
1993	42.9	5.0	5.6	7.3	1.5	1.3	8.0	25.1	5.4	5.9	1.5	1.0	17.7
1994	46.2	4.7	5.3	7.2	2.7	1.3	9.2	27.0	5.9	5.7	2.5	1.0	19.2
1995	56.3	8.2	6.7	9.0	3.7	1.4	10.9	30.3	6.4	6.0	3.3	1.1	26.0
1996	60.3	9.4	7.4	10.8	2.7	1.4	11.1	33.5	7.2	6.1	2.8	1.4	26.8
1997	57.2	6.0	5.2	12.1	2.7	1.6	11.3	36.1	7.5	6.5	3.9	1.5	21.0
1998	51.8	5.0	5.0	9.5	2.5	1.5	10.6	36.9	8.4	6.9	3.4	1.7	14.9
1999	48.4	5.5	4.7	8.1	1.0	1.3	10.4	37.7	9.3	7.3	2.9	1.5	10.7
2000	51.2	5.2	4.3	8.6	1.9	1.2	11.6	39.0	9.4	8.3	2.7	1.4	12.3
2001	53.7	5.2	4.2	9.2	2.2	1.3	12.4	39.4	9.9	9.1	1.7	1.5	14.3
2002	53.1	5.5	4.5	9.6	2.0	1.0	11.1	41.9	10.6	9.0	1.7	1.8	11.2
2003	59.4	5.4	5.0	11.7	3.4	1.0	12.2	47.4	11.9	8.9	2.0	2.4	12.0
2004	61.4	6.4	6.3	10.4	4.3	1.0	10.4	54.0	13.3	10.6	2.3	2.5	7.4
Jan-Nov:													
2004	55.7	5.9	5.9	9.1	3.9	1.0	9.4	49.1	11.9	9.6	2.1	2.3	6.6
2005	57.4	5.2	4.8	9.3	3.6	.9	11.1	53.9	13.2	10.3	2.7	2.5	3.5

¹ Total includes items not shown separately.
² Rice, wheat, and wheat flour.
³ Includes fruit, nut, and vegetable preparations. Beginning in 1989, includes bananas.
⁴ Less than $50 million.

Note.—Data derived from official estimates released by the Bureau of the Census, Department of Commerce. Agricultural commodities are defined as (1) nonmarine food products and (2) other products of agriculture which have not passed through complex processes of manufacture. Export value, at U.S. port of exportation, is based on the selling price and includes inland freight, insurance, and other charges to the port. Import value, defined generally as the market value in the foreign country, excludes import duties, ocean freight, and marine insurance.

Source: Department of Agriculture, Economic Research Service.

Table B–103.—*U.S. international transactions, 1946–2005*

[Millions of dollars; quarterly data seasonally adjusted. Credits (+), debits (−)]

Year or quarter	Goods[1]			Services				Income receipts and payments			Unilateral current transfers, net[2]	Balance on current account
	Exports	Imports	Balance on goods	Net military transactions[2]	Net travel and transportation	Other services, net	Balance on goods and services	Receipts	Payments	Balance on income		
1946	11,764	−5,067	6,697	−424	733	310	7,316	772	−212	560	−2,991	4,885
1947	16,097	−5,973	10,124	−358	946	145	10,857	1,102	−245	857	−2,722	8,992
1948	13,265	−7,557	5,708	−351	374	175	5,906	1,921	−437	1,484	−4,973	2,417
1949	12,213	−6,874	5,339	−410	230	208	5,367	1,831	−476	1,355	−5,849	873
1950	10,203	−9,081	1,122	−56	−120	242	1,188	2,068	−559	1,509	−4,537	−1,840
1951	14,243	−11,176	3,067	169	298	254	3,788	2,633	−583	2,050	−4,954	884
1952	13,449	−10,838	2,611	528	83	309	3,531	2,751	−555	2,196	−5,113	614
1953	12,412	−10,975	1,437	1,753	−238	307	3,259	2,736	−624	2,112	−6,657	−1,286
1954	12,929	−10,353	2,576	902	−269	305	3,514	2,929	−582	2,347	−5,642	219
1955	14,424	−11,527	2,897	−113	−297	299	2,786	3,406	−676	2,730	−5,086	430
1956	17,556	−12,803	4,753	−221	−361	447	4,618	3,837	−735	3,102	−4,990	2,730
1957	19,562	−13,291	6,271	−423	−189	482	6,141	4,180	−796	3,384	−4,763	4,762
1958	16,414	−12,952	3,462	−849	−633	486	2,466	3,790	−825	2,965	−4,647	784
1959	16,458	−15,310	1,148	−831	−821	573	69	4,132	−1,061	3,071	−4,422	−1,282
1960	19,650	−14,758	4,892	−1,057	−964	639	3,508	4,616	−1,238	3,379	−4,062	2,824
1961	20,108	−14,537	5,571	−1,131	−978	732	4,195	4,999	−1,245	3,755	−4,127	3,822
1962	20,781	−16,260	4,521	−912	−1,152	912	3,370	5,618	−1,324	4,294	−4,277	3,387
1963	22,272	−17,048	5,224	−742	−1,309	1,036	4,210	6,157	−1,560	4,596	−4,392	4,414
1964	25,501	−18,700	6,801	−794	−1,146	1,161	6,022	6,824	−1,783	5,041	−4,240	6,823
1965	26,461	−21,510	4,951	−487	−1,280	1,480	4,664	7,437	−2,088	5,350	−4,583	5,431
1966	29,310	−25,493	3,817	−1,043	−1,331	1,497	2,940	7,528	−2,481	5,047	−4,955	3,031
1967	30,666	−26,866	3,800	−1,187	−1,750	1,742	2,604	8,021	−2,747	5,274	−5,294	2,583
1968	33,626	−32,991	635	−596	−1,548	1,759	250	9,367	−3,378	5,990	−5,629	611
1969	36,414	−35,807	607	−718	−1,763	1,964	91	10,913	−4,869	6,044	−5,735	399
1970	42,469	−39,866	2,603	−641	−2,038	2,330	2,254	11,748	−5,515	6,233	−6,156	2,331
1971	43,319	−45,579	−2,260	653	−2,345	2,649	−1,303	12,707	−5,435	7,272	−7,402	−1,433
1972	49,381	−55,797	−6,416	1,072	−3,063	2,965	−5,443	14,765	−6,572	8,192	−8,544	−5,795
1973	71,410	−70,499	911	740	−3,158	3,406	1,900	21,808	−9,655	12,153	−6,913	7,140
1974	98,306	−103,811	−5,505	165	−3,184	4,231	−4,292	27,587	−12,084	15,503	−9,249	1,962
1975	107,088	−98,185	8,903	1,461	−2,812	4,854	12,404	25,351	−12,564	12,787	−7,075	18,116
1976	114,745	−124,228	−9,483	931	−2,558	5,027	−6,082	29,375	−13,311	16,063	−5,686	4,295
1977	120,816	−151,907	−31,091	1,731	−3,565	5,680	−27,246	32,354	−14,217	18,137	−5,226	−14,335
1978	142,075	−176,002	−33,927	857	−3,573	6,879	−29,763	42,088	−21,680	20,408	−5,788	−15,143
1979	184,439	−212,007	−27,568	−1,313	−2,935	7,251	−24,565	63,834	−32,961	30,873	−6,593	−285
1980	224,250	−249,750	−25,500	−1,822	−997	8,912	−19,407	72,606	−42,532	30,073	−8,349	2,317
1981	237,044	−265,067	−28,023	−844	144	12,552	−16,172	86,529	−53,626	32,903	−11,702	5,030
1982	211,157	−247,642	−36,485	112	−992	13,209	−24,156	91,747	−56,583	35,164	−16,544	−5,536
1983	201,799	−268,901	−67,102	−563	−4,227	14,124	−57,767	90,000	−53,614	36,386	−17,310	−38,691
1984	219,926	−332,418	−112,492	−2,547	−8,438	14,404	−109,073	108,819	−73,756	35,063	−20,335	−94,344
1985	215,915	−338,088	−122,173	−4,390	−9,798	14,483	−121,880	98,542	−72,819	25,723	−21,998	−118,155
1986	223,344	−368,425	−145,081	−5,181	−8,779	20,502	−138,538	97,064	−81,571	15,494	−24,132	−147,177
1987	250,208	−409,765	−159,557	−3,844	−8,010	19,728	−151,684	108,184	−93,891	14,293	−23,265	−160,655
1988	320,230	−447,189	−126,959	−6,320	−3,013	21,725	−114,566	136,713	−118,026	18,687	−25,274	−121,153
1989	359,916	−477,665	−117,749	−6,749	3,551	27,805	−93,142	161,287	−141,463	19,824	−26,169	−99,486
1990	387,401	−498,438	−111,037	−7,599	7,501	30,270	−80,864	171,742	−143,192	28,550	−26,654	−78,968
1991	414,083	−491,020	−76,937	−5,275	16,560	34,516	−31,136	149,214	−125,085	24,131	9,904	2,897
1992	439,631	−536,528	−96,897	−1,448	19,969	39,163	−39,212	133,767	−109,532	24,235	−35,100	−50,078
1993	456,943	−589,394	−132,451	1,383	19,714	41,040	−70,311	136,057	−110,741	25,316	−39,811	−84,805
1994	502,859	−668,690	−165,831	2,570	16,305	48,463	−98,493	166,521	−149,375	17,146	−40,265	−121,612
1995	575,204	−749,374	−174,170	4,600	21,772	51,414	−96,384	210,244	−189,353	20,891	−38,177	−113,670
1996	612,113	−803,113	−191,000	5,385	25,015	56,535	−104,065	226,129	−203,811	22,318	−43,147	−124,894
1997	678,366	−876,470	−198,104	4,968	22,152	62,674	−108,310	256,804	−244,195	12,609	−45,205	−140,906
1998	670,416	−917,103	−246,687	5,220	10,210	66,248	−165,009	261,819	−257,554	4,265	−53,320	−214,064
1999	683,965	−1,029,980	−346,015	2,593	7,085	72,943	−263,394	293,925	−280,037	13,888	−50,554	−300,060
2000	771,994	−1,224,408	−452,414	317	2,486	71,339	−378,272	350,918	−329,864	21,054	−58,781	−415,999
2001	718,712	−1,145,900	−427,188	−2,296	−3,254	70,009	−362,729	288,303	−263,120	25,183	−51,910	−389,456
2002	682,422	−1,164,720	−482,298	−7,158	−4,245	72,520	−421,181	270,792	−260,776	10,016	−64,046	−475,211
2003	713,421	−1,260,717	−547,296	−12,527	−11,736	76,745	−494,814	309,830	−263,526	46,304	−71,169	−519,679
2004	807,536	−1,472,926	−665,390	−14,485	−13,304	75,596	−617,583	379,527	−349,088	30,439	−80,930	−668,074
2004: I	193,789	−345,241	−151,452	−3,200	−3,212	19,012	−138,852	86,401	−71,379	15,022	−22,271	−146,101
II	200,072	−364,059	−163,987	−3,643	−3,014	18,602	−152,042	91,465	−85,543	5,922	−20,515	−166,635
III	204,801	−372,576	−167,775	−3,829	−3,394	17,533	−157,465	95,504	−89,250	6,254	−15,771	−166,982
IV	208,874	−391,050	−182,176	−3,813	−3,684	20,452	−169,221	106,154	−102,918	3,236	−22,374	−188,359
2005: I	213,840	−400,169	−186,329	−3,020	−4,499	20,796	−173,052	106,951	−106,308	643	−26,259	−198,668
II	223,540	−410,469	−186,929	−3,066	−2,770	19,166	−173,599	111,147	−112,688	−1,541	−22,641	−197,781
III *p*	225,226	−423,151	−197,925	−2,652	−1,676	19,458	−182,795	118,732	−118,220	512	−13,538	−195,821

[1] Adjusted from Census data for differences in valuation, coverage, and timing; excludes military.
[2] Includes transfers of goods and services under U.S. military grant programs.
See next page for continuation of table.

400

TABLE B-103.—*U.S. international transactions, 1946–2005*—Continued

[Millions of dollars; quarterly data seasonally adjusted. Credits (+), debits (−)]

Year or quarter	Capital account trans- actions, net	Financial account							Statistical discrepancy	
		U.S.-owned assets abroad, net [increase/financial outflow (−)]				Foreign-owned assets in the U.S., net [increase/financial inflow (+)]			Total (sum of the items with sign reversed)	Of which: Seasonal adjust- ment discrep- ancy
		Total	U.S. official reserve assets[3]	Other U.S. Govern- ment assets	U.S. private assets	Total	Foreign official assets	Other foreign assets		
1946			−623								
1947			−3,315								
1948			−1,736								
1949			−266								
1950			1,758								
1951			−33								
1952			−415								
1953			1,256								
1954			480								
1955			182								
1956			−869								
1957			−1,165								
1958			2,292								
1959			1,035								
1960		−4,099	2,145	−1,100	−5,144	2,294	1,473	821	−1,019	
1961		−5,538	607	−910	−5,235	2,705	765	1,939	−989	
1962		−4,174	1,535	−1,085	−4,623	1,911	1,270	641	−1,124	
1963		−7,270	378	−1,662	−5,986	3,217	1,986	1,231	−360	
1964		−9,560	171	−1,680	−8,050	3,643	1,660	1,983	−907	
1965		−5,716	1,225	−1,605	−5,336	742	134	607	−457	
1966		−7,321	570	−1,543	−6,347	3,661	−672	4,333	629	
1967		−9,757	53	−2,423	−7,386	7,379	3,451	3,928	−205	
1968		−10,977	−870	−2,274	−7,833	9,928	−774	10,703	438	
1969		−11,585	−1,179	−2,200	−8,206	12,702	−1,301	14,002	−1,516	
1970		−8,470	3,348	−1,589	−10,229	6,359	6,908	−550	−219	
1971		−11,758	3,066	−1,884	−12,940	22,970	26,879	−3,909	−9,779	
1972		−13,787	706	−1,568	−12,925	21,461	10,475	10,986	−1,879	
1973		−22,874	158	−2,644	−20,388	18,388	6,026	12,362	−2,654	
1974		−34,745	−1,467	366	−33,643	35,341	10,546	24,796	−2,558	
1975		−39,703	−849	−3,474	−35,380	17,170	7,027	10,143	4,417	
1976		−51,269	−2,558	−4,214	−44,498	38,018	17,693	20,326	8,955	
1977		−34,785	−375	−3,693	−30,717	53,219	36,816	16,403	−4,099	
1978		−61,130	732	−4,660	−57,202	67,036	33,678	33,358	9,236	
1979		−64,915	6	−3,746	−61,176	40,852	−13,665	54,516	24,349	
1980		−85,815	−7,003	−5,162	−73,651	62,612	15,497	47,115	20,886	
1981		−113,054	−4,082	−5,097	−103,875	86,232	4,960	81,272	21,792	
1982	199	−127,882	−4,965	−6,131	−116,786	96,589	3,593	92,997	36,630	
1983	209	−66,373	−1,196	−5,006	−60,172	88,694	5,845	82,849	16,162	
1984	235	−40,376	−3,131	−5,489	−31,757	117,752	3,140	114,612	16,733	
1985	315	−44,752	−3,858	−2,821	−38,074	146,115	−1,119	147,233	16,478	
1986	301	−111,723	312	−2,022	−110,014	230,009	35,648	194,360	28,590	
1987	365	−79,296	9,149	1,006	−89,450	248,634	45,387	203,247	−9,048	
1988	493	−106,573	−3,912	2,967	−105,628	246,522	39,758	206,764	−19,289	
1989	336	−175,383	−25,293	1,233	−151,323	224,928	8,503	216,425	49,605	
1990	−6,579	−81,234	−2,158	2,317	−81,393	141,571	33,910	107,661	25,211	
1991	−4,479	−64,389	5,763	2,923	−73,075	110,809	17,388	93,421	−44,840	
1992	−557	−74,410	3,901	−1,667	−76,644	170,663	40,476	130,185	−45,617	
1993	−1,299	−200,551	−1,379	−351	−198,823	282,041	71,753	210,288	4,617	
1994	−1,723	−178,937	5,346	−390	−183,893	305,989	39,583	266,406	−3,717	
1995	−927	−352,264	−9,742	−984	−341,538	438,562	109,880	328,682	28,299	
1996	−631	−413,409	6,668	−989	−419,088	551,096	126,724	424,372	−12,162	
1997	−1,014	−485,475	−1,010	68	−484,533	706,809	19,036	687,773	−79,414	
1998	−702	−353,829	−6,783	−422	−346,624	423,569	−19,903	443,472	145,026	
1999	−4,888	−504,062	8,747	2,750	−515,559	740,210	43,543	696,667	68,800	
2000	−929	−560,523	−290	−941	−559,292	1,046,896	42,758	1,004,138	−69,445	
2001	−1,223	−382,616	−4,911	−486	−377,219	782,859	28,059	754,800	−9,564	
2002	−1,363	−294,027	−3,681	345	−290,691	794,343	115,945	678,398	−23,742	
2003	−3,214	−328,397	1,523	537	−330,457	889,043	278,275	610,768	−37,753	
2004	−1,648	−855,509	2,805	1,215	−859,529	1,440,105	394,710	1,045,395	85,126	
2004: I	−428	−295,140	557	727	−296,424	423,023	147,401	275,622	18,646	11,010
II	−372	−133,886	1,122	−2	−135,006	304,937	77,039	227,898	−4,404	−3,747
III	−393	−137,525	429	−11	−137,943	254,228	75,792	178,436	50,672	−12,977
IV	−455	−288,957	697	501	−290,155	457,915	94,478	363,437	19,856	5,718
2005: I	−4,466	−81,510	5,331	4,487	−91,328	243,451	25,277	218,174	41,193	15,238
II	−315	−225,202	−797	971	−225,376	375,816	82,646	293,170	47,482	−7,710
III p	−311	−124,020	4,766	562	−129,348	396,919	38,394	358,525	−76,767	−16,265

[3] Consists of gold, special drawing rights, foreign currencies, and the U.S. reserve position in the International Monetary Fund (IMF).

Source: Department of Commerce, Bureau of Economic Analysis.

TABLE B–104.—*U.S. international trade in goods by principal end-use category, 1965–2005*

[Billions of dollars; quarterly data seasonally adjusted]

Year or quarter	Exports							Imports						
			Nonagricultural products							Nonpetroleum products				
	Total	Agricultural products	Total	Industrial supplies and materials	Capital goods except automotive	Automotive	Other	Total	Petroleum and products	Total	Industrial supplies and materials	Capital goods except automotive	Automotive	Other
1965	26.5	6.3	20.2	7.6	8.1	1.9	2.6	21.5	2.0	19.5	9.1	1.5	0.9	8.0
1966	29.3	6.9	22.4	8.2	8.9	2.4	2.9	25.5	2.1	23.4	10.2	2.2	1.8	9.2
1967	30.7	6.5	24.2	8.5	9.9	2.8	3.0	26.9	2.1	24.8	10.0	2.5	2.4	9.9
1968	33.6	6.3	27.3	9.6	11.1	3.5	3.2	33.0	2.4	30.6	12.0	2.8	4.0	11.8
1969	36.4	6.1	30.3	10.3	12.4	3.9	3.7	35.8	2.6	33.2	11.8	3.4	4.9	13.0
1970	42.5	7.4	35.1	12.3	14.7	3.9	4.3	39.9	2.9	36.9	12.4	4.0	5.5	15.0
1971	43.3	7.8	35.5	10.9	15.4	4.7	4.5	45.6	3.7	41.9	13.8	4.3	7.4	16.4
1972	49.4	9.5	39.9	11.9	16.9	5.5	5.6	55.8	4.7	51.1	16.3	5.9	8.7	20.2
1973	71.4	18.0	53.4	17.0	22.0	6.9	7.6	70.5	8.4	62.1	19.6	8.3	10.3	23.9
1974	98.3	22.4	75.9	26.3	30.9	8.6	10.0	103.8	26.6	77.2	27.8	9.8	12.0	27.5
1975	107.1	22.2	84.8	26.8	36.6	10.6	10.8	98.2	27.0	71.2	24.0	10.2	11.7	25.3
1976	114.7	23.4	91.4	28.4	39.1	12.1	11.7	124.2	34.6	89.7	29.8	12.3	16.2	31.4
1977	120.8	24.3	96.5	29.8	39.8	13.4	13.5	151.9	45.0	106.9	35.7	14.0	18.6	38.6
1978 [1]	142.1	29.9	112.2	34.2	47.5	15.2	15.3	176.0	42.6	133.4	40.7	19.3	25.0	48.4
1979	184.4	35.5	149.0	52.2	60.2	17.9	18.7	212.0	60.4	151.6	47.5	24.6	26.6	52.8
1980	224.3	42.0	182.2	65.1	76.3	17.4	23.4	249.8	79.5	170.2	53.0	31.6	28.3	57.4
1981	237.0	44.1	193.0	63.6	84.2	19.7	25.5	265.1	78.4	186.7	56.1	37.1	31.0	62.4
1982	211.2	37.3	173.9	57.7	76.5	17.2	22.4	247.6	62.0	185.7	48.6	38.4	34.3	64.3
1983	201.8	37.1	164.7	52.7	71.7	18.5	21.8	268.9	55.1	213.8	53.7	43.7	43.0	73.3
1984	219.9	38.4	181.5	56.8	77.0	22.4	25.3	332.4	58.1	274.4	66.1	60.4	56.5	91.4
1985	215.9	29.6	186.3	54.8	79.3	24.9	27.2	338.1	51.4	286.7	62.6	61.3	64.9	97.9
1986	223.3	27.2	196.2	59.4	82.8	25.1	28.9	368.4	34.3	334.1	69.9	72.0	78.1	114.2
1987	250.2	29.8	220.4	63.7	92.7	27.6	36.4	409.8	42.9	366.8	70.8	85.1	85.2	125.7
1988	320.2	38.8	281.4	82.6	119.1	33.4	46.3	447.2	39.6	407.6	83.1	102.2	87.9	134.4
1989 [1]	359.9	41.1	318.8	90.5	136.9	35.1	56.3	477.7	50.9	426.8	84.6	112.3	87.4	142.5
1990	387.4	40.2	347.2	97.0	153.0	36.2	61.0	498.4	62.3	436.1	83.0	116.4	88.2	148.5
1991	414.1	40.1	374.0	101.6	166.6	39.9	65.9	491.0	51.7	439.3	81.3	121.1	85.5	151.4
1992	439.6	44.1	395.6	101.7	176.4	46.9	70.6	536.5	51.6	484.9	89.1	134.8	91.5	169.6
1993	456.9	43.6	413.3	105.1	182.7	51.6	74.0	589.4	51.5	537.9	100.8	153.2	102.1	182.0
1994	502.9	47.1	455.8	112.7	205.7	57.5	79.9	668.7	51.3	617.4	113.6	185.0	118.1	200.6
1995	575.2	57.2	518.0	135.6	234.4	61.4	86.5	749.4	56.0	693.3	128.5	222.1	123.7	219.0
1996	612.1	61.5	550.6	138.7	254.0	64.4	93.6	803.1	72.7	730.4	136.1	228.4	128.7	237.1
1997	678.4	58.5	619.9	148.6	295.8	73.4	102.0	876.5	71.7	804.7	144.9	253.6	139.4	266.8
1998	670.4	53.2	617.3	139.4	299.8	72.5	105.5	917.1	50.6	866.5	151.6	269.8	148.6	296.4
1999	684.0	49.7	634.3	140.3	311.2	75.3	107.5	1,030.0	67.8	962.2	156.3	295.7	179.0	331.2
2000	772.0	52.8	719.2	163.9	357.0	80.4	117.9	1,224.4	120.2	1,104.2	181.9	347.0	195.9	379.4
2001	718.7	54.9	663.8	150.5	321.7	75.4	116.2	1,145.9	103.6	1,042.3	172.5	298.0	189.8	382.0
2002	682.4	54.5	627.9	147.6	290.4	78.9	110.9	1,164.7	103.5	1,061.2	164.6	283.3	203.7	409.6
2003	713.4	60.9	652.5	162.5	293.6	80.7	115.8	1,260.7	133.1	1,127.6	181.4	295.8	210.2	440.2
2004	807.5	62.9	744.6	192.3	331.5	89.3	131.5	1,472.9	180.5	1,292.5	232.5	343.5	228.2	488.3
2003: I	173.2	14.2	158.9	40.3	70.5	20.0	28.1	311.0	35.6	275.4	44.5	71.4	51.3	108.2
II	174.7	14.7	160.0	40.3	70.9	20.4	28.4	309.8	31.2	278.5	44.5	73.2	52.7	108.3
III	178.2	15.7	162.4	40.1	73.6	19.6	29.2	313.5	32.9	280.6	45.9	73.6	51.3	109.8
IV	187.4	16.2	171.2	41.7	78.7	20.7	30.1	326.5	33.4	293.1	46.5	77.7	54.9	114.0
2004: I	193.8	15.9	177.9	44.8	80.7	21.0	31.4	345.2	40.0	305.2	51.3	80.8	55.4	117.7
II	200.1	16.0	184.1	47.0	82.3	21.8	32.9	364.1	41.5	322.5	56.9	85.5	57.2	123.0
III	204.8	15.4	189.4	49.1	84.2	23.1	33.1	372.6	45.1	327.4	60.8	87.8	57.5	121.3
IV	208.9	15.6	193.2	51.4	84.3	23.4	34.1	391.1	53.8	337.3	63.5	89.4	58.1	126.2
2005: I	213.8	15.6	198.3	53.1	85.4	23.7	36.0	400.2	52.9	347.2	65.4	90.7	58.2	132.9
II	223.5	17.1	206.4	56.1	90.2	23.5	36.6	410.5	57.4	353.1	65.3	95.9	58.1	133.8
III *p* ...	225.2	16.8	208.4	55.7	90.8	24.6	37.3	423.2	67.5	355.6	65.8	96.1	60.6	133.2

[1] End-use commodity classifications beginning 1978 and 1989 are not strictly comparable with data for earlier periods. See *Survey of Current Business*, June 1988 and July 2001.

Note.—Data are on a balance of payments basis and exclude military.

In June 1990, end-use categories for goods exports were redefined to include reexports; beginning with data for 1978, reexports (exports of foreign goods) are assigned to detailed end-use categories in the same manner as exports of domestic goods.

Source: Department of Commerce, Bureau of Economic Analysis.

TABLE B–105.—*U.S. international trade in goods by area, 1999–2005*

[Millions of dollars]

Item	1999	2000	2001	2002	2003	2004	2005 first 3 quarters at annual rate[1]
EXPORTS	683,965	771,994	718,712	682,422	713,421	807,536	883,475
Industrial countries	401,525	438,292	406,148	381,132	398,763	441,562	479,901
Euro area[2]	105,474	115,826	111,049	103,860	109,958	124,798	133,411
Canada	166,713	178,877	163,259	160,916	169,929	189,982	210,192
Japan	56,073	63,473	55,879	49,670	50,253	52,288	53,364
United Kingdom	37,657	40,725	39,701	32,085	32,871	35,120	37,813
Other[3]	35,608	39,391	36,260	34,601	35,752	39,374	45,121
Other countries	282,440	333,701	312,564	301,290	314,658	365,974	403,573
OPEC[4]	18,315	17,625	19,503	17,808	16,556	21,592	29,309
Other[5]	264,125	316,076	293,061	283,482	298,102	344,382	374,264
Of which:							
China	13,047	16,141	19,108	22,040	28,287	34,639	40,009
Mexico	86,758	111,172	101,181	97,242	97,224	110,698	118,364
International organizations and unallocated		1					
IMPORTS	1,029,980	1,224,408	1,145,900	1,164,720	1,260,717	1,472,926	1,645,052
Industrial countries	557,249	636,311	599,330	591,844	622,073	702,264	759,656
Euro area[2]	144,928	164,002	166,190	172,474	187,608	209,393	226,392
Canada	201,287	233,676	218,726	211,756	224,249	259,034	284,217
Japan	130,873	146,492	126,478	121,426	118,034	129,807	137,704
United Kingdom	38,789	43,388	40,982	40,464	42,574	46,032	49,248
Other[3]	41,372	48,753	46,954	45,724	49,608	57,998	62,095
Other countries	472,731	588,097	546,570	572,876	638,644	770,662	885,396
OPEC[4]	41,952	66,995	59,752	53,246	68,346	94,105	120,357
Other[5]	430,779	521,102	486,818	519,630	570,298	676,557	765,039
Of which:							
China	81,789	100,021	102,279	125,189	152,426	196,674	237,275
Mexico	110,550	136,811	132,205	135,496	139,036	157,105	168,492
International organizations and unallocated							
BALANCE (excess of exports +)	−346,015	−452,414	−427,188	−482,298	−547,296	−665,390	−761,577
Industrial countries	−155,724	−198,019	−193,182	−210,712	−223,310	−260,702	−279,755
Euro area[2]	−39,454	−48,176	−55,141	−68,614	−77,650	−84,595	−92,981
Canada	−34,574	−54,799	−55,467	−50,840	−54,320	−69,052	−74,025
Japan	−74,800	−83,019	−70,599	−71,756	−67,781	−77,519	−84,340
United Kingdom	−1,132	−2,663	−1,281	−8,379	−9,703	−10,912	−11,435
Other[3]	−5,764	−9,362	−10,694	−11,123	−13,856	−18,624	−16,973
Other countries	−190,291	−254,396	−234,006	−271,586	−323,986	−404,688	−481,823
OPEC[4]	−23,637	−49,370	−40,249	−35,438	−51,790	−72,513	−91,048
Other[5]	−166,654	−205,026	−193,757	−236,148	−272,196	−332,175	−390,775
Of which:							
China	−68,742	−83,880	−83,171	−103,149	−124,139	−162,035	−197,265
Mexico	−23,792	−25,639	−31,024	−38,254	−41,812	−46,407	−50,128
International organizations and unallocated		1					

[1] Preliminary; seasonally adjusted.
[2] Euro area includes: Austria, Belgium, Finland, France, Germany, Ireland, Italy, Luxembourg, Netherlands, Portugal, Spain, and beginning 2001, Greece.
[3] Australia, New Zealand, and South Africa and other western Europe.
[4] Organization of Petroleum Exporting Countries, consisting of Algeria, Indonesia, Iran, Iraq, Kuwait, Libya, Nigeria, Qatar, Saudi Arabia, United Arab Emirates, and Venezuela. Previously included Ecuador (through 1992) and Gabon (through 1994).
[5] Includes mainly Latin America, other Western Hemisphere, and other countries in Asia and Africa, less members of OPEC.

Note.—Data are on a balance of payments basis and exclude military.
For further details regarding these data, see *Survey of Current Business*, July 2005.

Source: Department of Commerce, Bureau of Economic Analysis.

TABLE B–106.—*U.S. international trade in goods on balance of payments (BOP) and Census basis, and trade in services on BOP basis, 1981–2005*

[Billions of dollars; monthly data seasonally adjusted]

Year or month	Goods: Exports (f.a.s. value)[1][2]							Goods: Imports (customs value)[5]							Services (BOP basis)	
			Census basis (by end-use category)							Census basis (by end-use category)						
	Total, BOP basis[3]	Total, Census basis[3][4]	Foods, feeds, and beverages	Industrial supplies and materials	Capital goods except automotive	Automotive vehicles, cles, parts, and engines	Consumer goods (nonfood) except automotive	Total, BOP basis	Total, Census basis[4]	Foods, feeds, and beverages	Industrial supplies and materials	Capital goods except automotive	Automotive vehicles, cles, parts, and engines	Consumer goods (nonfood) except automotive	Exports	Imports
	F.a.s. value[2]							Customs value								
1981	237.0	238.7	....	....	....	....	....	265.1	261.0	....	....	....	....	....	57.4	45.5
1982	211.2	216.4	31.3	61.7	72.7	15.7	14.3	247.6	244.0	17.1	112.0	35.4	33.3	39.7	64.1	51.7
1983	201.8	205.6	30.9	56.7	67.2	16.8	13.4	268.9	258.0	18.2	107.0	40.9	40.8	44.9	64.3	55.0
1984	219.9	224.0	31.5	61.7	72.0	20.6	13.3	332.4	[6] 330.7	21.0	123.7	59.8	53.5	60.0	71.2	67.7
1985	215.9	[7] 218.8	24.0	58.5	73.9	22.9	12.6	338.1	[6] 336.5	21.9	113.9	65.1	66.8	68.3	73.2	72.9
1986	223.3	[7] 227.2	22.3	57.3	75.8	21.7	14.2	368.4	365.4	24.4	101.3	71.8	78.2	79.4	86.7	80.1
1987	250.2	254.1	24.3	66.7	86.2	24.6	17.7	409.8	406.2	24.8	111.0	84.5	85.2	88.7	98.7	90.8
1988	320.2	322.4	32.3	85.1	109.2	29.3	23.1	447.2	441.0	24.8	118.3	101.4	87.7	95.9	110.9	98.5
1989	359.9	363.8	37.2	99.3	138.8	34.8	36.4	477.7	473.2	25.1	132.3	113.3	86.1	102.9	127.1	102.5
1990	387.4	393.6	35.1	104.4	152.7	37.4	43.3	498.4	495.3	26.6	143.2	116.4	87.3	105.7	147.8	117.7
1991	414.1	421.7	35.7	109.7	166.7	40.0	45.9	491.0	488.5	26.5	131.6	120.7	85.7	108.0	164.3	118.5
1992	439.6	448.2	40.3	109.1	175.9	47.0	51.4	536.5	532.7	27.6	138.6	134.3	91.8	122.7	177.3	119.6
1993	456.9	465.1	40.6	111.8	181.7	52.4	54.7	589.4	580.7	27.9	145.6	152.4	102.4	134.0	185.9	123.8
1994	502.9	512.6	42.0	121.4	205.0	57.8	60.0	668.7	663.3	31.0	162.1	184.4	118.3	146.3	200.4	133.1
1995	575.2	584.7	50.5	146.2	233.0	61.8	64.4	749.4	743.5	33.2	181.8	221.4	123.8	159.9	219.2	141.4
1996	612.1	625.1	55.5	147.7	253.0	65.0	70.1	803.1	795.3	35.7	204.5	228.1	128.9	172.0	239.5	152.6
1997	678.4	689.2	51.5	158.2	294.5	74.0	77.4	876.5	869.7	39.7	213.8	253.3	139.8	193.8	256.3	166.5
1998	670.4	682.1	46.4	148.3	299.4	72.4	80.3	917.1	911.9	41.2	200.1	269.5	148.7	217.0	263.1	181.4
1999	684.0	695.8	46.0	147.5	310.8	75.3	80.9	1,030.0	1,024.6	43.6	221.4	295.7	179.0	241.9	282.5	199.9
2000	772.0	781.9	47.9	172.6	356.9	80.4	89.4	1,224.4	1,218.0	46.0	299.0	347.0	195.9	281.8	299.5	225.3
2001	718.7	729.1	49.4	160.1	321.7	75.4	88.3	1,145.9	1,141.0	46.6	273.9	298.0	189.8	284.3	288.4	224.0
2002	682.4	693.1	49.6	156.8	290.4	78.9	84.4	1,164.7	1,161.4	49.7	267.7	283.3	203.7	307.8	294.9	233.7
2003	713.4	724.8	55.0	173.0	293.6	80.7	89.9	1,260.7	1,257.1	55.8	313.8	295.8	210.2	333.9	309.1	256.7
2004	807.5	818.8	56.6	204.0	331.5	89.3	103.1	1,472.9	1,469.7	62.1	412.8	343.5	228.2	372.9	343.9	296.1
2004: Jan	62.2	63.1	4.6	15.3	25.9	6.8	7.8	112.1	111.9	4.9	28.7	26.9	18.0	29.4	27.3	23.5
Feb	64.8	65.7	4.7	15.9	27.2	7.0	8.2	114.7	114.4	5.0	30.9	26.5	18.7	29.2	27.6	23.6
Mar	66.8	67.8	4.8	16.7	27.6	7.2	8.6	118.5	118.2	5.1	31.7	27.4	18.8	31.0	28.4	23.7
Apr	66.1	67.1	4.7	16.4	27.2	7.3	8.5	118.9	118.7	5.1	31.0	28.0	19.0	31.4	28.3	23.9
May	68.2	69.1	4.8	17.2	28.3	7.3	8.5	120.8	120.5	5.3	32.4	28.2	19.2	31.2	28.2	24.4
June	65.8	66.8	4.6	16.5	26.8	7.2	8.5	124.4	124.1	5.2	35.1	29.3	19.0	31.3	28.5	24.8
July	67.8	68.5	4.6	17.4	28.0	7.5	8.4	122.8	122.5	5.2	34.0	29.1	19.0	31.0	28.4	24.7
Aug	68.1	68.9	4.5	17.0	28.1	7.8	8.7	125.2	124.9	5.2	36.6	29.0	19.1	30.7	28.5	25.5
Sept	69.0	70.0	4.8	17.4	28.1	7.8	8.8	124.6	124.4	5.1	35.2	29.6	19.4	30.9	28.7	25.0
Oct	69.3	70.2	4.8	17.9	28.1	7.8	8.9	128.7	128.4	5.2	38.0	29.9	19.5	31.6	29.3	25.4
Nov	68.6	69.5	4.8	17.8	27.6	7.6	8.9	131.8	131.5	5.4	40.6	29.7	19.2	32.6	30.0	25.8
Dec	71.0	71.9	4.8	18.4	28.6	8.0	9.3	130.5	130.3	5.4	38.6	29.8	19.4	32.7	30.7	25.9
2005: Jan	71.6	72.4	4.7	18.5	28.5	8.2	9.4	134.3	134.0	5.6	38.4	31.1	19.9	34.4	30.6	26.5
Feb	70.7	71.5	4.6	18.7	28.0	7.8	9.5	135.5	135.2	5.5	40.0	30.0	19.8	35.5	30.7	26.4
Mar	71.5	72.5	4.8	18.7	28.9	7.7	9.4	130.4	130.1	5.5	39.9	29.6	18.5	32.1	31.3	26.5
Apr	74.6	75.5	5.0	19.5	30.5	7.9	9.3	136.9	136.6	5.5	41.8	31.9	18.8	33.8	31.2	26.8
May	74.5	75.5	5.5	19.8	29.6	7.7	9.7	135.3	134.9	5.7	39.4	31.3	19.7	34.1	31.2	26.7
June	74.5	75.6	5.1	19.6	30.1	7.8	9.5	138.3	138.1	5.6	41.5	32.6	19.6	34.2	31.3	26.9
July	75.1	75.9	5.0	19.9	30.3	8.0	9.6	137.6	137.4	5.6	42.1	31.8	19.7	33.5	31.6	26.9
Aug	76.7	77.9	5.1	20.1	31.4	8.3	9.5	140.5	140.5	5.7	44.1	32.0	20.8	33.3	31.6	26.5
Sept	73.5	74.6	4.9	19.0	29.1	8.3	9.9	144.8	144.5	5.9	47.1	32.3	20.1	34.2	32.3	27.0
Oct	75.2	76.1	5.0	19.0	30.9	8.5	9.4	148.4	148.1	5.8	50.0	32.1	20.8	34.5	32.2	27.1
Nov p	77.4	78.4	4.9	19.4	32.0	8.7	10.0	146.2	145.9	5.8	48.8	32.1	21.0	33.5	31.9	27.3

[1] Department of Defense shipments of grant-aid military supplies and equipment under the Military Assistance Program are excluded from total exports through 1985 and included beginning 1986.

[2] F.a.s. (free alongside ship) value basis at U.S. port of exportation for exports.

[3] Beginning 1989, exports have been adjusted for undocumented exports to Canada and are included in the appropriate end-use categories. For prior years, only total exports include this adjustment.

[4] Total includes "other" exports or imports, not shown separately.

[5] Total arrivals of imported goods other than intransit shipments.

[6] Total includes revisions not reflected in detail.

[7] Total exports are on a revised statistical month basis; end-use categories are on a statistical month basis.

Note.—Goods on a Census basis are adjusted to a BOP basis by the Bureau of Economic Analysis, in line with concepts and definitions used to prepare international and national accounts. The adjustments are necessary to supplement coverage of Census data, to eliminate duplication of transactions recorded elsewhere in international accounts, and to value transactions according to a standard definition. Data include international trade of the U.S. Virgin Islands, Puerto Rico, and U.S. Foreign Trade Zones.

Source: Department of Commerce (Bureau of the Census and Bureau of Economic Analysis).

TABLE B-107.—*International investment position of the United States at year-end, 1997–2004*

[Billions of dollars]

Type of investment	1997	1998	1999	2000	2001	2002	2003	2004ᵖ
NET INTERNATIONAL INVESTMENT POSITION OF THE UNITED STATES:								
With direct investment at current cost	−820.7	−895.4	−766.2	−1,381.2	−1,919.4	−2,107.3	−2,156.7	−2,484.2
With direct investment at market value ...	−822.7	−1,070.8	−1,037.4	−1,581.0	−2,339.4	−2,455.1	−2,372.4	−2,542.2
U.S.-OWNED ASSETS ABROAD:								
With direct investment at current cost	4,567.9	5,095.5	5,974.4	6,238.8	6,308.7	6,645.7	7,641.0	9,052.8
With direct investment at market value ...	5,379.1	6,179.1	7,399.7	7,401.2	6,930.5	6,807.8	8,296.6	9,972.8
U.S. official reserve assets	134.8	146.0	136.4	128.4	130.0	158.6	183.6	189.6
Gold ¹	75.9	75.3	76.0	71.8	72.3	90.8	108.9	113.9
Special drawing rights	10.0	10.6	10.3	10.5	10.8	12.2	12.6	13.6
Reserve position in the International Monetary Fund	18.1	24.1	18.0	14.8	17.9	22.0	22.5	19.5
Foreign currencies	30.8	36.0	32.2	31.2	29.0	33.7	39.5	42.5
U.S. Government assets, other than official reserve assets	86.2	86.8	84.2	85.2	85.7	85.3	84.8	83.6
U.S. credits and other long-term assets ...	84.1	84.9	81.7	82.6	83.1	82.7	82.0	80.8
Repayable in dollars	83.8	84.5	81.4	82.3	82.9	82.4	81.7	80.5
Other	.4	.3	.3	.3	.3	.3	.3	.3
U.S. foreign currency holdings and U.S. short-term assets	2.1	1.9	2.6	2.6	2.5	2.6	2.8	2.8
U.S. private assets:								
With direct investment at current cost	4,346.9	4,862.8	5,753.7	6,025.2	6,093.1	6,401.8	7,372.6	8,779.6
With direct investment at market value ...	5,158.1	5,946.4	7,179.0	7,187.6	6,714.9	6,563.9	8,028.3	9,699.6
Direct investment abroad:								
At current cost	1,068.1	1,196.0	1,414.4	1,531.6	1,693.1	1,860.4	2,062.6	2,367.4
At market value	1,879.3	2,279.6	2,839.6	2,694.0	2,314.9	2,022.6	2,718.2	3,287.4
Foreign securities	1,751.2	2,069.4	2,551.9	2,425.6	2,169.7	2,079.9	2,953.8	3,436.7
Bonds	543.4	594.4	548.2	572.7	557.1	705.2	874.4	916.7
Corporate stocks	1,207.8	1,475.0	2,003.7	1,852.8	1,612.7	1,374.7	2,079.4	2,520.1
U.S. claims on unaffiliated foreigners reported by U.S. nonbanking concerns	545.5	588.3	704.5	836.6	839.3	902.0	597.0	801.5
U.S. claims reported by U.S. banks, not included elsewhere	982.1	1,009.0	1,082.9	1,231.5	1,390.9	1,559.5	1,759.3	2,174.0
FOREIGN-OWNED ASSETS IN THE UNITED STATES:								
With direct investment at current cost	5,388.6	5,990.9	6,740.6	7,620.0	8,228.1	8,752.9	9,797.7	11,537.0
With direct investment at market value ...	6,201.9	7,249.9	8,437.1	8,982.2	9,269.9	9,263.0	10,669.0	12,515.0
Foreign official assets in the United States	873.7	896.2	951.1	1,030.7	1,109.1	1,251.0	1,567.1	1,982.0
U.S. Government securities	648.2	669.8	693.8	756.2	847.0	970.4	1,192.2	1,499.6
U.S. Treasury securities	615.1	622.9	617.7	639.8	720.1	812.0	990.4	1,260.5
Other	33.1	46.8	76.1	116.4	126.9	158.4	201.8	239.1
Other U.S. Government liabilities	21.7	18.4	21.1	19.3	17.0	17.1	16.6	17.1
U.S. liabilities reported by U.S. banks, not included elsewhere	135.4	125.9	138.8	153.4	134.7	155.9	201.1	271.5
Other foreign official assets	68.4	82.1	97.3	101.8	110.4	107.6	157.2	193.8
Other foreign assets:								
With direct investment at current cost	4,514.9	5,094.7	5,789.5	6,589.3	7,119.0	7,502.0	8,230.6	9,555.0
With direct investment at market value ...	5,328.1	6,353.7	7,486.0	7,951.5	8,160.9	8,012.0	9,101.9	10,533.0
Direct investment in the United States:								
At current cost	824.1	920.0	1,101.7	1,421.0	1,518.5	1,517.4	1,585.9	1,708.9
At market value	1,637.4	2,179.0	2,798.2	2,783.2	2,560.3	2,027.4	2,457.2	2,686.9
U.S. Treasury securities	538.1	543.3	440.7	381.6	375.1	473.5	543.2	639.7
U.S. securities other than U.S. Treasury securities	1,512.7	1,903.4	2,351.3	2,623.0	2,821.4	2,779.1	3,408.1	3,987.8
Corporate and other bonds	618.8	724.6	825.2	1,068.6	1,343.1	1,531.0	1,707.2	2,059.3
Corporate stocks	893.9	1,178.8	1,526.1	1,554.4	1,478.3	1,248.1	1,700.9	1,928.5
U.S. currency	211.6	228.3	250.7	256.0	279.8	301.3	317.9	332.7
U.S. liabilities to unaffiliated foreigners reported by U.S. nonbanking concerns	459.4	485.7	578.0	738.9	798.3	892.6	454.3	581.3
U.S. liabilities reported by U.S. banks, not included elsewhere	968.8	1,014.0	1,067.2	1,168.7	1,326.1	1,538.2	1,921.1	2,304.6

¹ Valued at market price.

Note.—For details regarding these data, see *Survey of Current Business*, July 2005.

Source: Department of Commerce, Bureau of Economic Analysis.

TABLE B–108.—*Industrial production and consumer prices, major industrial countries, 1980–2005*

Year or quarter	United States [1]	Canada	Japan	France	Germany [2]	Italy	United Kingdom
	Industrial production (Index, 2002=100) [3]						
1980	56.2	57.2	72.2	76.7	75.8	78.7	76.8
1981	56.9	57.5	72.9	75.9	74.4	76.9	73.7
1982	54.0	53.1	73.1	75.3	72.0	74.5	73.8
1983	55.4	56.0	75.5	75.4	72.5	72.8	75.8
1984	60.4	63.0	82.5	76.7	74.7	75.2	76.3
1985	61.2	66.2	85.5	77.2	78.3	75.3	80.2
1986	61.8	65.7	85.4	79.1	79.7	78.4	81.9
1987	64.9	68.4	88.3	80.5	80.0	80.4	85.3
1988	68.2	73.0	96.5	83.4	82.9	86.0	89.7
1989	68.8	72.8	102.1	86.3	87.0	89.3	91.6
1990	69.4	70.8	106.4	87.5	91.5	88.7	91.6
1991	68.3	68.2	108.4	87.2	94.1	87.9	88.6
1992	70.3	69.1	102.2	86.0	92.0	87.0	89.0
1993	72.6	72.4	98.6	82.6	85.1	85.0	90.9
1994	76.5	77.0	99.8	85.9	87.6	90.1	95.7
1995	80.2	80.5	103.1	87.6	88.1	95.4	97.3
1996	83.6	81.4	105.5	87.4	88.3	93.8	98.7
1997	89.7	86.0	109.3	90.9	91.0	97.5	100.0
1998	94.9	89.0	102.1	94.2	94.4	98.6	101.1
1999	99.3	94.3	102.4	96.5	95.5	98.5	102.3
2000	103.5	102.4	108.0	100.2	100.8	102.7	104.2
2001	99.9	98.3	101.2	101.5	101.1	101.6	102.6
2002	100.0	100.0	100.0	100.0	100.0	100.0	100.0
2003	100.6	101.0	103.0	99.5	100.4	99.4	99.5
2004	104.7	105.0	108.5	101.8	103.5	98.8	100.2
2005 ᴾ	108.1	....	....	....	....	....	....
2004: I	103.1	102.8	107.0	101.1	102.2	99.9	100.3
II	104.4	104.5	109.3	101.8	103.6	99.7	100.8
III	105.1	106.2	109.1	101.5	104.1	99.2	99.8
IV	106.2	106.5	107.9	101.8	104.1	98.3	100.2
2005: I	107.2	106.7	110.0	101.8	105.0	97.3	99.2
II	107.6	106.7	109.6	101.3	106.0	98.4	99.1
III	108.0	108.0	109.3	101.8	107.5	99.0	98.6
IV ᴾ	109.0	....	....	....	....	....	....
	Consumer prices (Index, 1982–84=100)						
1980	82.4	76.1	91.0	72.2	86.7	63.9	78.5
1981	90.9	85.6	95.3	81.8	92.2	75.5	87.9
1982	96.5	94.9	98.1	91.7	97.0	87.8	95.4
1983	99.6	100.4	99.8	100.3	100.3	100.8	99.8
1984	103.9	104.7	102.1	108.0	102.7	111.4	104.8
1985	107.6	109.0	104.2	114.3	104.8	121.7	111.1
1986	109.6	113.5	104.9	117.2	104.6	128.9	114.9
1987	113.6	118.4	104.9	121.1	104.9	135.1	119.7
1988	118.3	123.2	105.6	124.3	106.3	141.9	125.6
1989	124.0	129.3	108.0	128.7	109.2	150.7	135.4
1990	130.7	135.5	111.4	132.9	112.2	160.4	148.2
1991	136.2	143.1	115.0	137.2	116.3	170.5	156.9
1992	140.3	145.3	117.0	140.4	122.2	179.5	162.7
1993	144.5	147.9	118.5	143.4	127.6	187.7	165.3
1994	148.2	148.2	119.3	145.8	131.1	195.3	169.3
1995	152.4	151.4	119.2	148.4	133.3	205.6	175.2
1996	156.9	153.8	119.3	151.4	135.3	213.8	179.4
1997	160.5	156.3	121.5	153.2	137.8	218.2	185.1
1998	163.0	157.8	122.2	154.2	139.1	222.5	191.4
1999	166.6	160.5	121.8	155.0	140.0	226.2	194.3
2000	172.2	164.9	121.0	157.6	142.0	231.9	200.1
2001	177.1	169.1	120.1	160.2	144.8	238.3	203.6
2002	179.9	172.9	119.0	163.3	146.7	244.3	207.0
2003	184.0	177.7	118.7	166.7	148.3	250.8	213.0
2004	188.9	181.0	118.7	170.3	150.8	256.3	219.4
2005 ᴾ	195.3	184.9	118.3	173.2	153.7	261.3	225.6
2004: I	186.3	179.0	118.3	168.8	149.6	254.2	216.0
II	188.9	181.1	118.6	170.3	150.7	256.1	218.9
III	189.6	181.5	118.6	170.6	151.2	257.2	220.2
IV	190.7	182.2	119.2	171.4	151.5	257.8	222.3
2005: I	191.9	182.9	118.0	171.7	152.3	259.1	222.8
II	194.5	184.6	118.5	173.2	153.2	260.9	225.5
III	196.9	186.2	118.3	173.8	154.4	262.4	226.3
IV ᴾ	197.9	186.3	118.5	174.2	154.9	263.3	227.5

[1] See Note, Table B–51 for information on U.S. industrial production series.
[2] Prior to 1991 data are for West Germany only.
[3] All data exclude construction. Quarterly data are seasonally adjusted.

Note.—National sources data have been rebased for industrial production and consumer prices.

Sources: National sources as reported by each country; Department of Labor (Bureau of Labor Statistics), and Board of Governors of the Federal Reserve System.

406

TABLE B–109.—*Civilian unemployment rate, and hourly compensation, major industrial countries,*
1980–2005
[Quarterly data seasonally adjusted]

Year or quarter	United States	Canada	Japan	France	Ger-many [1]	Italy	United Kingdom
	Civilian unemployment rate (Percent) [2]						
1980	7.1	7.3	2.0	6.5	2.8	4.4	6.9
1981	7.6	7.3	2.2	7.6	4.0	4.9	9.7
1982	9.7	10.7	2.4	[3]8.3	5.6	5.4	10.8
1983	9.6	11.6	2.7	8.6	[3]6.9	5.9	11.5
1984	7.5	10.9	2.8	10.0	7.1	5.9	11.8
1985	7.2	10.2	2.7	10.5	7.2	6.0	11.4
1986	7.0	9.3	2.8	10.6	6.6	[3]7.5	11.4
1987	6.2	8.4	2.9	10.8	6.3	7.9	10.5
1988	5.5	7.4	2.5	10.3	6.3	7.9	8.6
1989	5.3	7.1	2.3	9.6	5.7	7.8	7.3
1990	[3]5.6	7.7	2.1	[3]8.6	5.0	7.0	7.1
1991	6.8	9.8	2.1	9.1	[3]5.6	[3]6.9	8.9
1992	7.5	10.7	2.2	10.0	6.7	7.3	10.0
1993	6.9	10.8	2.5	11.3	8.0	[3]9.8	10.4
1994	[3]6.1	9.6	2.9	11.9	8.5	10.7	8.7
1995	5.6	8.7	3.2	11.3	8.2	11.3	8.7
1996	5.4	8.9	3.4	11.8	9.0	11.3	8.1
1997	4.9	8.4	3.4	11.7	9.9	11.4	7.0
1998	4.5	7.7	4.1	11.2	9.3	11.5	6.3
1999	4.2	7.0	4.7	10.5	[3]8.5	11.0	6.0
2000	4.0	6.1	4.8	9.1	7.8	10.2	5.5
2001	4.7	6.5	5.1	8.4	7.9	9.2	5.1
2002	5.8	7.0	5.4	9.0	8.6	8.7	5.2
2003	6.0	6.9	5.3	9.6	9.3	8.5	5.0
2004	5.5	6.4	4.8	9.8	9.9	8.1	4.8
2005	5.1						
2004: I	5.7	6.6	4.9	9.8	9.7	8.3	4.8
II	5.6	6.5	4.7	9.8	9.8	8.1	4.8
III	5.5	6.4	4.8	9.8	10.0	8.0	4.7
IV	5.4	6.3	4.6	9.8	10.0	8.0	4.7
2005: I	5.2	6.2	4.6	9.9	10.0	7.9	4.7
II	5.1	6.0	4.4	9.9	9.9	7.8	4.7
III	5.0	6.0	4.4	9.7	9.4	7.8	4.8
IV	5.0						
	Manufacturing hourly compensation in U.S. dollars (Index, 1992=100) [4]						
1980	56.0	49.5	32.8	51.7	46.1	43.8	46.0
1981	61.5	54.7	36.0	46.6	39.3	39.1	46.5
1982	67.5	60.2	33.5	45.6	38.8	38.4	44.1
1983	69.3	64.4	36.1	43.5	38.6	39.4	41.0
1984	71.7	64.8	37.1	41.2	36.3	39.1	38.9
1985	75.6	64.0	38.5	43.4	37.2	40.7	39.9
1986	79.0	63.8	57.1	58.5	52.4	54.4	49.1
1987	81.3	68.4	68.2	69.8	66.0	66.0	60.9
1988	84.1	76.5	78.4	72.8	70.4	70.6	70.6
1989	86.6	84.5	77.4	71.4	69.1	72.7	69.4
1990	90.5	91.6	79.2	88.4	86.4	90.1	84.6
1991	95.6	100.2	90.9	90.4	86.0	93.5	94.4
1992	100.0	100.0	100.0	100.0	100.0	100.0	100.0
1993	102.0	95.6	117.2	96.2	100.3	82.8	88.9
1994	105.3	91.9	129.9	101.9	107.0	81.7	93.2
1995	107.3	93.7	146.1	117.4	127.6	84.2	97.4
1996	109.3	95.2	127.2	116.2	127.2	95.0	96.9
1997	112.2	94.6	117.9	101.5	112.5	88.9	105.1
1998	118.7	91.9	111.7	101.4	112.5	86.7	114.7
1999	123.4	94.9	128.0	100.8	110.3	84.1	118.7
2000	134.7	98.0	133.7	91.9	100.5	75.1	117.7
2001	137.8	97.4	119.5	91.5	100.5	75.5	116.4
2002	147.9	99.2	116.2	102.2	108.7	81.7	128.7
2003	160.1	114.9	126.3	127.2	132.9	101.0	147.1
2004	163.6	123.5	136.0	143.2	147.0	113.8	170.7

[1] Prior to 1991 data are for West Germany only.
[2] Civilian unemployment rates, approximating U.S. concepts. Quarterly data for Japan, France, Germany, and Italy should be viewed as less precise indicators of unemployment under U.S. concepts than the annual data.
[3] There are breaks in the series for France (1982 and 1990), Germany (1983, 1991 and 1999), Italy (1986, 1991 and 1993), and United States (1990 and 1994). For details on break in series in 1990 and 1994 for United States, see footnote 5, Table B-35. For details on break in series for other countries, see U.S. Department of Labor *Comparative Civilian Labor Force Statistics, Ten Countries: 1960–2004,* May 13, 2005.
[4] Hourly compensation in manufacturing, U.S. dollar basis; data relate to all employed persons (employees and self-employed workers).
For details on manufacturing hourly compensation, see U.S. Department of Labor *International Comparisons of Manufacturing Productivity and Unit Labor Cost Trends, 2004,* October 27, 2005.

Source: Department of Labor, Bureau of Labor Statistics.

407

TABLE B–110.—*Foreign exchange rates, 1984–2005*

[Foreign currency units per U.S. dollar, except as noted; certified noon buying rates in New York]

Period	Canada (dollar)	EMU Members (euro) [1][2]	Belgium (franc) [1]	France (franc) [1]	Germany (mark) [1]	Italy (lira) [1]	Netherlands (guilder) [1]	Japan (yen)	Sweden (krona)	Switzerland (franc)	United Kingdom (pound) [2]
March 1973	0.9967	....	39.408	4.5156	2.8132	568.17	2.8714	261.90	4.4294	3.2171	2.4724
1984	1.2952	....	57.752	8.7356	2.8455	1756.11	3.2085	237.46	8.2708	2.3500	1.3368
1985	1.3659	....	59.337	8.9800	2.9420	1908.88	3.3185	238.47	8.6032	2.4552	1.2974
1986	1.3896	....	44.664	6.9257	2.1705	1491.16	2.4485	168.35	7.1273	1.7979	1.4677
1987	1.3259	....	37.358	6.0122	1.7981	1297.03	2.0264	144.60	6.3469	1.4918	1.6398
1988	1.2306	....	36.785	5.9595	1.7570	1302.39	1.9778	128.17	6.1370	1.4643	1.7813
1989	1.1842	....	39.409	6.3802	1.8808	1372.28	2.1219	138.07	6.4559	1.6369	1.6382
1990	1.1668	....	33.424	5.4467	1.6166	1198.27	1.8215	145.00	5.9231	1.3901	1.7841
1991	1.1460	....	34.195	5.6468	1.6610	1241.28	1.8720	134.59	6.0521	1.4356	1.7674
1992	1.2085	....	32.148	5.2935	1.5618	1232.17	1.7587	126.78	5.8258	1.4064	1.7663
1993	1.2902	....	34.581	5.6669	1.6545	1573.41	1.8585	111.08	7.7956	1.4781	1.5016
1994	1.3664	....	33.426	5.5459	1.6216	1611.49	1.8190	102.18	7.7161	1.3667	1.5319
1995	1.3725	....	29.472	4.9864	1.4321	1629.45	1.6044	93.96	7.1406	1.1812	1.5785
1996	1.3638	....	30.970	5.1158	1.5049	1542.76	1.6863	108.78	6.7082	1.2361	1.5607
1997	1.3849	....	35.807	5.8393	1.7348	1703.81	1.9525	121.06	7.6446	1.4514	1.6376
1998	1.4836	....	36.310	5.8995	1.7597	1736.85	1.9837	130.99	7.9522	1.4506	1.6573
1999	1.4858	1.0653	....	....	....	....	....	113.73	8.2740	1.5045	1.6172
2000	1.4855	.9232	....	....	....	....	....	107.80	9.1735	1.6904	1.5156
2001	1.5487	.8952	....	....	....	....	....	121.57	10.3425	1.6891	1.4396
2002	1.5704	.9454	....	....	....	....	....	125.22	9.7233	1.5567	1.5025
2003	1.4008	1.1321	....	....	....	....	....	115.94	8.0787	1.3450	1.6347
2004	1.3017	1.2438	....	....	....	....	....	108.15	7.3480	1.2428	1.8330
2005	1.2115	1.2449	....	....	....	....	....	110.11	7.4710	1.2459	1.8204
2004: I	1.3184	1.2499	....	....	....	....	....	107.24	7.3533	1.2552	1.8385
II	1.3590	1.2047	....	....	....	....	....	109.69	7.5968	1.2768	1.8063
III	1.3078	1.2227	....	....	....	....	....	109.94	7.4922	1.2569	1.8193
IV	1.2208	1.2991	....	....	....	....	....	105.67	6.9436	1.1818	1.8687
2005: I	1.2262	1.3112	....	....	....	....	....	104.54	6.9225	1.1817	1.8911
II	1.2438	1.2591	....	....	....	....	....	107.53	7.3190	1.2270	1.8560
III	1.2014	1.2196	....	....	....	....	....	111.24	7.6788	1.2742	1.7847
IV	1.1733	1.1890	....	....	....	....	....	117.28	7.9699	1.3015	1.7486

Trade-weighted value of the U.S. dollar

	Nominal				Real [7]		
	G–10 index (March 1973=100) [3]	Broad index (January 1997=100) [4]	Major currencies index (March 1973=100) [5]	OITP index (January 1997=100) [6]	Broad index (March 1973=100) [4]	Major currencies index (March 1973=100) [5]	OITP index (March 1973=100) [6]
1984	138.2	60.1	128.7	9.8	117.2	118.2	114.3
1985	143.0	67.2	133.6	13.1	122.0	122.0	122.1
1986	112.2	62.3	109.9	16.5	106.6	99.6	126.2
1987	96.9	60.4	97.2	19.9	97.9	89.0	123.6
1988	92.7	60.9	90.4	24.1	91.4	83.9	113.1
1989	98.6	66.9	94.2	29.6	93.0	88.2	107.7
1990	89.1	71.4	89.9	40.1	91.4	84.8	110.8
1991	89.8	74.3	88.5	46.7	90.0	83.1	110.3
1992	86.6	76.9	87.0	53.1	88.1	82.0	106.6
1993	93.2	83.8	89.9	63.4	89.5	85.2	104.0
1994	91.3	90.9	88.4	80.5	89.3	84.8	104.2
1995	84.2	92.7	83.5	92.5	86.9	81.0	104.2
1996	87.3	97.5	87.2	98.2	88.9	85.9	101.1
1997	96.4	104.4	93.9	104.6	93.7	93.2	102.2
1998	98.8	115.9	98.4	125.9	101.6	98.2	115.6
1999	....	116.0	96.8	129.2	101.0	97.9	114.2
2000	....	119.4	101.6	129.8	104.9	104.7	114.4
2001	....	125.9	107.7	135.9	111.0	112.2	119.0
2002	....	126.7	106.0	140.4	111.2	110.6	121.6
2003	....	119.1	93.0	143.5	104.5	97.6	123.2
2004	....	113.6	85.4	143.4	99.8	90.6	121.9
2005	....	110.8	83.8	138.9	98.3	90.5	118.1
2004: I	....	113.2	85.3	142.4	99.0	90.0	120.6
II	....	115.8	88.0	144.3	102.0	93.4	123.4
III	....	114.8	86.4	144.6	101.1	92.0	123.1
IV	....	110.5	81.7	142.1	97.2	87.1	120.3
2005: I	....	109.4	81.2	139.9	96.2	87.1	117.9
II	....	110.7	83.5	139.1	98.1	89.9	118.5
III	....	111.1	84.6	138.3	99.2	91.8	118.4
IV	....	112.0	85.8	138.2	99.7	93.3	117.5

[1] European Economic and Monetary Union members include Austria, Belgium, Finland, France, Germany, Ireland, Italy, Luxembourg, Netherlands, Portugal, Spain, and beginning in 2001, Greece.
[2] U.S. dollars per foreign currency unit.
[3] G-10 comprises the individual countries shown in this table. Discontinued after December 1998.
[4] Weighted average of the foreign exchange value of the dollar against the currencies of a broad group of U.S. trading partners.
[5] Subset of the broad index. Includes currencies of the euro area, Australia, Canada, Japan, Sweden, Switzerland, and the United Kingdom.
[6] Subset of the broad index. Includes other important U.S. trading partners (OITP) whose currencies are not heavily traded outside their home markets.
[7] Adjusted for changes in consumer price indexes for United States and other countries.

Source: Board of Governors of the Federal Reserve System.

TABLE B–111.—*International reserves, selected years, 1962–2005*

[Millions of SDRs; end of period]

Area and country	1962	1972	1982	1992	2002	2004	2005 Oct	2005 Nov
All countries	62,851	146,658	361,239	752,566	1,889,307	2,520,724	2,913,251	....
Industrial countries [1]	53,502	113,362	214,025	424,229	757,942	930,204	952,991	....
United States	17,220	12,112	29,918	52,995	59,160	58,022	50,083	49,690
Canada	2,561	5,572	3,439	8,662	27,225	22,173	23,633	23,980
Euro area:								
Austria	1,081	2,505	5,544	9,703	7,480	5,406	5,803	5,636
Belgium	1,753	3,564	4,757	10,914	9,010	6,962	6,660	6,656
Finland	237	664	1,420	3,862	6,885	7,987	6,991	7,001
France	4,049	9,224	17,850	22,522	24,268	26,098	23,738	24,197
Germany	6,958	21,908	43,909	69,489	41,516	35,301	36,440	36,006
Greece	287	950	916	3,606	6,083	888	686	623
Ireland	359	1,038	2,390	2,514	3,989	1,829	1,741	670
Italy	4,068	5,605	15,108	22,438	23,798	20,698	20,285	21,432
Luxembourg	....	....	....	....	114	195	195	183
Netherlands	1,943	4,407	10,723	17,492	7,993	7,380	7,620	7,378
Portugal	680	2,129	1,179	14,474	8,889	3,852	3,550	3,626
Spain	1,045	4,618	7,450	33,640	25,992	8,566	7,129	7,507
Australia	1,168	5,656	6,053	8,429	15,307	23,143	27,716	29,662
Japan	2,021	16,916	22,001	52,937	340,088	537,813	575,084	584,424
New Zealand	251	767	577	2,239	2,750	3,409	4,593	....
Denmark	256	787	2,111	8,090	19,924	25,241	23,064	22,487
Iceland	32	78	133	364	326	676	657	693
Norway	304	1,220	6,273	8,725	23,579	28,530	29,301	30,383
San Marino	....	....	....	....	135	229	....	....
Sweden	802	1,453	3,397	16,667	12,807	14,458	14,854	14,966
Switzerland	2,919	6,961	16,930	27,100	31,693	37,259	26,280	26,673
United Kingdom	3,308	5,201	11,904	27,300	29,305	29,548	29,455	30,262
Developing countries: Total [2]	9,349	33,295	147,213	328,337	1,131,365	1,590,525	1,960,261	....
By area:								
Africa	2,110	3,962	7,737	13,044	54,155	82,599	105,958	....
Asia [2]	2,772	8,130	44,490	190,363	720,289	1,041,653	1,268,949	....
Europe	381	2,680	5,359	16,006	139,325	214,557	277,398	....
Middle East	1,805	9,436	64,039	44,149	98,645	108,899	133,354	....
Western Hemisphere	2,282	9,089	25,563	64,774	118,953	142,817	174,602	....
Memo:								
Oil-exporting countries	2,030	9,956	67,108	46,144	110,079	139,674	175,138	....
Non-oil developing countries [2]	7,319	23,339	80,105	282,193	1,021,287	1,450,851	1,785,124	....

[1] Includes data for Luxembourg 1962–92. Includes data for European Central Bank (ECB) beginning 1999. Detail does not add to totals shown.

[2] Includes data for Taiwan Province of China.

Note.—International reserves is comprised of monetary authorities' holdings of gold (at SDR 35 per ounce), special drawing rights (SDRs), reserve positions in the International Monetary Fund, and foreign exchange.

U.S. dollars per SDR (end of period) are: 1962—1.00000; 1972—1.08571; 1982—1.10311; 1992—1.37500; 2002—1.3595; 2004—1.5530; October 2005—1.4458; and November 2005—1.4241.

Source: International Monetary Fund, *International Financial Statistics*.

[Percent change at annual rate]

Area and country	1987–96	1997	1998	1999	2000	2001	2002	2003	2004	2005[1]
World	3.3	4.2	2.8	3.7	4.7	2.4	3.0	4.0	5.1	4.3
Advanced economies	3.0	3.5	2.6	3.5	3.9	1.2	1.5	1.9	3.3	2.5
Of which:										
United States	2.9	4.5	4.2	4.5	3.7	.8	1.6	2.7	4.2	3.5
Japan	3.2	1.8	–1.0	–.1	2.4	.2	–.3	1.4	2.7	2.0
United Kingdom	2.4	3.2	3.2	3.0	4.0	2.2	2.0	2.5	3.2	1.9
Canada	2.2	4.2	4.1	5.5	5.2	1.8	3.1	2.0	2.9	2.9
Euro area	....	2.6	2.8	2.7	3.8	1.7	.9	.7	2.0	1.2
Germany	2.6	1.7	2.0	1.9	3.1	1.2	.1	–.2	1.6	.8
France	1.9	2.3	3.4	3.2	4.1	2.1	1.3	.9	2.0	1.5
Italy	1.9	2.0	1.8	1.7	3.0	1.8	.4	.3	1.2	[5]
Spain	2.9	4.0	4.3	4.2	5.8	3.5	2.7	2.9	3.1	3.2
Netherlands	2.7	3.8	4.3	4.0	3.5	1.4	.1	–.1	1.7	.7
Belgium	2.2	3.8	2.1	3.2	3.7	.9	.9	1.3	2.7	1.2
Austria	2.5	1.8	3.6	3.3	3.4	.8	1.0	1.4	2.4	1.9
Finland	1.3	6.2	5.0	3.4	5.0	1.0	2.2	2.4	3.6	1.8
Greece	1.4	3.6	3.4	3.4	4.5	4.3	3.8	4.7	4.2	3.2
Portugal	4.0	4.0	4.6	3.8	3.4	1.7	.4	–1.1	1.0	.5
Ireland	5.2	10.8	8.5	10.7	9.2	6.2	6.1	4.4	4.5	5.0
Luxembourg	5.2	8.3	6.8	7.3	9.2	2.2	2.3	2.4	4.4	3.1
Memorandum:										
Major advanced economies[2]	2.7	3.3	2.8	3.1	3.5	1.0	1.1	1.8	3.2	2.5
Newly industrialized Asian economies[3]	7.9	5.5	–2.6	7.3	7.9	1.3	5.3	3.1	5.6	4.0
Other emerging market and developing countries	3.8	5.2	3.0	4.0	5.8	4.1	4.8	6.5	7.3	6.4
Regional groups:										
Africa	2.2	3.4	3.2	2.8	3.3	4.1	3.6	4.6	5.3	4.5
Central and eastern Europe	.9	4.2	2.8	.5	4.9	.2	4.4	4.6	6.5	4.3
Commonwealth of Independent States[4]	....	1.1	–3.5	5.1	9.1	6.3	5.3	7.9	8.4	6.0
Russia	....	1.4	–5.3	6.3	10.0	5.1	4.7	7.3	7.2	5.5
Developing Asia	7.8	6.5	4.2	6.2	6.7	5.6	6.6	8.1	8.2	7.8
China	10.0	8.8	7.8	7.1	8.0	7.5	8.3	9.5	9.5	9.0
India	5.9	5.0	5.8	6.7	5.4	3.9	4.7	7.4	7.3	7.1
Middle East	3.4	4.7	4.2	2.0	4.9	3.7	4.2	6.5	5.5	5.4
Western Hemisphere	2.7	5.2	2.3	.4	3.9	.5	.5	2.2	5.6	4.1
Brazil	2.1	3.3	.1	.8	4.4	1.3	1.9	.5	4.9	3.3
Mexico	2.5	6.7	4.9	3.9	6.6	–.2	.8	1.4	4.4	3.0

[1] All figures are forecasts as published by the International Monetary Fund. For United States, advance estimates by the Department of Commerce show that real GDP grew 3.5 percent in 2005.
[2] Includes Canada, France, Germany, Italy, Japan, United Kingdom, and United States.
[3] Includes Hong Kong SAR (Special Administrative Region of China), Korea, Singapore, and Taiwan Province of China.
[4] Includes Mongolia, which is not a member of the Commonwealth of Independent States, but is included for reasons of geography and similarities in economic structure.
[5] Figure is zero or negligible.

Note.—For details on data shown in this table, see *World Economic Outlook* published semiannually by the International Monetary Fund.

Sources: Department of Commerce (Bureau of Economic Analysis) and International Monetary Fund.